The Improv Dictionary

The Improv Dictionary: An A to Z of Improvisational Terms, Techniques, and Tools explores improvisational approaches and concepts drawn from a multitude of movements and schools of thought to enhance spontaneous and collaborative creativity.

This accessible resource reveals and interrogates the inherited wisdoms contained in the very words we use to describe modern improv. Each detailed definition goes beyond the obvious clichés and seeks a nuanced and inclusive understanding of how art of the moment can be much more than easy laughs and cheap gags (even when it is being delightfully irreverent and wildly funny). This encyclopedic work pulls from a wide array of practitioners and practices, finding tensions and commonalities from styles as diverse as Theatresports, ComedySportz, the Harold, narrative long-form, Playback Theatre, and Boal's Theatre of the Oppressed. Entries include nuanced definitions, helpful examples, detailed explorations of the concepts in practice, and framing quotes from a leading practitioner or inspirational artistic voice.

The Improv Dictionary offers valuable insights to novice improvisers taking their first steps in the craft, seasoned performers seeking to unlock the next level of abandon, instructors craving a new comprehensive resource, and scholars working in one of the numerous allied fields that find enrichment through collaborative and guided play.

Each significant entry in the book is also keyed to an accompanying improv game or exercise housed at www.improvdr.com, enabling readers to dig deeper into their process.

David Charles, PhD, works as a professional improvisational practitioner, deviser, author, and improv scholar. A New Zealander by birth, David has called central Florida home since 2003, where he has served as a Professor of Theatre and Dance, Departmental Chair, Producing Director of the historic Annie Russell, and Founding Artistic Director of Rollins Improv Players at Rollins College. He is a former Equity improviser with Walt Disney World's Comedy Warehouse and a proud ensemble member, instructor, and director at the region's preeminent improv venue, Sak Comedy Lab.

The Improv Dictionary

AN A TO Z OF IMPROVISATIONAL TERMS, TECHNIQUES, AND TOOLS

David Charles

NEW YORK AND LONDON

Designed cover image: © Ensemble members of the long-form improvised show *The Lost Comedies of William Shakespeare* perform the welcoming number on the stage of the Annie Russell Theatre. Costume Design, Annie Trombo; Set Design, Lisa Cody-Rapport; Scott Cook Photography.

First published 2024
by Routledge
605 Third Avenue, New York, NY 10158

and by Routledge
4 Park Square, Milton Park, Abingdon, Oxon, OX14 4RN

Routledge is an imprint of the Taylor & Francis Group, an informa business

© 2024 David Charles

The right of David Charles to be identified as author of this work has been asserted in accordance with sections 77 and 78 of the Copyright, Designs and Patents Act 1988.

All rights reserved. No part of this book may be reprinted or reproduced or utilised in any form or by any electronic, mechanical, or other means, now known or hereafter invented, including photocopying and recording, or in any information storage or retrieval system, without permission in writing from the publishers.

Trademark notice: Product or corporate names may be trademarks or registered trademarks, and are used only for identification and explanation without intent to infringe.

ISBN: 978-1-032-42410-1 (hbk)
ISBN: 978-1-032-42406-4 (pbk)
ISBN: 978-1-003-36267-8 (ebk)

DOI: 10.4324/9781003362678

Typeset in Times Ten LT Std
by KnowledgeWorks Global Ltd.

Access the Support Material: www.improvdr.com

To my mother, Sheila (Shuttlebus) Charles, for giving me my love of the word and my passion for teaching. To Denise Walsh, for serving as my first fearless theatre mentor and deviser, and for launching me into my studies abroad. And to my improvising friends, colleagues, collaborators, and students (past and present) for continually gifting me a place to explore and grow.

This book, and the blog series from which it liberally draws, were made possible by sabbatical support and grant funding from my home institution, Rollins College, in Winter Park, Florida. Dramaturgical assistance for several of the original long-form productions pictured within these pages was provided by the Rollins College Student-Faculty Collaborative Scholarship Program.

For my son.

Contents

Introduction 1

The Ten Commandments 6

A 23

B 47

C 60

D 98

E 109

F/G 128

H/I 146

J/K/L 160

M/N 173

O 185

P 194

Q/R 213

S 225

T 269

U/V 286

W 296

X/Y/Z 305

Introduction

Thank you for opening this book! If we've never met, I imagine you'll want to know a little more about me and the rationale for this undertaking before embarking on this rather expansive series of improv musings. Read on... My name is David, or Dr. D. to a few generations of university students, and I've spent perhaps an embarrassingly large amount of my adult artistic and academic life in the world of improvisational theatre.[1] Whether I'm performing, directing, writing, or teaching, the inspiring theories that enable spontaneous creation are never far from my mind, and as we continue to forge our way into the twenty-first century, an ever expanding array of fields and disciplines are realizing what improv practitioners have known for a long time: an improvisational mindset can enrich and elevate almost any interaction or project. The following pages offer a (substantial) glimpse into the inner workings of spontaneous creation drawn from a decades-long pursuit of this sometimes maligned and misunderstood craft; after all, when improv works well, it looks easy. But there are well-tested methods behind the seeming madness, and this dictionary strives to provide you with some tools and techniques that can deepen and inform your play and interpersonal communication both on and off the stage.

ABOUT THE AUTHOR

I started my journey as an improviser in the late 1980s in New Zealand during an artistic heyday when Keith Johnstone's highly addictive Theatresports franchise received national funding from the United Building Society. This amazing boon provided funds for high school coaches, supported regional and national competitions, and enabled slickly produced underwritten professional shows, all of which, in retrospect, spoiled me more than a little in terms of what improv could look and feel like – from the use of great kiwi theatres, to polished technical and musical collaborators, to dedicated teachers and mentors for whom improv served as a significant facet of their artistic identities and incomes.

When my desire to attend university and a scholarship brought me to the United States to study, I coincidentally found myself in Chicago; although, I will freely admit I didn't really know just how lucky I was at the time as a fledgling and thoroughly addicted improvisational practitioner. Alongside more "regular" theatrical studies at Roosevelt University, I continued to hone my craft in the classroom and on various stages, joining Chicago ComedySportz, the Players Workshop of Second City, and creating my own opportunities on campus when my curiosity couldn't be satiated by the official offerings alone.

My formal studies then took me on a winding journey down the Mississippi River more or less – first to Western Illinois University for an MFA in performance, where I started to focus on improv pedagogy and devising, and then to Louisiana State University for a PhD in theatre history, theory, and dramatic literature. During my doctoral studies, my days were filled with research and eventually a dissertation focused on global improv practices and trends, and my nights with exploring short- and long-form applications and inventions.[2] Some of those discoveries and formats with The Improvisors and the various casts of *Making It Up* in Baton Rouge still infuse and inform my current practices and projects all these years later.

In 2003, I relocated again with my degree fresh in hand to Rollins College, where I still currently work as a Professor of Theatre and have served as the Chair of my department, Producing Director of the historic Annie Russell Theatre, Founding Artistic Director of Rollins Improv Players, and a Cornell Distinguished Faculty Member. On campus, a lot of my work directly or indirectly utilizes the rich storehouse of improv techniques that inspire personal, connected, and joyful play. Off-campus, I've called Sak Comedy Lab my professional improvisational

DOI: 10.4324/9781003362678-1

Figure 1.1 The author prepares for *The Lost Comedies of William Shakespeare* at the Annie Russell Theatre. Scott Cook Photography.

home for nearly as long, though I've directed, devised, and improvised in many other venues as well, most notably Walt Disney World's Comedy Warehouse, where I also received my Actors Equity card as a full-time short-form player.

Since that first intoxicating taste in the 1980s, improv has fueled my creative, educational, and professional being, challenged me to seek truth and inclusion in my work, pushed me to dance on the boundaries separating form and freedom, and reminded me time and again of the unmatched gift improv in all its guises can provide those who study and teach the craft with care and thoughtfulness.[3]

I have always been an improv hoarder of sorts – my undergraduate honors thesis consisted of my first crack at compiling an extensive list of improv games and exercises. The longer I have taught, however, the more I have craved a resource for my students that gathered the collective wisdoms of this vibrant field, many of which reside in the very terms most of us use to describe the helpful and less-than-helpful patterns that populate our stages and classrooms. Furthermore, I wanted to jump-start important conversations about some of the underlying tensions and pitfalls that can complicate how we use these performance strategies, for without nuance, it is easy for many individual techniques to potentially cause as much damage as delight. It's common for those of us who seek to pass down the insights of our forebears to oversimplify popular tropes, but when we discuss saying "yes, and…," or extol the glories of groupmind, we should also acknowledge that agency is crucial on the improv stage and that this might rightly require saying and hearing "no," and that as we aim to build ensemble, we should be wary of erasing difference or gravitating to the insular safety of playing only with those who share the same life experiences or are obsessed with the same pop culture trends.

What started as a seemingly simple project of exploring core improv terms from a more critical and aware perspective unexpectedly expanded into the sizeable book you're now holding or viewing on some form of screen. You'll undoubtedly see my academic and populist voices battling each other a little as I have sought to provide critical depth without needlessly puncturing the awe-inspiring playfulness that marks so much of what we do in the field of spontaneous performance. I hope this dictionary communicates more than a little of that passion that sparked my own journey as a teenager at Logan Park High School and offers you some delectable food for thought as to how the very words we use to describe the art of spontaneous collaborative creation can help us unlock powerful new pathways and potentials.

Welcome to the A to Z of improv terms, techniques, and tools!

ABOUT THIS BOOK

This project aims to include a wide variety of sources and improv theories drawing from short- and long-form, comedic and dramatic, entertainment and service-centered modes and practitioners. While I have worked to cast my net as broadly as possible, I wouldn't be so foolish as to claim that this dictionary could possibly be truly comprehensive nor objective (whatever that might mean). The first life of this manuscript was as an online blog where I drew liberally from my own experiences as a practitioner, improv historian, and theorist (with the vast majority of this work occurring on Western stages and in English). I cannot pretend these biases do not lurk in the background of my assumptions and advice.

That being said, I have endeavored to assume as inclusive a stance as my own geographic and language barriers would allow and, in particular, have sought to weave philosophies drawn from often overlooked practices inclined toward efficacy alongside acclaimed figures such as Johnstone, Spolin, and Close, who rightly continue to hold a great deal of sway in modern comedic forms. Scripted theatre has also always coexisted beside and informed my improvisational play, and I ardently believe that both traditions owe more to each other than is always openly admitted. Subsequently, you'll see I often incline toward a theatrical vocabulary when defining and situating core improv practices. I've also held a longstanding interest in allied traditions in the healing arts, such as Theatre of the Oppressed, psychodrama, and Playback Theatre, that prioritize community or social goals over aesthetics alone. I posit that this inclination is critical for successful and engaging performances in general and spontaneous theatre more specifically. Most of us who have stepped onto an improv stage are intimately familiar with the interpersonal gifts and lessons found therein. I would offer that when we neglect to recognize and fully exploit how our play can also elevate and build a greater community beyond our immediate ensemble that our work is stripped of much of its inherent value and cogency.

And speaking of the healing arts, just as many improvisational practitioners use the tools of improv in the hopes of affecting positive change, I also believe that improv used badly can cause harm, and I've endeavored to unpack this belief throughout the following pages. I do not subscribe to funny at any cost, or that improv and comedy are synonymous for that matter. And just like this dictionary, I too am a work in progress: while I have sought an inclusive approach and language and earnestly strove to interrogate my own biases, I acknowledge that I am still growing with and through the craft of improv too.

My career, especially in the academy, developed within a tension between colleagues who see an obvious value in the tenets and discipline of improv (often those not in my own department, ironically) and those who have been dismissive or wary of its worth and popularity among students (beyond, perhaps, its usefulness in preparing scripted performance). The joy of improv can sadly inadvertently diminish the perceived value of the craft as so much of formal education upholds a deeply ingrained belief that work must be humorless or perhaps even unpleasant in order for it to be seen as meaningful and important. This book unabashedly strives to take the joyful creative spirit of spontaneous creativity seriously without losing the whimsy and irreverence that also characterizes much of the field. One hopes, after all, that if we take our own craft seriously that others might become more inclined to do the same.

I provide this context to recognize the complex site that improv holds in our modern world and to stress that this compelling and provocative way of seeing and experiencing life has implications far beyond the formal performance venue. Whether your interests lie on the stage, in the classroom, within the community, or in the allied fields of communication, psychology, or sociology (to name just a few), the wisdoms of improv can unlock enormously valuable interpersonal skills needed to collaborate, create, and thrive.

ABOUT READING THIS BOOK

As this project continued to grow and grow and assume a life of its own, swelling to over 200,000 words, I became increasingly aware of how readers might meaningfully approach such a work. First and foremost, as the title suggests, this dictionary is designed to serve as a reference book. I imagine few will set about reading this tome in alphabetical order from cover to cover! Rather, it's written to kick-start inspiration, explicate unfamiliar strategies, and provide new ways (hopefully) of exploring old problems. In my efforts to avoid making this dictionary problematically self-referential, sending the reader in endless circles as they explore an area of interest, I confess you will likely find moments of gentle repetition as I thought this the less egregious though equally imperfect option.

If you're new to the study of improvisational theory and performance, I highly recommend starting with the introductory chapter on the Ten Commandments. It's in vogue to protest and question the rules of improv, but I find these fundamental concepts helpful when applied joyfully and without becoming a member of the improv police. The ten core concepts are then further elucidated and complicated in later entries. I've used this frame as a launching point as it's telling that many of these strategies arise across multiple spontaneous schools (even if the language used to describe such common patterns is a little different). The terminology utilized in my initial entries finds its inspiration in Keith Johnstone's Theatresports, although I encountered this language in New Zealand and cannot identify who originally penned the particularly pithy phrases, alas.

If you've been around the improv block a few times, the alphabetized entries are designed to scrutinize and complicate some well-worn tropes. Are there unintended pitfalls when we talk about making parallel choices, accepting our first thoughts, or asking questions onstage that warrant thoughtful investigation? I'm hopeful I can help you look at problems and patterns from a different angle and perhaps even challenge your underlying assumptions and expectations in the process. You'll find each entry is diligently cross-listed and will direct you to other thematically connected ideas and conversations as well.

If you've been playing in the improv world for a while and perhaps even teach or coach the craft, this work is designed to provide a possible resource that can facilitate a common working vocabulary. Most improvisers tend toward the phrasing they first encountered, and you'll soon learn that, for me, this evolved from Johnstone's teachings. The terms we might use to describe various concepts may differ a little – "You say 'negating,' I say 'blocking'" – but I've found there's a lot of consensus in general in regards to what types of choices best enable collaborative and generative play and those habits that make other improvisers avoid you. This work has grown in no small part from my own desire to offer my improv students an accessible resource for digging deeper into core competencies that also consciously reflects important discoveries and discussions that have further enhanced our field in the last few decades. I have also found it helpful to use targeted entries as prompts for individual journal responses as this enables richer explorations and discussions. I'm a huge fan of learning as much as you can on your feet and in real time. Moving some discussion online greatly helps this goal.

And, regardless of where you might place yourself in your own evolution, I've also linked each entry to a curated companion game that is currently available in the Game Library at www.improvdr.com. These supplemental exercises aim to provide a practical experience that can further reveal the dynamic in question or offer an alternate pathway if the concept being discussed is generally viewed as problematic. Many of these games draw from the ever evolving short-form canon as, whether or not you perform in this modality, these intentionally concise scenes provide digestible and discrete explorations with a clear point of concentration or focus that allows the dynamic in question sufficient room to reveal itself.

ABOUT DISTRUSTING RULES AND HOW NOT TO READ THIS BOOK

At the core of improv resides a healthy inclination toward questioning, bending, and breaking rules and norms. This skeptical attitude rightly extends toward many of the foundational ideas discussed within these pages. Some respected modern practitioners encourage their students to ignore or discard inherited rules altogether (often in much more acerbic or colorful words). The language and terminology of any field of learning, however, contains a great deal of the hard-earned wisdom of our artistic and pedagogic ancestors; and I would posit that it is foolhardy to dismiss such rich windows into the development of our craft needlessly.

Yes, rules that are deployed doggedly, understood poorly, or taught didactically are likely to result in constipated creativity. But it is shortsighted to blame the ideas themselves for burdening the act of collaborative play. The paradigmatic concept of "yes and...," for example, may lead to uninteresting improv lemmings inelegantly following each other off an improv cliff, or novice players becoming trapped in their mind intellectualizing every choice before they make it, or even chain improvisers into believing they must abandon their agency, dignity, and sense of good judgment. A carefully applied and nuanced application of this term, however, can provide players with a swiftly agreed upon scenic foundation from which to effortlessly build, encourage performers to delight in elevating the ideas of their peers, and remind an ensemble to see the value of every choice regardless of its source or initial sparkle. It is easy (and perhaps tempting) to dismiss an improv strategy when it is offered as a bludgeon rather than a precision instrument. And, frankly, most art gets at least momentarily a little clunky as artists start to consider and sharpen their skillset. Still, all disciplines – even one as apparently undisciplined as improv – benefit from insightful critique and focused contemplation of the ideas propagated and polished by those who helped define the modern movement.

And so, this dictionary earnestly seeks to helpfully define, unpack, and complicate the bounty of improv wisdoms that lurk within core concepts rather than reject (or celebrate) them outright, much in the spirit of embracing the momentum of all those trailblazers who have gone before rather than taking my own chisel to a new slab of rock to stubbornly make, at best, a modestly different wheel.

ABOUT GRATITUDE

It is truly humbling to contemplate the number of collaborators with whom I have shared the stage and classroom, or who, in their generous written accounts have spurred me into compelling theories and greater performance highs. Some of their names serve as my example characters here and in my accompanying Game Library. Other performers, designers, and fellow creators adorn the photographs scattered throughout the pages that follow. I am deeply indebted to the casts, companies, and classes that have shaped me, given me the space to fail and then try again and walked alongside me into wonderfully terrifying and unfamiliar improv terrain. In particular, I would like to acknowledge my two improv homes since 2003 that continue to fuel my sense of improvisation, play, and wonder. Sak Comedy Lab, in Orlando, Florida, has been a gem of a creative playground, allowing me both a regular opportunity to improvise alongside some of the best talent (scripted or non-scripted) in central Florida while also occasionally letting me commandeer their stage for my own long-form projects of love. And Rollins Improv Players, on the campus of my home academic institution, Rollins College, in Winter Park, Florida, continues to inspire and challenge me as I create and teach alongside the next generation of young spontaneous artists and activists who routinely push me to be bolder and better. Forgive my cowardice in not wanting to elevate a handful of names (such as Chelsea, Travis, Alexa, Chris, Emily…) for fear of who I might inadvertently omit but thank you all for making all that follows here possible.

NOTES

1. If you would like a more detailed working definition of improvisation, see the dictionary entry of that same name.
2. The terms "short-form" and "long-form" are often used to (partially and imperfectly) define the field of improvisational theatre. If you are unfamiliar with this language, these terms are considered at length in corresponding dictionary entries.
3. You can learn more about my journey with both scripted and non-scripted projects at www.improvdr.com.

The Ten Commandments

COMMANDMENT #1

As a high school performer in New Zealand during the late 1980s. I received a now dog-eared manual that included the "Ten Commandments of *Theatresports*," a series of guidelines to help inspire and motivate the novice mind. I'm not sure if these improvisational nuggets were ever quite formalized like this in other regions of the world that played in the franchise, but I distinctly remember them as part of my initiation into the craft of spontaneous performance.[1] Over 30 years later, I'm revisiting these foundational concepts as a way of framing this more comprehensive improv dictionary. If you're looking for a user-friendly summation of the key tenets that enable collaborative play, I still find these ideas cogent and provocative.

The first *Theatresports* Commandment is:

Thou shalt not block

For those of us who have played in the field of improv for any length of time, I'm certain we've all heard similar advice repeatedly throughout our training and careers. As I first encountered improvisation through *Theatresports*, I tend to defer to its terminology in my own teaching and directing, but many others use the term negating which is a direct equivalent. In its simplest sense, to block is to say "no" to your partner, to an offer, or perhaps even to the audience or general frame of the production. This choice, we are told, tends to grind the action of the scene to a halt, prevents discovery, and stops the flow of energy and ideas between the improvisers on the stage. We've all done it, experienced it, and winced as we've felt a scene's potential suddenly evaporate into a cloud of negotiation or half choices. It's a fitting first commandment, as most would agree that it is one of the cardinal sins of improvisation. For those who prefer emphasizing the positive, you could invert the rule to read, "thou shalt always accept" (or yield) which emphasizes our responsibility to take on the choices of our partners and make them work. This companion concept is addressed head-on in a later commandment (number five).

Complicating the Strategy

1. **Don't become the "no" police.** There can be a trap in over-emphasizing the danger of the word "no" itself, and a resulting temptation for novice improvisers to almost police each other when and if this shunned word appears in scenes. I know I'm not alone when I note that this is probably missing the point of the guideline, and in my own teachings, I stress that it is the *essence* or *energy* of a "no" that is problematic rather than the word itself. Here's an example I'll often provide: as an improviser I say to my partner, "You look ill. Are you feeling alright?" If my partner responds "Yes, I'm fine" with no sense of irony or illness, then this would actually block the intent and latent potential in my first choice. Here, a reply of "No, I'm feeling terrible, I haven't slept in days," would fully embrace my idea and help move the scene forward. The word "no" is obviously irrelevant in terms of accepting the premise as provided. As players and instructors, we must be sure we are offering this tool in its most helpful form and not making our fellow improvisers paranoid about a word.
2. **"No" energy is often worse than a block.** Similarly, *merely* responding in the affirmative but without any energy, conviction, or excitement is generally tantamount to a block or "no" as well. If you've improvised for more than a few weeks, you've likely experienced this situation on numerous occasions. You or your partner reluctantly say "yes" to a proffered suggestion, but the energy is so tepid or halfhearted that the scene is lucky to stumble forward with any grace or ease. This reemphasizes

the concept that blocking is not so much a word as it is a state of mind. For many, it may start with convincing ourselves to utter "yes" to our partners in a scene, but we're really aiming for a much more dynamic and energized level of acceptance.

3. **Using a "no" to add dynamism.** When we consider the energy of a block or "no," the path can become more fruitful and clear. If we seek to increase energy, tension, momentum, or interest by fully embracing the stakes and details offered to us, a block is rightly seen as a breach of this contract, or a moment when our fear gets the better of us and prevents us from opening the most powerful doorways. A parent-in-waiting confronts their child, "I forbid you from seeing that troublemaker again;" a boss interrogates an employee with stolen merchandise in their bag, "I believe you have company property on your person;" a childcare worker stands over a child and a poorly dug hole, "I was wondering if you knew the whereabouts of our class goldfish?" In each of these cases, and oh so many more, a strong "no" informed by a character's point of view would make for a solid next step if it clearly accepted all the givens provided. Our partners may even be hoping for a verbalized "no" in these cases to further the tension of the scene.

4. **A case for the transparent "no".** I also love "no" as a choice when the company and audience are all on the same page that this response is, in fact, a lie. In the three above examples of the love-struck teenager, the light-fingered employee, and the class-pet burying child, a seeming denial prefaced on clear stage action to the contrary, could unlock delightful potentials. Blocking is most destructive when it undermines the established given circumstances of a scene: "That's a really lovely boat you have, sis," "This isn't a boat and you're not my sister!" In the above three examples, a "no" delivered as a lie reinforces the given circumstances, creates a clear point of view, and also reflects an honest reaction to being caught. Such a move made with clarity and certainty is likely to activate rather than discourage the initial player.

5. **But perhaps say "no" to unnecessary conflict.** Something not to overlook in this philosophy is that pushing down your instincts or desire to block can also open up more interesting relationships and dynamics. The concept of conflict can be enticing as an improviser and grabbing at an energized "no" at the top of a scene can feel like a sure-fire way to jump-start the action. So often, however, such scenes devolve into negotiations, yelling matches, or stagnation when one character wants something and the other won't budge, or characters exchange a barrage of accusations without anyone accepting culpability. It's important to note that while conflict is often a key part of our theatrical stories, it isn't necessary for a scene to shine. Characters can be united in their efforts to overcome an unseen or environmental obstacle, pitting themselves against the world or a common enemy rather than each other. Or they can just be involved in a joyful and escalating dynamic filled with love and wonder. Emphasizing the need to embrace each other's early choices can be a form of preventive medicine in this regard, making it possible for something more nuanced than an argument to emerge.

6. **And definitely say "no" to ignorance.** When we teach accepting and yielding and the potential destructiveness of blocking, I'm not sure we always consciously or adequately discuss the import of the instigating choice or offer. If I'm aware that my partner is obliged to accept my choices on stage as an improviser, I believe that comes with a responsibility on my part to pitch situations and dynamics that will provide joy and agency. I don't ascribe to the notion that improv should honor *any* random or potentially hurtful, uninformed, or ill-advised thought or choice. This is how harmful stereotypes, racism, misogyny, homophobia, and the like can become perpetuated in our rehearsal halls and stages under a misguided chant of "always accept your partner's choice." In such instances, I would *strongly* advocate for a "no" onstage, *and* a candid post-show conversation where discomforts can be aired, heard, and acted upon. In this manner, we can commit ourselves to a process that is joyful and representative for all our collaborators and redouble our efforts to use the tools of improv (and *accepting* specifically) to embrace, elevate, and include.

The Bigger Picture

An even greater application of the principle, "Thou shalt not block" awaits when we consider that as artists we should not negate or limit the truths or experiences of our scene partners, and always be looking to more deeply understand, represent, and engage them in our play together on stage. This is not a small feat, but it strikes me that this is truly a worthy goal of a life spent in the art.

Related Entries: Accepting, Blocking
Connected Game: Reiterate/Repeat[2]

COMMANDMENT #2

Let us continue our stroll down improv memory lane with the second commandment that reads:

Thou shalt always retain focus

Focus stands as an integral and challenging element of improvisational theatre. In our scripted counterpart, you have a text, directors, and design team to expertly move focus around the stage and construct important moments so that the audience will, at least theoretically, catch the most significant details of the action. On the improv stage, the improviser assumes all these creative roles, and the likelihood is greatly increased that you'll encounter split focus (the dynamic of having multiple characters or areas of the stage competing for attention in a non-aesthetically pleasing fashion). Subsequently, focus provides a powerful tool and an important consideration in our work. Some of my own large-scale improv productions include as many as 15 improvisers all onstage at once, and so this has become an area of particular personal interest as a director.

Thinking about Focus

If we're in agreement that clear focus is an important aspect of our stage work, the question then becomes how do we navigate this effectively, especially in our larger scenes? Here are some ideas that I've been exploring of late.

1. **Know who the scene is about.** If you're operating in a more narrative/story-based mode, this can be easier than in more thematic or game-centered work. Generally speaking, if your protagonist is onstage (or antagonist), then the audience is likely to be interested in how they are responding to the action as it unfolds. Certainly, there can be sidebars and scenes that deliberately feature a supporting character or group, but it's easier to move focus around if there is a collective sense as to whose story is currently being featured. If this isn't you, or you are not directly involved in an exchange with this character currently in focus, your best bet is generally to exert patience unless grabbing the focus is highly deliberate and strategic.
2. **Pay attention to status.** In very large scenes, status becomes critical to move focus around

Figure 2.1 Chorus members of *It's All Greek to Me* generously throw focus elsewhere as the improvised action unfolds (Costume design: Kyra Wagner; Lighting design: Akin Ritchie). Photo credit: Tony Firriolo.

effectively, and if in doubt, players should defer to the highest-status character on stage, especially if this persona is currently unquestioned in their power. (This may or may not be the aforementioned protagonist.) Some warning here: this does not mean that the highest status person should monopolize the dialogue (which is a temptation and trap) but rather actively assess who may need some space or focus to move the story or game forward. In this way, the highest-status person can almost serve as a conductor, making sure all voices have a chance to contribute. In theatrical worlds, such as improv Shakespeare, where kings and queens tend to thrive, identifying the highest-status person is often a little easier than in contemporary pieces, where this might take a little more concentration on the unfolding action. It can also be extremely helpful for the high-status characters to leave larger scenes to ensure those who might not realistically speak in their presence have a chance to do so. If status is still a relatively new dynamic for you as a player and you want a primer, it still doesn't get much better than Keith Johnstone's chapter on the subject in *Impro*.[3]

3. **Defer to strong energies.** Connected to the status awareness above, players should also defer to large energies and emotions, especially as they enter the playing space. In addition to serving as a helpful theatrical strategy, this also can add an element of realism in that most of us would step back if an argument or confrontation suddenly stumbled into our path. This rule of thumb allows the actors who have taken focus to relish it for a while and pursue their truth without interruption. The high-status character can then help segue the focus elsewhere as the scene reaches its zenith or interrupt the action at an appropriate moment if this needs to occur in order to strategically suspend the ultimate climax of the scene.

4. **Stack your entrances.** Something that I've played with to some success in my long-form work is building the final scene by gradually layering entrances of the ensemble with those characters less connected to the greater problem or story entering first, and those most likely to be needed for the climax finally sharing stage as a later or final combination. This provides a growing stage picture and energy that helps the final steps of the rising action, while giving softer or simpler story arcs a chance to have their final moment before they are eclipsed by more charged hues. The key to this strategy is being brave if you consider yourself a supporting or more minor character and getting to the stage early, as it can create an odd energy lull if you wait too late in the game and don't have much of weight to offer to the rising action.

5. **Move, then talk.** In larger scenes, this is almost a must, but it can be oddly challenging if applying this wisdom isn't a tendency already in your improviser tool belt. While some actors might have a perfect sense of timing and be able to stealthily slip a Shakespearean droll aside into the mix without undercutting the scene's momentum, many of us do not, and there can be a true act hunger in larger group scenes. If characters move with clear purpose, preferably from weaker to stronger stage positions (from the margins of the stage toward the center, for example), this signals everyone that they are primed to take focus and make an offer. Such movements decrease the likelihood of improvisers interrupting or speaking over each other while placing the next speaker in a strong position to control the stage. This can also be a helpful trope when you're not in a large group scene and promotes varying the stage picture and utilizing the environment. The companion note would be that it's equally helpful for those who have had their moment in the sun to then move from stronger to weaker stage positions so as to make room for others.

6. **Choose your camp.** When there are clear and contrasting points of view emerging in the scene – perhaps between our protagonist and antagonist – it's helpful for you to know your camp as a character. Who do you side with and why? Whose fate is inextricably tied up to your own? Even if other characters are the primary drivers of the scene, this gives you an honest and active connection to the stakes and outcome of the action. This approach to crowd control has the added bonus of also informing your staging choices (should I go and stand behind my person to give their presence more volume?) and helps sell moments of tension and/or the climax of the scene (should I be rejoicing or commiserating at this moment?) It's certainly possible that there might be more than two camps, especially in larger ensemble pieces, but this strategy can lose its effectiveness if everyone becomes a camp of one.

An Exception

I'll confess I'm actually a fan of contained moments of chaos on stage where focus is not immediately clear or consistent; however, I'd preface that statement with some parameters. I think the dynamic needs to be used sparingly and with purpose. Focus needs to quickly return at the completion of a cluttered exchange. And any chaos needs to build and serve a greater purpose (such as intensifying energy before a significant structural or story moment). In this manner, the tight focus attained after the moment of discord possesses even a sharper edge in comparison. This dynamic serves as the focus of a later entry on Split Focus.

A Parting Thought

When we talk of retaining focus as improvisers, this also clearly extends to keeping our attention on the stage and the need to give all our energy to the action that is currently occurring in real time (as opposed to allowing our mind to wander away or start to contemplate our next choice or action). This is one of the greatest gifts and challenges in spontaneous theatre: prioritizing the here and now above all else as that will provide the doorway to the next honest moment. When we allow those other voices in our heads (our judges, our playwrights, our critics), we can easily lose the very foundational quality of our craft that drew us to this art form in the first place.

I've concentrated on larger group scenes above as these are innately more difficult, but these techniques are equally helpful in smaller scenic clusters: a third entrance shouldn't interrupt a clearly higher status character already onstage, for example, until acknowledged, unless this status bump is intended as a bold move. Moving focus poetically requires us to engage our director eye a little as improvisers and view a scene not exclusively through the lens of our individual character's needs and wants, or frankly, with the ego of our inner improviser craving maximum stage time.

Related Entries: Focus, Sharing Focus, Split Focus
Connected Game: All Together Now

COMMANDMENT #3

The third commandment states:

Thou shalt not shine above thy teammates

Improvisation is almost exclusively a team sport. A more recent development centers around the exploration of solo improv scenes and shows which strikes me as a mode that doesn't fully capitalize on the creativity that flows between different players, resulting in unexpected connections and discoveries. Perhaps this role of co-creator can be taken on by the audience to some degree – especially in interactive pieces – but my personal jury is out as to whether or not this is the most dynamic use of an improviser's craft. And yet, I digress. In *most* instances, improvisation is a team sport and the ethos of putting the team first is for many a critical underlying principle. The scene succeeds if and when the team succeeds. Individual success should not be placed above the success of the whole. To shine, in this context, does not honor your teammates.

There is a lot to like about this philosophy, and I'm not going to challenge it here as this is certainly an approach I esteem, endorse, and seek to follow in my work. But I do think there are some gray areas that deserve mention as they complicate this ideal in helpful ways.

The Nuances of Shining

1. **We should pitch and play to strength.** Whether it's a short-form game or a long-form structure, it is rare for every member of the team to have the same strengths and skill sets. It makes sense for the benefit of the show, our audience, and the craft for us to *set each other up to shine* and we shouldn't slink away from these moments. For example, most troupes have some members who excel at singing while others have strengths elsewhere. Audiences would greatly prefer to see the aforementioned members of the team step up for musical opportunities, while other teammates lean into character, staging, movement, narrative... It's important that we honestly know which of our tools are sharpest as improvisers, and that we use these to support the group and the show. I might relax this preference a little when we're in a workshop situation as this is a place for players to try and hone new skills, and I would also caution that pitching to strength should still include danger and not merely require an improviser to do that trick again that they did last week. In short-form shows, my favorite hosts find ways to pitch to the multitude of strengths contained in that evening's ensemble, thereby doing much of the work of sharing around the light in advance.

2. **Sometimes the show or scene isn't about you.** I come from both a scripted and improvisational background, and a lot of structural analysis in the former world has influenced how I see scenic work and narrative in the latter. Most stories (not all, especially in non-linear traditions) have a clear protagonist and this conceit can be extraordinarily

helpful when it comes to shaping our onstage action. If you are the protagonist in a long-form show, you are likely to have more – perhaps *considerably* more – stage time than those filling in supporting, cameo, or ensemble roles. It's always a good thing for performers to have an awareness of providing windows for under-featured teammates, but at times, the protagonist just needs to be onstage doing the next logical step. I don't imagine many of us would necessarily categorize this as "shining," but I think it's healthy and important for companies to embrace that, depending on the form and genre, some characters will appear more frequently than others.

3. **Don't conflate stage time with import.** In some ways, this advice connects to the above observation. I have directed and performed in many a long-form where the "leads" are much less interesting or memorable than the supporting players. It is a true gift to have the ability to know what a scene needs as an improviser, and to be able to execute this in a dynamic and succinct fashion. Most of us don't enter the field of improvisation to sit on the bench while others create, but it's an important patience to foster. If you're truly present in a performance, you will be ready to enter when the moment is right and know how to best serve the action.

4. **Don't write yourself out of a show.** If the energies of a performance are tending to favor another player or players, it can be tempting for us almost voluntarily to write ourselves out of the show, leaning back in our chair, or hiding in the wings with a sense of defeatism. This is very different to me in tone and intent than watching and relishing the successes and triumphs of our teammates with true joy and abandon. If we are lost in a cloud of cynicism, it is unlikely that our energy will be primed to make that quick Canadian Cross to establish environment, or provide a supporting offstage voice or sound effect, or rush in to help form the needed set piece or facilitate a fast scene change. If we are patiently observing with a sense of pleasure, we're more likely to be in the flow and the rhythm of the show, able and ready to make that little finesse that might seem small on the surface but is actually deeply enriching the work all the while reminding our teammates that we have their backs for anything they may need big or small. It's also, ironically, common for these contained moments of selfless finesse to open up larger performance opportunities later in the piece.

5. **Seek balance over the long stretch.** Depending on the style of play, there will be chances to achieve balance when you consider the bigger picture. In short-form pieces, it's not uncommon to sit out of a scene because you're not needed, and a thoughtful ensemble will find ways to pull less featured players more robustly into the action in subsequent games. In long-form pieces or runs, a quieter night might be offset with a shuffling of roles or opportunities for future performances. In both cases, I think a candid recounting of who had ample chances to shine on any given night alongside a joyful acknowledgment of those who may have facilitated these journeys can make sure the company feels equally invested and responsible for the process.

To Close

At its core, the third commandment is a great reminder for us to keep our focus on the group as a whole, to set each other up for joy and success, and for us to share wholeheartedly in the collective accomplishments of the ensemble. We shouldn't look to diminish or extinguish the lights of those around us, nor use our own to needlessly eclipse those with whom we share the stage, but rather combine our energies toward the common goal and good.

Related Entries: Shining, Winning
Connected Game: Raise the Stakes

COMMANDMENT #4

And the fourth commandment declares:

To gag is to commit a sin that will be paid for

Gagging is another of those omnipresent terms that appears in many modern improvisational schools and philosophies. It refers to the act of making a joke within a scene or improvised play merely for the sake of making a joke. It's generally an act of desperation from a player craving immediate and perhaps unwarranted audience approval. On a more insidious level, it can be considered as selling out the scene or your fellow players to get this immediate response in a way that is destructive rather than constructive – commenting or upending the premise or energy of a scene rather than reinforcing or elevating it. A subset of gagging is the act of pimping which generally gets this cheap laugh directly at the expense of a scene partner by making them do something – generally uncomfortable – for your own amusement. These tendencies are one of the quickest paths to undermining trust and cohesion within an ensemble. Again, it's likely that if you've been improvising for a while, you've certainly been the recipient of such a choice, and frankly, probably dealt out your fair share as well.

Modern improvisation is often conflated with comedy and most companies – save those that explicitly espouse a social justice focus – do tend to emphasize comedic products and strategies. This improv trap strikes me as being closely connected to this spoken or unspoken expectation. (It doesn't help our art form that there is a chain of stand-up comedy venues called "The Improv" for example.) To address this tendency, we need to scrutinize our goals as improvisers and calm the internal demon that craves the immediate feedback of audience laughter.

Assuaging the Gagging Beast Inside Us All

1. **Audience reactions come in all shapes and sizes.** I routinely remind my student improvisers is that there is a wide array of audience responses equally as desirable as laughter. You can't necessarily hear a smile of recognition when an audience member sees something familiar appear in the action. A nudge to a fellow audience member because they've said something recently like the line of dialogue on stage is similarly inaudible. As is a sigh of solidarity, a quiet gasp of surprise, or if the company is firing on all cylinders, a stifled sniffle if an audience member has been moved. Most of us would consider all these human reactions as markers of success, in addition to those moments of uproarious laughter when the perfect comedic connection occurs. If we only privilege and acknowledge laughter as a worthy outcome, however, we are undermining and diminishing the possibility of these other equally fantastic reactions.
2. **Invest and trust in your audience.** We often talk about playing to the top of our intelligence as improvisers: gagging usually (but not *always* as I observe below) works counter to this foundational philosophy. Depending on the venue we call home, or the explicit or implicit messages we send in our marketing and show theme, our audience may have built-in expectations, but I'm a fan and advocate of giving both a little of what the audience knows they want *and* pushing this boundary while at least gently challenging their expectations. You can train an audience to reward or discourage gagging in the way you frame these moments in a show. You can give them obvious humor *and* simultaneously mix in some thoughtful satire or social commentary. I fear that all too often we justify our own bad performance behavior with a wry "well that's what the audience wanted" when we haven't really given them an opportunity to want something else, something more nuanced, more astute, or more vulnerable. When I was introduced to *Theatresports*, it always felt like a serious scene might be just around the corner in any given show. This didn't always happen, and in fact it probably *rarely* happened, but I loved that the frame of the show allowed for such a possibility.
3. **Comedic patience is often rewarded.** I hope you've experienced the moment on stage when you have seen the obvious joke, the audience has seen the obvious joke, and there is almost a mutual agreement that it is too easy or cheap, and the gag is then skipped and replaced with a second or third choice. This creates improv magic and builds a connection and trust between the players and their patrons. Similarly, when a scene starts out with patience and confidence, almost ignoring any audience reaction or the lack thereof, seeds become planted for rich connections and laughter that will occur further down the line. Gagging, in this instance, can almost feel like "naming the game" and sap a scene, especially in its infancy, stalling it from finding an energized trajectory. Allowing the balance or platform of a scene a little room to breathe and find itself strikes me as particularly important.
4. **Shine the light on your partner.** If gagging lurks in your DNA, it can be helpful to shift your focus and think about ways to offer up comedic potentials to your scene partner instead. Such generosity can be under-appreciated and overlooked, but this approach also minimizes the potential for pimping or unwelcome offers and endowments. If you set yourself up as the target or butt of the joke, this whimsy offers a delightful sense of playful permission. This is almost the target rhyming equivalent of gagging, where you see the potential for a laugh but rather than take it yourself, you skillfully craft the setup or appropriate conditions for your partner to execute the moment (or, perhaps, as above, skip the obvious joke entirely to create an even richer moment).
5. **Double down on relationship and story.** Many improv traditions emphasize the importance of connections as a source of audience joy and laughter, and these conditions are much more likely to emerge organically when our attention is focused on our scene partner, our point of view, and the given circumstances of the world. When we are more deeply vested in our characters and not "wearing them lightly" we're also less tempted to have our mind wander off to construct a quip

or punchline. As many have said before me, we're typically funniest when we're most relaxed and ourselves – when we're just chatting with friends over drinks. We're less inclined to gag if we have that same sense of investment in the realities of our scene and relationships.

One More Thing

The fourth commandment also talks about the cost of gagging as it's a sin "that will be paid for," and relentless joking at the expense of a scene and your partners will certainly erode trust, interrupt momentum, dissipate story integrity, and possibly train your audience to want little else but a string of jokes. I consider some exceptions to the "no gagging" rule in a later "G" entry listed below and have linked a game that flexes our humor muscle as, ironically, I think joke construction is a seldom-taught skill that many short-form companies expect of their players. That being said, improvising in order to have a venue where you can gag strikes me as similar to buying a Ferrari just to drive it around the block on Sundays. Sure, you *could do that*, but why would you when it can do *so much more*?

> **Related Entries:** Gagging, Pimping, Shivving
> **Connected Game:** My Movie

COMMANDMENT #5

The fifth commandment extols:

> **Thou shalt always be changed by what is said to you**

So much of improvisational theatre requires combining and justifying the various ideas of those involved. This commandment voices a great reminder that it is not enough to merely give lip service to your partner's idea or offer, but that you must allow it to push you off your preordained course. For those of us inclined to planning or thinking ahead (I am certainly in this camp), we should probably indelibly tattoo this motto somewhere on our body so that we keep it front of mind in our work.

One of the earlier exercises I use when teaching novice improvisers is often Word at a Time Story. In this narrative game, each player, typically standing in a circle, provides the next sequential word to a spontaneous story. (You can read a full description of the exercise in my Game Library.) Among the many helpful lessons one can glean from this simple little game is that the more you try to drag the story back to your own vision, the more likely you are to destroy it or grind the process to a screeching halt. Conversely, while efforts may not construct the "best" stories known to humanity (especially if it's your first try), the results are nearly always something wonderfully unique that no *one* member of the group would have written alone. This little moment of improv narrative wizardry can't happen if we're not all willing to drop our personal agendas and be *changed* by the offers of our teammates and collaborators.

There can be so many things weighing against us in this battle to be flexible and resilient. If you've subliminally planned out a few next steps, an unexpected wrench in the works can throw you off your game and preconceived notion for how the scene "should" turn out. If you like control or struggle with trust, truly letting a new direction emerge can elevate your fear levels as you now must deeply invest your energy into your partner(s). If the proffered idea strikes you as inferior or bland or trite or over-original, it can be exceedingly difficult to abandon your seemingly more nuanced or colorful or unique or organic choice. But this is what improv and, one could argue, theatre in general is about: change. And improv specifically is about the risk of adding energies together in new and surprising ways and finding the unexpected connections therein. Otherwise, we'd just do these make-em-ups by ourselves!

Fully embracing new offers can be trickier than it sounds, especially if at first glance the choice is unusual or perhaps even seems unhelpful. Here are a few possible strategies:

Ways to Embrace Change

1. **Slow it down.** When a new idea enters the stream of our scene, it can be tempting – especially if you feel that you're in a groove – to pass over the unexpected element. Fight that instinct. If you're surprised as the improviser, then chances are you'd be surprised as the character as well. It's okay not to know how to react, especially if the new information strikes you initially as a non-sequitur. It's okay not to immediately make "sense" of this new choice. It's okay to take a breath and to process the offer. In fact, if the scene was hurtling in a certain direction, this may be the true gift of a less-than-predictable choice as it may break the routine.
2. **Take a gut check.** In some ways, these strategies are a little cumulative. After you've slowed down, take a breath, make sure you've really understood

the nuance and intent of your partner's offer, and then take a gut check. This term was game changing when I was introduced to it as it tackled an issue that I was struggling to address as an instructor. A gut check is a (usually silent) moment when as a character you allow yourself to have a true emotional reaction to what *just* happened. It marks a scenic moment that might have otherwise seemed trivial as one of great import. If you tend toward the intellectual as a player, this also encourages a heightened sense of emotionalism which can truly be liberating and exciting to experience and to watch.

3. **Avoid shifting blame or focus.** I might be splitting hairs here a little, and this advice is largely contingent upon the type of offer being provided by your partner, but if it has a revelatory or accusatory tone, it can be tempting as an improviser to quickly throw back a similar charge: "You just stole that donut," might be followed by, "Only because you ate all the cereal in the apartment...," thereby moving the focus back to the other player. I believe assuming an air of culpability, more often than not, opens new possibilities and allows your partner's choice room to really bloom and gain significance. When we instinctively rally back with an accusation of our own, the scene usually devolves into an argument and little more.

4. **Combine, don't discard.** If you're surprised by your partner's choice and already had something really interesting going, you don't need to completely disregard your prior choices and actions. In fact, if these were working well for you, the audience will probably feel quite disappointed if you then just throw them away. However, you will generally be better served if your immediate priority is tending to the new element that has emerged. Gut check and lean into that choice and trust that the prior reality will infuse and inform the scene. For example, if I am a parent in a scene caring for a child, and someone comes in and needs my services as a tax accountant, I should fully embrace this new pathway, but it would be remiss for me as an improviser (and as a parent) to forego my prior obligations to the established child. The tension between these two facets of my character is, in fact, likely to be a great source of energy in the scene that follows.

5. **Emotionally justify the new choice.** Especially if you're surprised by the offer, or you are inclined to intellectualize as a player in general, there can be a huge temptation to justify the unexpected new information dispassionately and rationally. This tendency can also lead to those dreaded talking head scenes that we all seek to avoid as improvisers. Again, building on the prior suggestions, such a cerebral stance will likely disarm or explain away the gift from your partner, as is potentially the case with my donut example above. When the choice lands, seek an emotional truth first, trusting that a broader justification will follow if it's necessary.

6. **Add stakes and urgency.** When your scene is faltering a little or struggling to find an organic path forward, we can diminish our chances of an enjoyable dramatic outcome when we sift or sort through the offers of our scene partners in search of something "good." Remember that almost any choice can generate a strong and dynamic reaction if we invest sufficiently. (The connected exercise below models this truth well.) Allowing ourselves to be changed with such gusto can truly serve as a great gift for the scene and is a dynamic way to honor and recognize the contribution of our scene partner.

A Final Consideration

The audience wants to see us go through the door previously unopened and embrace the choice that is at first glance seemingly implausible. Theatrical improv might adopt a competitive frame, particularly in short-form traditions such as *Theatresports* and *ComedySportz*; however, we must be vigilant as players that this conceit does not infuse our scene work together on stage. Performing with "emotional armor" or a stance that is never willing to cede the high ground can become exhausting to act opposite.

I would also muse that in a world that is becoming increasingly polarized, watching characters change and improvisers accept a multitude of possibilities is a pretty radical and dynamic act all in itself. If you subscribe to the practice of show postmortems, this commitment to deep listening, gut checking, honoring our partner's insights, and adopting a willingness to take on new information with grace and kindness, strikes me as an excellent model for enabling company change and inclusiveness as well. After all, if we are not ultimately willing to change based on what we hear from our artistic partners or the greater communities around us, we are doomed to have the same conversations and battles into perpetuity.

Related Entries: Breaking Routines, Bulletproof, Change
Connected Game: It's Tuesday

COMMANDMENT #6

In the spirit of this *Theatresports* commandment, I'll keep this introduction brief and just observe:

Thou shalt not waffle

I'm not sure that the concept of waffling has gained as much traction in North American improv as some of the more universal terms mentioned within *Theatresports'* Ten Commandments. Wimping – for me, a related term – is referenced later in this taxonomy and I think it is a more familiar phrase for many. I consider waffling as almost a subset of this broader concept. While wimping refers to the act of halfhearted engagement with a choice or providing a postponing energy, waffling is the verbal manifestation of this to the nth degree. To waffle is to become verbally effusive, filling any perceived empty stage space with an often-meandering diatribe that might only loosely have a relation to the topic and action at hand. My prior sentence might be an example! For those of us who are inclined to be more verbal than physical in our craft, this is a particularly common trap as it allows us to escape into the seeming safety of our words where we don't have to interact with our partners or be changed by their offers and insights (a trap discussed in my prior entry).

It's worthy to note that instructors often warn of "talking heads" scenes where actors essentially stand motionless, leaving the rest of their bodies disengaged while typically "witty" dialogue ensues. To my knowledge, there isn't an equivalent warning for excessively focusing on our physicality: "That was a great scene, but there wasn't enough dialogue and you were both just 'moving bodies' the whole time…" This might be the clearest indication of the veracity and ongoing import of this particular commandment that encourages us to talk less in our work.

Engaging Our Whole Selves as Improvisers

In the battle many of us face against our waffling tendencies on the improv stage, let's consider some strategies to increase our physical contributions. I've provided these in a loose ranking from most intense to less so…

1. **Don't speak.** This might not be the best approach to try without forewarning your scene partners, and perhaps it would be wise to initially explore this technique in a workshop or closed rehearsal, but if you are a lover of the word, challenge yourself to make it through a scene or a game with no dialogue. I think this is innately more interesting if your character *can* speak but is actively choosing not to, so it's not an invitation to do a series of scenes where your characters are all gagged and tied up or you're an animal or piece of furniture. If you're familiar with the communication concept of utterances (sighs, grunts, and other non-language-based speech acts), I think these are well within the spirit of this approach as you still want to be making clear and specific choices for your partner to incorporate into the scene. And obviously, you don't lose at the exercise should you break this pattern at the "perfect" moment and provide fitting dialogue when it's the strongest choice for the scene or if your partner needs your verbal presence for the story to move forward. Silent or Gibberish scenes are, frankly, a great training device in general if they're not currently in your repertory.

2. **Give yourself a word limit, version #1.** As the scene begins, give yourself a low word target for the scene as a whole, perhaps ten or twenty words. As with the strategy above, this isn't so much about hitting this self-imposed target precisely, but rather embracing the invitation to make strong physical, emotive, and full-bodied choices rather than focusing all your creative energy on your dialogue. How much can you communicate about your relationships to others on stage with a look, gesture, simple touch, or staging choice? Don't bother actively counting the words as this will likely put you back in your head, but rather aim for this approximate number, and make each word important, deliberate, and rich with meaning. Literally slowing down your speech and reducing your word count might also unlock interesting new characters and verbal patterns to add to your stock as a bonus.

3. **Give yourself a word limit, version #2.** This is based on the game I know as Sentences. In short, each player receives a number from the audience and that number denotes how many words will be in each of their sentences for the duration of the scene. Again, this is about the spirit of the technique rather than the letter of the law, so select a smaller number for yourself and strive to answer in sentences of approximately that number. As is the case with the challenge above, this strategy is about streamlining your speech acts and making every word count while leaning more heavily into *how* you say those words and the way your body supports your subtext. Gut checks (discussed in the prior commandment) further support this

goal of deepening your emotional commitment and connection.

4. **Deploy the "ten second" rule.** This is something I came up with for my on-campus troupe that tends to favor language over physicality. We'll occasionally use it as a training technique but there's no reason you couldn't self-impose it for some of your scenes on any given night. Simply put, for the first ten seconds of the scene you need to silently focus on creating your environment and your relationship to it and anyone else present on stage. In a workshop situation, I'll ring a bell or give a similar signal that dialogue can now start: the key in this moment is not to effusively announce all the things you wanted to say for the last ten seconds or painstakingly describe your past actions but rather trust that you've communicated sufficiently to just make the next logical and small step. The "ten seconds" is obviously very much a conceit and I'll allow this time to linger as long as it is helping the improvisers explore their physical reality in a dynamic fashion.

5. **Focus on the environment in general.** It's often the case that if we haven't created dynamic elements of the environment during the first phase of our scene, these elements will never make it to the stage. You can't realistically place a mimed billiards table center stage, for example, if characters have clearly been walking through that area for the first half of the scene, so we need to get these formative objects in place quickly. Viola Spolin utilizes a "three large objects to define a space rule" which is helpful in this regard. If you self-define as a verbal improviser, deliberately focusing on the environment can truly enable a whole new category of discoveries.

6. **Take a movement or dance class.** I have never been an able sports player – I've always described myself as an "indoors kid" – and am subsequently much more innately comfortable with verbal rather than physical skills. But as part of my formal theatre training, and as necessitated by casting, I have taken dance classes (predominantly ballroom) and had to perform choreography quite often in musicals. I'm certainly no solo dancer, especially as I get older and further from those days, but it did imbue in me a certain physical bravery. If you are a "talking heads" improviser, this probably won't change noticeably after a well-intentioned two-hour workshop: you need to step outside your comfort zone and put in the work. Whether it's directly connected to improv and theatre, such as a jazz, mask, stage combat, or contact improv class, or more generally focused, such as yoga, gymnastics, or martial arts training, it's likely to give you confidence and a movement vocabulary that can greatly elevate your craft. And you're likely to meet other artists or people who aren't improvisers which is a plus in and of itself as we can tend to get trapped into small improv clusters!

An Exceptional Circumstance

As I've mused on these commandments, the exceptions nearly always take a similar form, in that you should happily break the rule if it is the manifestation of a greater scenic game or the essence of a characterization choice. I believe it was at the Players Workshop of the Second City where I first encountered the concept of a Chatterbox scene where one character spews out a stream of consciousness in response to almost any prompt from their teammates. This would be a good example of using a tendency toward verbosity as an asset rather than a burden, but we should probably be aware of the warning signal if such a character emerges with surprising frequency in our scenes.

I continue to wage my own battle against my personal waffling demons, so I offer these suggestions as someone who still utilizes and needs these techniques in their own craft. I'm also aware of the irony that this consideration on waffling is one of my longer entries…

Related Entries: Physicality, Talking Heads, Verbal Skills, Waffling
Connected Game: Sentences

COMMANDMENT #7

Our journey through my dog-eared manual of *Theatresports* commandments continues with:

When in doubt, break the routine

Patterns are an interesting occurrence in theatre and art, often providing a foundation or backdrop for the journey that follows. Whether we call these initial story patterns platforms, routines, given circumstances, or the balance of a scene, this commandment observes that there is an innate value in disturbing or upending these initial scenic trends at opportune moments. In the scripted realm, I think of this disruption as an ignition – a spark that sets the rising action in motion – although such pattern ruptures are by no means limited to this particular dramatic moment. In the improv realm, there is a tension (perhaps unspoken) between schools of thought that prioritize perpetuation of the pattern in order to elevate a game, and those that recommend breaking these patterns to facilitate new story discoveries and directions. In the parlance with which I'm most comfortable, the former instinct serves as an example of **parallel action**, while the latter prefers **complementary action**: parallel actions tend to mirror or replicate prior choices, while complementary actions connect in causal, thematic, or justifying ways. There are certainly advantages to both approaches. Here are some that jump to mind:

Moments to Uphold the Routine

1. **You don't know what is going on.** If a scene is up and running, the audience is enjoying it, but you're unsure as to the specifics, a paralleling choice can be your best bet. If your entrance is needed to add energy and dynamism to the scene, mirroring and extending the energies already present will give you some time to "get up to speed" as a fellow player without inadvertently stepping on what has already been created. Obviously, this is not an ideal improvisational situation, and we should all strive to actively observe the scenes unfolding before us, but there are unquestionably times that we can clearly sense that a scene needs our presence from the wings while being equally unsure as to what exactly our presence should add or bring.
2. **A game is building that hasn't peaked.** Being the third chef overwhelmed by the dinner rush, the fourth student ill-prepared for the final looming in the morning, or the fifth clueless home repair specialist looking for the cause of the leak, are all examples of potentially elevating a clear game that is unfolding. In these situations, thinking different or adding a new color or nuance may, in fact, puncture the game or have the effect of "naming" or "calling out" (and thereby puncturing) the very dynamic that is creating great joy and energy: "It looks like none of you plumbers can find that leak…" These types of game-centric scenes might eventually benefit from a complementary action down the road to help them phase into a second wave or act, but a premature shift in focus might dissipate the very playfulness that served as the hallmark of the work.
3. **There are a lot of characters on stage.** I've written in my musings on the second commandment about the challenges of retaining and moving focus in large group scenes, but this strikes me as another important moment when parallel points of view are extremely helpful. If you're entering a group scene that is becoming fragmented or difficult to follow, immediately and boldly allying with an existing character, camp, or perspective can help elevate the choices of others already on stage and assist more successful focus exchanges. This may particularly help in the latter portions of a scene or long-form exploration when you might be focusing on your thesis and antithesis and finally looking for an out or "winner."
4. **A character or point of view needs an ally.** There are times that our best intentions as improvisers might lead us into scenarios where we inadvertently perpetuate an injury, uphold an archaic stigmatizing belief (without satire or commentary), or place a character in a role that may trigger the performer or audience. In these hopefully rare cases, I think redistributing the volume of the scene is critical and we can do this by clearly mirroring or sharing the point of view of the character at risk. Paralleling might not be the only viable strategy in these moments, but I can see it having value, especially if a more nuanced approach isn't immediately available.

Moments to Break the Routine

1. **The energy or dynamism of the scene is stalling.** It's not an uncommon feeling to be in a scene and for it to feel as if it's just *stuck*. We're making breakfast, and then we're making breakfast, and then we're making breakfast… Someone else enters and… making breakfast at this point probably isn't likely to put the exploration on a firmer footing. I'm a big advocate of complementary actions in these moments. I've given a rough and ready definition above, but in some sense, a routine break would be providing a new context, rationale, or element that is related to but not a duplication of the action already underway. We're out of eggs, our breakfast date has arrived early, the gas stove has set the curtains on fire… I sometimes use the (albeit strange) conceit of "why did the playwright choose to show us this action on this day" as a way of nudging the story forward to the thing that doesn't always happen or the unique spark that will offset the balance and create momentum.
2. **The scene is meandering over well-worn terrain.** Especially in the short-form tradition where it is not unlikely that we might face similar scene ask-fors or initiations, it's common to face improv déjà vu. If you're taking the first steps down an

improv path that you have been on many times before, I think breaking both the character's and the improviser's routine is critical if you are to keep the exploration fresh and playful. We want to be careful of being needlessly "original" (an upcoming commandment), but we should be receptive to opening new doorways and options that may reveal unexplored potentials.

3. **The scene or characters have not been ignited.** I think this advice is a little more contingent on a long-form setting as a three-minute scene can get away with remaining in stasis with charm and an emotional build. In long-form, however, especially styles that are narrative, linear, or character-based, we generally need the world as we know it to become tilted, threatened, or at odds. This isn't to necessarily suggest that the very first beat of the play requires a major break in routine – scripted plays may loiter in the balance for multiple scenes at first. But watching numerous vignettes in a row consisting of characters just doing what they always do is unlikely to start to generate energy and interest for you as players or for your audience.

4. **Your improv or scene has become complacent or predictable.** If we always play the same sorts of roles, or start our favorite games in the same way, or lead scenes into well-worn and previously successful shtick, then we're probably in need of some personal routine breaking. If you are fortunate enough to have a regular and frequent outlet, this is perhaps more likely to occur than those in our community who are playing infrequently, although I think unhelpful trends can certainly happen either way. This is perhaps the most meta interpretation of this commandment that can encompass our craft and tendencies on a more global level. There is a radical potential in improv to push toward change and the new, and we need to be wary of complacency and the expediency of the known. So, if your scenes are starting to become all too familiar, break up your own patterns and routines.

One Last Thing

As my bio divulges, I'm very much into devising complex narrative long-form (sometimes two hours or more in length) and so while I can see a value in paralleling others' choices at times, I generally would fall into the routine breaker column as I've found in my own work it is very difficult to stimulate new material and nuances if the company heavily favors "same" over "different." I think this also reveals my innate preference for teaching improv through the lens of story rather than game, although the older I get, the more these two terms seem to be almost interchangeable. Furthermore, there is something enticing about fully embracing this general philosophy of breaking established norms, practices, and approaches to our stories and our craft as a community. I think this is both the unique potential and challenge of improvisational theatre: we should always strive toward sharing new stories, including new voices in our casts, and merrily wrestling with new ways to tackle the fears and rewards of the unknown. Otherwise, we're just endlessly perpetuating a routine, which will inevitably become dull and ineffective.

Related Entries: Balance, Breaking Routines, Complementary Action, Parallel Action
Connected Game: CAD Bell

COMMANDMENT #8

The eighth commandment observes:

To wimp is to show thy true self

I find the phrasing of this statement particularly interesting as in many ways it implies that our "true self" is perhaps not laudable and that most of us are fear-based in our actions. (The next commandment offsets this a little.) As noted in an earlier entry, wimping is the act of not fully investing yourself in your own offers and ideas or those of your teammates. If we consider the ideal acceptance as the energy of a "yes, and…," and a block as that of a "no," the wimp splits the difference and is usually denoted as a "yes, but…" The "but" in this case usually provides conditions, modifiers, or postponements, all of which can have the tendency to whittle away the momentum and potential of the scene. I tend to use the image of someone at the gym who doesn't frequent it often (which would be me) and as a result struggles to lift the weights. One who wimps in a scene is equally unable to lift their weight and commit to the actions as they emerge.

As we become more experienced (and proficient?) as improvisers, the ways in which wimping can infect our work can become more subtle. You may be avoiding the actual "yes, but…" and yet still fall into other performance patterns that have a similar energy-sapping effect. So, for new and seasoned improvisers alike, I offer the following warning signs that you may need to return to the improv gym for a few extra rotations...

Signs You Might Be Wimping

1. **You like to discuss, at length, others' offers.** I've written about the trap of waffling, the sixth commandment, and this is the word lover's most likely wimping approach. Our partner makes a choice, and we then verbally weigh the pros and cons, point out inconsistencies or potential fallacies, or just generally stall the action with our language. More times than not this will have the probably unconscious but desired effect of postponing or dismissing the new idea that might have pushed us onto a path hitherto unexplored.
2. **Your response has an "or" energy.** It can be hard to let go of a preconceived notion or idea for a scene, and if we're not careful, we can use the preferred language of improv in ways that undermine its message or intent. If my partner, for example, offers "Let's go to the movies," and I respond with "Yes, *and* let's go to the museum first!" my "and" is really operating as an "or." I'm providing an alternative rather than supporting the instigating offer and the scene will now probably focus on the museum rather than the suggested movie theatre.
3. **Your standard scenic energy is deadpan.** As is the case with most of these foundational improv tools, they are as much about *how* we say something as they are about *what* we say. Our words might appear accepting, but if we routinely withhold our emotional storehouse, this suggests that we are not fully committing to the energy of our scene work. Of course, a deadpan character might be the pitch-perfect choice for a specific scene, but if you fall into this stance often, it's likely that it has become a mechanism for holding your partner's choices away at arm's length.
4. **You stood (largely still) for the whole scene.** Just as a deadpan character tends to limit the emotional exchanges and depth of a scene, a reluctance to fully engage your whole body might indicate that you are resisting the physical gifts of your fellow players. Not all premises will invite crawling through escape tunnels being chased by rabid rats, but just as we can deflect verbal offers and potential, so too can we ignore or dismiss ways to truly "yes, and..." the physical world as it appears before us.
5. **You end scenes largely as you started them.** As we unpack the final commandments, it becomes apparent that they all tend to inform each other and this observation very much snugs into the fifth commandment that promotes being changed in our scenes and craft. If it's not uncommon for you to play characters who, as the scene comes to a close, have not transformed, tilted, or developed, this may be a signal that you are not fully taking on the choices and endowments of your peers. For those of us who tend toward high-status characters, this can be a particular trap as such a position can almost empower us to rebuke or brush off ideas that may not align with our own expectations.
6. **Your scenes routinely end up where you hoped or planned they would.** Again, in a nutshell, if this is your norm, then you're probably not really embracing the ideas of those you play with to the fullest extent possible. If you're not being surprised, you're not paying attention.

Some Closing Advice

And this returns us to the initial phrasing of this commandment in that "our true self" in the cases listed above is probably performing from a place of control and fear, and that need for safety is what our potentially ingenious wimping strategies are revealing to our fellow players and audience. If you recognize yourself in some of these patterns (and I surely do), it can be helpful to recommit to simply prioritizing and using new ideas as they emerge. You can: **(1) reduce your reliance on language; (2) follow your partner's idea before your own; (3) explore characters with a wider emotional range; (4) begin scenes in unexpected physical positions; (5) invert your status tendencies and embrace comeuppances;** and **(6) spend scenes exclusively building on the ideas of your teammates.**

Let's all strive to lift our appropriate weight in our scenes together.

Related Entries: Fear, Postponing, Wimping
Connected Game: Ad Campaign

COMMANDMENT #9

It's the penultimate commandment and it declares:

Those who try to be clever are not, while those who are clever, do not try

I view this commandment as a reminder and a charge to just be yourself. Bring your own idiosyncrasies and perspectives to the stage and think less about trying to appear clever or funny. I touch on this concept a little in the fourth commandment that focuses on the habit of gagging or making jokes on the improv stage in ways that typically don't best serve the action or story. If your primary concern is trying to make the audience laugh, you are likely your own worst enemy in reaching success. When I'm in the audience, there are few energies that make me *less* inclined to laughter than this perceived desperation, and I do not think I am unique in this regard.

I have a theory that there are two ways we can approach our work as actors in terms of our relationship to the theatrical mask of performance. We can either *wear* this mask of characterization to hide ourselves as the improviser, escaping our own experiences and feelings by assuming those of another. Or we can use the theatre as an opportunity to *remove* the mask that society and convention have placed upon us, and spend our stage time revealing and exploring different facets of ourselves. Clearly, both approaches have merit and a place in our craft. The first, in particular, can be an important method of "Atticus Finch-ing" by placing ourselves in the shoes of others. In terms of the current commandment in question, however, I would offer that the second method of removing our masks might be a fruitful antidote to ill-advisedly elevating cleverness or the "funny" above all else.

Bringing More of Yourself to the Stage

1. **Don't wear your character "too lightly."** If you're assuming a character purely as a comedic device or prop, it will generally show. Even in a brief short-form scene, we can tend to a character's backstory and seek a portrayal based on our own experiences, fears, or dreams. A tell-tale sign that you may be falling into this trap is if you are overly aware of the audience or tend to break the "fourth wall" and look into the auditorium for approval.
2. **Lean into a personal passion or experience.** We're better situated to create interesting and revealing characters if we risk bringing facets of ourselves to the stage. A comedic frame may not be the most welcoming venue for our heavier stories and encounters but connecting to different roles you play in the real world (parent, friend, child, student, co-worker, lover, immigrant, sibling, etc.) will open up a different potential for discovery and connections. You'll also have a better likelihood of *earning* laughs played in this more personal territory than frantically *grabbing* for them in characters and scenarios that are completely alien to you.
3. **Trust that your honest reaction is enough.** You've probably had that moment on the stage when the audience has erupted into laughter, perhaps unexpectedly, when you just said something that was "you." Don't undervalue the joy garnered from moments of honest recognition. I've worked with a lot of improvisers who were initially dissuaded from exploring the field as they didn't think of themselves as "funny," and yet almost without exception when they were just being honest, they routinely crafted incredibly humorous (or provocative, or touching, or engaging) moments and situations.
4. **Know what's happening in the world.** Let's face it, if we don't know much, we can't bring much to our work. You have to understand the news, current affairs, pop culture, societal trends, and the like in order to access this material knowingly on stage. This is perhaps the biggest trap for those of us who come to improv from a theatrical or performance background as the arts can tend to exclusively consume our time and resources. But the more we grow and become multi-faceted and informed, the more we can access in our work. Know more so you can bring more.

In Summation

Take the risk of being yourself. The improv world doesn't have another you yet, so you're needed.

> **Related Entries:** Cleverness, Gagging, Obvious, You
> **Connected Game:** Passion Statements

COMMANDMENT #10

And we've reached the end of our journey exploring the gifts of *Theatresports'* Ten Commandments unless you've stumbled into this entry first, in which case, "welcome" and feel free to explore the other nine once you're finished here!

The tenth and final commandment opines:

When thy faith is low, thy spirit weak, thy good fortune strained and thy team losing, be comforted and smile, because it just doesn't matter!

It can prove difficult to retain a sense of perspective in our art, and those of us who have spent years working in this field may struggle in particular to balance a commitment to the art with a joyfulness in the execution of that art. I don't know where I first heard the adage that improvisers *play* rather than *work*, but this strikes me as an important reminder. I would like to think that our efforts could and dare I hope *should* matter, especially as theatre in general and improv more specifically are often maligned or undervalued in society, but I do agree with the overall tone of whimsy in this sentiment: we are *players* and we foster a collaborative world of play.

Some Etiquette Suggestions

So how do we retain a sense of joy and perspective in our work as improvisers?

1. **Take the competition seriously.** These commandments are very much focused on the specific improv event of a *Theatresports competition*, and this framing element is integral to the flow and climax of that particular franchise. There are teams, a host or umpire, guest judges, and an audience rooting on their favorites. You may not be playing this specific format, but a lot of short-form relies on similar tropes to create a dynamic and entertaining event. At the end of such shows, it's not unusual for audience members to commiserate a loss with team members or truly celebrate a well-secured victory. Some shows have a built-in "wink" that acknowledges that the competition is a conceit, but if this isn't the case, enjoy the opportunities such a frame provides. If your team has become the underdogs of the evening, relish that position. If you have generated heat and a rebel-like persona, that can add great value to the show if you allow it to grow and develop.
2. **Don't take the competition too seriously.** While many improv shows deploy this frame, I find fewer things more off-putting as an audience member or teammate than the improvisers *actually* becoming competitive. By all means, use the challenge of the evening as motivation to play at your highest level, but the audience experience, and frankly that of the cast as a whole, should always eclipse any lurking individual desires for success. Focus on the caliber of your collaboration, the arcs of your stories, and the journey of the evening as a whole. Scores, winners, and trophies should remain as gimmicks. Holding onto disappointments from the evening will only put you in your head for the next round or scene.
3. **Take the work seriously.** If we are committed to growing as performers, creating dynamic performances, and at least gently pushing the boundaries and possibilities of live performance, I do think we should take our pursuit of this craft seriously. By this, I mean we should conduct ourselves professionally, respect the process of creativity and that our collaborators might have different processes and needs than our own, and bring a sense of focus and commitment to our time together and our work onstage. I am particularly interested in improv frames that could rightly be described as challenging, ornate, and perhaps even a little impossible by design, and such work needs a reasonably high level of preparation and rehearsal. Dedication in these situations is vital.
4. **Don't take the work too seriously.** There are certainly moments when a rehearsal or performance may become tense. Performers may be developing a new critical skill or technique, material may move into more emotional or complex terrain, as a team you may lose the narrative thread or experience times when trust or listening has become eroded. It's important to take a breath in these moments and embrace the "failure," the difficulty, and the learning. Most of us love improv because the results are so unpredictable. Stumbling is part of the journey. I've been known to say in my classes that the mark of a professional improviser isn't that they stumble less often, but rather that they are able to bounce back from these stumbles with greater agility and joy. Strive to be the improviser who can laugh in the face of failure!
5. **Take feedback seriously.** I don't think there are many performance art practices that routinely hold postmortems or note sessions after every single performance: in the scripted world, this typically stops (excluding major catastrophes) after the final previews. We are much more likely to grow and develop in our craft if we honor this tradition and use this time well to reflect on our struggles and successes. Be present for these conversations. If you're in the development process (or perhaps just in general), take written notes. Remember that the note you need to hear most might come from anyone in the greenroom. Don't fall into the trap of not recognizing that the newest troupe member or an ancillary participant might have the observation that you need to hear right now in order to grow. Practice your generous and active listening backstage as well as on it.
6. **Don't take feedback too seriously.** Wild and uproarious applause and laughter from the

audience is great, but don't let this feedback mute observations from your team if their experience was quite different in that self-same moment. If you are confused by a note, or offended, or disappointed, take the risk of sitting with the feedback rather than becoming defensive, angry, or committed to a narrative of justification. We're improvisers, so most of us can provide a rationale for making any number of potentially awkward or injurious choices on the stage. You might still end up disagreeing with a note once you've gone away and mused on it for a while, but it's better that you model respect for your fellow company members and it's rarely worth getting into a battle over scenic minutiae. Ultimately, no specific note matters more than your relationship to the person who felt the need to express their experience or observation. And over the long haul, bad energy backstage will become more detrimental than the occasional bad choice onstage.

In Closing, One Last Final Musing

I know that I can personally struggle maintaining this balance between the serious craft and joyful abandon of improv. I often reflect on how fortunate I am as an adult to have a space in my life where I can truly and unapologetically play. This is something we should not take for granted nor undervalue. I agree wholeheartedly that any small moment or slip truly "doesn't matter" in the grander scheme of things, although I would add that developing communities of play, inclusion, and connection serves as an admirable and deeply worthwhile mission, and that this goal *matters greatly*.

Related Entries: Abandon, Postmortem, Rehearsal Etiquette, Speaking Your Truth
Connected Game: Three Sentence Scenes

NOTES

1. I have not been able to trace the original author of these guidelines as they were not attributed in that circulated photocopied document in the late 1980s. Lyn Pierse includes them years later in her *Theatresports Down Under.* 2nd ed. Sydney, Australia: Improcorp, 1995. p. 7.
2. Connected games can be found in the Game Library at www.improvdr.com.
3. Keith Johnstone. *Impro. Improvisation and the Theatre.* 1979. New York: Routledge, 1992.

A

ABANDON

For those of us who have spent any time in the field of improvisation, finding, nurturing, and maintaining a sense of playfulness in our craft serves as a central preoccupation. **Abandon** embodies a childlike sense of exploration, a joyful commitment to the process at hand, and an uninhibited embracing of the here and now that seeks to at least suspend (or at most silence) the voices of critique and judgment. To play in such a manner, as children often do, for the sake of playing itself is the hallmark of improvisational abandon at its most unfettered and free.

Viola Spolin nods to the enemies of playfulness when she writes,

> Abandoned to the whims of others, we must wander daily through the wish to be loved and the fear of rejection before we can be productive [...] we become so enmeshed with the tenuous threads of approval/disapproval that we are creatively paralyzed. We see with others' eyes and smell with others' noses.[1]

There are many factors that can contribute to such a paralytic state: our fear of failure or embarrassment; our need for approval or gratification from our internal judges or our external teachers, peers, or audiences; or our injuries from past stumbles or perceived failures. These strong influences can all conspire to take us out of the precious moment of creativity, and make us, instead, "see with others' eyes" as we navigate the unknown terrain that is improvisation.

Strategies for Nurturing Abandon in Your Play

1. **A judgment-free process starts with you.** Often, we are our own hardest judges or critics and it's important to note that if we bring this energy into our playing spaces, it will be difficult for others to shift the paradigm. It's not uncommon for self-judging to represent itself as negativity or for others to perceive (rightly or wrongly) that your critical eye is actually leveled at them rather than yourself. This energy will quickly erode any trust that is building. If you are feeling anxious, unhappy, or frustrated with your work, be sure not to reflect these self-perceptions onto your fellow ensemble members. It's one thing to share, "I just felt off in that scene;" it's another to say, "That scene was really terrible and nothing good was happening in it."

2. **Separate the playing from the evaluation.** Notes and assessment are an important part of every art, and it would be counter-productive to advocate for a position of *never* reflecting honestly on our work. However, if you are spending every moment on stage actively assessing your choices, you are unlikely to be present and connected deeply to your scene partners and the nuances of the story as it develops. Give yourself permission to turn off this note-taker until you're back in the greenroom or reflecting on the action after-the-fact. To return to the image of children playing above, they rarely assess the effectiveness of their playing during the game itself, as this would suspend the very act of collaborative creation.

3. **Lower the stakes.** If you have limited or infrequent opportunities to play and practice your craft, this can make the moments you *are* onstage feel disproportionately and unhelpfully crucial: "If this is *my only* chance to play this month, then *every* moment must be exceptional as I won't get another chance for ages." There is something to be said for the sporting model of "getting in rotations." If you're able to expand your network of performance groups and opportunities, this can abate that voice that wants every scene to be an

exemplar. In addition to exposing yourself to different energies and styles of improv, you are also building resilience and strengthening your skill set.

4. **Give yourself a small, discrete challenge.** I've become a big fan of a pre-show personal challenge, especially when working on some of my more complex long-forms that can feel overwhelming during the development process. If you have a hard time quieting your inner voice, then at least focus this self-scrutiny in a helpful way. Before performances, challenge yourself to something specific that you can review once the curtain has lowered. Avoid opaque or generalized objectives, such as "to do better" or "to knock it out of the park," and instead consider a personal trend you're wanting to elevate or adjust, such as "I want to have a strong character point of view," or "I want to give scenes room to breathe."
5. **Focus on the joy of others.** If you're a people pleaser, take this suggestion with a grain of salt, but if we're setting each other up for joy on the stage, then it's likely that some of this joy will find its way back to us. There are many improvisers in my current performance network that just bring such a wonderful, silly, and carefree energy to the stage that I want to mirror this playfulness back to them, even if I find myself a little in my head that day. Most players will quickly forgive a "less than fantastic" choice or move if it was generated from a generous and giving spirit. Just make sure you extend this same courtesy of forgiveness to others, and perhaps more importantly, to yourself.

Final Thought

I think it would be fair to say that many (if not most) of us are attracted to the craft of improv as it gives us a chance to reconnect to that childhood spirit of play and creativity that is so regrettably lacking from the world of adults. When we consciously or otherwise decide that we want to become good at this passion and take it more seriously, our sense of abandon can sadly become a casualty to this cause. But it's important that we hold onto this foundational energy and attitude. Improvisers, after all, are often referred to as "players" as this sense of play is so fundamental to

Figure 3.1 My current professional improv home, Orlando's Sak Comedy Lab, provides a much-needed venue that enables joyful play for improvisers and audience members alike. James Berkley Photography.

our art. So, by all means, take your improv seriously, just don't extinguish the very abandon that attracted you to the art in the first place.

> **Related Entries:** Commandment #10
> **Antonyms:** Fear, Judging
> **Synonyms:** Freedom, Playfulness
> **Connected Game:** Room at the Inn

ACCEPTING

If you have taken one improv class, read one book or article on the subject, or even just talked casually to your one improv friend, it's likely that you have heard of the concept of accepting or yielding, often referred to simply as saying "Yes and…" It's a deceptively simple tool, although as Johnstone notes, it can have a surprisingly significant influence on our craft:

> The actor who will accept anything that happens seems supernatural; it's the most marvelous thing about improvisation: you are suddenly in contact with people who are unbounded, whose imagination seems to function without limit.[2]

Accepting is this playful spirit of embracing the ideas and suggestions of others (and yourself). To accept is to attack the unfolding action with a positive and creative mindset and see the inherent good and potential of other's actions by assuming a "let's do this" attitude.

Example

The scene starts with Players A and B sitting, presumably at a table. Player A takes a moment to examine their food, then looks up to Player A.

Player A: "Pass the salt."

Player B sees that the salt is nearby and slides it across the table.

Player B: "There you go."

A Little Added Detail

Most improvisers would recognize the above exchange as a pretty simple offer ("Pass the salt") and acceptance ("There you go"). Player B has received and honored the premise, and in perhaps the simplest sense has said "yes" by fulfilling Player A's apparent need. This is a fine first move, albeit perhaps a little pedestrian. As you play with the concept of accepting more, however, the true import of the "and" becomes increasingly apparent. If we witnessed the above dialogue in an embodied scene, we could probably extrapolate small nuances from the performers that might offer doorways into a more dynamic next step; but here written on the page, the next step is probably that they will continue to eat their now slightly-more-salty meals.

The contract of the "and" in the omnipresent "Yes and…" is that players commit to taking the risk of adding something *of their own* to offers as they emerge. In this way, the humblest start to a scene can quickly become crackling with potential as offers are polished and elevated by our scene partners. This is the fuller and more fruitful variety of accepting and yielding that most schools of improv extol. The improv "yes" embodies the attitude of "do no harm" in that it will generally allow the momentum of our partner's choice to move forward, but the improv "and" adds our own fingerprints to the scene in a way that shares the joys and responsibilities of collaborative creation. (I consider some important nuances and exceptions to the "Yes and…" attitude in an earlier entry, "Commandment #1," that's worth checking out too.)

Let's review and explore some of the different ways to use this "and" so that every idea or initiation has an opportunity to bear fruit.

Some 'Andy Ways to Get More Out of Your And

1. **Yes and… emotion.** Even if you are not at all sure what your partner intends, you can always have an emotional response or point of view. In the above example, if we just added a strong emotion to Player B's response, the scene could quickly ignite. Player A asks, "Pass the salt." Player B looks up lovingly from their own meal and notices that the salt is right beside them, so gently and slowly pushes the shaker toward Player A. As Player A reaches for the salt, their hands touch and linger. Player B smiles sweetly, and eventually lets go, cooing, "There you go." Without changing a word, the scene suddenly feels like it is about something much more dynamic and playful than the salt, just by Player B boldly accepting the premise and then adding a clear emotional mood.

2. **Yes and... relationship.** The above examples may already be hinting at relationship, but this is another way to add to a partner's choice or inference. If we maintained the above text and emotional energy, but said, "There you go, wifee," as if this was one of the first times we'd uttered that word to our partner, this adds a whole new level of detail that our partner can now explore. Here the endowment is in keeping with the emotional choice, but there can also be great fun when you find contrast in these choices. A petulant or irritated energy followed by a newlywed endowment can open up some exciting new potentials and vistas for the scene as well.
3. **Yes and... backstory.** Here you can use the "and" to further elucidate the relationship or given circumstances of the world in which we're playing. Perhaps Player A asks, "Pass the salt," but now Player B elects to gently but firmly move the shaker further away while noting, "You know what the doctor said about your blood pressure," or stands up defensively bemoaning, "I'm never going to cook as well as your father…" The initiation has still clearly been accepted and embraced, but now the world has expanded with details and nuance. Novice improvisers can mistake accepting as just giving the salt as per the request, rather than accepting the ground rules that we are eating together, and that one player believes the food needs more salt.
4. **Yes and... environment.** Another possibility is giving some focus and attention to the greater environment as the first pieces of the scene come together. Perhaps Player A's "Pass the salt" is followed by Player B searching the booth table and then anxiously trying to get the attention of a passing waiter, apologizing all the while, "Sorry, the Yelp reviews were rather misleading." If it's not already obvious, adding a little emotion, endowment, or backstory to the mix would only heighten the moment further.
5. **Yes and... tension.** Yet another possibility is to add a little tension or mystery into the mix as the scene starts up. You'll notice I don't use the word conflict as I don't see these terms as necessarily interchangeable, although conflict may become the ultimate result of such a choice. In this instance, when Player A requests, "Pass the salt," Player B might quietly and deliberately pick up the salt, slowly stand, and cross to the other side of the table, all-the-while carefully unscrewing the shaker top, only to dump the entire contents of the shaker on the uneaten meal. "There you go," might still be nonchalantly muttered as they return to their seat. This is certainly not a small move, but it conjures a litany of interesting questions that the players now get to explore and define.
6. **Yes and... game.** The "and" can also serve as the next gentle move in an unfolding game. Here, after passing the salt, Player B might request that Player A passes the pepper as the second move in a discovered one-upping dynamic of various attempts to make the meal more enticing or edible (although, frankly, such a move could lead to any number of possible curves of absurdity). As the scene finds momentum, it's likely that some of the other strategies listed above will come into play as well to further flesh out the details of the world in which the game is emerging.

Final Thought

These strategies are offered to potentially unlock some new ways to get the most out of your improv "ands" especially if you've found yourself stuck or stalling as scenes take their first steps. It's important to note that as I offer written examples, there is a critical distinction between *creating* something regardless of the initiation and *discovering* your choice based on the subtle clues and inferences gleaned from your partner's work. The former would not serve as a good example of accepting and may lean into the territory of blocking or chasing the over-original, while the latter would be strongly preferred as it is honoring potentials found in the first moment (even if your read on that moment is substantially different than your partner's tentative intent).

I'm a big fan of front-loading scenes with at least a helpful handful of specifics, as this typically provides a more dynamic set of equipment on the improv playground. Making sure early acceptances are rich and nuanced assists in this endeavor and will set you up for more effortlessly successful play down the road.

Related Entries: Active Listening, Commandment #1, Consent, Heighten, Justification **Antonyms:** Blocking, Denial, Negating, No **Synonyms:** Agreement, Yes And, Yielding
Connected Game: That's Right Experts

ACCUSATION

An **Accusation** is a great technique for providing energy, interest, and dynamism to a scene that might be stagnating or stuck. It is part of the **CAD** trinity (the other two techniques being **confessions** and **discoveries**) and this strategy is a helpful move if you're looking to activate a scene that's been dwelling unproductively in a state of balance. As Jimmy Carrane and Liz Allen remind us in *Improvising Better*, "there's no doubt that there is a rule of improv: avoid conflict. But this rule doesn't mean avoid anger. It means avoid reacting to conflicts with disagreement."[3] Accusations offer up new information or context that places culpability on your scene partner in a way that reveals something (perhaps, but not necessarily, unflattering) about their character or past actions. An accusation, by definition, uncovers details that the character was hiding, avoiding, or evading. When such a move is met with acceptance (as opposed to deflecting conflict), the results are usually wonderful.

Example

Players A and B are deep into a late-night study session, shuffling papers and notes across the dorm room floor. Player A, obviously stressed, looks up from the turmoil:

Player A: "I don't understand why you're not panicking more. This exam is 50% of our final grade."

Player B: *(with disinterest and an eye toward the door)* "I'm getting tired. I think I'm going to call it a night."

Player B starts gathering up their things while Player A watches with incredulity. After a moment, they decide to casually comment...

Player A: "So, you're not going to share the exam answers you purchased from that senior?"

There is a tense moment as Player B pauses at the door, and then slowly turns...

Some Things to Keep in Mind When Making an Accusation

1. **An accusation is subject to the normal foundational rules of improv.** As the energy of an accusation is directed to your scene partner and it is incumbent upon them to accept this information, it's important that your offer comes from a place of helpfulness and integrity. Be wary of wandering into the territory of pimping and gagging; that is, providing a choice that you know will make your scene partner uncomfortable (as the performer *not* the character). If you're playing in a long-form modality, you'll also want to exhibit some care in terms of making sure that the choice tracks with other established facts and backstory. It can be dynamic to craft an accusation in such a way that creates tension or juxtaposition with known details – the model straight "A" student has some skeletons in their closet – but be cautious of making a revelation that *undermines* a played reality, especially if such a choice is primarily designed to get an easy laugh.

2. **Inherent accusations will often serve you better.** There is certainly a value to almost saying *anything* as a revelation if the scene is faltering and then figuring it out with your partner after-the-fact: this is improvisation after all! However, accusations that mine specifics from the prior established actions and scene in question will often land with greater impact and effectiveness. In the above scene, the characters were students studying for a final. An accusation that connects to these realities (and other backstory established in previous scenes) is more likely to open interesting doors than something that feels truly random, or dare I say, desperate. Player A could offer, "I know you're really a spy sent here to undermine our student body elections," but unless such a choice connected to a broader thematic mood or genre that was already brewing, this move might help less than something more obvious.

3. **Seek accusations that affect your character personally.** Accusations that have an influence on the status quo of the current relationship tend to offer gifts that will keep giving, as opposed to revelations about unseen or absent characters. It's definitely possible to still mine value from this latter category of offer, especially if you're in a voluminous long-form, but in our efforts to bring action to the stage, strive to offer a choice that not only upturns your partner but that also connects to your own fate and objective. It's helpful if there is a personal reason why your character is offering up this information *now*.

Some Things to Keep in Mind When on the Receiving End of an Accusation

1. **Take a moment (or five) to let the accusation land.** It's really important that we don't treat an accusation like just any other choice in the scene, especially if it's been offered up to add some heat to a story that is becoming dangerously cold. On a technical level, as the performer, we can make this offer stand out simply by pausing the scene for a moment to highlight that a significant action has just taken place, even if we're still not quite sure as the performer how this moment is significant

just yet. On a character level, this also affords us the chance to truly take a gut check to let the character process what has just happened and strategize their next move accordingly – as we would in real life. Taking such a pause means we're less likely to diffuse or pass over a moment that our partner offered with a sense of profundity.

2. **Avoid the temptation to return in kind.** When you're on the receiving end of an accusation, accept and savor this moment in the hot seat. It's human nature to want to squirm out of this new information or return the attack with a choice of your own that moves culpability back to your partner. Avoid this trap. An exchange of accusations typically results in an argument or debate where no one particular accusation maintains any heat or value. Embrace fully this gift from your partner by accepting the ramifications. Similarly, avoid the temptation to rationalize or justify the choice in a detached or intellectual way that diminishes the emotion of the moment.

3. **Allow the scene and relationship to tilt or change.** In addition to adding or revealing new information, an accusation is likely to upset the pre-established relationship between the characters. The accusation *should* shift how the characters view each other. On deeper levels, it's also likely to adjust status relationships and who has the power in the scene or situation. This holds true whether the accusation is "negative" ("You stole the answers") or "positive" ("I know you told Chelsea that you want to kiss me.")

Final Thought

It's important to remember that there are a *lot* of different ways to fully accept an accusation and a great deal depends on the scope and style of performance in which the scene takes place. If the dramatic arc provides sufficient time, for example, it can be effective and dynamic to vehemently deny an accusation if the audience *knows* you are in fact lying and there is sufficient time for this seed to be watered and ultimately exploded elsewhere in the action. There are also instances when an accusation may reveal as much about the speaker as the recipient: perhaps the accuser has been misled or manipulated by another character seeking to sow strife and discord. Choices of this type are less likely to serve if we're playing in a short-form scene and subsequently need to fully unwrap the gift of the offer in the next few minutes. It's also a trap to find a clever intellectual reasoning or justification for *not* taking on the new choice, especially if you wrestle with being changed or ceding the control or high ground in a scene. But if you find yourself in a scene struggling to find its next beat, an accusation may be just the improv tool you need.

Related Entries: CAD, Confession, Discovery
Antonyms: Balance, Stasis **Synonyms:** Revelation
Connected Game: Point/Counterpoint

ACTING

Carrane and Allen provide an apt warning when they observe,

> Improvisers don't want to act in their scenes anymore. Instead, they want to talk their way through them. Acting your way through a scene is becoming all but obsolete, and that troubles us. Being clever has become a substitute for acting.[4]

I work on both sides of the scripted/unscripted "divide" (as well as in the middle!) and it is abundantly clear that there is a wonderful reciprocity between the skill sets of these two closely related art forms. Performers more versed in the norms of text-based theatre can benefit greatly from learning how to embrace the unknown, developing a higher tolerance for process and "failure," honing and learning to trust their instincts, elevating and celebrating the import of the ensemble, as well as just experiencing the raw joy of unmediated collective creativity. These lessons, and many more, are readily available on the improv stage.

Just as many artists in the scripted tradition may have little or no formal improvisational training, it is also true that many improvisers find themselves on the spontaneous stage without having ever studied **Acting**. Yes, one can argue that improv and acting on some levels almost seem synonymous, but in reality, while improvisation does so much to free the inner player and voice, it does not always fully exploit the riches of a scripted tradition that benefits from a similarly long history.

As is the case with many of these entries, I am painting with some broad strokes here, identifying general trends that I've observed in the various improvisational communities in which I've taught, performed, and devised. The following thoughts are obviously generalizations with exceptions, but they also reveal some habits from the scripted realm that could further deepen and enrich our improvisational craft if they are not already doing so. It is also important to note that merely saying "take some acting classes" is simply said but does not recognize that such training may not be easily available or that there may be significant financial or societal barriers preventing access to this toolkit.

Scripted Theatre Techniques Worthy of Emulation

I offer here four performer tendencies found amongst scripted theatre practitioners that are not always equally present in the world of improv.

1. **Stagecraft.** An inescapable reality of performance is that it can take a while to find comfort on the stage. While improv training deals a lot with collaboration, content, and creativity, it does not always adequately or deeply address the nuts and bolts of good performance etiquette. Am I currently standing in an open position in a way that I can be seen by my audience? Is my staging choice dynamic and throwing focus to the current character who is most important? Can I maintain the nuance of my vocal choice while making sure I am still heard at the back of the auditorium? Am I using my whole body to clearly express my character's energy and subtext? Scripted actors are at a distinct advantage in that they get multiple chances during rehearsals to address these issues in any given scene while their improvisational counterparts may never face the same exact scenic parameters more than once. Honing these instincts through repetition, however, is invaluable, and as an improv director, it is usually a simple feat to determine who has found this innate comfort with the mechanics of stagecraft, and who is still figuring out the rudiments in a way that might be undermining otherwise exciting work.

2. **Vulnerability.** There are so many different types of actors who value and excel at different facets of the craft, but *many* actors trained in the scripted tradition have found increased ease in bringing their emotions to their work. Scripts usually demand deep character research and contextualization as actors seek to find themselves in their roles in order to forge emotionally rich connections. Ideally, this process also inclines scripted performers to nurture empathy and a sense of integrity in their work. Improvisational practitioners can rarely benefit from this particular process as, with few exceptions, there is no time to engage in character-specific research for personae that are literally created in the moment of performance. As Carrane and Allen note in the framing quote, improvisers can also tend to over-value wit or wordplay, often as a substitute for more grounded or revealing character work. To craft spontaneous characters that resonate deeply, it is important to harness the scripted tools of vulnerability, appropriate emotionalism, and connection.

3. **Training.** If you are fortunate enough to have studied theatre in a formal or academic setting, you were likely exposed to a wide array of training opportunities. If you viewed singing as an important string in your bow, you probably sought out voice lessons. If you were a little clumsy on your feet, you hopefully enrolled in a movement or dance class. If your training was in a university setting, you were also likely exposed to some theatre history, performance theory, and perhaps some of the design or technical aspects of theatre production. (I'm a big advocate of the liberal arts ethos of taking classes in a wider array of topics and disciplines as they give artists a broader and richer understanding of our world as a whole.) Such a comprehensive level of training is less common amongst improvisers if they did not also happen to pursue more traditional performance studies. This may be partially symptomatic of the rarity of explicitly comprehensive improv training programs that consciously reach into important sister disciplines. I'm not sure that I know of an all-inclusive improv theatre history course being taught anywhere in the United States, for example: it's generally lucky to get some scant *commedia dell'arte* coverage in a broader survey class. I think there can almost be an assumption that improv *isn't* or *won't become* your full-time gig which further dissuades this level of pursuit. But I can't help but wonder how the field of improv might further flourish if our ranks explored more opportunities to train across a broad array of topics and techniques.

4. **Discipline.** My observations under this heading are likely informed by very particular experiences and trends in my own improv circles, and there are obviously improv companies that follow "professional" models and best practices. For good or evil, a lot of improv is synonymous with "amateur" or "community" with many companies actively and rightly claiming such monikers with pride. Ensembles may include membership from a wide variety of day-jobs or

sources, and this is in many ways a true strength of our art. The scripted realm is typically much less fluid in terms of rehearsal and participation expectations, especially if you are working in a union or professional house. Whether it's punctuality and preparation expectations, engaging in show-specific research, or simply writing down any directorial notes or feedback for future reference, there are scripted best practices that could benefit our improvisational processes and rehearsals. An underlying tension frequently emerges when improvisers assume that our improv should always be *fun*: discipline or organization can unfairly be viewed as an antonym to *fun*. Improvisers can also become "spoiled" by the immediacy of audience feedback in performance which can make workshopping without this incredible energy much less appealing. Scripted performers, on the other hand, are used to the quiet tyranny of silence in the auditorium during rehearsals and understand that they must still give every moment their all.

Final Thought

There is much the improvisational world can steal from its scripted kin (and vice versa). As improv continues to grow and evolve, we can continue to look at the scripted tradition for helpful tools and techniques, and players that borrow indiscriminately from both performance practices often position themselves favorably for both joy and success. It is not uncommon for improvisers to hit plateaus in their work. Frequently, a helpful strategy can consist of crossing the divide and exploring scripted training which invariably offers insights and skills that simultaneously enable and unlock new acting heights on the impromptu stage too.

> **Related Entries:** Commandment #9
> **Antonyms:** Cartooning, Cleverness, Commenting
> **Synonyms:** Emotional Truth, Vulnerability
> **Connected Game:** Scene Ending in I Love You

ACTION

The choices and strategies characters deploy to push themselves closer to their objectives. A play – scripted or improvised – that assumes a linear or Aristotelian structure can be considered as the interconnected sequence of actions that combine to create a cohesive plot. If you are inclined toward a "stand and deliver" style of improvisational play, it is likely that your work would benefit from considering more active choices and journeys.

> **Antonyms:** Activity, Talking Heads

ACTIVE LISTENING

Active Listening is a common term improvisers use to denote a deep commitment to focused communication. Mary Crossan describes this critical skill when she observes,

> Improvisation's spontaneous nature taxes the basic skills of listening and communicating. It demands that individuals give their full concentration and attention to the moment, rather than being preoccupied by what happened, or what could happen.[5]

It is unfortunately rather easy to fall into the trap of listening passively, assuming that you have gathered the gist of your partner's comment or argument, while your mind wanders and starts to formulate your response or next move, or perhaps just wanders in general to life issues and decisions. Active listening, on the other hand, seeks to mine the deeper nuances, intentions, and gifts of each speech act, understanding that in the world of improv theatre, no choice or clue should be needlessly overlooked or wasted.

While we refer to this intense and deliberate heightened presence in the given moment as "listening," it would be misleading to consider it as merely an aural skill. In the scripted tradition, it's possible (though equally in poor form) to await our designated cue line somewhat absentmindedly, so that we can respond when it's our turn with the next line of text. A strong performer will undoubtedly make nuanced adjustments based on small changes in the antecedent actions each evening, but were they to tune out for a moment, as long as they hear the end of their cue line, the scene can still move forward with some success. In the improvisational tradition, tuning out for even a few seconds can completely derail the momentum and direction of the scene, and a failure to discern the subtle intentions of your partners can allow exciting potentials to dissipate into the sea of missed opportunities. As Crossan notes above, there is no room for preoccupation on the improv stage. After all, how can one truly embrace and accept an offer if it was never really received in the first place?

Elements for the Active Listener to Consider

As we all strive to become better and more engaged listeners in our work, here are some facets of our active listening to embrace:

1. **Consider your partner's emotional truth.** On a simple level, active listening embraces not just *what* is being said but also *how* it is being said. If there is something about your partner's delivery that is unexpected, passionate, or perhaps even suspicious, recognizing this reality is probably at least as important as hearing the specific words of their dialogue. There may be a dissonance between the line and its delivery, whether the improviser intended this or not. "You're home early" might be accompanied with unfettered joy, suggesting a pleasant and welcome surprise. Or there may be a hesitance or quality that suggests the surprise was less-than-pleasant. While the improviser may elect not to immediately name or call out this perceived emotional truth, they would be remiss not to recognize and process it.
2. **Subtext will often open more doors than text.** Yes, we should certainly listen closely to the text that appears in our scene work, but the hidden meanings being communicated under the dialogue as subtext will nearly always provide richer opportunities. If these undertones are neglected or ignored, we are increasing exponentially the difficulty of the path ahead. "I love you" can mean a multitude of different things in a scene, and it's important to comprehend whether a partner is confessing or affirming love, or perhaps setting the stage for an apology after disappointing you, or possibly even laying the groundwork for a difficult breakup. If you actively seek and receive this deeper meaning, you are more able to make choices that can further heighten and embrace your partner's point of view.
3. **Don't neglect body language.** Similarly, your scene partners are likely communicating a great deal even when they are not engaging in dialogue, or further complicating their meaning by the way it's framed with their physical choices. Are they keeping their distance even if their words are seemingly loving and friendly? Are they using the environment or an activity to avoid you, or finding ways to put themselves in your path? Again, such choices may not be conscious or deliberate on the part of your fellow players, but body language and staging patterns are nonetheless being received and translated by the audience, so we'd be foolish not to show the same care in our own perceptions.
4. **And then there are the eyes.** There will be times when organic staging may not allow you to seek a strong connection through eye contact with your scene partners, but at the very least, find moments to check in with them as the scene evolves. Emotional, subtextual, and body language choices are all amplified through strong eye contact and there are nuances that are difficult to communicate any other way. Some improvisers can struggle with honest eye contact: it definitely exposes you as a player and requires comfort with being open and vulnerable. Evasions of this ilk are a challenging habit to break, but an inability to connect this way with others on stage will diminish your onstage relationships whether you want it to or not, as your improviser habit and character manners will become conflated.
5. **Active listening isn't limited to the stage.** Remember that you never know when you'll be needed in an improv scene and so we cannot passively rest on our laurels when we're in the wings awaiting our turn. Position yourself in such a way that you can receive as much of the onstage subtlety as possible. (On my home campus, I always encourage players to crouch downstage of the scene so that they don't miss anything.) If you're actively listening offstage, this also equips you to assist if an onstage player may have had their back turned at an inopportune moment or missed a scenic choice that is clearly important or full of promise. I'd also offer that active listening is equally important when we're *all* offstage discussing or debriefing a scene. If we're checking in about a moment of onstage tension or a potential breach of our company's goals or performance parameters, it would behoove us to make sure we are accurately understanding the feelings and reactions of our fellow players.

Final Thought

Students who cross over from scripted to improv work with me have commented that they find improvisational theatre considerably more tiring – as well as invigorating, challenging, rewarding, and a whole other host of adjectives! We don't have "scenes off" in the improv world where we can relax in the greenroom and catch up on a little reading. The need to actively listen on the improv stage is essential, consuming, and unforgiving. This concept reminds us that we need to rigorously stay in the moment, avoid planning ahead, connect fully with those with whom we share the stage, and to joyfully assume the role of a detective, searching for latent clues in the simplest of actions or choices made by our fellow players.

Related Entries: Emotional Truth, Obvious, Postmortem, Presence, Subtext **Antonyms:** Blocking, Erasure **Synonyms:** Accepting
Connected Game: Beneath the Line

ACTIVITY

Not to be confused with action which describes tactics that create energy and momentum, activity is typically synonymous with stage movement and blocking. While activity might craft a novel stage picture, or heighten energy and motion, when performed without an understanding of objective and need, it rarely adds lasting fuel to the dramatic action.

Antonym: Action

ADVANCING

Advancing describes a key narrative and story construction term that defines the forward momentum of a scene. To advance is to take the next logical step in the rising action as our characters pursue their underlying goals or objectives. In simple terms, each advance in the story is another beat or plot point and when we string them all together you have a description of the scene's dramatic arc. The companion term, **extending**, adds detail and nuance as opposed to the skeleton of the story itself. I don't tend to think of extending as an opposite, however, as good storytelling and scenic construction require a thoughtful balance and tension between both elements.

Example

Player A enters the kitchen and notices a broken glass on the floor.

Reaching down to pick it up, they cut their hand on the glass and begin to bleed.

In discomfort, they move to the sink and start to rinse their hand under the faucet.

The cold water shocks them, instinctively making them step back carelessly in response.

The sudden movement makes Player A slip on the blood on the kitchen floor, and they fall, hitting their head on the kitchen table...

Some Thoughts on Advancing Your Advancing

I tend to frame advancing as a storytelling tool, but this device clearly applies to all our scenic work as improvisers.

1. **Small steps are key.** If we take small steps in our stories, the events that unfold are likely to take on greater significance and meaning. Sometimes our excitement as improvisers can make us rush through the narrative arc, especially if a sense of where the story is heading has become clear. Fight this instinct to leap ahead. So much of the joy and dynamism of improvisational storytelling involves true discovery in the moment, and we don't want to lose sight of the gifts of the here and now. In the example above, we could have easily just had Player A clean up the broken glass in one generic sentence. By breaking this larger action down into smaller steps, we invite the possibility of new discoveries. As the oft-quoted adage notes, so often in improv the scene occurs on your way to what you *thought* was going to happen.
2. **Reduce, reuse, recycle.** In addition to making needlessly large steps, improvisers frequently cram in too many ideas, actions, and events into their scenes, probably from the fear of being too boring or obvious. I would contend that stories, in general, suffer from *excess* rather than *lack*. This may be the result of each player wanting to make sure they've made a significantly noticeable contribution, or not trusting that there are enough elements already in play, or perhaps just an inability to actively listen so that rich ideas are carelessly dropped or missed. Regardless of the cause, the result is typically the same: a story that becomes overburdened with increasingly disconnected and competing actions. If you are improvising the first scene of a two-hour long-form, some excess might prove helpful and warranted as you'll have ample time to get back to it later; but if your goal is to craft a cohesive arc in a shorter amount of stage time, *less* is almost always *more*.

3. **Pursue the "inherent" move.** To return to the above example, after Player A stoops to pick up the glass, a flying saucer could pull the roof off the house and teleport them inside. This could certainly result in an interesting scene, but this offer could be inserted as a later move in almost *any* scene. You'll go on much more interesting, varied, and dynamic journeys if you privilege and honor the scenic ingredients already established. It's helpful to ask ourselves what elements are already known or what are the rules of this particular snapshot of the world that are in play. The arrival of a flying saucer would also be an example of offering a giant leap rather than a small step. Consider instead how you can elevate or heighten preexisting choices, which brings us to my last suggestion…
4. **If in doubt, look backward.** In our efforts to push a scene to the next moment, we can lose sight of all the gifts and ideas that are already at our disposal. This Johnstonian philosophy of looking backward to move forward in many ways links all the prior advancing observations. If we're rushing too quickly through the actions, we're likely to miss nuance and potentials. If we are anxiously bringing too much to the improv table, it will probably be at the expense of choices that have already been crafted and developed. If our offers are too "original" or disconnected from the given circumstances, then it's foreseeable that we might be erasing rich or nascent ideas that would benefit from patient focus and attention.

Final Thought

The above strategies emphasize the need for us to take our time with our storytelling and give every choice its moment in the sun. In our efforts to craft interesting scenes, we can fail to trust that exciting actions will emerge gradually and organically. These suggestions are somewhat predicated on the assumption that specific and nuanced work is occurring, which is where the companion concept of **extending** very much comes into play. But I'm constantly reminded in the improv workshop how captivated I can quickly become by a team deeply listening and moving the action along one small obvious move at a time. So, while the very concept of advancing suggests momentum and progression, keep in mind that it doesn't mandate that you need to rush to the end of each scene; in fact, mindful advancing encourages us to take our time to enjoy the unfolding process along with our audience, savoring each little victory along the way.

Related Entries: Chapter Two, Extending, Looking Backward, Obvious
Antonyms: Balance, Inaction, Stasis
Connected Game: Because

AGREEMENT

The act of believing and valuing the scenic offers and elements established by your scene partners. Characters may find themselves at odds due to contrasting or conflicting points of view or objectives, but the improvisers inhabiting the characters should fully embrace the established facts (even if their characters have opposing opinions about those "truths" or antecedent actions).

Synonym: Accepting

AMBIGUITY

Bernie Sahlins notes, "In creating, we rightly value the implicit over the explicit. The former is more subtle, more intelligent, more artistic, more worthy. Ambiguity is the soul of good work. It is more effective to show than to tell."[6] The relationship between ambiguity and specificity in improv is, needless to say, complex. If players are reluctant to name constituent scenic elements, it is highly likely that the scene will float in a nowhere limbo and may struggle to find a dynamic build and payoff. If, on the other hand, players name *everything* mercilessly, the scene can start to feel like a poor approximation of the human condition, lacking any sense of intrigue or nuance. In the context of this entry, I think it's important to note that this first example would not be illustrative of desirable ambiguity, but rather reflect vague or wimpy creation. **Ambiguity** for our purposes is not an absence of choice, but rather a delight in leaving room for playful mystery and subtle subtext. It is playing with an attitude of trust that every idea need not be spelled out immediately for your partner and audience alike, and that such a stance allows ideas to morph, develop, and mature as the action dances forward.

I have started using the phrase **specific ambiguity** in my own work to describe this fruitful approach to slowly developing deep relationships and backstories in improvisational theatre. I think I coined this phrase, although as is the case with so many of the strategies that have been in my lexicon for a while, it's also possible I subconsciously picked it up elsewhere. Utilizing ambiguity in this manner, particularly in expansive long-form pieces, can truly add depth and weight to stories and characters, providing the audience and players with intriguing questions and motivations that are worthy of our collective time and energy.

Example

Player A is washing dishes in the sink with a stern energy as Player B arrives home, obviously late, to their shared apartment. Player B carefully removes their coat and takes a timid step toward Player A by the sink.

Player B: "Sorry I'm late…"
Player A: (softly) "Again."

Player A pauses for a moment but does not look up from the dishes. Player B senses that this is not a typical exchange but proceeds regardless…

Player B: "You got my text?"
Player A: "Yeh, I got your *texts*."

Player A's final word and emphasis makes Player B reconsider what this moment is about…

A Further Consideration

It's possible that Player B's next line might now justify or explain the building tension, but there is also a dramatic value to letting this energy and mystery develop further. While the dialogue might feel sparse, the performers are clearly listening and observing each other carefully, and the emotional exchanges and details are rich. In many ways, the stage directions and subtext are carrying the weight and interest rather than the potentially unremarkable words. As audience members (and as players) we have an increasing list of questions that are steadily evolving. Why is Player A clearly so upset before B even arrives? Where does Player B work and why are they so frequently late home? Why does B mention a text singular, but A replies in the plural? What did these texts say, and are they the source of the tension?

As I was concocting the scene, I certainly had tentative specifics in mind, but if I was in this scene with another player, it's more than likely that their read on the situation and resulting gifts could be *quite* different than my initial assumptions. This is much of the joy of such an approach to scene making as if we're patient and connected, we can tease out when and how important details make it to the stage.

Striking the Balance between Richly Ambiguous and Problematically Vague

1. **Scenes generally thrive with context.** There is a marked difference between having your audience wonder, "Why is there so much tension between this couple?" as opposed to "Who are these people and why are they in a scene together?" In the above example, most would pick up on the kitchen location. There is room for debate about the relationship: I was intending a romantic or married couple, but as written the characters could just be sharing an apartment, or possibly members of a family. There is a familiarity between them, but the scene might need a few more beats for this to become clear. While the improvisational spirit is literally built on questioning and breaking rules, I would offer that ambiguity in our scenic work is much more helpful when it comes to the "why" of the scene as opposed to the "who," "what," or "where." Certainly, having an unidentified character lurking in the background of several scenes only to be revealed as a critical role later in a performance would be an effective use of this dynamic, but *generally* I think of ambiguity thriving in the domains of subtext, motivation, and backstory.

2. **Be careful of naming or calling out the ambiguity.** If a scene is becoming delightfully charged and dramatic with some gritty underlying unvoiced questions, be careful of prematurely or needlessly pointing out this fact. (This is a particular trap if you are a new entering character.) In the above scene, I could ask Player A as the next line of dialogue, "You're acting strange. What's going on with you?" but this move could well puncture the developing game, especially if neither of us wanted (or were able) to put the pieces together just yet. As is the case with pretty much *any* scenic game in improv, once we explicitly name it, we have usually edited or ended it. This is not to suggest that ambiguity *needs* to become the central device of the scene; in fact, a little touch of this concept can go a long way. But *if* it has bubbled up as the major gift, then perhaps exercise some caution before you unwrap it!

3. **Conversely, be careful of digging yourself into an ambiguity pit.** It can be such joyful fun to continue building a scene with rich ambiguity, but there is also a trap of adding so many vague elements that you, your scene partner(s), and the audience will struggle to keep them all sorted and connected. Consider exploring one color or avenue of ambiguity rather than a more scattershot approach. This way you can craft each step through your character's point of view and objective, and that makes it less likely that the scene will collapse under the burden of too many competing and potentially incompatible unknowns (dare I say, think of the last few seasons of *Lost*). To return to the above example, as Player A, I might begin the scene with the choice that I was the unintended recipient of a text from Player B that makes me question their motives and recent behaviors. Or it can be helpful to frame it as a question, "Who did "B" intend that text for, as it certainly wasn't me?" I might have something tentatively more specific in mind, but a central choice or question will allow me to flow with and respond to the pitches from my scene partner. And I can just throw that unvoiced choice away when and if a more inspiring dynamic develops.
4. **Don't be afraid to get specific when it's needed.** While you can obviously have an avalanche release of all your hidden thoughts and meanings in a CAD-like fashion if the elements are at your fingertips, the power of ambiguity is in its ability to build energy and intrigue. If the scene or relationship is losing dynamism and interest, don't stubbornly remain in the land of ambiguity, as this is a sure sign that the scene is looking for a new way to evolve. If the scene is struggling to find a next move, offering up at least a tentative piece of context for your prior actions will likely prove helpful. In a short-form modality, it's foreseeable that most ambiguity will need to be resolved or at least acknowledged prior to the blackout if these characters and scenarios will not have another opportunity to breathe. In a long-form modality, there's more room to leave your scene with that lovely ellipsis feel that makes the audience crave for the characters to return to the stage again. However, if it's late in the run, you'll want to be careful that you haven't left so much unresolved that your journey as a character lacks meaning or a payoff.
5. **Don't mistake vagueness for ambiguity, please.** As I noted in the definition, I think there is a big difference between making a rich choice with a tentative or partially conceived motivation informed from your character's point of view, and making an unsupported, random, or ill-defined choice from a place of fear or passivity. To return to Sahlins' opening quote, ambiguity still contains an implicit meaning or choice, as opposed to an explicit unnuanced statement or perhaps an offhand comment with little or no intention on the part of the improviser. (Curve balls are perhaps an exception to this rule and are discussed elsewhere.) Helpful ambiguity is still purposeful, well-crafted, and connected to the needs and wants of our characters. It is informed by the known parameters and context of the world that we have created together onstage. Such choices are still deliberate *choices* and not merely improvisational placeholders awaiting others to provide details.

Final Thought

While I think the concept of ambiguity is relatively accessible, its delicate application can create challenges. As improvisers, we find delight in seeing something exciting appear on stage but may not always have the patience or fortitude to allow it to unfold at its own pace. Fast-paced improv environments, in particular, can almost prove caustic to a gentler evolving scenic approach if we're not mindful. But I'd offer the rewards of specific ambiguity are many, and that this technique is a concrete way of building trust and connection with our audiences as such an approach, at its core, values their ability to piece together the breadcrumbs in real time alongside the performers they are watching on the stage.

Related Entries: Curve Ball, Specificity
Antonyms: Vagueness, Wimping
Connected Game: Conscience

ANTAGONIST

In traditional (read Aristotelian or Western) theatre, the antagonist refers to the "opposer of the action" or the character that seeks to thwart the progress of the protagonist. This is not to be mistaken for merely being antagonistic, which can become stalling rather than motivating. While a structural antagonist might on some level say "no" to the dreams of their rival, they are very much saying "yes" to the reality and complexities of the given circumstances and provide fitting obstacles accordingly.

> **Antonym:** Protagonist

ANTECEDENT ACTION

While backstory and exposition can theoretically occur anywhere in the dramatic arc, antecedent action refers to the events that have occurred before the main action of the scene or play begins. Such elements form part of the Given Circumstances or CROW and provide a powerful tool for bringing energy and interest quickly to the stage.

> **Synonym:** CROW

APPROVAL

It's likely that if you're an improviser and you're reading this entry that you have struggled or are currently struggling with the desire to obtain **Approval**. Whether it's from your teacher, classmates, director, fellow company members, that special someone in the audience, or the panel of judges and critics that reside in our heads like our own personal Waldorf and Statler, our unabated need for approval can linger like a storm cloud over our artistic endeavors. At "best" it might serve as an occasional nuisance or motivating force, at worst it can become debilitating, providing an unwanted barrier through which all our spontaneity must pass before it can make it bruised and limping onto the stage. Lyn Pierse aptly describes a pernicious source of this blight when she offers,

> The need for teacher approval is a problem. It does not facilitate 'creative independence', but its existence is not surprising given that most of our education is based on getting it right and keeping in the teacher's good books.[7]

In the workshop environment, the instructor often (willing or not) becomes a stand-in for many if not all these internalized voices of doubt and judgment. It's not uncommon for players to actually break the fourth wall and check in with the teacher mid-scene as the action progresses, seeking some small form of encouragement or acknowledgment. Pierse, quoted above, writes of a "Get lost Keith" exercise in which Johnstone, the founder of *Theatresports*, actually encourages his students to actively yell at him if they find themselves seeking his approval as they are performing in order to discourage this "need."

While seeking feedback and earnestly processing notes are critical elements of our craft as artists, if we want to grow and learn from those who have walked this path and stumbled before us, the act of consciously or unconsciously seeking approval during the act of spontaneous creation is sure to undermine our creative efforts. There is already plenty for an improviser to tend to during a scene: their partner(s), staging, characterization, story arc, games, and so on and so on. It is in our self-interest, then, to do our best to silence this internal beast that craves a constant diet of encouragement.

So let us consider some ways to harness this instinct and focus our lens instead on a more productive pursuit of self-appraisal. My earlier entry on **abandon** provides some general strategies for quelling the judges, so here we'll explore instead how personal goals can assist in this regard.

Goals in Pursuit of Gaining Your Own Approval

1. **What do I want from this scene or game?** You'll quickly note a trend in these posts that it's important to set your goals *prior* to the performance and then assess these challenges *after* leaving the stage. It's generally unhelpful to have a myriad of goals or notes floating through our brain as we improvise, but I think giving yourself a reminder or point of concentration (in Spolin terms) can help set you up for success. For example, the short-form game Moving Bodies tends to become a yelling fest, so I'll remind myself prior to this game that I want to focus on more grounded and nuanced dialogue. This doesn't guarantee that the scene won't still devolve into irrational yelling, but it at least allows me to start the scene with a fighting chance. If you've been receiving notes from your coach or director, or have noticed yourself falling into a trend you'd like to break (or achieving a trend you're keen to continue), then this is a good way to activate these observations and suggestions.
2. **What do I want from this performance?** Whether you're playing in a short-form competition or a long-form piece, there may be a more global challenge that you want to gift yourself before the performance begins. If I'm directing, I like to take a few minutes before a run or performance

for improvisers to share these goals. I find publicly sharing personal challenges a helpful tool on several levels: it gives each player a little accountability and asks them to commit to a focus; it allows the company to notice trends that may assist the performance as a whole; and it empowers fellow players to assist each other in meeting personal goals. If I know that you are committed to more dynamic staging and I find myself engaging in a talking heads scene with you, I am now more likely to look for helpful ways to break this staging pattern as well. When issuing a broader goal, be sure that it is still specific and, for lack of a better term, "measurable." It's a bit of a cop-out to say, "My goal is to have a good show," as we might all have a different idea as to what that might mean for you. Do you want to keep out of your head, or put away a stressful day, or keep your focus on your scene partners?

3. **What do I see as my mid-term goal?** If we consider the above goals as short-term or immediate, what are you hoping to achieve as an improviser in the next several months or year? Again, I'd recommend steering away from imprecise or unachievable objective statements. If I want "to be famous," that goal, while not unusual, is largely unattainable if we consider it as one step or move. Sure, there are accounts of someone being discovered, but then there is the other 99% of the industry that has worked tirelessly so that they would be trained and ready when opportunity knocked. Perhaps your goal is to perform in at least three different performance venues, or try your hand at four different forms or styles, or forge connections with at least another dozen players with whom you have not yet worked. If your goals are discrete and clear, you can easily assess how you're doing and then change or adjust them as you deem necessary. It's not a bad idea to write these down somewhere too that you can refer to and update as needed.

4. **What do I see as my long-term goal?** One of the beauties of the improvisational community is that it is a big tent housing people with so many different experiences and aspirations. Know what you want to ultimately get out of the craft so that you can also consider what you are willing to put into your pursuit of the craft. Are you seeking a sense of community, an outlet for artistic expression, a way to develop your communication and social skills, a pathway to a life in the arts, or all of these and more? Being honest with yourself about what you hope to achieve will also allow you to ally yourself with others in your performance circles who are working toward a similar end.

Final Thought

We can't grow without the nourishment of feedback and assessment, but we will never thrive onstage if we allow our desire for this approval to infect our work and make us second guess our actions. We must, instead, give ourselves permission to fall and trip and make glorious mistakes so that we may learn from these moments and may then, in turn, repeat the process while making newly informed falls, trips, and glorious mistakes. When our focus is on gaining approval from outside forces, we are likely putting ourselves squarely in our head and thereby diminishing the very likelihood of achieving this amorphic goal.

Related Entries: Abandon
Synonyms: Checking In, Judging
Connected Game: Eye Contact

ARCHETYPE

Amy Seham provides some important food for thought when she warns, "unexamined spontaneity, for all its pleasurable sensation of flow and connection, can serve to feed sexism and racism at the deepest levels of myth and archetype."[8] Exploring archetypes in performance is rife with potential opportunities to reify or reinforce uninformed or harmful assumptions. As Seham cautions, the line between archetype and stereotype can be murky at best, and non-existent at worst. Short-form with its tendency toward bite-sized scenes providing little room for complex examination or exploration of a trope or type is particularly problematic, although long-form traditions are by no means immune. Genre-based work, by definition, draws on commonly held assumptions and beliefs in terms of the rules of the game and how characters should be depicted and utilized, and ensemble-based pieces will typically only be as sensitive to issues of representation as their constituent membership.

How we depict and represent ourselves and others is a fraught and complex subject, and this consideration makes no claim to have sorted it all out. Instead, I offer some incomplete thoughts and strategies as I seek to gain greater awareness and sensitivity in this area. For the purposes of this entry, I would like to offer the following working definitions. A **stereotype** is typically an unnuanced characterization based on unquestioned and often inherited assumptions made from the "outside." In improv, such characters are usually worn lightly, embodied with little integrity, and can primarily serve to get an easy laugh or provide interactions to move the action along for other more privileged characters. **Archetypes**, on the other hand, are characters that are informed by a canon or body of work that serves as a *starting* point for exploration and that invites (if not demands) the performer to seek variance, differentiation, and integrity from an empathetic and insider perspective. While an archetype will evoke familiarity, it also leaves room for and expects critique, personalization, and conflict with inherited perceptions. More complex opportunities for humor generally emerge through this dialogue between the improviser and the role they are inhabiting.

Clearly, the well-intentioned pursuit of an archetype can certainly slide into the domain of the stereotype if we are hurried, careless, or uninformed as performers. I think few veteran improvisers could contend that they have not had many such moments in their career. In my own long-form devising, I have explored some ways to minimize this risk (with admittedly mixed results). Here are some lessons I've learned as I continue to explore fruitful and artistically responsible ways to utilize archetypes on the improv stage. I've referenced past projects a little more than I tend to, as they're helpful in providing concrete examples as to what approaches seem intriguing or promising.

Possible Strategies for Empowering Archetypes

1. **Consider archetypes free from physical identifiers.** This can be challenging in genre-specific pieces if you're seeking fidelity to sociopolitical circumstances, but many concepts might allow for the utilization of archetypal personae freed from signifiers such as sex, gender, race, sexual orientation, ethnicity, and the like. Types such as "the micro-managing parent," "the selfless best friend," or "the rebellious teenager" can all become embodied by as diverse an array of performers as your ensemble houses while still honoring character energies and functions that inhabit your source material. If you tackle this when you're devising your piece, you are a step ahead of reducing the likelihood of damaging stereotypes in the end product. I used this strategy to strong effect in *Murder We Wrote: An Improvised Whodunit*, where an ensemble of thirteen rotated into a cast of eight characters for each performance. Role assignments were literally drawn randomly in front of the audience, and subsequently, a legal partner, publisher, caregiver, and married couple became assigned by the luck of the draw in a way that avoided potential societal or heteronormative biases.

2. **Practice inclusive initial casting.** This approach almost needs no explanation as the more inclusive the cast is, the more voices there are present in the mix and the more opportunities there are to craft nuanced representations. In the sub-genre of parodic improv, this is particularly important as when it comes to period pieces, a commitment to casting in an "historically accurate way" can easily exclude all manners of difference. Modern audiences are quickly willing to accept "non-traditional" casting choices, and this can be either presented as is without commentary or woven into the greater concept and presentation of the piece. For example, my large-cast version of *The Lost Comedies of William Shakespeare* featured an "all-male" cast that was, in fact, two-thirds female identifying. This enabled some dynamic and complex layering as various bodies assumed traditional Shakespearean roles: on some nights, we would have one of many female actresses playing the role of a male Elizabethan actor who in turn assumed the character of a courtly female that donned male garb in order to escape into society…

3. **Enable flexible in-the-moment casting.** In pieces less constricted by historically situated mores, archetypes can be shared or self-assigned with a heightened awareness of societal and company patterns. A self-aware company can deliberately place different voices and bodies into positions of power, high status, as the protagonist, or in other archetypal roles. I've found with smaller cast shows this flexibility is essentially a necessity, as there may only be one available body to play the next "needed" character. *Lights Up: The Improvised Rock Opera*, a four-actor two-act musical tour de force, certainly falls into this category as improvisers all end up playing two or three roles each during most performances as deemed necessary by the vicissitudes of the evening. *It's All Greek to Me* required similar flexibility as players adopted the Attic tradition of having three improvisers playing all the featured characters alongside a ten-improviser chorus. In *Upton Abbey*, a 30-character homage to life in an English Manor, the audience randomly selected which recurring characters would be featured in any given performance, thus offering another built-in strategy to lift up voices that might not typically emerge as protagonists.

4. **Explore ways to satirize or critique tropes as they are used.** This is perhaps the most complex

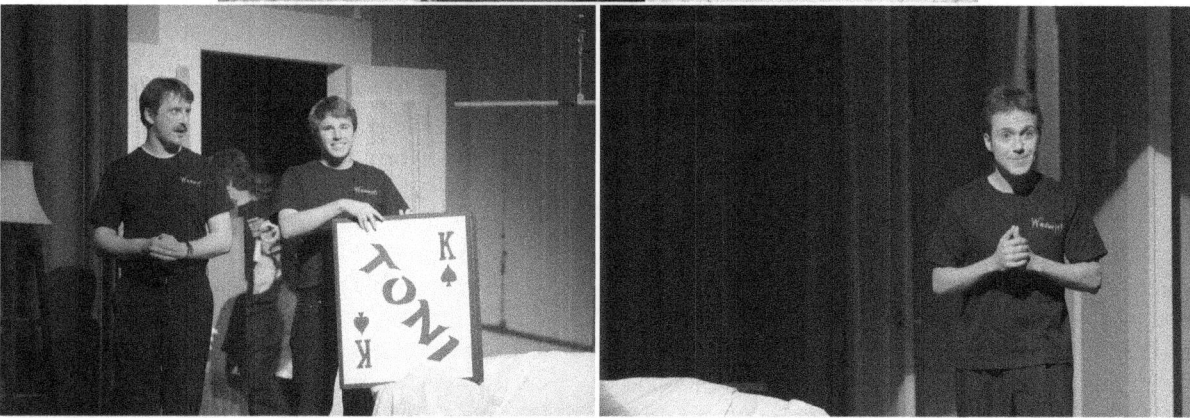

Figure 3.2 A row of costume bags drops from the ceiling, awaiting to become randomly assigned to the cast members of the Annie Russell Theatre's *Murder We Wrote* (Scenic design: Lisa Cody-Rapport; Costume design: Desiree Masucci; Improvising stage manager: Emily Russell nee Jarrell). Photo credit: Toni Firriolo.

approach aimed at reducing the likelihood of stereotypes populating your improv worlds. An almost-Brechtian technique of assuming the role of both the character while maintaining the artist's voice and point of view *behind* or *in tandem* with that character can create some fruitful tensions. Whether it's a wry comment or "wink" in a short-form scene as you are called upon to satisfy an unnuanced or reductive role, or a satiric contextualizing of a character in such a way as to highlight the harmful tropes that have bound them, there are ways to take on a potentially stereotypical persona so as to call out and deconstruct the underlying assumptions. I've explored this type of approach with mixed results, to be candid. It requires a subtle skill on the part of the ensemble, as well as an acceptance that such choices may not always be uniformly received, understood, or welcomed by sectors of your audience. My dramaturgical improv piece, *Private Lies: Improvised Film Noir*, danced in this terrain, embracing some central tropes of the genre, such as the whiskey-sodden private eye, mysterious and unknown crime boss, and a trapped smoky speak-easy singer, while also endeavoring to look critically at issues of class, politics, race, immigration, and poverty. It is a complex issue in the improvisational realm to represent such challenging issues on stage without succumbing to stereotypical presentations or potentially portraying unsavory themes without carelessly triggering your company or audience. But I don't think we should shy away from such thoughtful striving.

Final Thought

Improvisation by its very nature is deeply referential and innately connected to artistic and social antecedents. I would hold that it is therefore incumbent upon us as artists to seek nuanced and complex portrayals on our stages and to accept Seham's charge for *examined* spontaneity. I've endeavored to make a distinction between empathetically informed archetypes, and naïve or uninterrogated stereotypes. This line is unquestionably thin and potentially elusive. But just as the improv ethos would suggest that we forgive ourselves and others when we stumble or fail in our craft, so too does it charge us with creating an artistic community and performance mode that seeks deeper and more inclusive truths and forms of representation.

Related Entries: Groupmind, Inclusiveness
Antonyms: Stereotype, Wearing Your Character Lightly **Synonyms:** Emotional Truth, Empathy
Connected Game: Genre Rollercoaster

ASK-FOR

The audience ask-for has become a tried-and-true tradition for most improv productions in both short- and long-form modalities. On one level, it operates as "proof" that the resulting action is legitimately spontaneous: I still, surprisingly, encounter audience members for whom this is an issue. On another level, it breaks the fourth wall that often separates performer and observer, and places the spectator in the role of co-creator, or perhaps at least as the inspirational muse, potentially connecting them more deeply to the action that will ensue.

While some improv companies and performance practices have moved away from the tradition of eliciting audience suggestions, feeling perhaps that it is a needless tyranny, the majority of improv troupes still utilize the tool of using an **Ask-for** as a way of jump-starting the improv action. (On this point, Keith Johnstone, founder of *Theatresports* remarks, "I'd never imagined that improvisers would one day be asking for suggestions before every scene and enslaving themselves to the whim of aberrant individuals."[9]) Each troupe or format likely has a slightly different approach or philosophy when it comes to gathering inspiration. For example, in the long-form tradition, I've constructed formats that launched from one or two suggestions, while others have incorporated large (literal) slates of ideas and/or paused the action to elicit a new element to send the action reeling in an unexpected direction. And when I'm playing short-form, the way in which I interact with the audience also varies from show to show. In my current short-form home, Sak Comedy Lab, I'm much more likely to sift through choices in *Gorilla Theatre* as a director than during our competitive *Duel of Fools* or *King of the Hill* formats, where we *tend* to take the first thing we hear.

That being said, I think there are certainly some best practices when seeking suggestions from the proverbial or literal darkness of the auditorium. If you're a frequent player, I imagine most of these strategies are already in your tool belt.

Ways to Get the Most Out of Your Ask-For

1. **You get what you ask for (mostly).** If your prompt is "Can I, please have a small room in the house?" you shouldn't be surprised if you're met with a chorus of "Toilet" or "Bathroom." If our ask is too narrow, we're probably going to find ourselves getting similar results again and again, so find ways to provide a more open-ended question that's likely to yield different results from audience to audience. "Where's the last place you took a photo or selfie?" will still result in a location but you will probably get a wider variety of responses. Similarly, if you're playing a short-form show with a stock set of games and generally ask the same question *every* time, don't be surprised when you get one of three variants as the answer. Creating a deeper array of prompts for yourself is likely to quickly pay dividends by opening up whole new scenic possibilities.

2. **Be careful of needless insider jargon in the ask.** For a while, I performed with a troupe where we'd often ask for a "non-geographic location" in an effort to avoid getting a bunch of different country names. On the page, this ask-for can make sense, but for your casual viewer, that particular phrase probably doesn't hold too much meaning. We'd usually need to ask a follow-up question when we were predictably met with quiet consternation. Many of the locations where I perform are frequented by "regular" theatregoers, so we want to make sure our language isn't needlessly opaque or appealing only to the returning aficionados. In some of my period-specific dramaturgical improv, it's also become clear that some launching information is better provided through other means, such as a random draw or audience vote between pre-set options. For example, if I ask for a societal ill plaguing Prohibition America, it's more than foreseeable I might get nothing, the same thing every night, or something so anachronistic that it might puncture the stylistic homage before it has even begun.

3. **Burn common responses in the setup.** Some games or formats thrive or are designed with a very specific ask-for in mind: in the short-form game Crime Endowment, you need to assemble reasonably predictable elements (an activity, object, location, and accomplice are standards) so that the endowee has a road map for what they are trying to figure out. If you're unable to craft a new angle into the ask-for on the fly, you can always burn prior or common responses as examples. I might ask, "Can I have an outdoor activity such as mowing the lawn or walking your dog?" This way, you've hopefully dismissed options that will have you improvising over all-too-familiar terrain again. Note that *too many* examples are likely to stump the audience by putting them in their heads, and that it's not uncommon for someone to yell back the very thing you've just theoretically eliminated! It can also prove helpful to elicit a suggestion *prior* to explaining too much about the intended game or frame. In Crime Endowment, once the audience knows you're piecing together a crime that may needlessly narrow their imaginations rather than assembling the random components and *then* revealing that these seemingly inane choices will now form the dastardly deed.
4. **Don't let the over-eager monopolize.** This is probably more of an issue in the short-form tradition where you might find yourself seeking ask-fors multiple times throughout the evening, but performances can become dominated by an individual or smaller group during these pauses in the action. It could be a large group booking of pre-teens taking up the front rows and inadvertently serving as a barrier for the rest of the house with their excitement, current improv students trying to "help" by filling silences with well-worn offers for a particularly timid audience, a rowdy guest who has had a few too many drinks and now mistakes the stage for a television set, or someone who isn't reading the room well and is offering up inappropriate, vulgar, or demeaning ideas. I'll often let such a person or party get something into the mix but will then resolutely move to other sections of the audience with a comment such as, "Let's get this starting point from the back of the house." If truly disruptive behavior continues, that's when a host or member of house management should step in.
5. **Don't be afraid of the raised hand.** I've played in venues with huge floor plans, poor acoustics or sightlines, or thousands of guests. In these instances, it was almost unavoidable to ask for raised hands to make sure we could really hear the intended suggestion. This technique can also help if an audience has an unruly faction in its midst, as many people are less inclined to yell out that inappropriate thought if they are in full focus. A little loss of anonymity can go a long way in these cases! This is also a simple and helpful approach if you're looking for a slightly more complex or specific element, you're amassing a slate of many suggestions and you want to be sure you're getting to various parts of the room, or you would like to hear a few ideas before committing to one. A connected caution: sometimes I'll see fellow players select a "random" audience member who has not self-nominated, to offer up a prompt. While this can work (especially if the particular person has been clearly excited and participatory), I've also seen audience members squirm when they're the recipient of such focused and unwanted attention, so I tend to opt for letting folks volunteer with a raised hand instead.
6. **Establish clear expectations.** If you note at the top of the show that you are going to take the first thing that you hear, that's your contract and it'll take a little more wiggling to adjust if things inadvertently go awry. If you note that you're looking for something that you particularly like or find inspiring, then you've given yourself permission to sift through what you get. If you acknowledge that there are children in the audience and want a suggestion that is appropriate under those circumstances, then ignoring the racy option has already been justified. Or, to the contrary, if you've noted that this is a late-night show intended for adults where children shouldn't be present, you've warned any parents in the house that they might have some explaining to do after the show. Each company will operate under different expectations and parameters, but it's helpful to let the audience know those in advance, especially if you're working in a space that might house a wide variety of styles and formats.

Final Thought

At the end of the day, as Johnstone notes above, we need to give ourselves permission (if we haven't already) to take the suggestion that will best set us up for joy and success, or perhaps even leap into the unknown without a suggestion at all if that's our whim. There is no prize in nirvana for the improviser who *always* takes the first offer regardless of its helpfulness. Nor is there punishment in purgatory for quickly recognizing that an elicited ask-for might be problematic at best, or divisive and mean-spirited at worst. If you sense that the proffered idea won't suit, make the call, decline the gift (perhaps with a little humor or edge depending on your persona and what is warranted), and quickly move on to someone else. Yes, we want to honor our audience and allow them to feel connected and responsible for the resulting play, but we also want to enable scene work that excites and inspires us as players, as this will ultimately best serve *everyone* in attendance.

> **Related Entries:** Audience, Hosting, Initiation
> **Synonyms:** Get, Prompt, Suggestion
> **Connected Game:** Options

ASSUMPTION

There is unavoidable overlap when it comes to improvisational terms that describe the small units from which we build our scenes together. **Offers**, **initiations**, and **endowing** all share terrain with the currently featured idea of making assumptions: "The best initiations make assumptions, usually about their relationship, roles, or locations."[10] Each, in one way or another, refers to a singular idea, detail, or "move" that provides specifics for the evolving scenario. For the purposes of this entry, I would like to contemplate the concept of assumptions as it relates to asking questions in improv – something that is typically considered a no no (although I complicate this stance and muse on when it is a yes yes in my companion **questions** post). Through this narrower lens, the concept of **Assumptions** promotes providing scenic answers and context rather than pushing this burden onto your scene partner.

Example

Option 1

Player A takes great care in setting up a garden, obtaining a shovel, making sure that no one is looking, and then making the first few efforts to break the ground.

Player B enters nonchalantly and with little energy.

Player B: "What are you doing?"

Option 2

Player A takes great care in setting up a garden, obtaining a shovel, making sure that no one is looking, and then making the first few efforts to break the ground.

Player B slowly enters, with great effort, apparently lugging a heavy object behind them. They pause for a moment, clearly winded, and turn to look at Player A's progress:

Player B: "I don't know how I'm ever going to be able to repay you for this…"

Some Additional Analysis

In "Option 1," Player A is literally and figuratively doing all the work, and Player B's contribution is almost negligible. In "Option 2," Player B has now assessed Player A's actions and made some assumptions as to what might be happening. Rather than seeking permission, in this second example, Player B is making an additive choice, providing new information that is inspired by and supports the energy and details already established.

Variations of "Option 1" are surprisingly prevalent and pernicious, especially with improvisers who are still finding their footing in the craft. "What are you doing?" and choices of its ilk are often the result of fear: fear of making a big move, fear of getting it "wrong," fear of not making the "best" of all choices in a sea of almost endless possibilities. As a teacher and coach, I've seen a style of play that I would describe as a tyranny of deferring politeness. Players are so wary of stepping on each other's toes or upending another player's idea, that they hang back anxiously and add little to nothing. Meanwhile their partner, who often only began with the most tentative seed of a thought, similarly lingers in a state of deferment for fear of **bulldozing** or not leaving sufficient room for their fellow improviser to contribute. A perpetual loop of deferring politeness rarely results in joyous play and dynamic scenes.

What can we do as improvisers as we're walking into a scene and face a sea of questions that we are just dying to ask?

Techniques to Turn Your Questions into Assumptions

1. **Take a breath.** When we're not sure what to do or what's going on, we can quickly slip into "performer time" that makes three seconds feel like an eternity but that has little relation to the real "stage time" that steadily ticks forward. Taking a few extra moments, a deep breath, and really observing what

is happening is more likely to set you up for success than racing into the fray without having the time to process the nuances of your partner's actions. If you need an extra moment or two to understand what has been established, consider that the audience may be in the same boat. And frankly, part of the fun of improv is watching players squirm just a little if a choice isn't immediately transparent, so don't rob the audience of this pleasure.

2. **Start small.** You don't need to understand *everything* that is intended (assuming that your partner has, in fact, a clear intent in mind) to provide the gift of your entrance or addition when it's needed. If you're unsure as to the specifics of the bigger picture, concentrate instead on a smaller facet. Can you define a piece of the environment, add a new related prop, or assist in the creation of the mood or style? Choose one piece of the puzzle that intrigues and inspires you and make this the focus of your assumption. Also, keep in mind that your initial assumption need not be expressed verbally and that your thoughtful physical choices can just as easily enrich the emerging world.

3. **Lean into character.** If you're unsure as to your partner's choices or intent, you can still provide confidence and strength by sharply defining your own character, relationship, and point of view. In the above example, Player A is preparing the ground or burying *something*. If you want to allow some ambiguity or give some room for this to develop organically, you can still leap to a very specific emotional energy. If I'm excited, or nervous, or regretful, or amused, that color will provide an interesting new tone and help steer the scene into new or newly defined territory. I like this strategy in particular, as a character's point of view will rarely upend a partner's trajectory if they do have something loaded and ready to go.

4. **If in doubt, join.** I've written about parallel actions in an entry of the same name, but if your mind is flooded with questions, throw yourself into the established action. Grab another mimed prop and start digging, or start grabbing clumps of dirt with your hands, or moving rocks aside and out of the way. Find your own way of doing what you believe your partner is doing while adding energy and emotion. Such an approach of mirroring provides numerous benefits. It gets you off the sidelines and into the field of play, where you're more likely to have your creativity sparked. It gives your partner the gift of your presence and energy which in and of itself might reveal new pathways and options. And it is likely to push your own fear or misgivings to the side as your focus moves out from yourself and into the stage action.

Final Thought

My theory is that while we believe our deferring politeness is an act of kindness to our partners on stage, in reality, it is our fear getting the better of us and that our partners would nearly always prefer us to just take the risk of adding our idea even if we're not 100% sure it's what they had in mind. Making assumptions as a strategy isn't predicated on the notion that these assumptions will always line up perfectly with what our partner tentatively envisioned. As I noted above, our partner may, in fact, have *nothing* specific in mind. Rather, an assuming attitude acknowledges that many of the questions rattling around in our head may be simultaneously rattling around in the heads of our scene partners and audience, so why not just leap in and define what we see with richer context when we can rather than hiding in the shadows of the improv unknown?

Related Entries: Bulldozing, Endowing, Specificity **Antonyms:** Fear, Questions
Synonyms: Initiation, Offer
Connected Game: Scene without Questions

AUDIENCE

One of the simplest definitions of theatre is a person performing in a space in front of others: without the integral component of our audience, one could argue, we are essentially endlessly rehearsing. Or, in the words of Viola Spolin, "The audience is the most revered member of the theater [...] They are our guests, fellow players, and the last spoke in the wheel which can then begin to roll. They make the performance meaningful."[11] Especially in a mode as impermanent and collaborative as improv, the **Audience** takes on an even more critical role, donning numerous hats and functions in the shared moment of spontaneous creation. From source of inspiration or active participant, to communal partner, supportive patron, or honored witness, the function can vary widely from venue to venue. But regardless of their assigned or discovered role(s), their presence makes the whole theatrical affair *meaningful*.

I've directed and created works for professional, academic, and community markets and often think about how I am or how I could be better serving my varied audiences. Here are some current themes I've been contemplating.

Contracts We Could/Should Have with Our Audiences

1. **We should play at the top of our intelligence (and aim higher).** Most improv schools of thought promote this approach to the craft although, if I were to be a little blunt, I'm not sure that it is always consciously and rigorously applied and practiced. While it is incumbent upon us as artists to create material that will entice attendance, I think it's similarly incumbent upon us to use our positions on the stage in a thoughtful way, even if we're "just" trying to entertain. The most accessible crowd-pleasing improv still exists in the context of our current political landscape. I imagine that most of us working in more entertainment-focused modes are guilty of grabbing at some easy laughs, but we can also (or simultaneously) instill our improv with intelligence and care. Furthermore, if we are striving as artists to continually become more informed and aware of the issues and tensions in the world around us, then we are better equipped to knowingly reflect these realities back to our assembled guests. Some forms of improv are unabashedly pedagogic or radical in this sense, but I would posit that even the most seemingly benign short-form game can serve as an opportunity for astute observation.

2. **We should strive to reflect and represent our communities.** One of the gifts of improvisation is that it tends to make the tools of performance more readily available. For practitioners such as Augusto Boal, Viola Spolin, and Jonathan Fox, this is a primary element of their practices, but many "mainstream" improv companies embrace amateurs and new voices in a way that scripted theatre cannot due to the constraints of the written text and the highly hierarchical nature of scripted rehearsal processes. This is not to say that improvisational performance can't also be highly polished and professional, providing artworks that display careful crafting and practice, but companies often house multiple shows, ensembles, and performance opportunities. In addition to welcoming diverse audiences into our auditoriums, our craft benefits enormously from welcoming this same diversity onto our stages. We all crave to hear our stories told and see ourselves represented. We are more likely as a company to truly represent our communities if we are performing *with* and *amongst* them rather than merely *for* them.

3. **We should balance what our audience wants with what we find of value.** I create for a variety of companies and production situations and so my works are not always subject to the same financial pressures of the box office. In my free admission campus work, for example, we can take the risk of working on some projects that are more unabashedly about artistic development and exploration. When I craft pieces as part of a subscription season, I need to be aware that "regular" theatregoers will typically want something that looks a little more polished and akin to other scripted plays and musicals that are programmed in the same season. When I'm commissioned or invited to create works for professional or revenue-dependent partners, the need for having a sense of currently successful practices and programming looms larger. But in each of these instances, there should be a fruitful artistic tension between what we believe an audience will find joyful and what excites, intrigues, and inspires us as improvisational artists. Audience-pleasing work can quickly alienate or dishearten the company if they don't feel that this product is sufficiently challenging and artistically rewarding. Similarly, artist-pleasing work will quickly fold if it cannot find a way to attract and retain audiences. We should also keep in mind that an audience cannot know that they might like something different if we do not invest the time in exposing them strategically to new forms and approaches. It's all a matter of balance.

4. **We should nurture environments free from belligerence.** Whether belligerence or animosity is flowing amongst the players, within the audience, or between the stage and house, we should be attentive to addressing missteps and inappropriate conduct. Audiences should not be subjected to offensive material or representations without candid acknowledgment and redress. This may be framed "playfully" or "lightly" in the moment, but it should be clear that a flag of spontaneity is not being used as a cover for ignorant or reckless content. Similarly, fellow audience members should be held to reasonable codes of conduct as well. Allowing an insensitive, prejudiced, or bigoted suggestion to go unchecked can send loud messages to those who share our spaces and will quickly erode trust. As onstage improvisers, we are gatekeepers whether we embrace this role or not, and we should take this responsibility seriously as we seek to grow and honor

our audiences. This commitment to appropriate communication and content should also clearly apply to our educational programs and administrations as well.
5. **We should allow for mistakes while striving for improvement.** Embracing failure and mistakes is an important part of the improvisational ethos, and while my observations above stress accountability, we should also seek an environment that leaves room for stumbles and subsequent growth. There is a marked difference between an audience member yelling out an obscene or deliberately divisive suggestion or comment, and an uninformed patron using uninterrogated or lazy clichés or tropes. In my opinion, the former should most likely be escorted from the theatre, while the latter might invite an opportunity to gently educate or inform. Similarly, there is a stark contrast between a player who routinely assumes stereotypical or demeaning characterizations, and an over-eager neophyte whose anxiousness gets the better of them with an off-hand comment or simplistic portrayal. In my opinion, the former should most likely be escorted from the theatre, while the latter might invite an opportunity to gently educate or inform.

Final Thought

This entry became a little more serious and pedantic than I'd initially intended, but I believe we should be extremely wary of taking our relationship with our audiences for granted. I think it's important that improvisational practitioners show care in how they craft and frame improv events so as to maximize connections with and between audience members. As Spolin notes, they *are* what makes the art of improv meaningful. For those of us who have explored internet-based performance opportunities in the lost years of COVID, that reality – as we were faced with the silence and coldness of our computer cameras and screens – could not have been made more vitally clear and resonant.

And on a simpler note, make sure you graciously accept compliments from your audiences when you are fortunate enough to receive them. Nobody wants to give a performer praise only to have it awkwardly dismissed or ignored!

> **Related Entries:** Hosting, Inclusiveness, Trust, Volunteers
> **Connected Game:** Scene in the Audience

AUDITIONS

Auditioning is a necessary but seldom relished part of our craft as improvisers. I've experienced and led a wide range of different audition processes: from professional genre pieces and short-form ensembles, to community productions and collegiate troupes. While the details of these projects and processes vary from show to show and venue to venue, there are undoubtedly some helpful **Audition** strategies I've gleaned along the way that apply more times than they do not. So here they are…!

Putting Your Best Foot Forward

1. **Do your homework.** We rarely do our best and most playful work when we're uninformed going into an audition. In most cases, you should be able to find out something about the piece, style, or energy of the company or project. If audition materials are provided, read them thoroughly and jot down any questions you might have in case you get an opportunity to ask. If the company or production is currently performing, make sure you go and see them in action (and, if possible, briefly introduce yourself afterward). Have a look at any available online resources as well. While you cannot become a completely different kind of improviser overnight to suit a company's ethos, you *can* make an effort to lead with the most fitting tools currently available in your improv tool belt. And just having a sense of content parameters can save you the embarrassment of playing too G-rated in an adult venue or dropping your most colorful language in a format designed to entertain families.
2. **Listen and observe.** Generally, you'll be auditioned in small groups but there may also be an opportunity to observe others in the audition process. Take advantage of this chance every way you can. Listen to any feedback or adjustments provided by those running the auditions: often you can get a sense of their preferences or needs. Are they enjoying a more overtly comedic or ribald style of play, or nudging players toward scenes that are more connected and vulnerable? Does the audition space provide any challenges or unique opportunities for play? For example, are players struggling to stay open or be heard, and are there ways you can smartly adjust your choices when it's your turn to perform? You'll also want to make sure you're being a supportive and present audience member (this certainly will

be noticed as well) but don't completely disengage your directorial eye. And when it's your turn, make sure you're openly and receptively taking any notes or feedback you may be given.
3. **Focus on connection.** With a few very rare exceptions, improv is a team sport and it's likely that the directing bench is interested in how you connect and play with others. Don't let a desire to shine or "be seen" veer you off course from being a giving and attentive scene partner. As in any good improv scene, the interest and answers lie in the relationships you're creating and exploring on stage. This focus can be particularly difficult to pursue when our inner voices are fearful that we might not be doing enough or haven't been sufficiently noticed, but selfish improv will rarely be the *lingua franca*.
4. **Focus on play.** Yes, you should do your research and take the process seriously but remember to find joy and abandon in the audition itself. Be careful of relentless résumé-ing or name dropping, be sure to celebrate the successes and brave struggles of others and try to keep your competitive beast at bay. A lesson I keep learning as a director is that the "most talented" option may not always best serve the project or ensemble, especially if they bring with them pervasive negativity, a lack of resilience, or a deep fear of getting something wrong. In a field where the process *is* the product, displaying your ability to contribute joyfully and playfully even when the work gets tough or stressful will serve you well.
5. **Practice resilience and grace.** And speaking of resilience, this one audition may not work out in your favor. It's a really tough part of our industry that there will always be much more interest and talent than most improv stages could ever possibly satiate. Consider every audition as an opportunity to explore and learn something new about yourself or your craft. If your experience revealed a deficit, consider deepening your training in that area. If you're not cast this time but you made a strong positive impression, you might find yourself approached for a future gig. Improv practitioners are always looking for potential talent. Play the long game, especially if this is a company or creative team that you particularly respect and enjoy. Send a simple and sincere thank you note and see the finished product if you're able. And if you are cast, be sure to show grace and consideration for those who may not have had similar success. Our improv community is surprisingly small at times, and a poor "winner" is no more enticing than a sore "loser."

Final Thought

We can do a lot of harm to our own chances if we engage in too much second-guessing about a particular director's casting needs or preferences. Do your research, but then get your "play" on, taking joyful risks and lifting up your partners for similar success. Be the very best version of you – no one else can be better at that than you. And as Mark Twain mused in his autobiography, "We are always more anxious to be distinguished for a talent which we do not possess, than to be praised for the fifteen which we do possess." Focus on the latter!

Synonyms: Preparation, Professionalism
Connected Game: Three Through the Door

NOTES

1. Viola Spolin, *Improvisation for the Theater. A Handbook of Teaching and Directing Techniques*. 3rd ed. Evanston, IL: Northwestern UP, 1999. p. 7.
2. Keith Johnstone, *Impro. Improvisation and the Theatre*. 1979. New York: Routledge, 1992. p. 100.
3. Jimmy Carrane and Liz Allen, *Improvising Better. A Guide for the Working Improviser*. Portsmouth, NH: Heinemann, 2006. p. 15.
4. Jimmy Carrane and Liz Allen, *Improvising Better. A Guide for the Working Improviser*. Portsmouth, NH: Heinemann, 2006. p. 35.
5. Mary Crossan, "Improvise to Innovate." *Ivey Business Quarterly* 62.1 (Autumn 1997): 36(7).
6. Bernard Sahlins, *Days and Nights at the Second City. A Memoir, with Notes on Staging Review Theatre*. Chicago: Ivan R. Dee, 2001. p. 164.
7. Lyn Pierse, *Theatresports Down Under*. 2nd ed. Sydney, Australia: Improcorp, 1995. p. 53.
8. Amy E. Seham, *Whose Improv Is It Anyway: Beyond Second City*. Jackson, MS: University of Mississippi Press, 2001. p. 224.
9. Keith Johnstone, *Impro for Storytellers*. New York: Routledge, 1999. p. 26.
10. Charna Halpern et al., *Truth in Comedy. The Manual of Improvisation*. Colorado Springs: Meriwether, 1994. p. 57.
11. Viola Spolin, *Improvisation for the Theater. A Handbook of Teaching and Directing Techniques*. 3rd ed. Evanston, IL: Northwestern University Press, 1999. p. 13.

B

BACKLINE

The non-performing players watching the action standing ready to enter or support the scene as needed. In "Chicago-style" modes and improv performed in found or less theatrical spaces, this practice usually literally takes the form of a line of players leaning or sitting against the upstage wall of the theatre, although the expression can be more loosely used to refer to those members of the ensemble not currently involved in the performance.

Related Entry: Stage Picture

BACKSTORY

A term referring to (generally unseen) actions that occurred prior to those explored onstage. Such events and character histories can bring a lot of detail, stakes, and urgency to the improvisational plot, although many schools of thought warn that scenic work may become passive or static if characters *exclusively* talk about past events rather than actively explore and embody current ramifications.

Synonyms: Antecedent Action, Exposition

BALANCE

This serves as a slightly out-of-the-box entry in that there are four varieties of balance that are worthy of mention here. Instead of prioritizing one concept to stand alone, I'll address each in turn.

Definition #1

Balance can be used to refer to **the initial state of the world as our scene or improvised play begins**. In a structuralist or Aristotelian model this term describes the play before it has been ignited (or changed) in such an irreversible way that the rising action *must* begin. This momentum will then, in turn, eventually lead to the climax and, finally, the resolution. This is the varietal of balance referenced in *Truth in Comedy* when the authors note,

> To discover the potential games in each scene, players must pay close attention from the start. They must be especially careful to notice their own lines, since players often aren't aware of the games they are setting up themselves.[1]

It is indeed crucial to bring a high level of attentiveness to the opening moves of each scene because these details should provide helpful ingredients to assist in the formulation of the resulting action. While I love jump-starting scenes in the middle – and all the dynamic energy this choice brings – there is also something to be said for a more patient and deliberate opening, especially if you are working in a long-form modality where it is more likely that there will be time to really unpack ideas planted in these early moments.

Connected to this concept of balance is the tradition of **CROW** (Character, Relationship, Objective, and Where) or the related acronym WWW (Who, What, and Where). When these details are crafted with care and love during the opening of a scene, improvisers are more likely to have a strong and nuanced base from which to build their creative journeys. This dynamic is synonymous with the concept of a platform or routine awaiting something to interrupt or tilt the world into a new trajectory. It's important to note that the scenic balance does not suggest nor necessitate an initial lack of dynamism or energy. The given circumstances of your world may be quite elevated right from the get-go: you might already be in the grasp of the zombie apocalypse, your family might be in the thick of financial struggles and on the verge of losing their home due to staggering debts, or the colony of field mice might already be in the throes of escaping from the enemy brigade of cats. These energetic scenarios all may serve as a balance for a scene awaiting the discovery of what makes this day different from all the rest.

Player A: (entering their home with a heavy sigh) "Sorry I'm late for dinner. I hit that construction again on the highway…"

Definition #2

Balance can also be used to refer to **the way in which we work together as an ensemble**. When a group is operating successfully, there can be a sense that all the parts of the improv machine are functioning and interacting with ease, and that each cog is doing just the right amount of creative work, no more or less. It can prove truly challenging to address "act hunger" in improv: the desire for each individual to be seen and to contribute in a way that gives meaning and joy can be difficult to skillfully accommodate and nurture. And yet, if ensemble members routinely feel overlooked, under-featured, or poorly utilized, this will quickly undermine the cohesion that proves so integral to communal creativity.

I've written about **shining** as one of my commandment entries, and this earlier consideration provides frames and strategies for considering how we share the light of the stage. It's important to note that balance in this setting is not synonymous with equal stage time necessarily, although this certainly could be *one* measure, especially in performances such as short-form competitions where an attentive host or team can adjust their line-up or focus based on who has already enjoyed a featured opportunity to play. Rather, I would offer that balance is more a consideration of generosity and awareness. Was the company cognizant when players became under-utilized and was this addressed when it could be done so in terms of the established form or genre? Were acts of selflessness and generosity recognized and valued? Did the company as a whole fully support the central story as it emerged?

Player B: (looking furtively offstage to a patiently waiting fellow player) "I think I just heard my mother's car pull into the driveway. Please don't tell her about my terrible report card…"

Definition #3

We can also consider **Balance** in terms of **our company demographics and commitment to inclusiveness**. Are we actively pursuing balance in terms of who we see on stage, what stories we are telling, and whose voices we are uplifting and featuring? Improv has historically struggled with this sense of balance, and it has rightly been called upon to continue questioning its unchecked biases and charged with finding new ways to diversify its membership and leadership. Many movements, such as Augusto Boal's Theatre of the Oppressed, Viola Spolin's original theatre games, and Jonathan Fox's Playback Theatre, have defined themselves as movements committed to sharing the tools and power of creativity. Modern mainstream improv, though often influenced by similar philosophies, hasn't always displayed an equally strong track record of opening its doors and stages.

I explore this complex issue in greater depth in a later entry focused on **inclusiveness**, but it's worth repeating here that the health and vibrancy of improvisation's future is intimately connected to its ability to actively listen, include, and change. These tenets serve as the bedrock of our onstage craft and should similarly serve as calls to action for our offstage, organizational, and recruiting policies and practices.

Player C: (during a greenroom discussion) "We should invite this exciting new up-and-coming team to come and join us in a jam…"

Definition #4

And finally, let us consider **Balance** in terms of **our life and art**. It is unfortunately a rarity for improvisational practitioners to pay all their bills solely from their craft as a performer. Most professional improv artists that I know cobble together a living from acting in many forms, teaching, consulting, administrative work, devising and/or directing, and many (dare I say *most*) also maintain a full-time "day job" that is less often in the realm of improv theatre. As an industry, there exists a tension between what we personally find artistically satisfying and enriching, and what is marketable and therefore likely to attract a paying audience. (This is, perhaps, yet another facet of "balance" worthy of discussion which I explore a little in my discussion of the **audience**.) In the United States, at least, where there's a general lack of federal funding for the arts – especially those seen as fringe or marginal – the title of professional improviser can feel oxymoronic or, if I were to paint it in a more favorable light, aspirational.

It is an understatement then, to note that improvisers typically *do a lot*. Some modalities embrace and extol an amateur status – see the examples in definition #3 above. This nomenclature can sit less comfortably with those who have devoted a lifetime to the pursuit of spontaneous theatre forms and practices. As we contemplate our individual and collective place in the art and the greater artistic community, it is of equal importance that we pursue a sense of balance in our own lives. I will openly confess that this has proven a struggle personally. Exhausted artists are rarely sharp and joyful artists. Overwhelmed improvisers are seldom situated to lift up their teammates and fellow collaborators. We must remember to also live the lives that we seek to reflect on our stages.

Player D: "Just a heads up that I'm taking next month off to recharge a little…"

Final Thought

And so the concept of balance is clearly omnipresent and multifaceted in the realm of improvisation. Whether we are establishing rich and dynamic given circumstances, pursuing collaborative and inclusive modes of play and company demographics that facilitate crafting a chorus of stories in harmony, or seeking to successfully juggle the many facets and callings of our lives, balance provides a worthy and challenging goal.

> **Related Entries:** Commandment #3, Ensemble, Inclusiveness **Antonyms:** Breaking Routines, Shining **Synonyms:** Given Circumstances, Platform, Routine **Connected Game:** Four Sentence Story

BLACKOUT

In the most traditional sense, this refers to the lights plummeting (or possibly slowly transitioning) into darkness at the completion of a scene or improvised play. It provides perhaps the most resolute form of an **edit** or **button**. Some improv and sketch schools also use this term to indicate a dynamically brief scene (usually punctuated by a sudden or unexpected ending).

> **Related Entry:** Edits

BLOCKING

The scourge of blocking (not to be confused with the scripted theatrical concept of staging) recurs as an underlying theme in most modern improvisational practices. Lynda Belt and Rebecca Stockley observe the following:

> Blocking is a perfidious, recurring problem which appears in the work of the best improvisors. They may block to stay in control, or to stay safe. Many beginning improvisors block because it gets a laugh and it feels good to make people laugh.[2]

Blocking describes the practice of denying, negating, or dismissing the suggestions or offers of others on the improv stage (though one can certainly block one's own creative process as well). It often occurs as a voiced "no" although I prefer to think of it as an energy or lack thereof rather than a *word*. When you block, you hold your scene partner's choice at arm's length only to ultimately discard it. There are few habits in improv more likely to cause consternation or undermine the momentum and appeal of a developing scene, so much so that it is the first among the Ten Commandments of *Theatresports*: "Thou shalt not block."

Example

Player A has assumed the role of a parent working alongside their child (Player B) on repairing the family car.

Player A: (*Lying on their back as if under the car*) "Okay, just hand me that wrench on the workstation…"
Player B: "No."

OR

Player A: (*Lying on their back as if under the car*) "Okay, just hand me that wrench on the workstation…"
Player B: (*Ignoring Player A while on a phone*) "So I'm here at the mall but I can't see you anywhere…"

OR

Player A: (*Lying on their back as if under the car*) "Okay, just hand me that wrench on the workstation…"
Player B: "What are you doing lying on the ground like that anyway? Is that supposed to be a car?"

OR

Player A: (Lying on their back as if under the car) "Okay, just hand me that wrench on the workstation…"
Player B: (with no energy or commitment) "Ummm…" *They wander aimlessly around the space (and likely "through" the car) only to eventually return to their starting place without actually doing anything.*

Some Additional Analysis

As Belt and Stockley note, these parleys might garner a chuckle or two from the audience, but it is unlikely that any of these scenic variants are off to a good start. At the very least, Player A will feel a little ignored or rebuked. So why does this blocking energy so frequently appear in our improv if we are not vigilant? In many instances, it comes down to one simple and pernicious word: fear.

How Fear Can Lead to Blocking

1. **A fear of being wrong.** Improv is a rare performance tradition in which the process *is* the product and so the audience gets the joy and delightful agony of watching our fumbles alongside our successes. Most Western education systems, however, typically marginalize or hide the process of creation. Revisions or mistakes occur in private and educational systems rarely reward or recognize the importance of glorious mistakes. Keith Johnstone writes about the harms of formal education at length, and unfortunately decades later his observations still hold true for many students and their journeys. When we hide and devalue the pedagogic value of errors, and obscure the creative process, it follows that the fear of being wrong can loom large as a shadow over our work. The immediacy of improv does not coexist easily with a desire to sift through countless choices and options before adding to the scene. It demands that we follow our instincts and training and make the choice that feels "best" in the moment. Saying "no" would seemingly give us more time to weigh our options, although this brief pause usually results in little more than the improv train passing us by as we wait passively on the station platform.
2. **A fear of ceding control.** Just as many artistic and academic modes hide or undervalue the messy process, most of us also live in a culture that tends to praise the illusion of the individual genius. The innately collaborative nature of improvisation belies this mirage, but it is easily hampered by the persistent cobwebs of personal ego and desire. It can be difficult not to start to think ahead and contemplate how we as individuals would like to see a scene develop. "If I embrace my partner's choice, then the doorway to my 'great idea' will close and I don't know where we'll go instead." The world can make us feel as if we have so little control over our own destinies, but in prioritizing our own personal destination, we are missing the true creative value of the process. Saying "no" might appear to give us more control over how a scene develops, but in reality, it will likely thwart our fellow travelers, resulting in no one reaching improv nirvana.
3. **A fear of the unknown.** Threaded through the above fears is a reluctance to step willingly and joyfully into the creative void. If we don't know and control the path ahead, how can we possibly be right or have the action serve our personal goals as an artist or character? An ability to revel in such an expansive potential that can feel almost suffocating does not always come easily or quickly. In our day-to-day lives, it is probably wise that we don't embrace any opportunity without some reasoned consideration, but on the improv stage, we are giving the audience and ourselves the gift of suspending our survival instincts so that we may release our inner adventurers. Saying "no" allows us to remain on the precipice of action and discovery, but we will ultimately never learn what is beyond the ledge nor allow growth by welcoming earnest surprise into our work.
4. **A fear of revealing a lack of knowledge.** Unlike a traditional script, where we can spend our time researching a particular historical moment, cultural context, or character backstory, in the improvisational realm, we never know where our stories and scenes might take us. Often, a blocking energy can stem from the resulting uncertainty. Do I know enough about cars to join in the action of this repair? Will I reveal to the audience and my scene partners that I lack knowledge on an important subject? If I attack this scene with abandon, will I potentially embarrass myself? (As a teacher, I would argue this fear can also terribly undermine any candid sense of discussion in a classroom.) And yet, our audience so often applauds performer vulnerability and risk-taking, and we are likely to facilitate not only our own personal growth but that of our patrons when we make good-faith assumptions and choices. Saying "no" would appear to keep us safely on the sidelines, but instead, it robs the audience of the joy of our bravery and struggles as we embrace unfamiliar territory.

5. **A fear of assuming stances that might be mistaken as our own.** Improvisers do not have the protection of a playwright's script forming a screen between them and their characters. When we earnestly take on personae in front of an audience – especially those that might embody negative, undesirable, or caustic views – there can be a fear that anti-social views might be mistaken as belonging to the improviser underneath the mask. This tension appears more commonly in sincere styles of performance, but I have seen younger improvisers struggle with this dichotomy in short-form modes as well. There can be a power and release in embodying less laudable characters, and I personally enjoy seeking truth in points of view that are diametrically opposed to my own. (I would also confess that I was less able and willing to assume such roles when I was taking my first steps in the field.) Just as we encourage players to embrace the unknown in terms of where a scene might go, I think it is equally crucial that we embrace the unknown in terms of character views and systems of belief. Saying "no" to exploring the full range of our political world could appear to bolster our own convictions, but probably just prevent us from understanding societal tensions in a more nuanced and empathetic way.

Final Thought

When we follow the energy of "no" in our improv work, we are letting our fears get the better of us. It is not a small or simple thing to cast these fears out, and amassing additional experience does not mean that these battles have been fought and won for all times. Succumbing to the "no," however, provides us only with the most temporary of reprieves and the scene is likely to gallop ahead without us as we loiter in our desire to be right or in control. On the other hand, when we embrace the risk of "yes," accepting that invitation into the delights of the unknown, fear will often dissipate into the dust of our momentum. When we no longer dwell on every choice before we execute it, and rather bring our full presence into our bodies and the action of the scene, we begin to starve our fears from the time and oxygen they need to survive.

For some strategies on how to make the most of your "Yes And" onstage, see my earlier musings on **accepting**.

Related Entries: Commandment #1
Antonyms: Accepting, Agreement, Yes And, Yielding **Synonyms:** Denial, Negating, No
Connected Game: Rule Breaker

BRAVERY

The ability to step into the unknown with a sense of calm and grace in spite of the fact that you have no idea how things will turn out; an admirable improv skill worth nurturing.

Synonym: Abandon

BREAKING

A generally to-be-avoided habit of dropping the façade of your character and becoming your non-theatrical self during the unfolding improvisational action. In most improv cultures – especially those that incline toward a more realistic style of play – continuous breaking tends to diminish the stakes and intensity of the performance.

Synonyms: Corpsing, Mugging

BREAKING ROUTINES

Connected Game: Fortunately/Unfortunately
Related Entries: CAD, Commandment #7, Game of the Scene **Antonyms:** Balance, Platform, Routine **Synonyms:** Ignition

Final Thought

And so it can be helpful to overturn prior routines, if for no other reason than to allow yourself a chance to see things afresh once more. Routines and patterns are such an integral part of life, and therefore art; but it is when the balance is upended and the potential of something new is sparked that the power and poignancy of theatre begins.

Some Methods for Shaking Up the Routine

4. **Add significance by asking "What is different about today?"** In my improv workshop or class, I tend to use the language and frames of scripted theatre when it comes to considering

Figure 4.1 Cast members of *The Lost Comedies of William Shakespeare* break their established routine by going to sea (Lighting design: Akin Ritchie; Musical director: Stephen Merritt). Scott Cook Photography.

the structure and progression of our improvisational work. It would be rare (with the exception of some extreme variants of naturalism) to dramatize a *true* slice of life in which no notable event or journey occurred. Following this example, if our "play" begins with four friends eating fish and chips at the beach, typically something of import will happen or there will be a given circumstance that elevates this encounter beyond the everyday. (If we are working in a long-form modality, the exception to this rule would be if we are consciously establishing a **balance** for our play knowing that the routine will be broken in a future vignette.) The answer to "What is different about today?" is almost limitless and can support a wide range of moods and styles. We could have a gentle and heartfelt scene if this is the last day of summer before the friends depart to various universities. The gathering could take on a more absurd or whimsical energy if ravenous seagulls attempt to maneuver their way to the coveted food. Or we could embrace style if we learn that two of the friends are in fact lovers and planning to escape from their overbearing parents that very night. Initially, it's helpful if just *one* element is different today so as to enable everyone to explore facets of a similar game or story.

3. **Add interest with an inversion or tilt.** If the scene is meandering over well-worn routines, exploring an inversion or tilt can provide new life and interest. If the platform would typically mandate a power relationship (a teacher is instructing a student), finding a way to switch the expectation can offer a new pathway (the student has an area of expertise that the teacher does not share). If you enjoy status work, this break in the routine can be viewed as a status breach or scuffle: a mechanic is going through a lengthy car repair bill with a seemingly naive customer, only to learn that they are in fact a reporter doing an investigative piece on shady car repair shops. Or the concept of mapping can provide another interesting approach: the perfunctory scene at the breakfast table between family members slowly reveals itself to actually be anthropomorphized cockroaches preparing for their day.

2. **Add energy by heightening or climbing the curve of absurdity.** There are certainly times when the routine itself might be the most promising or charming component of the scene and disrupting

this joyfulness in a way that curtails it might erase a previously promising direction. In these instances, heightening the routine, adding stakes, urgency, emotion, intensified commitment, or all the above could prove to be a successful strategy for elevating the routine. Lucille Ball and the conveyor belt of chocolates come to mind as an example of this approach. While the routine may remain, it builds in such a way that it no longer exists in the realm of the mundane. If you are familiar with the curve of absurdity, this is an allied concept, with the routine initially beginning in a familiar way, but through the deployment of patient moves, culminates in an often absurd conclusion. I consider this concept more fully in my definition of the game of the scene.

1. **Add dynamism with a CAD.** CAD is an acronym for **C**onfession, **A**ccusation, and **D**iscovery and I deal with this concept and its constituent elements in other entries at greater length, but allowing your character to make a revelation will typically change the mood and possibly the direction of the scene. Powerful CADs tend to build off what has already been established (relationship, backstory, or environment elements) but perhaps in a slightly unexpected or charged way. By definition, they are disruptive, bringing something that may have only been brewing at the level of inference or subtext to the surface of the scene in a way that demands notice and address. If you are stuck in a loop, a well-placed CAD can be your best improv friend.

Example

A good example of breaking the routine would be inverting a well-established pattern...

As Johnstone notes, "Breaking the routine frees the improviser from the treadmill of always needing a good idea."[3] **Breaking Routines** is a helpful and liberating tool for generating material and interest in our work. Patterns and routines can provide a sense of familiarity and allow our audiences to connect to the characters and the worlds that we represent on the stage. But often the power of these routines resides in their function as launching pads. While an audience may find enjoyment in the repetition and fidelity of these patterns, it is generally when the routine is ruptured that such material truly takes on significance. If this initial breach occurs for the first time in our improvised play – thereby upending the balance – this moment can be thought of as an ignition that sparks the rise in the dramatic action. However, breaking routines as a strategy is not limited to this particular moment and will likely appear throughout your scenic work, providing interest and energy to your improvisational play (or lengthy book!).

BULLDOZING

Sharing is so integral to the craft of improvisation: when the ability to generously and deliberately move focus within the ensemble is off or hampered, the very act of collaborative creation becomes threatened. Paul Sills muses on this need in an interview with Jeffrey Sweet.

> ...actor's liberation is very important. For that you need a free space. A space where work can be freely done, in which a person is free to become. A space in which people share together and, in sharing, free themselves. But you have to have a way to enter into this space, to bring about the possibility of playing together in a reality that wasn't there before creating it together through sharing.[4]

I view **Bulldozing** in this context as it is fundamentally an inability to allow sufficient creative space for your teammates. The rationale or motivation for bulldozing can vary widely: it can be a manifestation of a lack of trust, a craving for acclaim or recognition, an inability to retain a greater awareness of other energies and possibilities on stage, a desire to move the scene in one specific direction that meets your individual whims, or a misplaced excitement to play that overshadows the critical need to allow others to "pong" to your "ping." Regardless of the intention, the result remains the same: a silencing of other potential voices, connections, and possibilities. As we become more confident and "stronger" as improvisers, this inclination can easily emerge, and it is certainly a beast that I continue to wrestle. While most would agree leading from strength is important, this improvisational attitude must always be tempered with generosity and active listening.

Example

Players gather around a table. As the lights come up, Player A assumes the role of the head of the household.

Player A: "Look, I know none of us want to tighten our belts, but I've been going over the family finances, and we are wasting a LOT of money every month on things that I just don't think we need."

The other players murmur and Player B stands as the precursor to speaking...

Player A: (interrupting) "Now I know what you're going to say. *Your* spending is essential, unlike everyone else's, but I've combed through everyone's credit card receipts. You spent over $800 last month on coffee alone..."

Player B begins to respond, but Player A has now moved their focus...

Player A: (talking to Player C) "And you! We all love snookums, but the amount you spend on dog grooming is astronomical. It's nearly as much as we spend on our mortgage."

They all grumble again. Player C lifts "snookums" onto their lap and begins to speak but...

Player A: (handing out various papers) "So, I have gone ahead and made up personal budgets for each of us. From this point on, we will all have to live off an allowance. Now I know what you're going to say..."

Some Additional Analysis

While bulldozing may not always appear in the form of a monologue or cascade of uninterrupted offers, this is frequently a telltale sign. Monologues certainly have a valid place in our work, but generally, these will expand upon a point of view or help add energy to the rising action during a pivotal moment. In the above example, other players clearly have the instinct and desire to contribute so as to help build upon the initial premise, but Player A is oblivious (or over-anxious) and unable to loosen the reins. While most of us enjoy playing alongside other improvisers who approach their craft and scenes with certitude and strength, as is the case with nearly all techniques in improv (and art) it is a matter of balance and awareness.

Ways to Siphon the Fuel of Your Bulldozer

As I've framed this problematic dynamic in terms of focus and sharing, let us explore ways to stop yourself in your tracks if you find yourself unwittingly playing the role of a bulldozer:

1. **Assume a lower status position.** When it comes to status in our improv work, it is innately easier to drive a scene if you assume a high status on stage. When you take on the role of the top dog, mafia boss, or big cheese, there is a power disequilibrium built in that can encourage or "excuse" a domineering energy or approach. However, if you adopt a lower-status character and truly embrace your position in the pecking order, this can help lessen the likelihood that your excitement as an improviser will get the better of you (and your teammates). In the above example, Player A could then bring forth the scenic starting point of overspending, but do so from a different perspective: "I don't know why Yvette wants to talk to us all about our spending. I've just been doing what I always do every week."

2. **Endow others as the protagonist.** When we perceive a scene as primarily *our* character's journey, this similarly sets up a temptation for monopolizing if we are already so inclined. Gifting the most pivotal or central role to another of our teammates should encourage us to direct our energy in a more helpful fashion. This may involve lifting someone else's status (as described earlier), although the protagonist need not be the highest-status character on the stage. So, Player A might offer, "Yvette, I know you've wanted us to watch our spending this month, and I really tried." It is certainly still possible to become voluminous and controlling, but if you are truly serving the journey of a protagonist, you should – at least in theory – be allowing sufficient room for them to react and experience that adventure.

3. **Restrict your verbal contributions (but not your breaths).** This is perhaps the most obvious suggestion and, frankly, is a helpful solution for nearly any focus or verbosity-related issue on the improv stage. Seek to maximize your clarity while minimizing your language and after each sentence take a true breath that invites and allows the next choice to come from another in the scene. "I've invited you all to this family meeting to discuss our financial choices." There is still a *lot* of richness and potential in such an opening choice. If we trust our own ability to communicate, and our teammates' abilities to co-create, the next choice should generally be a breath while we actively listen. In my experience, scenes are more likely to crackle if each character has a window to lock in their point of view in the founding moments, and this strategy aids in this endeavor as well.

4. **Find the love.** Again, I'm fond of this note for almost *any* scene or character, but in both a literal and metaphoric sense, love can help calm your internal metronome and remind you to focus on the experience of others. On a literal level,

building love into scenic relationships can inform your subtext, raise the stakes, and create an inner turmoil or tension that will hopefully enable you to trust the silences more. If Player A begins with nervous pacing and painfully announces, "I really don't know how to tell you this, but we can't afford to pay our bills this month," and infuses the line with love, the belligerence that can often accompany bulldozing has been diffused right from the top of the scene. On a metaphoric or perhaps meta level, when we add in a love for our fellow performers, this serves as a powerful reminder that we want to also set them up for agency and success. Bulldozing tends to appear when we're playing with a competitive rather than collaborative mindset.

5. **Delay your entrance (and look for your exit).** If you feel yourself revving up in the wings, anxious to get that *whole* idea to the stage, sometimes the best tactic is just to wait. In the short-form tradition, there are some games that I enjoy playing so much more than others: if a Shakespeare scene is offered, I'm much more likely to want to rush the stage than if Moving Bodies has been announced. In the former case, it can be helpful to resist the urge to start and defer to my teammates if they are primed and inspired. In the long-form tradition, if you know you are an important character or that there's a big move brewing, allowing others space prior to your entrance can make sure you are remaining receptive and reactive. Finding an appropriate exit is the other side of the coin and this is a helpful tactic if you've found yourself dominating or eclipsing others on stage. If you are the highest-status character, generous exits are particularly important as your "underlings" may not get to speak freely or engage in mischief while you are present.

Final Thought

Characters should dynamically fight for their objectives, striving to achieve their desired outcome in their life's story. *Improvisers*, on the other hand, should not be fighting or working in opposition to or at the expense of their collaborators. As we encourage and seek our strength and voice, bulldozing can and probably will emerge at times even among the most self-aware of companies: sometimes our excitement gets the better of us or we are sitting on a powerful move that needs a little room to fully materialize in a way that will serve the story and the company. But left unchecked, this energy can sap the creative spirit of your ensemble. It's important that we kindly acknowledge these moments when they occur so that we can continue to commit to each other and privilege the discoveries that can only occur when everyone has an opportunity to take a turn at the wheel.

Related Entries: Commandment #2, Give, Waffling
Antonyms: Passenger **Synonyms:** Steamrolling
Connected Game: Speak in Turn

BULLETPROOF

There's a lot of wisdom in Sahlin's observation that, "To believe that our ideas are true and incontrovertible, that they represent the only path of truth, is to cut us off from change."[5] It's interesting how alphabetizing concepts can frame them in certain ways. I view the habit of **bulldozing** as being closely connected to that of being **Bulletproof**. While the former often manifests itself as seeking control over the scene in a way that does not permit other players space for meaningful contributions, the latter seeks a similar control over the domain of your individual character. Bulletproof players tend to resist accepting any meaningful change or adjustment in their scenic role or function. They prefer to intellectualize choices rather than embrace them, with their characters almost standing outside of the scene looking in rather than joining the topsy-turvy abandon of the creative process. A bulletproof stance can also be indicative that a player has formulated choices (or punchlines) for several steps ahead of where everyone is *now* and so is reluctant to shift gears.

Example

Player A has donned the role of a supercilious store clerk at the register. Player B, in a panic, approaches the counter...

Player B: "Do you work here?"
Player A: (nonchalantly) "I'm standing behind this counter, aren't I?"
Player B: (distraught) "I can't seem to find my daughter..."
Player A: "And you expect me to do something about it...?"
Player B: "Couldn't you make some sort of announcement over the speaker system.?"
Player A: "My shift is over in five minutes..."
Player B: "Do I need to talk to your manager?"

Player A: "Be my guest."

Player B: (frustrated as both the character and player) "Can't you see that I'm a nervous wreck? Aren't you going to help me?"

Player A: (looking beyond them in the line) "Next."

Signs You're Wearing Your Improv Armor

1. **Your character resists change.** Change is around nearly every corner in the world of improv: a technical or musical improviser might offer a shift in mood, weather, or the environment; an emcee or director might provide a handle or recommend a different direction to explore; a fellow improviser might pose an unanticipated course of action to advance the story toward new rich soil. Most would recognize these as important offers and appreciate the responsibility to accept new ideas and fold them into the scene. Bulletproof armor, however, can make you adept at *acknowledging* these new potentials while staying firmly in your previously self-determined lane. Similarly, when a potential tilt emerges, while others may allow the given circumstances to adjust accordingly, a bulletproof stance usually results in discussing this choice rather than embracing its consequences. "Don't worry about the rain, it'll be gone in a moment. Anyway, back to that thing I was doing…"

2. **Your character repels endowments.** We learn so much about our characters by how they interact and grow through the relationships they embody onstage. Often our scene partners will provide well-intentioned gifts or endowments that add nuance and detail to our personae and backstories. Innate in these offers, once again, is an invitation to change or explore a hitherto undeveloped (or possibly unknown) facet of our characterization. If our bulletproof armor is fully equipped, this new information will undoubtedly challenge assumptions as to where the scene "should" be going. Rather than relish the opportunity to unlock a new potential of your character, you're likely to double down on the previously established qualities and norms. "Thanks for your concern, but it just turned out to be a headache. Anyway, back to that thing I wanted you to do…"

3. **Your character contests culpability.** Any accusations or blame will quickly deflect off your bulletproof persona. If your character is charged with any behavior or revealed to have been at fault, rather than gut check and take on this powerful choice, it's more likely to instigate a return attack or volley as fully accepting these offers will require a reconsideration of what the character is essentially about. To take on culpability also generally requires releasing some of your control or power in a scene, which can prove difficult once you're all suited up. "Sure I broke the window. You broke all the other ones first. So anyway, back to that joke that I was setting up…"

4. **Your character stifles emotional responses.** In my experience, improv armor is particularly adept at protecting the wearer from tapping into their emotional core as a performer. This attire adds distance between the occupant's words and any earnest emotional connection to the scene and its contents. I would posit that in many cases, this may have been how the armor was acquired in the first place if emotional expressions in general cause discomfort or have not formerly been valued or nurtured. To remain ensconced can become almost second nature and improv can (d)evolve into an almost exclusively intellectual affair. It's "safer" to stay emotionally disconnected after all. "I see that you are getting upset, but can we please get back to me just talking about things…"

5. **Your character avoids inconsistencies.** This is a more subtle trap and one that improvisers may fall into even if they generally don't perform in a bulletproof fashion. Consistency is an interesting dynamic in improv. On the one hand, it's helpful if characters uphold patterns, attitudes, and behaviors that they have established. Games often explicitly require this sense of mirroring, repeating, and heightening. On the other hand, in the "real" world, people are rarely consistent or "one thing." Our improvisational creations can take on whole new levels as our characters become internally dynamic and perhaps even contradictory: the hero who has a fatal flaw, the heroine who has a dark secret, the picture-perfect lover who has done something immoral in pursuit of their love. I've come to use the term consistent inconsistency to describe this more kaleidoscopic approach to character, where we explore how they are challenged and changed depending on their circumstances in ways that complicate or question their moral or essential core. A reluctance to take on this type of ambiguity can easily result in work that rarely transcends the one-dimensional. "I may have made a mistake but that was so long ago now, so let me just play my character this way again please…"

Final Thought

While I have prefaced each of the observations above with "your character…," the line between the persona and player is rather thin when it comes to assuming a bulletproof stance. The stage tends to magnify and accentuate our own interpersonal tendencies, especially in improvisational modes, and in my experience, this certainly holds true with this limiting approach to playing. It is no small feat to let down our guard as people and performers, but the deeper connections and journeys so central to improvisation may seem to stand away from us at arm's length until we let our fellow players truly affect us.

Related Entries: Ambiguity, Bulldozing, Commandment #5, Commandment #8
Antonyms: Change, Culpability
Synonyms: Wimping
Connected Game: Emotions

BUTTON

For such an omnipresent component of our improv scenes, I have surprisingly come across very little written about **Buttons**, those critical moments that (hopefully) mark the successful and dynamic completion of our game, scene, or vignette. I've had the good fortune to improvise predominantly in companies and spaces where there has been strong technical support and attentive technical improvisers who are indeed, as the authors of *The Improv Handbook* describe, adept at both acknowledging and *creating* strong scenic endings.

> The best, most elegant and simplest way for a scene to end is for the lights to come down, ideally accompanied by a burst of music from somewhere – musician or sound improviser. This means that the lighting improviser has a considerable amount of power, not just spotting endings, but actually *creating* endings.[6]

I'm not a huge fan of the sweeping edit as an improv staple for this reason, as it just doesn't feel clean or theatrical if you're performing on well-equipped stages (although I understand its pragmatic attraction when working in smaller "found" spaces).

The realities of our craft, however, are that we will not always improvise in ideal circumstances and so relying on expert technical support when it comes to crafting endings is likely a problematic approach. And even if we have talented musicians, hosts, and technicians in our venues, I contend that it is really the performers' *responsibility* to clearly pitch endings rather than meandering through the scene with the hope that someone else will rescue you when it's time to move onto something new.

Rehearsing buttons can certainly prove challenging as they are unavoidably so dependent upon the unique circumstances of the game or scene which they strive to punctuate. I offer here some potential ideas to enrich your current stockpile of approaches on the subject, as well as a few new ways to think about these pivotal improv moments.

Thoughts on When to Pitch That Button

1. **You've satisfied the promise of the game or scene.** In the short-form tradition, many games have built-in climaxes when the "rules" of the game or the central conceit have clearly been met. In First Line, Last Line, strongly delivering the last line as supplied by the audience offers a clear finale, as does using the letter "Z" to start the last line of dialogue in an Alphabet Game scene. These moments should be leaned into and fully embraced as the very construct of the game is handing us a clear and resolute ending – it is just up to us to honor and celebrate it! This is not always easily done and underselling such moments or losing clear focus on stage as they are offered rank highly on my list of improv pet peeves. More open or long-form scenes will rarely have such a guaranteed out, but the same philosophy can hold true: if we have made a contract or promise, meeting this expectation will suggest that the end of our scene should be in sight. For example, if a one-upping dynamic has emerged as the central device of the scene, when this game has organically reached its zenith, players should be actively seeking an ending. Or if we have been gradually building to the revelation of the puppet operator behind the curtain, exposing their identity will likely herald the scene's conclusion.

2. **The game or reality of the scene is suddenly tilted or inverted.** I tend to think of this as almost a "rug pull" dynamic in that something new is suddenly revealed to the audience (and maybe the players) in such a way that the central premise of the scene no longer holds true. Most improvisers are accustomed to breaking routines in order to add heat and initiate a rising action, and this approach is certainly related as it also breaks or re-frames the established given circumstances but generally in a way that stops the action rather than ignites it. While we are wisely warned against "naming the game" in

our improv, this would be an example of when doing so *could* serve as a doorway to the button. For example, three neophyte firefighters have proven themselves so incompetent equipping themselves for the call to the fire that eventually their captain enters to announce that they have missed the fire entirely. Or if we wanted to lean into the concept of a tilt, perhaps the captain enters and announces they have failed the drill, or that the fire station is now ablaze due to their inactivity. Successfully executed, this type of reveal as a button generally demands a fast blackout from the booth.

3. **The resolution or moral of the story has been made clear.** I consider the concept of a narrative resolution in my Game Library entry describing Four Sentence Story. Typically, a resolution in this context expands the audience's focus beyond the plight of the central characters to the greater world as a whole. What did this scene teach the protagonist that they will take with them from now on, or perhaps, what is the greater moral that we can all benefit from learning? In storytelling games, this may literally be spoken as a concluding thought or paragraph, while in scenic work, it might appear as a statement from a central figure, a physical action that makes the lesson manifest, or a rip-roaring culminating song in your musical! If our protagonist has spent the scene pushing away all their friends, a moment of them now entrapped in their isolation could prove dramatically effective. Or if they have just taken in that "one" stray cat too many, watching them realize that they can no longer find anywhere to sit in their own home. Softer energies can prove challenging as buttons, so don't be afraid to take that strong exit if need be or assume a soft freeze by staying in the moment until you're confident the lights are fully out (if you're lucky to have lights in your venue).

4. **A witticism, observation, or punchline landed.** In the short-form tradition, a strong laugh line is probably one of the more common doorways to a scenic button. Audiences at competitive shows often expect comedic work and so a particularly well-crafted or surprising punchline that garners a strong response will likely serve the trick. I've posited the question in an earlier commandment entry (#4), "When is a gag not a gag?" and noted that when used judiciously, this type of energy can serve to cap a scene. It's a tricky balance as if you're reaching clumsily for a punchline out of desperation – perhaps the scene has struggled on for far too long – there might not be a great chance of success. But even a groaner might be welcomed by an audience if the scene clearly outstayed its welcome. I'd caution against pursuing this strategy relentlessly, especially when working in a long-form modality where jokey buttons might actually cause harm to carefully constructed characters and storylines. And even in short-form performances, I think providing variety for our outs is important, as is honoring our function as storytellers. I've seen many a scene blacked out poorly on a line that received a burst of laughter when it needed a few more moments to reach its full story or game potential which would have provided a deeper sense of satisfaction for the audience.

5. **A clear moment of finesse has been achieved.** This is a little tricky to clearly define but I think most of us in the field of improvisation recognize and appreciate it when we see it. While a punchline might appeal to our funny bones, a finesse speaks more to our emotions, intellect, or artistic tastes as fellow storytellers. A simple example would be ending a narrative game or scene with the title as provided by the audience: if the final words of the scene consist of this elicited phrase (and the audience remembers it!), then there will be little doubt that you're pitching an ending. Similarly, if you're working in a genre piece, weaving a closing rhyming couplet (or sonnet) that is delivered with appropriate finality serves well, as would weaving together several plot points with strategic reincorporations or unresolved elements. It's striking how audiences revel in looking for our inconsistencies or plot holes, and smartly winking at or solving these slips can result in an undeniably dynamic out.

Final Thought

Perhaps the most important performance element of a successful scenic button is a delivery that marks it resolutely as such. Whether we build toward bold closing statements, intense emotional epiphanies, whimsical punchlines and inversions, or finesseful connections and wordplay, ultimately a button is a button because we have made it so. We need to give as much care and attention to this facet of our craft as we do to starting scenes. Yes, our fellow technical improvisers can save our necks and see potentials for scenic ends that might elude us on the stage, but as performers, it is really *our* responsibility to punctuate our scenes dynamically, with the full range of colors at our disposal: powerful exclamation marks, thought-provoking questions, definitive periods, and delightfully intriguing ellipses...

Related Entries: Edits **Antonyms:** Initiation, Starting Scene **Synonyms:** Conclusion, Ending, Resolution
Connected Game: Most Scenes in a Minute

NOTES

1. Charna Halpern et al., *Truth in Comedy. The Manual of Improvisation.* Colorado Springs: Meriwether, 1994. p. 86.
2. Lynda Belt and Rebecca Stockley, *Acting through Improv: Improv through Theatresports.* New Revised Edition. Seattle, Washington: Thespis Productions, 1995. p. 99.
3. Keith Johnstone, *Impro for Storytellers.* New York: Routledge, 1999. p. 84.
4. Paul Sills quoted in Jeffrey Sweet's *Something Wonderful Right Away.* 1996. New York: Limelight Editions, 1978. p. 18.
5. Bernard Sahlins, *Days and Nights at the Second City. A Memoir, with Notes on Staging Review Theatre.* Chicago: Ivan R. Dee, 2001. pp. 170–171.
6. Tom Salinsky and Deborah Frances-White, *The Improv Handbook.* New York: The Continuum International Publishing Group Inc., 2008. p. 314.

C

CAD

The acronym **CAD** stands for three helpful forms of revelation in our scenic work. Each is considered in greater depth as an individual entry (and companion game). If you are looking to break routines, raise the stakes, or increase the heat in your onstage relationships, CAD is an excellent tool to add to your repertoire. Dave Duncan considers the import of nurturing this spirit of surprise:

> It got to the point in the last few years that I played theatresports where we wouldn't even make up our own personal list [of challenges or games]. We would totally wing it off the bench. I guess that was our philosophy – always trying to surprise your teammates, always putting yourself at risk.[1]

Three Forms of Revelations

1. **Confession.** A character discloses a secret or personal information that isn't already explicitly known by their scene partner. Visit my entry of the same name to find some tips for crafting a dynamic confession.
2. **Accusation.** A dynamic piece of information or backstory is endowed upon another character in the scene. This focused entry offers things to keep in mind when making (and receiving) a revelation of this ilk.
3. **Discovery.** Something unexpected or surprising in the environment becomes discovered that changes the given circumstances for the characters. To learn more about how to get the most out of your discovery moments, review this stand-alone entry in the improv Ds.

Final Thought

If your scenes routinely become stuck or predictable, or your onstage relationships rarely deepen or evolve in helpful ways, exploring the gifts of a CAD can open up new vistas.

Related Entries: Accusation, Commandment #7, Confession, Discovery **Antonyms:** Balance, Platform, Routine **Synonyms:** Breaking Routines, Ignition, Revelation, Surprise **Connected Game:** CAD Bell

CALLBACK

Perhaps one of the most often quoted improv adages comes from Keith Johnstone when he writes,

> The improviser has to be like a man walking backward. He sees where he has been, but he pays no attention to the future. His story can take him anywhere, but he must still 'balance' it, and give it shape, by remembering incidents that have been shelved and reincorporating them.[2]

I find **Callbacks** (a type of reincorporation) one of the guilty pleasures of improvisation in that this seemingly simple device frequently elicits the most thunderous audience applause and appreciation. There is something inherently delightful about seeing material or scenic elements once placed to the side of the action suddenly making a return at just the right moment. If you've seen or participated in short- or long-form games where an audience member is interviewed about their life or day to provide source material, this device is central to the ensuing fun as the audience, now in the "know," finds great joy in seeing the cast weave these aforementioned facts into the action.

While the concept of a callback is relatively straightforward – recycle or reuse something that has already been established or shelved – expertly executing this tactic can make all the difference in performance.

Getting the Most Out of Your Callbacks

1. **You can't have great callbacks without great specifics.** The concept of callbacks and reincorporating is partnered with the technique of shelving for a good reason: if there are no details established and shelved in your scene work, then there won't be anything to reference or reclaim later down the road. It's important to spend sufficient time developing strong and clear given circumstances. Typically, we're unsure during the balance or early phase of a scene or longer format what *exactly* will prove important or of value, so it can be helpful to err on the side of generosity when it comes to crafting details. A little **ambiguity** can go a long way in this regard too, establishing some clear emotional energies or tensions without feeling the need to explain them away. While I don't think it's necessarily helpful to overwhelm the proverbial "improv shelves" with an abundance of random minutiae, taking a few moments to expand upon interesting elements of the emerging world can make an enormous difference. If characters are looking out a window, what is something *specific* that they can see outside? If you're working in an office, what is one *unique* activity that defines your profession? If your character is engaging in a physical hobby, what is a *quirky* characteristic of one of the related props?
2. **Generate your world and point of view first.** Callbacks can certainly occur almost anywhere within a scene (excluding perhaps the very opening moments), but I'd generally advise against them being your focus as the performance *begins*. Just as we need specifics and shelved ideas to draw from, we also need strong characters with well-defined points of view to populate the action. If your initial focus is on grabbing at callbacks, you're probably not adding much to the scenic inventory for your own later use and that of others. Successful reincorporations also tend to gain nuance and volume when they are in service of our character goals or reveal something dynamic about the relationships being explored. You're more likely to be able to use the tool of the callback with ease and finesse if you are performing from the comfort of a character that has a strong sense of what they are about.
3. **Callbacks aren't a substitute for good storytelling.** This is perhaps a trap for more novice improvisers, but the high of a well-received callback can quickly become a craving that can result in less-than-generous scene work. Be wary of all scrambling for a reincorporation the second it becomes possible or apparent, or racing to be the first one to point at the connection on stage. Ideally, such choices inform and enrich our storytelling first and foremost. Just because you *can* make a callback doesn't mean that you necessarily should. Sometimes, when a callback is *extremely* obvious, the audience will truly appreciate when the players just gently wink at it (or perhaps ignore it altogether) and then move on to more fruitful improv pastures. There is something innately generous and community-building about trusting that your audience sees what you see and doesn't need you to spell out *every* possible move. Which brings me to my final related thought...
4. **Callback patience is a virtue.** This might be an interesting topic for a scientific study, but I believe that often the power and pleasure of a callback can be directly proportionate to the distance between its first appearance and its later reuse. On the one end of the spectrum, immediately repeating or using an offer that has *just* been made wouldn't strike most improvisers as a callback at all as the idea hasn't spent *any* time maturing on the "shelf." This would generally be more aptly described as an **acceptance** or repetition. On the other end of the spectrum, a seed that was planted in the opening moments of a scene or show that may have only been gently or discreetly watered during the following action but then makes a featured reappearance at the opportune moment as the scene culminates can land gloriously well. In a related manner, if the focus of the callback has been repeatedly referenced or perhaps even elevated to a recurring gimmick, it strikes me that at least comically or structurally this may have also transformed from the realm of the callback into that of a **game of the scene**. In short, my instinct is that less is more when it comes to successful use of this device.

Final Thought

Allow me to share an important lesson I learned firsthand in terms of positioning a strategic callback as a long-form button. I'm always looking for a way to maximize the chances of a strong "out," especially when I'm working in two-hour long-form pieces as that's a lot of time for your audience to invest for the show just to fizz away at the last moment. I've used a common tactic for two shows, namely saving the title of the show or episode as the target rhyme for the final climactic moment. In *The Lost Comedies of William Shakespeare*, a title was obtained each night and written in full view on a slate that was lowered back to center stage for the final moment. While the title was definitely used to inspire each evening's journey, we went to great lengths to avoid saying it outright in any obvious way during the rising action. In a more recent piece, *Private Lies: Improvised Film Noir*, we similarly obtained a title for each "episode" in the form of "The case of the blanky blank." Again, this title deeply influenced the action but was never mentioned until the very last line of the piece. Now, there were undoubtedly a *lot* of factors in terms of how these two positioned callbacks played, but in the first case, the button landed without exception, while in the second, it garnered a mixed response at best. In the first production, the slate lowered with a visual reminder of our title; in the second example, so much time had passed since it was elicited during the opening that it likely lacked any memorability. The takeaway of this slightly meandering story is that a callback isn't a callback when no one can remember it…

Related Entries: Connections, Shelving
Synonyms: Looking Backwards, Reincorporation
Connected Game: Perspectives

CALLER

A **Caller** serves a frequent role on many short-form stages where games might require an outside eye to edit, adjust, or lovingly mess with the onstage players. Whether they are moving players through a list of emotions (as in Chameleon), demanding players change their lines of dialogue with the ring of a bell (as in Should've Said), or switching up the genre of a scene at whim (as in Genre Rollercoaster), the role requires keen focus and generosity.

Viola Spolin writes,

> It is the voice of the director seeing the needs of the overall presentation; at the same time it is the voice of the teacher seeing the individual student-actor's needs within the group and on the stage. It is the teacher-director working on a problem together with the student as part of the group effort.[3]

While Spolin's words were intended to describe the function of the side-coach, these observations hold equally true for improv callers. These collaborators often exist in a liminal position in the improv world, both participating in and standing outside of the improv scene in question. I've encountered several approaches when it comes to who assumes this integral role, a position that is somewhat unique to the short-form tradition but whose essential function can also be seen at play in other allied modalities, such as Playback Theatre's conductor or Augusto Boal's Joker figure. The role of the caller may be subsumed into that of the emcee or host of the event, an approach I'll typically take when working with a campus or emerging troupe. In competitive formats, a member of an opposing team may take on these duties for a scene as they are needed, or if you're performing in a more cabaret-style format where structural duties are shared among the ensemble, players may be assigned to don this hat as the playlist dictates.

While the identity of the caller may change from show to show and venue to venue, the inherent functions remain the same as they lend their offstage voice to help shape, steer, and amend the improvised action according to the specific rules of the short-form game in question. A scene can thrive or wither under the eye of this collaborator. Each format offers unique opportunities and challenges, but there are some basic principles and tensions that will typically remain in play.

Factors to Balance as a Caller

1. **Audience and players.** A good caller is working in service of both of these constituencies throughout the scene. On a simple level, to aid this dual function, a caller should be physically placed so that they can clearly see the action but can also be readily heard by players and audience alike. When performing in a proscenium arrangement, an optimal perch is on the lip of the stage or divide between the house and the performance space. It's generally wise to put your caller on a microphone if this is available so that their suggestions can be more readily heard and quickly applied. Regardless of amplification assistance, it's imperative that any calls are loud, clearly articulated, and concise.
2. **Game and scene.** The majority of called games consist of assigned handles for scenic explorations and it's important that both components of the action – gimmick and story – receive your attention (gimmick as it pertains to the unique hurdle or promise of the format; story as it pertains to

a satisfying and well-crafted narrative arc). Few scenes will do well if they cannot gain any momentum due to overly present calls; inversely, an audience may feel cheated if that "cool dynamic" that was introduced in the setup didn't really influence the scene in any meaningful way. To assist in maintaining the flow of the scene, I generally avoid freezing the action before offering adjustments. Instead, I favor repeating calls twice in a row: once to gain everyone's attention, and then again to ensure the information was heard. The exception to this rule would be games that require or benefit from more lengthy instructions that can't be provided in a pithy manner or require interaction with the audience, such as Song Cues or Options. Here, a call of "Freeze" is largely unavoidable as the caller needs strong focus to shape the next move. Remember that both the scene and game should be equally served and so it generally isn't helpful to make numerous calls before players have had a chance to establish the foundational elements of their characters and environment. Many called games are designed to challenge or throw off kilter the direction of the scene, so it's helpful if a solid base has been crafted first.

3. **Playful torturer and patient helper.** Often, short-form games frame the caller as a mischievous or possibly even undermining influence. While it is important to uphold this appearance to retain the integrity of the premise (and possibly the competitive frame of the show as a whole), generally, the caller also needs to serve the needs of the ensemble (and show) by enabling strong improvisational play. Subsequently, it's important to gradually ramp up the mischief making. This helps craft a dynamic rising action for the scene while also allowing the caller to make sure that their adjustments are proving helpful *and* surprising while simultaneously encouraging joy *and* risk-taking. It can easily dishearten a team (and audience) if impossible or seemingly mean-spirited calls prevent the scene from ever finding a steady footing and trajectory. On the other end of the spectrum, appearing *too* helpful can inadvertently lower the stakes of the affair and reduce the payoff of the built-in challenge. For example, in games such as Should've Said, it shouldn't appear as if the improvisers are setting up or actively want the caller to bell them out of a line of dialogue. If I'm on the bell, I'll deliberately let these moments pass without a call to retain the integrity of the dynamic. (The exception to this rule would be if a player has gotten themselves into trouble and is clearly asking for a lifeline.)

4. **Diagnoser and challenger.** My teacher might be showing here a little, but donning the role of a caller will also often afford you a chance to actively help the onstage improvisers and action. If players are falling into old or unhelpful habits, seize opportunities to nudge them into new or more fruitful territory. If I'm calling New Choice and characters are standing in an uninspired line without any semblance of location, I might call for a "new staging choice." In an Emotions scene, if a character is struggling with being heard or vocal production, I will likely offer up an extreme emotion to encourage fuller presence. The game Options provides an opportunity to unequivocally throw focus to a character that might have become marginalized or overwhelmed by others onstage by asking an audience member, "What is a big announcement that the flautist in the background is about to make?" Similarly, especially in companies with great trust and familiarity, the caller is empowered to challenge players who may typically excel or have a great deal of comfort in a particular game. If you play a lot of musical style games, for example, it can be tiring if you're only ever pitched the same handful of styles again and again. The caller can be instrumental in preventing such games from becoming clichéd or stale by working to push players out of tiresome patterns.

5. **In the moment and one step ahead.** Timing is so important in called scenes and if the caller becomes distracted or misses key plot points, they can quickly become a detriment rather than a helping hand. There is no substitute for giving the scene the gift of your attention as, in most cases, the most effective calls will truly emerge from the immediacy of the action. You don't want to be so busy planning your next move or addition that you miss the infinitely richer opportunity that just emerged organically. And yet, callers often also need to have some sense of the greater arc so that they can help the scene reach a well-crafted zenith. This balancing act undoubtedly becomes a little easier with experience as you'll start to have some backup strategies or call variants in your pocket in case something more intuitive doesn't materialize. There are small things that you can do, however, to help yourself. If you're working with a list as is the case in games such as Emotions or Genre Rollercoaster, it's a good idea to quickly identify a strong option or two that you can keep on reserve as the "out" or last call. If you're making calls on the fly, starting small and simply will similarly allow you room to save your most interesting or challenging idea for that last scenic moment.

Final Thought

Much like an improv host, I think a primary edict for a caller is to, first and foremost, *do no harm*. It's important to provide playfulness and unpredictability, but a caller should always have the best interests of the players and scene at heart. The mischief making function that is foundational to many short-form games that utilize this role certainly invites a little misbehavior or shivving, but we should exert care that we don't carelessly dance into the domain of gagging and pimping, asking the players to engage in behaviors purely for our own amusement. I've also seen such choices alienate an audience who may not feel "in" on the "joke" when a player is asked to do something that the company knows will cause them discomfort. Adept and generous calling can make or break an improv scene. I suspect that most audience members will have *no idea* just how much such callers have enabled the onstage players to shine, but I think this is also wholly appropriate praise.

> **Related Entries:** Hosting, Shape of Show, Shivving, Sidecoaching
> **Connected Game:** Song Cue

CALLING YOUR SHOT

This improv finesse consists of letting the audience know the challenge or impossibility of the current creative task at hand. Short-form game descriptions, for example, tend to outline the unique pitfalls that lie ahead, thereby letting the audience in on the difficulty of the game. Such an attitude allows observers to more deeply appreciate it when the pantomimed improv ball is then hit out of the proverbial improv park.

> **Related Entry:** Commenting

CANADIAN CROSS

I'm unsure why this improv strategy has been coined a *Canadian* Cross, but that's the term widely attributed to a style of performing where improvisers make a transitory offer intended to embellish, heighten, or provide context to the scene already in progress. Del Close alludes to this general style of play when he recommends, "Avoid judging what is going down except in terms of whether it needs help (either by entering or cutting), what can best follow, or how you can support it imaginatively if your support is called for."[4] By definition, a **Canadian Cross** moves through the space without the intent to stay or take focus for any length of time. It's a tactic that is equally useful in the long- or short-form tradition and is really a subset of the larger improv strategy of offering **side support**.

Example

Players A and B have started a heated encounter in a supermarket. They perform the first few lines standing toe-to-toe, almost in a talking heads fashion.

Player A: "I thought we agreed that you wouldn't shop here anymore so we didn't have to see each other."

Player B: "I think *you* agreed to that. This supermarket is a lot closer to my new apartment, so there's that."

Player A: "Oh I see, as always you're just going to change the agreement to suit yourself."

Player B: "And I see, as always, that you're making agreements without actually listening to anything I say."

Player C, gently acknowledging the awkward conversation, slowly pushes a supermarket trolley in the background of the scene and exits.

Player B: (starting to move) "If this is just going to be another argument, I don't need it today…"

Player A: (aware that they are being observed and reaching for a box on the shelf) "I just can't get the gluten-free crackers I like anywhere else…"

Some Additional Analysis

Player C in the above example has opted to make a quick walk through of the scene in order to support the established given circumstances. It's important that such a move does not needlessly steal focus, slow the action, or draw undue attention to itself as these moves will diminish the effectiveness of the choice which aims to essentially support rather than compete. It's also important not to get caught onstage for a protracted period of time as this will increase the likelihood of split focus or may imply to the featured players that you are waiting to make a more substantial offer or tilt. Effective Canadian Crosses are generally a light scenic touch rather than a dramatic turning point or revelation. They are frequently performed in silence, but *if* dialogue is offered it should be concise and not pull the featured players away from their current dynamic. Also, an adept contribution should strive to match the tone of the scene: an overly energized cross in a calm and grounded sincere scene is likely to do more harm than good.

Moments Ripe for a Canadian Cross

1. **The scene is set in a nowhere land (or no one land).** There is a lot to establish at the top of an improv scene and it is not uncommon for players to favor one element (relationship) over another (environment). During such moments, a Canadian Cross can provide a generous technique to help materialize a location that has only been implied or briefly mentioned. In the example above, the supermarket was discussed, but it wasn't yet a vibrant part of the scene. A gentle cross can bring this part of the world to life while also opening up new potentials for action and activity for those already onstage. It's also possible that the initial players have crafted a dynamic and detailed location but perhaps neglected character, relationship, or another given circumstance such as the time of day, weather, or season. A gentle endowment from a Canadian Cross could assist in these moments as well.
2. **The staging is stagnant or uninteresting.** It is a frequent improv trap to just end up standing and talking in our scenes. Even after a supermarket has been gifted, it's possible for the scene to continue to occur largely as an act of motionless dialogue as opposed to physical action. This is not to say that there may not be dynamic choices at play; but unless you're performing in the most intimate of spaces, theatre demands heightened presence and movement in order to fully communicate nuances to the back row of the audience. A well-timed Canadian Cross can offer up new ways to integrate the location into our action or orientate our bodies in the space. In this manner, our fellow shopper above could establish a display of carefully arranged imported limes that can become a (sour) focal point for later action between our quibbling couple.
3. **The game or stakes could be heightened.** Making the terse encounter in the supermarket markedly more public adds new layers of awkwardness and tension to the nascent scene. The scenario could certainly take place in a more private locale, but the given environment offers up opportunities to make this uncomfortable exchange even *more* uneasy. Once such a game has been introduced, it's incumbent upon those providing support to exercise great patience and self-control as an overabundance or poorly rushed chain of entrances will likely prematurely arc the scene and possibly "name the game" in a way that kills the dominant energy. When entering to expand upon a dynamic, it's important to leave sufficient room between each Canadian Cross to let the base scene react, adjust, and make its next logical step before nudging the game up another level if it's needed.
4. **The emotional weight of the scene could be deepened.** Related to the above strategy, a Canadian Cross can also be used to highlight or intensify the emotional journeys of the initial characters. There are manifold ways this could be achieved, but to offer two helpful examples, you can think in terms of a **parallel** or **complementary** choice or energy. A parallel choice would reflect and expand upon the energies already established. To return to our supermarket, we might see that other couples are similarly avoiding each other in the aisles as this shop *is just that good* that no one wants to lose it in the breakup. Alternatively, a complementary choice would contrast the established mood. In this situation, another couple might be cooing over each other while blissfully shopping together in perfect harmony. In either case, it's generally advisable to deepen the emotionalism of the original dynamic with choices that are building in *one* direction rather than an unrelated clutter of competing trajectories (so if the first cross established a *parallel*, subsequent crosses will typically prove more helpful if they also explore a *parallel* idea but in a new or elevated way).
5. **There is an opportunity to add playfulness or whimsy.** I offer this last scenario with some hesitation as I think this can become the most frequent justification for a Canadian Cross while, at its core, it may be the most problematic in terms of embracing the fundamental intent of this technique. An effective Canadian Cross should strive to keep the attention on the central characters, but there are certainly moments when a playful game can contextualize the scene in a dynamic way that momentarily shares the focus or adds new and helpful material. A passing shopper may start to discreetly video the encounter on their cell phone, suggesting that this may be a celebrity sighting, and this game may then be echoed by others crossing in turn. Or a series of shoppers might keep awkwardly needing the grocery item that is right between our protagonists no matter where in the store they go. (And perhaps each named item is also a commentary on their current relationship status: bread-for-one, a bunch of

sour grapes, a large box of wine…) Or a succession of shoppers might keep flirtatiously slipping one of the arguers their phone numbers in a way that elevates the emotional intensity of the scene. Some of these examples (and oh so many others) might appropriately invite a quick line of dialogue from the transitory player, but these need to be timed judiciously and with an eye to what the primary relationship ultimately needs to thrive.

Final Thought

There are some common traps with Canadian Crosses that deserve at least a brief mention here. Don't think of these supporting moments as necessarily laugh lines or comedic bits. This certainly *can* be the case, but there are so many other gifts that can be delivered through this technique, and we shouldn't consider these iterations as any less successful if they added something other than humor. Ideally, supporting players are elevating and framing choices that have organically emerged rather than offering up shtick concocted independently in the wings. It is also a trap to get caught on stage or overstay your welcome. Make sure you enter with the intention of quickly leaving or it is much likelier that you will find yourself struggling to find your exit. If you are inclined to speak, this should be concise, and you should assume that you'll get one line or so before you've served your purpose. The exception to the "get out quickly" rule may occur in the closing moments of the scene when a cascade or gathering of Canadian Crosses could help push the scene to its climax and offer up the potential for a dynamic group stage picture. But in general, the larger purpose of these crosses is to make a generous choice or endowment that will serve those who are doing the heavy lifting of the scene. Perhaps think twice about entering with a gift that is really intended for yourself in the form of audience laughter and appreciation!

Related Entries: Complementary Action, Give, Parallel Action, Side Support
Connected Game: Environmental Freeze Tag

CANCELING

Needlessly removing an established item from the field of improvisational play or making it irrelevant (often to pursue your own competing idea instead).

Synonym: Erasure

CARTOONING

I'm unsure how widely this term is applied in improv circles, but I've come to use **Cartooning** as a way to describe unnuanced or overly didactic onstage offers that describe rather than embody our choices. As Frost and Yarrow note, "improvisation is about order, and about adaptation, and about truthfully responding to changing circumstances, and about generating meaning out of contextual accidents."[5] An antithetical untruthful tendency primarily emerges when improvisers wrestle with the *seemingly* competing needs of crafting clear choices while also communicating these ideas in a way that feels natural and theatrically honest. This pitfall is related to the similar ill of **commenting** although, in my experience, a cartooning improviser often believes that their additions are helpful to the scenic arc and may not always recognize that there is a problematic lack of subtlety in their execution. Despite the difference in intent, the results are largely the same: we end up preventing the reality and emotions of our scene work from truly moving us as characters and players.

Example

Players A and B are given "siblings" to inspire their scene. Player A enters the space and immediately starts talking with little or no emotion…

Player A: "Wow, little sister, here we are back again in our childhood home in Michigan that neither of us have seen since we were pre-teens, and the place hasn't changed a bit, except, of course, for all the snow on the ground because it's the middle of winter. I sure hope the current owners will let us back into the backyard so we can see if that time capsule is still there that we buried on your fifth birthday…"
Player B: "Yes, and…"

Some Further Analysis

Now, arguably, there are a *lot* of interesting choices in this rant (likely, *way too many*), but delivering this information as an uninterrupted stream of consciousness will rarely provide any emotional depth or truth. This overly intellectual approach tends to appear more frequently at the top of scenes: Player A in this example is probably keen to heed their improv instructor's advice of clearly establishing the who, what, and where as quickly as possible. As noted above, I've found that cartooning is typically well-intended, but you nonetheless end up with something that feels like a summary or précis of a scene rather than a patient starting point rich with emotion, subtext, and detail.

Bringing That Third Dimension to Your Scene Work

1. **Increase your physical game and embrace silence.** It's more difficult to fall into the trap of announcing your choices if you lean more heavily into your physical game as an improviser. If you recognize yourself in the above example (I've certainly been guilty) privilege your physical work, especially as the scene launches. Rather than talking about winter, establish this with how you enter the space and your behavior in front of the house. In lieu of prescribing a future activity that your scene partner must obey such as the buried time capsule, allow your physical choices to unlock discovered potentials in the environment. Instead of just pronouncing that your scene partner is your little sister, explore what this might look like physically: are you comfortable in each other's space, is there a protective or nurturing energy, or perhaps a more sparring and competitive dynamic? There can't really be a "wrong" choice here, but there is a big difference between making a physical choice that starts to explore a specific type of relationship and merely just stating the title of the relationship in order to tick a box on some imagined improv checklist.
2. **Prioritize emotion over facts.** Cartooning tends to emerge more frequently among those of us who gravitate toward intellectual choices in our performance work, so it can be a similarly helpful approach to prioritize emotions if this is not your current habit or preference. Perhaps you have already formulated the rather complex backstory summarized above in your head as the scene begins; instead of voluminously verbalizing all of this, shift your frame into earnestly considering how does this make you *feel*? Were there good memories attached to your childhood and this house, or are you glad that those years are now firmly in your rear-view mirror? Is this trip something you've been excited about, or has it been a cause of stress or dread? Again, it doesn't matter what specific emotional choice you make, but bringing that energy (rather than just a list of facts) to the stage is much more likely to inspire your scene partners and intrigue or engage your audience.
3. **Share the responsibility of priming the scene.** If you're being more physical and/or relying more robustly on your emotional game this should also free up more room for your scene partner to have a meaningful influence on the opening moments of the action. Cartooning given circumstances may be intended as an act of generously "getting the basics out of the way," but it can also, unfortunately, minimize the opportunities for your partners to meaningfully contribute. Take the risk of sharing just one facet of that "great" idea you have brewing and then see what your partner does next. The more participatory and invested we all are as players in the opening moments of a new scene, the more we'll feel connected to the path that reveals itself one step at a time. Which snugs nicely with the next strategy of…
4. **Bring one brick.** This is a popular adage in improv: everyone should just bring *one* brick to the endeavor of creativity rather than the whole house. Cartooning can also be a way of exerting control over the action: if I clearly state at the top of the scene what *I* want it to be about then there is no chance of confusion or it moving in an unexpected direction. In short-form, when the clock is ticking quickly, this is a particular temptation as meandering scene starts can become challenging if they become a company norm. And I'm a fan of hitting the stage with a powerful and rich choice or context. But keep this ubiquitous advice in mind. Sure, bring one or two strong details to the stage, but make sure there's truly space for others to do the same.
5. **Build your subtext muscles.** Cartooning is also innately a trust issue: a lack of trust in yourself that you'll be able to effectively communicate your idea without laboriously spelling it out in every detail; a lack of trust in your teammates and audience that they'll read more subtle or nuanced offers; a lack of trust in the collaborative inner workings of improv to conjure helpful details even if they aren't precisely what you had in mind initially as an individual. If the vast majority of your improv resides in the land of your text (saying what you mean) rather than your subtext (playing what you feel), then it's worth your time to focus more resolutely on the latter. In many ways, this is a culmination of all the above tactics: increasing your physicality, leading with your emotions, releasing yourself of the responsibility of naming *all* the pertinent

details, and leaving room for your scene partners to add rich and exciting details of their own as the scene takes shape.

Final Thought

I think I've come to call this short-hand approach to performing cartooning because while such scenes are reminiscent of the human condition, they tend to feel two-dimensional: you've been told that the characters are siblings, but nothing in their behavior reflects that; someone mentioned that it was winter, but no one has taken this reality into their physicality… It's also certainly related to the concepts of showing versus telling (topics for future entries), although I tend to think of cartooning as an embodiment of the telling instinct taken to the nth degree. If you would self-diagnose that your improv is rich on detail but poor on connection or vulnerability, then perhaps some of the above strategies can help you make that next evolution.

> **Related Entries:** Commenting **Antonyms:** Showing, Truth, Vulnerability **Synonym:** Telling
> **Connected Game:** Stop! Think!

CENSORSHIP

As a public performance art, improv must address issues of content and appropriateness. While the term "censorship" undoubtedly has a negative connotation, in reality, most performances are shaped by artistic parameters whether these are set by the individual player, host company, or current societal norms. I would posit, however, that such forces should be faced and challenged when they primarily strive to silence truths – especially those that are complex, messy, inconvenient, or routinely marginalized.

> **Synonym:** Material

CHANGE

Writing of his work in the field of Theatre of the Oppressed, Augusto Boal observes, "if no one changes the play it will come to the same end as before."[6] A favorite definition of theatre notes that it is primarily a study of change and the ways that characters struggle to adapt (generally comedies) or fail miserably to do so at all or until it's too late (generally tragedies). Boal keenly applies this same notion to society in general. This notion of **Change** is central to many fundamental improv terms and strategies. Embracing and prioritizing change can be seen in philosophies such as **breaking routines** and tilts; the perils of resisting change is revealed in pitfalls such as being **bulletproof** or **commenting**.

As we balance the plethora of sometimes seemingly competing improvisational ideals, it can become difficult to know when or how to change without upending established games or energies that are successfully serving our scene work. Changes in the story arc are addressed elsewhere, so here are some character-centric ideas that can promote more well-rounded and dynamic performances:

Example

A parent (Player A) and adult child (Player B) are engaging in a driving lesson. It's several minutes into the scene, and Player B has been slowly but steadily improving in confidence and results.

Player A: "You're really getting the hang of this!"
Player B: "Well, I've certainly had a good teacher…"
Player A: "I don't think you're going to need my help much longer…"

A change awaits… to be continued below.

Changing Up Your Characters

1. **Change the inherent power dynamic or status.** If you are exploring a relationship with a clear power dynamic that has served you well thus far, consider inverting or complicating this component of your character. In the example above, the child is clearly the lower status character as they are in the role of student. Moving Player A into the higher status position will unlock some new energies and potentials. This can prove particularly effective if the scene has heretofore assumed a largely teaching or transactional quality.

Player A: "Dad, we need to talk about your vision. I don't think it's safe for you to drive any more…"

2. **Change your point of view on someone or something.** When your character learns something about themselves or the world that they occupy you are also opening the door to change, especially if this new knowledge is emotionally impactful or deepens the relationship we are currently

observing. This will also tend to make this particularly scenic moment more critical and dynamic rather than just another "driving lesson" or "conversation at work" or "chat on a park bench."

Player A: "Mom, I really had second thoughts about letting you back into my life, but this has been really nice…"

3. **Change your physicality, staging, or tempo.** If you're inclined to maintain the central dynamic as it is working well or enabling an effective game, explore a change in your character's physicality or tempo instead. If the driving lesson has been smooth sailing thus far, creating new obstacles or opportunities that will encourage a different use of the space can add another needed level to the scene. It could be as simple as literally turning the angle of the car, changing who's driving, or evolving the driving lesson into a full-fledged car chase in pursuit of a carjacker with a child trapped in the back seat.

Player A: "Oops, I must have taken a wrong turn onto this unsealed road; hang on, old man, it's about to get bumpy…"

4. **Change your stakes or urgency.** You can also change up a relationship or character energy by tinkering with the given circumstances or the consequences of the current activity. A scene that appeared to just be a calm lesson now assumes greater import and dynamism as we understand the "why" of the scene more fully. If you tend to assume a deadpan or even keel stance in your character work, this added spice provides a helpful addition to your tool belt as it will also encourage scenes that have a more driving energy (pun intended).

Player A: "Mum, I'm really regretting telling Amazon Prime that I already had my driver's license. I don't think I'm going to be able to do this…"

5. **Change your emotional truth.** Embracing a dynamic shift in your emotional center as a character is yet another helpful tactic that can elevate a scene to a new level. If the tone of the scene has been joyful or playful, introducing a touch of regret or suspicion will invite new content and details. Or, if you often find yourself stuck in argumentative dynamics, choosing to quickly shift gears (and then earning this shift) can prove highly effective.

Player A: (holding back tears) "Nick, this is the most time we've ever spent together. I don't think I want these lessons to stop…"

Final Thought

These approaches are just a handful of ways to encourage more flexibility and range in our character and scene work. At the top of a scene or larger performance such a change can facilitate moving from the balance to the ignition of the piece. Within the body of a dramatic arc, it can heighten the stakes, complicate the rising action, or add nuance and depth to your relationships. As a scene approaches an end, a dynamic shift can herald the final moments of your story and the button. While Boal is writing of the healing arts in my opening quote, a form that literally invites its audience to break the fourth wall and intervene with the unfolding stories, the advice holds true to most of our work in the theatre: "if no one changes the play it will come to the same end as before."

Related Entries: Commandment #5
Antonyms: Bulletproof, Commenting
Synonyms: Breaking Routines, Tilt
Connected Game: Status Swap

CHAOS

Action without shape, thoughtfulness, or purpose. While improv wrestles with the appearance of chaos, most spontaneous performance seeks to harness messiness to aesthetically or socially pleasing ends. Consequently, improvisation exists within the fruitful tension of chaotic freedom and graceful form.

Antonyms: Story, Structure

CHAPTER TWO

This is another phrase that I've adopted that may not be in wide circulation. If an improviser indulges in a **Chapter Two** offer, this refers to a narrative or story building inclination where players leap over the promise of the current moment in the action (our shared Chapter One, if you will) to move attention elsewhere, typically in the more distant future. Such a brusque move – deliberately or otherwise – ignores the current story or contracts in favor of something perceived as newer and more interesting. When players engage in a "Chapter Two," it's generally emblematic of overlooking the subtle or hidden potentials of the here and now, or perhaps not fully investing in these established details. It can feel like a re-set, "do over," or sudden shift in the mood or flow of the story. In other instances, this concept embodies **advancing** run amok, with the potential of several interconnected smaller choices being preempted or eclipsed by a leap to the beginning of a new but generally loosely related idea. In yet other cases, it describes the act of missing a strong ending by carelessly initiating another journey, particularly in a timed scenic environment where such an extension could prove problematic. I've come to use this phrase as a shorthand way of acknowledging that a needlessly large leap may have just squelched something of interest that was already percolating and worthy of our attention. Smith and Dean remind us of the importance and creative utility of small steps:

> The improvising process often makes the improvisor concentrate on small elements because (s)he cannot see the overall whole. This means that a multiplicity of elements is likely to build up, especially where a number of different improvisors are interacting with each others' small units.[7]

Example

A team is taking turns providing narration for a story based on the suggestion of "train."

Player A: "The rickety train was slowly and steadily making its way along the mountainous track, weaving through narrow valleys and winding trails deep within the dense forest."

Player B: "Inside, a collection of wary people huddled. The cold mountain breeze pushed against the train cars, occasionally intruding through an open door or cracked window, jolting the passengers back to reality with each chilly blast."

Player C: "The train engine started to audibly strain as the unfriendly path ahead became increasingly steep. The formerly steady rhythm quickly gave way to less predictable shudders and stammers."

Player D: "Jim excitedly met his younger brother on the train platform. He had a great day planned for their reunion, revisiting all their favorite childhood haunts."

How to Keep Your Story on the Same Page

1. **Know who your story is about.** The likelihood of a Chapter Two moment increases exponentially if we're unsure whose story we are telling or following (noting that, especially in the long-form tradition, we may be weaving multiple arcs together). In the above example, a strong sense of mood and environment was created, but we were pretty deep into the introduction without having any particular character of note. It is certainly possible that we might follow an unexpected protagonist – such as the train itself or the weather enveloping the mountains – but it's important that the team arrives at agreement as to this focus as soon as possible or else the story becomes more prone to the potential for a sudden and probably unhelpful shift in focus. Especially in narrative games, just clearly naming your protagonist early and often can dramatically reduce this risk.

2. **Know what your story is about.** Related to the above, if we've all embraced and added to a common goal or energy for the story, we're less inclined to upend our scene partner's efforts accidentally with a sudden ill-timed tonal shift. Player D's offer, while helpfully providing a specific character for us to follow and focus on, neglected to accept the overarching theme and energy of the train and its passengers struggling against nature. It's inevitable that the particular focus or theme of the story will continue to morph and develop, but jolting the scene out of the very energies that have inspired and defined the action thus far will typically confuse or disappoint your collaborators. Siblings reuniting is a choice rich with potential, but in this instance, it has largely **erased** what has come before.

3. **Know when your story is set.** My experience would suggest that a Chapter Two moment is also more likely to occur when the story is set in a "somewhere" or "general" time rather than a clear and specific moment. If you're talking about trains or mountains *in general* or weather patterns over an *unspecified* landscape or period of time, it can prove challenging to satisfy the above recommendations which, in turn, makes it more likely participants might be on radically different pages. On the other end of the storytelling gamut, if the scene rushes through *every* moment, leaping from what happened a month ago, to what happened last week, to what's happening today, it can also prove challenging to craft a unified arc. Sure, successful stories *can* exist under these circumstances, especially in more thematic or non-linear long-form modalities, but in more contained narratives narrowing your focus to a clear *now* will keep your story train on the tracks.

4. **Know where your story is set.** Similarly, darting between multiple or unrelated locations dissipates the momentum of most scenic explorations (unless, again, this is the very style of play you're engaging in). The above example includes such a leap in place. While Player D has provided us with "train proximity" through the creation of the station, this move leaped us through the potentially arduous journey that was only just starting to materialize. There are unquestionably times when scenes or shows essentially demand a location change in order to unlock the maximum potentials of the story in the most dynamic way possible, but every time you shift to a new locale, you might be leaving the most interesting thing that you've created behind you, especially if the location has almost become *a* or *the* character in and of itself.

5. **A possible exception (or two).** As with most improv strategies or dynamics there are always some pertinent exceptions. I would rarely advocate a Chapter Two move but have seen and used it myself when the story has meandered into needlessly problematic or potentially offensive material, especially when improvising in front of young or corporate audiences. In such instances, a re-set can serve the cast and audience and honor prior content expectations and parameters. Non-linear forms might also benefit from sudden tonal and focus shifts especially when there is a shared understanding that established elements have only been temporarily suspended and will be retrieved and recycled from the communal improv shelf later in the performance.

Final Thought

In general, a Chapter Two moment tends to be a symptom of vague-prov, poor listening, or competing visions for the "best" path forward. As always, dynamic improv is nearly always the journey rather than the destination, and we should resist carelessly leaping ahead.

> **Related Entries:** Advancing, Erasure, Over-Originality **Antonym:** Small Steps
> **Connected Game:** Shared Story

CHARACTER

Character serves as one of the four pillars of **CROW** (the others being Relationship, Objective, and Where) and is equivalent to the first "W" or **who** in WWW if you're more familiar with that acronym (the other two Ws standing for what and where). Both systems remind us to bring these important details to our scenes as quickly and dynamically as we're able, as in doing so we're more likely to have a strong and clear foundation on which to build a journey. Each of these elements will also evolve as the scene emerges, unlocking new discoveries and possibilities, but if players do not initially share a basic common understanding, it's more likely that the scene will falter or become needlessly contradictory.

I *love* basing both short- and long-form characters on my own experiences, foibles, and qualities as a person and if you were to ask me for *one* piece of advice when it comes to character it would be not to overlook the thousands of characters that you innately bring to the stage just by elevating one facet of yourself. (Explore Commandment #9 if you want to read a little more of that philosophy.) That being said, there is also great pleasure and growth to mine from deliberately moving away from our personal cores and donning roles that might not at first glance seem to share our assumptions and lenses. Boal discusses the value of connecting to our character's wants in particular:

> ... each actor must be directed to *live* the *desire* of their character intensely, rather than merely exhibiting that desire on the stage. As long as each character has an intense desire, as long as he or she intensely desires something – or does not desire something, which is also a form of desire, a negative desire – these desires will inevitably enter into conflict and from this conflict will spring the dramatic action. Theatre is conflict, not the mere exhibition of states of mind.[8]

Long-form and improv traditions in the healing arts are probably more conducive styles of play for building complexity and empathy with a wider range of personae, but we can consciously take this approach to much of our short-form as well.

Digging Deeper into Character

Relationship is a topic for another day so here I am exploring facets of character that start and emanate from the individual rather than that magical improvisational zone that exists between us as players. If you don't typically consider one or more of these dynamics in your work, giving some attention to a previously undervalued element of characterization can quickly reintroduce the potential for surprise and growth.

1. **Change your tempo.** Our character work can start to feel homogeneous if we bring the same rhythms to all our scenes. If you tend toward being a fast talker, slow down or change up your speech patterns; if you tend to remain stationary or assume a measured physical tempo, explore characters that are more dynamic or bring a sense of urgency to their staging. Laban movement qualities – such as glide, dab, and press – can further add new energies to your repertoire if you're looking for ways to alter your "typical" patterns. This can feel a little technical or artificial initially, especially when you truly step outside your previous comfort zones, so be sure to give attention to nuance and the "why." When we justify these behaviors through the lens of character, they normally take on greater detail and feel more grounded: this character tends to float through life because they are carefree and don't take on the stresses of their friends and families; this character exhibits a wringing energy as they are constantly in turmoil with both their own inner demons and the pressures of their environment…
2. **Change your age.** It's easy to have a tendency to predominantly breathe life into characters that are approximately our age (or, perhaps, are essentially "ageless" and therefore by default are approximately our age). It's important to keep in mind that age is only *one* facet of a person's identity and that there are, for example, a multitude of different octogenarians in the world that range from highly fit and physically active to more cautious or sedentary – to name just one possible metric. Assuming different ages, however, can encourage us to also explore characters who are in different phases of their lives on the stage, which can be really helpful if you tend to fall into premises from similar angles again and again. A first date scene that may have typically been played by two "twenty-somethings" will feel differently if you add a few decades to one or both of the characters; a first day of college will hold different meanings and possibilities for a middle-aged character restarting a career or a retiree looking for life enrichment and community than a more "typical" and expected teenager.
3. **Change your occupation.** Without necessarily placing your occupation front and center, committing to a specific job or type of work as a scene begins is another way to instantly spark your imagination and craft some backstory. Do you spend your days primarily working behind a desk in an office, or outside at a work site? Does your job come with social standing and mobility, or are you stuck in a daily grind? Does the work leave "evidence" on your body and the way that you move or interact with others, or are the scars more psychological? Is it a profession that defines you or that is merely one small part of your greater story? When we assume occupations that we may only know tangentially or from limited exposure through the media, it becomes important again to not settle at a surface understanding but, rather, use it as a prompt to consider how another type of experience might influence a character in the here and now. Even if this choice is never actively voiced or referenced within the resulting scene, it can add surprising levels, reactions, and motivations (or frankly, just add a new humorous lens in a "fish out of water" sense).
4. **Change your socioeconomic reality.** I've used Boal above to situate this entry; I particularly love his work in this area and often deploy exercises from his toolbox in my classroom to reinforce and complicate an understanding that social and economic forces can have a *huge* influence on what options characters may have at their ready disposal when facing a crisis or challenge. If we always assume our own socioeconomic reality, we are missing out on interesting opportunities to add specifics to our scene work and empathy to our tool belts. Losing a job, finding a $100 note, or facing a late mortgage payment can take on radically different tones and importance depending on where our characters are on this financial and privilege spectrum.
5. **Change your costume.** There is a wide variety of approaches to costumes in improv from more sumptuous and "rich" traditions in which characters appear in fully tailored and personal pieces to more "poor" traditions where costumes, if used at all, are constructed in the moment from found objects or are just imagined by the characters and audience alike. When working in this latter modality, unhindered by what might fit you on the rack backstage, there is truly no limit to what specific costume pieces we can bring to the stage through physicality, scene painting, and endowments. Entering a convenience store at the top of a scene changes substantially if we have donned an imaginary tuxedo, tutu, or chicken costume. Such a choice may or may not become explicitly relevant to the immediate action, but it is, at the very least, likely to invite new movement qualities and characterization traits.

Figure 5.1 Walt Disney World's Comedy Warehouse provided a beautifully curated and maintained array of costume pieces (and duct tape) that supported and inspired an endless variety of characterizations. Photo credit: Leesa Brown.

Final Thought

Some schools of improv actively encourage exploring different genders and sexes, which I think is certainly of value as well when done with care and empathy and not merely as a fast track toward a joke or gag. Exploring different ethnicities, races, or countries of origin is much more fraught, problematic, and (in my humble opinion) generally inadvisable, especially if you are in a short-form modality or moving from a majority or privileged position as a player into a minority or marginalized persona. There is one short-form game that my colleagues know I won't play for this reason, Dialect Rollercoaster (or, as I like to call it, Stereotype Cavalcade) as it invariably becomes a group of privileged improvisers doing quick hits and bits without any hope for depth or nuance. I think dialect work on the improv stage, in general, needs some careful consideration as well for the same reason. Host companies might have preferences or guidance on these more complex issues; if in doubt, the lenses above offer ample avenues to explore that are less likely to cause offense or ill will.

> **Related Entries:** Archetypes, Commandment #9, CROW, Experts, Objective, Physicality, Relationship, Where **Antonym:** Wearing Your Character Lightly **Synonym:** Who
> **Connected Game:** Character Walk

CHECK-IN

The practice of taking a moment before a performance or rehearsal to hear from each company member to forge connections, reestablish company goals, and develop an awareness of any unique or ongoing personal challenges (such as injuries) or limitations.

Antonym: Postmortem

CIRCULAR

A structural way to define a style of performance and storytelling that does not prioritize linearity or a refined plot but rather privileges theatrical elements such as theme, mood, or style as a governing creative principle.

Antonyms: Aristotelian, Linear

CLEVERNESS

The authors of *Truth in Comedy* rightly warn, "The most direct path to disaster in improvisation is trying to make jokes."[9] The concept of cleverness and the dangers contained therein receives some attention in an earlier "Commandment" post. Generally, **Cleverness** is viewed as a problematic habit where improvisers retreat into their heads to search for a witty or "original" contribution or punchline. As this very action takes us away from the immediacy of the scene and our fellow improvisers on the stage, it tends to disrupt more organic energies and flows, prioritizing the success of the individual over the discovered journey of the ensemble. Most would consider its antithesis (and a more desirable approach to the craft) as being **obvious** in our work – bringing our own innate and unique reactions and observations to our characters and scenes. Ironically, such an obvious approach may, in fact, result in *very* clever and original work, but this is a delightful byproduct rather than a consuming internally focused goal. Wit and astuteness certainly have a place on the improv stage, but an all-consuming desire to craft that perfect joke will prove troublesome in most improv settings that are committed to nuanced storytelling.

Example

The suggestion of "haunted house" inspires the scene.

Three friends, holding flashlights, gingerly make their way onto the stage.

Player A: "I should never have let you persuade me to do this! I don't care about the bragging rights anymore. This place is terrifying."

Player B: "Just hold my hand. We'll get through this. We just have to get something from the second story library as proof we were here."

Player A: "OK. There's the staircase ahead. Don't let go of me."

Player B: "I've got you."

Player C: "You think *this* is scary… [insert topical reference here]"

Signs That Your Cleverness May Be Getting the Better of You (and Your Scenes)

1. **You are still formulating a great retort for that line that happened 30 seconds ago.** We've all experienced that moment when the words didn't quite come when we wanted them to, but if you have a tendency toward cleverness, you're likely to formulate that response and offer it up later regardless of where the scene is *now*. The price of such a tendency is not only the disruption that you're probably causing but also your loss of all the details that were brought to the stage while you stood obliviously formulating that witticism in your head.

Player C: "…you should see the asking price on that sign we were talking about a few minutes ago when we were approaching the door."

2. **You are waiting for an opportunity to insert that zinger you thought about in the car on the way to the performance.** There are always exceptions to the rules, and I've worked with many players whose stand-up or sketch-writing chops allowed them to provide perfectly timed and well-crafted additions to the scene, but there is a trap in having material "at the ready" that you are actively seeking to insert into the action. It's foreseeable that you'll miss the nuances of your partners' offers if you are primarily waiting for a helpful "set-up." Depending on the style of your home venue, pre-planned material can also taste oddly different to an audience than humor that is honestly discovered. A similar trap awaits when we tend to blindly recycle bits and punchlines that have worked in prior shows regardless of what might be uniquely occurring in this performance (or co-opting a line that you've seen another player use in the past that you haven't earned in the present).

Player C: "…you should see the national debt figures just reported in *The Times* that are ballooning as we speak."

3. **You tend to hold back until you've had sufficient time in the wings to fully figure out and script your angle.** Few would encourage rushing to the stage completely clueless as to what is transpiring or how you can best contribute, but stubbornly waiting in the wings until you have it "all figured out" is an equally problematic approach, especially if it is at the expense of joining the scene when your energy and appearance is most needed. I won't deride a thoughtful and well-formed entrance, but there is also a true value in a well-timed entrance that contains a fitting and dynamic seed of an idea that invites others to play along. Improv erodes the gap between the moment of creation and performance, and you may not be fully capitalizing on the promise of the form if your instinct is to do all the work cerebrally and alone before joining your fellow players onstage.

Player C: "…you should see what's *downstairs* in the basement. I was reading in the newspaper that there have been a series of abductions. We should really do that instead… what were you two saying anyway?"

4. **You overly rely on your verbal gifts as an improviser and tend to comment on rather than participate in scenes.** This is a common theme that I explore in several other entries, so suffice it to say that unnecessary cleverness tends to pull the offending player out of the physical reality and flow of the scene. Don't overlook the value and import of throwing yourself physically and emotionally into the action alongside your peers. Don't mistake commenting *on* the action as being the same thing as contributing *to* the action.

Player C: "…you should both see yourselves in the mirror. Those outfits are so last year. I wouldn't be seen dead wearing that color palate. I'm just going to wait here."

5. **You often "know" the next five steps of the scene rather than discover one step at a time along with your character.** We can think of cleverness as being synonymous with gagging, but it also is a trap for the planner (a fact I personally know all too well). If you have been hard at work intellectually "solving" the riddle of the scene, willingly or not, you are now invested in seeing the action unfold in the manner your cleverness has envisioned. Such a stance can make a "clever" improviser prone to bulldozing or becoming bulletproof as you work to see the scene move toward a specific end.

Player C: "…it could only get worse if we go into the library and find an ancient, cursed book that, when we read from it, reanimates all the dead animals that are buried in the backyard, and then we accidentally drop the book out of the window and so have to go and find it to learn how to reverse the spell…"

Final Thought

There is an important distinction between allowing your knowledge base to organically infuse your work and privileging a cleverness in which you elevate internal mental gymnastics over embodied collaborative participation. There are certainly necessitated improv skills – such as target rhyming, punchline games, or clue-based endowing – that demand we balance an active intellectual process alongside our onstage presence. However, in general, there seems to be strong consensus that this should not become a standard way of playing as it can quickly erode other elements – such as story building, characterization, and emotional honesty – that will ultimately better serve your work in the long run. Allow your natural cleverness to infuse your process rather than wield it as a tool that dominates your actions and those of others.

> **Related Entries:** Commandment #4, Commandment #9 **Antonym:** Obvious
> **Synonyms:** Gagging, Over-Originality
> **Connected Game:** Player Interview

CLIMAX

Generally, a climax consists of the most dynamic moment in a linear story arc where the forces of the protagonist and antagonist finally collide.

> **Related Entries:** Antagonist, Protagonist

COMEDY

For many art-lovers the concepts of improvisation and comedy are almost interchangeable. While there are clearly modes of spontaneous performance that have more serious, earnest, or avowedly political ends (such as Theatre of the Oppressed, Theatre-in-Education, and Sociodramatic modes), a great deal of contemporary improv deliberately positions itself as an innately comedic enterprise. This inclination toward the comedic has historically cast a shadow over the value and efficacy of improv: humorous performance often becomes dismissed or undervalued as popular, low, or pedestrian as opposed to the elevated art of tragic or serious scripted work. Consider, for example, that Aristotle's work on the tragic form survived the sands of time, whereas his companion piece on comedy did not fare so favorably.

Acknowledging that improv is not inherently nor exclusively comedic in nature, it is *also* possible that we do not consider the multitudinous ways in which **Comedy** and improv intersect; comedy, after all, is not one static thing but rather a collection of ways in which art may elicit audience laughter toward an equally varied array of ends. Janet Coleman describes one such possibility in her examination of The Compass:

> Because the improvisational actor is trained, against his every acculturated impulse, to relax in the moment onstage without knowing what will happen next, the comedy that emanated from improvisational theatre was one of behavior, not jokes.[10]

All laughter is not made equally in the improv theatre. Laughter may serve as a sign of recognition ("I see myself in that moment,") appreciation ("I saw that connection coming,") surprise ("I *didn't* see that connection coming,") admiration ("I'd never feel comfortable doing that,") acknowledgment ("That was a masterfully crafted witticism,") alongside a plethora of other dynamics and energies flowing between the stage and the audience.

When we start to think of comedy as monolithic or "just one thing," we can simultaneously diminish the dormant and considerable powers of our improvisational craft. Comedy can certainly prove visceral and perhaps even inexplicable: most improvisers have experienced an earnest choice unexpectedly bringing the house down while other more deliberate efforts resulted in deafening silence. But we can also be highly deliberate and skillful in our application of the comedic spirit, providing our audience with an escape one minute, only to playfully challenge their assumptions the next.

Example

A customer walks into a shop... (to be continued below)

Equipping Our Comedic Tool Belt

1. **Physical comedy.** If we're not careful, improv can become, for many, a rather intellectual affair and it's good to remember that the way in which we use our bodies in the theatrical space can open up whole new comedic vistas. Is our character physically adept, or relentlessly clumsy? Does the environment work in our favor, or does it consistently impose new obstacles and barriers that thwart us in our intents? Does our physicality align helpfully with our objectives and desires as a character, or are there inherent contradictions or contrasts that unlock comedic juxtapositions? If we rely *solely* on our physical dexterity as performers, this can become pantomime, clowning, or slapstick, which may not be within everyone's reach (or everyone's cup of tea), but increasing our comfort in our bodies as performers will powerfully unlock new comedic pathways in our work.

A customer walks into a shop... and is so surprised by the jingle of the bell above the door that they trip over their own feet and try their best to recover with some sense of dignity...

2. **Wit and wordplay.** While **gagging** is rightly discouraged on most improv stages, this is not to say that verbal-based comedy isn't a mainstay of the genre. We must be wary of derailing a scene to throw in "that joke" that we have prepared, but wit, irony, and wordplay can all add to the joy of our spontaneous scenes when they are offered in a constructive (rather than destructive) fashion. I would distinguish this type of comedy from the practice of joke-telling as offers should still, ideally, provide scenic momentum, color, and detail, in addition to revealing and enriching the lives of the characters from which they emerge. Style scenes, in particular, can thrive with expertly crafted verbal exchanges that tap into theatre's rich poetic history.

A customer walks into a highly specific shop... and makes a witty observation based on the store's highly specific name... "Could you point me in the direction of your 'beyond' section please?"

3. **Parody.** Comedy has a long-standing tradition of merrily poking fun of other works of art, pop culture, television phenomena, and theatrical trends or indulgences. Whether you're working in a short-form improvisational format, or constructing a collection of sketches, a parodic scene can offer a fruitful shift of gears and an opportunity to explore a completely new energy. All comedy is highly

dependent upon the company and audience sharing foundational reference points, and this is most certainly the case when it comes to parodies. Without at least a general sense of the base material, a parody can quickly lose its relevance and charm, so it's important to know your audience well.

A television reality "star" walks into a shop... followed by their entourage... and a film crew...

4. **Farce.** Definitions of comedic sub-genres can tend to be moving targets as modern comedians are far less concerned with genre purity than our ancestors, but I tend to think of farce as comedy that explicitly considers some aspect of the human experience and holds it up for playful ridicule or examination. Farce might deploy the comedic "curve of absurdity" and start with familiar behavior that gradually escalates to the point of plausible implausibility. Exaggeration is often the hallmark of this comedic approach that may also contain broad physical comedy and slapstick. While we might recognize the art products or source material in a parody, we are more likely to recognize *ourselves* and our kin in a farce.

A customer walks into a shop... after attempting unsuccessfully to make a small purchase with an array of complex digital, online, and cell phone-related apps, they finally give up and offer cash...

5. **Satire.** This comedic approach rightly feels more overtly political as it tends to hold up human institutions for scrutiny. These institutions can be literal brick and mortar organizations such as big banks, the stock market, or the DMV (Department of Motor Vehicles), but can also be common experiences and human-made practices such as marriage, religion, or electioneering. Historically, much of the power and danger of comedy (and even more specifically, *unscripted* comedy) has belonged to this realm, where it can threaten systems of power, hierarchy, and oppression. Subsequently, governments have attempted to ban such work or limit its scope through forbidding the portrayal of clergy, the use of actresses, or creating unflattering depictions of the crown (or even wearing specific regal colors of fabric). It is certainly possible for satire to be used to "punch down," but this generally feels mean-spirited and politically "conservative" (in that in doing so it is seeking to maintain rather than question the "conserve" or status quo). **Punching up** toward formidable and powerful targets more typically serves as the norm.

A hungry working-class customer walks into an effete shop filled with wildly expensive and ultimately useless gadgets that can in no way help them with their current needs...

Final Thought

This is just a smattering of different comedic lenses and focal points: laughter undoubtedly can assume many exciting functions and guises. My brief list is primarily intended to encourage a reconsideration of the full range of improvisational performances that can tend to be homogenized under the banner of comedy. I fear our own community needlessly limits itself or underestimates the innate potential of comedic performance to encourage and instigate questioning and change. I'm indebted to my summer studies at the Players Workshop of the Second City many years ago with Eric Forsberg, who first elucidated this scope for me. Over 25 years later, I still utilize a similar approach in my own introductory improv sequence.

Related Entries: Commandment #4, Commandment #9, Gagging
Antonym: Drama **Synonym:** Punching Up
Connected Game: Demonstration Video

COMMENTING

Commenting is another improv habit that improvisers lean on to keep the stage action at a distance and takes the form of remarking (perhaps wryly) on the scene or choices of your partners rather than fully investing and committing emotionally to the story at hand. In his Washington Times article, Christian Toto critiques such tendencies: "Students should not tell their partners how to act or react, repeat something said earlier to stall, or make a comment on the action at hand since that doesn't allow for emotional response."[11] Some improv companies and schools look less favorably on this peccadillo than others, and it's certainly a "technique" that you may see seasoned improvisers deploying. Such a tool reminds me of scripted traditions like English pantomime that revel in a thin distinction between character and actor, and enjoy puncturing the fourth wall with direct audience interplay. In general, however, I'd categorize commenting in improv as a fear-based reaction that doesn't add energy or dynamism to the dramatic action; instead, it can tend to deflate your scene partner's offers in a way that necessitates that they assume the burden of keeping the story alive. Commenting suspends the theatrical conceit and contract, usually just for the sake of a witticism or observation that needlessly deflects an intended gift.

Example

Player A is waiting at a bus stop as Player B, clearly flustered, races into the space.

Player B: "I think that apartment building's on fire and there's a woman screaming for help from a third-floor window. We have to help…"
Player A: *(dispassionately)* "Well, that was some well-delivered exposition…"

OR

Player A: *(without moving)* "So I guess we won't be doing my idea then…"

OR

Player A: *(to the audience)* "Do I look like the firefighting type to you…?"

OR

Player A: *(sarcastically)* "I'm not sure how we're going to make *that* happen on this tiny stage…"

Some Commentary on Commenting

Consider reading my earlier "C" entry on **cartooning** for strategies that can help you bring that "Third Dimension to Your Scene Work," which will, in turn, tend to diminish the likelihood of this related trend. I'd like to use this opportunity to consider some of the reasons commenting can inadvertently sneak into our work.

1. **We're often rewarded by a disproportionate audience response.** There is no denying that a well-delivered and carefully timed rug-pulling comment on the action can elicit a thunderous audience reaction, but we must remain cognizant that not all laughter is created equal. If such a technique is ingrained in your company culture, the damage may appear minimal, but these types of choices can quickly become frustrating to your partner, especially if they have fully committed to the current premise. The audience may certainly enjoy watching this moment of improvisational squirming, but it is highly likely that our partners will not.

2. **We can maintain the safety of our position as a scenic observer.** As is frequently the case with less-than-laudable improv habits, commenting allows the offending player to dispassionately stand outside the action of the scene. When we don the hat of the "observer," we are less prone to explore emotion, vulnerability, and an honest connection to our character and their world. If the scene is moving into territory that invites culpability or emotional investment, commenting can allow us to retain the "safety" of distance – but at what expense? If you're prone to deadpan characters, this may be masking a fear of really joining the ebbs and flows of the impromptu journey.

3. **It buys us some time to process a new choice before committing to it.** It is not uncommon to truly feel surprised by ideas that emerge on the improv stage. Assuming a commenting stance during these occasions provides a postponing strategy. If we take a moment to literally describe the choice in a removed fashion, this buys us time to contemplate what we might want to add next. This is obviously a human and understandable response to the incredible uncertainty of the improvisational endeavor, but it also minimizes the very risk and adventure at the core of the genre. If you are truly surprised by a scenic development, chances are your character will be as well so why not just embrace this honest reaction?

4. **It provides the impression of tension or conflict.** Conflict is a topic for another day, but assuming the stance of a commentator can provide the *appearance* of conflict, especially if we embody a contrarian nature. This version of conflict, however, strikes me as a relative of good old-fashioned blocking in that it isn't an organic tension between the characters so much as a disagreement or struggle between the improvisers and how they perceive the rules of play. Commenting dryly on another's move might pose an obstacle of sorts, but it is rarely filtered through the world of the scene and so tends to stall *embodied* action in favor of conversation about *potential* action.

5. **Commenting on a choice is often easier than building on it.** Action and momentum are so important and can be notoriously challenging to

foster and build. Commenting will rarely assist in this scenic endeavor. Remarking on the choice of another player, or musing on perceived flaws, strikes me as low-hanging fruit in the meadow of spontaneity. It is riskier, more exciting, and ultimately more rewarding to climb that proverbial tree rather than merely stand beside it and assess whether or not it is a good idea for the tree to exist in the first place.

Final Thought

If a moment of commenting is going to happen in a scene, my personal preference is that it does so without suspending the point of view of the character entirely; that is, almost in a Brechtian manner, the statement offers the performer's *and* character's reality simultaneously. To use the example above, Player A might respond "I'm really not sure what someone of my stature can do... but count me in!" This can also be a way of playfully "calling your shot" as an improviser. Such a comment followed by a physically brave and adept pantomimic sequence would surely delight. Similarly, if a story arc has arrived at a complex climax that requires considerable finesse to resolve, a character noting, "I really don't know how we're going to solve this" could pleasantly add to the delight of the moment, especially if it is then accompanied by the first step toward a solution. In my opinion, commenting is most thwarting when it is offered in lieu of a "Yes, and..." rather than as a cheeky or playful bridge to the next bold scenic move.

Another variant of commenting is **speaking your truth** (or calling it onstage), where players provide important information to their teammates so as to address unhelpful patterns or habits. In this way, a player might note (as the character *and* the player), "Gee, I'd really like a chance to speak here..." While this may appear similar to commenting on the surface, the intent and spirit are markedly different as this is not a fear-based move designed to stall the action but rather a tool of empowerment and address.

Related Entries: Approval, Cartooning, Commandment #4, Mugging, Speaking Your Truth
Antonym: Commitment **Synonyms:** Corpsing, Gagging
Connected Game: Gibberish Scene

COMMITMENT

The concept of **Commitment** can serve as a stand-in for a host of important improvisational approaches and energies. A committed improviser might be viewed as passionate, present, and prepared, ready and willing at any moment to leap to the aid of a scene and their fellow players. A lack of commitment, on the other hand, could be marked by lethargy, hesitance, and inconsistent attention. An improviser that routinely embodies these latter traits is likely to serve as a source of frustration as they sap the excitement and attack from the collaborative creative endeavor. Those that give 100% of themselves to the process and journey, however, frequently emerge as audience (and fellow company) favorites, bringing energy and life to the stage. Libby Appel describes this state in the related field of mask work:

> ...the actor must be willing to let experiences occur without the full cognizance of where they are leading [...] There must be respect for the fact that solutions will evolve from the doing: commitment is essential to the technique.[12]

While we all have bad days and shows, commitment to our craft and companies provides an essential ingredient in the spontaneous *soup du jour* that is improvisation.

Commitments Worth Pursuing

Here are some facets of commitment that are worthy of attention:

1. **Focus.** Both on and off the stage, focus is critical as a performer (see Commandment #2). If we only passively give the work and our fellow players our attention, it is highly likely that rich gifts will be missed or misunderstood. There is truly no "time off" in an improv performance as we never know when our contribution may be most needed. It is embarrassing, to say the least, when you are the *only* person in the performance space who does not understand what is brewing or required because your mind has drifted elsewhere. Commitment or energy without focus and direction may prove equally as destructive as disinterested passivity. If your mind is too fraught or busy to offer such unfettered attention, perhaps consider taking the show off.
2. **Energy.** I don't imagine I'm unique in believing that improv is both energy draining and energy creating all at the same time. Especially in long-form modalities, it can be exhausting to give your

all for the entire duration of the performance, but withholding your energy and excitement is unlikely to leave you with additional reserves at the completion of the show. I've found the more I give to the stage in terms of energy, the more I acquire through the resulting performance: holding back provides less energy but also, oddly, seems to cost you no less in the long run as you don't get to fully draw from the generative vitality of the work either. And what's more, minimizing your energy contribution is dramatically reduces the oomph available to others on the stage. (In my opinion, blocking and commenting are often the result of players choosing to withhold their energy.) If you're having one of those days when your reserves have truly been expended, perhaps consider taking the show off.
3. **Trust.** Every time we step on an improv stage, we need to actively re-commit to trusting ourselves and the other members of the company. If we hold onto past injuries or ill will, play with a sense of leeriness or hesitation, or approach the event fearfully as we nervously wait for others' bad habits to reappear, we have largely lost the improv battle before it has begun. Trust is certainly more easily lost than regained, hence the import of dealing with any breaches in a timely manner during postmortems after the show. Similarly, it is equally critical that we exude a healthy trust toward our own work and choices, and do not needlessly carry the burden of our judges on our shoulders. If this essential trust is frayed in your performance group, or you are struggling to emerge joyfully from the injuries of thwarted self-expectation, perhaps consider taking some time off.
4. **Discipline.** Improvisation blends process and product in a dynamic and powerful manner, inviting our audience into the very moment of creation with all its splendor and clumsiness. There are few artistic pursuits that demand such an ongoing commitment to growth and discovery. To become complacent, overly comfortable, or inclined to rehash old territory with little effort to ignite new embers or potentials is anathema to the improvisational spirit. It unquestionably requires discipline to maintain this vigilance in our craft as improvisers, especially if we are working in more commercial enterprises that (seemingly) demand a certain level of repetition or predictability in the effort to win and maintain audiences. Stagnation, however, is the enemy of creativity, and it's important that we continually seek to push ourselves and our collaborators. To improvise is to grow. If you find yourself lethargically meandering through stale "bits" and recycled choices, perhaps consider taking some time off or enriching your work with additional training or experiences.
5. **Passion.** Related to the previous points, those of us who have been in the industry for a while can experience waxing and waning in terms of our passion and commitment. Improvisers who are fortunate enough to perform frequently are more likely to face this dynamic than those who are fighting just to make it to the stage once or twice a month. Improvisational theatre has the allure than every performance is an opening night, a quality that scripted theatre must fight to mimic. It is foreseeable and understandable that if you're wandering into the same building every night for long periods of time, your passion for the craft might suffer. Noting that passion need not be manic or over-the-top (neophyte performers can struggle shaping and controlling their newfound passion for the craft), it is important that we bring enthusiasm to our stages and audiences. If the play of improv has felt like work for a protracted period of time, perhaps consider exploring a new project or stepping away for a while to recharge.

Final Thought

I've semi-regularly co-facilitated an "Improv for Business" seminar with my home troupe, Sak Comedy Lab, where we'll posit the question, "What are you committed to as a worker or employee?" If, as a player, you are committed to creating community, this will undoubtedly infuse your work. If you are committed to growing as an improviser and developing your skill set, this will probably encourage you to push your boundaries as a player and encourage your teammates to do the same. If you are committed to challenging or representing the audience in sincere and dynamic ways, this will open up new ways to sharpen and utilize your craft. If you are committed to just getting through another show, then you may well become the albatross hanging around the neck of your company. No one commitment is necessarily or inherently better than any other, but *knowing* where our commitments lie (and what we are willing to give or sacrifice in order to realize them) is an important focus and compass for our work in this exciting and demanding field.

Related Entries: Abandon, Commandment #2, Focus, Freshness, Trust **Antonyms:** Cartooning, Commenting **Synonym:** Professionalism **Connected Game:** Act Harder

COMPLEMENTARY ACTION

Roberta Mock expounds on the essential qualities of improvised dance, noting that

> Contact improvisation stems from the idea that each body is unique. Dance is spontaneously created by the impulsive interaction of two different bodies […] Dance partners sustain physical contact and rely upon mutual trust and support. It is process, not product, which counts in contact improvisation dance.[13]

I love how this quote focuses on the unique relationship of bodies moving together in space. This dynamic strikes me as a core component of **Complementary Action**, a term used to describe the way in which characters or elements of the scene are related or connected. The companion (somewhat oppositional) concept of **parallel action** is a little easier to define as it typically refers to choices that are essentially mirroring or replicating each other. If someone enters the stage as a confident high school student reveling in their popularity, a parallel action would be to join the scene as another confident high school student, thereby supporting, elevating, and giving volume to the prior choice and any inherent games.

A complementary action is marked by the contrast or difference it adds to those energies already present in the scene. It is still firmly linked to the established world and given circumstances, but it is likely by design to add or emphasize a new facet or relationship. The confident high school student might be joined by an overwhelmed principal, authoritarian janitor, utterly perplexed new student, or disinterested former lover. Whereas parallel actions encourage us to think *same*, complementary actions invite us to think *different* but *connected*. For this reason, complementary actions are particularly critical in endowment games and exercises where improvisers endeavor to bestow predetermined suggestions on an unwitting recipient. When it comes to endowing, showing the desired elements (an equivalent to assuming a parallel role) would be considered particularly egregious in most improv circles. Subsequently, players must actively seek more creative ways (or complements) to guide their fellow improviser into the desired territory.

Example

Two slightly-out-of-shape runners and close friends (Players A and B) are in the midst of their first marathon race. It is clear that neither was quite prepared for this test of endurance, but neither wants to let the other one down. Their movements are pained and laborious, and each time they speak there is a clear sense of exhaustion and impending collapse.

A third player (C) enters...

How to Get the Most Out of Your Complements

1. **Think emotion or energy.** Third or later entrances into a scene can prove challenging for improvisers as it can be easy to inadvertently jerk the focus away from the established elements of the action that were proving engaging and dynamic. In such instances, it can prove helpful to offer a complementary energy that maintains some core elements of the status quo. If Player C enters as a fellow runner (a parallel at first glance) but is in *much* better shape, and so is having a delightful marathon experience, this can maintain the current game and activity but heighten the scenic energy by providing an emotional contrast. Perhaps the first two runners assume a façade so as not to lose face in front of their newly arrived friend, only to drop back into increased exhaustion once more as Player C sprints off effortlessly into the distance.

2. **Think action or staging.** A complementary mindset can also help add interest and dynamism to the physical components of the scene. Returning to our marathon runners, their movements may have degraded due to exhaustion with every step clearly proving to be challenging and highly deliberate. Player C, perhaps a rival runner this time, might pounce onto the stage with highly exaggerated gymnastic finesse, literally or figuratively running circles around their opponents. Here, I've elected again to maintain a relatively parallel *character* choice, but even greater staging freedom opens up if the character also assumes a more complementary role such as a reporter on the back of a motorcycle trying to conduct an interview or a marathon worker clearing up the racecourse just feet behind these last two runners.

3. **Think status or power.** I'm of the mindset that almost any scene can be improved with a careful consideration and application of status. Our marathon runners appear to be relatively equal in terms of status during this phase of the scenario. A new character (or perhaps a discovered tilt between the current two characters) can breathe fresh life into the scene by adjusting

or questioning this status relationship. Player C might join as a fellow runner who signed up these two friends to help raise money for a personal and highly worthwhile cause. This new character could be feeling remorse at the obvious pain they have inflicted on their ill-equipped friends (thereby assuming a lower status position) or embarrassed that their friends clearly did not train as much as they had stated (thereby assuming a higher status position). Once more, the central action and dynamic of the scene have remained unquestioned, but a complementary status has introduced some new spice.

4. **Think relationship or occupation.** And sometimes the running just isn't landing or has grown stale or generic and the scene would benefit from the infusion of a more dynamic complementary character. When I introduce this core concept in the classroom, I tend to start at this level as it is the most readily understood and appreciated. When we unlock the gifts of a complementary character or relationship, the potentials of the scene tend to multiply exponentially. Character C could be A's lover and is seizing this opportunity to break up with them. Or they could be a marathon worker that Player B accidentally hit with a discarded water cup that is out for revenge. Or they could be a former tennis partner trying to win their friend back to the ways of the racket. Or they could be a photo-snapping pedestrian who was a former crush from high school (who used to confidently revel in their popularity…).

Final Thought

While there is a somewhat oppositional relationship between complementary and parallel actions, I am hesitant to identify these terms as opposites per se as they both necessitate and reflect a close consideration of the choices and energies already in play. A truly oppositional choice to a parallel action would strike me as random or disconnected completely to the established given circumstances: our confident high school student, for example, might be joined by a time-traveling Franciscan monk. Some improv schools certainly voice a preference for one approach over the other, but most improvisers would agree that each technique has its time and place. I *tend* to prefer complementary actions in small cast or expansive long-form pieces as thinking *different* will typically unlock more dynamics and story potentials than an over-abundance of the same. On the other hand, if you're inclined toward exploring the "game" of the scene, parallels can definitely help sustain and elevate choices already in play, while a mistimed complement will likely puncture or disrupt the momentum. See Commandment #7 ("When in doubt, break the routine") if you want to further explore this interesting tension.

Related Entries: Breaking Routines, Commandment #7, Endowing, Parallel Action
Antonym: Over-Originality **Synonyms:** Different, Tilt
Connected Game: Gibberish Job Mime

CONFESSION

A scenic **Confession** serves as the second element (alphabetically) of the **CAD** trinity that also includes **accusation** and **discovery**. Each of these techniques is an example of a revelation or tilt intended to add dynamism to a scene that might otherwise find itself limping in an increasingly uninteresting stasis. While an accusatory revelation places culpability on your scene partner, a successful confession puts the speaker in the proverbial hot seat, providing new information about their past deeds, hidden desires, or unspoken secrets. Boal testifies to the value of such moments when he pens, "To surprise oneself means to learn something new, something strange, something unusual about oneself: something possible."[14]

Example

After a long road trip, married couple A and B approach the porch of A's childhood house. It is late at night, and they stumble with the luggage from the car.

Player B: "That unexpected traffic clearly cost us some time. I didn't think we'd get here this late."

Player A: "It's okay. I know you did your best, and I texted my folks to let them know we wouldn't make dinner."

Player B: *(nervously as they struggle with a suitcase)* "Well… we're here."

Player A: "Are you okay? You haven't been yourself since we hit the road."

Player B takes a deep breath…

Player B: "I'm not quite sure how to say this, but I got into a huge political argument with your father on the phone last week, and I called him some rather vulgar names…"

Crafting Your Confession

1. **Assume the role of the guilty or vulnerable party.** The gift of a confession is that it upsets the balance of the speaker's world (which, in turn, hopefully influences their onstage relationships and actions). It can be challenging when endowing backstory on another to find the balance between something that is provocative and also pleasurable for the recipient. With a confession, however, this challenge is markedly reduced as you have control over the tone and nature of the choice. To this end, make sure the power of the endowment truly lands on your own shoulders: it would be more accusatory, for example, to offer that A's father made the vulgar comments rather than taking the risk that you were the offending party. A confession needn't be negative, but it does offer the delightful opportunity to seize the role of the villain or miscreant.
2. **Give a confessional moment sufficient weight.** As is the case with the other options in the **CAD** trinity, almost *anything* could be a confession if you make the moment rich with import and suspense. Player B could have forgotten a seemingly meaningless item at home, stepped in something on the sidewalk, or told a white lie about A's cooking in the car. On some level, the initial specific doesn't matter so much as the way it is framed and presented – players will have the opportunity to polish and deepen the significance of the choice as the scene continues to build. So, even if your idea is only partially formed, if your intent is to offer your choice as a confession it's important to frame it as such. It may require that you emotionally preamble a little or adjust your tone and staging. Just don't needlessly undersell the choice, even if you're aware it'll need some additional help to shine. Ultimately, your character needs to deeply *care*: a seemingly lackluster confession can be extremely successful when delivered with sufficient pizzazz.
3. **Seek to make matters worse (or better) through timing or context.** The effectiveness of an attempted confession can change considerably depending on the placement of its delivery. Had Player B confessed about the in-law argument hours before arriving at the home, the power of the choice would be diffused. Sharing this knowledge just moments before the front door swings

Figure 5.2 Dramatic confessions are a staple of many genre-specific long-forms such as *Murder We Wrote: The Improvised Whodunit*, which culminated in a series of highly wrought monologues (Lighting design: Hannah Fry nee White; Improvising sound engineer: Brad Tehaan). Photo credit: Tony Firriolo.

open adds a whole new level of significance and drama. Endeavor to use any latent potentials of the present moment when crafting a confessional reveal. A confession burns less brightly if it focuses on characters or situations that are not actively involved in the current action (unless they are *just* about to enter). Instead, seek confessions that change the current onstage relationships, shed new light on pre-established facts, or utilize shelved details and offers as opposed to inventing completely new or disconnected scenic elements.

4. **Embrace the emotional risk of your choice.** Effective scenic confessions tend to come with some sense of personal cost or risk. "I like the snow" *could* be polished into a dynamic choice but is innately less charged than "I've never liked your parents." By definition, a confession is something that the character has elected to hide or obscure. It follows that there is an emotional toll when a character finally elects (or is forced) to share this inner turmoil. So let it land and gestate. Just as the recipient should take some time for a gut check, make sure if you're the speaker that you don't scramble to explain away your choice in lieu of taking that extra breath and really *feeling* the emotional potency of your words.

Final Thought

Confessions are such a powerful weapon in your improv arsenal and can reveal emotionally charged and dynamic doorways that will beautifully complicate your character and relationship work. Remember that they *needn't* be negative or embarrassing in nature and can also serve as an excellent way to increase the love and connections between characters. Take a look at the **accusation** entry if you'd like additional general pointers on how to deliver and receive CADs effectively.

> **Related Entries:** Accusation, CAD, Discovery
> **Antonyms:** Balance, Stasis **Synonym:** Revelation
> **Connected Game:** Inner Monosong

CONFLICT

Spolin provides sage framing advice:

> If players are simply absorbed with content, conflict is necessary. Without conflict, the scene gets bogged down, and little or no action can possibly take place. At best, however, it is titillation and imposed action and for the most part produces psycho-drama. However, when process is understood, and, further, that content is the residue of process, dramatic action is the result, for energy and stage-action are generated by the simple process of playing.[15]

Conflict – and the debate over whether or not it is needed for a scene to thrive – serves as a longstanding topic in improv. As Spolin aptly notes, conflict can be utilized as a short-cut to energy or action, although, ironically, it will often stall a scene when it is inexpertly or clumsily inserted. In the scripted tradition, **Conflict** is generally considered as the tension created between two opposing forces embodied by the protagonist and antagonist, respectively. The struggle between these parties culminates in the play's climax when one side eventually emerges victorious: in a classical sense, if the protagonist wins then you've probably experienced a comedy, and if they lose (painfully and publicly) it was likely a tragedy. If neither win, it may have been an absurdist piece!

On the improv stage, I would posit that conflict can be a little misunderstood and misapplied. Improvisers can rush to creating an approximation of conflict rather than mining this device in more subtle or surprising ways. There are, after all, *many* different forms of conflict and dramatic tension. It may take the guise of competing ideas or philosophies striving to answer a grand question, we might witness a thesis and antithesis slogging their way toward an uncertain synthesis, or follow two literal or metaphoric forces battling it out to claim the high ground. All-too-often in improvisational performances, conflict becomes synonymous with immovable points of view, or two characters yelling at each other. This is certainly a *type* of conflict, but it typically resembles blocking or postponing and will often bear similarly uninteresting fruit.

Example

Player A, serving as a parent, knocks on the door of their teenage child, Player B.

Player B: *(calling through the door)* "I don't want to talk to you!"
Player A: "Look, we agreed that if you didn't pull your grades up, you couldn't go to the dance with your friends…"
Player B: *(more yelling)* "Just leave me alone. You don't understand me at all…"

Player A: "There's no need..."
Player B: (even more yelling) "I said I don't want to talk to you!"

A scene of yelling ensues...

Underutilized Approaches to Conflict

While it's possible that the above scene might transform into something beyond a stalemate, it's highly likely that it will continue its current trajectory and result in little more than an all-out yelling fest unless the characters deliberately change gears. There are few energies on stage that are *less* appealing and inviting for an audience than unnecessarily protracted anger or animosity. So, while leaping to conflict might provide the stage with a type of energy, we must be cognizant that anger masquerading as conflict is unlikely a constructive or creative energy. It might *feel* good or cathartic for the players (which is part of its trap), but it usually results in scenes that ultimately prove ineffective and uninteresting at best, or tone-deaf and triggering at worst.

Here are some alternatives to consider if you find yourself on the anger train looking for a depot. Instead of argumentative conflict try...

1. **Passion.** I love investigating the concept of passion in my improv creations. There can be a tendency to think of darker hues when assuming an energized emotion, but the key to passionate characters is not their specific mood but rather the depths of their emotional storehouse. Conflict often becomes oppositional and stagnant as it can tend to be about what a character *doesn't* want, as opposed to positive and an actional pursuit of what a character *does* want. Player B is clearly upset that they have been grounded but has perhaps already given up on achieving their ultimate goal. The same scene would immediately strike a different tone if they built on their passion *for* the big dance rather than their anger or frustration with their parent. This may seem a little like semantics, but a shift in a character's objective can make a world of difference to how the story plays out.

2. **Allyship.** When most of us pursue conflict, we tend to explore it between our onstage characters rather than toward a common obstacle or focal point that both characters work together to overcome. If you're inclined toward confrontational relationships, shifting your mindset to that of a staunch scenic ally can truly become game changing. (Kenn Adams' *How to Improvise a Full-Length Play* unpacks this concept adroitly.) By uniting with your onstage partners, you can still benefit from the tension and dynamism of conflict while ardently and passionately striving toward a mutual goal. If Player A dons the hat of earnest sympathizer to their child, while they may still retain some frustration, the scene is more likely to uncover a variety of interesting hues. Likewise, if Player B agrees that their parent has gone above and beyond with encouragement and second chances, the scene will be less inclined to degrade into a screaming match.

3. **Mischievousness.** One of the challenges of unearned conflict is that it tends to stall the action and you may often look back on such scenes (when working in a long-form modality in particular) and feel that they could have almost been edited entirely from the dramatic arc without losing much value. If you find yourself repeatedly in these types of dynamics, a little bit of mischievousness can go a long way. Conflict can be the enemy of progress, especially if such moments prevent momentum. The teenager in the above example is certainly at a power disadvantage and their protestations are unlikely to quickly change their parent's position. So, try skipping the argument in lieu of a tactic more likely to give you success. Player B could apologize profusely, agreeing adamantly with their parent that they have not earned the right to go out, to finally re-establish trust... so that they can escape out their window unobserved. In holding tight to your character's true objective (going to the dance in this case) and deploying sneakiness, repetitive conflict can be avoided and replaced with skillful finesse.

4. **Internal Struggle.** Conflict often hits the stage between two heated characters, but we shouldn't overlook the dramatic and comedic potential of internalized conflict that is gnawing away inside a character. If Player A, as the parent, had *really* thought that their child would get their grades up and that barring attendance from the dance was subsequently a largely empty threat, anger will probably transform into an array of more complex and interesting emotions. Or perhaps Player B knows that they have been struggling balancing their schoolwork and social life, and they largely agree with this punishment but still don't want to miss the biggest night of the year. Take care that conflict that resides within a character doesn't translate into a different kind of stasis or inactivity and that it still manifests itself in a dynamic fashion; but investing in a complex inner life can prevent scenes and relationships from meandering aimlessly over barren terrain.

5. **Love.** This is a weighty topic worthy of its own entry but suffice it to say here that clumsy conflict is a poor scenic substitute for honestly portrayed love. As soon as our parent and teenager add love to the scene, it will undoubtedly become more dynamic and interesting. It is possible that the scene might still escalate into a moment of passionate confrontation, but if such an exchange has been contextualized and informed by love, the resulting conflict will typically ring truer. Perhaps Player B hates the thought of disappointing their ever-supportive parent yet again, or Player A feels that they haven't lived up to their obligations as a role model when it comes to helping their struggling child. Usually in life, it is those who we most love (or at one point loved deeply) that have the power to cause the greatest conflicts in our lives. As we construct our improv towers, we need to be wary of jumping to such conflicts without first investing in the love that bubbles beneath them.

Final Thought

Yes, sometimes you'll just need that moment of charged conflict. The story arc might be approaching its zenith, the show may need a bump of energy or raised stakes, or you're motivating an idling character to make a strong next step. In such instances, still seek finesse and moderation. Avoid pursuing conflict merely for its own sake. A little chewing up the scenery goes a long way, so look for a strategic exit if you've succeeded in upping the volume so that this dynamism can now transform into something new.

> **Related Entries:** Love, Objective, Relationship
> **Antonyms:** Agreement, Balance, Stasis
> **Synonyms:** Obstacle, Tension
> **Connected Game:** Alliances

CONNECTIONS

Callbacks, reincorporations, and connections all strike me as closely related concepts. The first two ideas tend to refer to the strategy of reusing formerly established facts or scenic elements at an opportune moment: callbacks are well-timed (often, though not exclusively, comedic) finesses that patiently weave theretofore shelved elements strategically back into the mix, while reincorporations include more practical narrative and story-based echoes such as simply repeating a character name shortly after its first appearance to keep it front of mind. While **Connections** can certainly include these types of improvisational recycling, I consider this concept as considerably more inclusive. When we seek or invite connections in our work as players, we are open to recognizing the *multitude* of complex ways that pre-established offers and patterns may interact and enrich one another.

> You just have to look. You have to open your eyes. It's a way of seeing. Just like any of the arts are. That's what makes it like life… you think of your life as a narrative when in fact it's probably a lot more like a Harold… You don't *make* order out of chaos, you see the order within the chaos.[16]

Example

A scene begins with an older character, Player A, baking cookies in their kitchen on a cold winter morning. They are patient and methodical, clearly an expert at their craft, and eagerly watched by a grandchild, Player B, awaiting an opportunity to taste the familiar fruits of this labor.

Later in the action, we see another character, Player C, in their own home kitchen making their famous grits and shrimp as their adult child, Player D, eagerly takes notes to record the process for future generations.

OR

Many scenes (and years) later, we see an adult Player B now teaching this familiar ritual to their own grandchild during an important shared moment in their lives.

OR

Several scenes later, we see a child being bullied on the playground. In a quiet moment, they open their lunchbox and pull out one of their grandparent's cookies, thereby revealing that they are Player B from the earlier scene.

OR

A few scenes later, we see an elderly character, Player E, in their home garage replacing a car battery that has died during a cold weather spell, all the while being observed by a young Player F with great attention and enthusiasm…

Opening Ourselves to Deeper Connections

Here are some ways to continue building an awareness and openness to connections as you approach your work as an improviser. I've provided these possibilities in a somewhat ascending order in terms of complexity.

1. **Use others' choices.** This might be the most obvious form of connection, but that does not mean that it is easily or excessively deployed. It is difficult to assume or exploit connections in our work if our primary focus is with our own ideas and offers. When we fully embrace the suggestions of our teammates, privileging their contributions above our own (or at least equally) then we are more likely to find dynamic and creative combinations and pathways. On the most basic level, repeating our partners' choices keeps these elements alive and well, be it a character's name, a feature of the environment, or the details of a mimed prop or costume piece. When we *actively* work to make these specifics important, whether they are used in the moment or polished and then shelved, we increase the raw material that can create and deepen meaning later down the road. From the above example, scenes might borrow the activity (baking), the environment (the kitchen or cold morning), the relationship (grandparent and grandchild), or a notable prop or emotion (cookies or anticipation).

2. **Appreciate and encourage patterns.** Patterns are a delight in improvisational storytelling and can assist us in many ways: we can elevate trends to help craft and build discovered games (my scene partner established a door that is hard to close that I should also fumble with at some point); we can lean into established routines or character mannerisms to heighten energy and playfulness (my partner has shown that they are nervous and have sweaty hands so I'll create another moment where that behavior will clearly emerge); or we can seek to disrupt or transform patterns to upset the scenic equilibrium so that our characters can go on new journeys (my partner placed everything precisely on their desk so I'll gently start to upend that sense of order). In each of these cases, our awareness and appreciation of recurring choices serve as a critical improvisational lens and technique. If we are oblivious to these emerging games and dynamics, we are ill-equipped to heighten, enjoy, and exploit them. Remaining studiously open to the emergence of patterns on the stage introduces new opportunities for thoughtful connections. Also, remember that a pattern or game more effortlessly builds when you actively reflect or add to it. Without a second "move" a pattern can't continue on to a third and fourth…

3. **Recognize rather than force connections.** As the opening quote attests, if we are working with awareness, we are likely to see potential connections with a surprisingly minimal amount of effort. If, on the other hand, we are working or striving to make such connections, they will often feel forced, unnuanced, or possibly even a little desperate. It strikes me as a deeply ingrained human tendency to observe and note patterns in our everyday world. Trust that these skills will also accompany you to the stage. If you are actively listening, and consciously looking backward (considering how the scene has evolved and what elements are already in play), combining the raw material of improv can become surprisingly effortless. To this end, trust that a well-timed and gently executed connection will typically serve you better than a clumsy grab or rushed comment. The audience enjoys seeing and discovering these moments as much, if not more, as we do as performers, and some of this appreciation can dissipate if we draw too much attention to the "trick" rather than letting the magic speak for itself.

4. **Explore skipping a step.** This device is a little difficult to describe, but there can be a joy in noting a clear connection but then skipping the most obvious next move or repetition in lieu of transforming the choice in an obvious but perhaps slightly less expected manner. Let me break that down a little! Rather than an explicit (first choice) connection, this might feel more like an implicit or "third" choice. It's perhaps clearest to model this in terms of word associating or repetitions. If Player A says, "I love you," and later Player B echoes, "I love you," but then the thread is completed by Player C announcing "Don't tell me that you love me…," the three vignettes or moments have still found a connection, but the third iteration has tilted the frame a little in a way that retains an element of freshness and surprise. A similar approach is to consider connections as thematic in nature rather than solely content or repetition based. In this manner, three vignettes might explore three *types* of love (or the lack thereof) and could still connect in a meaningful and perceivable fashion. In fact, I'd offer that such *implicit* connections are frequently the most dynamic, generative, and effective.

5. **Consider the (much) bigger picture.** If you're performing in an evening-long improvisational performance, then it's likely that the span of the entire event is included in the audience's frame of reference and is, therefore, up for grabs in terms of making connections. This attitude, when exercised with care, also holds true for short-form performances or events that might feature multiple disparate shows or scenes. In these instances,

the "first move" of a pattern could possibly lie in something outside the immediate frame in question and an apt reuse may also contribute to the evolving shape of show. Similarly, players can locate these first moves in current news events, pop culture happenings, or the prevailing zeitgeist, thereby making their actions connect to much broader themes and issues. On a more personal level, the same technique applies in terms of making connections to personal stories and experiences; although these more provocative moments may not contribute noticeably to the architecture of the event, they are nonetheless likely to add to the overall poignancy and power. The cautionary warning with all these less insular approaches is that the audience (or the majority thereof) needs to be *in* on the move, with the notable exception of personal connections designed to add character depth rather than collective meaning. Referencing or echoing that hilarious moment that happened in your closed rehearsal earlier that day or recycling those lazzi that brought the house down months ago are nearly guaranteed to alienate and exclude *this* particular audience rather than elevate the field of play. I refer to this as keeping the audience inside the circle of the performance.

Final Thought

There is also a second – equally important – facet of connection worthy of mention. The definition above focuses on the way in which material and content intersect and overlap, but it would be remiss to not also consider connection as it applies to the act of players engaging in the process of creating improvisation. Without this embodied practice of players sharing breath and space in an open and inviting way, and the resulting connection between the improvisers and their audience, improv would rarely amount to much, and so it is also vital that this unifying bond is nurtured and valued. In our excitement to play, we shouldn't neglect to see, hear, and connect to our fellow collaborators as it is through *them* that our journeys take flight.

Related Entries: Callback, Looking Backwards, Reincorporation, Third Thought
Antonyms: Randomness, Over-Originality
Synonyms: Patterns, Weaving
Connected Game: Phonebank

CONSENT

An undeniable tension exists in improvisation between playful abandon or freedom, and inner restraint or censorship. Frost and Yarrow speak to this dynamic when they write,

> The antonym of 'improvisation' is 'censorship', because while improvisation represents the permission (and self-permission) for artistic expression, and the acceptance of one's own as well as others' creativity, censorship self-evidently stands for denial and refusal.[17]

While some philosophies of play propose unfettered creativity at almost any cost, in reality, as we share the creative endeavor with others, guidelines and mutually beneficial boundaries are not only inevitable but, I would argue, innately healthy and helpful. "Play" shouldn't become an excuse for carelessness, insensitivity, or injury, especially as the central conceits of improv invite an attitude of accepting and embracing the choices of our peers.

With this commitment to work together comes a collective responsibility, particularly when our scenic choices and character endowments invariably enter the domain and freedoms of our partners. **Consent** in improv acknowledges that not all offers are made equally, and that individual players should unapologetically retain a level of agency over their own actions and characters. The banner of improv should not be used to create discomfort or encourage inappropriate behavior on or off the stage. We need to *purposefully* take care of each other. Furthermore, explicit consent is of particular importance when it comes to work that involves intimacy, staged violence, or potentially triggering material as such moments are rife with interpersonal complexities.

Consent Before, During, and After the Show

1. **Before the show…** In my home companies, it has become an increasingly common practice to incorporate a "check-in" ritual in the greenroom prior to beginning a show (or possibly a rehearsal). Here, players are encouraged to share anything that is happening in their lives that might influence their onstage comfort or choices, such as a new or recurring injury, if they're nursing a cold, or if something sensitive is occurring in their personal or home life. Standing companies might have developed a high level of rapport and know each other's boundaries

well, but this also serves as an opportunity to adjust these expectations as needed: a player who is typically comfortable with onstage displays of affection might not feel so inclined if they are getting over a cold or if there's a new guest joining the play for the night. This check-in also provides an opportune moment to address any lingering trends or issues that may be weighing heavily on a member of the ensemble. Perhaps they have felt silenced by their teammates, or unabashedly supported, or asked to play a cluster of roles that they find discomforting or offensive. Most greenrooms I've frequented are quite jovial and perhaps even a little goofy in the moments leading up to the formal performance, but it's important to give these pre-show rituals appropriate space and attention as they provide a chance to offer or define issues of consent before everyone is in the thick of the action.

2. **During the show (part one)...** Once the show is up and running, issues of consent become increasingly important as players are working in a fluid and real-time environment. First and foremost, players should seek to work in a spirit of love and consideration, offering choices and journeys designed to provide their partners with joy and appropriate challenges. Even if we've developed the utmost trust in our scene partners, we must also remember that our audiences don't know what may have been discussed backstage, and so we should also be mindful that we do not *appear* mean-spirited either. It's important that as characters *and* players we earnestly seek permission from our partners when approaching moments that might involve intimacy, intense emotions, or sensitive content. We often talk in improv circles about deploying slow motion when approaching stage violence: I believe the same tactic helps with passionate moments as well as it prevents suddenly springing an undesirable choice on a fellow improviser. In potentially challenging moments, I think it's generally more than appropriate to telescope our intentions a little ("If you're looking for a fight, just keeping pushing my buttons...") or asking our partner for permission to make our next choice if it might encroach upon their agency ("I've been wanting to kiss you since you walked through that door. Would that be okay with you?") In my books, asking questions in potentially heated moments such as these is *always okay*, as is *saying no*.

3. **During the show (part two)...** I also value having a safety valve in my pocket as a player that allows me to check-in with my fellow players as needed, especially in terms of material that might have wandered into potentially sensitive terrain. In recent years, I've started preferring "in truth" as an internal marker that my next sentence reflects both my character's and player's reality. For example, I might ask as my character, "In truth, would you like to stop talking about this?" to give my scene partner a chance to shift the focus of the scene if I sense it's getting unhelpfully raw. This is also a great tool to have in your pocket for emergencies: if I suddenly feel terribly ill on stage, I could inform my teammates with "In truth, I need to leave and I'm not coming back!" In this way, my exit isn't inadvertently viewed as the first move of a game that could then pull me back to the stage again and again. A good rule of thumb if you have any doubt as an improviser that the next perceived "logical" scenic choice will make your scene partner (or audience) uncomfortable is to follow the example of the ancient Greeks and, whenever possible, take the action in question offstage.

4. **After the show...** I'm considering the importance of the improv **postmortem** elsewhere, but just as the pre-show check-in allows for boundaries to be clearly set, the post-show notes session offers a chance to discuss when these boundaries have been broken or ignored. It is an industry norm for improv company leadership to play alongside other ensemble members, so it's also important to note that there may be a perceived or very real power disequilibrium that might discourage newer or more vulnerable members from speaking with candor. Developing avenues for advocacy and a culture of listening (rather than justifying or judging) can go a long way to help in this regard, but this intent must be actively fostered and pursued. A good first step is carefully modeling appreciation and acceptance in your own reactions to notes. In the (hopefully) rare case that a player may be engaging in repeatedly inappropriate conduct – willfully or obliviously – it's also important that the company has a clear mechanism for addressing this unwanted behavior. Trust is a critical ingredient in the improv endeavor, and it is worth our time as practitioners to rebuild this when the vicissitudes of spontaneous play stray into unproductive or unhealthy terrain.

Final Thought

While a consideration of intent seems admirable when pursuing issues of boundaries and consent, we must also acknowledge that *on some level* our intent as improvisers is almost irrelevant when it comes to how our choices have landed on our scene partners. My *intent* might have been to make a playful jab, or riff on a pop-culture motif, or give you an improvisational gift or challenge that I thought you'd enjoy.

The *result* of this choice, however, may have been frustration, embarrassment, or marginalization. If this is what my partner honestly felt, then that experience is what I need to hear, process, and honor. It's a given that, in most cases, the injury was accidental, but it's important that we don't allow our discomfort or guilt as the player who crafted this moment to eclipse the bravery and vulnerability of our scene partner as they share their honest experience. Recognizing the import of consent and its role in enabling a supportive and responsible performance environment is a critical tool to help us through those moments when the improv didn't quite live up to its fullest and most celebratory potential.

> **Related Entries:** Commandment #1, Postmortem, Questions, Speaking Your Truth, X-Rated **Antonym:** Carelessness
> **Synonyms:** Boundaries, Permission
> **Connected Game:** Sculptor Pairs

CORPSING

Corpsing, a concept closely related to **commenting**, refers to the accident (or tradition) of stepping outside of your character and undermining the scenic reality. This often takes the form of laughing *as the player* in reaction to what is occurring on stage. This is a newer term in my own improv lexicon: in the scripted tradition it would be synonymous with "breaking." I believe the phrase deliberately plays upon the most extreme scenario imaginable, which would be to laugh while reclined as a supposedly dead body or corpse, hence exploding any sense of theatrical realism. Some forms and genres deliberately play with this dynamic, such as *The Carol Burnett Show*, *Saturday Night Live,* or more presentational styles of performance, such as pantomime or interactive children's theatre where players happily step in and out of their dramatic personae as it suits. This dance between the theatrical and real world can certainly cause delight as we watch the performers fighting to maintain their composure in the face of increasing mayhem, and this is the dynamic McKittrick describes when he observes,

> Brechtian breaks are what make improv fun and exciting, because they remind us of the unrehearsed, instantaneous creativity of the performance and of the distance between the actor and the fictional character.[18]

Companies in both the scripted and unscripted tradition can, therefore, deploy this tool in order to add an element of whimsy and irreverence to the performance event.

While I understand why many see a value in this performance technique, I will confess that *in general* I am not a fan nor advocate. This stance reflects my preferred style of play and the more theatrically ornate worlds that I strive to build. Encouraging corpsing in these contexts will typically degrade the work of your teammates in ways that may cause unwarranted struggles to set the ship aright. That being said, I am also aware that this is, in fact, a tool I've perhaps unwittingly sharpened in my own improv toolbelt, and that finds its way into my work (even if I've only more recently discovered what to call it!) Short-form modes, in particular, tend to look more favorably on these slips as the improv constructions are more fleeting by design, and subsequently, the stakes are much lower if any one scene wobbles off target. So, while I am not entirely in favor of this tactic, I acknowledge that it has a time and place and that its effectiveness as a tool is largely dependent on the frame in which you are playing.

Example

A detective, Player A, stands over the body of a recently suffocated victim.

Player A: "After my close examination, it is clear to me that the butler was smothered in the pantry with this intricately embroidered pillow."

The murdered body laughs....

Keeping Life in Your Corpsing

To reiterate, I am not *advocating* shoehorning corpsing into all your improv, but if you find the mask of your character crumbling, here are some thoughts on ways to make corpsing additive rather than diminishing, especially in modalities or games where its presence isn't deliberately sought.

1. **Keep it real.** In my opinion, unless you're working in a broad or highly interactive form where the conceit of character is fluid and lightly worn, *deliberately* corpsing (or laughing at your own choices or discomfort) is a hard sell. Audiences can typically smell insincerity or manipulation a mile (or kilometer) away: if you're feigning a "break" for comedic effect, you could well end up

undercutting your own scene. Some improvisers have such an innate or polished charm that they can execute such a metatheatrical moment with finesse, but I fear that few of us are truly proficient at an effortlessly expert execution. Instead, attempted corpsing tends to feel amateurish or pandering – "I'm sooo funny I keep cracking *myself* up!" – or merely sabotages the emerging action through our misplaced efforts.

2. **Fight the good fight.** Instead of seeking these moments of breaking, consider that the witnessed fight *not* to corpse and break character is half the joy for the audience and players alike. If we play hard as improvisers, perhaps skating on a razor's edge of losing our cool, when corpsing *inadvertently* occurs it does so more organically. It's quite likely that as the improv stage is the cradle of surprise something might unexpectedly and utterly tickle our funny bone. Watching a player cheerily fight to maintain composure in such circumstances can serve as a riveting source of entertainment. However, over-playing these moments can quickly gild the lily, thereby destroying the very thing that was providing joy. Frankly, fighting to regain the character may, in fact, heighten a corpsing moment despite your best efforts; but again, this will generally appear more honest and play as such. The biggest audience laughs and reactions rarely come from the moments when we look (or beg) for them.

3. **A little goes a long way.** Corpsing is rarely a substitute for good storytelling and construction, and if you're building your improv castles from this quixotic sand, you are likely limiting your own chances of reaching any real heights. Yes, our work should be infused and powered by joyfulness – there are few things that I find more appealing as an audience member. Handled clumsily, however, corpsing can place the joy of the performer above that of the audience, especially if it appears (or has in earnest become) self-indulgent. If you consider yourself a novice or emerging improviser, I would caution against making this a go-to choice as it will definitely hamper your growth in other areas. At the buffet line of improv, I would liken corpsing to the parsley: a potentially welcome embellishment that few would consider a main course (unless you're a big fan of tabbouli!).

4. **Earn it.** Underlying all my observations above is the belief that successful corpsing needs to be earned. As a performer, you need to have developed a strong rapport and connection with the audience (and your teammates) if such a rupture is likely to land well. Corpsing tends to flourish when it emerges ultimately as a side effect of your efforts to retain character, or as an extension of your engaging and relatable performer persona. Be wary of striving to replicate others' success in this area, especially in unnuanced or mechanical ways. I have rarely seen corpsing work well when it becomes the *only* thing of value in a scene or monotonously present. More often, it weakens the narrative arc, thwarts your scene partner, and results in tepid and uncomfortable laughter from a needlessly generous audience.

Final Thought

If you're interested in developing the skill of corpsing, you are probably better served pursuing its opposite; that is, actively striving to stay in the moment at all costs and allowing slips to occur as they will. If you're working in a venue where corpsing is part of the culture, I'd still caution that it can easily become overused, poorly executed, or a mark of desperation. Yes, this device can add charm and whimsy but also know that this might be coming with a cost, especially if you're hoping to craft a multidimensional performance event.

Related Entries: Commenting, Mugging
Antonym: Emotional Truth **Synonym:** Breaking
Connected Game: Laugh and Go

CROW

Belt and Stockley provide a helpful definition of the current term:

> A process of defining offers at the beginning of a scene so that all involved in the scene have some basic information to base the scene on. CROW stands for Character, Relationship, Objective and Where. These are the essentials of a scene. The process involves including as much information about these in the first five lines of the scene. As soon as the players of the scene know who they are, where they are and what is happening they can improvise the story.[19]

The elements of **CROW** are extraordinarily helpful focal points for sharpening our craft as performers whether we are working in scripted or improvisational modes. Each element is sufficiently important and dynamic to warrant its own detailed consideration; here, I'd like to explore these concepts from a higher altitude.

I was introduced to this nomenclature through my initial studies of *Theatresports*, but Spolin's work with WWW (Who, What, Where) covers largely similar terrain. Our personae, desires, and environments can serve as a strong and empowering foundation for our creative work on the stage. When these components of our play are strongly established in a timely fashion, miscommunications and vague initiations are less likely to become compounded and hinder the forward trajectory of our stories. Belt and Stockley offer a specific challenge of landing such choices within the first five lines of the scene – which is certainly a worthy and admirable goal – although we should also tend to *how* such material emerges and not needlessly rush ill-formed ideas to the stage (which these authors are definitely not advocating either). Generally, more nuanced choices will offer richer pathways than hasty announcements that feel more like **commenting** than connected acting.

Example

Player A enters the space carrying a (mimed) large box that they carefully position on the floor and open. With clear affection, they pull one delicate object after another from the box, gently assembling them in a row on the floor in front of them.

Player B enters a few moments later carrying a large tray. They look lovingly at Player A and the activity that so consumes them. B places the tray down on a nearby footstool and retrieves two cups, offering one to Player A.

Player B: "I can't believe it's our first Christmas together in our *own* house!"

Player A pauses from their work for a moment to take one of the cups...

Player A: "Hot chocolate! You were listening to all those stories!"

Player B: "Not sure it's the best beverage for Florida, but my wife gets what she wants!"

Player B picks up one of A's carefully stowed objects...

Player B: "These are beautiful. Can I put the first one on our tree?"

Player A: "I actually have a bit of a system... No, sorry, what am I thinking? This is going to be *our* ritual now..."

Building Your CROW Foundation

1. **Split the "work."** There can be a tendency to strive to get the CROW "over with" as quickly as possible, perhaps with one player hitting the stage and almost reciting their idea rather than building it gracefully and gradually with their scene partners. (Such a panicked approach often embodies the pitfall of **cartooning** addressed elsewhere.) Don't rush your choices. Savor what your partner is creating, and let each idea have its moment so that it can bloom and grow. I appreciate the gift of having a more fully formed idea in your pocket as the lights rise on a scene, but it's exciting to offer one small part at a time so that there is truly room for your partner to process your offer and then add one of their own (good old fashioned "Yes, anding..."). Creating the CROW can feel like a burden if you needlessly take it all on alone. Alternatively, when you craft one aspect and trust that others will fill in the gaps, it's easier to find the pleasure and surprise in the process.

2. **Use all your tools as an improviser.** Exposition and the given circumstances can be tricky to establish under the best conditions – scripted playwrights struggle to elegantly define these elements as well. Be sure to deploy all your verbal *and* physical skills. It is asking a lot of ourselves to lay down great foundational choices with our words alone. If we place the "where" more dynamically in our bodies, in particular, our choices are more inclined to go the distance than when we merely declare our location. As is frequently the mantra of the improviser, strive to *show* rather than *tell* your audience and scene partner. For example, in the vignette above, the word "wife" might be almost unnecessary to define the relationship if we have clearly used our physical connection and staging to tell this story (and ultimately, the unique embodied energy of the relationship will probably serve you much better than just a descriptive title anyway).

3. **Specificity and import start here.** Look to make your own and your partner's choices detailed and important. A cup of hot chocolate is innately more interesting and likely to inspire than just some unnamed beverage. If I am assuming the role of Player A, it will add so much to the scene if I have particular images and choices in mind for each holiday ornament that comes out of the box rather than creating just one generic metallic Christmas ball after another. If you are inclined to rush through these first moments of creativity, you are less likely to find the unexpected small choice

that excites you and unlocks a new potential as a performer. So, take your time with each discovered object and element as this will increase the likelihood that you'll find those lovely little extra details.
4. **Define your ingredients.** Connected to the above, take the risk to make a definitive choice (or many) about the CROW components of the scene. There are some recurring traps that you should strive to avoid: nondescript friends, or two characters that just "sort of" know each other, are just a smudge away from **strangers** in terms of the dim spark they bring to the stage. Assume relationships that matter and demand passion and commitment. Imprecise actions are similarly problematic. If you're mopping the floor in big general movements without giving attention to where the bucket rests at any given moment, the weight and resistance of the mop, or what you're cleaning around (or cleaning up), the activity will quickly cease to have any additive value and will just become empty background movement. "Nowhere" scenes can't offer much in terms of staging either. Put something of note in the space or endow a more common feature with a peculiar characteristic. If you *initially* find yourself in a featureless hallway or street and neglect to quickly add a specific (furniture piece, weather condition, configuration…), it will become increasingly likely that the location will *remain* featureless (and unhelpful) for the duration of your action.
5. **Hide the magic.** If the creation of the CROW becomes a chore on any level, it can potentially take away as much as it gives. Relish the challenge of breathing new life into crafting these foundational elements. Sure, you may have played a scene with a spouse before, but there's no reason *this* relationship needs to be the same as any other you've embodied thus far. Explore ways to deploy subtlety and inference without sacrificing clarity and communication. The audience will quickly sense if scenes just hit the paces of quickly naming the basic assumptions; seek finesse so that they are unaware that your scene work is tending to these needs first. Emulate the stealthy magician that hides the foundational elements that are actually enabling the beautiful illusions that follow.

Final Thought

Some improv philosophies relish a more luxurious or patient approach to scene starts, encouraging players to find comfort in the unknown as the lights come up on the stage. It's not uncommon for the subsequent scenes to gently unfold with CROW ingredients remaining vague or disregarded, perhaps staying this way even as the lights come down. There is certainly not *one* way to frame the improv endeavor, and on the simplest level, it can be refreshing for all involved to break up the pattern of a show or series of scenes by varying the energy or dynamism of the launch. That being written, I have certainly seen many more cases of a scene struggling through the lack of a mutually agreed upon CROW than scenes thriving from the explicit absence of these ingredients. It's not uncommon for a scene to prioritize or excel in the crafting of one or two elements while others may recede into the background with less import (in my experience, the Where unfortunately seems to disproportionately suffer this fate). Ignoring CROW altogether, however, strikes me as inviting unnecessary chaos and confusion.

Consider exploring the constituent elements of CROW (listed below) for a deeper dive into how to maximize the creative potentials of each dynamic.

Related Entries: Character, Objective, Relationship, Where **Antonym:** Cartooning, Vagueness **Synonyms:** Given Circumstances, Initiation, WWW
Connected Game: Conducted Freeze Tag

CULPABILITY

As we advance in our craft as improvisers, I would rank few skills as more critical than that of embracing **Culpability**. Perhaps most simply and eloquently defined as the condition of "good people doing bad or regrettable things," culpability closely allies with the central improvisational philosophy of **change**. To embrace culpability is to fully accept rich but possibly unflattering endowments, take on responsibility for morally ambiguous actions, and savor opportunities to uncover complex character contradictions. Such a stance evokes the figure of the clown who is… "happy to appear stupid. He doesn't mind. He is not afraid of making a fool of himself. He is vulnerable, and happy to be so. His face is a disarming icon of happy stupidity."[20] Highly sought-after change on the macro or scenic level is heavily dependent upon culpability (and vulnerability) on the micro and personal level. In addition to helping action transform in new and dynamic ways, most audiences care more about a seemingly "good" and relatable character that finds themselves making a dubious choice than an overtly villainous persona replicating predictable depictions of right and wrong. Bringing an air of culpability to our work can serve as a powerful example of heightened and brave accepting, especially if it's connected to revelatory accusations or CADs.

Example

A nun, Player A, sits behind her desk as a nervous-looking novice, Player B, enters.

Player A: "I appreciate you coming to see me, Sister. I'm sure there has been some confusion."
Player B: *(anxiously)* "Of course. How can I help?"
Player A: "As I said, I'm sure she must have been mistaken – you've always been such an honest and moral woman – but another novice reported that she saw you taking some money out of the collection plate…"

Player B pauses for a moment and lowers her head.

Player A: *(gently)* "Sister?"
Player A: "I'm afraid what you've heard is the truth. I cannot deny that I took the money…"

The Gains of Culpability

1. **Less advising, more doing.** If advising scenes plague your work or relationships on stage, you may be falling into the trap of *discussing* dynamic or problematic choices rather than jumping right into the beautiful mess they will create. When we're asked to give advice on stage, it can be a very human instinct to give *good* advice, thereby pushing our scene partner away from a rich confrontation or discovery. Similarly, when we're receiving advice, we can tend to talk through all the options – especially bad options – that would be much more interesting to actually see. I teach a lot of improv on a college campus and a perennial scenario is getting dating advice or instruction on how to approach that appealing fellow student. It's very rare that such a scene amounts to much of anything (or much of anything *new*). Risk jumping into the inadvisable or unpredictable choice: ask out the most popular student on campus who doesn't even know your name, propose to your love interest on the third date, surprise your significant other with a visit from you and your parents (and grandparents… and three children from a prior undisclosed relationship…). So often the playful choice can be diffused or disarmed when we seek advice prior to its implementation.

2. **Less stagnation, more dynamism.** When you or your characters are disinclined toward culpability you may find yourself stagnating or trapped in a rut in your scene work. A lack of assuming responsibility keeps our characters "safely" away from change and growth. If the novice in the above example resists the charge of theft (or, perhaps worse, just assumes that she couldn't *possibly* have done it), then it's unlikely that the scene or greater story arc will continue forward with creative abandon. Instead, we're more likely to face characters stubbornly maintaining what they have established as their initial energy or essence. This, in turn, is unlikely to inspire dynamic scenic work. When we allow for the fact that our characters and their motives are truly a work in progress, open to transform and morph through the gifts of our partners and the given circumstances, it is much more likely that they will encounter excitingly unpredictable pathways. If you've found yourself stuck playing a limited cast of characters – ingénues can be particularly challenging in this regard – this pattern may actually be caused or compounded by an inability to see and embrace "bad" gifts that can facilitate compelling interruptions and shifts in your characters' deal.

3. **Less moralizing, more embodying.** I particularly enjoy theme-based improv that actively pursues an exploration of the human condition in all its chaotic wonder. An acceptance of culpability is central to such work. Without this mentality, scenes can easily fall into the trap of unnuanced "good" versus "bad" clichés, offering little that is truly new or engaging for the audience and players. If we're less concerned with espousing a particular viewpoint – most of us would agree that theft is generally a bad thing – and more interested in exploring the myriad of specific factors that might result in morally questionable or complex behavior, then our improv will come to life in rewarding ways. A scene about a "terrible" thief thieving yet again is innately less fascinating (to me at least) than a nun who has found herself in the unenviable position that this was deemed desirable or even necessary. I have found that newer improvisers can be hesitant to assume positions or philosophies that they deem "wrong" for fear that an audience might mistake their character's behavior or attitudes as being synonymous with their own. This type of theatrical bravery is certainly something worth encouraging and developing, and it comes with

the added advantage of building empathy as we assume positions and experience circumstances different than our lived truths.

4. **Less consistency, more ambiguity.** Humans are innately contradictory and inconsistent: a deeply loving friend can become hate-filled given cause, a shy co-worker can assert bold fearlessness if pushed, a highly intelligent family member can prove surprisingly dim-witted when faced with unfamiliar circumstances. When we seek misplaced consistency, especially at the expense of pushing away choices that at first blush don't feel "like" the character we're embodying, we will be "rewarded" by highly predictable and potentially monotonous dramatic actions. It's also easier for an audience to dismiss antisocial or morally suspect character traits when they are present in clearly "evil" portrayals. If we embrace **ambiguity**, on the other hand, and see moral corruption in characters we have come to love and with whom we identify, the dramatic and social effects are greatly enhanced. Most of us would like to consider ourselves as innately good people; subsequently, seeing similarly good people do bad things pulls us into the action as observers in entertaining and profound ways.

Final Thought

Characters and stories that remain in stasis will rarely reflect enticing experiences and conflicts. Personae that are virtuous beyond reproach don't demand much stage time and frequently lack agency or interest: villains who are devoid of any redeeming qualities or engage in only dubious actions will quickly become one-dimensional and stuck. Playing in the endless possibility *between* these two polar opposites by inviting change, surprise, inconsistency, and culpability, reinvigorates our work.

> **Related Entries:** Ambiguity, Commandment #5, Emotional Truth, Vulnerability
> **Antonym:** Bulletproof **Synonym:** Change
> **Connected Game:** Angel and Devil

CURVE BALL

While I had been familiar with the general tactic for a while, it was not until I read Mick Napier's *Improvise. Scene From the Inside Out*[21] that I came across the term **Curve Ball**. The concept connects several others, such as surprise, shelving, and randomness, and refers to the idea of strategically including some unpredictable elements in your scene work that do not initially seem pertinent to the current given circumstances. In this way, you're shelving potential choices that don't (yet) have an obvious meaning or thematic correlation, trusting that such a connection will emerge organically further down the scenic road. Throwing such a curve ball is a delightful example of being deliberately mischievous and raising the level of challenge. It requires trust (in yourself and your partners), patience, and playfulness, and serves as a helpful approach if you find your scenes losing that sense of "danger" that is the trademark of most great improv. For, as improv pioneer Jacob Moreno observes, "The first character of the creative act is its spontaneity, the second character is a feeling of surprise, of the unexpected."[22]

Example

A married couple (Players A and B) enter their apartment kitchen with laden bags of groceries balanced precariously in their hands.

Player A: "…it just seems that the basics go up in price every time we shop."
Player B: (starting to unpack) "I'm not disagreeing, it's just that the chili recipe is the chili recipe so there's no point in complaining to the cashier…"
Player A: "Did that make you uncomfortable?"
Player B: (playfully and without malice) "No, I'm used to it by now!"
Player A: (gently and lovingly nudging "B") "I know I need to let it go. But ground turkey just shouldn't cost that much…"
Player B: (getting out the "really big" pot) "I'm not disagreeing…"
Player A: (glancing absently out the kitchen window) "That moving truck is still parked on the corner…"
Player B: "This chili isn't going to make itself."
Player A: "Go easy on the peppers this time…"

Pitching Your Curve Balls

1. **A little goes a long way.** All improv rules are made to be questioned and broken, but I'd recommend that you don't overwhelm your scenic work with a flood of unrelated curve ball offers (as much fun as that sounds!) Yes, that certainly could be the game of the scene, but more often, judicious curve

balling will serve you better. It generally suffices to place one or two significant and memorable ideas upon the improv "shelf" awaiting greater context and use further down the line. If you overload the proverbial improv bookcase, each unexpected choice becomes ultimately less impactful and perhaps even less likely to be remembered and reincorporated. While a curve ball is a great way to keep a scene exciting and alive, it gains its value by being an *exceptional* choice.

2. **Pitch from strength.** I'd advise giving your initial attention to the basics (or CROW) of the scene and making sure these are dynamic and clear before throwing in an unexpected ingredient. If a scene is wrestling to find its footing, or the characters aren't firmly connected to each other, giving your attention to the deployment of a curve ball might not be the best use of your focus and time. Once the scene is up and running, and the players (and audience) know the "rules of the world," then an unexpected twist is a delightful way to forebode further adventures and keep everyone on their toes. If your scene feels like a delicate glass house struggling to find its way, this probably isn't the time to start throwing stones haphazardly.

3. **Add a new color.** My preference is for a curve ball to clearly add a new color or energy that noticeably differs from the prior established mood as this "marks" the choice as rich in spite of its apparent inexplicability. In the chili example, a food or cooking-related choice is more likely to feel like a CAD (Confession, Accusation, or Discovery) than a curve ball as it grows from the facts that have already been established. This sense of clear connection serves a CAD or revelation well but is somewhat anathema to the spirit of a curve ball, which is marked by its initial *lack* of connection. In this case, the moving truck portends *something*, but at this stage of the action, it really could be *anything*: a stake out of the couple, an in-law preparing to move in, an escape plan in its early stages... The choice in and of itself has no obligation to even vaguely hint at a specific meaning at this point; in fact, this would weaken its very gift which is considerably more long-term in nature.

4. **Don't needlessly point at it.** Similarly, an intended curve ball loses its dangerous future agency if it is quickly woven into the current action or hastily justified in an effort to have it make sense in the current scheme of things. It can be tempting to immediately contextualize an unexpected choice – "Oh, that's just the Johnsons. Their daughter is moving back from college." I'm not good at sporting metaphors, but this feels like bunting the ball rather than patiently waiting until the time is right and then expertly hitting it out of the park. It is certainly critical that all the players hear and process the choice that has been made but avoid the temptation to shift the focus to this new idea or carelessly comment on it – "Why are you talking about a moving truck?" As is evidenced in my vignette above, my preference would be to just let the choice sit and then continue without making it seem too unusual. If the choice is embraced without fanfare or question, it becomes an accepted part of the world ripe for exploring when the moment feels right.

5. **Honor the contract.** By definition, a curve ball tends to be memorable; subsequently, there is an expectation that such a choice won't be left sitting on the shelf unutilized when the improv scene or show draws to a close. If the moving truck doesn't find its way back into the story on some level, this earlier reference will feel unwarranted and unhelpful. As is the case with the related technique of callbacks, I think there is something to be said for deliberately prolonging the time between the idea's first mention and its later reappearance during a fitting moment: such patience can effectively add to the sense of tension, surprise, and (hopefully) enjoyment when it's successfully justified. This patience is harder to achieve if you're striving to weave multiple seemingly random elements into the scenic climax, hence the advice to show some restraint when pitching this type of choice early in the scene.

Final Thought

I am a big advocate for being obvious in your scenic work and letting an organic path emerge based on your innate reactions as a player and character. The concept of a curve ball provides a nice counterpoint to this approach, encouraging strategic risk and whimsy. If you tend to plan ahead or find yourself circling over painfully familiar improv terrain again and again, or perhaps even burning through material too quickly and running out of steam, this technique can reinvigorate your play, just make sure you don't start to "solve" or "unwrap" the random gift prematurely.

Related Entries: CAD, CROW, Justification, Reincorporation, Shelving **Antonym:** Obvious **Synonyms:** Mischief, Randomness, Surprise **Connected Game:** Should've Said

CURVE OF ABSURDITY

The narrative device of carefully pacing a scenic arc so that it begins close to the audience's known reality and then gradually becomes more and more removed and potentially absurd.

Related Entry: Game of the Scene

NOTES

1. Dave Duncan quoted in Kathleen Foreman and Clem Martini, *Something Like a Drug. An Unauthorized Oral History of Theatresports.* Alberta, Canada: Red Deer, 1995. p. 45.
2. Keith Johnstone, *Impro. Improvisation and the Theatre.* 1979. New York: Routledge, 1992. p. 116.
3. Viola Spolin, *Improvisation for the Theater. A Handbook of Teaching and Directing Techniques.* 3rd ed. Evanston, IL: Northwestern UP, 1999. p. 29.
4. Del Close, *Del Close Resource: On the Harold.* Del Close Resource. 28 Oct. 2000.
5. Anthony Frost and Ralph Yarrow, *Improvisation in Drama.* New York: St. Martin's Press, 1989. p. 3.
6. Augusto Boal, *Games for Actors and Non-Actors.* Trans. Adrian Jackson. London: Routledge, 1992. p. 20.
7. Hazel Smith and Roger Dean, *Improvisation, Hypermedia and the Arts since 1945.* Amsterdam: Overseas Publishing Association, 1997. p. 33.
8. Augusto Boal, *The Rainbow of Desire.* Trans. Adrian Jackson. London: Routledge, 1995. p. 5.
9. Charna Halpern et al., *Truth in Comedy. The Manual of Improvisation.* Colorado Springs: Meriwether, 1994. p. 26.
10. Janet Coleman, *The Compass.* Chicago: U of Chicago P, 1991. p. 280.
11. Christian Toto, "Improvisation Takes Practice." *The Washington Times* 30 March 2002: D01.
12. Libby Appel, *Mask Characterization: An Acting Process.* Carbondale, IL: Southern Illinois UP, 1982. p. xiv.
13. Roberta Mock, "Contact Improvisation Dance Uses Touch to Achieve Perfect Harmony Between Mind and Body." *The Independent (London)* 27 June 1994: 20.
14. Augusto Boal, *The Rainbow of Desire.* Trans. Adrian Jackson. London: Routledge, 1995. p. 141.
15. Viola Spolin, *Improvisation for the Theater. A Handbook of Teaching and Directing Techniques.* 3rd ed. Evanston, IL: Northwestern UP, 1999. p. 230.
16. Noah Gregoropoulos quoted by Amy Seham in *Whose Improv Is It Anyway: Beyond Second City.* Jackson, MS: U of Mississippi P, 2001. p. 54.
17. Anthony Frost and Ralph Yarrow, *Improvisation in Drama.* New York: St. Martin's Press, 1989. p. 146.
18. Ryan McKittrick, "Audience Becomes Spark For Boston Creem." *The Boston Globe* 22 Aug. 2001: C7.
19. Lynda Belt and Rebecca Stockley, *Acting through Improv: Improv through Theatresports.* New Revised Edition. Seattle, Washington: Thespis Productions, 1995. p. 200.
20. Anthony Frost and Ralph Yarrow, *Improvisation in Drama.* New York: St. Martin's Press, 1989. p. 67.
21. Mick Napier, *Improvise: Scene from the Inside Out.* 2nd ed. Meriwether Publishing, 2015.
22. Jacob Levy Moreno, *The Theatre of Spontaneity.* 2nd ed. New York: Beacon House, 1973 [1947]. p. 42.

D

DEADPAN

Reacting as if nothing matters or is of consequence. While this is a perennial dramatic type, its overuse in improv settings can quickly become problematic as such characters tend to lower the stakes, decrease urgency, and sap the momentum of a scene, placing the bulk of this constructive work on others.

Antonym: Emotional Truth

DEAL

The "Deal" of a scene or character typically refers to the unique quality or point of view that makes this particular dynamic or moment worthy of staging. Characters without a clear or compelling deal can tend to float through scenes and leave much as they entered them, often without making any lasting or noticeable impact on the story or audience. A simple strategy for discovering a deal is to reflect on what you have already done, and then making that choice again in new or heightened ways.

Synonyms: Game of the Scene, Point of View

DECIDER

The **Decider** serves as a traditional element of most short-form competitive formats and typically occurs after some sort of introduction and warm-up but before the main course of the games. It stands as a mainstay of franchises such as *Theatresports*, *Gorilla Theatre*, and *ComedySportz*, providing a means to determine the order of play when the show begins, or in the event of a draw between the teams, as a tiebreaker at the end of the night. There is a wide array of options, from line games to scenic battles, competitive songs, and timed endowments. Many will include a host serving in a facilitating or judging capacity, most will encourage audience interaction, and all – if executed well – should leave everyone clambering for more. While such moments tend to emphasize competitiveness, as Neva Boyd cautions, "Subordinate to fun, competition intensifies both fun and cooperation, but when distorted by extraneous rewards for winning, competition tends to create the reverse of all positive potential value."[1]

Example

Host: "And now that you've met the teams and know the rules, it's time to determine who earns the coveted advantage of playing first tonight…"

Decidedly Detailed Decider Dynamics

While the decider can feel a little perfunctory, when wielded with precision, this component of the show can serve multiple important functions.

1. **Modeling good improv tenets.** It can seem unfathomable for those of us who have committed decades to the field of improv that *anyone* hasn't seen this form of art, and yet if you're performing in a commercial venue, you're still likely to encounter some (if not many) first-timers in the house. A good decider offers an opportunity to model the basic principles and nature of improv, from its sense of playfulness and irreverence to its collaborative spirit and elevation of good sportsmanship. I am personally disinclined toward deciders that I would categorize as "parlor games" for this

reason, as they don't tend to put improv technique at the forefront of the event.

2. **Warming up the audience and players.** While a self-proclaimed warm-up often precedes the decider, this latter element of the show should continue the task of preparing the players and audience alike for the action that follows. When the audience directly participates in the process of eliminations, or serves as a continued source for ask-fors, their energy, excitement, and receptiveness will likely build. Seeking a decider that pushes the performers in their skill set will also (hopefully) sharpen their listening, attack, and abandon for the subsequent performance. There can be a fine line between pushing the players and overwhelming them and it's important that the decider models some finesse or impressiveness (alongside some delightful tumbles). I might think twice as an audience member about staying for a show if the company can't make it through an initial game with *some* modicum of grace. For this reason, I'm not a fan of deciders that reveal inherent skill deficits among the majority of the company. If the teams are not populated by strong singers, then don't sing; if you're not good at wordplay, then avoid punchline games...

3. **Introducing the players and frame.** As noted above, many short-form shows involve a competitive frame and the decider provides an important opportunity to establish this conceit. Some playful heat between the teams can color the action if this is your penchant, and players can further develop their individual and team personae (the underdogs, the braggarts, the newbies, the challengers...). You can also sow the seeds of a greater shape for the show: will the winning team continue their impressive feats of skill or face a comeuppance? As Boyd observes, true competition and improv strike me as odd bedfellows, but there is ample room here to playfully wink at the overarching "battle" through exaggeration, lampooning, and unbridled whimsy.

4. **Building momentum and connection.** Lastly, unless serving as a show-closer, deciders should also raise the energy and dynamism of the performance, making the audience want more. (Arguably, even as a tiebreaker at night's end, this goal holds true as you want to encourage the audience to stay for the following show or spill out into the street raving about the experience.) Meandering deciders that display little attack or finesse can do more harm than good. Some of my favorite deciders, such as Story, Story Die, I'll only slate if I have three or four players in the mix as it takes a *lot* of strength to keep a story artfully building over multiple rounds – you may be stacking the odds against yourself if you start with a luxurious bank of eight or nine. Furthermore, while I must admit that I can personally show reluctance in throwing a decider (I feel that the audience usually senses this choice and so it undermines the conceit), there are times that *someone* just needs to go out to keep the greater game alive. At the end of the day, we must be wary that the company isn't having more (often inexplicable) fun than the audience they should be entertaining. If the audience routinely grows listless or bored, you're doing something wrong.

Final Thought

In experienced and focused hands, a *lot* can occur in the seemingly simple moment of the show decider. Make sure you're not throwing away this opening element that is so ripe with potential and power.

Related Entries: Caller, Hosting, Shape of Show
Synonyms: Tiebreaker, Warm-up
Connected Game: Da Doo Ron Ron

DENIAL

Saying "no" to or otherwise negating a scene partner's offer or endowment, typically as the improviser (as opposed to from the vantage point of a character whose objective might conflict with a fellow player).

Synonym: Blocking

DENOUEMENT

In traditional linear storytelling, the denouement refers to the falling action that directly follows the climax of the story which, in turn, leads to the final balance or new status quo.

Related Entry: Balance

DEVISER

How do we describe an improvisational "maker," the artist who shapes and gives meaning to a spontaneous event? This role may be taken on by an individual, shared between a handful of co-creators, or broken into smaller interconnected roles within a collective. While the function of art maker *can* have a lot in common with our colleagues working in the scripted tradition, the scope and range of duties tend to have a broader and more inclusive reach, and the improvisational creator rarely resides neatly in one camp. I've personally explored using many different terms in my own work to describe this creative role and after some trial and error have settled on the nomenclature of **Deviser**. While the specific duties and responsibilities may alter from production to production and collaboration to collaboration, this term helpfully combines the multitude of hats that most improvisational practitioners wear as they approach the challenge and delight of crafting a new theatrical piece.

Faces of the Improvisational Deviser

An improvisational deviser might not assume *all* the following roles, but it is likely that many of these functions will at least partially fall under their purview:

1. **Creator.** Usually the seed of a new improvisational production will begin as a random musing. This initial inspiration may be teased out by an individual or collective who assumes responsibility for determining the intent and shape of the improvisational event. What artistic conversation does the show join or continue? How does it connect or react to other works of art (spontaneous, scripted, and from other non-theatrical disciplines)? Ultimately, what is the intended look, arc, and feel of the desired show? Depending on the circumstances of performance (such as the venue, producing entity, and intended audience), the initial spark may also include a strong consideration of the available production parameters.

    "I've got this idea of creating a fully improvised Molière French farce, utilizing rhyming couplets, a randomized stock set of *commedia*-inspired archetypes in period-appropriate costumes, and set in a drawing room location. I want to explore social facades and hypocrisy both then and now."
2. **Playwright.** Once an idea has been formulated and perhaps brainstormed, the next stage of improvisational show development frequently resembles that of a traditional playwright's function, although the process and product might look quite different. Previous training and experiences will undoubtedly inform the final shape, but the improv playwright determines the structural, textual, and framing elements (or lack thereof) for the piece. These may be formally collated and written down in a script equivalent, coalesced into a blueprint or pictorial chart, or polished and passed down primarily through oral notes and discussions. Or it may involve a mix of all the above. On occasion, "set" elements may also be included to frame the improv action that require a playwright's touch – such as an opening song, host banter, or introduction of the core conceit or characters. Alternatively, this voice may weave smaller improv units or devices aesthetically into a greater overarching form.

    "I'd really like to have a choreographed opening, reminiscent of the period, to introduce the company, present the possible archetypes, and then elicit votes or selections from the audience. The performance itself will resemble the dominant five-act structure of the period, with the events all occurring in the span of one day. Act One will utilize a *La Ronde* so we can meet the characters…"
3. **Dramaturg.** Depending on the focus and scope of the endeavor, the dramaturgic function could prove brief or expansive. If you are primarily interested in crafting a "modern day" piece, there will probably be little need for deep historical research, although you may elect to investigate and explore pertinent improv antecedents that connect to the work at hand. If you're looking to construct a specific genre piece or are setting your action in a distant time, culture, or location, intensive dramaturgical work could follow. While the playwright primarily solves the structural challenges and defines boundaries, the dramaturg provides content and sociopolitical threads and influences alongside story guidance and possibilities.

    "Let's read a strong cross section of Molière's comedies, mining them for character, story, and historical details that we can then use as inspiration. I'm also going to engage in some research focusing on early eighteenth-century France, and core tensions circling around religion, the aristocracy, gender roles, colonialism, and courtship as I can see these topics being particularly rich areas to bring to the stage."
4. **Director.** The above roles and work might precede or function in tandem with the actual process of mounting the production. If the desired work riffs on a well-known or accessible structure, or borrows liberally from a public-domain source, there may be little need to engage in a robust and separate development period. At its core, this director

function closely resembles its scripted equivalent in that the pertinent task is now getting the production up on its feet in a timely fashion. Unlike its scripted counterpart, however, the improv director tends to assume a deeply pedagogic role, providing strategies and techniques for crafting work within the desired frame and overcoming perceived challenges: they are equally concerned with the *how* as they are with the *what*. More often than not, they serve as teachers and coaches. The improv director's job also rarely concludes on opening night as they may continue to shape and craft future performances throughout the run with regular observations and notes.

"I see that we're struggling with the poetic element of the piece so today I'd like to focus on our verse. Let's get into two lines and we're going to warm-up with a rhythm and rhyme exercise to start those juices flowing…"

5. **Player.** Finally, it is not uncommon for improvisational practitioners to also perform in their own creative projects. They may lurk behind the scenes in a support or directorial capacity, serving as a resource or guide to the company (akin to a short-form host, emcee, or sidecoach), or may boldly trot the boards alongside their fellow cast mates as a co-creator (as is the case with *Playback Theatre's* Conductor, *Forum Theatre's* Joker, or *Gorilla Theatre's* Director). From experience, I would note that there are certainly pros and cons to also donning this hat, and while it is foreseeable that some of the above functions will helpfully persist (the director might lead post-show notes, for example), this conflation of roles can also prove problematic at times (fellow company members can needlessly defer to or seek permission from this collaborator in the moment of creation). Clear boundaries, expectations, and responsibilities are, therefore, a must.

"Welcome to *Wholly Molière* where we will attempt to improvise an entire full-length French farce based off your brilliant suggestions…"

Final Thought

These five roles strike me as the most common facets embodied by the improvisational deviser, although I've certainly taken on other obligations too, such as producer, designer, marketer, house manager, (ill-equipped) graphic artist, (equally ill-equipped) choreographer, and chief problem-solver. The improvisational impetus tends to elide and push boundaries, so it should probably serve as no surprise that this is also the case when it comes to re-envisioning the traditional theatrical production team. The title deviser, while imperfect, at least acknowledges and encompasses some of this fruitful messiness in a way that is more descriptive than the alternatives I've encountered in my own journey thus far.

And in case you're wondering, yes, the Molière format is a concept I'm currently musing on!

Related Entries: Dramaturgical Improv
Synonyms: Creator, Director, Dramaturg
Connected Game: Prologue

DISCOVERY

The third and final element of **CAD**, **Discovery**, serves as an environment-based form of revelation that tilts or heightens the scenic energy. Paul Sills provides a poetic tribute to this improvisational impetus:

> True improvisation is a dialogue between people. Not just on the level of what the scene is about, but also a dialogue from the being – something that has never been said before that now comes up, some statement of reality between people. In a dialogue, something happens to the participants. It's not what I know and what you know; it's something that happens between us that's a discovery.[2]

While a **confession** or **accusation** tends to shed new light on a character, relationship, or motivation, discoveries (when viewed through the narrower lens of CAD) use the greater setting as the source of improvisational inspiration. Such revelations are particularly unlikely to occur in ill-defined or poorly realized locales, so this facet of CAD also advantageously encourages players to imagine and build nuanced settings.

Example

Freshly dating Players A and B laugh jovially as they make their way down the pathway to the lodge in the woods.

Player A: "You're sure your parents won't mind us using their cabin? I haven't even met them yet!"
Player B: "I'd be surprised if they even remembered this place existed. We haven't spent a family holiday here in ages."

Player A: (looking around) "I can't believe how beautiful this view is… Oh, wow! When you said cabin, I was picturing something much less… grand."

Player B: "My family loves conspicuous consumption! The key should be in this lock box…"

As Player B fumbles with the lock box, Player A continues to investigate with awe.

Player A: "Is that a hot tub out back?"

Player B has become frustrated and then worried and finally a little embarrassed…

Player B: (after a moment, reluctantly) "The combination has been changed. I can't seem to get the key…"

Discovery Considerations

1. **Make it clear.** As is the case with the other two revelation variants, a discovery functions as a discovery because it is framed and presented as such. Be sure to "set up" an intended moment so that your partners and audience understand you are about to offer something noteworthy. Similarly, locate the source of your discovery clearly and resolutely. If there's a forest fire in the distance, indicate the specific direction. If someone has broken into the cabin, designate and embellish the features of a particular broken window. As I've said too many times, I'm sure, specificity breeds specificity after all.
2. **Make it different.** A discovery is a form of revelation which, by definition, needs to upset the scenic apple cart a little. An offer of this ilk should feel related to but ultimately different than the previously established status quo. When Player A notes the hot tub, for instance, this is very much in keeping with the established reality that the cabin is upscale and impressively decked out. If, on the other hand, Player A notes that there are three strangers *in* the hot tub, then that would likely read as an intended tilt. Thinking "same" works great for advancing a game; discovery tends to thrive in the land of contrast and complements.
3. **Make it important.** While the significance might not immediately seem apparent – as is also the case with accusations and confessions – a dynamic discovery should contain ripe potential for exploration. Successful discoveries can certainly start small and receive generous polishing and assistance from other players, but their first seed should unequivocally demand attention. In and of itself a changed lock box combination might appear a little mundane, but with some focus this idea can quickly raise the stakes and energy of the scene. Is it late at night and the couple is far from anywhere else they could stay? Are there highly vocal wild animals prowling in the nearby vicinity? Is there also a "for sale" sign in the driveway indicating perhaps that Player B's family finances have radically and suddenly changed?
4. **Make it personal.** Although a discovery will typically start out as an environmental, costume, or prop choice, it will prove most helpful and effective when it connects to or complicates the current relationships. Players are served well when they contemplate what this new discovery reveals about them or their motivations. Has Player B had their efforts to impress Player A now upended by this awkward moment? Does the changed combination suggest that Player B is no longer trusted or supported by their family? Or perhaps this small moment eventually leads us to learn that this was never B's family cabin in the first place and that their well-intending accomplice gave them the wrong information…
5. **Make it connect.** There is definitely a value in making a somewhat random or original find, such as noticing an unconscious paratrooper hanging from a parachute in a nearby tree, but large moves such as this may more closely resemble the form and function of a **curve ball** or a less desirable **erasure**. Helpful discoveries *tend* to emerge more organically from the previously established given circumstances rather than insert a *completely* different flavor into the mix. An over-original revelation can have a tendency to eclipse the very things that we were already relishing in the scene. Without some truly skillful crafting, it's unlikely that the focus will remain on the couple's budding relationship at the cabin if they need to rescue the stranger dangling from the tree – although now that I've written that, I would actually like to see such a balancing act attempted!

Final Thought

Remember that it is significantly more difficult to discover an object or facet of the environment that can ramp up the dynamism of a scene if you are performing in a "nowhere" land on an essentially empty stage. The more you craft an interesting location with a wide array of props and furniture pieces, the more you will ultimately have at your disposal to inspire a scenic revelation of note. While accusations and confessions can have a tendency to put characters at odds with each other, well-executed discoveries also have the added advantage of introducing common obstacles or objectives that promote greater physical presence and action.

Consider reviewing **accusation** for thoughts on how to successfully receive a moment of discovery.

> **Related Entries:** Accusation, CAD, Confession, Specificity, Where **Antonyms:** Balance, Stasis **Synonym:** Revelation **Connected Game:** Obstacle Race

DRAMA

Dividing improvisation into "comedic" and "dramatic" camps is a clumsy conceit (no better than "long-form" and "short-form" in most instances), but many companies at least loosely define themselves by these terms. Most competitive franchises and commercial ventures lean heavily toward the former light-hearted column, while the healing arts and markedly fewer improv companies opt to pursue the latter. **Drama** is also an imperfect and seemingly narrow term – I've grown to prefer sincere or honest as these descriptions do not preclude the possibility that improv crafted under this moniker may *also* include raucous laughter and mischief. For the purposes of this entry, I've defaulted to the term drama as this has historical precedence and is the standard nomenclature adopted by our scripted kin. Phelim McDermott offers a nice overview of this style of working:

> Theatre's about being able to examine things that are potentially difficult, or painful, or important, in a safe environment. Just seeing people on stage looking at themselves has an effect on an audience, because they see what power that has.[3]

When I was first introduced to *Theatresports* as a player in the 1980s, it was embedded in the culture that while shows were *generally* funny that it was always a possibility that an equally vulnerable and real scene could be just around the corner. Admittedly, these were few and far between in my fledgling days, but I have always valued this inclusive stylistic stance. After all, just as we should take our comedy very seriously (it's a powerful tool after all), so too can our dramatic work benefit from being taken not *too* seriously.

Example

Players A and B are exploring a difficult high school goodbye. The characters have been dating exclusively for several years but are now headed in different directions as university looms just around the corner. They have met at a favorite spot, a wharf jutting out into a pristine summer lake. This is where they first fell in love...

Thoughts for Elevating the Dramatic

1. **Embrace the light.** Whether it's a more dramatically inclined long-form, or a one-off short-form vignette, it can be a trap entering into a scene with the *intent* of being "dramatic." While it's certainly important to understand the tone and stylistic rules in play, it's equally important to fully utilize the playfulness and discovery inherent in the improvisational impetus. Even the most challenging scenarios or issues can find elevation through bringing all the facets of human experience to the scene. Humor, in particular, is a very honest reaction to stressful moments for many and accepting these lighter hues can also beautifully offset the heavier moves to follow. Humor – as opposed to comedy – is a little tricky to define but includes energies such as irony and self-deprecation, where the *character* sees their plight with a lighter or irreverent touch. If you have an inkling you're in one of those scenes with the potential for profundity, don't play the end (where you hope or think the scene is going) but rather relish the opportunities of the now. Seeing our high school sweethearts laughing and enjoying each other's company is only likely to make the outcome of the scene more meaningful and earned. Experiencing love and joy before possible heartbreak or loss makes the latter choices crackle. When we fearfully concentrate *only* on the drama, avoiding opportunities for joy or lightness, scenes can start to feel like approximations of real human behavior or resemble poorly executed melodramatic soap operas.
2. **Lean into relationship.** I've found that when scenes get too "plotty," they can have a tendency to lose cogency. Focusing too heavily on a story point (or, even more problematically, attempting to make *multiple* plot points and twists) tends

to overwhelm the scene: the more story that you push to the stage, the less time there will be for offers and themes to find enough space to breathe. Theatre isn't just *what* happens, but rather a detailed exploration of *how* these events unfold and change the lives of those involved. Alternatively, when players give focus to the central featured relationship, I've experienced that very little plot is actually needed for the scene to captivate; often a clear objective ("Player A is fighting to break up gently but resolutely") or juicy question ("Can this relationship survive a new long-distance phase?") is enough to create a riveting dynamic. Prioritizing plot too much also tends to put players in their heads and is another way of inadvertently encouraging end-gaming. While a breakup is possible (perhaps inevitable) for Players A and B, there is a lot to be gained from seeing these characters and the strength (or lack thereof) of their relationship. If they both deeply love each other, the stakes increase. If they are reminded of the thousand ways their partner brings them happiness as the scene progresses, the stakes increase. If neither of them has the strength to say what they both know needs to be said – you guessed it – the stakes increase. Perhaps they do or don't ultimately split, but if the audience witnesses this palpable tension, in many ways the actual outcome of the scene may have very little correlation to its perceived success and efficacy.

3. **Avoid emotional luxuriating.** Another trap I've witnessed in more dramatic improv is a tendency for improvisers to dwell in emotions. Sometimes, this is because it "feels good" or they believe that this is what it means to be a *dramatic* performer. Often the resulting emotions don't feel particularly organic or earned for the audience. Performers are nearly always better served by a "smaller" but connected emotional response rather than one that reads as "overt" but superficial. This is frequently a byproduct of focusing on the *portrayal* of emotions as opposed to reactively living in the reality. To this end, be sure to take a *moment* to gut check but don't then overstay in these more internal processes: react, feel, and then heighten that experienced truth. Keep your focus on your scene partners and leave room for the audience's own observations and journeys. If Players A and B are both fighting against becoming overly emotional so as not to cause their partner unnecessary anguish, this adds a new exciting tension. On the other hand, if both players are trying to "work up to tears," then they may well spend the whole scene without ever actually seeing or hearing each other. Luxuriating in emotions can also be a symptom of clumsy or ill-timed editing. It can be particularly difficult to edit dramatic scenes – fellow players may not want to step on a big moment or interrupt a build before it has reached its zenith – but these vignettes need the same generous shaping as their comedic counterparts and suffer equally from overindulgence.

4. **Use your whole self.** I'm unsure if this might be a unique pitfall in my own improv circles, but I've seen a disproportionate number of improv scenes that are aspiring to assume a dramatic tone launch with some variation of "Sit down, we need to talk." Such a move invariably nixes almost any interesting physicality or staging. Similarly, some improvisers take on a quieter (usually lower) and less supported vocal quality that telegraphs the desire to engage in "real acting now" but equally prevents verbal variety, nuance, and in the worst cases, audience comprehension. Dramatic scenes tend to thrive when we fully explore all the verbal, physical, *and* emotional components of the action. The innate trap of our wharf scenario would be to just sit on the edge of the wharf for the duration of the scene. Yes, this could work in adroit hands, especially if you're performing in a smaller space with limited staging options, but embracing activities, body language, and opportunities to *show* rather than *tell* the audience about the depth of the relationship and difficulty of this moment will likely add so much more to the performance. Perhaps A and B always used to feed ducks on the lake and have brought a loaf of stale bread. Or one of them has surprised the other with a basket of their favorite snacks. Or they enjoy fishing, birdwatching, or skipping stones. Almost *any* premise that invites movement will unlock whole new levels and allow you to fill any intentional awkward silences with subtext-laden action rather than solipsistic indulgence.

5. **Consider your intent and audience.** Furthermore, I'd recommend that our dramatic efforts don't trigger or needlessly bombard audiences or scene partners with "shocking" material. In the healing arts, there are often explicit social contracts between the performers as to how to address or represent sensitive material: this is much less common in more commercial performance enterprises, but there is unmistakable value in displaying equal care in terms of how we honor and welcome our audiences regardless of our preferred improv delivery system. It's important and generous to consider the

frame and expectations of all those in attendance. If they have gathered to blow off steam at an event advertised as a short-form laugh-fest extravaganza, it's probably not in good form to suddenly drop in triggering material without the time or intent to do so carefully and thoughtfully. Even when an audience is in the know that deeper themes and content are part of the performance parameters, I would hold that care should still be taken: there's a marked difference between tough material emerging organically from the flow of the action and players inelegantly launching content bombs for an ill-conceived shock value. Don't mistake taboo or controversial topics as being synonymous with drama; simple situations played with conviction and vulnerability will more often than not get you to the finish line. I'll heed my own advice and not provide potentially rough examples of how this might occur in our high school example. When it comes to challenging material, I'd also strongly advise against didacticism – presenting an issue in a slanted or simplistic light to uphold a pre-selected political stance. Such an approach can quickly lose an audience and undermine the established (and messier) realities and truths of your characters.

6. **Resist the temptation to solve everything.** When working in psycho-dramatic forms, such as Playback Theatre or Sociodrama, it could prove important that a reenactment finds a positive or uplifting outcome, especially when you're working with real attendees and their equally real narratives. In fictional modes, a well-intentioned desire to resolve complex conflicts or issues can result in saccharine plot points that undermine the integrity of the work. Magical or "Disneyified" solutions (a *Mickey ex machina* if you will) rarely ring true – finding a winning lottery ticket, miraculously getting offered the perfect job, the object of your unrequited affection suddenly loving you back... It's an understandable instinct to want to give our protagonists their unfettered dreams, and in some genre-based work, this may be built into the source material a little, but generally I find messier resolutions or denouements tend to ring truer. Yes, Players A and B could decide that neither of them will go to college but instead purchase the cottage by this wharf and now live here together in exquisite bliss. But successful and memorable drama generally emerges from tensions and questions that have no simple solutions. And when we frantically grasp at such solutions, we tend to assume a level of socioeconomic privilege or advantage that erases financial, cultural, and geographic differences. In long-form traditions, it's also innately more interesting to see characters make difficult choices that propel them toward new opportunities and challenges as opposed to clinging onto a status quo that leaves them as is.

Final Thought

I am personally drawn to improv modalities that allow for complex explorations of human themes through both dramatic and comedic lenses. Why not incorporate the best of these two deeply interconnected worlds? Such "impure" styles strike me as more representative of the world as we know and experience it. Whether you prefer one side of the style spectrum or the other, there is a palpable reciprocity between these energies, and I don't think it's coincidental that many of my favorite dramatic performers are equally expert comic improvisers: training in one area clearly reaps dividends in the other as well.

> **Related Entries:** Emotional Truth, Showing, Stakes, Subtext **Antonym:** Comedy
> **Synonyms:** Honesty, Sincerity, Vulnerability
> **Connected Game:** Fantasy Scene

DRAMATURGICAL IMPROV

Jacques Copeau inspires with the following hopes for modern improv:

> Improvisation is an art that has to be learned... The art of improvising is not just a gift. It is acquired and perfected by study... And that is why, not just content to have recourse to improvisation as an exercise towards the renovation of classical comedy, we will push the experiment further and try to give re-birth to a genre: the New Improvised Comedy, with modern characters and modern subjects.[4]

I've become inclined to use the term **Dramaturgical Improv** to define a subset of spontaneous play that tends to share certain characteristics beyond the more simplistic labels of long-form or narrative improv (although it tends to be both of these things as well). I'm indebted to Nicolas Zaunbrecher for first uttering the phrase in my presence at a conference where we were both presenting. The promise of the term resonated deeply with me in terms of encompassing a very specific and recurring type of improvisational approach and performance style that I have come to deeply value. The phrase itself warrants a little parsing:

Dramaturgy is a fluid term that can mean different things in different countries and to different companies. If you're unfamiliar with the role, on a simple level, a production dramaturg is often a researcher and creative collaborator who keeps an eye on the fidelity and accuracy of a play and its given circumstances. They are closely allied with the director and creative team, or, in some instances, serve as an audience-development and education resource. Dramaturgs also provide critical resources and critique for playwrights, especially when pieces are taking their first steps onto the theatre boards. Or their work spans all these areas, creating detailed resources for the company, working to fine-tune choices in the rehearsal hall as a "first spectator," providing historical context for the audience in program notes or displays, and developing educational materials for outreach programs.

And **improv** means make-em-ups...

Together, these words refer to a body of improvisational work that tends to place itself more consciously in conversation with other historical or stylistic trends and practices. Or perhaps put another way, it is improv built on a robust foundation or body of knowledge.

Qualities of Dramaturgical Improv

As a relatively new term, it is a little difficult to definitively articulate this particular approach to spontaneous theatre, but in general, the following tendencies tend to unify dramaturgical improv:

1. **Form and style.** Often focused on a particular genre or art product, dramaturgical improv tends to elevate and celebrate the source material that serves as its bedrock and inspiration. While a simple parody or brief short-form scene might happily skate on the surface, dramaturgical work, by definition, strives to paint a more hard-earned picture, incorporating emblematic devices, paradigmatic characters, and best practices while simultaneously mirroring key structural or formulaic components. Playful choices are inclined to emerge from a more informed vantage point as players engage in a theatrical homage rather than a hastily or ill-formed crafted pastiche. The resulting work may certainly assume an air of irreverence, but this will generally be born from a place of appreciation rather than distaste. (Most improvisers would not commit the necessary time to explore and inhabit a world or genre that they innately disdained!) *Showstopper! The Improvised Musical* and Free Associates' *Cast on a Hot Tin Roof* come to mind as examples of long-form pieces that display this sense of care and affection.

2. **Historicity.** While some dramaturgical pieces emphasize a genre or specific art product as the primary source of inspiration, others more overtly privilege a particular historical moment or period. Such works seek to acknowledge or replicate cultural and sociopolitical tensions that would have been in play during the time period in which the improvisational piece is set. There may be calls for "authenticity" or seeking informed perspectives and choices based on important historical trends and dynamics. This inclination can fold into a genre-specific piece and support structural and stylistic discoveries or become the unapologetic *raison d'être* of the event with the tools of theatre being repurposed to serve an explicitly pedagogic or edutainment end. In either case, such works generally acknowledge and privilege their historical antecedents and backdrops. Work of this ilk includes living history sites such as *Plimoth Plantation* that allows visitors to interact with early European settlers and indigenous peoples as they live their seventeenth-century lives, and the (sadly now defunct) *Astors' Beechwood* which offered visitors a tour of a Newport estate as if they were honored guests in 1891.

3. **Depth and detail.** I've likened the work behind this style of performance to the image of an iceberg: it's highly unlikely that on any given night or interaction with the event that you will be exposed to more than the tip of the knowledge, context, and research that has been amassed and lies dormant beneath the surface of the artistic creation. And yet, practitioners working in this modality tend to believe that this depth of preparation intrinsically elevates and enables the final product. Details and specifics are researched and pursued as they provide both dynamic launching points or scenic potentials, but also because they form a broad and solid common foundation from which to inspire play. Some improvisers may find this expected level of commitment off-putting while others enjoy the opportunity for personal enrichment and discovery. Polished improvisational parodies such

Figure 6.1 *Upton Abbey: An Improvised Comedy of English Manors* presented a serial long-form piece where random characters were drawn each night to serve as episode protagonists (Improvising stage manager: Grace Zottig; In-house dramaturg: Nicole Colangelo; Improvising Musician: Fletcher Wilson). Photo credit: Tony Firriolo.

as *Austentatious* and *Shakespeare Unscripted* (to name just two) embody this impetus and approach, and typically require company members to invest considerable time on research in order to gain familiarity and ease with the pertinent source material.

4. **Critique.** When dramaturgical improv situates itself in a particular historic moment or aesthetic frame, it also tends to offer a critique of the practices it replicates. This may or may not operate at as a primary goal and yet merely the juxtaposition of a bygone era or cherished form of the past alongside our modern mores will offer some food for thought in skillful hands, and in many cases this satiric or ironic tension is clearly desired and given focus. Whether it is revealing the limitations of gender roles, the blindnesses of powerful institutions, or the disparities faced by various segments of society, carefully etched homages offer a unique and powerful potential to reveal and question resilient societal inequities and contradictions. Such conversations may present themselves playfully, such as in *Some Like It Improvised*, or overtly, politically, and pedagogically, as is the case with Augusto Boal's *Forum Theatre*.

Final Thought

It is fair to note that some of the companies and productions mentioned above may not wish to choose the moniker of dramaturgical improv to define their own work; I offer these merely as reference points that share certain orientations and inclinations. As has often been the case with theatrical movements, they are most vividly and comprehensively defined well after the moment of their inception. But as we continue to contemplate the shape and scope of the improvisational impetus, I think it is important to make room in the conversation for works that combine spontaneity, structure, research, and efficacy in complex and nuanced ways. Such work has the potential to shatter the unscripted and scripted divide while serving and attracting a diverse and dynamic audience.

Related Entries: Deviser, Improvisation, Long-Form, Narrative
Connected Game: Sequence Game

NOTES

1. Neva Leona Boyd, *Play and Game Theory in Group Work: A Collection of Papers.* Chicago: University of Illinois at Chicago Circle, 1971. p. 123.
2. Paul Sills quoted in Jeffrey Sweet's, *Something Wonderful Right Away.* 1996. New York: Limelight Editions, 1978. p. 19.
3. Phelim McDermott quoted by Andy Lavender, "Whose Show Is It Anyway?" *The Times (London)* 19 June 1998.
4. Jacques Copeau quoted in Anthony Frost and Ralph Yarrow, *Improvisation in Drama.* New York: St. Martin's Press, 1989. p. 25.

E

EDITS

The improviser must wear and master many "hats" on the stage: director, playwright, performer, and in most cases, also an editor of the action, helping to shape the overall story arc through recognizing (hopefully) when it's time to move on or that a scene may benefit from an aesthetically apt nudge. Playback Theatre co-founder Jo Salas refers to this important task when she writes,

> We need to edit as we improvise, deciding in the moment which of all the features we have heard are essential for the story to be told. We must ask ourselves 'Why this story? Why here and now?' in order to feel its inmost meanings.[1]

In many short-form traditions, scenes are routinely edited by a host or technical improviser signaling that a moment is done and then the show essentially re-sets with a new offering. In most long-form styles, however, where the action is more fluid or continuous, ensemble driven **Edits** and segues are critical to the success and flow of the performance. Companies will typically have their own style preferences, but it's important to understand the foundational principles at play regardless of which genre you tend to call home as these techniques – when executed with finesse – truly enable some of the magic of improvisational theatre.

Example

Players A and B are performing the latter stages of a scene between an accountant (B) and their rattled client (A).

Player A: "…And you're absolutely positive that this isn't just some clerical error?"
Player B: "Look, I know this is hard to hear, but this kind of money just doesn't disappear through human error. Someone has been stealing a substantial amount of money from the company."
Player A: "But so few people would even have access to the books to try to manufacture a cover up. There's really only me, you, and my…"
Player B: "…your daughter…"

The scene awaits an edit…

Editing Options to Enhance Your Play

Here are some of the most commonly used editing possibilities. I've loosely ranked these from those requiring the least technical support to those that are a little more dependent upon the bells and whistles of a more traditional theatre space.

1. **Sweeps.** A sweep (less commonly known as a strike) involves another member of the ensemble marking the end of a scenic moment by running downstage of the action (in front of the current players) as if they were almost pulling an imaginary curtain. Upon receiving this signal, the players in the prior scene should move quickly to the wings or back of the stage depending on your staging practice. The sweeping player may exclusively embody this editing function and then recycle into the waiting ensemble as well or may culminate the motion of the sweep by then turning and beginning a new scene (or deploying one of the tactics below to keep an element of a previous vignette in play). I'll confess that I'm not a huge fan of this device as it can appear to attendees who aren't "in the know" as a peculiar tradition especially if you are working in a more theatrical space; but, in "found" or modest performance venues where you might not have a dedicated lighting operator (or theatrical lights at all) it can serve the purpose efficiently.

Player B: "…your daughter…"

Player C dashes across the downstage apron in a sweeping motion as Players A and B fade back into the ensemble. As C completes their cross, Players D and E have emerged and begin the next vignette…

Player D: (assuming the role of a doctor holding a baby) "Congratulations, it's a girl!"

2. **Clap in/tag out.** Another low-tech option is the clap in or tag out. If you've played the short-form mainstay Freeze Tag you're probably familiar with the basic premise: an offstage player essentially freezes the current action by clapping their hands (the **clap in**) and then quickly enters the stage. This new player has a variety of options once the scene has been halted and it is incumbent upon them to clearly conduct the next moment. As with the above example, they may use this technique to just edit the prior scene and then start one of their own alone onstage or with other new company members (although sweeps provide the more standard approach for enabling this move). They could also just join the scene as a new character and transport it in time or place. More often, though, the entering player will re-set the current configuration in some dynamic way. They might **tag out** a frozen player and have them leave so that a new scene or next step can occur with the remaining character or characters. This scenic adjustment may involve a shift in time or location as well. In more populated scenes, the incoming player may also "wave off" others who are not easily in reach to slim the cast down to just those desired. Another variant is a **revolving door** where typically one current character is physically pivoted to begin a different related scene while the prior vignette (and characters) essentially pauses so that they may be reanimated later. An extended series of quick tag outs or revolves can also build into a **run** of edits where you see a sequence of usually brief moments that build an energy or game. This series usually returns to the original character or combination that inspired the choice to mark the end of that particular dynamic.

Player B: "…your daughter…"

Player C claps their hands, freezing the action, and quickly moves into the scene tagging out Player B and assuming the role of the daughter in a new locale.

Player C: "…and I told them that the credit card machine had to be broken because there was no way my card should be declined… Anyway, long story short, I'm going to need an advance on my paycheck this week."

3. **Focus give.** Edits can be prompted by the onstage players with a strong and clear focus give. On the simplest (but arguably most effective) level, this may consist of an unequivocal **exit** after pitching a possible next step or vignette. On a slightly more nuanced level, current characters could instigate some of the dynamics above by endowing a new relationship or dynamic, thereby inviting a "clap in" style edit (with or without the clap) where an entering player now shifts the lens of the story. Another variant on the same theme would take the form of a **cut to…** offer where a character explicitly ruminates about a past or future event thereby throwing the action to this named moment. You can also utilize a **verbal tag** setup: here a character offers up a juicy line knowing that it will likely be taken and repeated by an awaiting player to shift the action. Successful focus gives require a little finesse and a common understanding as a company as to what to look for as a scene reaches its climax, but I like this approach when working with more seasoned and self-aware performers as it is steered by the current players and gives them some control over how and when their scene ends.

Player B: "…your daughter…"

Player A groans in clear discomfort at the thought.

Player B: (packing their things and exiting) "I'm not telling you what to do, boss, but if I was you, I'd talk to your daughter about this over dinner tonight."

Player C immediately sets up a family table as Player A turns and now enters their family home…

4. **Focus take.** There are also a variety of dynamics that involve a strong focus take while dispensing with the potentially jarring device of the offstage "clap." (Companies that have developed great comfort and trust, frankly, often deploy tag outs, revolving doors, and runs through clear **entrances** and intent alone.) Players can execute a physical **cross-fade** by entering and establishing their character in a new area of the stage, perhaps walking in front of the current action to make their appearance clear but, in nearly all cases, avoiding eye contact with the scene in motion so as to avoid being pulled into it. The prior scene should generally wrap up with the scene on deck then starting in earnest either pulling in a prior character or utilizing others from the bench. When this tactic is used more aggressively – by immediately beginning a competing and energized action – this

serves more as a swift **focus grab**. You can also make similar edits verbally: repeating or answering a line of dialogue in a new context as you enter the stage serves as a **verbal tag**; beginning your scene with a strong verbal offer from an offstage character provides a clear **verbal edit**; or depending on the style of the work, you could assume the role of a narrator or prologuer, talking on a god microphone or entering the space in a clear (and probably pre-determined) manner so as to **narrate** a new moment to explore. (Sometimes a **cut to...** leap is facilitated by a quick on- or offstage narration in this manner as well.) The key to all these focus takes is confidence, timing, and clearly communicating a particular intent.

Player B: "...your daughter..."

Player C as A's spouse speaks with great emotion while entering the space prompting Player B to leave the stage and Player A to pivot and join.

Player C: "*Your* daughter! *Your* daughter is stealing from us...?!"

5. **Supported edits.** If you have access to dedicated technical and musical improvisers, the potentials expand even further, although, in many cases, these dynamics are merely more polished versions of those listed above. **Sweeps** can now be heralded or replaced with musical play outs or dimming lights. (Music is such a helpful and gentle way to nudge players to get to the next thing!) **Clap ins** and **tags** can gain support from subtle or sudden lighting adjustments and soundtrack embellishments. Physical **cross-fades** and focus shifts now gain dynamism from the booth, which can even cue and sculpt these edits as needed. **Narrated** transitions shine with some technical polish that crafts a clear conceit to guide the audience's eye. And then there is the not-to-be-overlooked-or-underrated **blackout** (hopefully accompanied with a dramatic flourish of music) that allows the players to re-set and then deploy a strong entrance or edit from the lists above to jump-start the next scene.

Player B: "...your daughter..."

Players A and B pause for a moment as the music swells, and the lights suddenly plummet. Moments later a pool of light shifts the focus to a previously unused area of the stage where two new characters are soon seen driving a car on the highway.

Player C: "I don't think I can go on stealing from the company any longer. I think they're on to me..."

Final Thought

Successful edits have two things in common: they are clear conceits that are quickly understood by the ensemble and creative team (that is, *everyone* is on the same page that an edit is being offered up); and they are aesthetically pleasing and unambiguous for the audience, regardless of how many times they may have seen your work. Clumsy, inelegant, or frantic edits can unfortunately seriously hamper or diminish the effect of otherwise exciting work, so it is worth taking some time to determine and polish which approaches best suit your performance space, improvisational style, audience tastes, and technical abilities.

> **Related Entries:** Button, Entrances, Exits, Initiation
> **Synonyms:** Blackout, Sweep, Tag
> **Connected Game:** Verbal Freeze Tag

EMOTIONAL TRUTH

I've described improvisers as emotional superheroes to my students because our craft invites (if not demands) that we allow ourselves to go emotionally to places on stage that the average theatregoer would probably avoid at all costs. Some improv traditions clearly privilege this function, such as Playback Theatre, Forum Theatre, and the allied healing arts of socio- and psychodrama. Other styles of play might de-emphasize the emotional aspect of the improviser's craft, but I would argue that a pursuit of **Emotional Truth** can only elevate all our endeavors to a higher plane. "Play is not merely an outlet for surplus energy, but rather an outlet for those impulses and emotions knit up with the social interplay of group life."[2] Spontaneous theatre, after all, is a very human affair and benefits from exploring the full range of our foibles, fears, and passions.

Example

Player A sits on their adult child's bed.

Player A: "I'm really sorry that she didn't accept your marriage proposal. I can't imagine how you're feeling right now."
Player B: "She was out of my league anyway..."

OR

Player A, after pausing for a moment at the door to assess the situation, sits on their adult child's bed

Figure 7.1 Members of Rollins Improv Players light-heartedly explore getting emotional as they prepare for an on-campus performance in the dressing room of the now demolished Fred Stone Theatre. Scott Cook Photography.

and puts an arm cautiously but lovingly around their shoulder.

Player A: (after a long breath to summon the courage to speak) "I'm really sorry that she didn't accept your marriage proposal. I can't imagine how you're feeling right now."

Player B: (unable to make eye contact, the tears swelling in their eyes) "She was out of my league anyway…"

Inviting the Emotion In

There is no short-cut to portraying earnest emotions in our scenes – actors literally spend their professional lives pursuing and honing this skill – but there are some grounding techniques that can at least open a door to this more vulnerable style of play…

1. **Take some time.** When we rush through our scenes, expecting our words to carry *all* the meaning, we are much less likely to connect to our character and their situation in a more honest and potentially profound way. Take the risk of really breathing in your scene. This will encourage you to consider more earnestly *why* you are speaking, and *how* you might most effectively communicate your wants and needs as a character. (Sometimes, this may not be through your words at all but rather your actions or absence of words.) You'll want to make sure you are not just manufacturing silence for the sake of it – this time should be filled with energy and commitment – but use your breath to connect yourself to your emotional storehouse.

2. **Trust the audience.** This may be more of an issue in venues that consider themselves to be more overtly comedic, but most audiences will happily sit and observe a wide array of dynamic energies if they feel earned and honest. So even if our stated intent is comedy, we needn't fear material or a performance approach that might not result in belly laughs right out of the gate. When we grab at a joke, especially early in a scene, we may get that fix of immediate audience laughter, but it can come at the cost of a more nuanced or complex reaction further down the road. Trust that the audience will follow your exploration if

you are committed and present. This is not to say that an emotionally grounded scene should also be devoid of humor or lightness, but if our initial fixation as players is getting a laugh, the likelihood of emotional honesty decreases precipitously.

3. **Don't approximate or push.** The mark of melodramatic or amateurish performance is playing emotions artificially, exaggeratedly, or insincerely. There are certainly games and genres where such an approach might serve well satirically, but generally, emotionally "spending more than is in your wallet" will usually strain the credibility of the scene and the patience of your audience. I would posit that no one really wants to see someone *pretend* to cry, for example. I'd rather watch (or play opposite) a smaller and more honest performance than something grandiose but ultimately empty. Especially if you're approaching deeper or more sensitive material, overly indulging will likely ring untrue. It's more effective and theatrical to actually *fight* the swelling emotion rather than to over-eagerly welcome its arrival. (I consider this common pitfall a little more in my **drama** entry.)

4. **Bring yourself to the work.** I *strongly* believe that it is our right as artists to maintain a healthy separation between our lives and our work, and that we have no obligation to bring *all* of ourselves and our past injuries and failures to the stage. It's healthy for players to set boundaries, as it is to be skeptical of using our stages as public therapy sessions (unless that is their stated intent). That being said, I fear that it is equally problematic and potentially debilitating if we actively avoid bringing *any* of ourselves to our scene work. Our performances are unlikely to soar if we withhold our truths, interests, and experiences. Konstantin Stanislavski posited the notion of the magic "if" which loosely translates to asking yourself a series of related questions along the lines of "what would I do *if* I was in this situation?" Allowing this deeper connection to the world of our characters and their plights, with practice, can unlock a great cascade of emotional depth while also building empathy and imagination.

5. **Care more.** I deal with the concept of love as an improvisational imperative elsewhere, so suffice it to say that we're more inclined to become emotionally disengaged when we're pursuing stories and scenes that we do not care about or connect to, so bring the issues and relationships that ignite your passions to the stage. Fight for your character's happiness and for those that they love. When our onstage relationships become mere facsimiles of *real* relationships – dare I say unrelationships – we can more easily stand back and passively observe the work rather than roll up our sleeves and enter the fray. On a simple level, why should our audiences care about our characters and their fates if we don't?

Final Thought

Even the seemingly silliest of scenes or premises can benefit from a more emotionally grounded performance approach. We can tend to think of the more somber or negative end of the spectrum when we discuss emotional truth on stage, but the lighter hues of the human experience can equally gain depth and meaning with some earnest exploration. Why, after all, should we settle for being whimsical but removed observers when we could soar as emotional superheroes?

Related Entries: Comedy, Commandment #6, Drama
Antonyms: Cartooning, Commenting, Talking Heads, Waffling **Synonyms:** Acting, Culpability, Love, Vulnerability
Connected Game: Theme Scenes

EMPATHY

The gift of walking in someone else's shoes with an earnest commitment to understanding their journey in life. To improvise without empathy, arguably, is to limit your work to merely caricatures and two-dimensional approximations of the human condition.

Synonym: Love

ENDOWEE

A character who serves as the recipient of an unknown gift or attribute. In endowment-style games, this is the improviser who is not "in the know" and must fearlessly discover the pertinent hidden information.

Antonym: Endower

ENDOWER

A character who bestows unknown gifts or attributes on a naïve (but willing) fellow player. In endowment-style games, this is the improviser who is "in the know" and is charged with creatively communicating previously elicited information to the endowee.

Antonym: Endowee

ENDOWING

Endowing refers to the process of imbuing elements of our scenic world with dramatic detail. While this technique can inform and develop the imagined environment, props, or costumes ("When did this park bench get so rusty...?"), this subset of the critical improvisational **offer** often centers around the characters and relationships we build together. To endow, in this context, is to provide your partner with ideas and nuances that help them birth and sustain a character: it is a directed gift with an intended recipient. This process serves a critical function in endowment games – where one or more players aren't "in the know" and their teammates must steer them toward the hidden facts of the scene – typically with skillful **complementary actions**. However, in traditional improv scene work, endowing serves an equally important role as it quickly allows character qualities, relationship energies, and pertinent backstory and given circumstances to enter the flow of the narrative stream. Well executed endowing provides an on-ramp for players to move quickly onto the scenic improvisational highway.

Example

An as-yet undefined Player A enters the scene. Player B rushes over to them...

Player B: "Here, let me get you a chair, honey. You've been on your feet all day at the restaurant."

OR

Player B: "Grandma, thank goodness you're okay. I didn't realize you weren't behind us."

OR

Player B: "And what time do you call *this* young man? We agreed you'd be home by 10 pm sharp."

OR

Player B: "Kylen, you've got to stop following me around like this. I told you it's over between us..."

Elements of Effective Endowing

1. **Digestible specificity.** Some improv schools are a little leery of robust endowments as this tactic can become overwhelming when it is not deployed judiciously. As you would with any other scenic offer, be wary of an avalanche of endowing that provides your intended recipient with half a dozen facets to suddenly juggle and justify rather than a well-chosen one or two specifics that can help get the game going. If I endow my scene partner as my spouse arriving home from their restaurant, they still have ample room to make a lot of their own decisions based on their preferences, experiences, and instincts. What is their particular job at the restaurant and is it a high-end affair or a working-class franchise? Do they love their work or is it a necessary daily grind? What is the state of our relationship and marriage and is my gesture welcome or irritating? Remember that an endowment is intended as a pleasant addition rather than a restraining list of instructions. Making sure you leave room for your partner's own ideas and agency is critical in this regard.

2. **Pleasant surprises.** I like to use the concept of a gift when discussing endowments as it front loads the idea that we are offering up something that we believe our partner will appreciate and enjoy. Yes, this choice might embody a sense of playful whimsy and mischief – akin to **shivving** if you know the term – but endowments that push players into uncomfortable or ill-conceived territory would serve as an example of **pimping** or selling out your teammate to gain a quick laugh. It is undoubtedly easier to walk this line in a company where everyone knows each other well and respects each other's boundaries. When playing with a newer company, it's important to use pre-show check-ins and post-show postmortems to gain a deeper understanding of how choices are landing. In unfamiliar venues, it becomes even more important to avoid overloading your partner in one gigantic endowment dump as this also prevents any chance of adjusting your choice

based on their reaction on stage. For example, if I've endowed a fellow player as my grandmother and *then* have the cognizance that they have expressed they are always getting cast as older, I can then quickly follow up with making her vibrant and youthful as well.

3. **Emotional connections.** There can be a tendency to think of endowments as a factual verbal exchange, merely defining the biographical details of your scene partner. Don't overlook the emotional and physical connections as well. As I catch my teenage son coming home late, am I deeply disappointed in him, or is this a more jovial and loving kind of sparring? Is he excited to tell me of his adventures that evening, or does he feel smothered and trapped by my parenting style? Endowments can as readily be communicated through our staging and physical choices than just our words alone. If I hand my son a cup of hot chocolate (or a can of beer) when he enters, this adds a nuance and tone that is starkly different than if I pull out my handcuffs as an off-duty police officer. Similarly, leaping out of the shadows offers something different than just sitting calmly on the couch awaiting his arrival. As always, pay as much attention to the subtext and *how* as you do to the words and *what*. Closely considering the way in which we endow our fellow improvisers has the added advantage of slowing us down a little and leaving that much-needed room for responses and adjustments.

4. **Conscious choices.** Endowments also serve as a great opportunity to invert, question, or draw attention to assumptions and stereotypes in a critical fashion. Especially as a scene takes its first formative steps, a well-crafted endowment can jolt a scene out of stale or inelegant terrain. Kylen, in the example above, could evolve into a familiar stalking scenario (that was my loose intent when I crafted it) or this offer could enable a tilt into something a little more satirically self-aware. Kylen could become a cell phone provider trying to win back a customer, a parent who forgot their child's birthday yet again, or a best friend whose political insensitivity has finally gone too far. Thoughtful endowments can enable provocative and dynamic content, highlight dramatic (or comedic) contrasts, and encourage complex relationships and tensions.

Final Thought

Bite-sized, desirable, grounded, and aware are qualities that can elevate a simple endowment to the next level. If you are a "type A" improviser, endeavor to accept as many as you pitch as excessive endowing can be a sign of control-seeking bulldozing or waffling. If you can tend to go with the flow a little too much, then it's probably worthwhile to practice resolute endowments so that you can avoid the companion trap of routinely becoming a scenic passenger.

> **Related Entries:** Assumption, Complementary Action, Initiation, Offer, Relationship
> **Antonyms:** Bulldozing, Pimping, Waffling
> **Synonym:** Shivving
> **Connected Game:** Endowment Circle

ENSEMBLE

Most improvisational creation occurs in the ever-important **Ensemble**, a collective mishmash of participants that can lift each other to new heights and joys, or perhaps (in less ideal circumstances) hold each other's faces down in the messiness of spontaneity. The authors of *Truth in Comedy* echo a commonly held belief when they offer, "The only star in improv is the ensemble itself; if everyone is doing his job well, then no one should stand out. *The best way for an improviser to look good is by making his fellow players look good.*"[3] I've worked in ensembles that I have assembled and led, as well as companies where I have jobbed in or been hired, and I'm always struck that managing or maintaining a healthy group can prove so easy when things are going right, and so exhausting and all-consuming when there are underlying problems or issues. Even the "best" onstage improv work will leave a bad taste in your mouth when it's marred by offstage turmoil, problematic personalities, and interpersonal tensions.

Marks of a Healthy and Aspirational Ensemble

There are probably thousands of appropriate words I could use to describe a well-functioning ensemble, but here are some of the energies that I've found recur with frequency in groups where the collaboration flowed well.

1. **Accepting.** I'm using this term in its broadest sense. Healthy ensembles tend to accept and value a diversity of opinions, experiences, and approaches as well as just good old-fashioned diversity in general. Players accept their own failings and stumbles as well those of their peers,

ideas are floated freely and with gusto with a sense that they will be heard and assessed on their merits (rather than as a move in some hidden power game), and *all* the voices in the space are seen as intrinsically valuable.

Player A: (during the postmortem) "Yeah, I totally understand that my choice landed really weirdly and I'm sorry that I made you uncomfortable. I'm really going to think about what I did there, and I'll make a different choice next time. Thanks for being so honest with me about your experience."

2. **Joyful.** Regardless of the focus of the content or improvisational form, strong ensembles tend to find joy in their work together, even (or perhaps especially) when darker hues or stories emerge. Forgiveness is rarely sought as there is a deep-rooted assumption of good faith and that players are working generously for and with each other. Effective ensembles also tend to model the quality of resilience: players do not dwell needlessly in the fumbles but rather embrace and enjoy the process knowing that it will have both peaks and valleys in rehearsals and performance.

Player A: (during intermission) "We had some rough moments in our act one, but we really managed to push through them and lean on each other. Let's talk about how we can support each other *even more* going into the next act."

3. **Directed.** Improv ensembles deploy many different models of leadership so I'm not necessarily referring to a singular "director" or **deviser** but rather the notion that there are central principles and a direction that bind the group consciously together. Improv has *such* a wide reach, encompassing the healing arts, highly commercial enterprises, international franchises, and community-based groups. When members lack a foundational understanding of their mutual purpose and goals, it inherently causes ruptures and fissures. Knowing not just *what* you want your intended product to represent but also *why* you are working together can only help create creative cohesion and confidence.

Player A: (during the pre-show warm-up) "I've noticed some of our work has been ending on a rather dark or cynical note of late and our audience doesn't seem to gel with that unless we really earn it. Let's keep an eye towards finding the light and love in our relationships tonight."

4. **Dedicated.** Connected to the above concept, productive ensembles display commitment to their stated goals, whether it is creating and elevating community, providing an artistic outlet, pushing the boundaries of live performance, or a myriad of other possible objectives. I hesitate to use the term professionalism as there are many improv modalities that actively celebrate an amateur or volunteer status, but successful companies typically embrace the trappings of the professional in that they display focus and respect for each other and the craft and embody a dedication to building and sharpening the requisite skill sets.

Player A: (in an all-company email or correspondence) "Just a gentle reminder that we've all agreed to arrive in the space at least 45 minutes before curtain. Please do your best to honor that commitment and text the house manager if something truly out-of-the-ordinary has happened so that the ensemble knows when you'll be arriving."

5. **Creative.** Finally, I'd elevate the concept of creativity as it is difficult for a complacent or "stale" ensemble to truly thrive. Whether it is exploring old ideas in new ways or throwing out the old ideas altogether and attempting the completely untested, when improv becomes too risk averse, in my humble opinion, it may be marching in the wrong direction in terms of the genre's innate energy. My favorite projects are without exception those that I do not know from the outset are possible or guaranteed to succeed. My favorite performances are those in which new life is breathed into a game or scenario that I thought I knew like the back of my hand. My favorite players are those that continue to surprise with their ability to reveal something about themselves, me, or the human condition in general. Improv without a commitment to creative growth merely grasps the dull embers of spontaneity when it *could* dance dangerously in the crackling flames.

Player A: (in a note posted on the greenroom wall) "This is a list of some short-form games that have been heavily in rotation lately. As we encounter them on stage, let's make a concerted effort to launch into the scenes with new prompts or attitudes so that we don't overly rely on old material and bits."

Final Thought

When ensemble goes wrong it can take an enormous amount of work to right the ship, so it's worth taking the time to tend to the small slips and tensions before they have a chance to fester and escalate. This starts with us at the individual level owning moments where we have caused hurt or not lived up to the goals and standards of the group. If you're in a position of leadership, it's particularly important that you not only model this level of improvisational humility but also, as needed, communicate with others if they are routinely and problematically creating breaches in trust and joy.

> **Related Entries:** Commandment #3, Looking Good, Rehearsal Etiquette **Antonym:** Shining **Synonyms:** Professionalism, Teamwork
> **Connected Game:** Go

ENTRANCES

Why do we enter a scene: to raise the stakes or increase the energy; to help a featured character take the next dynamic step on their journey; to heighten a game or deepen an emotion or mood; to provide side support or playfulness as a **Canadian cross** or quick hit; or perhaps to embody the next needed character or complication? All meaningful entrances add, build, and shape the action and, unless avowedly surreptitious in intent, grab the focus to do so. To enter meekly, apologetically, or perhaps even unimaginatively can negate or undermine the very gift of your presence (with the notable exception of background work designed to gently embellish the environment). **Entrances**, then, are moments worth savoring and so are appropriately featured as the sumptuous main course of this entry.

Knowing that you're needed on stage for a scene is one thing, but knowing how to dynamically arrive is another altogether. Improv performance spaces run the gamut, and you might have limited staging options in terms of your arrival – perhaps little more than space to the sides of your performance space and a door in the back wall (if you're lucky). But regardless of the physical limitations of the stage, there are still a multitude of ways that we can make the most of our arrivals as performers. (Scenic starts, initiations, and effective scenic transitions are related topics that I deal with elsewhere.)

Example

A scene is in full motion with Players A and B engaging in a lovers' spat.

Player A: "… I just feel that you *never* even listen to me! What's the point of arguing with a brick wall?"
Player B: "Maybe I'd *listen* to you if you ever said anything new! What's the point of having the same argument again and again…?"
Player A: "Sometimes I could just…"
Player B: "Sometimes you could just *what*? Say it!"
Player A: (emphatically) "Sometimes I could just…"

And then an entrance occurs…

Under-Utilized Ways to Get Onstage

1. **Bring on a continuing offstage scene.** This works best if you can quickly elicit the aid of another player but can also prove effective if you deploy a cell phone or similar device as an absent "partner." Essentially, this dynamic feels as if you are picking up another story thread midway, almost in an editing fashion (although, ideally, you'll want to get the focus back quickly to the dominant action). This category of entrance is a great way of providing an energy shift or juxtaposition with the intent of shaking up the current status quo.

Player A: (emphatically) "Sometimes I could just…"

A and B's child (C) and their lover (D) dash on in giddy excitement.

Player C: (flashing a newly acquired engagement ring) "… scream about how much I've been waiting for this day. I can't wait to show the folks!"
Player D: "No ring could ever eclipse your inner radiance!"

2. **Announce your arrival.** An offstage equivalent to the above, an announced arrival typically involves an unseen voice or voices that relay the essence of the intended gift prior to the new characters materializing. This can be a helpful choice if you want to quickly pause or redirect an onstage energy that might otherwise overwhelm a more gentle or nuanced entrance. It also has the added advantage of warning the onstage players of what's to come so that they can adjust the staging or momentum as they deem appropriate. This technique stands in gentle contrast to the unequivocal focus take that tends to happen with the first strategy.

Player A: (emphatically) "Sometimes I could just…"

The neighbors (Players E and F) can be heard loudly whispering outside the apartment door.

Player E: "… tell them! You have to tell them honey. I don't think they realize just how thin the apartment walls are."

Player F: "It's just that they didn't respond very well when I asked them about their lawn maintenance last week… but here goes."

There's a knock at the door.

3. **Enrich the greater environment.** You can also embellish a more traditional walk-on entrance by giving extra attention to the bigger picture of the dramatic world. This can serve as a generous way of adding specificity or volume to a scene that might have been suffering a little from "talking heads" syndrome. These entrances can also reinforce a previously established element that may have become neglected or provide yet another means to elevate the mood or dynamic of the scene through heightened physicality.

Player A: (emphatically) "Sometimes I could just…"

Player G, wrapped in a drenched overcoat and holding a now-collapsed umbrella, bursts into the room.

Player G: "… Answer my phone calls please! I was waiting for half an hour on the side of the road in this thunderstorm before my cell battery finally died. I'm drenched!"

4. **Just don't walk or meander on (please)**. Sometimes, simply challenging ourselves *not* to just walk into the scene can unlock a whole new level of playfulness and creativity. So often, entrances can feel mundane or under-energized with characters almost sapping more energy from the scene than they bring. What's a different way to enter than through a real or ill-defined door? What's a new or atypical tempo you could employ physically, such as skipping, dancing, or even rolling? Is there a way of moving that offers up new staging patterns or potentials? How can we jump-start our own emotional commitment and energy? Yes, we must always be wary of over-originality merely for the sake of over-originality, but giving some consideration to the *way* you enter can also invite new character or story possibilities.

Player A: (emphatically) "Sometimes I could just…"

Player H, assuming the role of a young child, slowly crawls their way between the arguing couple who immediately change their tone and posture.

Final Thought

There are certainly moments when entrances do not and should not take strong focus by design: you're making a subtle **Canadian cross** to frame the action; you're gently offering up the featured characters the potential of side support from a marginal character if they should need it; or you're carefully sharing focus as a lurking character in the background patiently waiting for your moment to pounce. But in general, you should anticipate (and dare I say, unapologetically *want*) focus when you're the next player in. Don't throw away this inherent opportunity to add more than merely your passive presence: *make* an entrance! After all, if you're unsure about joining the action or what your insertion will add, the scene may, in fact, be better served by you remaining in the wings.

Related Entries: Edits, Initiation, Stage Picture, Take
Antonym: Exits
Connected Game: Key Word

ENVIRONMENT

I find Richard Schechner's description of environmental theatre suitably inspiring for this related consideration: "In environmental theater, if scenery is used at all, it is used all the way, to the limits of its possibilities. There is no bifurcation of space, no segregation of scenery."[4] Improvisational theatre has an extremely porous relationship with the greater environment, especially when performance takes to the streets, revels in outdoor festivals, or commandeers a found or public space. When we consider the **where** or location of our scene work, we can easily neglect the greater potentials of the **Environment** that extends beyond the literal or figurative fourth wall of the stage. Bringing such elements to the stage (or acknowledging those that are present whether we like it or not) adds new levels and dimensions to our work.

Example

Two roommates (Players A and B) sit on their apartment couch…

Considerations for Expanding Your Field of Play

1. **Time of day.** A conscious choice defining the current time of day can immediately take a scene from a tried-and-true trajectory into delightfully peculiar territory. Roommates sitting on a couch might typically conjure images of an evening movie viewing or weekend collapse after a long work week. Establishing the scene at five a.m. innately offers other possibilities. Perhaps they are both insomniacs, late shift workers, or locked in a persistent silence after a full-on argument that is finally about to break. Moving the setting in time to a Monday lunchtime might unlock a different set of inspirations. Do the roommates both work from home, are they such good friends that they race back to the apartment every lunch hour just to see each other, or are they awaiting the arrival of a new potential roommate and this was the only time they could all meet? Clearly and quickly leaping to a specific time can also serve as a great gift to your technical improviser if, in fact, such a decision is not prompted by their generous lighting and sound contributions.
2. **Time of year.** Selecting a definitive time of year can further expand the horizons of your explorations. If the apartment has seen better days and it's the middle of winter, the improvisers can immediately access a more intense physicality or emotion. It might be autumn and there is a particularly beautiful view outside the living room window, or the peak of summer and the air conditioning unit is broken, or the first gasps of spring with a cool and pleasant breeze drifting through the room... Considering the time of year can have the added value of bringing seasonal holidays and the like to the front of mind as well: have the two roommates just awkwardly and uncharacteristically exchanged Valentine's cards revealing a level of emotion that now neither knows quite how to handle?
3. **Historical time.** And why not focus the work on a specific time period? Such a stance invariably reveals nuances about the greater world that are likely to inform stock choices in new ways. The construct of "roommates" (or, for that matter, "apartment" or "couch") changes radically as we shift the sociopolitical, cultural, and historical frame around it. It's unlikely that a scene set in the European Dark Ages would replicate the same story as that played in a Singaporean high-rise complex of the 1970s. Similarly, a Bedouin oasis millennia ago invites different discoveries than a futuristic mountaintop landscape on Kilimanjaro. Add in time of day and year, and you've got an even richer tapestry inspiring your path.
4. **Fictitious offstage influences.** When you expand your circle of concentration and imagination beyond the elements within reach, other glistening potentials await. Weather provides perhaps the most obvious example of this strategy: if there's a huge storm outside the apartment of our two roommates, this should immediately add emotional volume. But you can also apply this concept to a broader array of environmental forces. Is there an incredibly busy street congested with angry traffic beyond the apartment window? Or perhaps an un-curtained room through the "fourth wall" where our dwellers can observe (and are observed by) the occupants of an identical apartment? Could the next-door neighbors that share a wall be undergoing major renovations that punctuate the action with blaring construction interruptions? Or the characters are sitting in an Airbnb knowing that there is a hidden camera somewhere in the room watching their every movement?
5. **Real offstage influences.** Some venues may turn the invented ideas above into actual unavoidable realities. If you're engaged in street performance or a highly interactive style of play, audience interruptions and comments will typically find their way into the developing action. Found spaces, especially those out of doors, will offer peculiar staging options alongside potential weather influences and distractions. Soundscapes can also invigorate or thwart the improvisation as players attempt to incorporate or ignore unanticipated car alarms, wildlife incursions, or noise pollution from oblivious passersby. While not all improv modalities equally embrace these real-world distractions, there are unquestionably benefits in viewing these moments as gifts and offers that can extend the greater environment as opposed to problems to quickly resolve or ignore.

Final Thought

Improv holds an innate inclination to blur boundaries: between form and freedom, inventiveness and tradition, players and audience (think of Boal's spect-actor). When we consider the environment, not only can we expand the reach and context of our work, but there's also a chance to deliberately blur the line between the fictional stage and the real-world spaces that we inhabit. And adding specificity to our scenes is always a good thing too!

Related Entries: CROW, Where
Antonym: Talking Heads **Synonym:** Location
Connected Game: Cooperation/Non-Cooperation Scene

ERASURE

I love the term **Erasure** as it evokes the image of someone drawing an ornate image on a chalkboard only for someone else to come along and wipe it off, but the concept is a direct equivalent to Johnstone's canceling (I just wasn't introduced to this particular term in my early days, so it never stuck). He writes, "Cancelling dismantles whatever has been established: you light a fire and a shower of rain extinguishes it; you feed a stray dog and it's flattened by a truck."[5] I consider erasing as a subset of blocking or negating with a notably unique facet: erasing usually *acknowledges* that an offer has been established and sees it for what it is but then elects to push it aside anyway; blocking more often neglects to recognize the intent or promise of a scenic choice and just responds as if it were not so. In both cases, improvisers tend to make such a move to pull the scene in their own preferred direction. While erasure is always problematic, it can prove doubly so in short-form structures where time is of the essence. In this fast-paced style of play, when detailed work is needlessly set aside there is not always time to replace it with something equally nuanced. Left unchecked, a tendency to erase can literally rob a scene of anything worth exploring.

Example

Player A begins the scene with a palpable sense of excitement. Romantic music plays in the background as they lovingly begin the task of preparing the dinner table for two. A large tablecloth is unfurled and then meticulously straightened. It is adorned with a vase of flowers, wine glasses, and silverware that were each gathered from various drawers and nooks in the dining room. Player A smells something cooking in the kitchen and darts off for a second only to return with a smile: the dinner is coming along nicely. They go to a cabinet and select a particular and very special bottle of wine, examining the label closely before reaching for the corkscrew and beginning the process of opening it...

Player B, presumably their special someone, enters.

Player B: "I grabbed some pizza on the way home. Don't forget it's my game night with the gang from work."

Some Additional Analysis

As I concoct this example, there are some (rocky) paths forward that might result in an interesting tension, but Player B's entrance (assuming that they were paying attention) has seen A's intent and decided to immediately upturn it. Player A is faced with the choice of fighting for their original premise and intent (which might predictably result *in conflict*), relinquishing their idea altogether and following B's concept (which in some ways wastes *all* of that great opening work), or carefully straddling a line between these two ideas in a way that accepts the game night *while* maintaining the desire for a romantic evening (which can be quite the challenge to pull off). When faced with an erasure, my preference would be for something of this third ilk if it's feasible, but such moments also beg the simpler question, why not just honor that initial instinct of your partner? Why not delight in using all those great specifics even if the scene ultimately takes a turn further down the road? In an ensemble with strong rapport, I could see such an erasing entrance skillfully executed as a playful challenge – "how can we joyfully keep these two competing ideas alive?" (This would be an example of mischievous **shivving**.) I think a more common result, however, would just be that of frustration.

If You Feel Yourself Erasing...

1. **Acknowledge.** If you sense you may just have been the perpetrator of an erasure, a good first move is to acknowledge this (either as the player or as the character). *Seeing* the beautifully set up dining table honors your partner's choice even if you have just proverbially stepped all over it. *Smelling* the delicious dinner in the kitchen (and perhaps naming it as your favorite) keeps these elements present and alive. You may elect

to play such moments naively, as if the *character* doesn't understand the importance, but it should be clear to your partner that the *improviser* very much understands and appreciates the current parameters.
2. **Shelve.** The more details you can track from the scenic initiation the better. Although it's important to note that an erasure can occur anywhere in the scene, they most frequently show up in those highly critical first moments. Remembering smaller details – such as the tablecloth or flowers as the centerpiece – provides more possibilities for later finesse. Of course, such an approach or recovery is less feasible if you weren't closely watching your partner's initial work, so such a maneuver reinforces the necessity of keeping our focus attuned to the stage at all times.
3. **Reincorporate.** If you're going full blazes ahead with a new choice, there are still ample opportunities to utilize aspects of the gifts formerly erased. As I noted above, this strikes me as one of the few strategies that is ultimately likely to prove palatable and successful. If the workmates arrive for game night, but you carefully acknowledge that the table is currently set for two, or need to move the flowers to set up the game board, or offer everyone some of that great-smelling home cooking, then at least the world of the scene is honoring some elements of the previously established premise. If we *never* get back to these rich potentials, then the improvisational loss is amplified.
4. **Combine.** Ultimately, the scene will feel the most cohesive and deliberate if all competing or disconnected elements eventually find some sort of creative logic for coexisting on the stage. To return to Johnstone's examples in the opening quote, if you discard the need or efforts to light the fire, or the inherent import of the dog, then the erasure has truly removed probably the most cogent and promising element previously established. It can prove tricky to maintain this original idea without it seeming like you are, in turn, blocking or rebuffing the idea of the entering player, but the audience has seen and hopefully become invested in what has already transpired, so they will be looking for its continued significance. Combining may take patience in many instances, and invite strategies reminiscent of improv callbacks and curve balls, but the audience gains great enjoyment from this form of improvisational recycling. Perhaps the intended recipient of the romantic meal was actually one of the coworkers?
5. **Post.** When erasure occurs in real-time on stage, there are often only partial solutions at best as to the path forward. If you are the recipient of this energy or blindness with any regularity, I would suggest that it's important to offer this observation in post-show notes. Your scene partner might be offering such moves in a spirit of mischievousness, oblivious to the way they are creating discomfort or undervaluing your artistry. Or perhaps worse, your partner may have no idea that they are engaging in this behavior at all.

Final Thought

Improv scenes tend to suffocate with excess rather than stagnate with scarcity. Erasure serves as an example of this former pitfall, as a player literally pushes the idea or work of a teammate off the stage to, at least in theory, make more room for their own. This irksome habit is less likely to infect our work together when we watch our fellow improvisers with loving attention, elevate their intentions and contributions, and joyously join in worlds and journeys that are not primarily of our own creation. That is the improviser I am working to become.

> **Related Entries:** Blocking, Bulldozing, Shivving
> **Antonyms:** Accepting, Justification
> **Synonyms:** Canceling, Negating
> **Connected Game:** Commercial

EXITS

While energized **entrances** add power and interest to our scene work, an inability to execute a timely **Exit** can quickly have the inverse effect. Some improvisers suffer from a condition I call **sticky feet** where they find themselves standing around in a scene no longer sure of their function or contribution. While there can be true value in adding our presence to climactic or large ensemble scenes, a cluttered stage generally takes away more than it gives. It's a true gift (and skill) to know when your exit is needed and then having the wherewithal to quickly act accordingly.

Example

A scene well underway struggles under the burden of an over-populated stage…

Should I Stay, Or Should I Go Now?

1. **Does your continued presence add energy and volume?** A simple question to consider as you're standing under the glow of the stage lights is "does my presence add anything to the current undertaking?" All-too-often I'll see improvisers just "sort of there," or even worse, a little bored and under-utilized so they've become distracting in the background with destructive rather than constructive games or asides. There are *many* ways you may be serving the greater story and earning your presence: you could be providing status or support for another important character on the stage (royalty needs an entourage); your conscious presence could assist in the crafting of a bold stage picture or energy; or your patient ensemble work could put the all-important hubbub into that pivotal crowd scene. If you are knowingly adding to a central dynamic such as these in a way that doesn't compete for focus, then you should probably *stay*.
2. **Will your exit facilitate clearer and more dynamic focus?** There's no denying that the more players there are on stage the more challenging it can be to effectively move the focus around. Even a seemingly benign third character can prove distracting if their arrival unhelpfully creates split focus and competes for attention. If you find yourself the fifth, sixth, or seventh player lurking in the limelight, the chances of disturbing the dominant story arc increase exponentially. When there is an over-abundance of characters on stage, players may strive to firmly grab the focus to direct the action, but it is often more helpful to *throw* the focus to others as you take a strong exit. It can prove *much* easier to know what a scene is really about when you aren't directly in the throes of it; if you find yourself primarily observing and suspect that there are other combinations present on stage (or anxiously waiting in the wings) that are more critical than you at this point in time, then it's a lovely act of improvisational largesse to *go*.
3. **Is your character important for the current action?** And then there are times that you'll probably serve everyone best by holding your ground. In a short-form scene if you have unmistakably emerged as the protagonist, or you are the teller's actor in Playback, or playing the role of the oppressed in Forum Theatre, then it's likely that an exit from a crowded stage may cause more harm than good. Similarly, as long-form pieces enter their last phases and may see multiple characters and stories intersecting and pushing each other to the climax, seek a heightened awareness of what energies have risen to the top of the improvisational pile and adjust accordingly. If all roads lead to your character and this is *the moment* for your world to crumble or find its footing, if you are part of a character combination that the audience has been craving to finally see together (perhaps the protagonist and antagonist, or the romantic leads), or if you are holding onto that one secret or piece of the puzzle that you know must be exploded for the play to reach its conclusion, then by all means, please *stay*.
4. **Does your ongoing presence hinder others from participating?** A lesson I've learned and re-learned multiple times in large-cast large-scale long-forms is that there are some characters who by their very nature may prevent others from speaking freely if your production is honoring social norms and decorum. High-status characters, especially those at the very top of the pecking order, can inhibit underlings from reaching their full potential if they are not extremely aware of how they use and share their stage time. It's unlikely that the servant would talk about their personal turmoil in front of the queen, that the temp worker might seek marital advice in the presence of the CEO, or that the uncool kids would have the gumption to plot their revenge while the high school elites lord over the cafeteria. When you are embodying a higher status role (or just a character that has experienced ample time in the action), it can be easy to forget that merely your presence alone could suffocate other interesting dynamics that actually need your absence to breathe and flourish. So, if you've enjoyed some unfettered stage time strutting as the big cat and see others waiting who are unlikely to challenge your right to speak, then let the mice play and *go*.
5. **Will an exit distract needlessly from the scenic build?** It is also a reasonably common occurrence to find yourself loitering in a scene as the action shifts into high gear. Perhaps the company is on the cusp of the final climactic moment, the competing forces are finally squaring off against one another, or there is a softer and earned vignette that displays vulnerability and emotional finesse. In these types of situations, even if you have become proverbial furniture in the scene, it is worthwhile to consider whether an exit might do more harm than good. In some instances, such as if you're working on a smaller stage, it might prove

a simple matter to step into the wings quickly and quietly in an unnoticed fashion. In other staging configurations, a subtle exit might prove largely impossible: perhaps the only established entrance might require you to pass between or in front of the characters who currently hold focus, or the quieter hues of the scene would be destroyed by any superfluous movement. Yes, such a dynamic might beckon as a comedic gold mine, but keep in mind any damage you might do in the process if the scene has established a different tone. In these latter instances, even if you feel your continued presence isn't crucial, the wiser course of action is to minimize any potential competition for focus and to gently *stay*.

6. **Have you fulfilled your intended function?** A final question that in some ways encompasses all of my previous musings is earnestly assessing if you are done as a character. If your intent was to make a Canadian Cross or provide some background support, is this environmental painting still serving? Perhaps you were facilitating or building on a game or playful dynamic; is there still any value (comedic, dramatic, or otherwise) in perpetuating that pattern further? If you're playing as a more featured character, are you still actively fighting for what you want or has this scenic unit served its purpose (did you win or lose this encounter)? As a supporting character, did you successfully provide your gift, tilt, or detail, and has it been fully accepted or incorporated by its intended recipient? When we linger too long as characters after completing our goal, it's not uncommon to find yourself a little stuck as others join the fray. Furthermore, if you know you're done remember that you can always re-enter later, but for now, you're probably best serving the narrative arc if you *go*.

Final Thought

Remember that a dynamic exit can serve a scene equally well as an energized entrance. It can sharpen the scenic focus, heighten the rising action, and generously provide others with some time on the improv playground. When improv fires on all cylinders, the allure of the stage shines strongly, and it is human nature to want to share in that joyful creativity. When we find ways to give to our scene partners in these moments, offering them up a magnanimous portion of this joy, we all eventually benefit.

Related Entries: Edits, Give, Stage Picture, Sticky Feet **Antonym:** Entrances
Connected Game: Entrances and Exits

EXPERTS

Expert games are a common feature of short-form improv show rosters and may include a handle such as an endowment, audience participation, or a physical or verbal restriction. The persona of the expert remains central to each of these frames and will typically involve an improviser feigning knowledge on a topic that is innately ludicrous or of which the improviser obviously has little true experience. Stepping outside of this particular scenic frame, however, the value of embodying **Experts** transcends this narrow improv subset and provides a powerful means of approaching characterization and scenic content generation. As such, this topic strikes me as worthy of a focused inquiry.

Example

The topic of lunar weather systems serves as the interview prompt.

Player A: "And welcome back to *Look Up!* If you're just joining the program, we're talking with esteemed astro-climatologist, Dr. June Piter."
Player B: "It's an honor to be on the show, Olivia."
Player A: "As we went to break, Doctor, you were just starting to explain your new discoveries regarding wind on the moon..."
Player B: "That's right, Olivia, it's been a long road to this particular breakthrough, but we've unlocked a mystery that has been plaguing scientists for decades: does the moon have wind?"
Player A: "And your revolutionary answer?"
Player B: "Just as the moon effects the earth's climate and tides, so too does the gravitational pull of the earth and other celestial bodies create movement on the surface of our nearest neighbor."
Player A: "Now you're going to have to walk me and our viewers through that a little..."
Player B: "It would truly be my pleasure..."

Figure 7.2 Whimsical expert games provide a mainstay of short-form venues such as Comedy Warehouse and Sak Comedy Lab. Photo credit: Leesa Brown [top] and James Berkley Photography [bottom].

An Expert Approach to Characterization

Certain qualities enable the persona of the scenic expert, each of which embodies an improvisational approach worthy of emulation.

1. **Confidence.** When you assume the mantle of an expert, it typically encourages a level of increased confidence and presence. Experts *know* their topics, which represent the pursuits of a lifetime, and they bring this grounded strength to their dialogue and interactions. By definition, if they are an expert, they have earned this reputation and title, probably from their peers in the field. Even if the scenic parameters are absurd or obtuse, an expert character should attack the material as if they have been living in this world for the bulk of their professional life.
2. **Passion.** While there is always the possibility of fatigue or burnout, experts generally *love* or find great excitement in their chosen field. Any opportunity to share their hard-earned passion is an opportunity to shine. Without this inherent joy and thrill, an expert character (or scene) can quickly lose its steam or playfulness. An expert should find delight in the chase of the conversation and savor the chance to educate those who may not yet fully comprehend the import and beauty of their field and unique findings.
3. **Knowledge.** Unsurety stands as the antithesis of the expert persona. Yes, they might willingly acknowledge a gap or limit to their field of study when it *rarely* occurs as they are equally experts on what they *do* and *don't* know, but such breaches should prove to be uncommon and largely inconsequential. Overwhelmingly, their knowledge emerges as broad and deep, representing the studious pursuit of a life's work. They know all the jargon and terminology (even if it's made up), all the most recent studies and findings (even if they're made up), and all the latest controversies and tensions in the field (even if...). After all, how could you really be wrong when everyone comes to you for the answers?
4. **Exactitude.** The expert's knowledge is most readily revealed through their powerful use of language. In addition to having the requisite vocabulary of their profession at their fingertips, experts are precise in their wording and responses. Stalling devices – such as "well," "um," and the like – appear infrequently as they merely postpone getting to the facts that are readily at hand. Approximations and estimates are used sparingly as why answer vaguely when you personally processed all the pertinent data? If a question is simple, it will be answered concisely to allow more time for the detailed narrative that will soon follow. Specificity is the preferred currency.
5. **Personality.** And then all these facets of character and communication find nuance through the guise of personality and point of view. While experts may all incline toward certain stylistic and linguistic devices, they are also highly individualized in nature. They could be child prodigies or long-in-the-tooth academics, revolutionaries on the cutting edge of the discipline or conservative traditionalists clinging to the ways of old, bookish recluses with poorly developed social skills or enthralling conversationalists who are always the life of the party. While some interesting characterization terrain might present itself by selectively undermining one of the essential qualities listed above (such as an expert who can never think of the right word), generally embracing these tools at face value will already result in a wide array of dynamic personalities.

Final Thought

The lessons learned and honed from embodying an expert persona belong in all our improv work. Characters and scenic choices thrive and take root when they hit the stage with confidence, passion, knowledge, exactitude, and a clear point of view. Experts make statements and choices unflinchingly and unapologetically as they *know* everything there is to know about their chosen field. This is a powerful place from which to play and create.

Related Entries: Character, Verbal Skills
Antonyms: Fear, Interviewer
Connected Game: Naïve Expert

EXPOSITION

A synonym for backstory or the unseen past events that influence current and future actions.

Related Entry: Balance

EXTENDING

American publisher William Feather cautioned, "Beware of the man who won't be bothered with details." **Extending** (some prefer the synonym expanding) works in conjunction with **advancing** as a storytelling and narrative construction tool. Advancing refers to the action of a scene, the events that occur one after another moving the characters toward a dynamic outcome. Extending serves the story by providing interest and nuance, painting details that ultimately increase the power of the story along with the likelihood that the audience may actually care or be moved by the journey. A story without sufficient extending will typically feel like a distant echo of the human condition, a mere facsimile, or undernurtured seed in desperate need of development. Arguably, there are only *so* many archetypal stories that we tend to retell again and again: person A meets and falls in love with person B, but they come from opposite sides of the tracks; travelers go on a long journey and face monumental hardships just to return home and ultimately discover themselves; an epic character seals their own tragic fate when they are unable to appreciate their deepest flaw... It is in the extending or the peculiar details of each retelling that familiar stories take on new and exciting faces.

Example

The boy walked down the road...

Details Worthy of Your Attention

As we tell and embody stories, almost *any* facet can benefit from a little additional attention and extending, but here are some of the more obvious targets:

1. **Environment.** Whether it's the weather, the topography, or the scenery, giving some early attention to the greater world of our stories invariably establishes rich details that will inspire our future actions. It is difficult, after all, to reincorporate strong choices later in the process if our improv shelf has been left largely bare. Selecting one or two elements for additional scrutiny will, in turn, make them richer and more memorable. We rarely know exactly where the interest or potential of a story will ultimately lie, so it almost doesn't matter what facet of the world you choose to feature so much as that you just commit to *something* with gusto and conviction.

The boy walked down the treacherous mountain path while the harsh wind dashed against his frozen limbs...

2. **Props.** Once you've considered the bigger picture, shift that lens to the smaller facets of the story. Hand props, pieces of clothing, or smaller items that populate the stage space provide rich vehicles for better understanding the world of the play and what might be at stake for our central characters. Any randomly selected object can become worthy of our attention if we merely imbue it with care and specificity. As smaller objects are more likely to move with our characters or reappear in a later setting, they are particularly malleable and useful. They can also reveal the inner life of our personae and promote action as they will often give our characters something to *do*.

The boy nervously clutched the trembling lamb as he walked down the treacherous mountain path; the harsh wind dashed against his limbs...

3. **Character.** The people that populate our stories are equally worthy of attention and extending. In scenic work, this extending tool allies closely with the technique of **endowing** where players generously bestow traits upon one another to provide backstory and complex relationships. This function remains crucial in narrative work, where the action resides primarily in our verbal choices. As most stories focus on a handful of characters to move the action along, we are much more likely to remember and connect to these people when they are well crafted and nuanced (and on a simple level, have *names*). Exploring the emotional state of a character further provides information that can jump-start the tension or rising action.

The terrified young shepherd, Kwame, nervously clutched the trembling lamb as he walked down the treacherous mountain path; the harsh wind dashed against his limbs...

4. **Mood.** Finally, extending can powerfully capture and create a unifying mood or tone for your scenic work. Are we living in a carefree PG-13 world, or a dark and brooding thriller? Does the story assume the fanciful and timeless air of a fairy tale or parable, or is it an urban dystopia populated by hopelessness and decay? Just as specific choices and character traits can be repeated and reflected by improvisers to craft a cohesive whole,

so too can mood and atmosphere. All it takes is for someone to elevate the style (perhaps even delightfully accidentally) and for the rest of the team to fully accept that this is now part of the deeper fabric of the story.

The foreboding moon loitered overhead in the cloudy night sky. He knew all-too-well the rumors that had been circulating about the fates of those who stayed out too late, and so the terrified young shepherd, Kwame, nervously clutched the trembling lamb as he walked down the treacherous mountain path; the harsh wind dashed against his limbs...

Final Thought

Details and joyful extending are the special sauce of improv: they just make everything better!

> **Related Entries:** Advancing, Endowing, Heighten, Scene Painting **Antonym:** Vagueness
> **Synonyms:** Details, Expanding, Specificity
> **Connected Game:** Advance/Extend Stories

NOTES

1. Jo Salas, *Improvising Real Life: Personal Story in Playback Theatre*. New Paltz, NY: Tusitala Pub., 1993. p. 23.
2. Neva Leona Boyd, *Play and Game Theory in Group Work: A Collection of Papers*. Chicago: University of Illinois at Chicago Circle, 1971. p. 42.
3. Charna Halpern et al., *Truth in Comedy. The Manual of Improvisation*. Colorado Springs: Meriwether, 1994. p. 37.
4. Richard Schechner, *Environmental Theater*. New York: Applause, 1994 [1973]. p. xxx.
5. Keith Johnstone, *Impro for Storytellers*. New York: Routledge, 1999. p. 118.

F/G

FALLING ACTION

The denouement or resolving action that follows the climax in a traditional linear story.

Antonym: Rising Action

FEAR

I make no claim to coining the improv adage "run toward fear," and if I had to pay a royalty every time I uttered these words someone would have a nice chunk of change in their pocket! I find that this advice has become central to my training philosophy because little of value will transpire on the improv stage (and one could argue in life in general) if we allow our **Fear** to get the better of us. Spolin observes, "Fear of spontaneity is common. There is safety in old familiar feelings and actions. Spontaneity asks that we enter an unknown territory—ourselves!"[1] I've written in a previous entry on **blocking** about some of the more prevalent sources of this anxiety and how an inability to break through these barriers is antithetical to the improvisational spirit of play.

All artistic enterprises likely include some wrestling with our inner creative demons, but as the improv process is so public, this battle typically stands front and center for improvisational practitioners. If there is to be pleasure, abandon, and attack in our work, running toward fear becomes not only a mantra but almost a requirement. Without taming this debilitating beast, we may spend much of our time as improvisers lurking in the wings or backstage (or even worse, on the stage itself) musing on what we might, could, or should have done in the scene that meanwhile passes us by.

Example

Carefree improv is happening, and then suddenly it isn't…

When to Run Toward Fear

Here are some particularly important moments to prod yourself to action:

1. **If you're a good kind of uncomfortable.** It's amply foreseeable that improv will push us outside of our comfort zones and I would contend that we need to identify and minimize this type of fear when it infringes on our work. Trying a game that you've never played before, stepping up and into a featured role that requires artistic stamina, or attacking material that feels alien or challenging to you all strike me as signs that you're heading toward growth and discovery. As I have become more experienced as a player and deviser, I find myself actually *seeking* these dynamics as the opposite of this type of fear can prove to be complacency.
2. **If you're unsure where the scene is going.** Again, this is a rather boilerplate scenario that could (should) describe most if not all improvisational undertakings, but fear can nonetheless creep into the work, especially if we *thought* we knew where a scene was heading and now it suddenly takes a sharp turn. When uncertainty beckons, it can be human nature to recoil or lean backward, but as improvisers, we must fight this survival instinct and instead lean *into* this glorious unknown. Fear in these moments feels synonymous with ceding control. Take one step forward trusting that your teammates will then do the same.
3. **If you're required to assume an unfamiliar stance.** Another moment to just "jump" is when the scene necessitates that we fill a role or function

with which we may not have much or *any* prior experience. In the real world, I couldn't fix a computer if my life depended on it, but on stage, my I.T. worker should exude a confidence and surety that belies my true incompetence. I also have a pretty pronounced political and spiritual point of view but should step resolutely into the shoes of different positions as the story dictates. I would contextualize this advice by noting that a fear of misrepresenting others is legitimate, and warranted, and demands that we seek empathy in our portrayals and an intellectual curiosity to research and educate ourselves when problematic blindnesses reveal themselves. Fearless improv should not become a cover for thoughtless improv. Consider exploring my earlier entry on archetypes for further thoughts on this complex dynamic.

When to Apply the Brakes

There are also valid moments when your "fear" might be a voice you need to listen to and honor:

1. **If you are putting yourself at unnecessary physical, emotional, or psychological risk.** Trust your instincts, honor your own personal boundaries, and retain your agency in a way that keeps you safe.
2. **If you are putting your scene partner at unnecessary physical, emotional, or psychological risk.** Make sure you are consciously and empathetically checking in with your scene partners as the scene develops and adjusting as needed.
3. **If you are putting your audience at unnecessary physical, emotional, or psychological risk.** Also, display care in how your choices are landing with the audience. There is a marked difference between challenging an audience to reconsider deeply held beliefs and triggering or insulting them obliviously.

Final Thought

Except for the three circumstances listed directly above, I would posit that "fear" can often serve as evidence that we're doing something right during our extemporaneous adventures. If we don't allow it to short circuit our creativity or make us retreat into our heads or the wings, fear can remind us of the awesome challenge of spontaneous performance. I wonder if seasoned improvisers ever truly tame fear or if, rather, they have found a workable truce in which they acknowledge the daunting nature of the work at hand and choose to transform the whispering voice of fear into bold action and energy.

> **Related Entry:** Blocking **Antonyms:** Abandon, Courage, Playfulness **Synonyms:** Inaction, Stasis **Connected Game:** Ballet

FOCUS

Gilda Radner offers some sage advice on the issue of focus:

> Del [Close] said to us, when you are onstage at Second City, you can always get all the attention, you can always steal the focus and be the funny one. Just stick your finger in your nose and you can get focus. But to equal the other people on stage – to give them their moment and then take yours and go back and forth – that was the much more difficult and greater thing. To really have a game of catch with somebody is the true excitement of improvisation, and it's so much more rewarding.[2]

Radner's recollection paints such an inspirational image of generous focus exchanges during an improv show. Her preferred dynamic invites a greater awareness of how and when the focus is moving, and a deliberateness in making sure there is a clear back and forth that allows room for everyone to play. I'm discussing the specifics of giving and taking focus elsewhere, so here would like to consider the concept of **Focus** holistically: what staging practices and techniques can we deploy that maximize the potential for elegant "games of catch?"

Oftentimes, in my introductory college improv course, I'll assign a scenario (such as spectators at a specific sporting event) and invite smaller groups to quickly and silently construct frozen images. I usually stipulate *not* to include sports players on the field but rather to concentrate on an image purely in the stands. This will provide a series of tableaux on a common theme that generally provides very different examples of how we create (or obfuscate) focus on stage. Many of the observations below tend to bubble up in the discussion prompted by these brief explorations.

Example

A line of excited movie goers waits in the early sales queue for the release of the next sci-fi blockbuster...

For Your Focused Consideration

1. **Levels and composition.** This is perhaps the most visual component and thus the trickiest to illustrate and discuss in a written medium. For those familiar with traditional theatrical staging tropes, I would consider these focus choices as largely "stage picture" considerations. Does a character assume a higher level or position on stage? Is someone standing away from the larger group in a way that gives them added attention? Is there a "chorus leader" who others are clearly deferring to in terms of their physical choices? In most instances, this featured character will emerge as the primary focus for that particular moment.

… Player A, a small child, scales their parent and sits atop their shoulders, now towering over the other movie patrons.

2. **Directionality and eye contact.** Once the stage picture has been crafted and populated, it is a relatively simple adjustment to transfer the primary source of focus. You might have a wide array of heights and poses, or characters scattered somewhat randomly across the stage, but if players turn or gesture toward a common character there will rarely be any doubt as to where the intended focus is flowing. While it is arguably the simplest focus giving technique, the straightforward act of looking where you want to throw focus has few substitutes in terms of its effectiveness. Even in the most potentially cluttered stage picture, if everyone resolutely makes eye contact with the same player, the audience will follow.

… the earliest arrival, Player B, suddenly drops the fistful of coins they have been feverishly holding and the rest of the line watches on casually as the panicked sci-fi fan scrambles on hands and knees to gather them all back up.

3. **Similarity and difference.** Another delightfully easy but important method centers on the concept of difference. If *everyone* in the scene assumes a higher level, or *everyone* is throwing their attention to a common target, but *one* character is doing something markedly different (they are crawling or hiding surreptitiously in the shadows) then this outlier, more likely than not, will become the primary focus or at the very least serve as competition. This is an effective tactic when used carefully and deliberately, and a focus challenge when it is a player's unconscious default. Less experienced players can tend to lack an awareness that their *different* choice in the land of the *same* might unduly create **split focus**. The more players there are on stage, the more problematic this lack of self-awareness becomes.

… an aggravated businessperson, Player C, paces frantically up and down away from the movie line, whispering loudly a litany of complaints into their expensive cell phone.

4. **Contained and dynamic emotion.** Regardless of the staging configuration, an emotionally bold or intense choice will nearly always reign supreme in the quest for focus. An audience will be drawn into a character whose emotional climate stands apart from those of their teammates or who has an intensity where others feel more contained or subdued. (The opposite also holds true in that if *everyone* is in full Greek chorus mode in the midst of heightened despair, *one* villager calmly counting their loaves of bread to the side will draw your eye.) When we talk about presence on stage, I think this is also shorthand for this level of emotional commitment and interest that pulls the audience into the performer's reality.

… a super fan, Player D, stuck uncomfortably in the middle of the queue, begins to frantically hyper-ventilate as the excitement of the whole affair just simply becomes too much.

Final Thought

There are unlikely to be many revelatory surprises in this list of focus shaping techniques, but in many ways that's the main take away. Most of us have an innate sense of what helps or hinders focus but having this knowledge alone isn't enough. We need to keep it front of mind in our work and use this "common sense" to help create the poetic focus exchange that Radner extols. If we retain awareness that a high stage position usually grabs attention, then we will probably exercise caution in striking such a pose unless we know it's an appropriate moment to shine. In scenes that become a little discombobulated, simply shifting our posture and giving strong eye contact can help set a scene partner up for success. Understanding that our quirky little side game will probably steal focus from where it's needed, or that we need to commit to a more dynamic emotionality when it's our turn to take the baton, enables us to sculpt focus rather than become subjugated to its whim. There is no inherently correct or incorrect way to move focus around the stage, but there are certainly purposeful exchanges and accidental or careless fumbles.

Figure 8.1 Cast members from *The Lost Comedies of William Shakespeare* encircle the Player King as he narrates an improvised prologue (in sonnet form) describing elements of the impending action (Scenic design: Lisa Cody-Rapport; Costume design: Annie Trombo; Props master: Molly Finnegan). Photo credit: Tony Firriolo.

For a reflection on some focus techniques that prove helpful in larger group scenes, review Commandment #2.

Related Entries: Commandment #2, Give, Sharing Focus, Stage Picture, Take
Antonym: Split Focus **Synonym:** Attention
Connected Game: Two Scenes

FOLLOWER

The mindful decision to elevate the choices of others on stage and join in their games and dynamics. An oft-quoted adage in North American improv is to "follow the follower," which is a rallying cry to suspend your own individuality in service of the ensemble and collective. Players who are inclined to pursue this improvisational approach are less likely to slide back into their heads in search of their own "unique" offer. While related to the concept of the passenger, an attitude of following generally holds a more positive connotation. Those that follow still gift all their energy and attention; those who tend to become passengers often do so to hide or avoid making substantial contributions.

Related Entry: Passenger

FORGIVENESS

Lovingly extending this gift to oneself and others engaged in the collective act of creation goes a long way to forging a robust, thriving, and joyful ensemble. When we hold onto prior missteps and hiccups, we are usually unable to recognize the beautiful new potentials that await in the current moment.

Synonym: Abandon

FRESHNESS

Most of my professional work for the last two decades has taken place at Sak Comedy Lab, where our shows are largely short-form structures with some hard-earned long-form scattered across the season. I have therefore played Moving Bodies (Puppets in the original *Theatresports* parlance) a *lot*. Too many times to count. We have great hosts that work hard to rotate games into the mix, but the reality is that some games are just crowd pleasers or fill a specific show need, such as bringing audience members up on the stage. Moving Bodies is one of these perfect storms for me in that it includes this sought after audience involvement as volunteers manipulate the improvisers' actions, and the results rarely garner anything *but* a perfect score regardless of execution. I'm not sure if I could even estimate how many times I've played the game as a result, and I will confess to having to stifle a groan some nights when it's announced in the lineup. I will also confess that it makes me laugh a little when students in my campus troupe complain that they've had to play a game *two* or *three* times in a semester, although I appreciate their desire to play something new. In reality, however, whether it's hundreds of times or just a handful, the question remains: how do we keep well-worn formats or games **Fresh**? Psychodrama pioneer Adam Blatner astutely notes, "Spontaneity is, above all, an *attitude of mind*, a commitment to thinking things afresh."[3] I'm using Moving Bodies as my paradigmatic example as it's my personal kryptonite, but I'm sure for many of you another game or structure immediately jumps to mind.

A quick sidebar: When we talk about keeping it fresh, that should go for us as performers as well, so always be sure to arrive clean and pleasant-smelling to rehearsals and performances.

Keeping It Fresh

I'm writing this entry primarily with short-form in mind although I'm confident some of these approaches apply to players engaged in open-ended long-form productions. Generally, my own long-form experiences have been set runs or shows that only play once or twice a month, so I'm always excited to get back to them, while on busy months I might play 15 to 20 short-form sets (down from 15 to 20 a week in my pre-parenting heyday).

If you're losing your improv mojo, here are seven suggestions for reigniting that spontaneous spark…

1. **Keep your attitude in check and your spirits high.**
   Going into any artistic endeavor with a foreboding sense of anguish nearly always proves to be a self-fulfilling prophecy. In this regard, while we may have played a particular game or premise multiple times, in most situations, the majority of our audience is experiencing it for the first time (or may, in fact, be relishing the prospect of seeing something a little familiar). In the scripted realm, we often seek this illusion of the first time in our performances, and it's an equally important factor in our improvisational work too; most would argue it is *the* defining feature of our discipline. No one pays to see a performer begrudgingly going through the paces or snidely commenting on how something has become stale or everyday. Also, in most communities, we shouldn't take for granted that there are far fewer performance opportunities than people keen to perform, so an attitude of gratitude can go a long way.

2. **Challenge yourself before the performance.** This is a tradition that I bring to a lot of my projects as I like how it bonds the company and allows players to see where everyone is at in terms of their energies and focus for the night. The challenge can be broad: "I want to make sure I'm setting up my partners for joy and success." Or it can be narrower, especially if there's a game on the playlist that you know might be a stumbling block: "I want to avoid turning Moving Bodies into a yelling **commenting** fest and really connect to my partner instead." In Spolin terms, this can give you a different point of concentration for the scene or evening, opening you up to more discovery and nuance. It also has the added bonus of giving you something to then consider post-show. Were you meeting your personal challenge, helping others to do the same, and did this open anything new up for you that you want to remember for future work?

3. **Look for ways to change it up.** If you're in a less-than-helpful groove with an improv game or show, look for ways to jolt yourself out of old habits and dynamics. To return to Moving Bodies, if you always tend to start the scene, position yourself to be a third entrance, or vice versa. If you always lean heavily into the physical activity of the scene, try instead to focus on the nuanced details of the relationship. If the scene always tends to be played in a modern context, throw some style or a genre onto the premise to open up a new approach. Some nights it might be as simple as having one audience puppeteer moving all the actors instead of the more typical two volunteers. This is one of my favorite things about how my troupe played *Gorilla Theatre*: we might re-visit some stock games, but they nearly always

had a new frame, premise, or handle that made them delightfully unfamiliar. There's no reason you can't take that same approach to other short-form performances and franchises.

4. **Launch yourself in a new way.** Most short-form companies inspire scenes with an audience ask-for before the lights go down, and yet many of us can get into predictable patterns in either how we solicit this material – "Can I have an outdoor activity that two people might do on the weekend" – or the way that we use this information to inspire the scene that follows. Mick Napier writes that every "dentist" ask-for needn't result in a scene in the dentist's office, and yet that's where we so often go first. It follows that if we're being predictable with our ask-fors and how we apply them, that the resulting work may quickly become predictable and uninspiring for us as improvisers too. I'd love to see a Moving Bodies based on a difficult family conversation or an emotionally vulnerable confession as that would push the game out of over-tilled territory quickly.

5. **Throw away the bits and stock devices.** This is a particular pet-peeve when I watch short-form. Routinely, teams or companies will lean heavily on tried and tested (usually comedic) devices that have historically worked in a game. Get your expert to create lists in your One-Voice Scene, have your guest name a variety of countries for your Universal Interpreter to pantomime (this one is problematic on multiple levels), or incessantly talk about how you can't see your partner in Moving Bodies to prompt your puppeteer to change your line of vision. I am sure I have done all of these, for the record. Yes, such devices *can* work, but if a game is feeling stale and you're relying on these devices, you are truly becoming your own worst enemy and risk merely moving through the paces of a scene without finding what is unique about the story on that particular night. You can always go back to well-worn devices as the scene culminates if it needs a Hail Mary to get you off the stage with some semblance of dignity, but if this is where you start your journey, it's *really* unlikely you're in store for a unique experience.

6. **Concentrate on story and connection.** This builds from the prior point that if you're concentrating on the gimmick of the scene, you are less likely to organically uncover the original story that quietly awaits. Build slowly and deliberately. Listen deeply and with care. Pursue the paths of highest interest. Exploit the novel and the unexpected as they gently emerge. Don't rush or push to the anticipated pay-off. When I trained in *Comedy-Sportz*, I remember that the manual they provided listed a series of comedic bits for many of the games, such as put a wig into a Slide Show and then have the narrator comment on "How did that fluff get into the projector?" before blowing it away. I understand the intent behind gifting new players with some game strategies, but underneath all the gags, most of us still just want to experience a good story well told. Every game is a scene; every scene is a story; and every story is constructed of small organically discovered beats.

7. **Don't expect any one show or format to scratch all your improv itches.** When I perform a short-form show (or any improv show for that matter) I know that there will be artistic compromises that need to be made in order to meet the specific expectations of our audience and venue. I love narrative long-form and exploring new improv concepts and structures. Generally, my short-form work doesn't fulfill all these personal artistic needs. But short-form creates an amazing connection to an audience, sharpens my skill set as a storyteller when I only get three or four minutes on average to get to the point, forges creative and lasting bonds with my fellow performers, and serves as an amazing opportunity to play – something that can be increasingly rare as you start to move through the decades. Even Moving Bodies can do all these things on a good night, although it probably is an awful lot to ask of one rather silly improv parlor game. And that's my broader point: keep a sense of perspective and look to have multiple projects going if you can if that's what you need to keep yourself challenged and satisfied as a player. It's not fair to ask any one game (or perhaps company for that matter) to satiate all your act hunger and artistic cravings.

Final Thought

I'm hesitant to give my last suggestion an official bullet point so I'm sneaking it in here, but sometimes it's also important to just take a break. If the thought of playing a certain game or working with a certain person is giving you undue stress, maybe that's a signal that you need to step away for a while to recharge and find that passion again. Most of us had that reality dropped upon us during the lost COVID years with mandated social distancing, and perhaps there is a small silver lining in that even Moving Bodies can prove a delight now audience members are finally able to safely play on the stage again.

> **Related Entries:** Abandon, Commitment, Presence
> **Antonyms:** Fatigue, Staleness
> **Synonyms:** Excitement, Joy
> **Connected Game:** Game Lab

GAGGING

To gag or not to gag, that could be the question, although, in most instances, the answer would be a resolute "not!" **Gagging** generally throws the proverbial wrench into the scenic works, stalling or diminishing the reality of the scene in order to grab at a joke or witticism. Or, as Johnstone pens, "A gag is a laugh that you get by attacking the story."[4] Most modern improvisational traditions favor (at least in theory) humor that evolves organically from the narrative and characters. Gagging tends to stand in opposition to this approach with its self-conscious and potentially destructive energy that usually expresses the performer's point of view or observation rather than that of the character they're (in this case, *lightly*) assuming. A performance that succumbs to unbridled gagging instincts might garner considerable laughter but will rarely thrive as a well-developed *scene*. More often than not, any deeper connections, observations, or emotions will have been cast aside in the quest for that immediate fix of audience approval.

Example

Any scene in the history of modern improvisation…

Player A: *(generally smiling at the audience)* "That's what she said!"

When Is a Gag Not a Gag?

Assuaging the ravenous gagging beast that lurks inside most (if not all) of us serves as the important subject for my earlier entry on the subject in my "Ten Commandments" series. I think one of the challenging mixed messages that short-form, in particular, sends in terms of gagging is that there are clearly moments when the ability to wittily assemble a zinger is lauded and applauded. These notable exceptions deserve some thoughtful exploration and so I give you four circumstances that come to mind for when is a gag not a gag…

1. **When it's the game.** Most franchises have games in the rotation that are essentially gag fests: "99 Jokes," "World's Worst," "There's a Blank in My Soup…" and their kin essentially demand the ability to quickly construct a punchline or groaner. As these are also standalone moments (as opposed to beats within a singular scene), each gag essentially serves as its own vignette and does not degrade or diminish the overall arc of a more significant journey. In addition to rewarding clever word play, these line games also encourage throwing any idea up against the wall in the hope that some will stick, and this sense of bravery is definitely a quality worth developing and emulating. A significant trap of such games is that players can tend to form "Rolodexes" of gags-gone-by ("We're fungis…"), which diminishes the risk and creativity. While most improvisers would confess to recycling material at times, avoid making this your stock approach.

2. **When it's a character.** When we think of parental figures making endless "bad Dad jokes" or Michael Scott-esque workmates desperately trying to forge bonds through terrible puns, we see recognizable human behavior that certainly has a place onstage. Here, the gags may support the point of view of the character as opposed to the external and removed observations of the player. Care is needed when executing this type of persona as there is a thin and elusive line between using the device of gagging to enrich the character and merely using the guise of a character to indulge your gagging proclivities. As is the case when assuming a high-status character, a character prone to bad joke riffing should exert extra generosity in terms of sharing focus so that the greater story can grow and evolve. A little of this character type goes a long way.

3. **When it's the style.** In the long-form tradition, gagging salvos can emerge as the "game of the scene" or may be woven into a larger comedic structure to serve a particular end. In the two-act long-form *Murder We Wrote: The Improvised Whodunit*, the murder weapon was always revealed with great import in the second act. The character who discovered the object would bring it to the stage with the charge to craft a (typically delightfully bad) pun to add humor and significance to the moment. It was a guilty pleasure that some improvisers delighted in more than others, but here a gagging energy served the greater purpose of the show. Shakespearean pieces might similarly deploy bawdy word play as part of the fun. Whether it's structural or discovered, it's generally wise to make sure these stylistic moments

are self-contained so that a gagging tone doesn't begin to pervade the work as a whole unless the work is defined by this tone, although I must admit I wonder how long such a work could last without caving in on itself!
4. **When it's a button.** I'm not sure if this is a universal position, but particularly in the short-form tradition I find that closing lines that have a gagish quality can provide clear outs to a scene, especially if the story has been stagnating or struggling and is looking for a little energy boost to go out on. As gags often undermine the credibility of a scene, they strike me as particularly dangerous in the foundational moments; as a scene looks to finish, a "rug pull" or sudden perspective shift or tilt is less likely to undermine the action going forward, especially if this world lives and dies in that one scene. I wouldn't recommend this as a *standard* device, but I have seen experienced improvisers rally a faltering scene with such a move.

Final Thought

To be crystal clear (as I write about when to execute gags in an entry that rightfully condones the practice of gagging in general) when we discourage gagging as a scenic choice, we must also acknowledge that joke telling is a special skill that some games demand. As is the case with all the improvisational tropes and guidelines that we hold dear, context and self-awareness are *everything*. Relying on gags because you don't know what else to say, or you're scared the audience hasn't laughed in a while, or you're uncomfortable bringing your real self to the stage, are all fear-based scenarios that will lead to shallow and anemic performances – especially if you're working in a style that privileges story. Using a carefully selected moment of whimsy to add spice to a scene or evening might, on the other hand, provide just the right playful finesse.

Related Entries: Commandment #4, Pimping, Shivving **Antonyms:** Endowing, Offer
Synonym: Joke Telling
Connected Game: World's Worst

GAME OF THE SCENE

Neva Boyd aptly defines the broader concept of a game as "… a situation set up imaginatively and defined by rules which together with the prescribed roles, is accepted by the players."[5] The **Game of the Scene** tends to be an explicit concept more pervasively used in long-form traditions. In short-form shows, scenic games or dynamics are prescribed and governed by the inherited rules: in They Said, They Said, two onstage players will provide dialogue while their offstage counterparts offer verbalized stage directions which the onstage characters must carry out. In long-form settings, the game of the scene is typically discovered organically as the result of players making moves or choices and others recognizing the potential of leaning into these energies. This is not to say that a short-form game might not *also* include an additional unique game that is the product of the moment, or, for that matter, that long-form shows may not *also* utilize set games co-opted from the short-form canon. And on an even more meta level, improv involves foundational games and techniques (accepting, justifying, connecting…) that provide a common language and approach that enables both prescribed *and* discovered games to thrive. Ultimately, regardless of the improv style at hand, players should always seek to recognize and join novel games as they bubble up in the scene. In some instances, such games might explicitly serve the narrative arc; in others, they might add equally valuable dynamism and delight.

Especially when you are taking your first steps as an improviser, the idea of intuitively finding games in the raw material of an improv scene can feel overwhelming: my experience with the ubiquitous North American long-form Harold would suggest that most players are more quickly able to wrap their heads around the recurring trio of scenes than that "other thing" that happens between the rounds. It is both liberating and terrifying that the game of the scene can truly be *almost anything* if the players bravely make it so. For this entry, I'd like to offer a non-exhaustive and glaringly incomplete list of *some* different categories of games a trained eye might notice in the hopes that these examples can help you also recognize other potentials in the sea of seemingly endless possibilities…

Example

Several players have positioned themselves on stage in chairs as Player A enters the movie theatre holding a large tub of popcorn. They look for a suitable chair and carefully make their way through the auditorium while trying not to disturb the silence…

A Non-Exhaustive and Glaringly Incomplete List of Some Different Categories of Games

1. **Curve of Absurdity.** Often, a discovered game will begin firmly planted in our known reality or everyday world. As the scene continues and the game is recognized by others and subsequently heightened, the moves or behavior become increasingly exaggerated and more absurd or distant from our daily experience. The curve of absurdity is a helpful shorthand used to describe this arc of escalation. For the 17% of improvisers who also enjoy math, think of the x-axis as time and the progression of the scene and the y-axis as representing reality at the point of origin and an increasing departure from this reality as it extends upwards. Scenes that follow this approach would be drawn as a parabola. The more firmly the scene is originally grounded in our observable world, and the more patient the build, the steeper the final destination can stretch the conceit without breaking it. Ideally, each new move or step should connect explicitly to the former as the team climbs the arc together. Many discovered and canonical improv scenes benefit and find structure from some variant of this approach, such as Inappropriate Behavior.

As Player A takes their seat it omits a small squeak that is quickly shushed by the other movie patrons. Player A then tries to quietly chew their very crunchy popcorn, but each bite is surprisingly loud. Again, more disdainful shushing. Then Player A's blaring cell phone goes off... Then, an ex-lover storms into the theatre and begins a loud argument... Then a secret service detail arrives to protect Player A from their lover by loudly securing the theatre...

2. **Mapping.** This is a popular scenic dynamic where one scenario is critiqued or heightened by using the tropes and clichés of another familiar situation. For example, parents might have an intervention with their teenager after discovering they have been dabbling in drama but frame the scene with the stakes and intensity of having discovered that their child has been dabbling in drugs: "Look, we know that it looks fun and all the other kids are doing it, but this can only ruin your life in the long run..." Strong mapping scenes tend to overlay a more dramatic or intense situation on top of a rather mundane occasion, and they generally thrive when you deploy careful **specific ambiguity**. If you explicitly say "drugs" instead of "drama" (or for that matter keep saying "drama" when you are overlaying the idea of "drugs"), the dynamic becomes punctured and less effective. The same is true with any other words that would *spell out* the game rather than imply it. Mapping works best when everyone is playing with the same juxtaposition – you don't have one parent exploring the "drug" connection while the other is playing at cross purposes with "dating." When mapping scenes emerge organically, they require a great deal of active listening and trust as it only takes a small misstep to explode the game prematurely. Mapping can also be pitched as a scenic game in its own right which is something we did with joyful regularity in *Gorilla Theatre*.

Mission Impossible music comes from the booth as Player A engages in increasingly acrobatic moves in an effort to silently make it to their seat. They skillfully avoid laser sensors, the gaze and flashlight of an over-anxious movie usher, hazy smoke pouring out of the glitchy A/C unit, and "enemy" patrons who try to stop them with overly carbonated beverages and skittle attacks...

3. **Competition.** Another subset of organic games consists of competitive dynamics. These may or may not also include a conscious curve of absurdity (or mapping element for that matter) but tend to have characters that are trying to gain the upper hand. One-upping is an excellent example of this tendency (or one-downing if you prefer). In this scenic game, players each try to gently outdo each other by being the best, the bravest, the wealthiest, the most popular, or practically any other trait that is deemed valuable as the scene develops. As with most improv games, while *characters* should appear as if they are fighting to win at any cost, *players* should focus squarely on the build of the game allowing opportunities for their partner to progress and win points as well. When players are also focused on the win, the resulting scene tends to lack the subtlety and nuance that makes it feel human and recognizable. If a one-upping energy bubbles up, be wary of leaping ahead several moves: "This is the best cup of coffee I've ever tasted" probably shouldn't be followed by "I just bought all the remaining coffee beans in the world, so enjoy that cup while it lasts!"

Once Player A has finally settled in, a second Player (B) enters with a larger bag of popcorn and makes their way in a similar fashion to a more luxurious seat in the premium seating area. Player A notices that their smaller popcorn is a little bland and pulls out a flavoring sachet that they sprinkle on the contents. It is now clearly delicious. Player B finds their own popcorn unsatisfactory so eventually signals a theatre worker who drags in the hot butter dispenser...

4. **Character behavior.** Character behavior, in general, opens promising doorways into a game for the scene. Mirroring, reflecting, and exaggerating moves and patterns can provide scenic energy and discoveries. In many cases, an improviser might have inadvertently made a seemingly unimportant or innocuous choice that, with some love and attention, can evolve into the core of the scene. Again, these behavioral games could then assume an absurd, mapping, or competitive nature, but they can also thrive in the land of parallel actions or "doing the same thing but in a different way." Language-based dynamics or those that invite word play or stylistic overlays provide strong examples of this instinct, as do Character Quirks and contagious scenes where mannerisms are recognized, cherished, and given space to develop.

Stealthily, Player A looks around before surreptitiously pulling out their cell phone to record the movie. Another patron, Player B, similarly checks that the coast is clear before pulling out a hip flask and spiking their movie soda. The game of contagious bad behavior continues with Player C slowly assembling a meal they have hidden on their person…

5. **Physicality and environment.** Related to the previous concept are more overtly physical and environmental dynamics. Perhaps the location conspires against (or assists) the characters in unexpected ways, characters explore unique but connected ways of entering or moving through the space, or the configuration of the "set pieces" necessitates that characters incorporate a complex assortment of obstacles. If your improv tends to float in a location-less world, these types of games are unlikely to appear as they require a physically rich and detailed style of play. Animal Kingdom and other games of its ilk explore this general approach, with characters using a varied array of animal essences to inspire their physical and interpersonal dynamics.

Player A finally manages to situate themselves and with a peculiar dog-like quality circles around their chair before finally coming to a rest. Slowly this animalistic quality spreads to others in the auditorium: Player B sits up with a start any time there is a sudden noise; Player C starts to lap at their drink with an audible pant; Player D develops an itch in a place that they can't quite reach…

6. **Referential.** My first steps as an improviser were in the short-form tradition so I will gladly admit that I tend to view the game of the scene through this lens a little. As my earlier examples suggest, often (though by no means always) discovered games in a long-form setting tend to have at least loose equivalents in the short-form canon and I think it's wholly appropriate to tap into these latter reserves explicitly. I would caution that *forcing* a short-form handle clumsily into a scene will prove woefully less effective than *discovering* that it is appearing of its own accord or *recognizing* that the scene's given circumstances invite the connection in a fruitful way. I also would contend that an audience will sense the difference between an enlightened choice and the desperate repetition and re-creation of inorganic shtick. As we deepen our knowledge of scenic structures and dynamics from a wide cross section of improv traditions, and share these discoveries in our improv communities, it becomes more likely that we'll make that inspired connection when the opportunity presents itself. A more recent addition to my own lexicon – Can I Talk to You for a Second? – provides a good example of what might delightfully offer a next step in our movie theatre example.

As the scene unfolds, Player B who has been irritated by A's late entrance, approaches the latecomer and whispers, "Can I talk to you for a second?" in a high-pitched resonance while pulling them to the aisle for a passive-aggressive scolding. A few beats after both of them have returned to their seats, Player C, who has been sitting with B, feels the need to call them out on their snoopiness and repeats the dynamic whispering "Can I talk to you a second?" Throughout the scene, players continue to pull each other aside for not-so-private exchanges of critique and discussion while using the emblematic phrase…

Final Thought

The game of the scene begins with *one* move that is noticed and built upon. All it requires to flourish is a specific choice, whether that choice was deliberate and intentional or subtle and accidental. Any one initiation that is given focus and attention opens multiple possible paths and outcomes. There isn't one *right* game of the scene waiting to be unlocked, but *a* game will rarely emerge and thrive if players are not fully present, enveloped in the given circumstances, and generously listening to and observing their teammates. A game is also less likely to take hold if it is only pitched and played by the same improviser; as is the case in real life, most games become dynamic when others notice them and join in their own unique way. Exploring a scenic game is the definition of process as it is not about leaping to a predetermined

Figure 8.2 Street Urchins Bucko, Billy, and Bean engage in playful games in the prohibition-era improvised serial long-form *Private Lies: Improvised Film Noir* at the Annie Russell Theatre (Costume design: Annmarie Morrison; Hair and makeup design: Jen Lang; Improvising stage manager: Samantha Clarke). Photo credit: Tony Firriolo.

destination but rather encourages experiencing a journey in lockstep *together* and arriving somewhere eventually *as an ensemble*.

> **Related Entries:** Accepting, Active Listening, Ambiguity, Handle, Heighten, Physicality, Verbal Skills **Synonym:** The Deal
> **Connected Game:** Bus Stop

GET

Also sometimes known as the "get-for," this refers to the initial suggestions (usually obtained from the audience) that serve to jumpstart and inspire improvisational stories.

> **Synonym:** Ask-For

GHOST CHARACTER

When an improviser embodies multiple roles at once within an improv scene or play, those that they are not currently voicing become "ghost characters." These characters, while still present, are not physically manifested until their original improviser (or perhaps another teammate) steps into their vacant space once more and gives them corporeal form.

> **Related Entry:** Character

GIBBERISH

In addition to serving as an important technique for a subset of short-form improv games, **Gibberish** sharpens many skills in the improviser's tool belt. Ironically, by utilizing this non-sensical language that is made up by players on the spot, communication and presence can actually improve in our scene work. William Stavru describes Paul Sills' use of gibberish in his process:

> To keep his players open and responsive to the present, he uses Spolin games. To keep the intellect out of the games, Sills makes his students talk and move in slow motion or speak in gibberish in the hope that they can duck their intellects and stay focused in the present.[6]

And Keith Johnstone lists a smattering of the benefits of utilizing such a tool in his *Impro for Storytellers*: they include developing stronger listening skills, a heightened ability to be changed by what your partner says to you, and a more refined sense of physical or non-verbal communication.[7] It can be tempting to dismiss the use of gibberish as a gimmicky conceit that primarily serves as a short-form handle, but as Stavru and Johnstone remind us, there is a deeper training value to be gleaned from exploring this approach to language on stage as well.

Example

Player A assumes a professorial demeanor and steps before the assembled students. They point towards a projector screen and begin...

Player A: "Parleavy qualahte. Gashumba dow franeetee powlay na tapitee."

A student, Player B, raises their hand and gets the professor's attention.

Player A: (pointing to the student) "Ba? Twaylee?"
Player B: (sighing and heavily confused) "Dabak zeshie kalumbo!"

The rest of the class snickers. The professor calms them with a gesture.

Player A: (reassuringly) "Twaylee, panefee laht noomba na tapitee."

With a gesture the professor invites Player B ("Twaylee") to come and join them by the projection screen ("tapitee")...

Bableshing Kadool Galoney (Strengthening Your Gibberish)

As you explore gibberish in your scenic work and training, here are some pointers to keep in mind.

1. **Make sure you're speaking the same language.** I appreciate the seeming absurdity of this subtitle, but gibberish is not a "set" language that recurs consistently from performance to performance. Rather, it is a collaboratively evolving and scene-specific form of communication. Within any given scene, then, characters should be speaking the *same* gibberish language – or dialect if you will – rather than their own predetermined variant that they brought with them individually before the scene even began. With the notable exception of scenes in which groups of characters are foreign to each other and therefore deliberately speaking gibberish that is not understood by all their scene partners (a delightful scenic premise), characters who are speaking the same language should sound similar to one another. I think most of us have a default set of sounds that we tend to go to when we're playing a gibberish scene, but if we're really committed to connecting to our partners, these sounds should start to unify and mirror each other. To this end...

2. **Repeat, repeat, repeat.** Language serves as language because it utilizes repetition to create shared meaning. While gibberish can be defined as a non-sensical language – that is, a verbal form of communication distinct from the 6,500 or so languages currently in use – it is a *language* nonetheless and should endeavor to replicate the basic systems and structures of language. First and foremost among these is repetition. Characters should echo the sounds and words that their scene partners establish. It's particularly helpful and effective to assign and reuse randomly created gibberish words for important names, nouns, and features of the scene. If a character's name becomes "Kazumae," it gives great joy to hear this used more than once *and* to see the assigned character respond or enter appropriately. Be mindful not to just blindly repeat *everything* that others have said, or no particular words or phrases will stand out as important, but strategic recycling serves as a relatively simple device that pays disproportionate dividends.

3. **Engage your whole body.** A pitfall of gibberish scenes and exercises is to craft essentially talking head dynamics with players drolly uttering incomprehensible language. As English (or your national tongue) has been stripped away, it becomes increasingly critical to use the other forms of communication at your disposal such as body language, intonation, and subtext. Gibberish alone, without these elements, is unlikely to offer much to your scene partners or the audience. Use your language sparingly and carefully,

making sure that you are fully physically engaged. If you're not mindful this can become pantomimic or resemble a game of charades which strikes me as overshooting the target a little. Keep in mind that in the fictional world of the play your fellow characters onstage actually *understand* what you are saying even if the actor behind the mask may not. But if you're prone to a rather stationary style of performance, gibberish work invites – if not demands – that you now act from the neck down as well using gestures, staging, and activity to further heighten and illustrate your intent.

4. **Avoid Charlie Brown-ing.** Some actors will tend to slip into a "wah wah wah" style of gibberish that I refer to as Charlie Brown-ing as it resembles the mumbling of the often-unseen adults in the Peanuts world. Gibberish can certainly feel alienating and scary when you make your first effort to construct a whole new language soundscape and many improvisers go through a stage of almost swallowing their own verbal offers. Gently nudge players away from this trap. On the one hand, it is largely a manifestation of fear and wimping: "I don't know how to say what I want to say so I'll just minimize my vocalizations." On the other hand, it further (and drastically) reduces the likelihood that anything of value will be communicated. Savor each peculiar word that you utter, making each and every one of the utmost import. Use the vowels to deepen and express your character's emotions and subtext. Attack your consonants to shape your intentions and objectives. When gibberish devolves into "wah wah wah," all these rich potentials are lost along with the ability to just say what you want in your native language.

5. **Follow typical speaking etiquette.** Another trap that tends to surface in early gibberish explorations is that the more general societal rules of communication can disappear. For example, people don't *typically* talk all over each other (and do so even *less* on a theatrical stage). Know who is the speaker in focus at any given moment and make sure that you let them finish their thought; or, if you do interrupt a fellow player, that doing so is deliberate and tactical. Generous and clear focus gives and takes are critical for the success of these challenging scenes. As a general rule of thumb, I'd also advise talking *less* than you might usually in a scene in terms of actual word count and seeking to say *more* than you might usually with your expressions, reactions, and other non-verbal forms of communication. Effusive chatter, run-on sentences, and talking over one another are no more laudable in a gibberish scene than

they are in a traditional vignette and are often a symptom of what I would call "empty speech" where characters are making sounds, but there is little true meaning or thought behind them.

Final Thought

As is the case with all skills in the improv arsenal, the only guaranteed way to build greater comfort and "success" with gibberish is to explore the dynamic with greater frequency and fearlessness. If you are more inclined toward word play and verbose characters, gibberish can feel very much like an Achilles' heel asking you to abandon those parts of your craft that provide you safety and comfort in order to explore an alien landscape of physicality, subtext, and emotion. Lean into the initial discomfort, and graciously accept this challenge and all the subsequent gifts it will bestow.

Related Entries: Physicality, Subtext, Verbal Skills, Waffling, **Antonym:** Talking Heads
Connected Game: Subtitles

GIVE

In everyday parlance, I imagine most improvisers would like to be thought of as *giving* performers. In this general context, the phrase conjures images of generosity, selflessness, and an ability to suspend personal ego for the benefit of the scene or the ensemble as a whole. This is, in many ways, Augusto Boal's exemplary performer:

> the actors must be dialectical, must know how to give and take, how to hold back and lead on, how to be creative. They must feel no fear (which is common with professional actors) of losing their place, of standing aside.[8]

When we talk of the specific technique of **Giving** in improv, we tend to frame it in terms of focus transference on stage. In partnership with the complementary skill, **taking**, it refers to how we move the players' attention – and thereby that of the audience as well – to where it is most needed or will do the most good. Successful focus giving, however, also has much in common with the more generic use of the term, and by moving attention carefully and lovingly we can, in fact, embody many of the admirable improvisational qualities listed earlier. This is not to suggest that strong focus takes cannot likewise serve as an act of kindness and care, but moving the lens of the scene to another when you sense it is wanted or helpful is one of the "simplest" but also most important skills we can develop and wield as we play together. To give focus in this manner is to simultaneously give trust, agency, and the precious space needed to create.

For some general ways of strengthening focus on stage consider exploring Commandment #2, and my earlier post on **focus** provides guidance on crafting stage pictures with a strong sense of purpose and directionality.

Example

A clutter of characters populates the high-powered boardroom. There are murmurs that the PR company is struggling and that it may be in irreparable trouble. In the excitement, characters are inadvertently talking over each other and creating multiple competing areas of focus...

Ways to Give

Here are some seemingly basic but undeniably effective ways to pitch the focus to a teammate particularly in moments where the action may have become ill-shaped:

1. **Verbal gives.** Verbal clutter onstage often results from multiple players unsuccessfully trying to take the focus from others who are engaged in a similar tension themselves. In such instances, assuming a *stronger* take may result in just magnifying the verbal cacophony rather than assuaging it. A pointed verbal give, on the other hand, can hopefully encourage other players to also throw their weight and energy behind another character thereby providing a more singular focus. There are several simple examples of this move: simply saying or repeating another character's name with conviction might suffice. If this offer is accompanied by a loaded question, request for information, or a call for a more prolonged speech act, the move will take on even more power. Once this verbal redirection has landed it is then equally important to provide silence so that the assigned character can then unwrap the proffered gift.

Player A: (above the boardroom din) "Chelsea, you promised us with the last round of cuts that we'd be out of the red..."

2. **Physical gives.** If you find yourself in a truly chaotic soundscape, it might not prove viable to offer up a unifying verbal cry. In these circumstances, a clear physical offer can similarly redirect scattered scenic focus. If strong eye contact with your intended recipient is not enough or is going unnoticed, you can add physical volume by pointing, gesturing, or shifting your posture toward them; hopefully, others will mirror this choice (or just simply turn to see where you're looking) which can be enough to provide one character with sufficient attention to take the scenic reins. When gestures or gentle turns are insufficient, consider more boldly adjusting your stage picture and relationship with your endowee by assuming a weaker or lower position onstage (taking a knee, sitting on the ground, bowing your head...) or coming downstage so as to keep them open and in the prime real estate. All it takes is for a few teammates to see your choice and replicate it for the intended focus to now have sufficient critical mass to proceed.

Player A looks to Player B (Chelsea) and recognizes that they are displeased by the ruckus. Player A then nudges those around them to relay this information, looking back to B each time. Soon the majority of the room has thrown the attention to Chelsea and are awaiting their response...

3. **Energy gives.** While this subset of gives typically involves both verbal and physical components, it often embodies a more multifaceted dynamic. Focus throws can be imbued with status relationships – generally, taking on a clearly lower status position will give more space to your designated scene partner. Or you can color your relationship with an empathetic emotion marking the endowee as someone who is particularly or uniquely affected by the current situation. If we boldly make someone else's feelings or needs preeminent this does a lot in terms of gifting them the focus in a crowded moment. This may take on a positive or uplifting hue when we display love, care, or concern, or may explore a more antagonistic dynamic if our character shows fear, envy, or disdain. Regardless of its specific intent, a clear subtextual energy can quickly help direct a scattered focus.

Player A, who has been sitting at the head of the table, suddenly turns to look at Player B (Chelsea?) standing at the door and quickly gathers their things to vacate the chair.
Player A: (nervously) "I'm sorry. I didn't see that you'd arrived."

They move aside with deference and purpose. As B assumes their seat, Player A procures B a glass and pours them a water.

4. **The biggest give of all (sometimes)...** And sometimes, the most elegant and effective form of giving focus is to simply take the improv leap and leave the scene. If you sense that the interest and potential of the story lies elsewhere (or *could* with some generous space) and that this player is comfortable and "in the zone," then an **exit** may prove the most successful give of all. I think it's important in such a moment that you are consciously pitching to strength or else it may feel more like an abandonment or lack of support rather than a magnanimous present; although, frankly, the remaining character can always call back on their desired scene partner if you have overshot the mark. Particularly if you are in a scene that is more bustle than content, using your own exit to encourage others to follow suit can further magnify the helpfulness of your choice, although there is undoubtedly a merit in just taking a low focus exit as well if you sense your presence is part of the problem rather than offering a path forward.

Player A suddenly stands up and looks to the door.

Player A: (darting for the door) "Chelsea is here. I was just finishing up my break. Don't most of us still have jobs to get to...?"

Final Thought

Skillful giving serves as a reminder to elevate the choices and journeys of others and that we need not (and should not) seek to govern the action alone. This strikes me as a helpful embodiment of Boal's charge to be willing to "stand aside" as artists to empower the voices, stories, and journeys of others.

> **Related Entries:** Commandment #2, Edits, Focus, Take **Antonym:** Split Focus **Synonyms:** Exits, Sharing Focus
> **Connected Game:** Focus Ball

GIVEN CIRCUMSTANCES

The general accepted assumptions of the fictive improvised world that support and inform creative play. These elements are often infused into the platform or balance and can be loosely summarized by the concepts of WWW and CROW.

Synonym: CROW

GOOD FAITH

Assuming that everyone involved in the creative event is making choices from a place of love and playfulness. When this belief becomes strained or questioned, trust can quickly become broken.

Synonym: Trust

GROUPMIND

The concept of **Groupmind** refers to a seemingly magical condition where the ensemble walks together in creative lockstep. It can feel tantamount to a collective flow state where ideas and moves cease to have individual authorship and are, instead, apparently products of a unified consciousness. As an improv conceit, it defies clear definition on the page and can tend to feel a little mystical or esoteric; yet, most improvisers can point toward numerous instances when they have felt this sense of effortless connection and creativity, when the same choice inexplicably seemed to bubble up for everyone in the ensemble at the same exact moment, or when players became completely immersed in the fictional world of play.

In many circles, groupmind is praised as a pinnacle of improv practice and a goal worthy of our utmost efforts and endeavors. And not without reason. If you've had the good fortune of visiting this creative nirvana you'll understandably want to return as much as possible. But as Seham rightly observes, complex tensions underpin most foundational improv philosophies:

> Improv's excitement comes from its internal contradictions. Improvisers are challenged to be at once unthinking and quick-witted; to be unselfconscious, yet aware of the audience, the scene, and the other players; to express individuality within a groupmind; to channel cosmic truths while parodying contemporary hypocrisies; to let go and at the same time to make do.[9]

It's important to keep in mind the potentially unintended (or unquestioned) consequences of an unnuanced pursuit of this improv state of being. Just as an overly simplistic cry of "accepting" at all costs can encourage stereotypes, diminish agency, and potentially promulgate all manner of injuries, so too can elevating groupmind without a careful consideration of what group we may be inadvertently centering or, alternatively, blindly marginalizing.

Example

The ensemble creates an effortless scene riffing on a pop-culture reference. Each player intuitively knows the game and how to gradually ramp up the dynamic until a joyous climax is reached. The team celebrates together afterward ...

OR

The ensemble creates an effortless scene riffing on a pop-culture reference that is shared by many of its members. Most players intuitively know the game and how to play it with one notable exception who hasn't experienced the source material in question. As the scene approaches its climax, this increasingly alienated player becomes further and further isolated. After a joyous climax shared by the majority of the group, the team questions why everyone was in the "know" and playing along except for one member who just wasn't "fitting in..."

Groupmind Dynamics Worthy of Interrogation

Here are some inherent tensions at play within the concept of groupmind:

1. **Exclusionary versus inclusionary.** Any "group" activity, creation, or membership can be defined by those who fall within its purview or those that are excluded from the event. In my introductory examples, the sense of effortless flow may further tighten the group dynamic or possibly serve (generally unintentionally) as a way of making some members feel unwelcome or unheard. If we pursue moments of "everyone being on the same page," we must also realize that some people may not be starting with the same book and that, in fact, this latter reality is more likely to create complex and interesting stories. If we esteem work that revolves around a common set of references or pop culture knowledge, we should also recognize that these cultural touch points are rarely truly universal and might alienate company members (and audience members) in a way that obfuscates difference. When we *accept* that groupmind doesn't mandate *one* common experience, we reduce the likelihood that its pursuit will create an environment where only sameness is valued.

   A company member joins a game in an unexpected way as they have not seen the television program that everyone else is utilizing in the scene. Company members embrace this novel and brave approach and weave it into the action...

2. **Dismissive versus self-aware.** Related to the first dynamic, it can be tempting (and destructive) to ignore or dismiss choices and energies that do not, on first impression, "gel" with the dominant mood of the scene. This is a particular trap in larger group scenes where parallel choices have become the game or focus of the moment. Just as we seek full involvement in our warm-ups and exercises so that everyone feels engaged and welcome, so too should we extend this philosophy to our scenic work and games. There is an innate value in recognizing that someone may *not* be experiencing the action in the same way or is retreating as others are scaling the bastion. If we succeed or fail *as a team*, then leaving fellow players behind should be avoided, especially if they are clearly expressing a desire to play. (The notable exception would be players self-selecting out of material or a game that they view as triggering or unhealthy.) Oblivious groupmind can tend to focus only on the experience of the majority; aware groupmind seeks to acknowledge and include.

   Several company members display discomfort as they can't join the word play frenzy riffing on the popular 80s sitcom. Team members joyfully incorporate them into the game focusing on their other skills in the realms of character and storytelling...

3. **White washing versus informed.** I've hummed and hawed about using this term in the subheading, but especially when summarizing the modern history of North American improv, it hits the nail squarely on the head as groupmind tended (tends) to express a young white heterosexual male perspective. I'm unsure if there have been similarly pervasive monoliths in other global improv communities, but in general, there is a heightened onus on those of us who have experienced the privilege of occupying dominant

cultural positions to educate and develop ourselves so that we are better equipped and more sensitive to the experiences of others. Left unchecked, groupmind can tend to demand that those whose stories and experiences have unfortunately often existed on the peripheral of society abandon their points of view in order to join the pervasive "majority." So much is lost if this becomes a subconscious or unspoken expectation. The fluid and immediate nature of improv allows *any* story to emerge, and it strikes me as a tragic waste of this power to merely regurgitate stale and familiar platitudes that have been amply amplified in performances past.

A company (that reflects the diversity of its greater community) consciously rotates protagonist and leadership positions in scenes, including who makes initiations and assumes high status roles, to ensure that one voice or set of experiences doesn't dominate from performance to performance.

4. **Coercive versus celebratory.** Another trap to avoid when elevating the concept of groupmind is extolling unity *at any cost*. It can be liberating and dynamic when everyone on stage shares a common vision and plays a scenic game in largely the same way. Such a dynamic can also be a coercive act that demands the subjugation of the individual. Yes, on some level, the improv ensemble can thrive when its members are able to defer their unique whims and story ideas for the good of the whole: not everyone can serve as the scenic protagonist or focus whenever they would like to assume this position. But especially when engaging in complex themes or societal issues, it can quickly become problematic if players are expected to "go with the flow" even if they find "the flow" uncomfortable, unnuanced, or unethical. There is a marked difference between subversively playing a position different than your own or assuming a stance with an air of informed satire or commentary, and being bullied into a function or portrayal you find distasteful, damaging, or an embodiment of prejudice. Stripping players of agency and self-determination rarely results in crackling scene work or a healthy ensemble.

As players recognize that the scene has moved into troubled waters, they allow the game to shift and morph providing space for voices that might have otherwise been edited, subsumed, or ignored, thereby noting their own assumptions and sitting in that discomfort in a playful but honest way...

5. **Clique reinforcing versus ensemble building.** At the end of the day, groupmind can tend to encourage us to play with those who think and act and respond in ways that we can almost predict. It can reward familiarity and homogeneity as has been seen in the faces of early (and more recent) long-form teams and companies that adorn the walls and websites of many trailblazing improv houses. We must display a wariness of mistaking cliques for healthy ensembles or complacency with inclusive creativity. Stories have a tendency to trot over well-worn terrain when they are only ever approached from the same voice or positionality again and again and again. We are ultimately serving our art, our audiences, and our companies when we actively pursue making the tent as big and inclusive as possible. And we are more likely to become more well-rounded, interesting, and accepting *people* at the same time.

A company elevates numerous different voices and perspectives as an integral part of its mission to develop an inclusive groupmind...

Final Thought

As a white man from New Zealand, I have generally worn the shoes of the "majority" in my work on the improv stage. I recall first playing with *ComedySportz* in Chicago during my college days. Part of the ballgame gimmick of the show includes singing the national anthem before the official competition begins. During my first performance, I had the uncomfortable experience of trying to mouth along the words with my American counterparts. After the show, I was rather incredulously met with disbelief that I *didn't know the words to the national anthem!* To which I replied, "Well, it's not *my* national anthem." A kindhearted company member (Phil Granchi) later sat me down and wrote the words out on a napkin, but this moment has stuck with me all these years later. There was no intended malice in my peers' reactions, but I *very much* felt like an outsider in that moment. I think it behooves us all to keep in mind that we don't have the same anthems, childhoods, and shoes and that, frankly, our improv and world are so much the better because of that.

Related Entries: Ensemble, Inclusiveness
Connected Game: Counting Circle

GUT CHECK

The important habit of taking a moment to honestly assess and then *feel* significant revelations provided by your teammates onstage.

Related Entry: Accusation

NOTES

1. Viola Spolin, *Theater Games for Rehearsal: A Director's Handbook.* Evanston, IL: Northwestern UP, 1985. p. 11.
2. Gilda Radner quoted in Jeffry Sweet's *Something Wonderful Right Away.* 1996. New York: Limelight Editions, 1978. p. 367.
3. Adam Blatner, *Foundations of Psychodrama, History, Theory, and Practice.* 4th ed. New York: Springer Pub. Co., 2000. p. 87.
4. Keith Johnstone, *Impro for Storytellers.* New York: Routledge, 1999. p. 125.
5. Neva Leona Boyd, *Play and Game Theory in Group Work: A Collection of Papers.* Chicago: University of Illinois at Chicago Circle, 1971. p. 47.
6. Describing Paul Sills with the Compass Players, William N. Stavru, *Second City and Story Theater Founder.* 28 Oct. 2000. <www.paulsills.com/doc_stavru.htm>.
7. Keith Johnstone, *Impro for Storytellers.* New York: Routledge, 1999. p. 214.
8. Augusto Boal, *Games for Actors and Non-Actors.* Trans. Adrian Jackson. London: Routledge, 1992. p. 237.
9. Amy E. Seham, *Whose Improv Is It Anyway: Beyond Second City.* Jackson, MS: U of Mississippi P, 2001. p. 224.

H/I

HANDLE

Handles provide an added spice or challenge to a scene and in many cases are largely synonymous with specific short-form games or devices – although their implementation can look quite different depending on the context and need. These additive elements can be discovered organically from the game of the scene (we're all moving as if we're in a zero-gravity environment, so let's keep doing that), may become imposed from an external host or director once the scene has begun ("Freeze! From this point on Player A has to finish everyone else's sentences…"), or may be issued up front as an additional challenge or conceit that frames the event or round ("When I ring this bell, the rest of the scene must be performed silently with a musical soundtrack.") The first approach most typically appears in long-form or more "open" performance traditions, the second in directed work such as *Gorilla Theatre* or *Micetro*, and the latter in more traditionally hosted short-form competitions when you have an emcee shaping the flow of the show.

And, of course, there are hybrid approaches. For example, with my current university troupe, Rollins Improv Players, I'll often deploy an emcee challenge round where team members begin an open scene (typically as a pair of characters) and once the action and central dynamic are clearly established, I'll pause the players and overlay a short-form game that is in our repertoire in the hopes that doing so will further add to the fun. I've also deployed handles in competitive shows to shake up well-worn and familiar formats so that now a Typewriter might involve all the characters speaking in gibberish, or an Entrances and Exits scene now also includes audience Options. Handles, as a general conceit and philosophy, can provide a playful porousness that allows a new sense of inventiveness with scenarios or structures that have become a little predictable. For, as playwright Aphra Behn attests in *The Rover*, "Variety is the soul of pleasure."

Example

Players A and B have begun a scene with the ask-for "flea market" inspiring the action. Player A begins the scene packing up for the day as B enters.

Player B: *(with kindness)* "Another rough day?"
Player A: "I don't know what I was thinking quitting my day job for this…"
Player B: "Honey, your art is beautiful – perhaps an acquired taste – but beautiful…"
Player A: *(holding up an etching)* "No one seems to value original work anymore. Everyone looks and says they could find it cheaper online…"
Player B: *(gesturing to the piece)* "That's one of my favorites!!!"
Player A: *(jokingly)* "Wanna buy it? Discounts for spouses!"

A handle is introduced…

Getting a Handle on Handles

Here are some possible types of handles that can enhance your play:

1. **Language handles.** If the characters and premise are strong, a verbal overlay can be a nice way of heightening what is working without unnecessarily impeding the action. There are a wide array of possibilities that fall under this heading: one or more players could be asked to switch into gibberish; the team might be instructed to continue by scrolling through the letters of the alphabet sequentially as in the Alphabet Game;

a language-centric genre could be offered to frame the scene such as a Greek tragedy or Elizabethan comedy; or particularly brave players can be given the challenge of continuing the scene in rhyming couplets…

Player B: "I can't explain how others see your art; For me, each brush stroke represents your heart."
Player A: "It seems that no one else here feels that way…"
Player B: "But should we really care what halfwits say?!"

2. **Character handles.** Many handles focus on the ways that characterizations and relationships are developed or presented. If you've fallen into an archetypal dynamic that doesn't have much nuance or spark, a well-chosen handle can reinvigorate the work or perhaps just add some delightful whimsy or panache! Some potentials include: characters could become imbued with an animal or other essence that now informs their mannerisms and traits; everyone might be invited to adjust their speaking style with a "baby talk" challenge or similar; a status arrangement can magnify or upturn an existing dynamic; or a playful game such as one-upping might add some edge or spice…

Player B: "That's a lovely offer, but you know I prefer my own artistic creations…"
Player A: "There are certainly a *lot* of them lying around unsold at our house."
Player B: "It's just so hard to part with something that has truly captured your vision. I'm sure you know the feeling, or maybe not…"

3. **Physical and staging handles.** These additions can prove quite helpful if a scene has become static or a little under-energized by encouraging players to interact with the world around them in a new or perhaps unusual way. Examples of this approach include: players adopt an Entrances and Exits limitation and may now only have two characters present in the scene at any given moment; the stage picture could become embellished with a Levels challenge requiring that no two characters can assume the same height; if there is a particularly important activity occurring this might become further heightened with a call that moves the action into slow motion, hopefully with a suitable soundtrack from the booth or musician; or players can be encouraged to explore different ways of interacting with a Contact (or "touch to talk") add-on that demands that characters must be physically connected with someone else on the stage before they can speak…

Player B: (gently placing their hand on A's) "This is your dream, and I support you 100%"
Player A: (placing the last etching in a box before collapsing their head on B's shoulder) "I don't know. I'm just starting to feel like the reality of this dream is much harder than I thought it would be."
Player B: (with playful jabs on A's shoulder that punctuate each word) "Hang… in… there… honey!"

4. **Called handles.** A called handle will likely prove a little more intrusive than some of those above because it requires further interruptions or adjustments as the scene continues. That being said, it also allows the caller (or callers) multiple opportunities to course correct or nudge the scene as its central dynamic evolves and becomes clearer to all involved. As is the case with the handles above, there is a large stock of short-form frames from which to gain inspiration: a Word Ball dynamic offers players an ever-changing number of words that must be featured in each sentence; characters might explore a rollercoaster of emotions offered up from the wings that now flavor their choices; lines of dialogue may be singled out as worthy to turn into spontaneous songs; or perhaps fellow company members are enlisted to serve as stage direction authors who introduce a series of specific actions into the mix…

Player B: "Here, let me help you with that last box."
Player D: (from the side of the stage) "They said as they clumsily reached for the box."

Player B does so and inadvertently drops it on the ground.

Player A: "Well, that just pretty much sums up my day so far."
Player C: (from the side of the stage) "They said as they clasped their face in disbelief…"

Final Thought

When handles are discovered or pitched from within the scene, players are more likely to offer up dynamics that provide a fitting balance of challenge *and* joy. It's important when an outside eye or voice offers up an overlay that they also seek this dynamic, allowing the performers an opportunity to stretch their improv muscles in a new way while *also* giving a good faith possibility for playful success. Handles can tend to innately lean into shivving or pimping territory and while the former of these energies can certainly be appropriate if your team or venue values such a mischievous energy, needlessly scuttling a scene rarely lands well for the audience or the players involved. My one-upping adjustment upended the previously rather supportive and loving tone which might have been the most cogent and promising dynamic at play, for example. A handle can *radically* change the trajectory of a scene. Therein lies both the value *and* the cautionary tale of this improvisational tool.

And a closing word of warning. There can be a tendency in improv to chase the *new*: "if we add together these *five* short-form improv games or pitch multiple 'games of the scene' then that'll *really* create interest and dynamism." Often, this just overwhelms the scenic action in such a way that suffocates the potential for any story or connection of note and substance. No ornate tower of handles will ultimately serve as a substitute for focused play and patient storytelling. While it's helpful to be on the lookout for when a handle might add to the fun, it's equally important to hone the skill and discipline to recognize when such a move might take away more than it gives.

> **Related Entries:** Caller, Game of the Scene, Long-Form, Short-Form **Synonyms:** Hoop, Overlay
> **Connected Game:** Oscar-Winning Moments

HEALING ARTS

An inclusive term to describe improvisational forms that prioritize efficacy over aesthetic (which is not to suggest that this style of play can't also satisfy both criteria with aplomb). Performance modes that define themselves in such a fashion include Psychodrama, Theatre of the Oppressed, and Playback Theatre.

> **Related Entry:** Improvisation

HEAT

Leaning into the (generally faux) competitive frame or energies of a show – especially in the short-form tradition – to add dynamism and playfulness.

> **Related Entry:** Winning

HEIGHTEN

Heightening is such a pervasive and all-encompassing term that it's a little tricky to define. To **Heighten** is to build, to add volume or attention, to increase interest and momentum, or to elevate the emotional consequences. Without heightening, many a scene will limp along anemically, while the characters fail to evolve or deepen, and the potential for action drowns in an ocean of indistinguishable possibility. Boal warns, "… faced with a conflict which is too weak and uninteresting, our creativity will not be stimulated."[1] When we heighten elements of a scene as improvisers, we make them important, memorable, and worthy of further investigation. When we fail to do so, we can experience scene work that never really seems to go anywhere or mean anything. Yes, it's critical to make (and accept) **offers** as players, but it is equally important that we make these choices count.

Example

Player A stumbles into the meeting already in progress, carrying their laptop under their arm.

Player A: "I really appreciate your patience this morning. I had a minor disaster at home and then traffic was…"

As Player A scrambles to set up, Player B gently interrupts…

Player B: "Kaitlyn, I'm not sure if you've met Ms. Wright from the head office."
Player A: (*now a little more frazzled, offering their hand*) "Oh, no. We've emailed a *lot,* but this is the first time I've had the pleasure…"
Player C: (*while shaking A's hand*) "It's nice to put a face to the name!"
Player A: (*struggling to turn on their laptop*) "And you! Sorry, this doesn't seem to want to boot up…"
Player C: "And our CFO apologizes that they are unable to attend in person, but we have them set up via video conference…"

Player D waves as if behind a large monitor.

Player D: "We're starting a little late, so we'll need to jump right into this."
Player A: "Of course. My coffee seems to have spilled on my computer case!"
Player B: "So, we're just waiting on you Kaitlyn…"

Taking Heightening to New Heights

1. **It usually starts with someone else.** Of course, you can heighten your own game and character choices, but I would argue that heightening tends to prove more engaging and successful when you build off someone else's instinct or offer. A game or energy starts to crackle when it emerges *between* the players and each of them assumes some ownership and responsibility for keeping the momentum building. When we pitch and play our own games in isolation, they can tend to become solipsistic and ineffectual, existing as more of an extension of our character than a manifestation of a greater story arc. While this character-driven boldness is undoubtedly a skill worth fostering as well, the technique of heightening is more likely to take hold when it is shared: Player B has seen that Player A is frazzled and adds to that dynamic. Player A reflects that back and the idea is furthered by C and then D. What was initially an individual choice is now a collective dynamic. Just keep in mind that as you explore this newfound direction that...

2. **It's about small steps.** There can be a temptation that once an energy or choice has been recognized and elevated for players to sprint to the finish line with abandon. After all, it's great fun when you know where the scene is heading! When you're in the "know" and can identify the central dynamic, it requires some paced self-control not to explode the conceit. Heightening is most helpfully considered as a process rather than a destination (in keeping with the world of improv in general). If Kaitlyn, in the example above, is *completely* overwhelmed in one or two moves (and, frankly, the illustration may be getting close to that in its pursuit of clarity), the scene can fail to grow beyond the first obvious initiation. To knowingly slow down the trajectory, consider that...

3. **It doesn't have to be a straight line.** As we look to heighten scenic elements and games, it can prove helpful to remember that our focus needn't be exclusive. If every subsequent move heightens the same idea, it is foreseeable that the story might quickly run out of steam or interest. We can continue the journey of frazzled Kaitlyn while also tending to other facets of the scene. What are some of the other relationships and dynamics in the board room? Are there details about the physical location that will further support the action? Are there subplots or side games that we can also pitch and invest in as Kaitlyn sets up her computer? If you're playing in a long-form modality, this more expansive (but deliberate) approach also sets up richer details that may resurface or become reincorporated later in the action. Heightening needn't mean that we are only working on *one* dynamic at the expense of all other scenic considerations or that we can't step away from a dynamic for a while, knowing that we'll return to it with added gusto. (Loosely speaking, this is core of the "step out, step back in" philosophy.) A more patient and inclusive approach also gives a little creative room because...

4. **It's not just more of the same.** While heightening will often include a mirroring or parallel energy – "what is happening to our protagonist Kaitlyn and how can we do more of it?" – merely replicating prior choices will only move the engine *so* far along the train tracks. Parallels provide the "yes" of accepting but there is still ample room for thoughtful "ands." Thoughtful heightening enables games or energies to *evolve* as the scenic needs and opportunities dictate. Moves or steps should be filtered through the unique lenses and traits of your character if for no other reason than to invite *new* ways of developing the *same* dynamic. What are some other aspects of Kaitlyn's life or day that can be pulled into play, as well as the pending presentation? If we all heighten in exactly the same manner, the game will quickly become stale and predictable. The fun is so often in the delight of discovering *how* we can heighten in our own unique way while keeping in mind...

5. **It's not purely an intellectual affair.** Heightening, especially when it takes on the guise of a game, can become a rather heady experience if we are not careful. In our efforts to calculate that next iteration or dynamic shift, we can easily find ourselves retreating away from the embodied action. Effective heightening should have an emotional component: why do we care about this particular game or the developing situation if we are not vested in any of the characters or their plights? If a character, such as Kaitlyn, emerges as the subject of the game, it's important that we give them room to explore an emotional journey as we construct our edifices around them. (This is yet another reason to remember that not every contribution needs to be a "move" so that there is ample room for reactions.) When the characters' emotional state or desires are elevated alongside the scenic patterns, we're more likely to experience a noteworthy journey. Without this emotional investment, heightening can feel like it's a

great dynamic that ultimately leads nowhere. As improvisers, we might get away with this once or twice in a performance, but an evening of such moments will quickly grow anticlimactic. Which brings me to my…

Final Thought

I can tend to think of heightening as a tool used primarily within a scene, but it's helpful to remember that games, energies, character foibles, and story tensions can all be heightened over the more luxurious course of an entire performance arc or long-form piece. Recognizing the gifts provided by our scene partners and then inviting them to continue along these dynamic paths through our reflections and reactions provides one of the fundamental building blocks of improvisational play.

> **Related Entries:** Accepting, Extending, Game of the Scene
> **Antonyms:** Commenting, Deadpan
> **Synonyms:** Stakes, Urgency
> **Connected Game:** Heightening Circle

HOOP

A gimmick, challenge, or additional obstacle added to an improvisational scene for entertainment purposes.

> **Synonym:** Handle

HOSTING

It wouldn't be an overstatement to say that an improv **Host** can elevate or suffocate a performance, especially in the short-form tradition where their presence and guidance can steer a show headlong into joy or frustration. Jonathan Fox provides an interesting perspective on this critical function through the lens of Playback Theatre, although I think it aptly transcends that one performance site: "It is an objective of the artist to entertain and delight the audience; the host to establish trust and put people at their ease…"[2] I suspect that many of us have a tendency to notice ineffective or uneven hosting, as when this task is performed well, it can feel seamless and perhaps even a little invisible. Such a sense of *ease* should not suggest that excelling in this role is by any means *easy*. The able host must expertly juggle multiple complex duties and hats and so it's worth looking at some of these functions in turn…

Hosting Hats

1. **Cheerleader.** I like this title as it conjures images of enthusiasm and support, but *your* version of this function needn't also take on the high-octane exuberance and screaming – unless that's your style! I'd note that I'm not a huge fan of the highly understated or casual host that feels like they just stepped off their couch and onto a stage that suddenly appeared in their living room. If the improvisational event becomes *too* mundane, I think we're throwing away some of the magic of the ritual of performance. Regardless of the tone you're hoping to achieve (Playback Theatre's earnestness will require something different than a roaring competitive short-form match), the host generally assumes the responsibility of establishing this tone. Their demeanor sets the stage – literally and figuratively – for the action that will follow, and so it is important that they send clear messages of playfulness and engagement. Whether you work on the healing arts or popular entertainment side of the improv spectrum, I would posit that the host needs to frame and nurture a space that is safe for creativity and abandon: this may look like a heartfelt invitation to share or an energized rock concert that gets everyone excited. I would include any efforts to warm up the audience under this heading: this component of the show should clearly reflect both your greater intent and the realities of the audience in front of you (it can be rather off-putting when a host uses the same elevated energy that they would for a crowd of hundreds when there is a smattering of dozens in attendance). It's similarly important that the host elevates the event and the players; by this, I mean that they should be visibly rooting for success and celebrating victories. On rare occasions, I've seen a more pugnacious persona work in a hosting position, but this takes a deep understanding of your audience and how to build rapport. I wouldn't recommend it as a starting point if you're new to the craft.

Host: "Well done team! That is undoubtedly one of the most difficult games in our roster. Let's go to the judges to see what they thought of it…"

Figure 9.1 The host of Sak Comedy Lab's *King of the Hill* conducts an audience vote to determine who will reign as champions (Lighting improviser: Charlie Downs; Musical improviser: Chris Leavy). James Berkley Photography.

2. **Editor.** In its simplest sense, I use this term to indicate that a host should have the ability and skill set to call down a scene or vignette, especially if it is wandering the woods aimlessly in search of a button. In a more aerial sense, the host should also be concerned with the overall pace and shape of the show as it is unfolding. The way in which you approach this task will likely vary from venue to venue. On campus, I have developed strategies to gently sidecoach or assist student players, offering up cloaked time warnings to nudge the action along: a "10 seconds" generally means that this should probably lead to your button; "30 seconds" is a more gentle invitation to start looking for an out, and "55 seconds" or any other seemingly random number is my cue that something on stage needs attention – players may be upstaging each other, or speaking too softly, or crowding the stage… Most professional houses don't deploy such a stealthy method, but the host can still utilize subtle signals that gift the players the benefit of their experience and vantage point. After all, the host often gets to watch the scenes alongside the audience and has an outsider's eye able to assess if the action is faltering or causing discomfort. Standing or moving toward the stage space can offer a similar nudge toward buttoning the scene, especially if accompanied with an arm at the ready to cue a blackout. Communicating with the booth to flash the lights or slowly start a fade is an oft-used tool at festivals to push an improv set toward an ending. Checking in with players at intermission or during postmortems about staging difficulties can help iron out these wrinkles in future performances too. And on a pragmatic level, the host should also keep a *close* eye on the length and rhythms of the show as ends of acts can make or break the audience experience, hence the import of editing scenes that are struggling needlessly so as to allow time to move onto something with fresh potential.

Host: "Okay teams, this next round is going to be a true two-minute challenge round…" [read: "We're running a little over, so I'd like to pick up the pace in this next round to buy us back some time…"]

3. **Translator.** The label of "improv" or "unscripted" can be applied to a wide variety of performances and it is not uncommon for our audiences to

wander into something that they might not have experienced before. A thoughtful host should aid in this process of welcoming and serve as a translator and ambassador for nervous neophytes in the auditorium. While I hope that most audiences don't need the obligatory definition of what improv *is* anymore ("So who here has seen the show *Whose Line Is It Anyway…?*"), in most cases, they may need some help knowing what you are doing with *your* improv. For those outside the bubble, "We're doing a Harold" or "Who's ready for an… [insert opaque long-form title here]" probably isn't sufficient to set them up with a blueprint for success, particularly if our intent is to appeal to a broader audience demographic (which I'd argue is key to our survival as an art form). The host should help define important features or facets of our work which, in turn, better equips the audience to enjoy the improv on its intended terms. If you're aiming for a laugh riot, an irreverent satire, or a sincere exploration of the human psyche, that target should probably be named upfront. If you want ongoing audience suggestions and interactions or are just going to start from zero while maintaining the fourth wall separation, the audience will benefit from this information. If your venue has house rules in terms of content (from the stage *and* the audience), then give your attendees the benefit of knowing these as well: we can't fault them for breaching standards they didn't know. The business of defining the show, setting expectations, and presenting the ground rules for participation or collaboration are probably not the most glamorous host functions, but when these are executed with care and finesse, they can add significant dynamism to the overall experience and so shouldn't be overlooked or undervalued.

Host: "For this next scene I've selected a rarely played game from our archives as I think this team is up for the challenge! You've seen some great improv tonight, but I think it's time we added some improv music into the mix…"

4. **Architect.** While the editor function is largely responsive, I view the related role of architect as more proactively engaged in the bigger picture. My favorite short-form hosts are deeply vested in their game roster for the night, often selecting scenes well beforehand that they feel will allow players to stretch and excel (while remaining flexible enough to change things on the fly if the given circumstances require it). Ever with an eye to the greater shape of the show, they prioritize variety by mixing "standards" with some calculated risks, audience favorites with games that appeal to the players, and more open scenic structures with those that are inherently gimmicky or restrictive. If they have a hand in casting (in short- or long-form traditions), they work to provide balance and joy, avoiding needlessly combative or stale combinations in lieu of groupings that will complement each other's energies and skills. I also view this hat as being the "adult" in the room as needed. They should keep the players and company free from harm, whether it is calling down a scene before that "impossible feat of skill" might injure the players or addressing and containing a belligerent audience member who thinks they are at a stand-up show. They should keep the audience and theatre staff safe too, whether it is acknowledging content parameters or material that may have strayed off the mark or addressing and containing a belligerent audience member who thinks they are at a stand-up show. I believe strongly that if a corrective voice or action is needed (and a member of house management or security is unavailable, absent, or unsuitable) that the host is best positioned to be this person as they serve and represent both the company and the audience. This protects the players from having to wear any negative energy as they continue to play. For this reason alone, it can be problematic when you have some of your least experienced or least resilient players serving in this role.

Host: "And as we go to intermission, I'd encourage you to take advantage of our restrooms (located through that door), or our concessions stand and bar. Unless you're that gentleman in the third row who, I think we all agree, has had plenty to drink already…"

Final Thought

In some instances, a short-form host also takes on the role of a caller and there are many common dynamics and strategies that apply equally to both functions. I've addressed "Factors to Balance as a Caller" in my earlier entry.

The face of hosting can look quite different in long-form and narrative shows where the requisite duties may also be split between multiple members of the company. But even in a more limited role, the responsibilities of the host are critical and deserving of attention and, dare I say, (greater) appreciation. I've worked in companies where the emcees were literally paid less than the fellow improvisers they guided and elevated. This hopefully archaic practice reflects that hosting can easily become a rather thankless or underappreciated task despite its unquestionable role in our improvisational endeavors. An audience may not always appreciate the subtle magic that the host enables, and in fairness, the host probably shouldn't be the most interesting or attention-grabbing thing in an improv show, but those who are collaborating on the stage should certainly acknowledge the artistry and generosity required to keep us safe and make us all look good.

Related Entries: Caller, Ensemble, Shape of Show, Sidecoaching **Antonym:** Audience
Synonyms: Conductor, Director, Emcee, Improviser, Joker, Referee, Umpire
Connected Game: Good, Bad, Worst Advice

ICK CHECK

A tradition of checking in at the completion of a show or rehearsal and giving space for players to openly express moments of discomfort while their fellow members actively listen.

Synonym: Postmortem

IGNITION

Often the first major tilt or shift in a linear story that shocks the world out of stasis and into action. Such a dynamic moment marks the end of the balance and the beginning of the rising action. Without an ignition (or inciting incident), the scenic world would remain stuck in its everyday rhythms and generally offer little of interest.

Synonym: Breaking the Routine

IMPROVISATION

This is a surprisingly difficult entry to begin even though (and because) it really serves as the starting point for all the entries that have come before and will follow. (If you're looking for a bite-size description, I quite like Lynn Pierse's "When we improvise, we act spontaneously, without preplanning, using whatever is at hand to invent stories and characters to create a world of make-believe.")[3] Oftentimes it feels difficult to define theatrical improvisation without resorting to a description of what it is *not*: at the simplest level, improv is *not* scripted, *not* a set product, and is *not* repeatable. In most Western theatre histories, improv is also relegated almost solely to its relationship to the scripted world: it's a tool for developing new (later-to-be-textualized) material, researching or deepening a repeatable character, or getting you through an onstage slip-up and then safely back to the lauded scripted action. Yes, improv can be all these things, but those who have dedicated themselves to this craft would quickly argue that these reductive tropes barely scratch the surface of this often-overlooked art form.

I endeavored to research and define improv on its own terms (freed from the shadow of the script) in my doctoral dissertation and I'm drawing liberally from those musings here while also trying to reduce the Bakhtinian theory that infused my work in a way that appeased my thesis readers but also sadly pretty much guaranteed that few in my chosen and cherished field would slog through the final result! I still maintain, however, that looking at the spirit of **Improvisation** as it has appeared across multiple times, places, and cultures reveals some striking tendencies that unite a wide-reaching and diverse performance style. There are, as one would expect, exceptions to all these improvisational facets, but I believe there are poignant and recurring themes that serve as helpful ways to consider what it is we do and value as spontaneous practitioners.

Five Improvisational Values

1. **Elevating play in a shared space.** Improvisation places a high value on the actual site of performance, crafting rich relationships with audiences in spaces that are often found or transitory. While improv can certainly mirror its scripted counterpart in erecting imaginary fourth walls between the players and the attendees, this is a less common orientation and performances often take place in streets, bars, public spaces, or on itinerant or portable stages. When improv does occur in more traditional theatre spaces, it still tends to deliberately challenge the separation of the event's participants by drawing attention to the physical means of the hosting space with players willfully crossing the great divide of the real or imagined proscenium.

The resulting creative space is typically communal and shared, whether this is in the vein of Richard Schechner's Environmental Theatre, Augusto Boal's Invisible Theatre, or South Korean Madang Theatre. In short- and long-form traditions, which serve as the focus of many of these entries, players often incorporate or refer to the constituent elements of the host venue and communities, and audience members frequently find themselves involved directly or indirectly with the improvisatory action.

Improv theatre values the potentials and details of the specific locations in which it appears.

2. **Esteeming the importance of the now.** Improv pioneer Jacob Levy Moreno defined this style of play as performance in the "here and now" and that the present is both the form's moment of birth and death. While many scripted traditions appear to seek or elevate a sense of timelessness or universality, improv is unavoidably and unabashedly committed to *this* very time and place. Its malleability embraces (if not demands) a responsiveness and reactivity. Improv that does not or cannot change or reflect the specifics of the historical *now* tends to become stale or a pale facsimile of the spontaneous spirit. This inclination toward process and change in and of itself can undermine more capitalistic models of art that demand reproducible and predictable products. A commitment to an evolving process serves as both improv's power and its burden: traditions such as the ancient Roman mime (and frankly, most pre-twentieth century or oral traditions) remain largely obscure to us as so little remains that can help us understand the nuanced nature of the work. In the modern period, some improvisation has been digitally captured or televised but, I would posit, that recorded improv quickly loses the magic of "presentness" and unrepeatability that is a defining feature of the form.

Improv theatre responds to and reflects the historical moment in which it's set.

3. **Raising the voices of the many.** Forgive me for slipping in a little Bakhtin here but he has the lovely concept of the prosaic (everyday) that stands in contrast to the poetic (elite). Improvisational theatre historically and globally tends toward the former rather than the latter. Most improv embraces labor-intensive models of performance (the work and skill reside primarily in the bodies of the players) as opposed to capital-intensive approaches, as one often sees in the scripted realm (the product requires complex technical and financial resources to succeed). It's not uncommon for an audience member to observe an improv show and become inspired to join the company – or pursue their own performance opportunities – and for these two moments to occur with little time separating them. An audience member attending an ornate Broadway-style production, on the other hand, rarely leaves with the same expectation that this form of art and venue is immediately available or welcoming to *them* in the foreseeable future. Improv theatre frequently presents itself as art by, for, and/or with the communities in which it appears, and with some few notable exceptions – Japanese Renga Poetry is a favorite – strives to include participants that may find themselves on the margins elsewhere. (This is not to suggest that there have not been painful failures or blindnesses in this regard as a quick consideration of modern North American improv will quickly reveal.) Many traditions, such as Playback Theatre, Spolin Games, and Theatre-in-Education, actively embrace those who might be considered amateurs, while other modes, such as Commedia dell'arte, Theatre of the Oppressed, and the Kawuonda Women's Theatre of Sigoti, illustrate moments when otherwise marginalized voices found a stage.

Improv theatre provides the means for inclusiveness, access, and representation.

4. **Privileging dialogue and flexibility.** I think it can be a common misconception to view improv as formless or without structure, and while it is defined by its lack of a set script, this does not mean that it may not incorporate other complex, ornate, or inherited structures, rules, and blueprints. The more important distinction perhaps lies not in the presence or absence of structural components but rather in the way they are utilized and viewed. To sneak in a little more Bakhtin, he provides the concept of the dialogic which means that multiple voices interact as equals to define and chart the artistic journey. Whereas the playwright's vision (or in some theatrical movements, that of the director, auteur, or designer) typically reigns supreme in traditional scripted realms, improvisers routinely inhabit the stage as empowered co-creators. Guiding hands may certainly assist or shape the action – Spolin's sidecoach, Boal's joker, Moreno's director, Johnstone's host, or Playback's conductor – but improv players enjoy considerable agency as co-authors. A great deal of modern improvisational theory focuses on ways to better enable the ways in which self-aware and generous collaboration can occur so that (ideally) voices are not needlessly or carelessly excluded from the process. Similarly,

improvisers are encouraged to actively and bravely balance form and freedom, structure and chaos, the familiar and the unknown.

Improv theatre seeks to create a space where the responsibility and joy of creativity are shared.

5. **Questioning the status quo.** Lastly, due to improv's reluctance to create a predictable and stable product, its very presence stands in defiance of the establishment as it uses laughter or pathos (among other tools) to question, ridicule, or undermine the systems of power with which it coexists. Whether it takes the form of overtly political performance on the streets, satiric commentary in the cabaret, or seemingly benign short-form games in a high school auditorium, the very fact that improv evades control and censorship – nobody can *really* know what will happen next – gives it an unmistakable power and potential that uniquely defines the genre. Cogent examples of this political tendency include Moreno's sociodrama with its merging of art and healing efficacy, Boal's Legislative Theatre that embodies spontaneous interplay as a means for changing and creating political reform, and Nigerian Apidan Theatre with its complex balance of numerous contradictory and oppositional elements. To return to the site of short- and long-form modern improv, most traditions acknowledge the power and importance of "punching up" as a foundational approach; that is, choosing worthy and deep-rooted societal powers as the targets of our work rather than the marginalized or dispossessed.

Improv theatre, with its innate unpredictability, provides a mechanism for challenging power.

Final Thought

I offer these five qualities as a way to understand and unify the broad array of performance styles that rightly self-define as improvisatory and also, on some level, as a charge to recognize the special power and tools that improv theatre possesses. Spontaneous theatre has a unique relationship to the here and now that inspires and informs our play, offers the rich potential to value and elevate voices and stories that may not find themselves welcome in more conventional performance modalities, provides the flexibility and means to enable collaborative and dialogic creativity, and holds the power to playfully or pointedly call into question inherited oppressive systems and norms. This is certainly an exciting artistic field worthy of our utmost attention and efforts!

If this lens intrigues you, a digital copy of my full dissertation is available online at the link included in this endnote.[4] It includes a strong bibliography and timeline, although these reflect what was available in print in English in 2003 and the world of improv and the internet have changed greatly since then!

Related Entries: Audience, Groupmind, Long-Form, Punching Up, Short-Form
Antonym: Repeatability **Synonym:** Spontaneity
Connected Game: New Choice

INCLUSIVENESS

Unlike our scripted kin which tends toward singularity in terms of the voice or perspective it propagates through the pen of the playwright, improv invites polyphony – the act of placing multiple voices in active conversation. The breadth and diversity of this dialogue, however, clearly depend upon the experiences and bodies present in the creative process; while the genre of improv enables inclusion, the realities of its practice can easily fall short of this ideal without conscious efforts to maximize this important and defining potential. Adam Blatner speaks to the critical nature of this mission of making spaces where we can all share stories and listen when he writes, "People need to give voice in order to feel more authentically alive, and we need to construct contexts in which we are willing to listen, and to share our own stories."[5] I ardently believe that all improv – regardless of its packaging or stated intent – has the inherent potential to meet this need *if* we display care and thoughtfulness in our endeavors. I would by no means assert that I have unequivocally succeeded in my own earnest efforts to foster and develop performance spaces that embody **Inclusiveness**; rather, I offer the following questions and observations for those of us who have assumed leadership responsibilities. These are some goals and tensions that I continue to wrestle with in my own endeavors to become a better ensemblist, collaborator, and ally. (I consider some possible strategies for *onstage* inclusion in my discussion of **groupmind**.)

Questions to Consider on the Path to Inclusiveness

1. **What messages are we sending our audiences and patrons?** Whether it's falling into needlessly gendered language in our introductions and

announcements, presenting homogeneous teams or troupes time and again, or performing in spaces that are clearly inaccessible to guests or performers with mobility needs, before we have even started to perform, we have likely sent profound and clear messages to our audiences. Someone who feels (or *is*) unable to join the stage action as a volunteer is unlikely to feel fully welcome, no matter what we might *say* or intend. Exclusionary signals also extend to publicity and promotional materials that establish an expectation and commitment to diversity (or a lack thereof). As they say, a picture is worth a thousand words: are our thousand words *still* centering white, cis, heterosexual, young men as has been the case for so much of at least North America's history? It's asking a lot of a potential audience to patronize our spaces if they feel there is very little chance their stories or experiences will be honored or understood. When we do include diverse voices on our stages, is this treated primarily as a gimmick – "we're going to have the men battling the *women* tonight!" – or are all participants valued for their host of talents and abilities?

2. **What messages are we sending our talent?** Are we consciously or unconsciously rewarding and advancing sameness? Do our casting practices seek and model inclusion or do we happily create product after product with the same demographics on our stages and in positions of creative control? Are we falling into patterns of tokenism – pushing company members who embody difference to the forefront for publicity purposes but not actively seeking to increase their voices as stakeholders or presence in the decision-making processes? Whose stories are being told on stage? Depending on the genre of performance, can protagonists appear from anywhere in the ensemble or, if we're engaged in shows with unavoidable hierarchies in terms of roles (leads, supporting players, ensemble…), are we committed to complexity and empathy in representation? Are there dramaturgical ways to acknowledge stylistic "norms" while simultaneously pushing back and elevating previously silenced voices and positionalities? Casting can prove particularly difficult if you are operating in a "closed" system – such as on a university campus or creating a show from a pre-existing talent pool at your resident company – as diversity challenges in your host organization may quickly become magnified in your smaller project. Hence the importance of also considering…

3. **What messages are we sending our students and future collaborators?** Most companies in the Western short- and long-form traditions rely *heavily* on attached training centers to support (if not subsidize and make viable) their public performances. For many of these students, advancing onto the mainstage or esteemed student ensembles serves as a primary motivating factor. If these aspirational companies (or the bank of instructors with which they'll work) are relentlessly homogeneous, students may quickly lose heart. As training centers are often feeders into more professional company positions, this further impacts the likelihood that ensembles may remain imbalanced or unrepresentative of the communities from which we draw. Companies should also examine barriers that may hamper enrolment from under-featured sections of their host communities. Are there scholarship or advancement opportunities for those who may not have the financial or schedule flexibility needed to follow the previously established pathways, for example? It follows that if your current training system is not attracting or retaining dynamic and diverse candidates that you may have inadvertently institutionalized impediments to company growth and inclusion. Also, have you implemented clear pathways for redress that encourage candor and deep listening, and are these avenues well-known for when we fall short as artists or facilitators?

4. **What messages are we sending our greater (artistic) communities?** Do our companies look like and fully represent our audiences? Do our audiences similarly reflect the breadth and depth of our larger communities? Do our training centers and leadership teams embody these voices and experiences? These questions are all complexly interconnected, but companies are more likely to excel when they appeal to and represent a broad cross-section of their host communities. In addition to welcoming new groups and organizations *into* our spaces, are we also showing up and building bridges by going *into* others' spaces when invited? Are we serving a greater artistic community and responding to the needs, joys, and struggles of our fellow collaborators and patrons? Do we allow or encourage material on our stages that is ill-informed, harmfully stereotypical, or blind to the world around us: are we using our craft and our skills to elevate and advance the conversation or merely hiding behind the façade of escapism? Are we *actively* working to reduce barriers to make our spaces more inclusive, or have we become complacent and content to play in places created primarily to make *us* feel welcome?

Final Thought

Although the tools of improv contain the potential for incredible creativity and inclusion, this theatrical nirvana is not a given but rather a beckoning destination. If we want a more dynamic and representative art and companies – and I certainly hope we all do – we must deliberately move forward along this path, accepting when we mess up or fall short and pledging to recommit ourselves with even greater passion and empathy.

> **Related Entries:** Ensemble, Groupmind, Improvisation **Antonym:** Cliques
> **Synonyms:** Yes, And...
> **Connected Game:** Identity Circle

INHERENT

Seeking story choices that have an organic connection and fully utilize previously established facts and elements.

> **Antonym:** Over-Originality

INITIATION

An often-intoned improv rallying cry consists of some iteration of Spolin's "Don't initiate! Follow the initiator! Follow the follower."[6] While an **Initiation** can refer to almost any inspiring **offer** or move in an improv scene that provides a new piece of information or opportunity, here I'd like to primarily consider some best practices and strategies for the very first moments of an improvised scene, or the *initial* initiation if you will. Scene starts are ripe with potentials *and* pitfalls: a grounded and elegant opening will often lead to joyful abandon, whereas a clumsily or rushed first salvo can proverbially sink the ship before it's even set sail. I've mused on story and character-based strategies in my **CROW** entry so will take this opportunity to discuss some more technical stagecraft practices that can set you up for success as the lights start to fade and you make your way to the stage. While I'm gently assuming a short-form frame for these comments – there are a *lot* of first moves in a short-form show after all – these strategies also hold true with slight adjustments to other improv modalities as well.

Example

The team has received the suggestion of "spelunking" for their scene. The host leads the audience in a countdown as the lights fade and the players ready themselves for the scene ahead...

Strong Scenic Starts

1. **"I'll start."** Whether it's literally uttered by a player or gently signaled by a look or established signal, I *strongly* advocate that a player clearly self-selects to begin a scene. In short-form workshops, I offer the mantra that the first two words of every scene should be "I'll start" as I am such a believer in this conceit. This cue, or similar, prevents teammates from all scattering to the wings, as no one should (ideally) move until someone has happily nominated themselves to begin. There are few things more off-putting as an improviser than having the first moment of a scene consisting of your fellow players abandoning you onstage without even a thread of an idea in your pocket. For a scene to start from strength, it's crucial that the first initiation comes from a place of strength and excitement. (In my own long-form work this "I'll start" has evolved into a simple gesture – such as a hand over your heart – to let the cast know that you have something brewing.) Once a player has marked themselves to begin, it's a simple matter for them to quickly select a scene partner (if one is required) with a light tag or look, or to ask fellow players to quickly help them set up a needed element ("Make me a car...") Such an attitude reduces the likelihood of a scenic false start with the lights rising on a glaringly empty stage or multiple players obliviously making competing and contradictory initiations. The latter scenario *can* prove charming occasionally as players now must skillfully combine disparate elements, but I find a cascade of tepid scene starts ultimately does little to aid the spontaneous event.

As the host leads the countdown "3, 2, 1..." Player A mouths "I'll start" and gestures to Player B to join them downstage...

2. **Place yourself.** Whether you're dashing to the wings as you're not initially needed or positioning yourself purposefully onstage for the first moment, make sure your first staging choice is deliberate and definitive. If a teammate has bravely offered themselves up to get the ball rolling and you aren't currently needed, get yourself to the edge

of the performance area quickly. Whenever possible you should position yourself in such a way that you are able to see all the unfolding action without drawing undue attention to yourself or obstructing the view for the audience. I'll often advocate for crouching downstage of the action if this is feasible and aesthetically pleasing, as this posture typically allows for jumping into the fray immediately when you're needed. If you're in a more traditional theatre space with a backstage and wings, make sure you are still able to view the action and don't become needlessly distracted rifling through costumes, props, your cell phone, or the like. I'm not a big fan of standing against the "wall" behind the action as this has the double disadvantage of making it difficult to see the more nuanced expressions and gestures of your teammates if they're appropriately playing to the audience, *and* it's easy to distract from the scenes in progress. It can also create confusion as to who is actively involved in the scene. (I appreciate in some venues, there may not be an obvious alternative.) If you see an opportunity to quickly arrange a few chairs or blocks to support the initial premise – or perhaps even use your body as a set piece depending on your style of play and the tone of the scene – endeavor to have this in place as efficiently as you can. If you volunteered to start, or have been nominated by a teammate to join them, position yourself robustly on stage with an eye to how the stage has been used thus far: if all the scenes have been center stage, perhaps change it up and begin near the wings; or if several games have involved players standing and talking then grab a chair or block instead and orient it (and yourself) in an interesting way.

Player C and D, confirming that their teammates are excited to begin, quickly move to either side of the stage, taking a knee at the lip of the performance area. Player B accepts A's invitation to join them downstage and they both lie on the floor in dynamic positions...

3. **Do something.** Whether you're establishing an activity, making the first contributions to the environment, or defining the core relationship, do something *active* rather than just talk or call on another player. Part of the gift of embracing an "I'll start" philosophy is that it empowers players to seize the beginning of a scene without fear that they may be stepping on the ideas of their teammates. It remains good form, however, for the onstage players to then adequately share this task of setting the given circumstances. The self-nominating player – Player A in the above example – will typically also make the *first* offer which tends to set the tone of the scene that follows. So, as the literal or figurative lights rise on the scene, it's incumbent on the first player to offer up something *specific*. It's important to note that this doesn't mean that the initiating player has a fully fleshed concept for the whole scene (most would agree this is likely to be more destructive than helpful), but rather that they can provide the initial spark of inspiration with care and confidence. Many improv schools of thought would recommend that this connect to the **CROW** (Character, Relationship, Objective, or Where) of the premise, but it could also be as simple as a well-crafted mood, emotion, or energy: Player A is clearly enamored by their underground adventure, or in the middle of a panic attack, or having an epiphany about how caring their partner has been... If you're able to make this first choice with your whole body and being (rather than as a cartooning commentary – "I'm loving this spelunking..."), you have already placed yourself on a firm scenic footing, hence my encouragement to *do* something rather than merely *say* something. This approach also increases the likelihood that you'll start to shape the environment which becomes increasingly unlikely if it remains undefined in the opening moments of the scene.

As the lights come up, Player A squeezes themselves through a narrow passageway as Player B crawls closely behind. Both use precise movements, carefully adjusting their physicality to accommodate the equipment tied to their bodies. Player A can be heard audibly breathing – a mix of exhaustion and excitement...

Player A: "The guide said the cavern should be right around this corner..."

4. **Don't overthink ask-fors.** Whether you've just elicited an ask-for from the audience to inspire your play or are reacting to the offers embedded in your ensemble's prior scenes, trust these impetuses to inspire your work in both obvious and new ways. If you're using audience prompts to launch your work, there is certainly no need to *begin* with this information: there is undoubtedly a creative value in taking a tangential approach or gently building up to the proffered idea, especially if this increases the likelihood of action or activity. (The "I'll start" approach also affords the first player a little space to develop a more out-of-the-box idea that might not have been front-of-mind for their teammates.) However, there

can also be plenty to mine from just grabbing the suggestion head on as this allows you stage time for the offer to morph into a multitude of less linear possibilities. After all, if the audience says spelunking and then immediately sees you spelunking, they're not likely to feel ignored! Just be cautious of taking an exciting offer and then disarming it by crafting a scene where you talk about possibly "doing the thing," traveling to the site of potential activity, or gathering the necessary equipment. I might feel a little cheated as an audience member if I called out spelunking and then watched a lethargic scene about a couple considering but never actually going into the cave… At the end of the improv day, it matters less how you use or find inspiration from the initial prompt than the intensity of the energy with which you prime the creative furnace.

After one final gymnastic twist, Player A finally emerges into an opening, adjusts the lamp on their helmet, and looks around them with a sense of awe and wonder…

5. **Elevate the initiator.** Whether you've been invited by the first player to begin the scene, or join the action later as it unfolds, seek to elevate and polish the choices that clearly hit the stage first. Built into the "I'll start" philosophy is the gift of providing the first initiator a little room. Generally, this first player wouldn't have offered themselves up for this function if they didn't have a glimmer of an idea. It is foreseeable that several company members may become inspired to start the scene, but it's unlikely to prove fruitful if the opening moments become a confusing competition of cluttered concepts. Accept and elevate the initial choice as best you understand it. Trust that if you have a dynamic idea that it will find its way into the scene if that's what *this* scene needs. Scenes often struggle under the burden of excess when too many ideas rush the stage and compete rather than connect: this tendency can be particularly destructive during the critical first moments when the story seeks to find its footing. Spolin's notion of following the initiator (or follower) feels particularly pertinent during these crucial first steps.

After a few more moments of twisting through the tunnel, Player B finally emerges. A moment later their eyes adjust to the space and they are filled with similar wonder. They gently take Player A's hand…

Player B: "Wow! This really is like a cathedral!"

Final Thought

I will happily confess that I can be a little persnickety when it comes to establishing etiquette for starting scenes – especially with novice improvisers – but those initial seconds as we prepare and begin our scenes have the power to make or break the explorations that follow. If we abandon others onstage who are ill-prepared to start, we have eroded trust before the first word has even been uttered. If we dash backstage as the action begins and cannot see the nuances of the first scenic choices, we are less likely to be able to contribute knowingly and meaningfully when we're needed. If we begin a scene in our heads and are oblivious to others' initiations or scenic intents, we may spend much of the scene scrambling to get on the same page as our collaborators. I've found that one of the clearest indicators of how well players will connect and communicate within a scene resides in these first opening moments, so it's well worth taking the time to consider and rehearse how to successfully get the improv ball rolling.

Related Entries: Ask-For, CROW, Offer
Antonym: Button **Synonyms:** Launches, Starting Scenes
Connected Game: Bell's Kitchen

NOTES

1. Augusto Boal, *The Rainbow of Desire*. Trans. Adrian Jackson. London: Routledge, 1995. p. 60.
2. Jonathan Fox quoted in Jonathan Fox and Heinrich Dauber's *Gathering Voices: Essays on Playback Theatre*. New Paltz, NY: Tusitala Pub., 1999. p. 124.
3. Lyn Pierse, *Theatresports Down Under*. 2nd ed. Sydney, Australia: Improcorp, 1995. p. 29.
4. David Alfred Charles, *The Novelty of Improvisation: Towards a Genre of Embodied Spontaneity*. Dissertation. 2003. https://digitalcommons.lsu.edu/gradschool_dissertations/76
5. Adam Blatner, *Foundations of Psychodrama. History, Theory, and Practice*. 4th ed. New York: Springer Pub. Co., 2000. p. 107.
6. Viola Spolin, *Improvisation for the Theater. A Handbook of Teaching and Directing Techniques*. 3rd ed. Evanston, IL: Northwestern UP, 1999. p. xiii.

J/K/L

JOKES

What new players often mistake as the primary content or focus of improvisation. While many practices value and incorporate wordplay, wit, and repartee, few prioritize the "joke" above all else, valuing instead concepts such as connections, emotional truth, and story.

Related Entry: Comedy

JUDGING

The tendency to hyper-critically evaluate oneself or others during the creative process. An inclination toward judging tends to place players in their heads rather than in the shared embodied space.

Antonym: Abandon

JUSTIFICATION

Justification stands as one of the foundational tools of improv as it imbues our work and stories with meaning and dynamism. To justify choices involves combining seemingly disparate or unrelated offers through providing context and pertinent backstory. Improv guru, Del Close, includes this tool as one of his key tenets: "Don't deny either verbal or physical reality […] The actor's business is to justify."[1] It can be tempting to think of this technique as primarily a strategy for assisting the scene when things are going awry – such as is the case when players and their choices are not uniting in a playful and helpful way; but justifying also supports most of our more run-of-the-mill storytelling efforts as we work to make sense of the potentially random elements that populate our fictive worlds. This performance approach likewise provides a preferred alternative to merely calling out or **commenting** upon inconsistencies in a way that might provide laughter but doesn't ultimately work to bring ideas into alignment (or make our partners look good during the creative process).

Example

As the lights come up on the start of a new scene, Players A and B have both taken the field and initiated without an awareness of their scene partner's presence or intent.

Player A is pulling a heavy roast out of an oven downstage right…

Player B is intensely digging a hole with a shovel downstage left just a few feet away…

Justifying as a Source of Creative Strength

Here are some ways to unlock the hidden potentials of apparently contradictory scenic moments…

1. **Hold onto your own gift (or that of your partner).** Be wary of needlessly throwing away the richness of your own reality in order to embrace that of your scene partner. If the audience has *seen* you pull something out of an oven it will feel anticlimactic for you to immediately drop that reality completely and join your partner's digging. Likewise, throwing away the digging choice and just coming inside without ever returning to this rich idea will also probably disappoint. Justifying is, first and foremost, about combining

our ideas rather than casually throwing some of them away. This isn't to say that our actions and choices will not morph and transform: perhaps Player B is digging a hole to bury yet another disastrous roast in the backyard. In this way, our scenic work becomes unpredictably and delightfully cumulative rather than unhelpfully reductive and monolithic.

2. **Engage more than just your brain (or your wit).** Another temptation that can occur when faced with choices that aren't immediately compatible is a tendency to over rely on our dialogue to "fix" these ruptures rather than deploy our entire skill set as performers. If Player A calls out "Stop digging and come have dinner," for example, while B's choice has been recognized, it hasn't really been embraced. If, on the other hand, Player A continues to prepare dinner for their partner who *always* starts a new household project moments before they are about to dine and infuses the scene with this well-worn emotional truth, now both choices have been honored more fully in a way that also heightens the physical and emotional stakes of the scenario. Seek an emotional as well as an intellectual truth and connecting rationale.

3. **Avoid calling out the rupture (or dismissing its potential).** I've mentioned the trap of commenting above as this tendency strikes me as a way of diffusing the potential of starkly different choices rather than maximizing the risk and beauty of such moments. Some companies and performers elevate and enjoy this often deadpan or wry style of play: "I see you clearly didn't notice that I was cooking before you decided to make that digging choice…" Such call outs are likely to get an audience laugh; but, in my opinion, will rarely do much to ultimately fuel the engine of the scene. And they also have the very real likelihood of deflating your partner's attack and eroding trust. Astute audiences will recognize misfires or challenging contradictions, and there is arguably some value in gently "winking" at these scenic detours, but to openly mock such moments routinely saps them of any latent creative tension.

4. **When in doubt, make one small step (as you don't need to "solve" it all in one move or alone).** Relish the struggle. Unlike most forms of art, improv allows the audience to witness and enjoy the messiness of the process. There's no expectation that all choices will immediately find their way effortlessly into the greater narrative arc. Perhaps our scene above bravely moves forward for several minutes with neither player providing an outright justification for the two opposing actions as they trust that they will eventually get there. (Is it finally revealed that Player B is burying the last guest who made a rude comment about A's cooking?) It's also helpful to relieve yourself of the burden of holistically solving any disparity: offer one small connection or piece of context. Player A might playfully note that "The neighbors are going to be home in half an hour" to add urgency to B's digging without defining its nature or purpose. Player B could call "Your pot roast smells absolutely divine" as a way of acknowledging A's clear intent. Such a patient approach is reminiscent of an improv **curve ball** that offers something new without any rush to weave it immediately into the known context trusting that a richer connection awaits further down the line.

5. **Honor stated realities over inferences (or yet-to-be defined elements).** While there are moments when an action can be repurposed or morphed into a more connected choice, I find that it's helpful to err on the side of fully embracing any *stated* reality. If Player B announces, "All this digging is making me thirsty," it's unhelpful for Player A to wrestle with this established fact now awkwardly in order to further a preconceived intent: "Why do you always call the vacuuming digging? The living room looks great!" Once Player B has named their activity, that needs to be honored. We might learn that Player B has, in fact, been digging through the floorboards of the kitchen, or that Player A has been cooking in an outdoor brick oven, but as would be the case with any improv offer, it's important that we don't negate or start to argue about the building blocks of the scene as improvisers. Justifying is an invitation to bring us together rather than have us doggedly hold onto our own preferred path or preconception.

Final Thought

While justifying is an improviser's bread and butter on the stage and a critical tool for crafting stories and journeys, there is one place that it can prove less than helpful: in our postmortems and note sessions. When a director or fellow player offers feedback on the effectiveness of a scenic choice, or perhaps raises a concern about how they felt on the receiving end of a plot point, avoid feeling the need to justify your actions. In improv it's a given that the path emerges before us as we go and that it's likely you had a (really good) reason for making the choice that you did, but it's good form to also realize that our (really good) intentions may still have resulted in an unhelpful or inorganic moment, or that we may have inadvertently thwarted a fellow player. Take the note.

> **Related Entries:** Accepting, Commandment #1, Curve Ball, Offer, Postmortem
> **Antonyms:** Blocking, Bulldozing, Commenting
> **Synonyms:** No Mistakes, Weaving
> **Connected Game:** Justify Circle

KINDNESS

I will freely admit that the initial impetus for this entry was a desire to find a suitable "K" for my improvisational stroll through the alphabet! But the more I've mused on the topic of **Kindness**, the more I've realized that we probably don't talk about (and practice) it enough. Whether a desire to serve or forge community is inherent within your performance practice (as is the case with Theatre of the Oppressed and Sociodrama modes) or your work assumes a more commercial or competitive edge, we should consciously consider how we are interacting and collaborating. One of North America's improv pioneers, Viola Spolin, explicitly connects this concept to the craft itself when she writes, "Theater games do not inspire 'proper' moral behavior (good/bad), but rather seek to free each person to feel his or her own true nature, out of which a felt, experienced, actual love of neighbor will appear."[2] So, let us consider how to…

Practice Kindness Toward…

1. **Yourself.** Improvisers, alongside artists of all stripes, tend to be harder on themselves than anyone else could possibly be. In the realm of spontaneity, struggles and slips are not only inevitable, but most would agree are actually key to the live creative process. When we are unable to forgive ourselves for our missteps the very act of holding onto this negative energy undoubtedly increases the chances of ongoing heady struggles and fumbles. Allow yourself room for growth, acknowledge that there will be good choices (scenes, shows…) and not-so-good choices (scenes, shows…) and strive to set your focus on the emergent present rather than the stumbles of the fading past. When we're unable to show ourselves this form of kindness, we can become a source of creeping negativity that can infect the whole company or performance. Such a flagellating stance also closes us off to receiving notes and learning from our mistakes in a way that can arm us for future victories.

2. **Your characters.** In our pursuit for onstage conflict and dramatic tension, we can accidentally default to a stance of meanness or contrariness: "My scene partner's character loves this item, choice, or activity, so I'll hate it or find it mundane to add some energy…" While these dynamics certainly have a place in our work, we shouldn't overlook the power of embodying characters and relationships that display joy, love, and empathy. Some of my favorite scenes as an audience member involve watching characters who are clearly finding pleasure in each other's company or who unite in the face of conflict rather than become at odds (typically inexplicably artificial odds, no less) with one another. An attitude of kindness and empathy also invites more complex and dynamic representations that are less likely to fall into stereotypes or clichéd one-dimensionality. What's more, when we're endowed as a *seemingly* villainous persona, exploring a greater variety of shades that reveal an inner turmoil or beauty helpfully adds all manner of depth and relevance to the scene.

3. **Other improvisers.** Just as we should give ourselves a break when our work doesn't meet our own expectations, so too should we display generosity with our collaborators. In my experience, when we are on the receiving end of a clumsy or problematic offer, the initiator is typically more than aware of their misstep (the audience will often let them know this immediately). When debriefing the work, assume good faith in your castmates' intentions and leave room for their own artistic journey and development just as you hope they are displaying the same kindness to you and your craft. If a teammate is *clearly* aware that they broke a trust or carelessly crossed a boundary, little is to be gained from a public flogging. And even in circumstances where a fellow player *isn't* aware that their actions were hurtful or unwelcome, a gentle discussion is much more likely to induce change than an angry confrontation. In a proactive sense, also be aware of your fellow players' needs and hopes going into a performance: if you can set them up for joy and success, why wouldn't you do that?

4. **Your audience.** Lastly, let us not forget our audiences – please! I use improv in a wide variety of settings ranging from high octane laugh fests to edgy and sincere narrative long-forms. Regardless of where you are performing on this inspiring spectrum of improv, it's important that we are aware of our audience's needs and expectations.

From simple factors, such as are there any young children present in the auditorium, to more complex factors, such as has there been anything disturbing in the news that could be triggering, we should strive to take *informed* and *deliberate* risks. While some of my long-form work tackles rather intense themes at times (bigotry, poverty, mental health...) our audiences are forewarned and we strive, albeit imperfectly, to explore these issues with care and complexity. It is certainly *possible* to tackle weighty topics in a short-form modality, but care should be shown in raising sensitive subjects, especially if the form does not allow more than the briefest nod or players are grabbing at potentially offensive material for mere shock value. Knowingly satirizing societal blindnesses or conventions is also markedly different than carelessly reinjuring parts of our audience for an easy response or cheap laugh. One approach resembles the adage of being a little cruel to be kind by appropriately ruffling the feathers of complacency, while the other can just feel plain cruel...

Final Thought

All four of these focal points are highly important, but I suspect that practicing kindness first and foremost to ourselves and our craft will quickly enable this energy to emanate toward our other collaborators. As they say, a little kindness...

> **Related Entries:** Archetype, Audience, Ensemble, Postmortem **Antonyms:** Anger, Pettiness
> **Synonyms:** Empathy, Forgiveness, Love
> **Connected Game:** Nicer Than You

LEVELS

Gene Kozlowski, a theatre professor in my MFA program, astutely noted that no one wants to watch a character angrily yell or indulgently whine for any protracted length of time. In the scripted tradition, this can be a particular trap when we approach monologue work as it's tempting to find one energy or emotion and then just sit in it because it "feels good." This same cautionary wisdom holds true when we improvise. If we want vibrant performances, then we must embrace **Levels** – physically, verbally, emotionally, and in terms of how we approach our content.

Example

Four players stand awkwardly in an unintentional line as they engage in under-energized banter...

OR

An angry premise between rival lovers results in a three-minute uninterrupted yelling fest...

OR

Players perform a scene in which characters bemoan their relationships without any shades of humor, irony, joy, or satiric commentary...

OR

A scene unfolds exploring the issue of peer pressure at a college party, but characters are worn lightly and never develop beyond cheesy stereotypes...

Ways to Level Up

1. **Physical levels.** Performers working in the scripted tradition will generally spend *hours* exploring and polishing scenic staging, crafting images to steer the audiences' focus, or placing characters in particularly strong positions for climactic moments. We are undoubtedly at a disadvantage in this regard when it comes to improvisational staging – our physical choices are unavoidably more fluid and contingent upon the vicissitudes of spontaneous play. But there are simple adjustments that we can deploy in order to make our physical presence more interesting and engaging. We can avoid standing in lines (or just standing passively in our scene work altogether) in lieu of exploring more pleasing angles or clusters. While we want to avoid the trap of needlessly sitting in our scenes (it can prove oddly challenging to launch yourself from this perch if you're not careful), a few well-placed chairs or blocks can afford helpful new possibilities so that everyone isn't on the same plane. Similarly, while we must be mindful that we remain in our audiences' sightlines, remember that the floor, too, is our friend, and we can crouch, recline, or take a knee to add variety. A simple but helpful tip to remember is that if you are making the same physical choice as your teammates (and this isn't intentionally assisting the story or game) then try a different choice to break up the pattern.
2. **Verbal levels.** Some performance venues pose acoustical challenges, especially if you are working

in found or outdoor spaces, but it's equally important to explore levels and range in your vocal work. Players who tend to over or under-project may frustrate their viewers. If you're working in a new space, it's helpful to test the acoustics with some of your fellow performers – with or without microphones – so you have a sense of any potentials or pitfalls (noting that a space can change significantly once an audience is present). Recalling that unrestrained yelling can quickly prove off-putting (and perhaps even triggering), be cognizant to explore your full range: stark contrasts in volume and tone are dynamic and effective. On the other end of the volume spectrum, if your default vocal energy is timid or reserved, explore passions and characters that encourage greater vocal presence. Thunderous proclamations or hushed confessions are beautiful contributions, but if they become monotonous norms or stale routines, then, like any other unexamined pattern on the improv stage, they will benefit greatly from being deliberately and dynamically broken.

3. **Emotional levels.** Just as we should strive to find levels in our physical and verbal choices, so too should we seek emotional variety and depth. There isn't *one* way to play a given emotion, and most humans don't stay in the same shade of any emotion for an extended period of time. Anger can prove the most dramatic when it has climaxed into a whispered threat; passion can transform from a soft smolder to an exuberant celebration; pride can manifest as a subtle knowing look or a boisterous proclamation! A character needn't (shouldn't) feel obliged to present any given emotion in one static manner. Also, consider taking this approach of varying emotional magnitude when it comes to mirroring or sharing your partners' state of mind – they might be furious while you are mildly perturbed, or passionately enamored while you are quietly happy… The concept of opposites can prove helpful in this regard as well. (Michael Shurtleff writes vividly about this in his *Audition*.) Sure, we might be exploring a scene between rivals that invites a good dose of jealousy, but if there are tinges of admiration as well the emotional landscape will deepen. Inversely, a courtship scene between two lovers will likely include attraction or passion, but some shades of agony or indifference could unleash an even broader spectrum of interesting hues.

4. **Content levels.** Finally, consider levels when it comes to the material and characters we are inhabiting. Some modes of improv more explicitly demand multi-faceted portrayals – such as performances in the healing arts – but even mainstream commercial enterprises can (should) benefit from looking beyond the surface of a scenario or character. Mining our work for new and cogent discoveries will also keep our content fresh for ourselves, our scene partners, and our patrons. When faced with a tried-and-true premise or relationship, we can look to unlock new facets or elements: what is a contradiction that our character might embody; is there an important side of an issue or theme that is rarely given voice; can we humanize through empathy a character that might otherwise become a simplistic or damaging stereotype? As improvisers, it can feel as if we're often returning to the same well to drink once more, but we can level up by jarring ourselves out of past ways of looking at stock material.

Final Thought

Another professor in the same acting program, Sonny Bell, would often note that performers should all have two tattoos (on their posteriors) reading "must be seen" and "must be heard." Ultimately, it will not matter if we are crafting beautifully nuanced work if it does not effectively communicate to the back rows of our auditoriums. Pursuing appropriate levels certainly assists in this regard. But beyond this embracement of craft, it's equally important to pursue the full range of human expression. Exploring levels, in all the facets of our work, encourages a greater awareness of our partners, breaks us out of unhelpful ruts and patterns, and adds depth and dynamism to the characters and actions that populate our imaginary worlds.

Related Entries: Commandment #7, Emotional Truth, Stage Picture **Antonyms:** Talking Heads, Upstaging **Synonyms:** Physicality, Verbal Skills **Connected Game:** Stand, Sit, Kneel, Lie

LINEAR

A term to describe a style of storytelling that prioritizes plot and connected action. Such works are also known as Aristotelian in more traditional playwriting parlance.

Antonym: Circular

LOCATION

The physical setting and parameters for a scene or play.

Synonyms: Environment, Where

LONG-FORM

Mick Napier offers a popular take on a common means for dividing improv styles: "Time is a context to describe the *art form* of improvisation. There is *short form* and *long form*. (Bizarrely, it's the only *art form* which categorizes itself in length of time.)"[3] Theorists before me have noted that there are, in fact, other genres of art that also classify themselves by time or length (one-act plays/full-length plays, short stories/novels, haiku/renga poetry and the like), but the nomenclature of **Long-Form** (in contrast to **short-form**) remains widely used at least in North American improv circles. Many, myself included, seek to deliberately elide or soften the boundaries between these two spontaneous impetuses as, increasingly, improvisers train and utilize skills from what were once, at least in theory, sparring camps. Players may prefer to perform in one modality over the other: this typically corresponds with how they took their first steps in the art form. But it's undeniable that these improv schools have thoroughly cross-pollinated, and rightly so, as both approaches have a great deal to offer.

The easiest distinction between long- and short-form is that the former tends to craft a connected piece while the latter provides discrete scene units that often take the form of competitive improv games or a cabaret-style revue. Even this description, however, quickly reveals how problematic (and pointless) it is to seek to draw a solid line separating the two spontaneous instincts. *Gorilla Theatre*, for example, features a series of improv scenes or games much like its kin *Theatresports*, but some scenes *may in fact* be connected through the directors' themes or visions. And even franchises such as *Theatresports* and *ComedySportz* – which tend to serve as the poster children for short-form – frequently develop meta-narratives that grow and intertwine over the entire course of the competition: "Will the underdogs ever seize victory from the seasoned professionals," or "can the improvisers appease the impossible-to-please judge to finally gain a perfect score?"

That being said, whether we like it or not, we have now inherited these prolific defining terms and improvisers tend to use them as a shorthand to explain their conceit or passion to friends and audiences (although I remain unsure as to whether an audience ultimately cares if a show defines itself as short- or long-form so much as they are concerned with experiencing a performance that is *good*). "Long-form" increasingly has become an ill-fitting title that loosely describes a multitude of approaches to structuring and crafting an improvisational event. So, in an effort to further elucidate this energy, I offer an incomplete list of inspirations that can serve as a centripetal force uniting our "longer" spontaneous efforts.

Systems to Structure Your Long-Form

1. **Theme-based structures.** Many Western improv long-forms embody a thematic approach to storytelling, providing a series of scenes that are connected by an over-arching concept or idea that may be provided by the audience as the original inspiration or that emerges gradually from the scenes themselves as they play off one another. These pieces often feel like an anthology of loosely connected and fragmented short stories amassed around a commonality. A major plus of such forms is that, by design, they are porous and inclusive: many ideas and characters can be thrown against the proverbial improv wall as there is ample room to edit and discard elements that aren't particularly strong or don't "stick" (to continue my pasta analogy). Examples include the omnipresent *Harold* where typically one word or phrase gets the ball rolling, the *Armando Diaz* where a guest monologist provides fragments of a true story that morph into original scenes, and the *Lotus* in which thematic connections are organically discovered as players rotate between three different premises. I would also include most "organic" or "free-form" improv in this category too as it typically seeks to weave emergent threads and ideas throughout the duration of the play.

Host: "All of our scenes tonight are going to be – at least loosely – inspired by an idea that we get from you, our audience. So, who here has a favorite word that they don't mind sharing...?"

2. **Location-based structures.** Other long-forms rely heavily on location as a defining feature. In some

instances, this is a fictional or theatrical locale that unites all the action and characters. In other cases, the action may take place in literal locations that are crucial to the performance conceit. Many long-forms assume a "poor theatre" approach to the craft, with physical elements, costumes, and props all being manifestations of the players' and audiences' imaginations. Location-based structures allow for the possibility of a more sumptuous design approach (although this is by no means the norm). Incorporating more "traditional" theatrical design elements can, in turn, enable art works that are more easily recognizable and accessible to patrons who aren't improv aficionados. *Close Quarters* provides a good example of a theatre form contained in one greater location that replays the same few minutes in time from multiple perspectives. Interactive and site-specific performances, such as *Tony n' Tina's Wedding*, *Finnegan's Wake,* and theme park strolling players engaged in *Streetmosphere*, illustrate modes that use actual "real" spaces to craft immersive events. While some of these forms definitely incorporate highly structured elements or moments, the very presence of an audience that is invited to play along demands an improvisational ethos and commitment.

Cast member: (*welcoming audience guests into a real church*) "We're all so glad that you could make it to witness this special event. So, which side of the church will you be sitting on today? The service should be starting shortly…"

3. **Relationship-based structures.** A third unifying possibility is that of character and relationship. While this element is undoubtedly featured in (most) other long-forms as well, in these particular cases, the concept of exploring relationships stands clearly at the center of the endeavor. Often, characters are deliberately shuffled into new and/or pre-set combinations that allow for the audience to see the cast of players in different lights and scenarios. Such forms allow performers to dig deeper into their characters as they tend to only play one each for the duration of the piece. There is also great mileage in seeing how different facets or faces of a character emerge depending on their company. *La Ronde* strings together a series of two-person vignettes with each character performing in (initially) two scenes in a row with a different partner. *Family Reunion* utilizes a location-specific frame with a series of family members escaping onto a back porch or similar in dynamic combinations. *Pass-Off Scene* (you may know it as *Follow the Leaver*) explores a similar energy but with characters now in motion, moving through various rooms or parts of a greater location in real time.

Director: "For tonight's show, I'm looking for an event or occasion that might bring members of an extended family together, such as a baby shower or funeral…"

4. **Narrative and dramaturgical-based structures.** I've grouped these two long-form approaches together as they share an interest and commitment to "the canon." Narrative improv typically seeks to replicate the tropes, structures, and story arcs of literary traditions, while dramaturgical improv digs deeply into historical antecedents and customs to inspire play. These two approaches may or may not be combined in the service of the one project. The resulting structures tend to be more linear – echoing their models in theatre, film, television, and literature – although this is not to say that there may not be *many* threads and characters that the audience follows. These works can have the advantage of appealing to more "traditional" theatregoers and art consumers as attendees often have a better chance of understanding the central premise and basic rules of the game, especially if they are familiar with the source material in question. Parodies, style-work, and homages generally fall squarely into this category. Examples include the wide array of improv Shakespeare, murder mystery, and musical pieces that appear on many improvisational stages.

Player King: "The bard has penned many famous epic tragedies and comedies. What is an original title that has never been seen before that can inspire our Shakespearean folly today?"

5. **Efficacy-based structures.** Finally, I don't believe that it is common (yet) to also include service-focused practices under the heading of long-form, but many of the healing arts certainly belong here as well. These approaches may also incorporate some of the structural devices listed above, but their unabashed focus is on efficacy and personal or social change. Playback Theatre organizes a series of warm-ups, short scenes, and reenactments that are performed in the service of those in attendance. Players talk about the "red thread" that emerges in any given performance connecting stories in an organic and meaningful way. Boal's Theatre of the Oppressed forms similarly deploy the tools of live performance

as spect-actors can interrupt staged scenarios, replacing performers in the hopes of finding new more satisfying strategies and endings. While Viola Spolin and her contemporaries are often recognized for their contributions to more "mainstream" theatrical improv and sketch comedy, many of her games were initially developed with an eye toward increasing play and communication between children from different cultures and backgrounds. In each of these cases, although performances might include smaller units or scenes, there is an undeniable connective tissue uniting the events that reflects a long-form lens.

Conductor: "Did anyone come to the performance today with a story that they wanted to see enacted, or perhaps you've been inspired by one of our earlier shared experiences…?"

Final Thought

Obviously, this is not an exhaustive list, and many practitioners are actively pursuing and developing hybrid forms that combine these artistic impulses in exciting and new ways. And there are unquestionably other organizational taxonomies one could use to describe this type of work (language-based, movement-based, music-based…). But I think there's a value in recognizing past historical trends and successes as we seek to chart an enticing and effective improvisational path forward.

> **Related Entries:** Dramaturgical Improv, Improvisation, Short-Form **Antonym:** Chaos
> **Synonym:** Narrative Long-Form
> **Connected Game:** La Ronde

LOOKING BACKWARDS

Bernie Sahlins suggests, "… if you can't find an ending, look at your opening."[4] **Looking Backwards** is a common improv mantra and strategy. I tend to think of Keith Johnstone's teachings when I stumble back into this notion as this was where I first encountered the concept. (I've quoted his paradigmatic passage on the subject in my **callbacks** entry.) The thought of shaping the future path of an improv scene can truly feel overwhelming as there are almost endless possibilities. When one considers past actions and events, however, the next scenic move frequently appears without this same sense of panic or strained effort. This theory of looking backwards also resonates with what we are told about human behavior in general; namely, that the best predictor of someone's actions is what they are known to have done in the past. It would follow, then, that what characters have *already* done can shed considerable light on what they could do next when the scenic path ahead feels unsure.

Example

Three players have begun their scene by standing in line to get their books signed at a Barnes and Noble. Player A is hugging their well-worn copy of the book in question as if it were their child; Player B appears to be more interested in their cell phone and scrolls through screen after screen; Player C seems jittery which may or may not be explained by the coffee cup they are nervously clutching. Player D, a store employee, stands somewhat dispassionately at the front of the line that ends at a currently empty table.

Player D: "One more minute…"

Reverse Psychology

1. **Look backwards… at what you've just done.** Sometimes, the most interesting choices are instinctual moves that we may have contributed almost unconsciously. As players consider what to do next, they should not neglect the small things that they have already created. Often, a strong next choice is merely repeating or amplifying what is already happening: Player A can heighten their parental relationship to their book; Player B might adjust their physical position in an effort to get better cell phone reception; Player C could take one more gulp of coffee and experience the hyper-caffeinated results. I'd add that even if your actions are subtle, you should commit to them with attack and specificity. It's difficult to build energy and interest (for you, your fellow players, *and* the audience) if you are blasé about your own first choices.
2. **Look backwards… at what your partners have done.** It's certainly good form to build upon your own game or dynamic, but even greater joy can be found in enabling the journeys of other players and characters. It's not uncommon for an improviser to miss the richness of their own accidental "move," and in such instances, it's an act of improv generosity to give fellow teammates a playful nudge. I've also found that a game or trajectory is

more likely to build when players join *each other's* game rather than only play their own. Be mindful not to name the game or explode it by jumping ahead multiple steps – Player B announces to A "Your book is on fire!" as opposed to simply eyeing the treasured tome with disconcerting curiosity. A gentle echo can be enough to start – Player A pulls out their own cell phone and joins B's efforts to connect to the store Wi-Fi, thereby making everyone's connection slower…

3. **Look backwards… at what's been shelved.** Clearly, this isn't typically applicable to the formative moments of the scene, but as the action continues to grow consider what elements have been well-established and then set aside. In some performance situations, this tactic might also apply to what has occurred in seemingly unrelated scenes or games that occurred *much earlier* in the evening. As is the case with the approaches above, this strategy (essentially a **callback**) is highly contingent upon players creating and remembering *specific* choices. Perhaps Player C sits their coffee cup down on the author's table early in the scene and it is eventually knocked all over Player A's beloved book, or Player B's omnipresent phone, or the esteemed author once they finally arrive. It could also be as simple as Player D continuing to punctuate the scene with unenthusiastic time updates, "One minute late…"

4. **Look backwards… at your contract with the audience.** This is another thought for later in the scene, but the philosophy of looking backwards should also apply to any contracts that have been explicitly or implicitly made with the audience. In the short-form tradition, it can feel anticlimactic if the audience suggestion used to inspire the scene doesn't actually materialize or connect with the action (not to say that we have to shoe-horn ask-fors into *every* scene and can't use them more metaphorically or tangentially to inspire our choices). Your scene or play may have received its launch from a title, which can likewise serve as a compass setting when the path ahead becomes obscured. Improv games will generally come with a set of expectations as well – someone needs to die in Death in a Minute – while similar expectations may emerge from more open scenic forms. Whether you fully honor these contracts (the author arrives, and everyone gets their books signed), or playfully subvert and thwart them (the super fans have lined up at the wrong store), remembering and acknowledging foundational conceits can powerfully enable your next move.

5. **Look backwards… at how this all started.** Lastly, as Sahlins recommends in the opening quote – which I invite you to look back at now – if you feel the scene has lost its thread, sense of direction, or is unable to find a button, consider how your story started. There is usually still something vibrant in the story's residue that you can resuscitate or simply parallel. Does Player A now clutch their *signed* copy of the book even more closely; is Player B desperate to get cell reception so they can post their selfie with the author; does an over-caffeinated Player C vibrate at an even higher frequency? While one would hope that at least one of our protagonists ultimately changes because of their adventures and conflicts, this doesn't mean that they have lost the idiosyncrasies that make them unique. And, frankly, audiences are often tickled when they recognize the return of pre-established behaviors or patterns.

Final Thought

Look at your opening if you can't find an ending… (I'm taking my own advice!)

> **Related Entries:** Advancing, Callback, Reincorporation, Shelving **Antonym:** Over-Originality **Synonyms:** Content, Material, Offer **Connected Game:** Word at a Time Story

LOOKING GOOD

I will confess that this topic title is a little opaque, but I couldn't find a more elegant abbreviation for "making our scene partners look good on stage." Although, in terms of the more obvious definition of looking good, it is also important that improvisers practice good hygiene, dress appropriately to their venues and means, and select clothing that isn't needlessly distracting or prone to infringe upon their movement in unhelpful ways. It's challenging to be fearless if you don't want to get close to some scene partners (or they don't want to get close to *you*), or you spend most of your scenes fidgeting with apparel in a way that isn't enriching your characters.

Looking Good in my intended context here, however, is a shorthand for one of the golden rules of improv: Johnstone observes, "The art of improvisation is to make the other person look good."[5] If everyone on stage is focused on the joy and success of their partners, then ideally, everyone leaves the experience happy and satisfied. Such a performance stance also has the benefit of moving the focus away from ourselves – which tends to create solipsistic and heady improv – and places it on our fellow players – which tends to forge more dynamic relationships and stories.

Example

Player A: (as a parent while they leave the scene) "OK, now don't do anything I wouldn't do."

OR

Player B: (throwing the focus to their primed scene partner) "Well, you know what your mother always says in moments like these…"

OR

Player C: (entering the room with a finger against their ear) "I've finished the sweep, Madam President. The Oval Office is secure."

OR

Player D: (joining an abandoned teammate who has been left awkwardly alone on stage) "I'm so sorry I'm late. Please tell me you haven't been standing outside the restaurant this whole time…"

OR

Player E: (backstage in the greenroom during intermission) "I've had a lot of stage time already. Is anyone else craving more?"

Implementing the Golden Rule

1. **Do less, give more.** This first suggestion is primarily for type A improvisers who enjoy starting scenes and leading the narrative charge. (I very much fall into this category myself.) If no one else is hankering to launch the next scene, sure, step into the fray, but make sure you are giving that extra second to allow players with different performance tempos a chance to do so as well. If you're about to enter as your *third* character in a three-minute scene, consider deferring to teammates who have generously waited in the wings instead. If you've had your moment of finesse in a called game, look to enable others to rotate into the spotlight rather than seizing such opportunities again and again. Improvisation is *exciting* and it's easy for players to let this excitement get the better of them when it comes to sharing the wealth. I *know* I still fall into this trap, but you normally have a whole evening of scenes to course correct. Just as stories suffocate under the burden of too many offers, so too can scenes ultimately suffer from too much of *you*.

2. **Gift the payoff.** Competitive shows and companies can put players at odds with each other a little: who can come up with the quickest punchline, or offer the most novel variation in the scene? While some games need this sporting energy to thrive (most line games, for instance), I believe taking this mindset into our scene work wholesale rarely serves our ensembles or final product. Some of my most cherished moments onstage have been the result of gifting the payoff. Target rhyming is a lovely example of this where you set up a fellow teammate further down the line with a fantastic word by offering up a lesser or more challenging relative – if we're singing a song about nurses the first player might end their line with "machination" to allow their partner the superior rhyme of "vaccination." This wonderfully generous strategy can apply to many other situations as well, such as setting up a punchline for another to land, seeing a connection but allowing a teammate (or even the audience) to make it explicit, or embracing an opportunity to pitch a moment of finesse to a fellow player as you know it's in their wheelhouse.

3. **Play second fiddle.** And sometimes it's important for the scene, quite simply, just not to be about *you*. If we keep elevating the same people into the role of protagonist again and again, we're likely to get the same narratives again and again. Even if you start the scene there is no reason that you can't use this time to literally set the stage for the arrival of another, more important, character. If you tend to play high status characters your voice will often become more central to the story's arc, so exploring lower status sidekicks, confidants, and underlings will add a whole new array of supporting tactics to your improv arsenal. As our community continues to strive toward the ideals of inclusiveness inherently ensconced in the DNA of improv, it's not enough to just include diverse voices in the background; instead, we must seek meaningful ways to enable new stories and experiences to stand front and center. Rotating who wears the mask of the protagonist regularly is one simple step in this direction (as is exploring forms where the very notion of a singular protagonist is challenged or dismantled).

4. **Make the sacrifice.** It is so tempting to race into the scene that is playfully thriving and probably

doesn't need your presence while hiding in the wings when another scene struggles and desperately needs an injection of assistance. When we are committed to making others look good, we need to rewire these common instincts. If a scene is succeeding uproariously, support your teammates by *not* entering so that they can play through their own premise unhampered – or perhaps exiting if the scene is becoming clumsily crowded. There will certainly be times when a cascade of entrances mirroring the current dynamic *becomes* the game of the scene, but this needn't be a default. Similarly, a lot of trust can be lost when a struggling scene doesn't receive the help it needs (even if no one really knows what this help should look like). Merely feeling that your teammates are continuing to stand beside you in a mucky scene can send a loud message and forge camaraderie within the company and with your audience.

5. **Check in often and openly.** Finally, commit to checking in regularly and frankly with your fellow improvisers. Unlike scripted pieces, an improv show can change paths during the actual performance and address imbalances or missteps. In some of my own long-form pieces it has become standard practice to simply ask a few open questions backstage at intermission: "Is anyone feeling under-featured or shut out?" or "Is anyone feeling overused or unsupported?" More weighty conversations regarding improviser choices or habits are generally best left until the postmortem as "scolding" an excited improviser for monopolizing the action just moments before they return to the stage isn't likely to do anyone a favor. (Not that scolding should serve as a tactic in healthy postmortems in general.) But taking a moment to quickly assess trends and rhythms usually proves helpful: I think this is particularly important when there is no outside coach or director eye to offer such observations. For example, in *Lights Up*, a musical format that uses four singing improvisers, we'll routinely want to make sure that someone hasn't ended up singing four ballads in act one while another player has done little more than some background weaving. It can be daunting for improvisers to speak up so it's important to work as a company to build this trust and to honor what has been shared.

Final Thought

Many of my own favorite and cherished improv moments have occurred when I have been on the receiving (or, as noted above) the giving end of this philosophy. Moving our focus onto the success of our partners so often results in a confidence and clarity of choice that simultaneously elevates our own work. Ego in improv is a complex dynamic, and many of us pursue performance because it fills some innate need or desire in our own psyche; but, when we're able to harness this passion for the benefit of others, everyone wins.

Related Entries: Commandment #3, Ensemble, Hosting, Postmortem, You **Antonyms:** Shining, Winning **Synonyms:** Balance, Inclusiveness **Connected Game:** One-Downing

LOVE

If you were to ask me on any given day what one ingredient is commonly missing from run-of-the-mill improv scenes my instinctual answer would most definitely be **Love**. In our quest toward dynamism – which often regrettably takes the form of conflict – love and its many splendid manifestations are easily overlooked. And yet, while there are certainly no cure-alls in improv, it strikes me that it would be a truly exceptional scene that could not benefit from adding love, deepening its presence, or finding greater nuance in how we are applying it to our actions and scene partners. Many improvisers are comfortable bringing anger and its darker companions to the stage; those that are equally adept at displaying heartfelt love are, sadly, less common unless you're fortunate enough to be routinely playing in service-oriented forms.

Spreading the Love Around

1. **Find love in your own characters.** As the (admittedly problematic) saying goes, "you can't truly love someone else unless you love yourself" and I believe this also applies to our characters. Narrow characters that are merely "humanesque" will rarely have the depth to go the distance, especially if you're working in long-form structures. When we wear our characters lightly, it can seem tempting to see them as simple creatures; but when we explore their inner vitality and humanity, such personae can quickly become more vibrant and relevant. What are their qualities that you admire? Are there struggles that you share with your creations? What do those closest to them find worthy of adulation? If we are taking

on characters that, at first blush, are villainous or antagonistic, it becomes even more important to nurture these facets worthy of appreciation, even if these details are left largely beneath the surface. Pursuing more sympathetic hues also serves as a defense against sliding into uninterrogated stereotypes that typically display an outsider's curt summation (rather than an insider's understanding) of a person.

2. **Find love in your onstage relationships.** The dramatic canon is filled with scenes between characters that are deeply invested in each other whether they are romantically involved, fellow family members, or boldly united in a cause or struggle. We're often warned about placing strangers at the center of our action: a primary reason for this well-founded leeriness is that such characters rarely have sufficient backstory to forge a meaningful bond. And yet, with novice and more experienced players alike, improv scenes between close lovers, loyal relatives, and cherished friends can all start to resemble lackluster stranger scenes when no attention is paid to exploring deeper emotional connections. Remembering that love can assume many guises – attraction, intense devotion, deep respect, and oh so many more – it is worth our time as players to invest in these dynamics. It can be as simple as reflecting on the performer's qualities that you admire or esteem to begin the process (noting important personal boundaries and the like). Finding the love between you and your partners also increases the likelihood that you'll have the presence of mind to make sure they're looking good and enjoying themselves on stage as well.

3. **Find love in the moments of conflict.** While I tend to think of love as being – to some degree – an antidote to conflict, the relationship between

Figure 10.1 Some of the many faces of love as seen in *Upton Abbey*, *It's All Greek to Me*, and *The Lost Comedies of William Shakespeare* (Set design: Lisa Cody-Rapport; Sound design: Robert Miller). Photo credit: Tony Firriolo [left and right]; and Scott Cook Photography [center].

these two scenic elements is considerably more complex. Adding love *to* a conflict is actually a fantastic method for raising the stakes and heightening interest. When you think about the people in your own life who are most likely to cause conflict, frequently they also currently or once held places of great affection (or perhaps thwarted such opportunities). If we don't need or want anything from our opponent anymore and have given up completely on finding any redemption or reconnection, it would follow that we'd have little to lose by just leaving the scene there and then. It is the love that gives us the reason and stubbornness to stay and fight. Keeping this emotional vulnerability front of mind can add poignancy and prevent familiar scenarios from becoming trite. Love such as this can also add internal tensions and conflict *within* the character which is a powerful addition to any scene.

4. **Find love in the craft.** There is something palpable and invigorating about being in the presence of company members who *love* to play. While we are surely allowed down days and moments of nonchalance (no one can exude "chalance" all the time!), I think it's important to explore ways to stay connected to this passion. For most of us in the field, improv is a labor of love providing rewards that are often less about remuneration and more about community, connection, and expression. If the craft becomes more labor than love, this can have an influence well beyond our own work and progress. And it's markedly more difficult to find the love in the scene if you have very little joy being on the stage in the first place. It's critically important that we do not infect our improv communities with our own negativity or complacency. You can read a little more about this challenge in my entry about **commitment**.

Final Thought

I considered including the audience as a potential focus here too, but I think it's easy for performers to be led astray by seeking a fickle audience's love and accolades. I also don't think I'm alone in finding that trying to impress an audience (or a special someone in the audience) nearly always results in inferior work and play. Perhaps rather than striving to earn an audience's elusive love, we would all be better served by sharpening the ways in which we display our love *for* the audience, whether this is providing them with a respite from a challenging week or news cycle, offering them an inclusive venue in which they feel seen and appreciated, or crafting characters and stories with empathy and nuance in mind. Or, actually, a delightful cocktail of all these dynamics now that I come to think of it!

I'll close with one last variant of love as articulated by Paul Sills:

The irony is that the art which is most exciting today is impermanent and not meant to last except as an act of love [...] It just comes out between people. It doesn't want to be written down. It passes in the moment and disappears.[6]

Related Entries: Consent, Emotional Truth, Freshness, Kindness **Antonym:** Conflict
Synonyms: Empathy, Joy, Passion
Connected Game: Mantras

NOTES

1. Del Close's key improv rule as recalled by Rob Kozlowski, *The Art of Chicago Improv: Shortcuts to Long-Form Improvisation.* Portsmouth, NH: Heinemann, 2002. p. 27.
2. Viola Spolin, *Improvisation for the Theater. A Handbook of Teaching and Directing Techniques.* 3rd ed. Evanston, IL: Northwestern UP, 1999. p. xv.
3. Mick Napier, *Improvise. Scene From the Inside Out.* 2nd ed. Englewood, CO: Meriwether Publishing, 2015. p. 5.
4. Bernard Sahlins, *Days and Nights at the Second City. A Memoir, with Notes on Staging Review Theatre.* Chicago: Ivan R. Dee, 2001. p. 171.
5. Keith Johnstone as quoted by Lyn Pierse, *Theatresports Down Under.* 2nd ed. Sydney, Australia: Improcorp, 1995. p. 37.
6. Paul Sills quoted in Jeffrey Sweet's, *Something Wonderful Right Away.* 1996. New York: Limelight Editions, 1978. p. 21.

#YatesItUp

M/N

MAKE MATTERS WORSE

Raising the stakes and energy of a scene by introducing strategic and proportionate obstacles and context. In theory, making matters better serves a similar energizing function, although it is markedly less common.

> **Synonyms:** Heighten, Obstacle

MAPPING

Using the language and tropes of one situation as subtext and inspiration for another only loosely related premise.

> **Related Entry:** Game of the Scene

MATERIAL

The reach of improvisational performance repeatedly proves itself to be considerable and all-encompassing. While scripted works, by necessity, become static and subsequently slow or unable to purposefully respond to changes in the sociopolitical landscape, improv's immediacy can quickly weave news and cultural shifts into the performance event. This ability to adapt provides both an innate strength and challenge as improvisational **Material** is simultaneously enticingly responsive and potentially overwhelming in its limitlessness. A playwright can rework and privately reject earlier attempts; improvisers, however, do not enjoy this level of premeditation nor after-the-fact reflection and revision. Furthermore, content parameters are often moving targets with boundaries being reset after new infractions or ruptures have been discovered in the heat of performance.

Janet Coleman articulates the ideal improvising state of mind when she describes the paradigmatic performer:

> The habit of responding to audience suggestions and accepting all premises make improvisational actors curious, informed, and keen to the changes in their cities, their country, their cultural landscape. The practice of tapping into their own supply of subconscious material opens new territory for them as writers, directors, and as lone performance artists.[1]

Although embracing this sensitivity can feel daunting as a practitioner when it comes to accessing and molding creative inspiration and content, there are tried and true approaches to help shape and direct this potential limitlessness…

Example

Two improvisers stand on an empty stage…

Sources of Material Inspiration

Content can emerge with ease as you respond and react to numerous impetuses, including:

1. **Your life.** It's an oft-quoted adage that authors should "write what they know," and this is also excellent advice for aspiring improvisers. While fantastical adventures in fictional worlds certainly have their appeal and place in our craft, it is frequently sufficient for players to just bring

themselves – their stories, passions, fears, and experiences – to the stage for exploration. When unsure how to react or respond, an improviser's honest and personal reaction will nearly always be enough to keep the creative spark thriving. That being said, improvisers are best served by not settling for just bringing what they know *today* to their work. Players benefit from actively pursuing a spirit of intrigue: improvisers who are *interested* in the world typically make *interesting* players and characters. If a scene reveals a lacuna in your knowledge, by all means accept this as an invitation to find out a little more about the topic at hand and do a little (or more than a little) research.

2. **Your scene partners.** A potential pitfall of the above advice is that you might privilege your own knowledge base or experiences over those of your fellow players. When crafting spontaneous material, also actively look for ways to prioritize and support the stories of others. Whether you play as allies, foils, or foes, there are ample opportunities to elevate others' voices and narratives. In these moments, it remains helpful to merely react openly and honestly as the action emerges. And don't overlook the importance of simply giving others' material the space it needs to flourish – some scenes will thrive more fully when collaborators knowingly and lovingly support it from the wings. When you throw yourself bravely into the unfamiliar fray, also be open to adjustments and feedback. If a fellow player observes a blindness or limitation in a character (or, perhaps, in your assumption or knowledge as a player) recognize this as a chance to learn more about the human experience from a perspective other than your own.

3. **Your audience.** Improvisational theatre often receives a launching point (or many) from the audiences it serves in the form of ask-fors and suggestions. These provide a great way to push you out of tried and tested patterns and scenarios if you are imaginative in how you both elicit and then utilize these prompts. As I discuss at greater length in my earlier **ask-for** entry, the way you pitch your question will greatly influence the range – or lack thereof – of outcomes, so it's worth your time to consider how to help your audience keep the improv inspired and fresh. Similarly, while it's a wise approach to trust your obvious instincts and reactions when responding to these prompts, there can also be a value in "skipping a step," especially when it comes to launching the scene. Not all scenes inspired by "plumber" need to begin in a bathroom, nor do all scenes responding to "elevator" need to feature a mechanical break-down between floors. As you strive to make material vibrant, throwing out the stale opening salvo goes a long way to keeping everyone on their toes. Maintaining a heightened awareness of your audience, their expectations, and reactions *during* your scene work can also helpfully create content parameters. If a family audience encourages more "wholesome" content, embrace this as a challenge and frame your storytelling accordingly.

4. **Your frame.** Content inspiration and guidance frequently emerge from game or show structures and their inherent potentials. It's important to know and honor expectations built into the improvisational event. It generally won't prove effective or helpful to drop an intensely heavy topic into a Canadian Cross during a short-form giggle-fest, or share your most trivial or scatological observation during an earnest healing arts performance. Just as it's important to know your audience, it's equally important to know the intent and spirit of your event and to let this inform your content choices. In many cases, specific games or improv dynamics will also unlock new material in exciting and dynamic ways. Rhyming games, for example, can open up delightfully unexpected pathways as players juggle story and language needs. If an improv structure invites a new way of looking at or organizing your material, happily capitalize on this opportunity to approach familiar problems in unfamiliar ways.

5. **Your world.** Lastly, as Coleman observes, improvisers should find inspiration in the very world and spheres that they occupy. Improv is a theatre of the *here and now* and is subsequently framed by current affairs and events whether or not this is the explicit intent of the performing company. A scripted piece can't suddenly change to address a tragedy in the news (although it might call for a modified curtain speech or lobby announcement); an improv work, on the other hand, will be marked (or marred) by the company's ability to take such an event into consideration. An effective improviser needs to be informed if for no other reason than to avoid pulling a scene into terrain that will cause your patrons undue injury (or to phrase this as a positive, can mine a whimsical recent event for its comedic gold). So, I repeat, pursue a spirit of intrigue. Watch or read the news. If a recent event potentially casts a new light (or shadow) on an established game, character, or approach, apply your best judgment and reassess the most responsible and responsive path forward.

Final Thought

As you contemplate how to best coax and shape material, boundaries may feel suffocating or restrictive, and yet creativity exists in a fruitful tension between boundless chaos and sculpted form. Some traditions esteem "saying the first thing that pops into your head" regardless of whether this "first thing" is well-informed, hurtful, or perhaps even just distastefully ugly. I believe it's possible and healthy to pursue spontaneity and new material while simultaneously acknowledging certain parameters that can help shape and elevate the journey. Improvisers should feel no compunction, for example, editing out thoughts that might cause self-harm or carelessly trigger other participants. What's more, playfully accepting some artistic boundaries – whether these come from our partners, audience, the structures through which we create, or the sociopolitical world around us – should inspire rich new reactions and stories.

The concept of censorship in improv is complex: it is important that players do not edit their choices based on debilitating fear, and most of us seek spaces where passionate voices can be emboldened rather than silenced or further marginalized. When it comes to content, I think it is prudent, therefore, to acknowledge that as we serve as our own playwrights, we also assume a degree of responsibility for what we present to the world *and* what we willingly or absent-mindedly exclude from our stages.

> **Related Entries:** Obvious, Speaking Your Truth, You
> **Antonyms:** Cleverness, Over-Originality
> **Synonym:** Content
> **Connected Game:** Word Association

MISCHIEF

Not taking the work of improv too seriously; allowing inspiration to playfully introduce unanticipated detours and pleasant hurdles.

> **Synonym:** Abandon

MIME

The art of making the physical elements of performance out of nothing more than air and imagination.

> **Synonym:** Space Objects

MISTAKES

Most improvisers concur that there are "no mistakes in improv," thereby acknowledging that even unintended slips and fumbles can create rich potentials and gifts when viewed with joy and then embraced with open arms.

> **Antonyms:** Justification, Weaving

MOTIVATION

The desires and dreams that push a character forward into the dramatic action.

> **Synonym:** Objective

MOVE

An improvisational choice, offer, or contribution to an unfolding game or story progression.

> **Synonym:** Offer

MUGGING

The most prevalent form of **Mugging** takes the form of performers staring and smiling out into an audience as they are – at least in theory – also actively engaged in a scene. It evokes images of young performers peeking out from behind the grand drape as the performance occurs, checking to see if their loved ones are present and enjoying the show. Only on the improv stage, there isn't generally a grand drape and this form of checking in occurs in full view of the company and audience. This habit resembles its improv kinfolk – corpsing, commenting, and breaking – and is typically the nervous manifestation of a performer seeking approval or anxiously taking the temperature of the house. On the surface, it can appear as though the performer is cheating out, assuring that they can be seen or heard; but in practice, muggers are reducing the effectiveness of their work by draining the connection to their characters and the onstage action. Subsequently, as is the case with the related terms above, this improv technique invariably becomes problematic and should be avoided as it takes away more than it adds in all but a few instances. Belt and Stockley provide an alternate, more widely lauded ideal, when they write, "They [improv players] must be concentrated, listening, playing truthfully and honestly, playing off the actions and reactions of others. They must be able to create a reality out of nothing."[2]

So, noting that this tool is generally inadvisable, here are some of those few instances that are worthy of mention where mugging might actually serve the greater improv good...

Example

Player A, a bullish security guard in a department store, approaches a hapless customer (Player B) with a disproportionate sense of aggressiveness...

Player A: "I need you to show me the contents of your bag."

To be continued below...

When Is a Mug Not a Mug...?

1. **When it's an accepted convention.** I tend to assume a representational style of performance when I imagine modern theatrical improv, but there are certainly historical and contemporary traditions that celebrate a more presentational approach, such as period and style-infused pieces, street theatre, or interactive modes. In these cases, overt breaks of the fourth wall may, in fact, be part and parcel of the event. Shakespeare's fool, Molière's maid, or Commedia dell'arte's servant are all more than likely to connect to the audience in such a fashion with a knowing look, eye roll, or perhaps even a more protracted aside or soliloquy. These devices are woven into the very fabric of such genres. This is also the case when characters are deliberately lightly worn in a Brechtian or Boalian fashion so that the performer's point of view is present alongside that of the character they have assumed. In these cases, mugging is no longer a distracting actor habit but rather a dramaturgical tool, stylistic nod, or theatrical weapon.

   Player A: "I need you to show me the contents of your bag..."

   Player B, representing a marginalized societal group that is often berated by oppressive capitalistic mouthpieces, turns to the sympathetic audience and rolls their eyes in recognition of the injustice about to play out...

2. **When it's a tip of the hat.** There is also a recognized tradition of "tipping your hat" in some modern improv circles. This phrase refers to acknowledging an improvisational slip, finesse, or perhaps even an easy laugh. In some ways, this is an after-the-fact equivalent of "calling your shot" when an improviser frames a particularly noteworthy improv move beforehand. As such, a "tip of the hat" consists of a brief pause in the onstage action that playfully winks at a clever or silly move. Some schools even explicitly include the hat tip gesture – imagine you're a Dickensian street-vendor acknowledging a passing member of nobility, if you will! In these playful moments, the offending player (or successful player depending on your point of view) lets the audience know that they recognize the folly that they have just committed. After this brief shared moment of collective appreciation, the prior action resumes relatively unhampered by the self-aware metatheatrical lull. This derivative of mugging will struggle to find a home in heavier or more dramatic pieces seeking fidelity or verisimilitude but can add joyful whimsy in less august environments.

   Player A: "I need you to show me the contents of your bag..."
   Player B: (with an exaggerated and ribald air) "And I need *you* to show me the contents of your head..."

3. **When it's a deliberate critique.** I'd also advocate a mugging variant in moments when it feels appropriate (if not outright necessary) to address something awkward or problematic on stage. This connects with the improv concept of **speaking your truth** or calling it onstage when something currently unfolding is creating unwarranted discomfort or injury to you, your fellow improvisers, or the audience. Players may inadvertently be perpetuating harmful stereotypes, punching down rather than up in a mean-spirited fashion, or oversimplifying complex issues in a way that further marginalizes. In cases such as these it can prove

helpful (if not critical) for the audience to see that the company understands what it has done or is still actively doing. If an older company member has been endowed as a grandparent for the umpteenth time in an evening, or a foreign player's accent has been used once more as the butt of an easy joke, or a teammate has been cast as the "beloved" or "object" without any agency yet again, looking to the audience in commiseration will likely land as being wholly warranted and appropriate.

Player A: "I need you to show me the contents of your bag…"
Player B: "So, just because I'm young you assume that I'm here to steal something…?"

4. **When it's a teacup.**

The author tips his hat…

Final Thought

One could fairly argue that the exceptions I have listed above are quite different than a run-of-the-mill mug where an improviser gormlessly breaks character to look out into the audience. As is so often the case with improv and art in general, context and intent are everything. These exceptional examples all may *look* the same as a nervous glance seeking approval, but in reality, they are functioning in a much more complex way reinforcing stylistic traditions, playfully acknowledging unforced errors, or adding complexity to stale tropes. Mugging, after all, is just another improv tool and it is not so much the tool that is at fault, but rather whether its owner is deploying it from a place of solipsistic panic or informed strength.

> **Related Entries:** Approval, Commenting, Corpsing, Gagging, Speaking Your Truth, Wearing Your Character Lightly
> **Antonym:** Cheating Out **Synonym:** Breaking
> **Connected Game:** Asides

MUSIC

I have always been attracted to musical improvisation and luckily my career has been graced by working with and learning from an array of exceptional improv musicians – from my earliest days with Dunedin Impro, to Chicago *ComedySportz*, Disney's Comedy Warehouse, and now my current home venue, Sak Comedy Lab. Boal observes, "…if one can use music, it should be used a lot; if one can use dance, there should be as much dancing as possible! If one can play with colours, why limit oneself to black and white?"[3] And I couldn't agree more! While my on-campus work generally can't afford a resident musician, these troupes and projects have also benefited from some formidable visiting talent. Helpful communication patterns and performance strategies have emerged from this multitude of short- and long-form experiences. I am writing this book under the assumption that my readership most likely consists of improvising performers and directors rather than musicians, so I offer these observations with that vantage point in mind. However, I acknowledge my considerable debt to the long list of my musician collaborators who have shaped my practices in innumerable ways, and hope that these performer-based tips might also make the impossible task of composing on-the-spot masterpieces a little easier as well!

Example

Player A has just professed, awkwardly, their love for Player B. After a moment, lush music begins to swell, signaling that a song is about to start. Player A takes a breath…

Releasing Your Inner Muse-ic

1. **Breathe.** This is a simple and critical lesson that I keep relearning as an improvisational singer. Don't be afraid of silence in your musical creations. Whether it's the song's preamble or you're taking a lull between verses as you seek inspiration, use these silences to breathe deeply and fully. Your musical work will always benefit when you start from a grounded place of strength as opposed to leaping into a song out of panic. As you breathe, listen *closely* to the clues and signals that your musical collaborator is offering: is there a gift in terms of tempo, mood, pitch, or emotional dynamic? In all likelihood, several of these elements will be in play. Process this information as you breathe while also keeping in mind that these staged moments should be filled with acting and action. Breathing also connects you to the emotions and core of your character, which is generally the best source for dynamic and interesting material. And, as an added bonus, adept musicians can read your breathing and sense when you are prepared to take the leap into lyric.

2. **Communicate.** Don't be afraid to actively communicate with your musical ally as the song develops. The specific tools available to you are likely to heavily depend on the stage configuration of your venue. If the musician is in easy view, you can probably say a lot with a simple look or nod; if you're separated by a considerable distance, you might need to lean more heavily on sweeping gestures, staging, or even verbal cues. Just as musical improvisers should make strong offers, it's more than appropriate for singers to do so lovingly as well. If you want to launch into a sweeping bridge, make a sweeping gesture or change in staging. If you're circling back to the chorus, telescope this with your lyric or maybe just whimsically gesture to players or the audience "chorus!" depending on the style of the production. It's also possible to speak (sing) your truth if your mind can tackle the lyric logistics fast enough. Perhaps the tempo is getting too brisk: you could request a slower pace by singing "My thoughts are speeding so fast that I can't catch my breath…" There are a lot of moving pieces that interact when improvising songs – don't be afraid to playfully let others know what you are experiencing or needing. (More significant or recurring challenges should be addressed during the postmortem.)

3. **Accept.** Just as improvising singers hope that their musician collaborators are setting them up for joyful success, so too must performers strive to empower and make musicians look good. Recognize and accept offers pitched from the piano (or your instrument of choice) just as you would from any other artistic voice engaged in the performance. If we don't view the musician as an equal partner in this magical act of creation, then improvisational trouble will lurk just around the corner. My specific pet peeve in this regard is when a musician senses that the action would now be best served by a sung interlude and so begins to vamp… only to have this offer loiter painfully in the background of the scene – largely ignored by the players – so that it must eventually fade away into nothingness. A similar issue can occur at the end of songs when the musician provides a grand ending only to have the singer push on regardless as they wanted to go for "just one more verse." If a song is pitched (or edited) embrace it. If you're working with underscoring rather than songs – a truly priceless scenic addition in its own right – and a mood shift emanates from the keyboard, be sure to enjoy and justify it. Especially as a company develops knowledge and rapport, it is probable that a well-intended musician may push you outside of your comfort or ability zone. Give it your best shot trusting that everyone is working toward the same goal of playful excellence.

4. **Structure.** It's inherently more difficult for players and musicians to be on the same page if there aren't some shared assumptions when it comes to terminology, game strategies, and song structures. I like to use the language of verse, chorus, and bridges as a rough template, but it doesn't matter what terms you use as long as they are mutually agreed upon. Use structure as your communicative friend. When verses meander unpredictably or choruses change drastically with each appearance, this increases the chances that singing improvisers and the musician(s) will end up working at cross purposes. Establishing and reusing a verse frame, on the other hand, or setting a catchy and easily repeated chorus or hook, provides safe harbors in the song that everyone can return to if inspiration leads you awry. Rhyme and rhyme schemes are another important tool in this regard. If you're able to mirror prior efforts – the first verse was "ABCB," so the second becomes "DEFE" – this helps others see and repeat the patterns to keep the song moving forward. There are numerous examples of composers and songs that use structure (or rhyme) loosely, if at all, but these are probably unhelpful templates at least for initial explorations.

5. **Train.** Professional singers spend lifetimes honing their craft and developing musical prowess and they *know what they're going to sing*. Improvising singers strive to replicate this while also *composing their songs at the same time*! If musical improv is important to your trajectory – perhaps it's heavily featured in the venues in which you want to play – instinct and moxie may not be sufficient to get you to the finish line alone, especially if you have fundamental deficits such as matching pitch or healthily supporting your voice. It can prove challenging to secure training if you have limited time or financial resources, but this may be the next step you need to take to unlock new opportunities. A better understanding of vocal production and music will only help you communicate more effectively with your musicians as well. In commercial venues, it's asking a lot of our audiences to frequently sit through unpleasant vocal efforts once the novelty of well-intended attack wears off. It may not be the wisest strategy, therefore, to rehearse this skillset in front of a paying crowd. Some risks are better suited to the privacy of closed workshops or tutorials.

Figure 11.1 *Lights Up: The Improvised Rock Opera* and *An Improv Revue* performances at Orlando's Sak Comedy Lab. (Musical directors: Anthony Riley [top] and Ryan Goodwin [bottom]; *Lights Up* band in shadows: Frank Filipo and Jim Young). Photo credit: Charlotte Breanne Brown [top] and Mariah Clinkscales [bottom].

Final Thought

My first long-form experiment took the form of a musical, *Insta-Musical: Just Add Water,* in the early 1990s and since then, I've crafted more original pieces that use these skills than any other, including *(Your) Opera in a Trunk, FourPlay: The Improvised Musical, Family Drive, Lights Up: The Improvised Rock Opera,* and *An Improv Revue,* as well as featuring this skill in numerous other pieces and formats. There is something rather special about the intensity and appeal of this style of storytelling. I've also found in short-form houses that an ability to show comfort and knowledge in this area can make all the difference between advancement and stagnation.

> **Related Entries:** Rhyme, Verbal Skills
> **Antonym:** Emptiness
> **Connected Game:** Tag-Team Song

NAMES

Specifics are the lifeblood of improvisational creation, and so it would follow that naming people, places, and objects is critical if we want to maximize interest and develop nuance. Character **Names** are a particularly rich site for both detail and – less ideally – confusion. I am inclined toward Salinsky's position on the subject.

> Audiences love details, but some details are more easily remembered than others. Details which have little bearing on the plot are easily forgotten, especially by improvisers in the heat of the moment. Particularly when people are starting to improvise, I'd much rather they called each other by their real names, instead of having to stop and think up a name which they (and the other improvisers) are only going to forget a minute later.[4]

Hurriedly assigned fictional names can quickly disappear into the improv ether never to be heard again, and subsequently add little of lasting value to the event. Salinsky's co-author, Deborah Frances-White, makes a contrasting and meritorious case for invented names and the resulting connections they can spark in the players' imaginations. I don't believe there is a one size fits all solution when it comes to this practice, and I deploy both approaches depending on the form, style, and venue. Regardless of your standard tactic, however, using names deliberately and effectively on stage stands undeniably as an important improv skill to foster. Players visibly struggling to recall a critical character's name might garner a chuckle once or twice by a generous crowd reminded of the transient nature of improv, but this lazzo quickly becomes stale and will stall the action when it becomes a performance norm. And so, with this in mind, I offer some tips that have served me well in the past when it comes to naming your all-important scene partners.

Example

Half an hour into a long-form performance an important character is needed, but no one remembers their name…

What's in a Name?

1. **The case for using your own names…** I agree with Salinsky that using our own names is a good place to start, especially if we're working in relatively new ensembles. This has become the standard approach in my campus troupes, particularly when we play long-form, as we strive to bring more personal material and stories to the stage. Using real names, in this case, removes one more potential barrier between the improvisers and a connected sense of sincerity. Not everyone likes this approach – it can *theoretically* limit the types of characters you might play. And in some cases, such as when you're assuming an unflattering or narrow-minded persona, it can be nice to have the camouflage of a name other than your own. But all things being equal, I have come to appreciate the mental energy such a simple approach frees up as it's exceedingly rare that there are miscommunications or name slip-ups when this is your performance norm. I'll also tend to keep surnames fluid so that these can adjust as family relationships and the like deem it necessary (acknowledging that many families have a beautiful variety of surnames too).
2. **The case for naming each other (rather than yourself)…** If you are more inclined toward the equally esteemed tradition of using original character names, I find it extremely helpful to default to naming each other rather than yourself. Yes, there are social situations in which it's common for us to introduce ourselves – although these are often stranger moments which aren't typically strong improv starting points. But I've found that when

I endow or give another player a name it's more likely to stick than when I assign myself a new one (and you can always introduce your fellow scene partner if the scenario warrants it). In most instances, it's much more common and natural for scene partners to use and reuse fellow character names than their own – unless your character tends to talk about themselves incessantly in the third person! In this way, it's easier to keep a new name alive and active than if the character in question just throws out their invented name and the scene moves on. Which brings me to…

3. **The case for burning a name in…** Regardless of whether we're using our own real names or fictitious inventions, it's unlikely that our audience or fellow players will easily recall these offers if they are only mentioned once in passing. When we first meet a new character of note or start endowing an unseen character in preparation for their later entrance, it's enormously helpful to keep their name alive by making it important. This could be as simple as passing the name around a few times as seasoning to your regular dialogue, or (preferably) it could become emotionally or dramaturgically significant. If every time you utter your parent's new romantic partner's name you do so with dripping repulsion, you and your audience are better equipped to remember this choice. Or if your character comments on the familiarity of the name – "That was my best friend's name in high school" – then you're also forging a connection that will hopefully stand the tests of time. Improvisers can become needlessly self-conscious when it comes to repeating names in scene work, but this is something we all do in our everyday life, especially if we're meeting someone for the first time and we want to make a lasting impression or connection.

4. **The case for evocative names…** There's also no need to pursue randomness when it comes to creating names onstage; in fact, it's helpful to recycle names that are evocative from your own life and experiences. If a character exudes an energy that reminds you of a family member or co-worker, *why not* give yourself the gift of this memory and emotional shortcut? (Assuming, of course, that this person isn't present in the audience if it's a less than flattering portrayal!) It's amazing how stumped many improvisers can become when tasked with assigning a name, as if there could really be a wrong choice. Why not use the storehouse of names that you already have at your fingertips? Depending on your performance mode, you could also benefit from the emotional cobwebs these names bring with them and use these experiences to color your relationship or subtext.

5. **The case for representation when naming…** Character names unavoidably reflect our heritages and cultural experiences. I grew up in a country where Anglo and Polynesian names were the most common. When I moved to America, I've tended to drop the latter, sadly, from my performing repertoire for fear (perhaps misplaced) that these names wouldn't be recognized or understood. Subsequently, I've now lost comfort with an important part of my own identity and background. Don't be a David. (Be a Rawiri!) Enjoy the opportunity to populate our stages with a vast array of names that reflect the diversity of our companies and communities. When we allow others to name us on stage, this empowers our fellow players to bring their families – literally or metaphorically – into the center of the action. Especially if you are accustomed to improvising from the vantage point of a dominant culture, it can be easy to forget that this easily results in others' differences being erased if we are not aware and open. So, strive to joyfully accept as many names as you bestow. And check in with your company afterward to make sure name endowments aren't restricting the types of roles fellow players are receiving or revealing cultural blindnesses.

Final Thought

One small warning I'd add is to perhaps be wary of assigning current players' names to others in the action. I have a teammate for whom David is a default endowment and it always throws me off a little when it's assigned to someone else on stage! Although now that I've committed that suggestion to print, I would offer one notable exception to this preference. In my campus troupe, Rollins Improv Players, we always have company members rotated into tech and house management positions. We've developed a tradition of occasionally using a non-playing company member's name when referring to a previously unseen character that may or may not become important to the action. In this way, other available players don't become benched for a relationship that isn't eventually needed. In situations when this shelved character would serve the onstage action, either a slated troupe member will just take on this name and role or, if we've exhausted our current casting pool and we're playing in a "one improviser one role" mode, the named player might leave their other assigned duty and make a cameo.

In many theatrical and literary traditions names provide snapshots of a character's inner nature or a humorous commentary – Sir Andrew Aguecheek and

Toby Belch spring quickly to mind. The improv stage can certainly continue to strategically learn from and share in this custom. Embrace the risk of assigning names (both fictitious and true), enjoy the connections doing so might unconsciously unlock, and relish the details they will add to your characters and scenes.

> **Related Entries:** Character, CROW, Endowing, Inclusiveness, Relationship, Specificity
> **Antonyms:** Gagging, Pimping, Vagueness
> **Synonym:** Details
> **Connected Game:** Name Circle

NAMING THE GAME

The universally frowned upon gimmick of pointing at and describing the scenic game or dynamic rather than joining and elevating it. Assuming the former stance invariably and abruptly punctures the very element that was providing amusement and creative energy; assuming the latter allows the scene to continue to grow and evolve.

> **Synonym:** Commenting

NARRATIVE

While **Narrative** can reference a style of long-form performance that tends to mirror Aristotelian or linear scripted models, the term can also more simply refer to the spoken (or embodied) storytelling elements of our play. Whether or not your work explicitly incorporates an individual or shared narrator role, narrative skills and techniques serve as the bedrock of improv disciplines committed to convincingly sharing well-crafted stories. Narrative, after all, is the study and application of what gives stories shape, cohesion, and power. Johnstone's contributions to this spontaneous element are undeniable and significant. He posits, "Once you decide you ignore content it becomes possible to understand exactly what narrative is, because you can concentrate on *structure*."[5] Improvisers are wise to study and closely consider this aspect of their craft. As I elucidate in my **hosting** entry, narrative skills also resonate with many of the strategies deployed by an adept emcee in terms of how they structure and steer the course of an improv event or enable the arc of the greater show.

Example

Player A: "The window shutters strained against the relentless chilly breeze as the grand old house stood shivering on the Atlantic beach front…"

Qualities of Strong Narrative

I often base my introductory improv lessons squarely in the domain of storytelling as I've found this familiar element facilitates focused and team-oriented play. In such instances, I'll wrap up workshop sessions with some version of the question, "What did you see or experience that struck you as particularly effective?" The answers are surprisingly consistent from class to class and apply with good measure to both performance style and substance:

1. **Confidence.** Johnstone nods toward this quality a little in his observation above in that if we become obsessed with the what or material of improv at the expense of the how or structure, the process and results tend to suffer. It's rare and perhaps even destructive for an improviser to "know" exactly where a scene or story is heading, especially during the initial moments of inception. As some sense of uncertainty is a given, there is something bracing about watching improvisers face this reality with calm confidence. When we feel that the story is in good hands, we can also relax as audience members as those crafting the action at least *appear* to know what they are doing. On the other hand, narratives constructed with an air of fear or panic are much less likely to draw the audience into the creative act. The popular adage "fake it until you make it" would seem to directly apply here.
2. **Point of view.** Whether a narrative explicitly traces the arc of one character or voice, or is a collective amalgam, a story can quickly lose steam and effectiveness when it lurches inelegantly from one perspective or attitude to another. While confidence embodies an awareness of the "how" or delivery style, a unified point of view invites us to consider the "why" behind a story. Why is this story being told *now*? Why is this narrator or cast of characters focusing on these particular elements or issues? Why should we be paying attention to this journey? Now, in reality, once again, this "why" is rarely known or explicit when the story launches, but as the scene evolves, it's important that subtle clues are mined and honored. As tentative answers present themselves to these questions above, it's helpful for team members to keep these front of mind. Pursuing

a unified point of view also invites individuals to cede their personal agendas to serve the greater narrative that has become centered.

3. **Detail.** Narratives lacking in detail quickly become tiresome or clichéd as specifics will imbue the most well-worn scenario with completely new shades and potentials. Just as a story's point of view will emerge gradually as the scene unfolds, the significance of any one detail is likely to remain obscure until the narrative has enjoyed sufficient room to expand. So, as Johnstone notes, it's less critical to puzzle over the nature of any one specific rather than commit to a storytelling approach that provides an assortment of rich specifics in general. There are certainly moments when we might deliberately add an element of foreboding to the story arc, but it is more common for shelved facts to become dynamically important after-the-fact as we look backward for options to help us move the narrative forward. Be wary of an overabundance of buckshot details as this can make a story drown, but a dearth of detail or nuance robs narratives of their generative spark.

4. **Consistency.** I write a little about the concept of consistent inconsistency in my consideration of **bulletproof** and I'm not advocating for characters or storylines that are devoid of change, ambiguity, or internal contradictions; however, narratives tend to soar to greater heights when they develop and uphold stylistic conventions and behavioral norms. If you have created a world in which animals speak and this is an accepted part of that story universe, then it's important that this reality remains in play (or if animals now suddenly *can't* speak then this is recognized as an incredibly significant plot twist). If your narrative takes place in an everyday modern world, then be wary of radically shifting the tone and inserting aliens (unless, again, this is a deliberate move that everyone accepts unquestionably and is pitched as an earned *surprise* from within the established context). Stories that are a little of this and a little of that but not a whole lot of one thing in particular (perhaps inadvertently reflecting the competing preferences of the players) rarely coalesce in pleasing ways. As a narrative finds its own voice, be sure to elevate this quality.

5. **Connection.** In terms of connection, I think it is helpful that, as storytellers, we give at least some attention to our tone and content. I concur with Johnstone that structure unlocks multitudes of options by deemphasizing the stifling need to elevate content to the point that we become imprisoned by the impossible task of finding the one "right" detail. However, I also hold that there is value in understanding your audience's expectations, experiences, and preferences. While a children's fantastical story might please a younger audience, it could have a limited shelf life in front of a more ribald nightclub crowd without adjusting its tonality or focus. And erring in the opposite direction – crafting edgy mature content for a grade school gathering – is guaranteed to elicit a parental letter-writing campaign. Know your audience – although this doesn't mean you shouldn't strategically challenge or surprise them as well. On a simpler level, also truly *connect* to your audience when it's appropriate: make eye contact generously through the fourth wall as the narrator if this is in keeping with the format's premise; play *with* the audience and not merely in front of them.

Final Thought

One of the most profound gifts of improv narratives (in comparison to our scripted kin) is that they are much more likely to prove porous and multi-vocal. An editor doesn't go back and cut away the delightful transgressions or messes that may, in all actuality, be some of the moments that most resonated with various sections of the audience. As tellers and players, we needn't ascribe meaning immediately to each choice as it is born; rather, we can let each idea grow at its own pace trusting that if we explore narratives with bravery and attention, our structures of play can do a great deal of the heavy lifting. Allowing our audiences to connect the dots alongside us as performers is part of the appeal of the improvisational craft, as is the tacit understanding that, on some level, we have eschewed the illusion that theatre can produce a singular narrative in favor of an appreciation that ultimately significance is in the eye of the beholder.

Related Entries: Advancing, Bulletproof, Extending, Hosting, Long-Form, Looking Backwards, Shape of Show, Specificity
Synonyms: Storytelling, Structure
Connected Game: Pop-Up Story Book

NEGATING

A rough equivalent to the improvisational concept of blocking, although negation may contain a more aggressively erasing energy that destroys or punctures a fellow player's choice rather than more passively ignoring or tabling it.

Synonyms: Blocking, Erasing

NEGATIVITY

A tendency to leap to unearned conflict, assume a contrarian point of view, or to dislike your fellow characters, scenarios, and activities. Defaulting to such a mindset can quickly create needlessly caustic onstage relationships and scenes that struggle to develop.

Antonym: Love

NO

A word sometimes erroneously considered as an equivalent of blocking or negating. While such an utterance *can* embody a player's fear of ceding control, it can also be strategically used to accept offers or reinforce important personal and artistic boundaries.

Related Entry: Commandment #1

NOTES

1. Janet Coleman, *The Compass.* Chicago: U of Chicago P, 1991. p. 299.
2. Lynda Belt and Rebecca Stockley, *Acting through Improv: Improv through Theatresports.* New Revised Edition. Seattle, Washington: Thespis Productions, 1995. p. 1.
3. Augusto Boal, *Games for Actors and Non-actors.* Trans. Adrian Jackson. London: Routledge, 1992. p. 235.
4. Tom Salinsky and Deborah Frances-White, *The Improv Handbook.* New York: The Continuum International Publishing Group Inc., 2008. p. 123.
5. Keith Johnstone, *Impro. Improvisation and the Theatre.* 1979. New York: Routledge, 1992. p. 111.

OBJECTIVE

A character's **Objective** is the "O" of the improv concept **CROW** or a "W" in the equivalent WWW that corresponds to the "what" of a scene (for me it's the second one!) You may use one of its many synonyms – such as goal, motivation, desire, or want – and in my acting classroom, I tend toward the robustly energized phrase "What are you fighting for?" as it demands an equally vibrant answer.

In scripted theatre, a character's objective is typically parsed from an extensive consideration of their actions, dialogue, and all the clues and exposition scattered by the playwright throughout the text. This is a very backwards looking process in the service of discovering a forward looking energy to help your character strongly navigate the trials and tribulations of the plot. In our improv constructions, however, we rarely have the benefit of knowing where our characters will end up, and their backstories are typically invented as we go along. Regardless, both traditions (and all those in between these two poles) benefit greatly from characters who are actively pursuing *something* as they move through their scenes. As Spolin aptly reminds us,

> Any game worth playing is highly social and has a problem that needs solving within it – an objective point in which each individual must become involved, whether it be to reach a goal or flip a chip into a glass.[1]

A lack of an objective or focused involvement typically translates into a lack of energy, purpose, and commitment.

Although many others have certainly made similar observations and connections, I've used Charles Waxberg's *The Actor's Script* in my classroom for many years and want to acknowledge that his codification of essential objective ingredients has become almost second nature to my own approach. I also widely utilize a hierarchy of character wants. If you're unfamiliar with the term super objective, this usually refers to the greater goal that summarizes your character's want over the whole dramatic arc, with smaller (sub)objectives typically steering any given scene, and then smaller yet tactics applying to a specific moment or scenic beat. When you're playing in a long-form mode, having at least a generalized and evolving sense of what your character is trying to accomplish provides a much-needed touchstone as the improv swirls around and through you.

Example

Two players sit on a park bench.

Player A: "Hi."
Player B: "Hello."

An awkward silence ensues...

Earmarks of a Strong Objective

When you are formulating your objective as a character, strive to make sure it is...

1. **Active.** The gift of an objective is that it propels us into the onstage action. Therefore, a passive or static objective will largely undermine this beautiful potential for motion. If your character's want is internalized – "to be left alone" – or weak – "to be happy" – it's unlikely that it will inspire exciting journeys or choices. I'm a fan of framing your objective with the language "I am fighting to…" for this reason as it tends to promote the deployment of powerful verbs and actions: "I am fighting to… enrapture… escape… impress…" Verbs of this ilk will encourage dynamic tactics, while meeker or intellectual verbs (to wait, to consider, to wish…) will more typically withhold energy and attack. It can prove helpful to lean

into actions that have a strong physical energy or connotation. Exploring an objective such as to think, contemplate, or muse will just have you standing passively rather than interacting with your world and fellow players.

Player A: (to interrogate) "Hi."

2. **Positive.** Pursuing positive objectives provides additional fuel to the above. It's an easy trap to fall into playing what we *don't* want in a scene, and this is a likely culprit for artificially manufacturing a lot of unhelpful improvisational conflict: my scene partner wants to go to the movies, so I'll make my objective *not* going to the movies. This might feel dynamic, but at the end of the day (or scene), if we ultimately succeed, our characters end up with nothing new or just continued stasis. Subsequently, it's much more interesting to pursue an objective that is positive and embodies something that you *do* want (even if this is escape or freedom). Both scripted and improvised plays seldom allow every character to achieve their desires, but the pursuit of even seemingly impossible dreams provides characters with an impetus to keep moving in spite of the odds. Objectives may not be *rational* – trying to pry appreciation out of that impossible boss or parental figure might never happen – but they must be worthy of your character's time and energy.

Player A: (to get the truth) "Hi."

3. **Connected.** Strong objectives will cease to prove effective when they are not relevant to the current action and characters. In the scripted realm, it's a helpful trick to simply include your scene partner's name in your objective statement: "I am fighting to reveal that Greg is a fraud." Connecting explicitly to our fellow players onstage works equally well in the improv tradition; after all, if you don't actively want *anything* that involves your scene partners, why would your character choose to stick around for any length of time? Even an insignificant server in the background is probably angling for a good tip or some job security at the very least. So while our improviser minds should strive to function as giving and generous scene partners – setting others up for success – it's also important that our character minds are a little unapologetically solipsistic in an effort to figure out how other characters can best serve our dramatic agendas (or, perhaps, how we can serve theirs as an objective can also very much be framed to assist the journey of another).

Player A: (to force a confession from my lover) "Hi."

4. **Dynamic.** I've written about some of the pitfalls of this improv element in my entry of the same name, but **conflict** is also a central tension in most crackling objectives. For our purposes, it's helpful to consider this ingredient as a source of tension or suspense. Objectives that lack some perceived conflict, in theory, could be immediately accomplished. If one character wants to kiss another character, and they, in turn, want to kiss them back, then the scene could very well fulfill this promise within moments of its initiation. But, if both characters *perceive* that their scene partner is ambivalent or uncertain in their feelings, then this same scene will likely have room to flourish. Here, it's the perception of conflicting objectives that makes the world of difference. So, when formulating your character's want, keep in mind that they should assume some form of obstacle or challenge in their path (even if this belief is based on fear or misinformation). Similarly, if you become aware of your partner's objective in a scene, you needn't immediately provide this pathway. It's important that we **accept** the facts and circumstances, but letting everyone easily have what they want is unlikely to increase stakes and energy, especially if such a move doesn't ultimately serve our own character's goals.

Player A: (to trick a confession out of my lying lover) "Hi."

5. **Evocative.** This objective facet might feel a little intangible, but in some ways, it is the most important. Once you've pursued an active, positive, connected, and dynamic goal, you'll want to make sure that it interests and inspires you on a personal level. You can "satisfy" all the other ingredients but still remain lackluster if the resulting pursuit isn't something *you* particularly care about. Even if you are proverbially hiding under several layers of stage makeup, your work is unlikely to shine if you do not bring something (important) of yourself to the role and the stage. Attaining this goal can prove challenging to coach as, frankly, no one else can really solve for you what ignites your own passions and interests. But if you find yourself routinely playing characters that don't seem to have any significant spark or pizazz, consider that you may be inadvertently leaving your own spark or pizazz behind as you enter the playing field. This also applies to the language that you use to define your goals. I might personally love the energy of "I am fighting to destroy the competition on the battlefield of love," but this might not speak to you *at all*, in which case this should

Figure 12.1 Characters in *Murder We Wrote: The Improvised Whodunit* required life and death objectives and stakes as everyone needed to function in the dramatic action as a viable suspect. Photo credit: Tony Firriolo.

not be your objective statement even if it ticks all the other boxes.

Player A: (to gently coax a confession out of my soon-to-be ex) "Hi."

Final Thought

Waxberg provides "consistency" as a sixth ingredient noting that a character's goal can't negate established facts and clues provided by the playwright. This notion is a little trickier in improvised works as, by design, they do not have one author or unifying voice, and this wonderful polyphony often results in some messiness or contradiction. It is a noteworthy goal to seek character consistency (and some consistent inconsistency too as I talk about in my **bulletproof** discussion), and I think it's helpful to also seek unity when it comes to the rules of the world and style of play. Furthermore, it's good to keep in mind that we shouldn't bend a character's core unduly so that they resemble our own ideals or experiences when the action clearly expects or needs them to be something else. This can be particularly tempting when a character acts in ways that shake up our own moral compasses.

If I were to add one last objective facet that's a little unique to the improv setting – as we can generally make our characters say or do anything we want – it would be that with very few exceptions in the healing arts, we should make sure our objectives reside behind the fourth wall of performance (or "within it" as Spolin notes above). If our character is fighting to "impress that casting director" or "win back that ex-lover sitting in the third row," then we've undermined our scene work before it's even uttered its first breath.

Related Entries: Character, Conflict, CROW, Relationship, Where **Antonyms:** Obstacle, Passivity, Stasis **Synonyms:** Desire, Goal, Need, Want **Connected Game:** Get Them To...

OBSTACLE

An element or choice introduced into the narrative stream designed to thwart or intensify the characters' journey and objectives.

Synonym: Conflict

OBVIOUS

Instructors like to task their students with being **Obvious** on the stage – a seemingly simple concept that undoubtedly serves as a surrogate for many interrelated improv concepts. Consider Johnstone's advice:

> The improviser has to realise that the more obvious he is, the more original he appears. I constantly point out how much the audience like someone who is direct, and how they always laugh with pleasure at a really 'obvious' idea.[2]

Such a rallying cry can coax improvisers into pursuing more personally connected and real choices or "using themselves" on the stage; it may serve as a stand-in for exploring immediacy and reactiveness in our scenes, quickly saying our next thought rather than retreating into our intellect and sorting through multiple possibilities; or it might reference having faith that a simple and honest choice will garner more productive pathways than a needlessly clever or ornate construction. While there is perhaps some variety in how the term is deployed, the central idea remains that improvisers should seek to privilege honoring innate reactions and ideas rather than worshipping at the altar of **over-originality** or **cleverness**. This *seems* easy enough, but tapping into and trusting our raw creative instincts is no small feat.

Example

Player A enters Player B's office for a high-stakes job interview at a leading advertising firm.

Player A: *(with a light and welcoming energy)* "Sorry to keep you waiting. We've had such an impressive array of candidates, but I'm excited to get to know you a little better."
Player B: *(after much painful deliberation)* "Where would be a good place for me to put... my pet cheetah...?"

Obvious Pointers

If you are an over-thinker, meticulous planner, or verbal-centric player, consider adding some of the following strategies to your toolkit:

1. **Leap before you look.** While this may not be the best advice in the real world, in the land of improv such a mantra can break us free from our minds and launch us into the here and now. If you have a tendency to search for the "perfect" line of dialogue or scenic contribution, you may routinely edit out simple yet effective responses. Bypass this intellectual process by challenging yourself to make your first choice *now*. If you find yourself judging or assessing a scene partner's choice, rather than leaning backward and thinking, make the active choice of just leaping in and physically joining them. If you tend to intellectualize and internalize before committing to a move, start speaking as soon as your character is in focus and just let the words flow (without being needlessly verbose as that's another issue altogether!) On a purely technical level, it's more challenging to be over-original if your mind and body are too busy actively engaging in the task at hand with all your energy and attention. Which brings me to...
2. **Keep your focus on the stage.** When our focus is truly on our scene partners and the physical world that is being created before our very eyes we are also less tempted to bypass our immediate instincts. Watch, listen, and then make a small move or contribution. Trust that you are not solely responsible for "solving" the scene, or bringing "all" the energy, or providing the "most" dynamic choice alone. Over-originality tends to raise its anxious head when players forget that they are engaging in a team activity and that there is usually ample material already present on the stage at any given moment to find the next

small step forward together. Keep your focus on your relationships, activities, and *this* particular unique action. (On a related note, when our focus drifts offstage – perhaps seeking approval from a coach or judge – then we're much more likely to miss the improv smorgasbord of potential laid out before us.) This snugs nicely with the concept of…

3. **Acting is reacting.** This is an oft-quoted axiom in the scripted theatre world, but it applies equally (if not more so) to the improv stage. At this truism's core is the notion that the answer to determining our own choices lies inextricably in the energies we receive from our scene partners. When we needlessly focus on creating (specifically, *individually* creating), we can neglect the inspirational source of reacting. In addition to forging stronger connections and energies between characters, this approach is also highly generative. When we react passionately, honestly, and organically, this will likely provide ample material for our partners to then do the same. If, contrarily, we eschew visceral reactions for measured and more intellectual responses, the energy and dynamism of the scene tends to suffer. An obvious and immediate reaction will nearly always serve you better than an artificially concocted "move." And, after all, you don't need that out-of-the-box addition because you are typically better served when you strive to…

4. **Add importance rather than something new.** Over-originality is often a manifestation of an improviser's desire to make sure they are being seen doing *enough* by making recognizably "significant" contributions. More times than not, however, such an instinct squelches more subtle offers and burdens the scene rather than elevates it. Taking on the mantle of being obvious also means embracing that every improvisational move needn't bring something *new* and that, on the contrary, there are generally plenty of great ideas already percolating in the scene. The most obvious choice might actually prove to be elevating the idea of another that is already in play (or has been previously shelved) rather than shoehorning in that thing that you were wanting to do regardless of the fact that the scene doesn't really need it. The "and" of "yes, and…" rarely soars when it's disconnected and completely original. Rather, remember that the "and" can add volume, stakes, nuance, and substance to something that is currently actively in play. Not to mention, this has the added bonus of making your scene partners *look* and *feel* good.

Final Thought

As I discuss in Commandment #9, in being our own version of obvious we will usually reveal our innate and unique creativity. In reality, no two players will have the same exact organic response to any given situation or prompt with any regularity as we all bring to the stage our own peculiar stories and experiences. Trust that your obvious reaction and choice will prove enough. Let this source of effortless creativity shine through in your work.

> **Related Entries:** Commandment #9, Curve Ball, Material **Antonyms:** Cleverness, Over-Originality
> **Synonyms:** Emotional Truth, You
> **Connected Game:** Death in a Minute

OFFER

An **Offer** is the smallest improvisational unit. It is an idea put into motion, a single move in a game or story, an instigating action or instinctive response, or one proverbial brick given to assist in the creation of the larger improv edifice. Pretty much *anything* we do when we improvise (arguably consciously or even accidentally) serves as an offer in the service of the greater collective act of spontaneous storytelling. Lyn Pierse adds, "Some offers are richer than others, but there are no bad offers. No longer are players searching for the secret or correct answer that only the teacher knows."[3] While Pierse notes that there are no bad offers – a common improv sentiment – it is certainly fair to say that there *are* problematic ones. Choices that perpetuate harmful stereotypes, needlessly offend (as opposed to astutely satirize), or carelessly puncture or negate the established given circumstances are unquestionably to be avoided. As are offers that put yourself, fellow players, or the audience in physical or psychological peril. But to Pierse's point, there is rarely a singular "correct" offer as each player will process and react to onstage impetuses in their own unique way.

As we work to embrace the multitude of ideas that present themselves in our improv productions, it's helpful to remember that there are different *types* of offers that will serve our scene work and partners in correspondingly different kinds of ways. It can prove helpful as a player to also recognize whether or not you may be leaning toward one type of contribution again and again at the expense of developing comfort in other areas of artistry. To this end, I offer several subsets and tensions that can infuse our play with maximum potential. I am not suggesting that one end of any given spectrum is intrinsically better than the other, but rather that purposefully leaning in one direction or the other may prove more effective in addressing the peculiar needs of any one particular moment or could dynamically enhance the prevailing tone of the piece in which you're working.

Example

Player A steps forward and delivers the first line of a story...

Player A: "Once upon a time there was a wise old woman who lived high in the mountains of Tibet..."

Player B steps forward to contribute...

Surveying the Vast Terrain of Offers

1. **Physical and verbal offers.** While this may appear a rather obvious or simplistic distinction, many improvisers find greater ease on one end of this spectrum than the other and so might almost exclusively reside in one preferred sphere. Most choices we make on stage will probably contain both of these elements to some degree, but it's not uncommon for players to largely favor one mode of creativity. Just knowing your innate predilection can encourage you to break your own recurring patterns. Leaning into physical choices can go a long way in short-form games or scenes that tend toward verbosity or static stage pictures; prioritizing verbal choices can embellish scenes that have relied heavily on embodied characterization but might now benefit from the specificity and nuance that rich dialogue can provide. (In fairness, the first deficit is much more common in my own improv circles than the second.)

Player B steps forward and silently assumes the role of the wise old woman, meticulously assembling an array of personal items before herself as she prepares for the day. She looks out on the expansive vistas that extend from her home...

OR

Player B: "She was renowned for her kindness and insight, and would greet each stranger that traversed the rocky path outside her abode with a warm smile and equally warm nourishment..."

2. **Emotional and intellectual offers.** Emotional offers tend to elevate the import and stakes of our work on stage, connecting our stories to personal human narratives and experiences. Intellectual offers, on the other hand, more frequently appeal to our rational selves and might tease out abstract or cerebral themes. Again, there is no argument that both types of offers (and the myriad of choices that combine these tendencies in complex ways) have an important place on the stage, and clearly, work that appeals to both an audience's heart and head is likely to prove most effective and memorable. If your work is marked by esoteric chatter, however, upping the emotional volition of the scene will add consequence and connection. Similarly, scenes that have inadvertently become self-indulgent or emotionally excessive will benefit from offers that elevate or frame the material from a more aerial or logical stance.

Player B, assuming the role of the wise woman, carries on a small parcel with great care and affection. As she painstakingly moves the earth with her bare hands, she palpably mourns a great loss...

OR

Player B: "Banished from her homeland since she was a child, the woman looked keenly into the distance. Little could escape her piercing view as she counted the days until she could avenge her family."

3. **Contained and expansive offers.** There is a lot of talk in improv circles about making small steps and breathing careful life into the simplest of choices – and this would certainly be akin to a "contained" offer approach that typically polishes an existing idea rather than adding a whole new element. Alternatively, expansive offers, or those that propel the action forward with fresh complications and greater momentum, also hold a crucial place on the improv stage. The former category of choices is great for adding detail and embellishment, raising up minor details and making them important. The latter serves when a story may have become bogged down in minutiae or needs a leap forward to reinvigorate the process. If material has become inappropriate, stale, or overly self-referential, an expansive approach can also open up dynamic new potentials. Tightly timed scene work (as one often sees in short-form traditions) benefits from nuanced smaller moves as there is rarely time to chase multiple seemingly unrelated

threads. Improv that has more room for luxurious exploration (as one often sees in long-form pieces) *also* thrives off strategic expansive strokes that provide raw material for the mill that can be fleshed out and connected (much) later as needed.

Player B: "The trek up to the beacon was long and arduous, but it was a task that the wise old woman completed every morning with unwavering regularity."

OR

Player B: "Below her in the valley, a young boy started his morning chores – corralling a particularly stubborn herd of goats that viewed him more as a nuisance than an owner."

4. **Advancing and extending offers.** Advancing refers to the *active* elements of the story – the plot features that move our characters from one event to the next. Extending adds detail and significance to the raw elements of the story, be they characters, places, or objects. There is some correlation to the tension above as expansive offers *tend* to assume an advancing function, leaping the story to a new moment, character, or locale, but contained offers can certainly take on an advancing or extending function: you can add a small descriptive detail or a closely connected but minor subsequent action. Effective stories generally contain a dynamic and ever-evolving balance of these two impetuses. If your scene is stuck in a status quo, advancing will likely do the trick to raise the heat. Extending can prove helpful when scenes are racing from generic action to generic action without adding sufficient details to create and sustain interest.

Player B: (*assuming the role of the wise old woman, and pushing a boulder before her*) "I've warned you all before that no one shall pass this way, and now you've given me no choice but to bar the path myself…"

OR

Player B: (*continuing the narration*) "The blustering wind lashed against her weather-beaten skin. She pulled her ragged cloak around her aging shoulders as a futile gesture to keep warm…"

5. **Presentational and representational offers.** Finally, offers can assume various stylistic or theatrical features. Presentational theatre gladly steps in and out of the performance frame, with players directly addressing the audience (as characters, or themselves, or a Brechtian combination of the two) or playing scenarios with an air of critique or distance. Representational performances more rigorously and deliberately maintain a "fourth wall" separation, often in the pursuit of creating a "realistic" experience replete with verisimilitude. Devices that would appear playful, inclusive, and engaging in productions committed to the former style might be viewed as mugging, breaking, or commenting in the latter. Players working in modes that embrace a presentational feel might incorporate offers that explicitly connect to or utilize the audience or greater performance space – immersive and interactive modes use these tools to great effect as well. Improvisers in more representational venues typically incorporate factors beyond the fourth wall in more subtle or understated fashions, such as leaning into material that is clearly garnering a favorable response, or adjusting stage pictures so that sightlines are appropriately maintained. Improvising musicians and technicians can similarly lean into drawing attention to the theatricality of the event or work to more subtly support and elevate the mood and focus of the story.

Player B: (*as themselves, talking directly to the audience*) "Now, who would like to come and join us to play the role of the wise old woman…?"

OR

Player B: (*assuming the role of the woman and mumbling under their breath while preparing for the day*) "I'll never understand why a relentless stream of visitors disturbs my peace on this mountain. Why can no one understand that I am happiest when I'm alone?"

Final Thought

I hope these examples amply demonstrate that merely by considering the *type* or *category* of offer we are about to contribute we can productively spark our imagination in new and interesting ways. For example, I personally love language-centric improvisation, so I like to challenge myself to focus more pointedly on my physical offers so as to keep this element of my scene work vibrant and engaging. Building an awareness of both your own habitual choices and the greater stylistic needs of your company and productions also increases the likelihood that you'll unlock some of the "richer" hues that Pierse references above. For while I agree that nearly *any* offer can effectively add to the play when met with sufficient joy, love, and acceptance, it would also be fair to note that offers informed by the peculiarities and specific needs of the here and now are more likely to memorably elevate the creative act too.

> **Related Entries:** Advancing, Assumption, Endowing, Extending, Justification, Physicality, Specificity, Verbal Skills **Antonym:** Stasis
> **Synonyms:** Choice, Initiation, Move
> **Connected Game:** Stop and Go

OPPOSITES

The useful technique of exploring contrasting energies within a character or scene to avoid sliding into stereotypes or stale storylines.

> **Synonym:** Levels

OVERLAY

Introducing an unexpected or additional hurdle for the players to navigate within the scene.

> **Synonym:** Handle

OVERLOAD

Inundating the stage with a surplus of usually unrelated and unhelpful choices, typically to avoid committing to any one of them in a meaningful and connected way.

> **Synonym:** Waffle

OVER-ORIGINALITY

Improvising from a place of fear is unlikely to result in joyful play and it's not uncommon for one such fear pulsing through an improviser's busy mind to be that of not appearing creative enough. This desire to seem brilliant or inspired can sadly result in the blight of

Over-Originality. While the pursuit of cleverness can stymy players as they crave the non-existent "perfect" contribution, a desire to appear original may result in improvisers throwing out random, disconnected, or needlessly different offers that ultimately smother, negate, or muddy the creative streams already in motion. Although the over-original player hopes to reveal their brilliance for all to see, they invariably stand out for less admirable reasons as their solipsistic actions decay group trust and cohesion. It's fair to note that players who are not seeking this stance may also – on occasion – surprise their teammates with a seeming non sequitur, but there is an important difference between stalking originality at all costs and being open to where inspiration might unexpectedly take you. The first is an unhelpful focus and goal; the second is the byproduct of a carefree process.

Generally, focusing on **achieving** *unexpected* RESULTS just leaves *and the audience* your partners need- less- ly confused or irritated while adding little value to the process.

I've dealt with this improvisational habit from multiple angles in other sections: **commandment #9** examines the pitfalls of *trying* too much or in the wrong ways; **cleverness** offers some tell-tale signs that this tendency might be infecting your process; **obvious** suggests pointers for addressing an inclination toward over-originality; and **curve ball** provides a potential exception to the rule by offering a more productive avenue for wielding an appetite toward randomness. So here I will heed my own advice and not pursue an overly original perspective but rather simply ask, "Why be over-original when you can be…?"

Example

Players have formed a circle and are constructing a Word-At-A-Time Story.

Player A: "Once…":
Player B: "Upon…"
Player C: "RHINOCEROS!!!!!"

Why Be Over-Original When You Can Be...

1. **Present.**
2. **Effortless.**
3. **Reactive.**
4. **Honest.**
5. **Yourself.**

Final Thought

Worshipping at the altar of over-originality manifests a poorly constructed belief as to what creativity should look or feel like in the improvisational endeavor. "Creative" need not be synonymous with unique, random, or gobsmackingly surprising. Rather, it can (and should?) just be an honest reaction or expression of you and/or your character. "… the more obvious an idea seems to you, the more clearly it will express your uniqueness, but if you try to be creative, you'll be forever dredging up the same fashionable stupidities."[4]

Related Entries: Commandment #9, Curve Ball, Offer **Antonym:** Obvious **Synonyms:** Cleverness, Randomness
Connected Game: Hesitation Speech

NOTES

1. Viola Spolin, *Improvisation for the Theater. A Handbook of Teaching and Directing Techniques.* 3rd ed. Evanston, IL: Northwestern UP, 1999. p. 5.
2. Keith Johnstone, *Impro. Improvisation and the Theatre.* 1979. New York: Routledge, 1992. p. 87.
3. Lyn Pierse, *Theatresports Down Under.* 2nd ed. Sydney, Australia: Improcorp, 1995. p. 88.
4. Keith Johnstone, *Impro for Storytellers.* New York: Routledge, 1999. p. 88.

P

PARALLEL ACTION

Mick Napier remarks, "The biggest reason people screw up a three-person scene is that they think 'different' when they could have thought 'same.'"[1] While he doesn't use the term explicitly, Napier's words advocate the use of **Parallel Actions**, especially when it comes to entering a scene as a third (or later) player. In the simplest and purest sense, assuming a parallel action to your teammate involves replicating or mirroring their choice (as opposed to crafting a connected but different offer which would be considered a **complementary action**). In practice, parallels are rarely true mirror copies of the original: explicit parallels – or offers that seek to do the same thing in *exactly* the same way – are only really helpful in a limited handful of situations. Large Shakespearean crowd scenes, epic Wagnerian battle parties, or wailing Sophoclean choruses could certainly benefit from strongly unified ensemble work.

Figure 13.1 Chorus members watch on with concern as the action heats up in *It's All Greek to Me: An Aristophane-Slapping Comedy of Tragic Proportions* (Props design: Brianna Banales; Improvising stage manager: Lyndsey Delk nee Goode). Photo credit: Tony Firriolo.

Here, the group is largely operating as a singular entity or is primarily tasked with giving focus, status, or both, to their protagonist. In cases such as these, or when you're engaging in well-populated background side support, clear parallels in energy and intent avoid creating distracting distinctions and behaviors that would likely pull focus from the intended featured action.

More commonly, however, parallel actions do not seek to do the same thing in *precisely* the same way but rather aim to perpetuate the present action or game through riffing on the dominant energy in slightly different but clearly *similar* ways. Parallels uphold the established mood or premise rather than significantly disrupting or complicating it. If you are playing a destitute and impoverished serf craving to catch a glimpse of your lord, I too will assume a servant character whose plight and nature are closely aligned to yours (as opposed to becoming the lord, or a constable, or a fellow serf who loves life at the bottom of the pecking order). Frankly, even in the large group examples listed in my opening paragraph, subtle nuances that reflect your character's point of view will typically and appropriately add reality and life to the scene – unless you're literally playing automatons or a well-trained militaristic mass stripped of all individuality. It's a matter of degree and knowing when to and when not to *heighten* or draw attention to your individual perspective or difference. Thinking "same," therefore, shouldn't imply that you are merely mindlessly doing the same thing in the same way at the same time.

Example

Two slightly-out-of-shape runners and close friends (Players A and B) are in the midst of their first marathon race. It is clear that neither was quite prepared for this test of endurance, but neither wants to let the other one down. Their movements are pained and laborious, and each time they speak there is a clear sense of exhaustion and impending collapse.

A third player (C) enters…

How to Get the Most Out of Your Parallels

1. **Mirror and heighten the emotion.** To Napier's point, if the scene is firing on all cylinders and the players have locked into powerful and playful perspectives that the audience is eating up, Player C coming in with a whole new deal could easily destroy the current elaborate improv house of cards. Alternatively, Player C could painfully limp back into the race, echoing the exhaustion created by their fellow improvisers. If Player C merely reflects back the same level of fatigue as their predecessors, one could argue that their entrance probably wasn't needed, so it is helpful that they continue to play the established game while *also* adding some new details that can heighten the emotional reality – in this case, perhaps embodying a woeful version of one-downing. If Players A and B are a little short of breath, for example, perhaps Player C is now visibly gasping for air. Parallel actions are uniquely equipped for setting and extending games. When coupled with a new entrance, a parallel choice also frequently provides an opportunity to highlight stage dynamics that may have not been fully appreciated by those subconsciously crafting these foundational elements in the trenches.

2. **Mirror and embellish the physicality.** In the above example, Player C has focused on the emotion of exhaustion or fatigue, but they could also double down on the physical component of the scenario. (Although, one would hope that our entering player above would instinctively add to *both* the emotional and physical specificity of the scene.) If Player A has commented that they have developed blisters from the running, and Player B has countered that they may have ruptured their Achilles tendon, Player C might limp on with a makeshift crutch that they have fashioned from discarded water bottles. If the characters are, all the while, fighting to put on a brave face in front of their friends by minimizing their pain, this third entrance adds more fuel to this particular fire. Or, perhaps, they are all equally determined not to be the very last person to cross the finish line despite their ever-escalating injuries and obstacles. Again, Player C has offered up a "same" but in a slightly different way that tightens the focus and direction of the subsequent action.

3. **Mirror and deepen the point of view or objective.** Assuming the same point of view or objective can have the wonderful side effect of forging scenic allies united in a common bond. (Adopting an equal status can have a similar result as it tends to place characters on an equal footing free from obstructive competition.) If Players A and B are unwavering in their goal to finish this race as it's a fundraiser for a co-worker's treasured charity, Player C joining and amplifying this imperative raises the stakes even further. Now, all *three* runners (one with blisters, one with cramps, and one with a makeshift crutch…) must egg each other on so that no one will let down the team and their much-loved colleague. Artificial conflict can so

easily hamper scenic progress: a parallel objective provides a fruitful gateway that unites the characters on a dynamic path forward instead.

4. **Mirror and enrich the occupation or activity.** Lastly, consider the element of occupation or activity as a possible source for mirroring. If the scene occurs in a work environment, it can add interest to engage in at least different facets of the occupation at hand even if the characters all share a similar job title or function. (You'll probably want to avoid throwing in a superior or manager if you're looking to maintain the prior pattern.) Or, if you're in a workplace that is defined by sameness – such as a secretarial pool where everyone is at a typewriter or computer by definition – consider exploring idiosyncrasies in the equipment or how your character performs their job functions. In our runner example, assuming the persona of another runner is probably a given, but you could also build other parallels to further unite the characters: do they all work together at the same coffee shop, or are all members of one extended family, or all go to the same gym, or are all first responders…? Each of these choices adds nuance without undermining or upturning the game in play and offers a specific common lens through which to process the story elements.

Final Thought

And here's a fifth parallel possibility that might also come in handy, although it feels quite different in tone, so I've not included it with my list above. While I wouldn't recommend this as a standard choice, mirroring others' language can also serve as a helpful tactic, especially if you are a little lost or unsure how best to contribute to the scene. In a "Reiterate/Repeat" kind of way, you can parallel prior dialogue while still adding your presence, point of view, and energy. This can buy you a little time to get up to speed without vampirizing your scene partner's attack with unhelpful stalls or questions.

I've deliberately mirrored this discussion and its examples with my earlier **complementary action** entry to emphasize that both scenic tactics can bear rich improvisational fruit. If you read these entries back-to-back, you can also sense the inherent differences in how both of these approaches can nourish a scene. Astute parallel actions invariably water ideas that are already currently in play, and so my examples above all taste a little similar as they look to augment the same opening moves of the exhausted runners. Complementary actions, on the other hand, cast a wider net by design as they seek connection to and inspiration from what has gone before and do not feel obliged to heighten or mirror this world as is. Subsequently, Player C, in my earlier entry's corresponding examples, assumes a much broader array of characterizations and relationships. Both approaches, thinking the same (in a different way) or thinking different (in a connected way) have intrinsic and stage-tested value. Depending on your preferred style of play, you may esteem one over the other, but I have no doubt that achieving fluency in both improv languages serves the craft in the long run. Both choices are, after all, clear manifestations of the "Yes, and…" philosophy: parallels just tend to emphasize the "yes" while complements lean more resolutely into the "and."

Related Entries: Breaking Routines, Commandment #7, Complementary Action, Endowing, Extending, Offer
Antonym: Over-Originality
Synonyms: Mirroring, Same
Connected Game: Diamond Dance

PASSENGER

While **bulldozing** often occurs as a misplaced manifestation of excitement or desire to take control, assuming the role of a passive scenic **Passenger** embodies the opposite energy of relentless giving that can prove equally unhelpful. The mark of a bulldozer is an inclination to over-participate at the expense of their teammates; passengers tend to shirk their responsibility to contribute meaningfully to the action, thereby shifting all the weight of scene building to others. Seham describes this second tendency when she writes,

> …the women [in the all-woman improv team, Jane] soon learned that constant deference or passivity in improv was just as damaging to the ensemble as bulldozing and that sometimes the best way to support the scene or the troupe is to lead.[2]

This is not to suggest that scenes require everyone to equally participate at all moments in the same ways in order to achieve improv glory. There are certainly times when accepting a support or background function (or not entering at all) stands firmly as an act of generosity as it allows other collaborators sufficient space and focus to craft compelling journeys. Most plays, after all, have designated leading roles, supporting roles, and ensemble members because these distinctions allow the skillful construction of engaging story arcs. But, donning the hat consistently of a scenic passenger is another matter entirely as it places the burden of creativity solely on the shoulders of others, denying our fellow players and patrons the chance to experience and enjoy energy and ideas from all members of the ensemble. So, while it's desirable for us all to hang out in the back seat of the improv car on occasion quietly enjoying the view, it's problematic if this becomes our standard mode of operation, *especially* if we're working alongside others with similar scenic inclinations.

Example

Players A and B are crafting a scene based on the suggestion of "burglars." As the lights rise, Player A is carefully cracking open a window to an estate while Player B waits behind them.

Player A: (whispering) "I think I've managed to bypass the security system. If we don't hear anything in the next five seconds, we should be in the clear."

Both players wait with varying degrees of trepidation. After a pause to see if Player B is going to make a choice, Player A continues…

Player A: "Alright, hand me the tool kit and I'll spray the room to make sure there aren't any infrared detectors."
Player B: (nonchalantly) "Here you go."
Player A: "Now you're positive that the famous 'Jewel of the Euphrates' is being kept in the study safe?"

Player A meticulously sprays the aerosol into the room and then begins to move Catherine Zeta-Jones style between imagined beams. Player B follows but without any of this physical commitment or finesse.

Player B: "That's what I read."
Player A: "We're lucky my contacts knew the owners were going to be travelling this week and that we'd finally have a chance." *(They suddenly change their posture as if they've heard something.)* "You didn't tell me they had a dog!!"
Player B: "I didn't know…"

Some Additional Analysis

It's conceivable that Player B is doing no harm in the above example: they are, after all, allowing the story to move forward. While it's difficult to capture performance energies in a written approximation, it would seem, however, that Player A is making several moves that are actively inviting (if not craving) B's contribution. A failure to contribute consistently in such circumstances makes Player A unduly have to conjure one new detail after another with little support. There are certainly more aggressively destructive habits than being a passenger – such as negating or contradicting established elements – but Player A is largely being robbed of B's energy and inspiration, which will quickly start to impede the joyfulness of the story if this dynamic continues unabated.

Ways to Jump into the Driver's Seat

The antidote to playing as a scenic passenger is by no means becoming a dictatorial driver, but if you're inclined to let others make the formative choices time and again, there are lessons to be gleaned from placing yourself more squarely in the thick of the action. If you've found yourself falling into passive roles and choices, consider challenging yourself to do one (or more) of the following:

1. **Assume a higher status position.** I more often see players falling into the role of a passenger when they self-select low status roles and relationships as a default, so it can prove helpful to break this cycle by adopting the guise of someone higher up the status ladder. While there are *many* ways to play high status – and status needn't be exerted by barking orders – when status is played well, lower characters should defer to their superiors when it comes to making final decisions. It follows that if you happily assume a higher status, you will feel more empowered and encouraged to make strong assertions and contributions. In the burglary scenario, if Player B takes on the stance of an experienced robber, then it would follow that they will need to offer up more substantial elements of the plan. Assuming the function of Player A's sidekick, to the contrary, allows B to spend most of the scene hiding unproductively in the shadows. Similarly, choosing to be a neophyte – "this is my first time robbing a house" – discourages bold character choices as you can now ask your partner to lead pretty much every major moment.

2. **Offer yourself as the protagonist.** Passengers tend to thrive in the role of the best friend, lackey, or underling as these functions cast the spotlight on *another* character. If the scene above continues along its current path, Player A will surely emerge as the leading character as they are more fully and clearly invested in the action. Without becoming needlessly selfish or dismissive of other players, Player B can reduce the likelihood of insignificance by making their fate critical to the action. In the scripted realm, it's not uncommon for actors to analyze a text exclusively from their own character's perspective in such a way that imagines themselves as the star (even if from a structural perspective they are obviously a supporting player). This attitude alone can prove helpful. If B's burglar pitched this heist due to their own extreme financial situation, their investment in the action will increase exponentially, as will their desire to make contributions that will maximize the chances for success.
3. **Increase your verbal presence and contributions.** This is a generalization, but I've found that passengers are often more comfortable physically and emotionally on the stage rather than verbally. Obviously, rich and fully articulated physical and emotional offers can add amazing things to the scene and may be more than enough to keep the story building and developing. There are times in the action, however, that a specific choice with an energized verbal component may be the next offer required to push the scene forward. Player A, for example, made several strong offers that could have readily benefitted from a good old-fashioned verbal "yes, and…" What specific tools were they using? What was so important about the "Jewel of the Euphrates?'" Who were the owners, and why were they out of town? Player B's minimal responses do little to add more colors and textures to the emerging painting. If you can fall into this pattern of verbally absent characters, take the risk of exploring more verbose characterizations, or at least make sure your responses transcend the most basic of agreements by providing new details and additions. "I believe they have *five* blood-thirsty guard dogs that they deliberately keep hungry while they're out of town…"
4. **Find the self-love.** I've noted the importance for bulldozers to find the love in their scene work as this tends to reduce belligerence and increase human interactions that organically invite generosity and connection. For passengers, I'd advise a more robust sense of self-love and appreciation for your own ideas and instincts. Passengers can tend to undervalue their own voices, privileging those of their teammates who *appear* more confident and spontaneous. It's difficult to take up stage space when we are prejudging the success of our offers before they have even left our mouths. Just as we are charged with treating our scene partners as if they are geniuses – full-throatedly embracing anything and everything that they might contribute – so too must we apply this attitude of audacious acceptance to our own musings and reactions. There is no expectation that every improv offer will emerge as a fully constructed masterpiece. Bring your individual detail or brick trusting that the ensemble will find how best to use it.
5. **Be the first to the stage.** Lastly, passengers can find disproportionate comfort waiting all-too-patiently in the wings. Break this routine by grabbing your fair share of scene starts. It's probably not wise to rush to the stage from a place of fear or obligation, especially if this is going to put you firmly in your head as the lights rise. But when you have that seed of inspiration, don't be afraid to inform your fellow players that you want to step up. There's also no need to be alone for these scenic initiations – by all means, designate a scene partner to join you – but take the risk of making that first defining choice. On a purely technical level, this can firmly set you up to apply some of the strategies above as you can establish your status, centrality, or verbal confidence. On a structural level, this puts you in the driver's seat right from the get-go, even if you are inclined to rideshare and happily pass the wheel shortly after your first few retorts.

Final Thought

Supporting and supportive players are critical to the art of improvisation and few performances will profit from overly competitive performers aggressively fighting for scenic supremacy. Just as bulldozers benefit greatly from learning how to cede control so as to raise the voices and journeys of others in the ensemble, so too can passengers gain from finding ways to bring their own stories and suggestions to the forefront with unapologetic confidence. Ideally, improvisers shouldn't bullishly lead with obliviousness nor sheepishly follow from fear but rather share the responsibility and joy of collectively creating a vast array of stories.

Related Entries: Commandment #3, Commandment #8, Take **Antonyms:** Bulldozing, Steamrolling **Synonyms:** Passivity, Wimping **Connected Game:** Double Speak

PATTERNS

Recognizing and elevating the organic structure that slowly presents itself as the scene takes shape.

Synonym: Connections

PHYSICALITY

Frost and Yarrow provide a beautiful launching point for this consideration:

> ... improvisation, if it does extend knowing, does so because it unblocks inhibitions and prejudices, encourages participation and learning to take responsibility, enhances observation and body awareness, and develops verbal, tactile and other physical skills – it makes use of the whole body as a resource of channels of sensitivity and response, intelligence and insight, expression and articulation.[3]

There are many rich and historical movement practices that provide highly physical examples of performed spontaneity, such as contact improv, mime, and the wide array of clowning traditions that have appeared across multiple cultures and time periods. In North America, at least, modern popular improv doesn't always fully exploit **Physicality** and left to its own devices, can become a little intellectual, static, or ponderous. Needless to say, this is a shame as such heady tendencies undervalue the incredible communicative potentials of the human body. I consider space objects (props) and conjured locations elsewhere, so here I would like to muse on the ways that we can increase our sense of playful physical abandon when it comes to the site of character.

Example

Two nervous soon-to-be adoptive parents (Players A and B) wait anxiously in a small official office. Both players sit, and then sit, and then sit some more...

Tactics for Increasing Your Physical Vocabulary

1. **Mimic or parallel.** If you consider yourself a little less equipped or inclined to add physical energy to a scene, there is no shame in observing and using the choices of more body-centric players as a source for inspiration. I would offer this as one of my favorite forms of **parallel action** as it tends to add volume and energy to a scene that might otherwise prove unhelpfully stationary or mundane. If Player A gets up and starts to pace the room out of a sense of nervousness, Player B can certainly stand and perform a similar dynamic in their own character-specific way. If Player B picks up a magazine from a coffee table and starts to idly flip through the pages, Player A can benefit from grabbing a magazine or something else as well – perhaps a brochure, a child's toy, a box of handkerchiefs... Such choices have the added benefit of defining the location in greater detail while also providing characters ways to *reveal* their feelings and subtext through behavior as opposed to merely announcing or **cartooning** these contributions.

2. **Change your center.** Some actor traditions deploy the concept of a character "center" or a physical source from which energy or movement emanates. If you typically just stand as some ill-defined version of yourself, changing your physical lead or center will quickly unlock new movement potentials. I've explored this concept with or without adding emotional energies and both approaches have clear merit. Player A may process their nervousness predominantly through their fingertips, rolling their fingers on the arm of the chair, constantly adjusting their clothing, or scrolling through screen after screen on their cell phone. Player B could utilize aggressive shoulders that jut them into the space, causing sharp posture adjustments or a tendency to expansively consume the room. If you're playing in an overtly comedic style, taking on unexpected leads can inspire dynamic relationships or portrayals: how do panicking feet, judging elbows, or lustful nostrils influence the world of the play? In more subtle genres, this approach has equal merit although you might elect less overt or peculiar manifestations.

3. **Apply an essence.** Another way to jolt yourself out of your habitual movement qualities (or lack of movement altogether) is to assume a physical essence as a foundation for your character. There's really no limit as to where you might look for inspiration, although animals (fox, eagle, hamster) and environmental qualities (cloud, fire, stream) work uniquely well as they innately suggest ways to *move* as opposed to items that are inherently more static (brick, book, cup). Essence work invites both verbal and movement-based adjustments as part of the fun is holistically embodying your perception of the inspirational source: what

does a fox really want, how might such an animal use their words, and where in the room would a fox prefer to wait? If you find greater comfort in your verbal play, be wary that your application of an essence doesn't focus *exclusively* on the language components – as tempting as this may be – but rather risks exploring the movement qualities as well. Essence work can also quickly create dynamic and unanticipated relationship energies. What might transpire in the scene if Player A has taken on a jaguar essence while their partner Player B explores that of a deer?

4. **Add an idiosyncrasy.** In some ways, this is just another iteration of the well-worn improv advice to *do something specific* and then use this as a doorway for future behavior and scenic choices. Characters can tend toward the mundane when we do not create or embrace anything uniquely peculiar about them. These personae peccadillos may be organically discovered (Player A just straightened a magazine so now leans into this choice) or more consciously inserted into the action (Player B continually twirls their wedding ring between their fingers). It's possible that such embellishments may remain small and serve primarily to add specificity and color, but if they are heightened or featured, they can also provide the first move of more significant games or story elements. Is Player A worried that their need for organizational perfection will cause issues with a new child in the house? Does Player B's fidgeting eventually reveal that they raced somewhat reluctantly into this marriage to increase their attractiveness as potential adoptive parents?

Final Thought

Thoughtful movement can do much to increase the vibrancy of our stage work and characters. What may start as a rather obligatory effort to add some staging or character flair can quickly evolve into a more central or formative element of the scene if it is given sufficient love and space to grow. For those of us who are movement hesitant, sometimes it is

Figure 13.2 Rollins Improv Players explore a physical warm-up designed to get them out of their heads and into their bodies. Scott Cook Photography.

really as simple as challenging ourselves to make *one* out-of-the-box physical choice as an improvisational leap of faith and trusting that this will lead to others and greater comfort overall.

More helpful strategies for enriching your character movement toolbelt can be found in my entry on **character**.

> **Related Entries:** Character, CROW, Game of the Scene, Verbal Skills, Where **Antonyms:** Talking Heads, Telling **Synonyms:** Movement, Showing **Connected Game:** Animal Kingdom

PIMPING

Pimping is a rather unflattering name for an equally unflattering improvisational habit.

> One of the big no-no's in improv. A typical pimp would be saying to your partner, 'Say, why don't you do that little dance you used to do!' Since it would be un-improv-like to deny your line, your partner is then trapped into doing what you tell her to do. Pimping is never good.[4]

When this energy infuses your scenic choices, you are likely selling out your improv partner for an easy laugh at their expense. While the concept is related to that of **offers** and **endowing** in general, it is primarily this self-serving or scene-sapping spirit that makes all the difference. Offers provide constructive story building blocks, endowments joyfully define your fellow players in welcome ways, but pimping adds little of value to the work. Instead, such moves corrode trust and put teammates in the squirmy position of either declining your idea (and perhaps looking like a poor sport in the process) or taking it on only to feel diminished or demeaned.

Example

Players A and B, assuming the roles of a teenage dating couple, begin the scene both sitting on Player A's family couch.

Player A: "You'd better be going soon. Dad will be getting home any minute now."
Player B: "I really wish you'd tell him about me."

The sound improviser provides the cue of a car pulling in.

Player B: "Are you embarrassed by me... by us?"
Player A: "No, not at all. You'll see. My father always brings his work home with him. He works at a strip club and treats the front door as if it's his stage. It's the tear away clothes that really make me uncomfortable, but he has to do it *every single time* he comes home. Quick, hide behind the couch."

Player C stands behind the offstage door, contemplating whether or not to even enter.

Do This Instead...

If you think the choice you're about to make might be heading into this unsavory terrain, or you fear you might be carelessly pushing another improviser outside of their incredibly appropriate comfort zone, do this instead...

1. **Take a moment and assess.** Just because you've had a thought – and perhaps this thought has tickled your funny bone – doesn't mean that you *need* to contribute it to the scene. Some delightfully silly or outrageous thoughts best serve us when they remain as delightfully silly or outrageous *thoughts*. You can share it with your troupe backstage after the show, and everyone can chuckle with relief that you had the wherewithal not to scuttle a scene to serve your whimsy (especially the person who was about to be sentenced to wear your creativity). If the *only* reason you are making an offer is to get a laugh, and you *know* that your scene partner is the butt of the joke, then don't say or do that thing. No one laugh is worth causing irreparable damage to your creative relationships. Improvisation should not become synonymous with a scorched earth approach to interpersonal creativity.
2. **Test the waters.** It's certainly foreseeable that a well-intended offer might inadvertently stray into the domain of a pimp despite your intent to helpfully add dynamism or specificity to the scene. In cases where you feel you might be dancing around this line, *do less*. Part of the damage of a pimping offer is that it strips away the agency of the recipient: they can do the pitched action and feel nasty, or they can push it away and risk appearing like a bad improviser. In the above example, Player A has pretty much mandated a rather explicit choice, especially by using language such as *every single time*. If the intent is to provide an unexpected or jarring parental energy, there are many ways to do this while allowing Player C to fill in the details. "My Dad isn't like all these other suburban dads,"

"I'm really anxious about what you'll think about my father," or "You have to promise you won't tell anyone at school about my dad," all set up a dynamic tilt, but now Player C can make a choice that honors your need *and* retains their dignity and agency as a collaborator.

3. **Redirect the offer.** If you're unsure whether your intended gift is, in fact, an actual gift and not a curse or improvisational albatross, don't send that choice to someone else. Rather, if you feel your idea has the potential to really serve the scene, step into the fray yourself and take on the endowment that you know another might not find joyful. I'm not sure why this might be the case, but if Player A *really* believes that this dating scene will be served by some dancing, then they should take on this character trait or task. Player C might then decide to enter and establish that dancing is in the family DNA by embracing this choice *as well*, but now they have the option to heighten, shift, or provide a complement to your idea. I'd add that if your choice is clearly tacky, tone deaf, or punching down rather than up, this approach might still provide a problematic outcome, so it's not an invitation to just embody all the most tasteless tropes you can conjure.

Final Thought

But what should you do if you're on the receiving end of a pimp? There isn't a large assortment of helpful responses, hence the pernicious nature of such choices. In short, I'd advise saying no as creatively as you can and then addressing this moment with the initiator and the company during the postmortem. Ultimately, you shouldn't feel obliged to take on any old nonsense that another improviser throws at you, especially if you find it problematic or mean-spirited. If you are Player C in the above example, you could acknowledge what has been said about your dancing entrances but choose that *today* is significantly different and mark it as such by *not* performing your typical celebratory dance. Perhaps you've lost your job or found out something concerning about your teenage child. You could also use Player A's words to define *them* rather than you – making a mundane entrance as an accountant with a briefcase – suggesting that Player A doesn't want their romantic partner to know anything real about them. Or, you could just say no and do something else completely and figure it out later. There can be a temptation to try to spin or turn a pimp on itself and have it land back on the initiator – "Come and join me in our traditional Daddy's home dance!" – but I'm not a big fan of meeting problematic improv with more problematic improv, and this can often have the unwanted side effect of encouraging more of this behavior, especially if it results in the audience reaction that the instigator craves.

If the proffered idea is playful and you don't mind embracing it, I would contend you've moved out of the domain of the pimp and into **shivving** territory, which is defined by this sense of welcome mischief rather than dreaded obligation.

Related Entries: Commandment #4, Gagging, Shivving **Antonyms:** Endowing, Offer
Synonym: Selling Out
Connected Game: Furniture

PLAYER

A ubiquitous term used by improvisers to describe themselves.

Related Entry: You

PLATFORM

The beginning of an improvised scene or play that establishes the given circumstances and foundational reality. Generally, the platform is synonymous with the unbroken routine or balance that sets the stage for more interesting action when this stasis becomes tilted or challenged.

Synonym: Balance

PLOT

The essential and typically connected actions of a story.

Related Entry: Advancing

POINT OF CONCENTRATION

A Spolin expression that refers to the primary focus, gift, or challenge of a given game or exercise. Neglecting or forgetting this focus may result in scattered or unproductive play.

Related Entry: Objective

POINT OF VIEW

It's common improv parlance – at least in my current circles – to talk about filtering the events of a scene through your character's **Point of View**. This phrasing refers to the specific way your personae approach the world, their primary attitude or "deal," if you will. In our quest for content, a strong point of view can open the floodgates for generative material as choices become largely responsive – and perhaps even effortless. A character needs only to react with some thread of consistency based on their earlier behaviors rather than frantically search for a unique contribution. If you've ever found yourself floundering in a scene without an anchor, it's likely that you hadn't locked in a strong attitude or, perhaps, let it go prematurely. Finding a dynamic character perspective can at times prove easier said than done. Roger Bowen paints a less-than-rosy picture of the challenge:

> ... the on-the-spot improvisation is truly the most ephemeral of the work we do. It's very rare that you get something that, in addition to being funny and displaying virtuosity, also makes some kind of statement, has some point of view.[5]

Here are a few potential keys for unlocking this powerful scenic doorway...

Example

A group of characters has been waiting on an exposed elevated train platform for the last train of the evening. They have been engaging in small talk to pass the time. The booth improviser offers storm rumbles, and it starts to rain...

Find Your Point of View by...

1. **Wanting something.** Characters devoid of objectives typically become characters devoid of energy and action. If you don't want something specific, after all, you can coast through a scene with very little at stake. Theatre explores winners and losers, those who obtain their dreams and those who are punished for striving to do so. In long-form explorations, there may be some considerable time to test and adjust your greater goal for the dramatic arc; in short-form scenes, the action might culminate before you've managed to articulate your character's goal if you're not careful. It's helpful to grab something – large or small – even if you revise it multiple times throughout your journey. This may be as simple as allying yourself with another significant character, pitting yourself against a common foe, or pursuing a deep desire that may never explicitly surface in the dominant story arc. It matters less whether you achieve this goal than that you have a goal at all.

Player A has established that they are going to an important late-night job interview – an opportunity to finally prove themselves to their overbearing parent and enter the world as an adult. As the rain starts to fall, this need to make a professional first impression necessitates that they ask a fellow traveler if they can share an umbrella.

2. **Feeling something.** Another pathway to an immediate point of view is assuming and deepening an emotional energy or climate. There are many ways to formalize this: your character might have a mantra, ethos, or words that they live by such as "there's no day like today." Digging into a deep emotion or quality can also get the improv ball rolling: perhaps you are overly sensitive, or extremely introverted, or you feel an underlying sense of envy for how others always seem to have an easier life than you. Strong feelings activate games, encourage the development of dynamic backstories, and provide onstage relationships with energy and interest. Feeling a strong emotion doesn't dictate that this energy must remain static, unnuanced, or monotonous in its execution. Just as a strong objective should be explored through a vast array of tactics, so too can an emotional center find expression through a multitude of shades. And a sudden and earned shift can provide a breathtaking climax or tilt, especially when it changes or challenges the core of a character we have come to know and love.

Player B has spent the earlier phase of the scene exploring a wide-eyed optimistic energy that finds the good in everything and everyone. As the weather takes a turn for the worse, they kick off their sandals and start to dance in the puddles, laughing all the while.

3. **Loving something.** Loving something or someone adds another potentially profound level to an emotional point of view. Many emotional cores can prove self-serving, introverted, or even isolating. This is not necessarily unhelpful – a relentlessly paranoid character that feels the world is out to get them could provide some nice power to a scene. Choosing to honestly and earnestly love something or someone, however, adds a whole new level of vulnerability and stakes. There are *many* kinds of love, and this need not necessarily be romantic in nature, although theatre is filled with these kinds of stories for a good reason. Characters might embody parental devotion, or profound loyalty to a friend, or passion for a workplace, occupation, or sports team. As I discuss in my **love** entry, this powerful ingredient is often absent or poorly approximated in spontaneous storytelling, and yet when it appears, it can elevate the most mundane premise into something quite astounding. Loving someone also tends to push you into the scene in actionable ways as opposed to retreating into your imagination.

Players C and D have been gently cooing for the duration of the scene, clearly sharing a literal or metaphorical lovers' honeymoon. When the rain appears, Player C, without hesitating, lifts their jacket so that it covers both of their heads. It's just another excuse for holding each other tight.

4. **Believing something.** An additional source for a strong POV can reside in a powerful conviction or belief. If you're leaning toward a more comedic tone, these may be quirky or slightly odd in nature: a character might have a deep-seated fear of stepping on any cracks in the train platform having taken to heart too seriously the chant that such behavior might result in their mother suffering bodily injury. If you're exploring more complex hues, character beliefs could embody some of the more intricate societal issues of the day: a bystander might be silently protesting the plight of working-class citizens who struggle to pay for the train to get to and from their minimum wage jobs that don't meet actual living expenses in an industrialized city. Bowen, in the quote above, recognizes that improvisation's ability to question or mock the world as we know it as a unique (although unfortunately, in his opinion, rarely executed) quality of the form. I ardently believe that we needn't silence astute critiques when we play. Sometimes, such a stance is viewed as being "political," but, in reality, when we avoid such stances, we are also being political, just in the service of the status quo. Even in more whimsical performance modes, portraying characters that believe something important can encourage valuable discourse through satire or parody.

Player E, who has revealed themselves to be an environmentalist to the nth degree, has perched beside the train benches. When they hear the rain approaching, they produce a small drinking canister, which they use to discreetly collect the rainwater.

5. **Bringing something.** Finally, a point of view can become quickly established by bringing something with you to the stage. While I'm not really meaning grabbing a prop or costume piece as you enter, this actually can jumpstart the process too. Rather, I would advocate for using what you have at your disposal. In most cases, this will be our own real-world experiences and histories. Perhaps you have worked a late-night shift in a particular job and can bring this reality (and its physical remnants) to the scene, or you're *always* leaving your umbrella at home when there's an unexpected rainstorm, or you've had some less-than-pleasant experiences using big city mass transportation systems. In long-form pieces, also be sure to bring the performed history of your character to the scene if this moment occurs later in the arc, along with any pre-established point of view elements such as a want, feeling, love, or belief. Your character might begin as someone quite different from you, but even a small commonality can connect us to our work in profound and helpful ways. Don't be afraid to use what you know by bringing your "obvious" to the work.

Player F, a regular elevated train rider in real life, has a visceral image of the train platform and its sights, sounds, and smells. Almost unconsciously, they grab a free real estate paper from a nearby stand and hold it above their head when they sense the rain is about to fall.

Final Thought

Investing quickly in a clear point of view will soon pay improv dividends. There isn't one correct pathway to finding your scenic filter, but the longer you wait to make a definitive choice, the more likely that you'll find yourself wandering a little as an improv passenger. Whether you grab an objective, mood, passion, conviction, or part of your own life story, this vantage point can add flavor and flair to your character work. And to Bowen's point, as artists we should be mindful that our character point of views can *also* serve a greater socio-political perspective that can meaningfully serve our communities.

> **Related Entries:** Comedy, Emotional Truth, Game of the Scene, Love, Objective, You
> **Antonyms:** Passenger, Passivity
> **Synonyms:** Deal, Perspective, POV
> **Connected Game:** Rashomon

POSTMORTEM

"He listens well who takes notes." — Dante Alighieri, *The Divine Comedy*

Due to the unpredictable and ever-evolving nature of an improvisational production, it is common practice to conduct detailed note sessions or **Postmortems** after each performance (unlike our counterparts on the scripted stage). This has been the case with all of my professional and collegiate companies although the look of these debriefs changes between venues. When there's a resident director or you're working in an educational setting, it's common for postmortems to be more unidirectional – with feedback moving primarily from the artistic team to the improvisers. In professional settings, this can also be the case or note sessions can prove a little more multivocal with responses moving between players perhaps facilitated by the evening's host or a senior member of the troupe. When this post show ritual is handled well and with finesse, it can further unite the players in a common mission; when it is fraught or needlessly divisive, it can do more harm than good. There is no guaranteed approach to unpacking the soaring successes and fumbling fractures of a performance, but I've found that a commitment to listening and learning from our discoveries and mistakes stands as a crucial element of a thriving improvisational environment.

Here are some pointers on the two equally important functions of both *giving* and *receiving* thoughtful analysis in your improv debrief sessions:

Thoughts on Giving Notes

1. **Seek conciseness.** Focus on what will benefit the company and individuals moving forward, patterns that need elevating or breaking, and adjustments that will serve the greater vision or mission. It can prove disheartening for all involved when undue attention is given to a misstep that was *so* situational that it will never happen again. In most cases, improvisers have already mentally given themselves the note when such fumbles occur, so don't needlessly dwell on these struggles but rather briefly acknowledge them if it's necessary to offer up future prescient strategies. (If they're truly oblivious or in meltdown, this is better addressed in a one-on-one anyway.) Also, be wary of lengthy musings as to what *you* would have done in that situation – offer a tool rather than an after-the-fact personalized and ultimately inapplicable blueprint.
2. **Seek balance.** Strive to find a balance between constructive and positive notes. (It's a shame that most artists experience this binary when well-articulated suggestions are *also* acts of appreciation and support.) I've noticed that there can be a tendency to over-emphasize the former category, especially if time is tight, but players are generally more receptive to critique when they also feel adequately and sincerely celebrated. Admittedly, this can add volume to the postmortem session, so also consider after-the-fact ways of helpfully continuing the conversation. In some of my devised pieces, I have explored distributing written notes and just sharing the high points in person (although this certainly adds a time burden on the company director). With my on-campus troupe, we'll utilize social media platforms to allow players to give supportive shout-outs and personal musings as well.
3. **Seek empathy.** Especially if you are leading a note session (or are a senior player or more regular participant) keep front of mind how challenging these endeavors can be and don't focus on unhelpful minutiae. Be careful of your tone or preambles that will make the listener defensive or on edge, such as a foreboding "This note is for you…," "I've noticed that you *always*…," or "If there's one thing I hate it's…" It can be easy to forget how impossible it is to improvise and balance so many competing needs at once. It's also important to practice empathy during moments of discord or when a fellow player shares feeling marginalized or hurt by a choice. Sometimes, it can prove helpful to simply offer the note from a more personal (rather than high status) place in these moments: "I've experienced a similarly difficult moment. While I couldn't find a path at the time, afterwards I thought about…"
4. **Seek joy.** Read the room and set a tone accordingly. If it's been a bit of a challenging show and

the company is clearly beating itself up a little, this might be a good time to emphasize growth and lean into the successes. After a performance where company members are riding high, this might provide an opportunity to consider some more nuanced or granular issues that can open up even new heights for the future (although be wary that you don't cast an unnecessarily large shadow over the glow of success). I believe it's important to acknowledge the dominant mood: if everyone knows the show was rocky it will feel disingenuous and ultimately unhelpful to doggedly insist otherwise. But it's also probably not a good time to heavily lay on feedback that will be perceived as negative. Failure is inherently *part* of improv and it's healthy to find ways to laugh in the face of our slip ups. Joyful notes can go a long way toward building up a troupe's tolerance and acceptance of risk and fumbles.

Thoughts on Receiving Notes

1. **Take the note...** even if you have a pressing justification or reason for your choice. As improvisers, most of us can quickly come up with a string of *great* justifications for why we did what we did, but at the end of the day, a note is responding to how we did what we did landed or the way it was received by our partners or the audience. Be open to the reality that your choice may have had an unintended consequence despite your efforts to the contrary.
2. **Take the note...** even if you don't agree with it. If you don't *understand* the observation, seek a moment with the director or company member after the session (or perhaps sit with it for a night and then approach them if it's still pertinent). Ask for clarity in the note session only if it'll benefit *everyone* present. I can struggle with keeping notes contained as a director; assuming a "thank you" approach as a player can go a long way to help in this regard. Those providing feedback are just as fallible as those receiving it, and sometimes an offering will be opaque (or kindhearted but not particularly apt) just as is the case on the stage.
3. **Take the note...** even if you have to pass up a great opportunity to show how much you know, or who you've studied with, or why you should be appreciated more... When postmortems become status battles you've headed off the map into dangerous territory. There are certainly appropriate places to muse on the greater philosophical ramifications of our craft – in my circle, this is typically at a bar after the show – but strive to avoid intellectual flights of fancy during the postmortem itself. If you make a one-upping move in a company of improvisers, someone is more than likely to quickly join the game – perhaps without even consciously choosing to do so – while the minutes will continue to tick away.
4. **Take the note...** literally consider taking the note and writing it down so you can review it later, especially if you are working on a new or complex piece. In addition to being a mark of respect for the creative team – "I value your feedback enough to record it to look at again later" – it also allows you to self-diagnose trends that you might not immediately catch when you are no longer in the heat of the moment. Are you constantly being praised for certain choices or behaviors that you can now lean into? Are there skill sets, games, or structural components that keep tripping you up that might warrant more training or a conversation with your director or mentor?

Final Thought

I've reflected on the import of well facilitated postmortems elsewhere when it comes to dealing with ruptures in how we treat and represent each other on stage (see **consent**). As I continue to grey, I am increasingly of the opinion that complex interpersonal and habitual performance issues rarely find fruitful solutions in a public or community note session. Regardless of the sensitivity of the facilitator, such moments invariably can feel shaming or become mired by other well-meaning improvisers either trying to kindly dull or less kindly sharpen the message – some conversations are just best handled one-on-one. In my experience, postmortems infused with respect, playful professionalism, and dare I say love, can actually capture some of the creative joy and camaraderie that hopefully defines our onstage successes as well. If your note sessions routinely feel angsty or cynical this may, in fact, suggest more systemic issues in your company.

Related Entries: Acting, Commandment #10, Consent, Ensemble, Rehearsal Etiquette, Sidecoaching **Antonym:** Check-In
Synonyms: Debrief, Feedback, Notes
Connected Game: Best and Worst

POSTPONING

Postponing or deferring the scenic action serves as a prevalent form of improvisational procrastination. Smith and Dean offer helpful context when they describe a common human instinct:

> We are conditioned to avoid taking risks, to 'play safe', to avoid failure, and to produce commodities [...] we are encouraged to be well prepared for any public task and to keep any element of unpredictability to an absolute minimum.[6]

Viewed through this lens, postponing provides an opportunity to cling onto the known for just a little longer. Many terms and techniques have emerged to describe and mitigate this tendency. Like so many other to-be-avoided tactics, postponing manifests a player's fear or nervousness: "but I don't know what will happen if we follow that big choice or plot point!" Some styles of play are more embracing of talky scenes than others, but few would espouse putting aside rich story potentials in favor of just musing about theoretical possibilities ad nauseam. Bear in mind that you should not confuse postponing (which stalls momentum and any likelihood of advancing) with the important story function of extending (which adds stakes, detail, and context). The first instinct adds little to the dramatic action while the second serves a critical storytelling purpose.

Example

Player A is faced with a difficult employment choice. They have just been offered a life-changing opportunity as a consultant, but this new position would require frequent travel and they recently started a family with their partner. Their current position as an in-house I.T. specialist is safe and can pay the bills but does not provide any challenge or potential for advancement.
The lights rise on Player A and...

I'll Get Around to Giving This a Clever Title Later

If you find yourself falling repeatedly into one of these postponing patterns, consider "don't do *that* but do *this* instead..."

1. **Don't discuss, do.** In real life, we often assemble our support network to help us navigate complex decisions. It follows that some of this behavior belongs on the stage, but I've found that it can quickly become disproportionately cumbersome. If Player A discusses this employment dilemma with their spouse, and then a few scenes later muses about it with their parent, and then a few scenes after that chats about it with their best friend at the pub, much of the dramatic "action" may have been expended with essentially *nothing* actually happening. In most cases, much more interest awaits when the audience gets to see a character *do* rather than *discuss*. As is frequently the case in the best theatrical scenarios, there probably isn't a "right" decision to select, so why not give the character (and the audience) the joy of the journey? Take a first step and *see* where it goes. So, instead of Player A talking with their spouse about what to do, let's see their first fraught airport goodbye.

2. **Don't seek advice, beg forgiveness.** Connected to the above, seeking advice in some ways extinguishes the heat of choices that could have been realized. If you talk about the potential of causing marital strain (perhaps in *multiple* scenes), then it's less impactful down the line if this is what eventually transpires as you've already essentially dress rehearsed the scene to some degree in front of the audience (perhaps in *multiple* scenes). On the other hand, if your character leaps into the metaphorical snake pit (why does it always have to be snakes?) knowing that there will likely be ramifications, the stakes and danger of the choice will invite more emotionally vibrant realities. Player A might be *very* aware that their spouse would not be on board with losing their financial safety net now that they have a child. So, instead of Player A asking for approval, let's see them go ahead and secretly quit their current job so that there's no option other than to pursue their career dream. A scene in which Player A is now confronted with this behavior after-the-fact will surely prove more dynamic than a blasé discussion about what to do. This is undoubtedly *not* a sound approach for your real life, but it certainly adds fireworks to your stage personae!

3. **Don't contemplate, activate.** If you're the scene partner in the above examples, you also hold a great power to disrupt postponing tendencies. If you find yourself cast in the problematic role of an advice giver, fight the urge to have a sit and talk scene. Rather than carefully weigh through all the options, impetuously grab one and sell it with all your might. Better yet, grab an option that you *know* is ripe with complications or serves your own self-interests: bring fuel rather than water to

your scene partner's burning problems. Perhaps you can personally benefit from the guilt created by Player A experiencing some marital strife, or you have an eye on their old (or potential) job. In general, you and your stories will be better served by championing change over perpetuating stasis: if in doubt, push the scene in the direction of the unexplored territory. So, instead of rationally and dispassionately talking through all the potential pros and cons with Player A, grab their cell phone and make them call their employer *now* with their spontaneous decision.

4. **Don't half commit, over-commit.** Postponing shares much with the improv habit of **wimping** and usually manifests its sedentary "Yes, but..." energy. Mundane and everyday scenarios can crackle when approached with an "all in" attitude instead. If you and your characters don't care about their plights, then it's equally likely that those watching will only be minimally invested too. In traditional acting lingo this connects to the stakes and urgency of your character journeys. If the job decision isn't particularly significant or pressing, then you'll be served by making it so. Increase the voracity however you can. Perhaps Player A isn't *only* unsure about their career path but is experiencing a full-blown mid-life crisis and this is just the first step on that pathway of realization. So, rather than having a scene in which Player A wonders about their career options, let's see them buy an overpriced convertible on credit and then leaving the grid altogether!

5. **Don't begin, continue.** I apologize for the inelegant title language, but I couldn't find a better concise alternative! The habit of postponing can be short circuited merely by changing the way we begin our scenes. All too often, improvisers instinctively start at the beginning – sitting down to dinner and revealing the new work potential, arriving at a friend's house with a six pack and a conversation agenda, walking into the office of their spiritual adviser for their weekly appointment. Obviously, these can all provide fine starts to a scene, but if you're inclined toward postponing, you may have already lost the battle a little with such a choice as these initiations are unlikely to hold much heat. It will be easy to sit and chat, gently work your way up to the topic of intended conversation, and then muse a little collectively on what to do next; that is, if you're not edited before you've finally narrowed in on your focus. Alternatively, if you start in the middle or "continue" prior unseen actions, it's more likely that momentum will keep your character moving forward. So, instead of Player A gently easing into their desired topic or content, they could immediately rip off the band aid by announcing "I've quit my job," or "I've made a terrible mistake," or "You've never wanted me to be happy...!"

Final Thought

In short, if you know postponing is in your bailiwick consider shocking yourself out of improv habits designed to keep you static and safe. Don't waffle, risk. Don't hesitate, attack. Don't look before you leap, leap bravely into the great unknown before you look. Your characters (and scene partners) will thank you for it.

> **Related Entries:** Commandment #6, Commandment #8, Telling, Waffling, Wimping
> **Antonyms:** Abandon, Advancing, Leaping, Showing **Synonym:** Inaction
> **Connected Game:** Word at a Time Crime

PRESENCE

When we refer to a performer as having **Presence** on stage, we are often referring to a quality that, on some level, can feel a little amorphic. Without exception, such an observation is intended as a compliment, and many a casting director has credited this characteristic or the lack thereof as a determining factor in their decisions - "I like them, but they just don't have any presence..." Spolin notes the import of this quality: "Acting requires presence. Being there. Playing produces this state. Just as ballplayers in any sport are present in the playing, so must all theater members be present in the moment of playing, in present time."[7] It is extremely difficult to embody and refine a quality that many consider almost intuitive or second nature, but there are certainly improvisational tendencies that contribute to the present improviser's success. Here are a few:

Attributes of the Present Improviser

1. **Existing in the moment.** As Spolin observes, improvisation is a theatre of the present moment and successful improvisers must thrive in the here and now. Despite the multitude of competing needs and stimuli, players with presence exude a

sense of comfort and belonging. Yes, they might occasionally let the audience see them sweat, or fleetingly acknowledge the impossibility of the task at hand, but their focus is the current process and journey. The improv world around them may seem topsy-turvy, but they are grounded or at least give the audience the impression that they know what they are doing. Just as one wouldn't want to go to a professional sporting event and ponder whether or not the players know the rules of the game, this holds equally true of the improvisational player. Engaging performers at least *appear* to know the rules and so can just playfully explore where the scene wants to go next. The improviser with presence lives on the tightrope; the performer without spends their time worrying about the potential fall.

2. **Engaging actively.** To pursue presence is also to fully commit to the current events and actions. Regardless of whether you are standing in the limelight as the protagonist, or happily to the side as an ensemblist, enthralling improvisers are themselves enthralled in the original stories of their imaginations. When our attention wanders on stage, it should be no surprise that the audience's commitment might do the same. Or worse, an improviser who has temporarily "checked out" might grab the focus but for all the wrong reasons. Active engagement, on the other hand, *gives* heat and emotion to the stage, especially when it is dynamically filtered through the lived reality of the character. The improviser with presence finds a way to care about the ebbs and flows of the action; the player without often only has their attention turn on when they have a "good idea" or know they are in focus.

3. **Heightening energy.** I consider good theatre as heightened and well-edited life. With very few stylistic exceptions, scripted playwrights work diligently to minimize or cut out the mundane human moments and interactions so that their dramatic arcs have maximum effect. When improvising in realistic modes the same should hold true with players looking to imbue their scenes and characters with an emotional depth worthy of the stage. Present actors successfully "fill the space." On a technical level, this means literally eschewing filmic nuance when performing in larger venues where such choices won't carry to the back wall. If you're not seen and heard, then it's unlikely that you're communicating effectively. On a more visceral level, this means that improvisers embody characters worthy of populating the stage, and that these personae have important stories and dreams. The improviser with presence makes brave choices of emotional weight and significance that connect to the audience; the actor without withholds.

4. **Embracing receptivity.** And a present performer fully accepts the given circumstances and the intentional or subliminal offers of their partners by reacting honestly and fully. This orientation allies with the improvisational commitment to change and flexibility. It is not enough to stand and bear witness to the events on stage. Instead, fully present players embrace the scenic vicissitudes and use them to dig deeper or soar higher. Without sacrificing their commitment to the here and now, such players gain fuel and inspiration from their awareness of the multitude of factors framing their performance, joyfully justifying changes to the stage from fellow technical improvisers, incorporating and adjusting to the audience's reactions and contributions, or pausing for the unanticipated airplane flying overhead during their outdoor show. The improviser with presence doesn't flinch from interactive creativity; the artist without becomes rattled.

Final Thought

The accolade of presence can serve as a stand in of sorts for confidence and the way in which we present ourselves to our audience and fellow collaborators. The more experience we gain, the more likely that this confidence will build correspondingly. But there are also definite skills and habits that we can actively nurture: silencing our internal judges to focus on the current moment, investing fully in the improvisatory action, seeking strong connections to our characters and work so as to raise our commitment and stakes, and playfully taking the unexpected in our stride.

Related Entries: Abandon, Change, Commitment, Focus **Antonyms:** Absence, Distractedness, Passenger **Synonym:** It (as in, they have "it") **Connected Game:** Ritual Scene

PROBLEM

An obstacle encountered within the course of a scene that warrants the characters' focus and attention. Alternatively, an attribute that can be assigned to an improviser who should be avoided at all costs.

Synonym: Conflict

PROCESS

The antithesis of product. Improvisational theatre is somewhat unique in that – at least theoretically – process and product occur simultaneously. It is commonly believed that placing too much focus on the finished product will inadvertently hamper a joyful and creative process and may be essentially biting off your improvisational nose to spite your improvisational face.

Synonym: Improvisation

PROMPT

An initial idea to inspire improvisational play.

Synonym: Ask-For

PROTAGONIST

In traditional scripted theatre, the person who "carries the action" of the play. This is not to be mistaken with the hero of the action, although historically this has often been one and the same. Protagonists need not be admirable, or likable, or good, but we do tend to view the world from their vantage point and experience the action somewhat vicariously through them.

Antonym: Antagonist

PUNCHING DOWN

Generally, a cheap or bullyish comedic shot that blindly seeks a laugh at the expense of another who is not present or given an opportunity to present themselves with any sense of truth or empathy.

Antonym: Punching Up

PUNCHING UP

The notion of **Punching Up** in our improv work undeniably utilizes a moving target that is highly subjective and situational in nature. The gist of this approach is that richer journeys await when we aim our collective comedic barb at the powerful or privileged rather than the powerless or marginalized. (This is not to be confused with crafting scenes where potentially marginalized groups are given agency as subjects rather than suffer ridicule as comedic objects.) As Sahlins observes, "… the wit and effect of the parody goes down as the target goes down […] your parody form must be worthy because you are, perforce, reducing it anyway."[8] There is an issue of effectiveness when as performers we seek to pull down to size a comedic object, but the import of choosing our material consciously and with an appropriately developed social conscience should also loom large. Our choices when we perform, after all, have the innate ability to uphold *or* question societal norms. Punching up reflects an understanding of this power and responsibility while its antithesis, punching down, tends to perpetuate problematic stereotypes and social inequities.

Example

A group of New Zealand improvisers, on their home turf, riff on dominant perceptions of what it means to be a kiwi in front of an audience who wrestles with these tropes in their own day-to-day lives.

As opposed to…

A North American troupe of improvisers, on their home turf, riff on dominant perceptions of what it means to be a kiwi in front of an audience that does not include any self-identifying New Zealanders.

Choosing Our Comedic Target

The spirit of punching up is challenging in that such an improvisational stance or attitude will not look or function the same from venue to venue, performer to performer, or culture to culture. Rather than a "one size fits all" litmus test, a commitment to punching up is more about a willingness to interrogate our choices (particularly in comedic venues) and learn from our past attempts and stumbles. Here are some provocative questions to keep in mind when aiming our shots as improvisational practitioners…

1. **Whose voice or story are you representing?** It is important for artists to consider whose stories we are telling. If we routinely have protagonists with unexamined privilege leading our journeys, we increase the likelihood that other characters in the mix may become little more than stage dressing or the butt of the joke. In such instances, there may be few opportunities to punch up in any meaningful fashion as, literally, there may not be anything "up" for our protagonist to punch at! On the other hand, if we actively seek a variety of perspectives and stories (hopefully coming from an equally varied ensemble of players) then our stages will become populated with a polyphony of potent agency.
2. **Is your subject part of the establishment or usually disempowered?** The "establishment" may look a little different from location to location although historically it has assumed a depressingly monolithic appearance similar to that on my own driver's license. If our work upholds these institutions of power, then our improv may well be serving the status quo or conserve (in the Moreno sense of the word). When our art champions the under-served or under-represented and elevates these stories and experiences, then we are more likely functioning as empathetic or satiric agents of social change even if this is on a micro level. Even the gimmickiest short-form game can blindly reinforce or playfully critique the world around us. When we relegate the disempowered to the margins of our work (as objects rather than subjects) then the likelihood of punching down increases exponentially.
3. **Are you questioning or reifying stereotypes?** Building from my first two bullet points, when we typically see difference in our scenes as brief or supporting encounters there is significantly less time to offer portrayals of substance. Short-form modes struggle with this reality just by the very nature of their reliance on a rapid-fire succession of disconnected scenes that rarely allow for characters to reappear and deepen. Subsequently, such appearances can feel slight or resemble punchlines rather than fully fleshed characters in their own right. Punching up would invite us to center a wide range of voices so that we can experience the world through their eyes rather than merely catch clichéd glimpses of these "others" in the shadows.
4. **How do your company and audience demographics frame your intent?** In my opening example above, little has changed in terms of content, but the performance parameters that frame the event clearly make all the difference. In the first example, the scene may feel like a communal act of bonding over a shared experience between the improvisers and their audience; in the second (unlikely as it might be), the same exact choices could easily appear mean-spirited or tone deaf. This is also the difference between affinity improv where an otherwise marginalized group wields the tools of performance together often for a like-minded audience, and mainstream homogeneous troupes that primarily consist of a metaphoric Mount Rushmore of privilege. While the first experience lifts up those who may have been voiceless, the second is much less likely to do so. Punching up recognizes that we all don't have an equal right to make fun of the same things in the same ways.
5. **What kind of laughter are you seeking and achieving?** Ultimately, the final test of whether we are punching up or down often resides in the laughter of our audience. This can prove problematic in and of itself if we view any and all laughter as desirable and equal. However, there is a marked difference between a group laughing from recognition as they commiserate or empathetically acknowledge a shared experience, and a powerful privileged majority uncritically laughing at tropes or portrayals of those usually not in attendance or without a staged voice in the conversation. Improv certainly can and has enabled both of these forms of laughter, and so many other kinds as well, as it is a tool in the service of the producers' and players' whims and goals. Punching up asks us to unequivocally examine these goals and course correct when we fall short of the intended mark.

Final Thought

Punching up reflects the nuances of our ever-shifting reality and demands of us as players a heightened awareness and honed sensitivity. Improvising with this lens in mind can reveal personal and company norms and assumptions that are ill-informed, problematic, or just plain bigoted. When we have the benefit of revision and rehearsal, as is the case in a sketch or scripted environment, walking this delicate line can feel less daunting. In our theatre of spontaneity, it's a given that most of us have had moments (probably *many*) where, with the benefit of hindsight, we know that our target was poorly chosen, or our comedic punches were clumsily executed.

When I improvise, I tend to take a larger degree of comedic latitude when embodying characters with whom I clearly share commonalities and experiences. Only embodying our narrow perspective, however, has its own set of problems and will limit how we present the wealth of human experience. But when our intent is to assume roles and stances that are further from our own lived realities, there is a greater risk that we might slip into unnuanced or even harmful over-simplifications. Here, a commitment to empathetic portrayal (and an openness to feedback and personal growth) is a must.

Self-deprecation can almost feel like a national obsession as a New Zealander, but if in doubt, this attitude can prove helpful in instances when you're unsure if you're punching up or down. Assuming an almost "punching sideways" or "at yourself" approach – making fun of our own identities and communities – minimizes the risk of causing harm rather than crafting humor. Admittedly, this isn't always a clear path either, especially for those facets of ourselves that are complex or contested: for example, as an immigrant who has called the United States my home now for over 30 years, I am *very* aware that my foreign-sounding speaking voice can frame any critique of my new home nation in unintended ways for a local audience. However, in general, I've found punching sideways provides at least a good starting point when another path isn't readily available. Also, if in doubt, consider *why* you have chosen your target. If it's easy, commonplace, or in vogue, that's perhaps a good signal to reconsider your strategy: as Sahlins contends, our target "must be worthy."

Related Entries: Archetype, Comedy, Inclusiveness, Material **Antonym:** Punching Down **Synonyms:** Awareness, Responsibility **Connected Game:** Inappropriate Behavior

NOTES

1. Mick Napier, *Improvise. Scene from the Inside Out*. 2nd ed. Englewood, CO: Meriwether Publishing, 2015. p. 73.
2. Amy E. Seham, *Whose Improv Is It Anyway: Beyond Second City*. Jackson, MS: U of Mississippi P, 2001. p. 71.
3. Anthony Frost and Ralph Yarrow, *Improvisation in Drama*. New York: St. Martin's Press, 1989. p. 163. This work is now in its 3rd expanded edition: Anthony Frost and Ralph Yarrow, *Improvisation in Drama, Theatre and Performance: History, Practice, Theory*. London: Palgrave Macmillan, 2016.
4. Rob Kozlowski, *The Art of Chicago Improv: Shortcuts to Long-Form Improvisation*. Portsmouth, NH: Heinemann, 2002. p. 155.
5. Roger Bowen quoted in Jeffrey Sweet's *Something Wonderful Right Away*. 1996. New York: Limelight Editions, 1978. p. 36.
6. Hazel Smith and Roger Dean. *Improvisation, Hypermedia and the Arts since 1945*. Amsterdam: Overseas Publishing Association, 1997. p. 23.
7. Viola Spolin, *Theater Games for Rehearsal: A Director's Handbook*. Evanston, IL: Northwestern UP, 1985. p. 3.
8. Bernard Sahlins, *Days and Nights at the Second City. A Memoir, with Notes on Staging Review Theatre*. Chicago: Ivan R. Dee, 2001. pp. 125–126.

Q/R

QUESTIONS

There are a lot of improv "rules" floating around that are oft repeated in an effort to assist novice improvisers as they take their first steps on the stage. Some practitioners express an overt skepticism about such rules in general, noting that they don't necessarily lead toward more successful improv but instead more in-your-head improv. However, when taken with a grain of salt, I believe that such guidelines are more helpful than hurtful, offering up players some best practices to increase the likelihood that everyone is working together in a helpful fashion and in a similar direction. I think that there is also something to be said for the fact that most experienced players can rattle off these inherited norms that provide some semblance of a foundational philosophy uniting improvisers when we get together for festival jams and all-plays.

One such rule is the frequently touted notion of "Don't ask **Questions**" in your scenic work. The authors of *Truth in Comedy* observe, "He who gives information is a gift-giver; he who asks questions is a thief."[1] The underlying rationale for such a sentiment generally observes that this habit puts all the generative work on your scene partner's shoulders while the questioner essentially steals away the momentum and spark of the scene. As with most less-than-helpful improv habits, asking questions tends to emerge from fear: fear of not quite understanding what your partner was intending; fear of not coming up with the *perfect* addition to the scene; fear of being vulnerable or looking out of control for a moment.

I have frequently seen this type of fear-induced improv onstage and in the rehearsal hall. It usually takes the form of lackluster dialogue – such as "How are you?" or "What do you want to do?" – often at the top of a scene when little of value has been established. I imagine these moments are familiar to us all. And, generally, such moments *don't* add energy or interest and *do* punt the ball back to the other player without any resonating potential or detail. While I agree that this type of question asking doesn't typically lead to joyful scenic work, I would offer that the improv community doesn't talk enough about when questions in our scene work *are* helpful or perhaps even critical for our creative success. Yes, I agree that mundane questions lead nowhere, and furthermore that **assumptions** are typically more dynamic, but not all questions are created equal nor used in the same energy-draining way.

Example

Some oft-appearing unhelpful questions:

Player A: (pointing at a mimed object that their scene partner has just created) "What is that?"

OR

Player B: (entering a scene having barely looked at their partner's initiation) "What are you doing?"

OR

Player C: (standing idly beside their partner with a minimum of energy) "Do you want me to do something?"

OR

Player D: (standing as the first player on an empty and undefined stage, turning toward a teammate who is neutrally waiting in the wings) "Who are you?"

Setting aside these irritating examples for a moment, then, here are…

Six Great Times to Ask a Question

1. **You didn't understand your partner.** I'll start with perhaps the simplest scenario (and one that probably occurs with greater frequency for those of us who have faced teaching or performing improv online). If our partner has made a rich and grounded choice, and the acoustics, audience applause, internet connection, their accent or dialect, other onstage business, or perhaps even just our own inattentiveness, obscured this offer in such a way that we just didn't receive it, I strongly believe a check in along the lines of "What was that?" or "Would you mind repeating that?" is wholly appropriate. A quick question strikes me as infinitely more helpful than making an ill-conceived assumption that might completely negate the intent or nuance of our partner's choice. Sure, our response based on a misheard fragment might get a laugh, but especially in a long-form or narrative setting where we're striving to build an arc more patiently, this will often be inferior to a more honest reaction stemming from what our partner was intending. We don't hear each other at times in real life, so we can certainly have that happen to our characters onstage too. Here, I believe a question is an act of honoring our partner's gift and making sure we are fully appreciating the intent behind it. As an improviser predominantly working in the United States who still very much has a New Zealand idiom, I've also included dialect and accent on my list of potential contributing factors as I'm aware that, despite my efforts to the contrary, I have been the source of miscommunications and I'd always rather have my fellow improviser (as their character rather than as the actor preferably) seek quick clarification so that the scene can then continue to dance merrily forward.

2. **You immediately answer the question yourself.** Though this perhaps isn't a good reason to ask a question in the first place, it is a helpful strategy for those moments when a bland one slips out. If you inadvertently ask your partner, "What is that?" and then immediately follow up with "You found my missing engagement ring," or "That is the answer sheet to our history test this afternoon," or "We agreed that we weren't going to bring home any more stray animals," then you've quickly taken a dull choice and given it some added luster and specificity. If the initial dull question was primed with a strong emotion or point of view, then this works even better with the second choice adding content to the tension or dynamism of the first. Essentially, you're playing "yes, and…" with yourself at this point, noting that your "yes" wasn't the most inspiring offer at first.

3. **You are playing a role that would usually ask questions.** This is perhaps the most obvious exception in my mind, and while many would agree that we want to avoid **transaction scenes** and that questions tend to lurk at the core of these dynamics, some scenarios almost demand that we embrace our function (at least initially) as the questioner. A teacher calling in a student to a conference, a mechanic examining an unfamiliar car, a doctor giving a patient their annual exam – it is not unlikely that each of these scenes might take its first steps with some paradigmatic questions… "Did you get any help writing this paper?" or "Do you know where the clunking sound was coming from?" or "So what brings you into my office today?" I would suggest that we wouldn't want the scene to typically consist *only* of one-sided open questions, but it is not unforeseeable nor unhelpful for this dynamic to emerge and help provide the platform or balance of our world. In these scenarios, it could also be a fun inversion to use questions but have them come from the unexpected character, so now the patient asks the doctor about their health issues. You could also apply the above strategy to up the heat so that "Did you get any help writing this paper?" is quickly followed by "Because I wrote one *exactly* like it when I was an undergrad." Or use the strategy below…

4. **You are asking a loaded question.** In terms of question strategies, this is probably the approach I recommend most in my own classes. Acknowledging that questions will slip out and that we don't want to get in our heads about it, I offer that it is the intensity of the question that is important. Most of us would agree that a "How are you?" is less likely to get creative juices going than "Have you been managing okay at home alone after your back surgery?" There is no reason that the question can't in and of itself make nuanced assumptions about the world and relationship we are creating. The first question likely evolved from fear, while the second clearly presents interesting opportunities for the partner and scene, especially if it is accompanied with a thoughtful physical action and perhaps justifies any previously established energies or circumstances. I would offer one warning about loaded questions that is somewhat embedded in the surgery example above: improvisers should pay as much attention to *how* they are saying their question as to the details of the question itself or it can start to feel as if you are

cartooning or announcing choices rather than giving them full emotional weight. In this way, our inquiry about recovery could be showing great care for our partner, frustration that they keep calling for us to come around, or a more sinister hope that our plan to off our rival is finally working. Emotion and subtext here make all the difference. In short-form interview games where questions are central to the premise and structure, loaded questions are also an excellent way to give the interviewer a little more dynamism and weight as a character in their own right rather than *merely* a facilitator enabling the fun of the expert.

5. **You are using questions to heighten a game.** Some scenes thrive on questions. The appropriately named short-form game Questions Only or any of the multiple Expert variants serve as obvious examples, but there are many other situations where questions might add to the style or finesse of a scene. A cascade of questions can prove thoroughly successful in a Shakespeare or period-specific scenario when they escalate and create tension or playfulness between characters. I can't imagine *Private Lies: Improvised Film Noir* without a good dose of detective questions, for example, as that's part of the gumshoe's raison d'être. If a scene is exploring a more complex dynamic, such as in a mapping scene (where one scenario is played with the intensity and tropes of another) questions especially of a vaguer variety can help prolong the game and delight. If we're playing a scene in which a parent has discovered a comic book but is mapping this moment with the energy of a parent discovering illicit drugs, a carefully pitched "What is this?" along with a suitable gesture will serve the scene well. Here, the audience and players alike know the identity of the "this" so there's nothing problematic about the choice. We often played a version of Old Job, New Job in our *Gorilla Theatre* show at Sak Comedy

Figure 14.1 Questions are part and parcel of many style-based improv shows, such as *Private Lies: Improvised Film Noir* (Associate director: Travis Ray; Lighting designer: Kevin Griffin). Photo credit: Tony Firriolo.

Lab which similarly deploys this mapping concept, and I could certainly happily watch a whole sceneful of questions coming from a doctor who used to be a mechanic: "Do you know where the clunking sound was coming from?"

6. **You are checking in with your scene partner.** I've worked with many companies that deal with this issue in different ways, but there are times as we create together (moments inviting stage violence, intimacy, or potentially triggering or sensitive material) when I would argue it is not only appropriate to ask a question, but it is critical that we do so. We're improvising, and especially if you're playing in a context where "mature" or "adult" themes might emerge, we need to keep the safety of our partners front of mind. I think it's important to note that I don't really mean racy when I say "mature" or "adult," although sadly I think that's what a lot of improv inclines toward when it says it's pushing boundaries or is edgy. What I mean by these terms is that we're exploring material with sincerity and nuance in such a way that it might resonate deeply with our partners or audience. This is the type of *edgy* improv I'm personally most interested in. In these instances, a careful question can be an important way to check in with our scene partner, especially if this is someone we don't know particularly well yet. If I ask, "Do you want to fight me?" in a heated exchange then my partner can have me take that action offstage if that is what they need to do. If I ask, "Would you mind if I kissed you?" then my partner can frame a response that can honor the energy of the scene while maintaining their personal boundaries: "I desperately want to kiss you, but let's do it inside so the neighbors won't see…" If I nudge into material that I can see is stirring my partner, I can ask "Do you need me to leave now?" and then can honor their response while upholding the integrity of the scene. I've found this to be a less commonly needed tool in troupes that have developed a deep rapport and know a lot about each other's comfort zones and backstories, but I think this is an important strategy to have in our pockets to maintain a safe and playful stage. It's worth noting that this approach should also be applied to potentially "racy" material if the company hasn't previously agreed upon performance parameters prior to the show.

Final Thought

Yes, with some mental wrangling many of the questions illustrated in the above examples could be word smithed into statements, but I'm not sure that is a good use of our energy and concentration as improvisers; and furthermore, modeling consent on the improv stage strikes me as an important result of not needlessly demonizing the act of asking a question in and of itself.

Related Entries: Cartooning, Consent, Initiation, Offer, Speaking Your Truth, Specificity, Subtext
Antonym: Assumption
Connected Game: Questions Only

RANDOMNESS

A seeming kin of improvisation, randomness doesn't innately privilege connection, story, and structure, which are fundamental components of most improv practices. In this light, randomness offers an almost oppositional force, although some surprises and inexplicable inspiration certainly add to the creative process.

Synonym: Over-Originality

REHEARSAL ETIQUETTE

When I first read Mick Napier's *Improvise: Scene From the Inside Out*, I was inspired by his "Tips for Success" to collate my own **Rehearsal Etiquette** pointers. I've used the resulting document for most of my on-campus long-form work since and a gently adjusted version for my scripted shows too. As my university improv shows exist under a "conventional" theatre model – with directing and design teams, and five to six evening rehearsals each week – you'll feel these production circumstances and assumptions pulsing through the language. I'm by no means advocating a wholesale adoption of these guides as each venue and project has a different face and needs. Ensemble created pieces, for example, don't always utilize a traditional singular director or artistic team distinct from the troupe itself. But I hope that these hard learned lessons and approaches might facilitate your own formalized (or informal) practices. I found it extremely helpful just to go through the process of committing these to paper and imagine that the same might hold true for you.

Ten Rehearsal Etiquette Pointers

1. **Rehearsals are an apology free zone.** The rehearsal hall is a space for exploring and trying things out, so don't apologize for your stumbles or contextualize your work with an air of apology. Forgive yourself and others quickly and move on. There will be many other opportunities to fall and get up again.
2. **Focus on the work.** Refrain from bringing other reading, homework, or projects into the theatre space. There is plenty of learning to be had from the work of others as well as your own efforts. Undivided attention is a sign of respect and encouragement, and the bedrock of a collaborative rehearsal period. The creative team is committed to releasing you from the rehearsal space if you are not actively needed. Phones need to be put away during rehearsal until official breaks; stage management will keep everyone on schedule, so you won't need to keep checking the time.
3. **Fully commit.** Jump up to participate, join warm-ups, volunteer with excitement, and be the first to try the scene or dynamic that scares you most. Don't make others drag you along for the ride or perform the role of "tired" or "sick" company member. Don't fall into the trap of being "an opening night" performer who doesn't give it their all until an audience is present thereby denying your fellow players the necessity of your fully engaged energy. Full commitment extends to your punctuality and attendance as well.
4. **Notes are for directors.** Avoid giving fellow company members notes or unsolicited feedback. (An exception to this rule is if you felt unsafe or unsupported, or if something truly rocked and needs to be celebrated.) Let fellow company members learn through the doing and allow feedback to flow through the director and directing team. If you have a question or observation that will assist the whole team, by all means ask it. If you have a question or observation that will only primarily benefit you, wait until rehearsal is over and bend the director's ear privately.
5. **Positivity is contagious.** Relish the struggle. Applaud your own efforts and those of others. Celebrate that each "mistake" brings the ensemble one step closer to finding a more promising and joyful path forward. Don't let negativity or outside rants lurk in the background of the work. Find the love both on and off the stage.
6. **Try it.** If you find yourself on the verge of asking permission to try something or asking a question of clarification out of the fear of getting something "wrong," pause for a second and just allow yourself (and the rest of those in attendance) the gift of putting your question into action. Great discoveries are made through happy accidents or out-of-the-box approaches that weren't hamstrung by circuitous pontificating or misplaced efforts of getting it "right."
7. **Find your own type of improviser and celebrate it.** An ensemble is made up of a selection of players with various talents and strengths. You will not be good at everything; you don't have to be. Don't fall into the trap of disparaging comparison. Work on your deficits, but be sure to recognize your own assets (and those of your fellow improvisers).
8. **Exercise patience.** When fellow players are struggling with something that comes as second nature to you, model patience and attentiveness. Everyone works at different speeds, and you'll appreciate it when this attitude of grace is returned during your own moments of stress. Also, be careful of "helpful suggestions" during the heat of struggle as these can add to frustration rather than serve as an antidote to it. Leave room for everyone to have their own process.
9. **Leave your day at the door (as best you can).** Or use your day to help you mine deeper truths. Or use your day as a source of finding connected material. Or use your day to heighten your emotional storehouse… Just don't use your day to separate or isolate yourself from the process or the rest of the group as a whole. If you are truly not in a healthy space to work and need to be absent, contact the team prior to the rehearsal as early as you can so that any necessary adjustments can be made.
10. **Choose to be a contributing member of the team.** Be wary of sitting apart from the group, or always stepping outside when others are working, or sleeping, or constantly checking your phone, Facebook, or email as the rehearsal is in session. As in any good improv scene, exist in the real here and now with your fellow players.

Final Thought

Spolin rightly attests that "The techniques of the theater are the techniques of communicating."[2] Improv is communication made manifest, and poor interpersonal communication during the process and behind the scenes is more than likely to spill out into the onstage work as well if left unattended. These written thoughts are part of my earnest attempt to start rehearsals on a promising footing. As is the case with most classroom syllabi, the above ideas are a living document and in no small part responsive to issues or trends I've noted in the improvisational rehearsal hall to date. While it might be revealing my teacherly side, I think it's helpful to read these aloud and share them during the first rehearsal when possible as this embodies a clear commitment to the value and centrality of these (or your own) tenets. Although these were written with a student population in mind, as I have reviewed them for this undertaking, I would observe that many of these tensions emerge equally in non-academic venues as well.

More detailed thoughts on post-show notes and a collective feedback model can be found in my consideration of the **postmortem**.

> **Related Entries:** Acting, Ensemble, Postmortem **Antonym:** Bad Habits
> **Synonyms:** Teamwork, Professionalism
> **Connected Game:** Simultaneous Clap

REINCORPORATION

Reincorporation, the practice of reusing previously established story elements and facts, provides a critical improvisational tool for constructing coherent and cogent stories. Frost and Yarrow consider this technique as a particularly defining element of Johnstone's work:

> Johnstone abandons the notion of content, and concentrates instead on structure – the key to which is reincorporation [...] Free association takes care of invention and development; reincorporation takes care of structure.[3]

There are several important related terms and strategies connected to the current subject of discussion, the first and foremost being **shelving** which consists of creating details and momentarily setting them aside. Two other similar ideas deserve quick mention as well: **callbacks** generally display great patience before weaving shelved elements optimally back into the mix, while **connections** often reflect a greater sense of the whole by adding to an overarching design or underlying motif. The skill of reincorporation undeniably enables both these practices, but here, for the purposes of leaning into the distinctions rather than the similarities of related improv tools, I will consider the more foundational aspects of this broader term; namely, the simple (at least in theory) process of seeing or hearing something and then keeping this offer alive and in the flow of the scene. Reincorporating, in this wholistic sense, can be viewed as the act of conscious and deliberate repetition.

Example

A nervous Player A enters a formal office for their crucial job interview. They mime removing a rain-drenched coat and hanging it inelegantly on a coat stand in the corner of the room. As they approach their seat at the edge of the ominous boss's desk, they place their equally drenched briefcase on their lap, awkwardly fumble with the locking mechanism, and then eventually pull out a copy of their curriculum vitae, all as Player B (the boss) patiently watches on from the comfort of their oversized plush chair.

Player A: (extending their right hand to shake and their left hand with their résumé) "It's such an honor to meet you, Ms. Kojic. I'm Joseph Shoemaker..."

Repeat After Me...

1. **Repeat it.** To repeat a choice – either your own or, even better, someone else's – exponentially increases the likelihood that it will helpfully stay in the scenic mix for future use and reference. Improvised names, in particular, can tend to quickly evaporate if they are not deliberately and frequently echoed. Such a failure can particularly cause problems down the road in more substantial long-form pieces. Just as one would in a social situation meeting a new colleague for the first time, it's good form to keep newly proffered names (or any detail for that matter) alive and well through the simple act of repetition...

Player B: (happily taking the résumé) "I've been greatly looking forward to finally meeting you in person, Mr. Shoemaker..."

2. **Use it.** Reincorporations are obviously not limited to the verbal components of a scene, and similar repetitions can be utilized when it comes to physical offers and creations. Player A has crafted several rich choices in their first scenic salvo – the coat rack, the briefcase, the résumé – all of which singularly or combined can provide exciting next steps and possibilities. Ignoring these potentials for too

long will, once again, increase the chances that they may be forgotten (or misplaced in the case of mimed space objects). Even if you don't draw attention to your move, honoring the nuances of physical gifts keeps them in play even if you place them temporarily on the improv shelf for later use.

Player B: (gingerly taking the now soggy résumé) "I'll just let this dry out a little before giving it a closer inspection…"

3. **Mirror it.** More global or environmental choices – the time of day, temperature, outside influences – are also rich sites for recycling and reincorporation. A seemingly throwaway choice, such as noting that the interview is happening on the weekend, may open up interesting pathways, especially if you find yourself in a familiar scenic trope or dynamic. If a scene partner offers up a contextualizing choice, honor it by taking it fully on board and reflecting it back. This also applies to any "stage geography" that emerges – the placement of the office door, the location of the coat rack, the size of the boss's desk. The sooner your character utilizes these elements, the more likely they will remain credible and creatively useful.

Player B: (stepping out from behind their grand desk and going over to a window on the "fourth wall," pulling it firmly closed as they shudder from the cold) "Sorry you had to come out in this terrible weather. I got drenched as well driving into the office earlier today."

4. **Frame it.** When it comes to character or object behaviors and quirks, another potent strategy is reincorporating an idea by setting up the conditions for its reappearance as opposed to just repeating the detail yourself. Player A has provided a lot of specific behavior with their entrance, offering up inclement weather, a rather drenched exterior (and probably equally nervous interior), as well as a wet résumé and idiosyncratic briefcase. Rather than replicating or commenting on these ideas, an observant scene partner can provide a choice that invites the reappearance of a previously established dynamic. In many ways, this could serve as the second move of a "game."

Player B: (with a gesture toward the now locked briefcase) "You wouldn't happen to have another copy of your C.V. in there for my assistant who'll be joining us shortly, would you?"

5. **Elevate it.** Lastly, a reincorporation mindset can be used to elevate a prior choice by making it special or memorable. Arguably, all the above approaches could or should include a little of this ingredient as repeating an offer, by the very act of selection, indicates that the recipient has deemed it potentially worthy of some extra improv love and attention. A creative embellishment, however, can take something that may have seemed mundane at first glance, and move it powerfully front and center. In many instances, this is even *more* delightful and impactful when the initiator was not particularly intending their contribution as a significant move.

Player B: (gesturing to the apparent storm outside the window) "This frightful weather really is a reminder of how critical the work is we want to do here at the Environmental Initiative…"

Final Thought

To reiterate, this entry considers the simplest and most foundational subset of reincorporation: callbacks and connections embody the utility of a more patient or calculated approach. Immediate reincorporation does start to resemble basic "yes, anding" in its form and function which is, by all means, a laudable improv attitude in its own right. However, if you start to feel like an inelegant parrot, waiting a few beats to recycle a choice again serves the same purpose in a slightly less obvious fashion. Weaving your partner's name into the dialogue, referencing the wet résumé, or crossing over to the established coat rack to get your keys a minute or two into the scene will equally assist the creative endeavor, especially if you're working in a more expansive or leisurely style of performance.

When we improvise, we never know where the interest or creativity will come from; we increase the chances that these energies will emerge when we carefully use what has already been crafted (rather than fish for that "perfect" something that isn't actually there). In this sense, to reincorporate is to trust that, in most cases, the great choices you are looking for have probably already happened, they just need us all to pay appropriate attention to recognize them.

Related Entries: Accepting, Callback, Connections, Looking Backwards, Names **Antonym:** Shelving **Synonyms:** Recycling, Repeating, Reusing **Connected Game:** Word Association Reincorporation Story

RELATIONSHIP

The second pillar of **CROW**, **Relationship**, closely interacts with and enriches the earlier concept of **character**. With the exception of solo pieces (and even then, there are often implied or absent scene partners) an audience typically understands our characters based on how they engage with others in their environment. Through the lens of relationship, characters are rarely static or *one* thing: how a parental character treats their child will differ from their energies on their job site with fellow co-workers, or when dealing with poor service at a restaurant. Enjoying these energy shifts and contradictions – rather than clinging onto a misplaced desire for consistency – allows for the emergence of rich portrayals worthy of our collective time and attention. So much of who we are reflects how we are shaped by the diverse array of people we encounter on a daily basis. The same should hold true for our stage creations. And as Izzo notes, "We hunger today for the mirror of human relationship and personal interaction. We yearn to play."[4]

Example

Player B, Ms. Kojic, a powerful and confident executive, has just completed conducting a job interview with Player A. (See my previous entry on reincorporation for a refresher.) In the prior scene, we saw her in her element, exerting gentle but nonetheless recognizable control over the workplace.

The stage transitions into a new location, B's home. As they enter their palatial living room – the rainstorm still rattling in the distance – they are greeted by their new scene partner, Player C…

Making the Most Out of Your Onstage Relationships

1. **Want.** Strong objectives typically seek something specific from our current scene partners (as I discuss in my related "O" entry). If we do not want or need anything from those with whom we share the stage, then there is very little honest impetus for our characters to connect and build energy. It follows, too, that as our scene partners change so will our wants, or at the very least, the tactics or ways in which we actively try to achieve these desires. While character "B" might have been seeking to "woo over a highly desirable new employee" at the office, it's unlikely that this will also hold true when they arrive home and play out a scene with their teenage child. There may be some commonalities – "B" might seek some form of respect in both cases – but the tonality and specifics are likely *very* different. If you float from scene to scene and partner to partner with only one generic objective in play you are probably painting with just a small sampling of your character's available pigments. So be sure to want something clear, specific, and suited to your current circumstances.

2. **Echo.** This advice can hold true in most situations, but it's particularly helpful for a character that might have fallen out of rotation for a few scenes or who was previously somewhat ancillary: consider echoing an emblematic behavior or scenic element that connects you to your prior appearances. If Player B was painfully organized during their job interview, exerting strong control over every inch of their world, it will probably prove helpful to the performers and the audience if some semblance of this energy reappears, even just fleetingly, so that we can connect the scenic dots and guarantee that everyone is on the same imaginary improv page. On a simple level, just mentioning a prior scene can do the trick – "I think I've secured our top pick for the firm" – although this can feel like **cartooning** if you're not careful and grounded. (There can also be a dramatic value in withholding these connections strategically as a reveal, but this is still honoring the general echo philosophy.) This is not to suggest that such echoes should then dominate the current action: talking ad nauseum about that job interview you just had in a way that essentially replicates the earlier scene won't add much. But carrying the cobwebs of this encounter can provide some nuance even when (ideally) the next appearance assumes a very different tone and purpose as you…

3. **Complicate.** While echoing helps establish a character baseline through recognizable habits, too much behavioral or energy repetition (especially in long-form modes) can become limiting and redundant. If your high-powered boss is the same high-powered boss in *every* scenario, then they will risk becoming an unmelodic one-note symphony. Subsequent character appearances benefit from an attitude of complication: how can this new scene challenge or add flavor to what we already know? This may involve exploring a similar character choice but in different ways: what blindness, limitation, or strength that we have previously established also manifests itself in this new relationship? Is our authoritative boss similarly controlling or confident in their family sphere? If this is the case, what does this particular brand of power look like? Are habits that serve character "B" well in

the office less welcome or even detrimental if they are not turned off upon arriving home? Even if you elect to hit the stage as largely the same person we saw before, just your change in relationship *should* shed some new light on your characterization.

4. **Reveal.** To dig a level deeper, in addition to complicating our character foundation, new relationships have the profound potential to open up whole new facets and features. It can prove helpful simply to inquire as you take your first scenic steps "what can I show or explore in *this* relationship that I'm unable to openly reveal in others?" There are countless forms this can take from vulnerability and weakness to certitude and control. Our boss, Ms. Kojic, who appeared as the picture of professionalism and aplomb might reveal a frazzled or tumultuous interior when she returns home to her invalid mother and a stream of taxing requests. Or perhaps the cool but approachable exterior seen in the job interview gives way to a passionate tryst with her former high school lover who is only in town for a few days. It is perhaps asking a lot for *every* character in an ensemble piece to reveal new shade after shade, but those with whom the audience has become most invested – our protagonist and antagonist, for example – benefit from as broad an array of relationship energies as the company can muster.

5. **Evolve.** Finally, especially in pieces with more substantial room for exploration, characters benefit from using their onstage relationships to evolve. A story arc in which an underdog remains an underdog without any glimmer of hope for advancement can quickly strain interest, as can adventures in which gallant heroes and heroines never truly face a challenge or the potential for failure. In short-form modalities, the pursuit of evolving can feel unlikely, but even here, characters can mine their onstage relationships for meaningful tilts and discoveries proportionate to the stage time they occupy. When selecting scene partners (and energies) this focus provides a helpful casting tool: what relationship can reveal our protagonist's fatal flaw or bring out our villain's redeeming qualities? It may prove that a character is ultimately unable to change, reflecting a more tragic style of play, but even if their attempts to evolve are finally thwarted, the embodied *struggle* should prove stage worthy. In epic pieces, the evolution might also span historic passages of time: perhaps we learn that our environmentally conscious employer is the heiress to a family fortune earned through mass pollution and exploitation. Here, our protagonist's development is as much comparative to their ancestors as it is to their own actions, but the stakes and import are raised through such context, nonetheless.

Final Thought

Carefully chosen and executed relationships can add volumes to the improvisational endeavor, empowering our characters to go on worthy and complex adventures. While at first glance it might appear that the specific choice of a relationship is critical to enable this type of dynamic play, in reality, most characters can fulfill one or many of the above functions given the opportunity and some degree of thoughtfulness on the part of the improviser. What's important at the end of the day is forging energized connections that are ripe with opportunities for discovery and development.

Related Entries: Bulletproof, Character, CROW, Objective, Where
Antonym: Strangers **Synonym:** Who
Connected Game: Here Comes the Bus

REVELATION

Surprising your partner (and possibly yourself) with an offer that shifts the balance or power of a scene.

Synonym: CAD

RHYME

There once was a young man from Lyme
Who couldn't get his limericks to rhyme.
When asked "Why not?"
It was said that he thought
They were probably too long and badly structured and not at all very funny. – Anonymous

I must admit I'm a little obsessed with **Rhyme** and how it can infuse and elevate musical and style-based improv. Pursuing rhyme is also a wonderful way to unlock unexpected plot and narrative twists – I've been known to joke that I can't be held fully accountable for where rhyming takes me on stage! While rhyme might feel like a tangential skill, it appears in many deciders, short-form games, and augments a wide array of elevated scene work, from the Greeks, to Shakespeare, to contemporary hip-hop and slam poetry battles. As Smith and Dean describe in their *Improvisation, Hypermedia and the Arts since 1945*, rhyming games are also a well-established form of modern Western improv. They write that

> Richard Tarleton, the famous Elizabethan clown active in the late sixteenth century, often improvised at the end of a play and engaged in contests with the members of the audience who would throw up rhymes which he was expected to better, but he would also sometimes add improvised speeches in the course of the play.[5] Even if you feel this skill will never be solidly in your wheelhouse, a familiarity with the basic strategies involved in crafting spur-of-the-moment verse can only help your verbal acuity and attack.

Example

Two farmers work in the field on a hot summer day. One is tinkering with their tractor while the other is mending a damaged fence.

Player A: "This scorching sun is not our friend."
Player B: "I fear this day will never end.
           The tractor's dead. It will not start."
Player A: "The fence is rotten – every part."
Player B: "The world conspires to do us harm…"
Player A: "Yet all we have is this old farm!"

Climbing the Rhyming Mountain

Like all skill sets in the improv canon, it might take you a while to find comfort in the land of rhyme, and some players are innately more adept than others. But each journey begins with a few brave steps, and I offer these foundational approaches with that in mind.

1. **Play from a place of joy and calmness.** When you approach rhyming situations, it's helpful to remind yourself that not every rhyme will be a "winner." If you expect *every* couplet to zing, you may have set yourself up with an insurmountable hurdle. It's okay to sweat a little, and, in many cases, this struggle adds great charm and performance value to the whole affair. When you play with abandon and joy, even your stumbles can land like amazing successes. I also always remind my students that every word has one perfect rhyme – namely, the word itself. Now yes, you don't want to overuse this failsafe method (or your rhyming scene will no longer feel like a rhyming scene) but knowing that there's *something* in your pocket for even the most challenging situation can go a long way in reducing anxiety. A slightly more advanced variant of this approach is to keep the final word but rhyme the penultimate one – so "blood orange" could be rhymed with "dud orange…"

2. **Don't forget the basics.** It's extremely difficult to rhyme with something that hasn't been clearly heard – especially when you're playing in a setting where rhyming couplets or clusters are shared – so be sure to speak (or sing) with clarity and in a way that unmistakably features the rhyming offers and responses. On a technical level, punching that final intended word a little can make a world of difference. It also doesn't hurt to pitch the pertinent word to the likely next speaker as usually we're able to clear up any confusion when we can see our scene partner's mouths and expressions. If you're inclined to verbosity or cramming excessive words into your allotted time or sentence, be aware that this habit may be causing others undue and unnecessary stress. Especially when you're establishing the scene or game, less is more in terms of words and will allow you a little extra space to really sell and act your offer.

3. **Structure and rhyme schemes are your friend.** Whether it's in the pursuit of an improvised song, playing a highly patterned decider like Da Doo Ron Ron, or sharing couplets between characters in a scene, structure can be your best friend or worst enemy. There is so much tempting us as players to retreat into our heads in search of new choices when rhyme is part of the equation, but if you lose the greater thread, your perfect rhyme could create more turmoil than acclaim. I'll often see an excited player throw on that third rhyme (which they've proudly formulated in their head and can't let go of) when a couplet pattern has been established as the norm, thereby throwing off the rhythms of the scene. This typically causes confusion as to whether this third line ("… flight" followed by "… night" followed by an unexpected "… plight") marks the first offer of a *new* couplet or should be left as an exceptional third in its own right. When a clear rhyme scheme or pattern has been set up and maintained, it behooves everyone to follow this blueprint unless a departure serves as a deliberate and rich breach – this may be the case for the final exchange in a scene, for example. This holds true for line lengths as well: a line of eight syllables followed by a meandering line of 20 is unlikely to hit the ear as a strong rhyme even if the two last words are beautiful lyrical matches.

4. **Keep an eye on what greater purpose rhyme is serving.** In some cases, rhyme is the name of the game, such as when you're playing in an elimination warm-up, but more times than not it is *one* element of the scene that seeks to serve story and character. If this is a less comfortable skill set, it is understandable that it might consume much of your focus, and perhaps this is a somewhat unavoidable stage in most improvisers' pathway toward rhyming confidence. However, few improv scenes will thrive if we're *only* concentrating on our language finesse. Make sure you're confidently bringing all your other gifts to the improv party as well and that rhyme is serving a greater scenic purpose or goal. Through the lens of character, a great deal can become justified or contextualized. A fluency with verse can reflect a lover's unfettered passion; a more plodding use of language could conversely suggest a character's simplicity or earnestness.

5. **An open vowel can go a long way.** If you are starting to scramble, embrace the gift of ending on an open vowel ("oo," "ay," or "ee") or a common word ending ("ate," "at," or "in.") While it's a strong choice to head toward a specific word or set up (as noted below), an open sound will leave multiple options available to you or your fellow players. Such an approach can also unlock the delightful generative quality of rhyming as well as there is a sense of true uncertainty as to where the next line will land and how this will influence the action or narrative. My only caution would be not to keep going to the same well over and over again. This can become particularly problematic if a memorable rhyming couplet or exchange has been crafted and then players return to these same sounds or words again (and again). Often, this will result in little more than a clumsier and less effective echo of the prior moment. Unless you're engaging in a truly epic long-form rhyming extravaganza, it's helpful to consider prior rhyming partners "burnt" whenever feasibly possible. The exception would be if you're pitching to a recurring hook or chorus phrase where the game can become finding *new* ways to rhyme with the established line. This would also serve as an example of this last strategy…

6. **A little targeting adds finesse.** Lastly, as you find greater ease with the tenets of rhyme, incorporating some target rhyming will greatly add to the impressiveness of your work. When you target rhyme, you set up a strong potential that is clearly linked to the current story or topic by providing the less on-the-money rhyme *first*. So, if the scene or song is about elephants the first speaker might opine "I'm so in love, I'm almost drunk" to gift the next player the elephant-inspired target word of "trunk." In group games, this is a great way to not only add value but also make your partners look good. The payoff, however, is equally joyous if you're setting yourself up for such a moment in a song or spoken couplet. This philosophy of reverse engineering a little – that is, thinking initially of the word you'd like to end on – is a strong approach in general, especially if you've clearly landed the other foundational elements of the scene. In this manner, you can focus on getting to your desired word or rhyme rather than suddenly arriving at the end of your thought and throwing out something opaque, poorly articulated, or just plain impossible to use. If I'm personally a little anxious or in my head, target rhyming will feel less manageable for me as a player, but even a little of this ingredient can really elevate your play, especially if it's used strategically to highlight verse endings, scenic buttons, or moments of emotional import.

Final Thought

If this skill scares you a little (or a lot), rhyming is one of the few improv subsets that you can effectively rehearse alone in your spare time as you walk between classes or meetings or while doing your laundry. In some ways, there really isn't a fast-track superior to just getting in some rotations when the stakes are low and no one else is watching!

Related Entry: Verbal Skills **Antonyms:** Not Rhyming, Prose **Synonyms:** Poetry, Verse **Connected Game:** Rhyme Fire-Line

---

RISING ACTION

The events of a linear scene or play that span the distance between the ignition and the climax, generally increasing the stakes and peril of the protagonist as they are met by the opposing force of the antagonist and their agents.

Antonym: Falling Action

ROUTINE

An uninterrupted pattern that generally invites disruption in order to launch the story into compelling action.

Synonym: Balance

RUG PULL

The typically comedic device of suddenly inverting or upending the reality of a scene. Such a move may "name the game" or starkly shift or adjust the assumed context so that the prior action is now viewed in a new way.

Related Entry: Gagging

RULE OF THREES

A widely held belief that three appearances of a story dynamic, element, or specific is innately joyful and possibly humorous. A widely held belief that three appearances of a story dynamic, element, or specific is innately joyful and possibly humorous. A widely held belief that three appearances of a story dynamic, element, or specific is innately joyful and possibly humorous.

Related Entry: Reincorporation

RULES

Inherited techniques and wisdoms that can help inform improvisational play (or potentially suffocate it when they are applied poorly and without nuance).

Related Entry: Commandments

NOTES

1. Charna Halpern et al., *Truth in Comedy. The Manual of Improvisation.* Colorado Springs: Meriwether, 1994. p. 57.
2. Viola Spolin, *Theater Games for Rehearsal: A Director's Handbook.* Evanston, IL: Northwestern UP, 1985. p. 5.
3. Anthony Frost and Ralph Yarrow, *Improvisation in Drama.* New York: St. Martin's Press, 1989. p. 135.
4. Gary Izzo, *The Art of Play. The New Genre of Interactive Theatre.* Portsmouth, NH: Heinemann, 1997. p. 6.
5. Hazel Smith and Roger Dean, *Improvisation, Hypermedia and the Arts since 1945.* Amsterdam: Overseas Publishing Association, 1997. p. 11.

S

SCENE PAINTING

I think I might have been a little late to the scene painting party in terms of my own personal improvisational journey! My early training was primarily through short-form games and the particular tradition under consideration strikes me as more common among Chicago-style long-form practitioners. I'm also inclined to add fully realized theatrical elements when I'm able in my own devised pieces. But that being said, there is undeniably something wondrously freeing about a purely imaginary approach to creating your improv worlds. Halpern describes this creative state when she notes, "Since real props cannot be transformed, they become a burden: when actual physical props are sitting around on stage, they limit the improvised creation of other props."[1]

Scene Painting literally allows *anything* to manifest on stage through the illustrative narrative efforts of the company (as opposed to a more mimetic or "space object" creative approach). The way in which scenic elements are spoken into being varies. Ensemble members might pause the action to briefly describe a physical detail such as a noteworthy prop or facet of the environment. This is relatively common in Harold-esque structures, where players routinely assume both character and editorial functions. In other cases, scene painting can serve as a dramatic preamble of sorts, initially establishing the given circumstances and then giving way to more traditional embodied action: this is the basic premise of the short-form game Prologue. Formats with built-in narrators, directors, or sidecoaches – such as *Gorilla Theatre* performances or the scenic game Typewriter – might combine these first two approaches with an outside eye offering up helpful scenic embellishments when and where they're needed. In my own work, I've also used this device as an overtly theatrical choral function in a long-form Greek tragedy where members of the chorus poetically described the scenic elements throughout the action. And it's become a defining feature of a more recent undertaking, *Lights Up: The Improvised Rock Opera*, that incorporates company members alternating into narrating epic contexts and stage effects for a show with no real props or costume pieces. Needless to say, scene painting can add a *lot* of detail to your improv under a wide variety of circumstances and with minimal expense!

Example

Three players (A, B, and C) assume various positions in a line across the stage adopting the personae of dreary subway passengers...

A few beats into the scene an offstage player, D, strategically enters the space (or perhaps speaks from the lip of the stage) to further describe the action as the performers gently pause...

Player D: "The florescent lights flicker on and off as the subway car lurches clumsily forward..."

OR

As the three subway improvisers place themselves, a teammate or director narrates an introduction...

Player D: "It was much later than Casey preferred to ride the subway home, and so as the cabin shuddered over the rickety track he clung extra tightly to his freshly finished manuscript..."

OR

One at a time the chorus of players pontificates on their surroundings...

Player A: "Oh, slow-moving A train, sleepily carrying your last impatient haul of the day..."

Player B: "Dim shadows of impersonal buildings flick past your grey dusty windows, slowly becoming sparser as the dense metropolis gives way to suburban sprawl..."

Player C: "Your wary cast of regulars busy themselves with idle distractions – a cell phone, newspaper, earbud music – avoiding eye contact or communication, until the arrival of the stranger..."

OR

Players slowly populate a dimmed stage as an offstage voice sets the scene...

Player D: "Sharp beams of light punctuate the darkness. Eerie train clicks undulate through the auditorium as several lonely figures can be seen in the brief flashes of stage light. From the orchestra pit, the drummer joins the rhythmic cacophony as the subway travelers slowly start to pulse to the loudening beat..."

Pigments of Your Imagination

1. **Get in and out quickly.** Unless the intent is to create epic narratives, scene painting generally aims to augment the action quickly rather than grind it to a halt. You'll want to be careful about voluminous or clumsy additions that awkwardly interrupt the flow of the story or impede the characters from building and sustaining momentum. Sparsely produced improv is particularly well-suited to this stealthy approach with its bank of improvisers usually lurking on the back wall or sides of the stage with quick access to the action as needed when inspiration hits. More often than not I've seen such moments delivered essentially through the fourth wall with direct address to the audience, perhaps with some directional gestures to indicate specific placements and the like. Such a style deliberately contrasts clearly with the more representational delivery of the characters within the world of the scene (which also prevents any confusion as to the intent behind the addition). When in doubt, follow the common adage that "less is more" and strive to deliver your offer as concisely as you can. I've seen a succession of scene painting contributions become the game of the scene, and this is certainly a fun and playful use of the dynamic, but usually these metatheatrical additions serve better as gentle nudges rather than riveting opuses in their own right (unless that's the goal of course).

2. **Create rather than repeat.** By design, scene painting offers should add new elements or circumstances rather than merely reiterate what has already been well established. There's no need, for example, to say that a young passenger stands beside the subway train door if this is a reality that has been clearly embodied and that the audience has already seen. The innate value of scene painting is that it can be utilized to introduce or heighten choices that might feel a little clumsy or resemble **cartooning** coming from the characters themselves. In this manner, such narrative inserts can jumpstart a scene that might be floundering a little in its balance or provide (or draw attention to) a promising spice or texture that the onstage characters will find invigorating. What environmental influence or addition might intensify the scenic energy, or warrant further investigation, or appeal to the improvisers' imaginations in a way that can spark new adventures and relationships? As scene painting can become a little addictive – it is such an enticing way to contextualize and shape the stage action – it's helpful to keep in mind *why* you're contributing to the scene to minimize your chances of overwhelming the players. If you're heightening a game, will your "move" further this dynamic or merely postpone the story arc? Are you surprising your fellow improvisers in ways that open new doorways, or has the device become a form of **gagging** or **pimping** for your own pleasure and amusement?

3. **Consider your tone and delivery #1.** Quick-hit scene painting tends to assume a metatheatrical tone as opposed to coming through the voice of a character. Most companies that commonly use this tool have developed a clear approach to avoid creating onstage confusion and it's a relatively simple matter for the audience to quickly learn these cues – whether it's a specific staging choice or tone of voice. There is certainly plenty to be mined from enjoying this juxtaposition to the spoken dialogue within the scene proper. Furthermore, there's a wonderful opportunity to introduce rich idiosyncrasies when describing props and scenic elements. What makes this particular train a little out of the ordinary? How does this evening differ from all the other evenings for the passengers? What does this character do or wear or carry that makes them stand out a little from the crowd? Embracing poetic or nuanced language can craft inspiring and original offers that will jolt a scene out of the everyday.

Scene painting is a theatrical conceit in and of itself so enjoy this opportunity to utilize less pedestrian language and energies.

4. **Consider your tone and delivery #2.** While scene painting often serves more traditional "realistic" scene work by providing a touch of presentational finesse, in more stylistic pieces this impetus can become filtered through the lens of character as a way of adding to the overall tone or feel of the piece. I've attempted to give a little taste of this in my third example above where the train passengers evoke the grandeur of a mythic chorus narrating the entrance of their protagonist. This particular approach might not serve your own needs or tastes, but there are *many* ways to exploit the potentials of this descriptive device. Whether it's folded into the narrative of a film noir detective, incorporated into the poetic musings of a Shakespearean prologue, or becomes adeptly woven into the expositional dialogue of your first act, the conceits of scene painting can bear many fruitful gifts when it comes to establishing the greater world of your play. If you're inclined to explore narrative long-form modalities, it's well worth your time considering how you might incorporate this tool to serve your greater goals.

5. **Take full advantage of all your senses.** Lastly, I'd offer that while it's fair game to provide character-based details (moods, motivations, staging), one of the greatest gifts of scene painting is that it can materialize scenic elements that the onstage players can't easily tend to themselves such as sounds, smells, and epic sights. Enjoy the opportunity to use all your senses while also expanding the boundaries of the stage itself. In addition to telling us what a character may be wearing or holding, scene painting can describe the greater surroundings in a way that contextualizes and elevates the current action. What is happening in the room next door that might encroach upon our story? Are there weather or environmental forces at play? If you're working in a venue with limited technical abilities, can you paint features of the soundscape such as busy streets, rowdy crowds, or hectic construction sites? In *Lights Up* we've also developed the successful custom of using this device to define and describe the audience in a way that invites them to join the conceit of the show: are they discerning critics, boisterous high-schoolers, or rabid super fans ravenously consuming their favorite show? When it's worked well it adds an almost *Rocky Horror* dynamic to the show that empowers the audience to assume their own personae in the greater event.

Final Thought

Scene painting provides a helpful reminder for those of us who tend toward a more language-based style of play that there are so many physical facets of our improv worlds worthy of exploring. If your available venues are modest in terms of their technical abilities, these techniques will truly explode any perceived limitations as, ultimately, space can become anything if the company simply invests the creativity to make it so.

Related Entries: CROW, Extending, Narrative, Physicality, Space Objects, Verbal Skills, Where **Antonyms:** Emptiness, Talking Heads, Undefined Space
Connected Game: Typewriter

SECOND SUPPORT

Providing background or supplemental choices designed to assist or frame the primary action.

Synonym: Side Support

SECRETS

When it comes to the use of **Secrets** in our improv, one size does not fit all needs and situations. I've explored numerous approaches in my short- and long-form work and now deeply appreciate how hidden information can add to the detail, tension, and arc of spontaneous storytelling. In our battle against **cartooning** or overtly didactic choices, carefully utilized secrets provide mystery, dimension, and complexity. Especially in long-form pieces where we may encounter a smaller set of characters for a larger period of time, these elements can also prove crucial for sustaining interest and momentum. I've heard some instructors warn that unexploded secrets, in particular, can actually steal energy and stall the action if they become too internally focused thereby serving *only* the needs of the individual actor. While there is clearly some wisdom in these words, as I outline below, I believe there are many fruitful strategies for making sure secrets are generative rather than diminishing. As is frequently the case, it is less likely a fault of the tool rather than its clumsy or uninformed application.

Example

Player A: (with a disproportionate sense of defensiveness) "Nothing is going on with me. Why would you even ask that…?"

Secrets Secrets Are So Fun

I'm not sure I fully realized just how much I've deployed secrets in my own productions until contemplating this dictionary entry. Here are some potential strategies that I've found useful. I've bundled them by the different spheres of who is (and isn't) in the know…

1. **Everyone, including the audience, is in the know.** In this situation, the key information may have been elicited as an ask-for prior to the scene in question or enacted by a player in full view of the audience and fellow company members. Even when a secret is common knowledge, it can create energy and playfulness as the company enjoys exploring how this "hidden" information influences and frames the unfolding action. "Known" secrets unlock the wonderful potential of improvisational lies where *everyone* knows that false information has been proffered; this, in turn, encourages dynamic and creative storytelling and justifications. If the audience has provided the suggestion of "plagiarism" and, subsequently, we all *know* the protesting student has clearly engaged in this activity, the resulting scene becomes much more about their tactics than the simple presentation of this known truth. Similarly, if a scene begins with a character onstage alone accidentally breaking a prized possession, when they spend the majority of the scene carefully shifting the blame to another unsuspecting candidate this can enable dramatic (and comedic) mischief. Yes, there can be a power in jumping to culpability through an earnest confession, but prolonging the revelation of commonly held information when played with finesse adds suspense and interest while also complicating characterizations and motivations in nuanced ways. To a certain degree, improvisers exploit a similar dynamic when riffing on or alluding to historical or pop culture storylines (thereby placing everyone in the collective know), although care should be taken if most of the audience may not, in fact, be familiar with the referenced source material.

2. **Everyone except a featured player is in the know.** This configuration is most common in endowment games where one player leaves the performance space while critical elements are obtained from the audience. Games such as Crime Endowment, Chain Murder, and Home Late all utilize this approach to strong effect. Here, the secrets are often somewhat metatheatrical in that they are structural or game conceits rather than strictly based on the characters' perception of reality. Endowment games thrive on this disconnect between what the audience *knows* and what the endowee struggles to comprehend. The contrast between the seeming transparency of loaded offers or clues and the oft-resulting bewilderment of the player who is in the dark provides a joyful and typically humorous juxtaposition. This dynamic is particularly well-suited to the stop-and-start dynamic of short-form shows where it's possible to remove a player for the allotted time as the pertinent elements are assembled. If you're familiar with this type of endowment game, it's a common adage that it really doesn't matter if the endowee is ultimately successful or not as long as they attack the scene with conviction and maintain some sense of improvisational composure and narrative. The audience will relish the struggle if it's undertaken with charm and delight. Such scenes also serve as palpable reminders that audiences savor the *process* and gain satisfaction from a game well-played as well as a game well-won. While the game examples listed above lean toward the comedic, I also use a similar device for training purposes where paired characters are provided secrets known to the audience but not each other. (For a favorite example, see Mantras in my Game Library.) With some carefully constructed scenarios, the dynamic routinely results in weighty dramatic explorations.

3. **Only the pertinent player/character is in the know.** Secrets of this variety provide rich character motivations and backstories. In most improvisational traditions, it's possible for players to craft their own secrets as scenes unfold in such a way as to increase the dynamism or tension at play. If a character is struggling with unknown abandonment issues from their past, a looming breakup may take on additional intensity, or a character that has been secretly harboring and suppressing an unrequited love for a long time will likely feel more deeply if their passions are suddenly reciprocated. Such secrets may also be provided or imposed by an outside hand or system. For *Murder We Wrote,* I compiled a large array of secrets into a shuffled deck of cards with each character drawing one before each performance just to add a little extra spice and complexity to the action. As each secret was random, they typically had

Figure 15.1 Secrets abound in the productions of *Murder We Wrote* and *Upton Abbey* on the Annie Russell Theatre stage (Scenic design: Lisa-Cody-Rapport). Photo credit: Tony Firriolo.

little or nothing to do with the greater plot of the murder but rather served as red herrings or engaging subplots. In these cases, private secrets ally closely with the concept of a character's objective, informing the shades and specifics of their tactics and subtext. Subsequently, many of the preferred facets of an **objective** apply here equally as well, specifically pursuing choices that are active, connected, and evocative: *active* in that the secret propels the relevant character into the scene rather than encourages them to retreat into their unseen imagination; *connected* in that it forges bonds and needs embodied by the other characters present within the stage action; and *evocative* in that the hidden information inspires the player in question to engage in the communal act of creation. (The concerns expressed in my introduction above strike me as inabilities to construct secrets that meet these key criteria.) While I think it's possible that *some* secrets can effectively remain as such as the curtain falls on the production, unless the genre demands it, I think leaving *too many* motivations unresolved or hidden might also frustrate rather than captivate the audience.

4. **Not even the pertinent player/character is in the know.** This is territory I've been exploring with some more recent serial long-form work. Such a strategy is largely unworkable in shorter modes that are more on-the-spot and don't allow for some behind-the-scenes orchestration. An omnipresent hand is required for this system to thrive as they assume the responsibility to curate and plant potentially intersecting secrets into the backstories of the improvising stock characters. This is not a small feat, but such an approach can provide a rich and contrasting array of dramatic possibilities that are unlikely to emerge organically. While some of the other secret methodologies offer more immediate payoffs and pleasures for the audience that are well-suited to shorter improvisational scenes, this more dramaturgical angle can provide exciting and buried powder kegs that can reveal dynamic twists and turns more suited to action that seeks to develop over the course of many hours or multiple viewings. In my own work, *Upton Abbey* would serve as a full-throated commitment to this experiment. Here, a cast of 30 characters – 15 upstairs and 15 downstairs played by a cast of 15 improvisers assuming two roles apiece – each received carefully researched and constructed character biographies in which both explicit and dormant secret information was carefully embedded. As the eight-episode show developed, and when characters randomly rotated into featured story positions, an in-house dramaturg would carefully reveal pertinent secrets to the characters in question as mandated by the action. This level of preparation was undeniably considerable (and might fly in the face of some practitioners' view of what is and isn't improv), but the results were often riveting as characters, players, and the audience all experienced honest moments of surprise and revelation together.

Final Thought

If you find yourself passively floating through the action without purpose or investment as a character, a little dash of secrecy can go a long way. Be wary of pursuing an inner life that is too "inner" and not "lively" enough – a well-executed secret should complicate and motivate action rather than squelch or minimize it. And don't under-estimate the value of letting the audience in on the game. Played carefully, a secret can have many phases of usefulness until it is ultimately exploded at the most or least opportune moment thereby shaping a climax or anagnorisis. And much like an effective **CAD**, a strong secret gains utility through its impactful delivery; after all, the character has decided to hold onto this information for a reason and shouldn't just carelessly throw it out into the scenic waters where it might be swept away.

Related Entries: CAD, Character, Commandment #1, Dramaturgical Improv, Objective
Antonyms: Cartooning, Truth **Synonym:** Lies
Connected Game: On the Back Word Endowments

SELFISHNESS

Though most improv philosophies espouse a dogma of looking after your scene partner, there is also a recurring belief that it is difficult to help others if you are not operating from a place of groundedness and strength. To this end, a little selfishness or self-centeredness can serve the needs of a scene when this permits players to hit the stage with a strong idea or point of view already in play.

Related Entry: Character

SHAPE OF SHOW

Formulae and structures house the creative freedom of improvisation, giving it meaning and direction. Dean and Smith observe,

> An important element in improvising is the balance between using procedural formulae and pre-existent material, and creating new material, new combinations of material and new procedures. Improvisations are not entirely self-generating and most improvisors have a bank of 'personal cliches' to which they resort.[2]

In short-form traditions, it is common to talk about the **Shape of Show** or the ways in which organizational and rhythmic choices influence the greater audience experience. Well-crafted franchises, such as *Theatresports* and *ComedySportz*, incorporate ingredients and benchmarks that greatly assist in this regard – the host welcomes, the scoring of competitive scenes, the declaration of the ultimate winner... Similarly, long-form and the healing arts utilize rituals and traditions to frame and shape the performance event in such a way as to (hopefully) maximize effectiveness and appeal. While spontaneous shows address issues of pacing and build in their own unique ways, I contend that the elements built into polished short-form structures can offer helpful guides and focal points for the broad array of other spontaneous works that self-select the label of improvisational theatre. Through this lens, a consideration of the shape of show can become synonymous with the concept of building a dynamic dramatic arc, artistically arranging a collection of improvised scenes, or aesthetically crafting the frame of a long-form piece.

Shaping the Show

1. **Set the scene...** I think we all hope we are fast approaching the day when we don't have to define the very concept of improvisation for our audiences before each show (I'm not sure we're actually there *yet*), but it is important, nonetheless, that our shows are framed and contextualized. An audience may struggle to enjoy and appreciate the skill of our work if they are not given the tools to do so, especially if our goal is to play to a diverse audience demographic as opposed to a gathering of insiders who are already in the know. It's difficult to appreciate something you don't know that you should be looking out for, so it's helpful to have an attitude of "calling your shots" a little. This may involve explaining the general rules or conceit of your improvisational enterprise, introducing the major characters or roles, or outlining what you are hoping to accomplish or create. If there's something particularly unique or impressive about your take on the art of improv, there's no harm in making that known too. While much of this framing work is typically done from the stage, it's also important not to overlook what can be achieved through your marketing materials – including online campaigns, graphics, programs, and lobby displays – that can help quickly establish a mood or sense of focused expectation. If we don't want to exclusively perform to fellow improvisers, some effort needs to be made to open the door to our world for those who are uninitiated.

2. **Warm the lights...** Not everyone enjoys the short-form staple of the audience warm-up, which generally functions to get the crowd laughing, engaged, and ready to freely share their own energy with the stage and players. I appreciate that this can appear pandering or ill-suited to pieces that don't crave a more sports-like interactivity. And there's no denying that such a full-throttle audience energizer would rarely serve more august or thoughtful performances with an eye toward service or social change. That being said, however, in most instances, it strikes me as important that companies consider how to invite the audience into the improvisational performance. In lieu of host banter and applause rituals, there is value in finding a mission-appropriate way to introduce the audience to the company of players or characters and to give them a user-friendly taste of the play that will follow. In short-form shows, this usually consists of a playful warm-up and **decider**; in Playback Theatre, you might utilize gentler audience introductions and simpler exercises that don't yet demand more lengthy or vulnerable narratives. On a simple level, while the explanation noted in my first bullet point might describe the puzzle to follow, this performative phase strives to give the audience some rudimentary pieces or examples.

3. **Pace the build...** As the performance takes off, it's helpful to consider ways to increase the apparent challenge, finesse, or substance of the event. To return to the metaphor of a short-form show, it's unlikely that the *most* (seemingly) difficult game will be slated as the very first offering of the competition: the arc of the show needs somewhere to *go*. The same holds true for long-form pieces. If you are weaving together smaller discrete units,

there is an innate value in saving something a little more dynamic or impressive for later in the work to help propel you toward the climax. This is not to suggest that players shouldn't be challenged earlier in the performance. Firstly, I'd argue without some sense of challenge or risk you're probably not inspiring your players nor enabling particularly fresh improv to emerge. Secondly, some well-planned (but honest) stumbles early in the programming serve as important and palpable reminders of the true impossibility of improv for the audience. But a full evening of improv where there are few peaks and valleys will quickly cause restlessness. In my current home venue, we'll usually end our short-form shows on one of a small handful of games (currently Crime Endowment, Scene Three Ways, or Lines from the Audience), but this is because these games have a record of giving us a thunderous out for the evening.

4. **Pursue helpful contrasts...** An additional strategy for crafting a dynamic shape of show is consciously looking for opportunities for contrast and variety. One of the great values of a pattern is that it makes ruptures all-the-more effective and dynamic. Look for chances to surprise or tilt expectations. In either short- or long-form traditions, scenes that become *too* uniform in length or style can start to feel oddly monotonous or even oppressive. Throwing in a well-situated quick-hit vignette can keep everyone a little on their toes. If your standard scenic casting unit has been two characters, seeing a larger ensemble moment (or a solo vignette) provides a new spice. (I'd argue that the same is true when it comes to character energies in our long-form too and that it can become tiring to see a character *always* in the same context and emotional climate.) In short-form shows, good hosts always have an eye on shuffling through a nice variety of scenic handles, bouncing between musical, physical, expert, narrative, called, and open scenes – to name just a few bundling potentials. Once the audience has learned and feels comfortable with the overarching rules of the game, there is something innately delightful about setting everything off-kilter a little with an element that doesn't, at first glance, replicate the patterns experienced thus far.

5. **Tell *this* story...** When we talk about the "shape of show" this often refers to the inherited norms and rules that have been passed down which provide a somewhat reliable and successful outcome. Franchises are particularly adept at this as they strive to provide a product that contains unpredictability in ways that maximize entertaining risks while minimizing clumsy failures. Such "quality control" can feel ill-suited to an artform that privileges process; but, in reality, aimless work that needlessly eschews the lessons of the past may quickly alienate and lose its audience. Yet, while there is clear value in embracing and exploiting the structures that have served us and our projects well in the past, shape of show *also* embodies a commitment to elevating what has distinctively occurred during this *one* performance that sets it apart from the expectations entrenched in the inherited structure. To return to Playback Theatre, some practitioners speak of the "red thread" that invisibly ties together the seemingly disparate narratives of the audience during any one particular event – the greater theme, tension, or communal story, if you will. I love this image and believe whole-heartedly that it can apply to most improvisational endeavors. So, while we uphold structural wisdoms, we should simultaneously embrace newly forged pathways and games that are unique to this specific undertaking.

6. **Provide some closure...** I've scattered pet peeves through many of these entries and here's another one! There is a recurring "out" for many long-form shows that loosely consists of some variant of "... and that's our time" often following a decent laugh line or pay-off. This probably speaks to my own preference toward forms with more narrative instincts and my parallel background in scripted theatre, but especially if I'm watching numerous sets in a row that leave the stage in this manner, I start to feel rather unsatisfied and even a little cheated as an audience member. Just as shape of show considers how to best wade into the waters of improv, so too should this thoughtful mentality prioritize a clean and fitting extraction. There are many looser forms that do tend to riff on a theme or idea without intending to land on a holistic or climactic payoff (and I like many of these forms greatly), but even if your preferred style of play doesn't privilege a pivotal moment of peripeteia there are still ways to frame an outro with some sense of pizzazz. Short-form competitions typically wrap up with quick acknowledgments and a celebration of the winning team so that even if the final scene of the night was a little iffy, there is still a greater celebration to provide closure and energy. Improv forms should consider seeking an equivalent to this dynamic out, whether it's tying up and honoring any contracts of the performance, exploiting structural components more likely to afford a climactic exchange, or providing a robust and playful curtain call.

Our audiences have invested considerable time in our enterprises by the time they arrive at their final destinations and an abrupt or almost apologetic button can needlessly call the value of this journey into question.

Final Thought

I began this entry quoting Smith and Dean's observations regarding how improvisation balances both the old and the new. The old, for many of us, consists of our designed or inherited frames and games, and all the lessons contained therein. The new embodies the relentless spontaneity of the here and now that seeks to explore hitherto unknown pathways. A healthy consideration and appreciation of the shape of show marries together these two creative impetuses, providing patterns that have stood the tests of time while also encouraging us to strategically disrupt or seek out new designs when they can serve the moment more effectively.

> **Related Entry:** Hosting **Antonym:** Chaos
> **Synonym:** Structure
> **Connected Game:** Home Shopping Network

SHARING FOCUS

Among the many critical communication issues inherently involved in the craft of improvisational theatre stands the necessity of elegantly **Sharing Focus**. Without a definitive text, carefully etched and repeated blocking (staging), or an outside eye polishing movement patterns and stage pictures, the improviser assumes a lot of responsibilities when it comes to crafting effective focus maneuvers. Pioneering game theorist, Neva Boyd, aptly articulates this critical function:

> A game is life in miniature. The play group is society epitomized. When the child attempts to take more than his share of 'turns,' the protest is immediate and expressed in terms he understands. When he makes a poor choice of conduct the group reaction and the consequences are immediate and definite.[3]

Focus provides such a multi-faceted and rich issue that I've addressed it from multiple vantage points throughout this dictionary.

Tools, Tips, and Traps When It Comes to Sharing Focus

1. **Moving focus in group scenes.** For a consideration of some best practices for clean focus shifts in those all-too-challenging ensemble scenes, explore **Commandment #2**, "Thou shalt always retain focus."
2. **Shining the focus on shining.** Keep reading my introductory chapter with **Commandment #3** to examine the nuances of shining, and explore when a scene or company may be best served by giving others the focus needed to excel.
3. **Focusing on stage pictures.** The titular entry on **Focus** looks at commonsense approaches for consciously constructing stage pictures that effectively and aesthetically direct the audience's gaze and interest.
4. **Ways to give focus.** My dictionary entry entitled **Give** examines time-tested methods for moving attention toward others on stage.
5. **Ways to take focus.** Inversely, **Take** explores the complementary improvisational skill of taking focus.
6. **When focus goes awry.** Lastly, **Split focus** refers to the failure to share attention onstage effectively. Explore some exceptions to this unhelpful improv habit in the entry of the same name.

Final Thought

At the end of the day, it doesn't matter how inspired our work is as improvisers if we present it in such a way that our audience cannot easily digest our choices free from unnecessary or careless clutter and confusion. In theory, the two most helpful tools to prevent such chaos are all variants of focus gives and takes. In practice, finding comfort and fluency with these techniques and applying them skillfully to the wide array of challenging situations that frequently emerge on the improv stage requires patience, dedication, and vigilance.

> **Related Entries:** Commandment #2, Commandment #3, Give, Take
> **Antonym:** Split Focus **Synonym:** Focus
> **Connected Game:** The Café

SHELVING

Shelving describes the improvisational act of strategically storing the pertinent details and offers that shape spontaneous stories in meaningful and satisfying ways. "A crowd delights in seeing a player pull out a forgotten scenic element just in time to solve a problem – like a chess player suddenly executing a checkmate, apparently out of nowhere."[4] This skill innately connects to that of **reincorporation** and its many variants discussed elsewhere. Without potentials planted on the improvisational shelf, the likelihood that anything of substance will grow diminishes considerably. However, to perhaps stretch this creative metaphor to its limit, not all shelving units are built to serve the same scenic ends and there are subtle but important distinctions as to how you can use this storage system to enhance your craft.

Example

Player A sweeps open the imaginary hotel curtains on the fourth wall while calling to their beloved.

Player A: "Darling, you really must soak in this astonishing view of the Pacific. I've never seen such glistening tranquility in all my life…"

Player B: (calling from an offstage bathroom) "You really have outdone yourself! You could fit a family of four inside the hot tub, *and* there's a complementary bottle of champagne and cheese board awaiting us on the marble counter." *(They join Player A at the window affectionately)* "I don't think I'll ever want to go back to the office…"

Stocking the Improv Shelves

As you assemble the raw material of improvisation, consider that shelving can serve several distinct and equally important creative functions.

1. **The lower shelves…** When it comes to the foundational elements of improvisation – names, locations, relationships, and character foibles – these offers shouldn't stray too far from arm's reach. With few exceptions (perhaps a grand identity reveal in a crime show), there is little value in having character names stowed away for protracted periods of time. Doing so will invariably lead to them being forgotten or laboriously reinvented. The same goes with fundamental scenic elements. If a fellow player has established a door on stage, ignoring that door for too long will make it vanish in the memories of the company (although ironically not the minds of the audience who have a knack for picking up on the smallest of inconsistencies). Moreover, noteworthy character behaviors left unattended will frequently dissipate into the land of lost improv choices. While we typically think of the "improv shelves" as a device for putting choices aside, in these cases, important offers should only reside here temporarily if they are providing the raw material for the current scene or story arc. Frequent physical use or verbal repetition will keep such ideas cogent and relevant. In long-form pieces where we might then step away from a premise or character combination for a while, a healthy dose of **reincorporation** burns in these choices so that when they need to rest on the shelf for a while before their next appearance, they have been polished in helpful ways to make them memorable.

2. **The middle shelves…** If we consider the lower shelves as providing easily accessible storage for our immediate and short-term scenic needs, the middle shelves are a great place for peculiar specifics, outliers, and idiosyncrasies. In many ways, this function takes care of the creative surplus that marks much of the craft of improvisation. In the moment of creation, it is typically uncertain just *what* will prove critical for the path ahead and significance generally becomes clearer with the benefit of hindsight. The cumbersome locking mechanism on the door that never works on the first try, the unique character quirk that grates against the protagonist's nerves, or the unexpected birthday present that doesn't suit the mood of the party – such choices are ripe in their own rights but may or may not ultimately prove instantly valuable. This is the domain of **callbacks** and **connections**. As the story develops, these shelved options provide grist for the creative mill and allow players to recycle and reuse prior memorable offers to elevate or contextualize the current action. If the proverbial cupboards are bare, these types of moves become challenging or unfeasible. Such moves also require that previous elements were well-established – a callback won't land if no-one recalls the original appearance. So, gently keeping these behaviors or ingredients alive during the rising action will typically serve you well. Generic choices – a window that just *is* – will provide much less spark when recalled than those that have a unique flair – a disproportionately loud laugh that reveals to the protagonist the hideout of their nemesis.

3. **The upper shelves…** And then some shelving is actually designed to hold onto those items you only rarely use or need. In some genres, such as a mystery or thriller, these shelves may hold significant dramaturgical weight as the play develops multiple threads and possibilities knowing that ultimately only one or two will prove "correct." More commonly, this storage houses the

seemingly random or throwaway suggestions and those scenic elements that have been introduced and then willfully set aside. Such choices resemble the function of the **curve ball**, unanticipated or somewhat random offers that at first blush appear out of place but that provide opaque investments for future discoveries and journeys. These offers are marked by their incongruity, while other shelved material generally supports the more obvious flow and energies of the work. It's helpful to note that curve balls, in particular, seek to stand out from the narrative waters and, as such, invite saving for later reuse. Other ingredients benefit from at least occasional reappearances before an intended payoff, but upper shelf additions can become punctured if they reappear too often with more than the most subtle of winks. Doing so can feel like providing multiple decreasingly successful punchlines to the same joke setup. It's also possible to structurally reserve a key element for a place of honor on the less frequented top shelves, such as the title of your show or a particular audience ask-for that summarizes the dramatic action, especially if you intend to use this information as a featured moment or dynamic button.

Final Thought

Each of these imagined shelves serves a related function, but they each benefit from a slightly different tempo and application. Raw base material will move on and off the lower shelf with great ease and frequency, while items on the middle shelves are used more sparingly and luxuriously, and those on the highest shelves of all are patiently incorporated with discipline and self-awareness. I imagine it's rather a common improviser fear that there won't be enough material for the scene or show and yet it strikes me that careful work will nearly always provide a surplus of potential shelved ideas. Yes, it's worthwhile to consciously place a few things of note on the improvisational bookcase, but ultimately, our work is better served by simply developing an awareness of what has organically emerged and stored itself for our future attention.

Related Entries: Callback, Connections, Curve Ball, Looking Backwards, Names, Reincorporation
Antonyms: Over-Originality, Randomness
Synonym: Offer
Connected Game: Chapters

SHINING

Eugene Van Erven cautions,

> Genuine theatre of liberation can never provide more than subsistence wages. It requires a lifetime commitment and a willingness to shed star complexes as well as high material expectations. Its only payoffs are moral, social, and cultural, never monetary.[5]

It strikes me that the habit of bulldozing and the desire to shine are improvisational relatives. The former generally emerges out of a misplaced taste for control, while **Shining** reflects an insatiable act hunger that inadvertently places the individual's ego and desire for accolades over the greater good of the show and ensemble. I don't view either improv trap as intentionally malicious but rather as a manifestation of misdirected excitement. We've all succumbed to these temptations, I'm sure. And, as I discuss in my third commandment, moments of creative finesse certainly have a valued place in the craft: we shouldn't become needlessly paranoid of stepping into the limelight when the scene invites us to do so. Problematic shining, however, occurs when players actively seek or create such moments repeatedly despite what might best serve the storytelling process. If we liken our improv abilities to those of a superhero or heroine, the shining player frequently uses their powers for their own advancement rather than the greater good of the community. (This may, in fact, serve as an interesting definition of villainy!)

I've dealt with facets of the current theme in several other entries: **bulldozing** offers some strategies for upending your own attention-seeking patterns; **looking good** provides helpful ways to throw the attention and joy to your scene partners; and **commandment #3** considers when shining might actually serve the greater artistic mission. So, for this current musing I'd like to illustrate some subtle and not-so subtle manifestations of the shining impetus that represent simple moments to disrupt your own less-than-ideal habits.

Example

Just as the action is about to fittingly follow Player B on a revealing journey of self-discovery, Player A steps forward…

Player A: "But first let me just give you some unsolicited advice…" *(to the musician)* "Hit it, Steve!"

A long solo song ensues that doesn't pertain to anything of note or consequence, although Player A is unquestionably a gifted singer...

Signs You May Need to Reduce Your Luminosity

1. **You typically play to win...** Some improv formats utilize a competitive frame to make the event more accessible and structured for an audience. With few exceptions, however, this is merely a conceit that shouldn't eclipse a more collaborative style of play. Even in short-form **deciders**, where players are clearly pitted against each other, there are ample opportunities to make others look good and to elevate the ensemble over the individual. And audiences will rarely savor a meandering twelve-minute opus that has long since outstayed its welcome because players wanted to win at *any* cost. In non-competitive frames, a "winning" attitude can also infect an otherwise collective affair with players seeking to dominate the stage action, aggressively pushing to beat fellow improvisers to connections and punchlines, or maintaining a character's upper hand regardless of the need or consequences. If you're not joyously celebrating the victories of others – often and earnestly – then you're probably falling into this camp.
2. **You always take the strong position...** While this heading could easily apply to the habit of using a high-status position to force your own agenda on fellow players, in this setting, I am using this language at its face value: literally don't always put yourself in the strongest stage positions thereby forcing your teammates to **upstage** themselves. For those with some traditional theatre training, it can become second nature to gravitate to center stage in order to keep yourself "open," but in an improvisational setting where an outside eye can't adjust and set these staging choices, making others assume weaker stage positions time and again can become symptomatic of not wanting to cede the scenic high ground. Arguably, if you don't consciously engage in strongly giving focus on stage it is foreseeable that you are consistently taking focus from others instead.
3. **You're the first to grab the call or shift...** Although this habit occurs primarily in the specific subset of called short-form games, it serves as an apt metaphor for a more pervasive improvisational approach as well. In called games a scene is punctuated by a series of prompts from an offstage player that invite immediate changes and justifications. These provide built-in micro shining moments as whoever makes the first choice generally has an unobstructed playing field with the most low hanging fruit available. If you *always* claim the pole position in such moments, this is likely at the cost of sharing the light around. This can also upset more organic scenic rhythms if another player has been situated to make the next choice, but you leap into the fray anyway. (Even in games where calls have a singular recipient, such as one-person emotional rollercoasters, it's still possible to share the latent opportunities provided by these moments.) In non-called games or scenes this over-eagerness can have a similar effect if you lunge at the next moment whether or not it makes sense for your character to make the next move.
4. **You heavily rely on a known stock of characters or tricks...** Some improv schools and projects have a greater appetite for stock or set characters than others, and most players happily revisit tropes or personae that have served them well in the past – this could be likened to the theatrical concept of "type" (although I have a *lot* of issues with this pervasive theory). While it makes sense that we might lean into character terrain that has the comfort of familiarity, we should also be mindful that we're not using our bag of tricks as a crutch that prevents us from taking strategic risks or supporting the work of others. If we're *only* willing to enter the fray when we can assume one of our polished personae or manipulate scenes so that we can present one of our surefire improv tricks, it follows that we may be missing many opportunities to serve the specific needs of any particular story more selflessly. The same holds true if we're only willing to play the games that are firmly in our own wheelhouses without supporting others in their preferred formats.
5. **You routinely have more fun than your fellow players...** This last point is a little tongue-in-cheek, but I think it warrants some rumination. I *know* I have performed in shows where in the moment I felt like I was "on fire" and then after-the-fact have realized that this heat had singed some of my castmates. That's not a good feeling for anyone involved. Alternatively, I've watched performances where improvisers have so clearly been trying to individually impress me as an audience member that they have done exactly the opposite, leaving me instead with the ponderous question as to whether or not they were actually having much more fun than those watching them. So many of us improvise because it is a source of joy and freedom and gives us a chance to share our voice and vision. And improv certainly can

and should serve these needs. But there is value in also keeping in mind when our more personal goals (and desires) are impinging upon the joys and journeys of our collaborators on both sides of the stage divide.

Final Thought

Van Erven is writing of a particular branch of improvisational performance, but these observations hold true for most of us involved in the profession. There are few improv-related avenues that can promise wealth or fame (although many training companies point at the well-known outliers as motivation). The social and community-building rewards of improv, however, are usually substantial. While it's understandable that we all have our egos involved in these enterprises – and it's always nice to be congratulated or noticed – it's a worthy endeavor to strive to use our individual lights in the service of others as well as ourselves.

> **Related Entries:** Bulldozing, Commandment #3, Ensemble, Upstaging **Antonyms:** Looking Good, Sharing Focus, Teamwork
> **Synonyms:** Competitiveness, Selfishness, Winning
> **Connected Game:** Emotional Door

SHIVVING

The line between an improvisational character and the improviser themselves is often thin and ambiguous, and many traditions delight in the entertainment potentials of watching the players squirm while they create as much as they appreciate the theatrical fruits of this strenuous labor. **Shivving** refers to a variety of meta-theatrical playfulness in which improvisers joyfully mess with each other a little to add some mischief into the mix. Seham notes such a tendency when she writes, "Discouraged in many improv settings, pimping is an accepted part of many ComedySportz games. The audience almost always responds with delight."[6] A type of **offer** or **endowment**, in experienced hands shivving results in heightened energy and whimsy. Used less adeptly, it can quickly resemble the **gagging** or **pimping** described above by Seham in its form and function, diminishing the scenic reality for little more than a droll observation or easy laugh. Shivving tends to target the performer under the character's façade rather than the character or story itself, drawing upon personal knowledge or observations of the player rather than their dramatic construction. As such, this device strikes me as innately less problematic in venues where the improviser is never far from the vantage of the audience as opposed to those improv houses that privilege a more overtly representational or "realistic" approach. In the former setting, shivving can irreverently add to the fun; in the latter, it risks collapsing the dramatic conceit altogether.

Example

Player A, as is their wont, enters the scene with a recently acquired wig from backstage.

Player B: *(upon seeing A in wig)* "I see you decided to wear a wig *again*…, David…"

Minimizing the Risk of Injury When Shivving

As the very phrasing suggests, shivving provides a sharp tool that wielded carelessly may cause unintended injury. If this performative approach calls to you, consider the following elements as you deploy its power…

1. **Rapport.** In my personal experience, shivving tends to miss the mark when it occurs in environments where deep trust has not already been firmly established. When I'm the target of this style of choice, a cheeky comment from a fellow player that I know well is likely to land much differently than from a new or guest teammate. Arguably, perhaps the source of a shivving retort *shouldn't* matter, but, in reality, teasing can feel quite differently coming from someone inside your circle of trust as opposed to an outsider – just like in real life. For example, an improviser who knows me well might poke fun of my New Zealand-ness, but it feels cheap or inelegant from an improviser who has just met me moments before if they decide to do the same. It's similarly important that players have built a clear relationship with the audience and that they understand some spirited misbehavior is part of the contract of the game or overall experience. I tend to avoid shivving in general as it can be challenging to assess these subtle ingredients in real time, especially if I'm not working alongside players where the trust is already deep and unshakable.

2. **Tone.** Although I've seen some well-seasoned improvisers deploy bullish or curmudgeonly personae onstage with surprisingly appealing results, these energies illustrate exceptions rather than the rule and when it comes to shivving an overly aggressive tone or style can make a barbed choice read as mean-spirited. Pursuing a more kindhearted or joyous approach generally yields less problematic results. This energy is a little difficult to quantify but often includes a rather clear "wink" to all those in attendance that your intent is to playfully jab rather than saltily injure. If you're inclined to deploy shivving to pointedly address *actual* performance concerns or frustrations (rather than to jovially mock trivialities or patterns), then it's possible that the audience will pick up on these darker hues and the choice will land accordingly. Consider saving corrective notes and observations for the postmortem backstage rather than lacing them into your scene – or if an adjustment is warranted, utilize the tradition of **speaking your truth** or calling it onstage which typically retains the POV and façade of your character.
3. **Irreverence.** I nod to this facet in my opening definition, but it's also important to honor the foundational conceits and energies of your specific performance event. Shivving feels more on point when the general environment and style of play are a little lighthearted and boundary blurring. If the players are never far from sight during the performance, playful breaches are more likely to add some delightful interplay. (Shivving can resemble "heat" in this way as players might taunt each other between the rounds of a short-form match.) On the other hand, if your venue goals are to craft detailed realistic worlds with finely etched characterizations that mask the performers' identities underneath, frequent shivving might starkly interrupt the dramatic action and plunge the audience into some proverbial ice water for little artistic payoff. With the notable exception of the healing arts, improv without *some* strategic mischief can easily become pretentious or posturing, but in some situations, shivving may not prove the most successful tool for accessing this creative playful spirit. So, pay some heed to the stylistic conventions that serve as the bedrock of your particular improvisational enterprise.
4. **Timing.** And also consider when and why you're deploying this technique. Shivving tends to encourage side games where players riff or circle around a singular moment with comedic musings and repartee. Many consider these flights of departure as having an innate entertainment value in their own right, but when this occurs in improvisational scene work it can problematically deflate the drive and energy of the parent scene. Loitering in such moments indulgently or detouring the story abruptly at a pivotal moment may result in some great laughs but ultimately degrade the narrative arc beyond repair. Specifically, shivving might cause more harm than good during the crucial opening moments of a scene as you're establishing the given circumstances, when the story is building steam toward an energized climax, or as a scene reaches for its closing moment or button. In each of these cases, a playful metatheatrical departure can sap the momentum and create unnecessary challenges for players when they inevitably strive to reassemble the scattered scenic jigsaw puzzle pieces.

Final Thought

Linking all the above observations is the underlying need for heightened awareness: are shivving moves being coded and received as playful by the intended recipients? Shivving without considerable charm is rarely pleasing for anyone involved. Does the audience understand that such choices are part of the greater conceit and are they empowered to equally enjoy these moments? If shivving becomes too "insider-y" it's much more likely that it will alienate rather than engage your guests. Lastly, is this manifestation of mischief serving the desired tone of your venue and project, or is it abruptly undermining other narrative or artistic goals?

This entry probably reveals my general ambivalence toward this improv tradition. In part, I think this is because it's awfully difficult to exercise this multifaceted awareness while simultaneously balancing the long list of other elements required for generative improvisational play. And, to speak my own truth more pointedly, as an improviser who predominantly plays in a country different from my birth nation, I've been on the receiving end of a panicked or neophyte player using my otherness to grab an easy laugh when nothing else came to mind. That quickly feels icky and marginalizing. In my improv kitchen, I'd liken shivving to the ground red pepper on my skill spice rack: a little can certainly add some fun flavor or heat to a scenic dish, but it doesn't take much to make the whole meal inedible. But to continue the metaphor, I'd also acknowledge that some players can handle and relish much more improv spice than I can!

Related Entries: Commandment #4, Commenting, Endowing, Gagging, Offer, Pimping
Synonyms: Heat, Mischief
Connected Game: Here They Come

SHORT-FORM

I've tackled the thorny issue of self-designated improv labels in an earlier entry (see long-form). Kozlowski voices a common distinction when he observes that "The most important distinction of short form is that none of the improv games connect in any way whatsoever to any other games,"[7] thus suggesting that **Short-Form** tends to consist of standalone scenes while long-form weaves together scenic elements in more complex ways to craft greater arcs and connections. There is unquestionably some (albeit simplistic) truth in this definition, but just as long-form has become a term that clumsily describes a vast array of performance styles, short-form deserves similar unpacking and complicating. So, here goes…

Common Short-Form Features

1. **Discrete units.** Kozlowski observes that short-form games don't *connect* – which can be the case – but I would tweak this definition to note that scenes do not generally require knowledge of previous improv vignettes to be understood and appreciated. Many short-form shows take on the format of a competition or sketch revue, and in these cases, a performance will consist of a series of different *seemingly* unrelated frames. This is the modus operandi of *Theatresports*, *ComedySportz*, and *Spolin Games*. Yes, each scene will generally be *discrete* – inspired by unique parameters, audience suggestions, or director prompts – and yet this does not mean that connections will not emerge between the apparently disparate offerings. Characters or locations may recur, common themes can emerge and deepen, or material from a whimsical Gibberish Scene in act one might reappear in the lyrics of a Tag-Team Song in act two. Unlike many long-form performances, however, experiencing these earlier moments may not prove crucial to gaining enjoyment from a later scene (this is frequently not the case in more linear narrative traditions). So, while individual scenes are designed to provide fulfillment in their own right, connections are still possible, pleasurable, and privileged, nonetheless.

2. **Meta frames.** Long-form performances can assume many various organizational frames – deploying thematic, location, or relationship-based foci, among others. In many cases, these structuring devices resemble other "traditional" theatrical genres and best practices. Short-form shows tend to utilize more meta framing devices that are not explicitly story or character centric. They are improv delivery systems rather than blueprints for creating dramatic meaning. In many cases, as noted above, shows utilize the tropes of professional sports and competitions: which of these great improv teams can ultimately emerge from the battlefield victorious by the end of the evening after tackling a series of increasingly difficult improvisational challenges? In other instances, such as Disney's Comedy Warehouse, individual players might perform in various shuffled combinations in an array of different improv games each set. While some specific scenes may deploy a faux competitive hook – such as Schmeopardy or Conducted Story – such shows don't heavily rely on the conceit of a declared winner for a payoff. There are exceptions, of course, yet short-form shows rarely utilize more conventional narrative frames to provide a sense of completion or closure but rather exist within an accepted construct that tacitly provides a loose rationale for enabling play.

3. **Player centric.** It's also extremely common for short-form shows to embrace the personae of the performers as part of the overall event. In competitive shows, for example, improvisers happily step in and out of character between the scenes (and sometimes *within* the scenes as well) becoming themselves or a close approximation thereof as they interact with the audience, gather suggestions, or introduce the next improvisational high wire act about to begin. While this impetus can be seen on occasion in long-form modes – *Harold* players often line the back wall of the stage watching the action as themselves before donning a character to enter the scene – in short-form traditions, the *player* is frequently elevated as a featured and fundamental component of the performance. The audience enjoys seeing this slippage between character and improviser that the scripted tradition, in particular, usually strives to hide in the service of realism. This impetus can also be seen in service-inclined practices such as Forum and Playback Theatre, although these modalities do not "celebrate" their participants so

much as "recognize" their efforts on behalf of a greater community.

4. **Stop and start.** Most long-form pieces seek an audience suggestion or input in the opening moments of the performance (if at all) but then will happily dance forward without further interruptions. Short-form shows are typically punctuated by multiple moments of rupture where the action pauses while players or a host elicit new ideas from the audience to inspire the next playful creation. Such pauses can be overt and inherent to the overall framing device – as is the case with *Gorilla Theatre* and *Micetro* – or, in hybrid forms with an avowedly short-form aesthetic, more stealthily woven into the performance event – as is the case with free form improv and some iterations of *Life Game* (where an audience member's recollections can inspire a series of varied vignettes). One could argue that in addition to being player centric – as each pause allows players to reset to their own personae – this stop and start energy also prioritizes the audience in a qualifiedly different way than the majority of long-form pieces. Most short-form improv has little interest in elevating a "suspension of disbelief" but rather deliberately points at the act and conceit of theatrical creation. Which brings me to my final defining feature…

5. **Accessible.** I *love* unwieldy and ornate long-form, especially of the dramaturgical ilk as I opine in my definition of this subgenre, but I also struggle with the reality that a lot of long-form almost demands that our audience has an insider's knowledge. Whether we're exploiting the tropes of a niche genre, riffing on the archetypes inspired from a pop culture trend, or exploring the preferred frame variant of our improv training home, the resulting long-form can struggle to appeal to those beyond our immediate improv circles. In contrast, short-form traditions generally embody more avowedly and unapologetically populist ends. Performances provide the tools for enjoyment and teach pertinent framing devices as the event unfurls. New games or elements are defined and modeled as they enter the stream of the evening: "You haven't seen this specific game before? Don't worry. We'll tell you everything you need to know before we play it!" This is not to say that long-form shows don't seek accessibility; in fact, an inability to find and maintain an audience is a surefire route to closure for an improv show regardless of its long- or short-form trappings. But I think it is telling that if you ask an "average" theatregoer on the street about improv they are more likely to reference a short-form franchise than a long-form piece.

Final Thought

Although I don't believe it's always intentional, there can be a tendency to use the defining language of improvisation to create unhelpful performative duchies. Specifically, as a professional practitioner of short-form for over three decades (and long-form a little less) at times it can feel as if the very term short-form is used by fellow improvisers to dismiss or diminish the value and craft of this fruitful branch of the improv tree. I hope this is changing. Understanding the inherent values and gifts of all improvisational modes and practices can only ultimately elevate our own work and better equip our tool belts regardless of the style we currently call home.

Related Entries: Game of the Scene, Improvisation, Long-Form, Shape of Show
Connected Game: Famous Last Words

SHOWING

Viola Spolin lists the following attributes as facets of her preferred non-acting:

> Involving one's self with a focus; detachment; a working approach to all the problems of the theater; keeping one's personal feelings private; learning to act through 'non-acting'; showing, not telling; 'Stop Acting!'[8]

While this is all excellent advice, for this discussion, I'm primarily interested in the final section that addresses the concept of **Showing** rather than **telling** – a common improv (and theatrical) adage. To show on stage is to allow ideas and offers to become revealed through behavior and action. Such an approach invites a richer and more nuanced style of play and facilitates discovery. This contrasts with telling which over-relies on language to state or describe scenic contributions. Telling encapsulates a performative instinct that frequently results in **cartooning** or two-dimensional scene work.

As many improv traditions take full advantage of imaginative and imaginary scenic elements, telling can present a particular temptation in our efforts to clearly define our surroundings and given circumstances. But we need not choose between a false dichotomy of "clear" telling and "opaque" showing as clarity *and* precision can also be the domain of improvisers who thoughtfully show their choices.

Example

Players A and B begin a scene based on the audience suggestion of a "hot air balloon ride…"

Show Your Choice By…

In the spirit of this advice, my examples come first:

1. **Doing something rather than considering it**

Player A extends their arm to B who uses it as leverage to leap over and into the balloon basket. A unties an anchor rope before B returns the favor and they both find themselves gently ascending, laughing all the while.

RATHER THAN

Player A: (standing) "Well, I think we've got everything for our hot air balloon ride. Do you want to do one more safety check?"

One definition of theatrical play that whispers in my ear as I write this is that theatre is a sequential list of (generally related and intensifying) *actions*. Yes, there are undoubtedly branches of the art that also highly prioritize thought and theory – George Bernard Shaw springs to mind with his epic stage direction notes – but there's a reason we use the verbiage *dramatic action* to describe the moves in a play. These actions shouldn't be mistaken for stage business or activity, although they can at times be synonymous, but rather tactics that strive to get characters one step closer to what they want or need.

2. **Experiencing something rather than describing it**

As Players A and B feel the balloon slowly rise from its previously tethered perch, they clutch each other's hands with sheer delight. Player A spontaneously dances a little happy jig that adds to B's amusement as their gaze slowly moves to the scenery around them.

RATHER THAN

Player B: (standing, but now theoretically in a balloon) "Our balloon is taking off. You can see everything gradually getting smaller…"

While there are foreseeable improv situations where some well-timed description may help get everyone on the same page, be cautious when this instinct is used in lieu of committing fully to the current experience. Allowing the audience to *witness* the characters' awe and excitement will invariably prove more engaging than merely hearing an all-too-often dispassionate narration or dose of **cartooning**. Experiencing instead of describing also unlocks the powerful improv tools of silence, subtext, and ambiguity.

3. **Creating something rather than pontificating about it**

Player B reaches into a picnic basket that they'd previously secretly stowed in the balloon, revealing a large bottle of champagne and two flutes. They meticulously pop the cork while A's attention is distracted by controlling the burner. Upon hearing the champagne popping, B turns with a smile and is greeted with a half-filled glass.

RATHER THAN

Player A: (still standing but now apparently in a balloon and a little hungry) "It's a shame we didn't pack any food. That would have made this extra special."

The second example could well result in a bracing scene about our couple becoming stranded without any resources, but more often, such language provides an unnecessary distraction from just crafting cogent props and scenic elements that can then add a myriad of nuances and possibilities. Does the popping cork ultimately puncture the balloon, or could the resulting champagne intoxication throw the couple off their predetermined course? Or, frankly, does just the act of sharing the drink simply but beautifully reveal and heighten the love and connection? Creating an array of scenic pieces (and then not talking incessantly about them) can go a long way toward encouraging a "showing" attitude.

4. **Feeling something rather than announcing it**

The couple laughs and smiles broadly as they ritualistically interlock their arms to enjoy the champagne toast. Captured in the moment, A throws the now empty champagne flute off the side of the balloon basket. Without skipping a beat, Player B mirrors the gesture as their eyes meet. The laughter transforms to passion as they seize each other in a loving embrace.

RATHER THAN

Player B: (standing some more in that balloon basket but now a little hungry and happy but speaking nonetheless without conviction) "I love balloon rides."

A tendency to "tell" is often further problematized by an equal tendency to shy away from **emotional honesty** and earned passion. Yes, our players can *say*, "I love balloon rides," but this will prove vastly inferior to feeling and embodying that reality. This advice holds even more wisdom when it comes to assertions of "I love you." Announcing our emotions can reveal a performer's anxiousness or discomfort with assuming the broad range of human experience, but such declarations will frequently call into question the very veracity of the utterance if these powerful words are not accompanied by an earned connection and heartfelt depth.

Final Thought

An added advantage to adopting a "showing" improvisational stance is that you can essentially double the communicative potentials of your scene work. When our *acting* and subtextual choices enrich the greater environment and core relationships, our *dialogue* can now explore other ideas and dynamics or introduce fruitful tensions and contradictions. In this manner, while the behavior of our hot air ballooners expresses affection and adoration for each other, the language could now show disdain for all the rest of humanity and the less fortunate scattered below them as they engage in their luxurious ascent – or a myriad of other satiric or whimsical ideas.

See my earlier thoughts on **cartooning** for related tips on "Bringing That Third Dimension to Your Scene Work."

Related Entries: Acting, Ambiguity, Love, Subtext
Antonyms: Cartooning, Telling, Wearing Your Character Lightly **Synonym:** Emotional Truth
Connected Game: In A, With A, While A…

SIDECOACHING

In *Theatre Games for the Lone Actor: A Handbook,* Spolin provides a helpful articulation of the **Sidecoaching** impetus: "Side coaching is a guide, a directive, a support, a catalyst, a higher view, an inner voice, an extended hand, you might say, given during the playing of a game to help you stay on focus."[9] As spontaneous play is rarely repeated or revisited, real-time adjustments can prove essential when seeking to introduce new strategies or while exploring unfamiliar terrain. A quick and astute word provided in the moment will allow instantaneous adjustments or course corrections unlike traditional theatrical notes which can easily become highly theoretical: what would have happened if you had tried "a" instead of "b?" No one will ever know as it's highly unlikely that scenario will ever play out again in quite the same way! Expert sidecoaching nudges players out of ruts or perceived traps and gently empowers their latent instincts, thereby keeping the scenic focus and momentum flowing.

I recognize and deeply value the tradition of in-the-moment coaching but must also candidly share that it is a tool I personally wrestle with a little for a variety of reasons. As I primarily teach and work in a university theatre department and well-established professional company, I've found that players in both communities are not always well versed nor receptive to this creative paradigm unless it is conducted with great gentleness. When playing *Gorilla Theatre,* the director role necessarily assumes this function as they "fight" to get their vision to the stage, although I wouldn't offer this as a typical model for sidecoaching as most would rightly consider the needs of this format as a little more aggressive and director-focused than a more typical sidecoaching relationship. I certainly deploy a more conventional variant of this tool when workshopping skills that require consistent momentum such as rhyming and musical sessions. Here, a quick word at the right time will assist much more than a lengthy discussion after-the-fact. In my day-to-day instruction, I find myself balancing sidecoaching with more traditional postmortem notes, although as I sit down to write this entry I also realize that in-the-moment coaching probably characterizes my style more than I might realize – it just sometimes takes hybrid forms, such as when I wander around the classroom space between various playing groups offering up little words of help or focus realignments.

I present the following observations with this context in mind. These thoughts stem from my own experiences and preferences on both the receiving and coaching side of the equation. Sidecoaching is unquestionably an expression of our personal artistic and pedagogic journeys and aesthetics. Finding your coaching groove is the pursuit of a life in the art and will undoubtedly reflect your own (positive and negative) experiences in the rehearsal hall as well.

Example

Players A and B are lost teenagers on a deserted beach. After several exchanges establishing their CROW, they now take their first nervous steps toward a menacing cave entrance. Player A struggles to turn on an unreliable flashlight while B looks on with terror. The sidecoach has patiently remained silent during these opening moments...

Player B: (stopping dead in their tracks) "I don't think we should do this..."
Sidecoach: (with gentle excitement) "Do it!"

OR

Sidecoach: (with anticipation) "What was that sound?"

OR

Sidecoach: (egging on Player B) "Why are you so nervous?"

OR

Sidecoach: (with relish) "Lean into that great sense of panic!"

OR

The sidecoach visibly leans forward in their chair with heightened attention and joy, and silently smiles.

Coaching Considerations

1. **Get in and out quickly.** By definition, sidecoaching pauses the scenic action to offer up some words of wisdom or encouragement. Lengthy musings decrease the likelihood that the players can maintain the dramatic integrity while listening to and processing the offered adjustment, so it's important to seek efficient brevity. If you need more than a few words and your advice isn't critical, I'd recommend holding onto the feedback until the scene has finished rather than grinding everything to a halt (unless injury – physical or otherwise – is imminent). When on the receiving end you can also do a great deal to minimize any negative side effects of these interruptions: assume a soft freeze as the sidecoaching occurs, don't feel the need to turn to or address the director, and strive to apply the new information through action rather than starting a sidebar discussion. There is also a lot to be said for assuming good faith on the part of the coach: if something strikes you as odd or unexpected, embrace it anyway – the director may have observed a potential that escaped your view.

2. **Nudge rather than solve.** It's my strong preference for a sidecoaching insert to encourage the players to uncover a potential pathway rather than explicitly dictating a specific course of action. A gentle exception to this "rule" might be the oft-uttered feedback of "do it!" when improvisers are stalled in a mist of contemplation, but even in this scenario, the coach is typically pushing players to do the thing that they themselves have posited rather than an imposed outside idea. This nudging approach snugs nicely with Spolin's concept of the "catalyst" that adds heat and momentum to the experiment already in progress. It's also reminiscent of the "teach a person to fish" analogy in that providing solutions will tend to create a codependency with the coach rather than strengthen the improvisers' own abilities to get into and out of playful trouble. Using questions rather than statements can provide a simple mechanism to make sure major offers are emerging from those engaged in the action as it allows the players to retain the agency of finding their own unique responses.

3. **Elevate the players.** Asking loaded questions from the sidelines also has the crucial effect of raising up the creativity of the scenic participants rather than inadvertently reflecting and privileging the skill of the sidecoach. *Gorilla Theatre*, discussed above, offers a unique exception in this regard in that the overarching premise frames each scene as the manifestation of the director's vision or conceit, but even here *in reality* effective coaching will very much recognize and encourage dynamics that emanated from the onstage players. Truly puppeteering the action will quickly become tiring for all involved. In simple terms, this requires the coach to as boldly commit to a "yes, and..." attitude as any other player in the space, reserving more oppositional direction for the most exceptional of circumstances. When these more potentially jarring course corrections are warranted, it can be helpful to exude an air of your own fallibility – "sorry, my last adjustment was clearly so poorly articulated" – rather than judgment of the players – "why are you unable to do what I've

instructed?" Like any other collaborative scene, if the story wraps up and you're left thinking "that was *exactly* what I wanted or coached," you've probably smothered a lot of the creativity and may be entering the realm of the **bulldozer**.

4. **Support rather than scold.** I've certainly worked with improvisers who prefer unadorned critique, but generally, the flower of improvisation blooms most impressively when it's watered with positivity and encouragement. Most improvisers will quickly become disheartened or stuck in their heads when greeted by a string of feedback that feels like harsh criticism. This is a direct equivalent to working alongside a negating or blocking energy on the stage as a fellow player. Liberally sprinkling sugar with the salt helps maintain a joyful environment. It's easy to fall into an unintended rut of primarily pushing players to make new or different choices rather than paying equal attention to encouraging and reinforcing successful and helpful dynamics as they play out. While it is unlikely that *all* critiques can be congratulatory, it is possible for corrective adjustments to also be offered with the spirit and tonality of joyful excitement. If players start to associate *any* sidecoaching interruption as a foreboding signal of negative feedback, it's unlikely that they will be open and receptive to the advice that follows. You don't want players experiencing a negative Pavlovian reaction to your very presence! It's no small task to develop and maintain this creative rapport so be aware that needlessly aggressive observations or energies can harm more than just the current scene.

5. **Enable joyful play.** Finally, embrace the sidecoach's role of ally (or the "extended hand" in Spolin's parlance). Sometimes, it's not worth interrupting the scene *yet again* for that clever observation that isn't really needed. It can be easy to forget that well-structured struggle can teach as much, if not more, as heavily directed "success." Spolin extols the coach's duty to facilitate focus; when feedback begins to actively pull the players' attention further and further from the stage action, the requisite focus on the improvisatory task at hand will quickly diminish. It's also important to read the room and individual players. I'm sure I'm not alone in encountering improvisers who find nearly any interruption – regardless of its positive tone or content – as off-putting and thwarting. Others bounce back with immediate and good-natured resilience. As is the case with all pedagogic instruments, one tool does not work the same way for all students. If sidecoached scenes are routinely resulting in bruises, then consider rebalancing your approach and taking some time to explicitly discuss and model the preferred application.

Final Thought

I'll end this entry with an anecdotal account of a sidecoaching style that I find a little disingenuous. On occasion, I've encountered a rather bullish energy where the coach regularly stops the action to aggressively push the players to a new action or beat. The instructions are, more-often-than-not, artistically legitimate but presented with an air of authority: "this is the best path forward and you really should have seen it." At the end of the exchange, the players will arrive at an interesting outcome, but they're usually a little jangled and unnerved, buffeted by the constant tirade of input. The coach will then frequently button the experience with some jovial iteration of the feedback, "look at what you just accomplished!" without any shred of irony that to even the most casual observer it has been very clear that the players have, in fact, accomplished very little *themselves* other than just anxiously following the series of barked directives. I know I've fallen into well-intended iterations of this dynamic – I just *really* want the players to experience some success or break out of deeply entrenched habits that are getting in their way. In reality though, any benefits from such an encounter will be fleeting. Effective coaching requires patience, rapport, and an ability to subjugate your own desire for quick results to the greater and messier calling of enabling a rich and imperfect process.

Related Entries: Caller, Deviser, Ensemble, Hosting **Antonyms:** Bulldozing, Judging
Synonyms: Directing, Mentoring, Teaching
Connected Game: Bad Extra

SIDE SUPPORT

I'm returning to improv trailblazer Keith Johnstone to jumpstart this definition. He describes an ideal working (playing) environment:

> Normal schooling is intensely competitive, and the students are supposed to try and outdo each other. If I explain to a group that they're to work for the other members, that each individual is to be interested in the progress of the other members, they're amazed, yet obviously if a group supports its own members strongly, it'll be a better group to work in.[10]

Effective improvisational **Side Support** directly embodies this enticing group mentality. When engaged in these performed acts of support, players strive to elevate, contextualize, and sharpen the journeys of their featured teammates for, as the very name suggests, side support does not seek to claim the spotlight of center stage but rather provide tactical assists from the margins. This is not to imply that such supportive improv moves are inconsequential – insightful side support can easily make the difference between a scene sailing and stalling – but the express intent is to ultimately serve the central players or situation. Any success or focus is typically fleeting as attention is deliberately thrown back to the dominant action. The rewards garnered for such supporters are less of the moment but rather from the forging of a generous ensemble that will return the improvisational favor when the spontaneous shoe is on the other impromptu foot.

Example

Coworkers and possibly soon-to-be life partners A and B sit nervously at an outdoor café table. While hopeful, neither is certain whether or not this is actually a first date as the focus of the conversation has meandered thus far around a common work project at the car dealership. This small talk has been endearing, but the scene feels as if it is searching for its next beat and neither player has this choice quite in reach…

The moment is ripe for some side support…

Putting Side Support Front and Center

Here are some ensemble-building ways to help (rather than overwhelm) the onstage action…

1. **Transitory support.** A favored form of side support is the highly effective **Canadian cross** that features transitory improvisers delivering a gift and then making a timely exit. (I deal more extensively with this subset of side support and how it can prove most helpful in an earlier entry of the same name.) This flavor of choice can embellish virtually any facet of the ongoing scene, may or may not include dialogue, and ideally functions as a playful nudge or step in an evolving game or dynamic. As the initiating player will exude an "I'm just popping in" energy, focus should quickly and easily return to the original dynamic after the intended delivery.

Player C: (entering as a member of the waitstaff and interrupting as gently as possible) "Just wanted to check in to see if you'll be ordering off the regular menu or our special couples offering tonight. The 'surf and turf' is proving extremely popular amongst lovebirds…"

2. **Energizing support.** Thoughtful side support can also provide focus and energy to the scene (Canadian crosses can certainly be used this way too). On the simplest level, fellow players can model audience behavior by avidly watching the stage action: it's easy to overlook the value and energy of unflinching attention and one of the most crucial gifts we can give our fellow improvisers is our commitment to their work even when we're just observing from the wings. In other situations, this function of focus or status enhancing may be needed on the stage itself with support now assuming the role of a riled crowd or throng of studious servants, for example. A scene might also benefit from more overt but less conventional efforts to raise the temperature or attack…

Player D: (standing over A's shoulder and assuming the function of their inner voice) "The evening is getting long. If you don't test the waters soon, you'll still just be awkward coworkers tomorrow…"

3. **Environmental support.** There are also ample ways to support your fellow players through enriching the greater environment. These additions may be character-centric – a resident violinist could start to make their way between the café tables while playing sumptuous music. They can also take more metatheatrical or presentational hues, especially if these are in keeping with your ensemble's aesthetic. To this end, players might offer **scene painting** adjustments, arrange or physically become set pieces and props, or heighten the mood with pertinent sound effects (whether or not this role is typically assigned to an improvising technician).

Player E: (stepping to the side of the stage and narrating to the audience) "A pair of cooing doves lands in the shadow of the couple's table. Their necks intertwine in a nurturing gesture…"

The sound technician adds to this choice by providing the sound of gentle cooing…

4. **Functional support.** Another important form of side support consists of keeping the players

safe or *physically* supported. This may be triggered by the dramatic twists and turns of the scene or the greater performance parameters. For example, if our café became transported to an orbiting space station, supporting improvisers might assist by enabling props (or perhaps some very game players) to *literally* float across the stage. Or, if you're working in a found space or have commandeered an actual café table, players might need to run interference as unforeseen challenges emerge. There can be a tendency to view side support solely through the lens of the characters' world, but addressing real-world needs strikes me as an equally valid and helpful application of this tool as it allows the featured players to concentrate on their reality freed from unhelpful intrusions.

Player F: (*in response to the jeering interruptions of a belligerent audience member, as "the manager"*) "I'm terribly sorry about the unruly table: they're just about to leave. Please allow me to comp you a bottle of our sparkling wine…"

Hopefully, such a move would then be followed by a member of house management politely escorting the rabble-rouser out of the auditorium…

Final Thought

As side support wanders into more competitive or solipsistic territory I fear it loses much of its generosity and ensemble-raising energy. This distortion echoes the model of "normal" schooling that Johnstone so ardently rejects, where players are primarily concerned with their own choices and accolades. I've noted elsewhere that there is, of course, a time and place for shining and playful competition in most improv venues, but when we code choices that explicitly seek to celebrate an individual's finesse as *side support* we may be missing the innate collaborative rewards of making our choices solely in the service of our teammates. And, in at least my experience, it is very much this latter dynamic that is frequently wanting in the art.

Related Entries: Canadian Cross, Environment, Heighten, Scene Painting **Antonym:** Shining
Synonyms: Assists, Second Support
Connected Game: From an Object's Point of View

SILENCE

A powerful (and sadly under-utilized) gift that can add stakes, energy, and interest to a scene when deployed strategically and from a place of strength.

Synonym: Gut Check

SOLUTION

Providing the answer to an onstage game or tension. Solving problems can tend to sap the energy of a scene when it is done too quickly or easily but will push a story thread or arc to a final state of resolution when applied with care and expert timing.

Antonym: Problem

SPACE OBJECTS

Space Object work refers to the craft of creating imaginary or mimed props and set pieces on the improv stage. "The improvisation is mimed: in this way sensitivity to objects is renewed and many objects can be conjured up without the encumbrance of a single real object."[11] It is, admittedly, a rather peculiar term when you stop and consider it – I think Viola Spolin coined this particular phraseology that has since taken root in many performance circles. Improvisation's delight and frequent reliance on imaginary set elements – as is also the case with many related clowning traditions – requires improvisers to give some thought and attention to how they summon an endless array of theatrical accoutrement from thin air. Props that are imbued with detail and finesse will add much to the improvisational endeavor; those that are only roughly approximated or carelessly abandoned will quickly degrade the magical spell that can so enthrall the audience. I think we've all cringed with disappointment when an inattentive player suddenly walks through a mimed set piece that was just moments ago so *real* in our imaginations due to the diligent efforts of a patient performer. Professional mimes and pantomimes literally spend a lifetime honing this craft of making something captivating materialize out of nothingness, but there are certainly some best practices that even those of us who are less physically adept can also exploit in their favor. Here are five…

Example

Players A and B, soon-to-be-parents, are struggling to assemble a "do-it-yourself" crib on the floor of their soon-to-be-born child's room. Player A, on the verge of giving up, is scrutinizing the instruction booklet one more time while brandishing in their hand the one meager tool the company provided. Player B, equally overwhelmed, has balanced the three-quarters assembled frame precariously on their arms as they catch a breath of air from the overhead fan.

Player B: (with strained patience, but affectionately) "Any new signs of hope in that booklet…?"
Player A: "I know they say a picture is worth a thousand words, but perhaps they could have also included a *few* words in the instructions as well…"

Mining Your Mime Work

1. **Slow it down.** Improvisers with a disinclination toward physical work can compound their ineffectiveness by rushing through any needed mime. I don't think I can imagine any circumstances where an increased tempo assists in the creation and communication of space objects. This impatient tendency is magnified by most players' inability to distinguish anxious "stage time," or how long something *seems* to last, from "actual time" experienced by the observing audience. The few seconds it takes to slow down and mime a scenic element with care is well worth the energy investment and seldom stalls the action as much as one might fear especially as this contribution is rarely the only thing of interest occurring in the moment. When we savor this physical work, we're also more likely to consider core attributes such as mass and weight, which make all the difference when it comes to believability. Just like those empty coffee cups on a long string of TV shows and movies can take you out of the action, so too can an airlight box strain realistic credulity when a litany of pretend objects is revealed to live inside it.

Player A with excruciating meticulousness slowly unfolds the opaque instruction booklet matching their held tool to each and every image. They glance at the scattered hardware on the floor around them.

Player A: "How do we have so many pieces left over?!?"

2. **Keep everything in its place.** In our anxiousness to deploy mimed props, players will frequently have the needed item magically materialize out of nowhere at their beck and call. Once items have been hastily crafted, they can then become tethered by imaginary elastic: "This cup is in my hand but now I've forgotten all about it while I was frantically gesturing, oh, and look now it's sprung back into my hand now that I've realized I need it again…" The figurative and literal step of going to acquire the item from *somewhere* adds so much to your world building. Placing objects slows you down, creates helpful and rich stage geography, and introduces opportunities for movement, activities, and games. All these benefits are then further amplified when you return the prop to its resting place (or conspicuously *don't*) later in the scene. Most companies caution against carelessly combining real and imagined hand props to support this imaginative spontaneous set design: if you pull out your real cell phone and moments later want to set it on the mimed coffee table where you had placed your pretend computer, you'll have few workable solutions that don't puncture the established reality awkwardly. A good and common rule of thumb for sparsely produced shows is to only utilize weight bearing pieces – a chair, bench, or bed – so as to avoid unhelpful inconsistency. (Occasionally, I've deliberately tweaked this rule and incorporated "hero props" that define particular characters or locations of note while leaving other needs purely mimed.)

Player B, still balancing the incomplete crib, reaches out with their free hand to the imagined near-empty glass that they perched on the awaiting equally imagined mattress a few minutes earlier. As they shake the fragments of ice cubes from drinks gone by…

Player B: "You are going to need to get me another iced tea if you want me to continue with this exercise in humiliation."

3. **Find the unique qualities.** Once you feel comfortable with the pacing and placement of common scenic props, a great deal of their value can emerge from making the items a little not-so-common. In the spirit of pursuing specificity, space objects become increasingly dynamic when they are imbued with idiosyncrasies and defining qualities. If the portrait is just inconveniently a little wider than the installing character's arm span, the toaster lever always requires two consecutive pushes to catch, or the official sterling silver pen never writes on the first stroke, not

only have the props become more interesting and memorable, but they are likely to add energy and joy to the scene. Unique props used in this fashion delightfully reveal character subtext and heighten emotions; although such gifts must be observed, received, and echoed by others as well for such choices to land strongly. A well-crafted item can also open up unexpected plot twists and surprises: if the expensive pen is stolen, repeating the established quirk could reveal the identity of its thieving owner later in the action. If you're utilizing a collection of similar or identical objects (moving boxes, library books, cans of corn…), a lack of uniqueness can quickly turn a potentially rich activity ripe with discoveries into a carelessly bland pattern that adds little or nothing to the work. Making even just one of the seemingly identical objects just a little peculiar – heavier, dustier, dinted – makes all the difference.

With renewed purpose (but no new ideas) Player A presses the small assembly tool into a series of bolt heads. The tool is clearly too small and unmanageable for their clumsy hands and each belabored effort results in several unsuccessful attempts to use the tightener in a less-than-painful way.

Player A: (grimacing) "If in doubt, tighten everything again…"

4. **Keep your eye (and hand) on the prize.** Space objects have a habit of problematically disappearing when they are not actively in use, which makes sense if you think about it as imagined objects are only present when we are consciously aware of them – invisible creations literally vanish when they are not being utilized in some concrete way. While I advise against **sticky feet** (an inability to find a timely exit once your contribution has landed) sticky fingers, on the other hand (!) is a helpful technique. When players loiter a little longer as they grab or stow an object, keeping it in their possession for that extra moment, space objects benefit from this added attention and are subsequently more likely to retain critical mass. This approach snugs nicely with the above concept of slowing down while adding the lens of careful deliberateness when it comes to those critical moments of introducing, shelving, and reincorporating relevant props and set pieces. In most cases, the longer an item is left unattended or unreferenced, the more likely it is to be forgotten or misused. Gently keeping such choices vibrantly alive with sticky fingers and occasional referencing goes a long way toward remedying this improv ailment.

Player B adjusts their hold on the increasingly cumbersome crib components in the futile hope that comfort is just around the corner. They place the drained glass back on the beckoning mattress.

Player B: "OK, three more minutes before I say we turn this into a bonfire instead of a three-quarters crib…"

5. **Build with your friends.** And as is the case with most improv strategies, space objects shine even brighter when they are not exclusively the domain of one player. As an object changes hands from one player to another, multiple characters join together to move or manipulate a common imaginary set piece, or a late entrance displays the wherewithal to reuse mimed pieces already established by their teammates, the effectiveness of such work exponentially grows. This is doubly so if such moments *retain the original qualities* of the space objects in question, or playfully upend them in thoughtful ways so that the pickle jar sat on the kitchen counter that one character has struggled in vain to open for hours is suddenly casually opened with a simple twist by their entering younger and frailer sibling. So, once you've tended to your own physical creation, be sure to join another player by using their mimed offerings.

With a frustrated sigh, Player A tosses the instructions over to B and scoots closer to take a turn on holding duty…

Player A: "Here, you give it another try. Everything is starting to look the same to me."

Final Thought

If mime is new or unfriendly terrain for you, consider conducting some firsthand space object research during your day-to-day activities. A lot can be discovered by simply breaking down and assessing how you use mundane objects. How do you brush your teeth, wash the dishes, or organize the recyclables? When you then bring these tasks and your own unique habits to the stage – and we all have them – you will be surprised by the delight and recognition they afford.

Related Entries: Environment, Where
Antonym: Real Props! **Synonyms:** Mime, Object Work, Props
Connected Game: Many Objects

SPEAKING YOUR TRUTH

Speaking Your Truth is a safety valve mechanism committed to maintaining the beauty and inclusiveness of our collaborative storytelling. The concept is synonymous with "calling it onstage," and I tend to use both terms interchangeably. To speak your truth is to momentarily conflate character and player (if this is not already your stylistic norm) so as to provide timely feedback to your teammates. You may elect to utilize such a response if you are physically in peril, emotionally triggered, artistically thwarted, or morally offended. This practice shouldn't be confused with **commenting** which inelegantly suspends the dramatic contract for a cheap laugh or reaction. Rather, it is an appropriate utilization of a player-based sidecoaching device designed to maximize safety and candid communication. When used with this intent in mind, a player can express discomfort, frustration, or critique of an in-the-moment improvisational decision that needs addressing *now*. It shouldn't be used lightly – hopefully, breaches that warrant such interventions are not commonplace on your stage – and whenever possible, it's helpful if this correction is utilized with a light touch. There are certainly moments when a no-holds-barred reaction is warranted: for example, blatant or harmful stereotypes demand a quick slap down, especially if this is a repeated behavior. Retaining a playfulness in less egregious or more run-of-the-mill situations, however, can provide the opportunity for course correction while also maintaining a sense of joyful momentum. Especially when we seek to explore challenging terrain together, this method can quickly assist us in support of our artistic efforts. "This is what stories can do, this is what art does: describe the most difficult truths in a way that we can bear to remember because the rendition is beautiful."[12]

When approaching this topic, it was tempting to focus on how to speak your truth, and this act is certainly complicated, vulnerable, and fraught with the potential of unintended consequences. (On a simple level, I utilize the phrase "In truth…" as a marker for company members that the next statement expresses the needs of the player.) In sensitive moments and during the fragility of improvisational creation, speaking your truth is truly a brave act. For this reason, I actually want to focus on the craft of *receiving* such an adjustment as it is in this moment of allyship that we either forge stronger collaborative bonds or retreat into defensiveness and bad behaviors. When we are trained as a company to engage in deep listening and empathy, missteps can serve as moments for growth and connection. If truth telling, on the other hand, is met with caustic push back, it is unlikely to function as an effective tool in the service of our art.

Example

As the scene has unfolded, Player A has become increasingly uncomfortable.

Player A: (standing atop a platform as they are being urged to jump) "In truth, I could really hurt myself doing this…"

OR

Player A: (after a well-intended teammate accidentally offers a backstory element that is too close to home) "In truth, that's really not something I want to talk about right now…"

OR

Player A: (having patiently waited for a minute to make a verbal contribution to the scene) "It'd be nice, in truth, if you all would listen to me for a change…"

OR

Player A: (responding to an offensive or reductive off-the-cuff endowment) "In truth, I don't see anything of value coming out of exploring that."

How to Fully Accept a Fellow Player Speaking Their Truth

1. **Listen without judgment in the moment.** When a teammate takes the risk to "in truth" you, make sure you are listening deeply and carefully to both their text and tone. Especially if they are endeavoring to keep an air of their character in play, it's feasible that you might need to read a little between the lines. Perhaps in our physical danger example above the player in jeopardy has been playfully egging on the game *up to this point* but is now cueing that the "obvious" next step can't happen. Trust that your teammate knows their own needs and limits. Unequivocally, let them know that they've been heard and understood.

Player B: (to their teammates and partner atop the platform) "Don't move a muscle, Jenni. We can help you."

2. **Assess your course correction good-naturedly.** Ego can be tricky when we're creating our own worlds on the spot and it's easy to become deeply invested in a scene's current trajectory. In fact, while we should assume a flexible attitude in our play, a complete lack of investment in our choices probably isn't the best standard mode of operation. Subsequently, caring is usually an admirable quality. If your partner requests a halt, it can be jarring. You might not understand their reasoning (it doesn't matter), agree with their reaction (it doesn't matter), or have a *really* cool next move that you *really* want to make (it doesn't matter). What does matter in such a moment is that your partner feels heard and safe. So, if their response leaves you creatively reeling a little, take a breath and assume a supportive and good-natured energy.

Player B: (to their scene partner who has unexpectedly bristled at a choice about their character) "Yeah, you're right. Let's talk about something else."

3. **Adjust your path accordingly.** Once you've taken a breath (if you need it), make sure you help to steer the scene into less troubled waters. It's not uncommon for almost *anything* to become a game or opportunity to riff on many improv stages, but this irreverent response really isn't in the spirit of "calling it onstage." Also remember that just because your partner has expressed the need for a new direction, this doesn't mean that they have another option loaded and ready to go. Be sure to roll up your sleeves in the pursuit of a door number two. That being said, it's also generous to leave some room – especially initially – for the effected player in case they need an opportunity to remedy the situation in a way that addresses their primary concern.

Player B: (in response to Player A's observation that they have largely been silenced thus far in the scene) "Sorry, my excitement got the better of me, Jamie. The floor is yours…"

4. **Listen without judgment after the fact.** There will be instances when this communicative device will fully serve its function on stage with players accepting the proffered adjustment in the spirit it was intended thereby enabling the scene to gallop forward into richer pastures. However, when more complex issues arise – such as recurring antisocial behavior, micro (or macro) aggressions, or choices that are uneducated or perpetuate ignorance or harmful stereotypes – it's likely that these highlighted moments will need further redress after the show in a **postmortem** or similar. Just as it's important not to become defensive on stage when nudged by a fellow player, so too is it incumbent upon players to listen openly when debriefing. We should be as willing to change off the stage as we are on.

Player B: (to their teammates as the scene in question is being discussed) "I know I messed up in that scene. I'm listening…"

Final Thought

There are a wide range of situations in which the tradition of speaking your truth can prove invaluable, from minor confusions to more significant unforced errors. I personally see little value in shock improv that seeks cachet from offending merely to offend, but if we pursue Fox's vision above of beautiful "difficult truths" then it is foreseeable that our own biases and blindnesses (and those of our partners) may become exposed or challenged as we wade together into uncharted waters exploring material worthy of our time and attention. Speaking your truth in such moments offers a tool for addressing slips as well as a priceless opportunity to learn from our mistakes.

Related Entries: Commenting, Consent, Mugging, Postmortem, Trust **Antonyms:** Obfuscating, Suffering **Synonym:** Calling It Onstage **Connected Game:** Narrator

SPECIFICITY

One of my teaching catchphrases would definitely be "specificity breeds specificity" – only rivaled by the equally ubiquitous "putting on my pedantic pants" when offering some nuanced specificity of my own as an instructor. Improv without details is like pizza without toppings: it might get the job done, but it's unlikely to result in any memorable flavor, experiences, or reviews. If we consider structure and story arc as the domain of **advancing**, details support the equally critical function of **extending**. What was the protagonist wearing or holding in their hand? What was the weather and terrain like on the eight-hour road trip? What type of bird interrupted the lovers' sleep? **Specificity** encourages interest, connection, and effectiveness by making our stories relevant and relatable. It puts the flesh on the bones of our creations. And, as Boal insightfully posits, there can be even wider reaching ramifications of assuming a specific mindset:

> the theatrical will should not be reducible to vague statements of desire – to want happiness or to seek the good of all mankind and universal peace and harmony – but must be concrete: to desire the good of this particular person, in this form and at this time.[13]

Example

Player A lumbers awkwardly onto the stage wearing an imaginary oversized wallaby mascot costume, its enormous head tucked uncomfortably under an arm... as opposed to... *Player A walks on stage sorta tired.*

OR

Player A: (frantically switching the windscreen wipers on full as they squint in a panic onto the obscured curving road ahead) "I think it's the next left if I can see it..." as opposed to... "I think it's the next left."

OR

Player A: (awakening) "I fear the jealous rooster pines on high/alone atop his chapel perch this morn/and wakes us with his plaintive screeching cry/A-cursing to the heavens he was borne..." as opposed to... "A bird woke us up."

Questions to Unlock the Details

As we pitch ideas to each other and place possibilities atop the improv shelves, it's helpful to consider how we can create offers that are particularly rich with latent creativity and potential. Any one or two of the following questions can increase the vibrancy of your creative palate during these moments. So, ask yourself...

1. **Why is this choice important?** There's a big difference between carrying an umbrella just "because" and carrying an umbrella because there's a torrential thunderstorm currently underway. The umbrella in these examples remains the same, but the conditions surrounding and contextualizing it can raise the value of the choice dramatically. Sometimes, this context is actually inspired by what was at first the seemingly random choice of committing to having an umbrella in your hand at the top of the scene; in other instances, your new offer results from and adds to a broader scenic frame that is already underway. If we populate our scenes with an endless array of mimed props or details, but *none* of them are imbued with importance, then we are likely doing more scenic harm than good (in terms of overburdening the stage with unnecessary offers). It's a given that we don't generally know just exactly why or how something that we've introduced is important until *much* later in the scenic arc, but if we offer choices as inconsequential throwaways then that is invariably what they will become.

2. **How is this scenic element unique?** If we enter the scene with an umbrella and imply foul weather outside, our work isn't necessarily done in terms of specificity. There is much to be mined from exploring the details of the umbrella itself. Yes, it's workable for the umbrella to be *just* another store-bought umbrella, but there's great fun to be had by adding at least one little finesse to the choice. Is it just broken enough that you can never get it closed on the first try? Perhaps it's clearly much too small to provide its owner any semblance of adequate protection. Or it could be one of those giant golfing umbrellas that you have to contort through the doorway until you find just the right angle. As I note in my prior discussion about **space objects**, an idiosyncrasy adds a delightful touch to an improv offer and potentially sparks the improvisers' imaginations in new and surprising ways.

3. **What makes this addition memorable?** Connected to the above, specificity can also increase the memorability and thus utility of a choice. Offers that are haphazardly thrown out to the abyss of the improv stage can easily fizzle away if they have not inspired further attention or play. I think of character names, in particular, as an example of this in that if a player names another character quickly and perfunctorily, in most cases, this name will soon vanish in the memories of everyone in attendance (with the potential exception of the entire audience who always seems to remember the one thing that the improvisers on stage cannot). If a choice is polished and given a little loving attention – especially as it is first introduced – this increases its staying power in the long run. If our umbrella-holding character struggles to get it through the office door and then places it (still opened and malfunctioning) problematically in the corner of the room, the details

of this choice are sufficiently enticing that they might herald a playful series of reincorporations throughout the resulting action.

4. **Does this material resonate with me?** Yet another level of specificity can helpfully aid the greater improv cause when we pursue elements that reflect our own experiences and passions. It's possible as you read this entry about umbrellas (apparently) that you are conjuring an umbrella in your own life. I currently live in an area of Florida that routinely sees almost tropical downpours on an afternoon basis (typically between 4 and 5 o'clock) and it took me a while to fully embrace just how predictable this occurrence was during our excessively endless summers. Finding an umbrella that was sturdy enough and provided adequate coverage but could also be crunched down sufficiently to fit into my teaching bag was an undertaking, so I am *very* protective over the couple of umbrellas that I've found that meet all these needs. These specifics can heighten the reality of my onstage umbrella in fun ways, bringing shades that others might view as original or creative but that, to me, are simply manifestations of my lived truth. And if you can make these types of connections to a relatively mundane prop, the power of such an attitude is amplified even further when you apply it to relationships, themes, and stories that are more personally poignant and significant.

5. **Can I bring more of myself to this moment?** And this segues nicely into my last suggestion, which is to actively look for ways to forge these more complex and revealing bonds with your scenic choices and offerings. It's not cheating to incorporate facets of your known world into your fictitious landscapes. To the contrary, this can provide one of the most effortless strategies for bringing details and nuance to our play. In addition to augmenting the action, you can deepen your emotional presence through (appropriately) accessing personal memories that unlock new story threads and subtext. My seeming obsession with umbrellas might translate into other facets of the scene or aspects of my character's behavior: if I'm paranoid about my umbrella then what else might hold true in my schema of the world? If you're not passionate or invested in *any* component of your character or the story then, it follows, that your energy, commitment, and creativity could deeply suffer as well. In our efforts to find new journeys and jumping off points, sometimes the best specificity begins by revealing (ourselves) rather than inventing (impersonal) random facts.

Final Thought

As I look for a way to wrap up this entry, I can't help but recall one of the more unique pieces of advice I received when I was becoming a parent for the first time. It went something along the lines of "use the most accurate words with your child that you can" so that rather than going "that's a nice dog" you should say "that's a nice French poodle." I think this is equally cogent advice for those (consciously) becoming improvisers for the first time. Even as I write this, the French poodle has become much more vibrant in my imagination than the ill-defined dog. Such an attitude improves our vocabulary while also hardwiring a preference toward peculiarity and fidelity. On the comedic stage, these situational peculiarities do wonders for breaking old performance patterns and tropes. In more dramatic venues, and in Boal's context above, the antithetical habit of universalizing can be seen as ineffectively and dangerously reductive. It's in the specifics of a person's life, passions, and needs that we better understand them and the world that swirls around them. It's the specifics that build doorways to empathy, understanding, and recognition. And as I say (when I have my pedantic pants on) this wonderful specificity will, in turn, breed more specificity.

Related Entries: Ambiguity, Discovery, Extending, Offer **Antonyms:** Generalities, Vagueness
Synonyms: Details, Nuance
Connected Game: Crime Endowment

SPLIT FOCUS

I love large cast improv projects and one of the built-in challenges of these productions is the curse of split focus. When things are flowing well, the players and audience are in accord as to where focus should be placed. As the cast number increases beyond one, the potential for inelegance and confusion increases accordingly. As Peg Jordan observes, this challenge exists on the improv dance stage as well: "Exercises for understanding form and context are part of [Action Theatre's Ruth] Zaporah's tools. She shows you how to value the container, 'everything has a form, even chaos has form'."[14] **Split Focus** refers to a company's inability to quickly address these moments of competing efforts to gain and hold the audience's attention. If the company can't decide where the action is most cogent, it follows that your patrons won't figure it out either and it's likely that serious structural or story challenges are brewing. Sharing focus through gives and takes provides the necessary direction and form to ameliorate what can otherwise easily degrade into unintelligible improvisational chaos.

Example

A scene begins between Players A and B as they are loading hay bales onto their tractor.

Player A: "We're going to have to get up to the high pastures early this morning. I heard some wolves last night and I want to check on the cattle…"

Meanwhile, Players C and D have started making out in the background…

OR

Meanwhile, Player E mimes falling from a great height in a parachute…

OR

Meanwhile, Player F is making their way to the stage through the audience while encouraging everyone to sing the national anthem…

Splitting the Difference

Hopefully, it's a given that 99 percent of the time protracted split focus won't do you any favors. (Consider exploring my other multiple entries collated under **sharing focus** for ideas on addressing these challenges.) The contrarian in me thought it worthwhile to muse here about those rarer occasions where unclear focus might serve your greater agenda. So here are some moments and ways that intentional and orderly chaos can support your creative needs.

1. **When one unified experience isn't the goal.** Keeping the wide breadth of improv practices in mind, there are many performance traditions where a linear or common narrative isn't the primary intention. Environmental or interactive shows, in particular, privilege individual and unique experiences over the illusion of one totalizing narrative. One can easily argue that no theatrical piece really succeeds in telling all its audience members the same story as each spectator in attendance brings something different to the table that frames and informs their experience in a different way. This reality of multiplicity is front and center in experiential pieces where my interaction in one corner of the space might be unwitnessed by anyone else at the greater performance event. In such instances, competing foci is part and parcel of the design, although many shows in this tradition, such as *Sleep No More*, also seek to craft more climactic moments that might require and benefit from steering focus to one singular happening.

2. **When it serves as a greater metaphor.** Improv that doesn't restrict itself to the style of realism can also successfully deploy split focus toward specific artistic ends. The chaos of unmediated focus can enable emotionally charged moments that creatively reflect greater societal ills or, perhaps, metaphorically reflect the fragmented mind of a character or situation. Here, chaos is embraced as its presence enhances or reveals greater truths and tensions. Perhaps there is a swirl of a cluttered stage to highlight a moment when our protagonist cannot find a helpful path forward, or the stage is densely populated by Boalian figments voicing all-at-once competing thoughts or demands as a crisis unfolds, or a character that has been made to feel invisible suddenly becomes obscured by a chaotic relay of focus-grabbing entrances and exits. When you step away from the conceits and strictures of realism, split focus certainly has an innate power to communicate a powerful array of emotions and psychological realities.

3. **When it is used deliberately to build energy or tension.** There are yet other useful possibilities where split focus functions as a means for generating theatrical energy and drive. The key word in this description is undoubtedly "deliberately" as clumsy split focus is more inclined to dissipate energy and thwart the audience. But when executed with a clarity of purpose or carefully woven into a greater structural arc, split focus can provide a much-needed punch of dynamism. This can particularly be the case in long-form pieces that might heavily rely on patterns such as two-person scenes or intimate locations that, after a while, might start to lull an audience due to their predictability and repetitiveness. Throwing in a well-placed ensemble-based moment can break such patterns and provide a helpful jolt. To some degree, the group scenes between the various rounds of a *Harold* can function in this capacity, or a high-octane crowd scene insertion that raises the volume of a story at a critical moment. I've come to use this strategy in several of my theme-based long-forms where personal narratives culminate in seemingly competing cacophony only to suddenly give way to focus and

calm once more. The contrast between these two experiences – chaos and stillness – manufacturers a crispness that can prove quite effective when executed with finesse.

4. **When it is orchestrated or conducted.** Lastly, and a little cheekily, I would contend that split focus can work on the improv stage when it is carefully housed and conducted. Now, I will concede that *strictly speaking* this might not quite meet the textbook definition of split focus that I have proffered above, as in conducting the focus you will typically clean up unhelpfully conflicting stage choices. But in some improv modes and pieces – such as the Café which I deal with in my Game Library – some element of split focus can become an inherent part of the improvisational tapestry, providing a background from which sharper moments of focus emerge, shine, and then become subsumed once more into the primordial ooze of the greater stage machinery. As is the case with some of my prior observations, this approach might belong more seamlessly in experiential pieces where the lived reality of the participants is of optimal concern (rather than any off-stage witnesses to the event). Many of Boal's ensemble-based exercises might fall into this category as well such as Cops and Guerillas, and Murder at the Hotel, especially if an outside eye or director periodically manipulates the action by prioritizing or unifying specific events or actions.

Final Thought

Improvisation wrestles with the eventuality that it could descend into complete chaos at any given moment – this is unquestionably part of the appeal of the form. But when left unintended, split focus can hasten this creative disintegration. Like so many other improvisational concepts that, on the surface, appear destructive, we should not lose sight of the fact that we can also harness this power in aesthetic and interesting ways. What's more, inviting a little of this madness into our work can encourage us to explore different theatrical styles, tones, and agendas.

Related Entries: Commandment #2, Give, Take
Antonyms: Focus, Sharing Focus **Synonym:** Chaos
Connected Game: Invisibility Scene

SPONTANEITY

The ability to effortlessly respond to your own ideas as well as those of your fellow collaborators.

Synonym: Improvisation

STAGE

The physical site of performance. Many improvisational modes delight in found or unconventional spaces, and even when more "traditional" venues are deployed, the line between players and audience members is often playfully and deliberately blurred.

Related Entries: Environment, Where

STAGE PICTURE

If a (stage) picture is worth a thousand words, I fear many improv productions may only routinely communicate a handful of syllables with their proclivity toward a stand (or sit) style of performance. How we arrange ourselves onstage alongside our imaginary or real set elements can add volumes to our scenic narratives. A thoughtful **Stage Picture** deepens meaning, detail, and dynamism while simultaneously directing focus and energy. An uninspired smattering of players on an ill-defined set, on the other hand, will have a contrary effect, distracting from even the most riveting or connected material. Ignoring our staging drastically reduces our options and effectiveness as performance artists. Spolin unequivocally elevates the need for this heightened awareness: "Every actor on stage is responsible for everything that happens. If some actors are not aware of the stage picture, other actors must move them."[15]

Example

Player A, a teacher, enters their office to find Player B, their student, sitting comfortably and defiantly in the chair behind the teacher's desk.

Player B: *(without vacating the teacher's chair)* "I've been waiting for you."

Player A takes a moment to assess the situation, takes off their jacket and casually hangs it on the hook on the back of their door. They conspicuously push the door fully open.

Player A: (nonchalantly) "I was held up at a meeting."

Player B starts to toy with various papers and books on the teacher's orderly desk, as if daring them to respond.

Player B: "You asked to see me."

Not taking the bait, Player A crosses instead downstage to look through their window out onto the campus green.

Player A: (without looking over their shoulder) "I want to talk to you about your performance in my class…."

OR

Player B: "I've been waiting for you."
Player A: "I was held up at a meeting."
Player B: "You asked to see me."
Player A: "I want to talk to you about your performance in my class…."

Some Additional Analysis

While the text of both of these vignettes is identical, the tone, details, and tension are night and day. The first iteration resembles a **status** battle as the characters fight to upend or uphold the expected power relationship between a teacher and student. The second version stripped of any staging or set details *could* evolve down a similar path but is equally inclined to become a sit and talk exchange devoid of any initial spark. Stage pictures and blocking (in the traditional theatrical sense of the term) make all the difference.

Picture This

1. **Help through strength.** When you are the featured character or engaging in a scenic moment of significance, place yourself in a position of strength. If you can't be seen or heard by the audience (and fellow players) the brilliance of your choice may become extinguished rather than further ignite the action. In many cases, the strongest position can default to downstage center, but if overly used, this orientation quickly becomes creatively dull, so invest in crafting well-furnished environments that provide levels, power positions, and interesting staging potentials. In any case, you should be unobstructed by other characters and set pieces. Assuming a traditional placement of the set pieces in the above illustration with the desk facing the audience, Player B has made a powerful choice with the simple gesture of waiting behind the desk in the teacher's chair as this is usually where the energy of a teacher's office naturally flows.

2. **Help through weakness.** To Spolin's point, we also have a responsibility to help our fellow players stay out of staging trouble. Some performers can tend to gravitate to a strong stage position regardless of whether or not it's appropriate for their character or the rising action. When we assume a weaker stage position, we actively help our teammates by giving them a robust physical opening to claim as their own. This doesn't necessitate that a generous staging "give" requires the improviser in question to **upstage** themselves or make it difficult to be seen or heard either (although if you're taking on a true ensemble or crowd role, a staging choice such as kneeling or having your back to the audience can display true magnanimity). In most cases, a self-aware player can enable a stage picture that throws focus to their partner while keeping both characters visible. The teacher's decision to cross downstage and look through the imagined window without turning back to talk provides such an example of gifting your partner an easy way to remain open and seen.

3. **Help through design.** The stage picture battle can be largely won or lost in the opening moments of a scene as hastily made set arrangements can haunt the scene that follows. Assuming a proscenium stage for our office scene above, if the teacher's desk is oriented so that it directly and flatly faces the audience, you might be in for some trouble. If the student establishes the teacher's seat facing the audience – the logical configuration – there won't be any good options if another character needs to sit opposite them. (The only silver lining to this predicament could be that imaginative players might accept this challenge and find novel ways to avoid problematic staging choices.) This often happens when making improv cars out of seats too: if four chairs are clumped in a square face on to the auditorium, the backseats

Figure 15.2 A lot of juggled furniture and malleable set pieces encouraged creative staging choices in *Upton Abbey* and *The Lost Comedies of William Shakespeare*. Photo credit: Tony Firriolo [top] and Scott Cook Photography [bottom].

become almost unusable. Exploiting angles, adjusting for sightlines, or gently raising otherwise obscured areas will generally ease this dilemma. It's also common improv practice to place large imaginary set pieces on the "fourth wall" (or between the company and the audience). Doing so can motivate staging without obstructing the improvisers. Player A utilized this practice by placing the office window in a downstage position.

4. **Help through contrast.** Returning to the office scene above, Player B has made a dynamic power move by sitting in the high-status chair, but even if they had initiated an uncontested status relationship by sitting where they "should," there is still a great value in the teacher not mirroring this choice. Stage pictures quickly become mundane when there is no variety or contrast. As a small scene, these improvisers might get away with sitting opposite each other for a while, but such a predictable choice is unlikely to add much to the overall experience. Especially as the onstage number of characters increases, a helpful mindset is to seek ways to break or augment the patterns around you. This can be particularly challenging in environments where there is a strong expected norm – such as movie theatre seating, a traditional lecture classroom set up, or passengers riding on a long haul bus – but even here, a little ingenuity can reveal staging potentials. I advise that if you look to your left and right and see fellow players standing or sitting *exactly* the same way you are posed, then it's your responsibility to find a playfully appropriate way to shake it up a little. This may need to be subtle, especially if your intent is to serve as part of a larger supporting crowd – shifting your body angle or sitting on a chair in a character-specific way – or could open the door to a bolder choice entirely – safely climbing a sturdy set piece or luxuriously lying on the ground.

5. **Help through decluttering.** Finally, while this suggestion wouldn't apply (yet) to the two-hander scene above, work to unclutter the playing field of superfluous characters, and unnecessary set pieces too if your venue incorporates real furnishings and props. The first simple but important step in this latter process is making sure your company has a good practice in place for efficiently striking prior scenic elements so that the next scene doesn't find itself awkwardly performing in an inherited amalgam of furniture from scenes gone by. In terms of characters, always be on the lookout for opportunities to leave, especially if your work is done. I further consider the critical question of "Should I stay, or should I go now?" in my entry on **exits**. As we strive to construct beautiful and helpful stage pictures, however, it's difficult to successfully frame characters and conduct focus when there is an excess of non-contributing human bodies. If Player B (or Player A for that matter) started the scene in the office with their posse (an idea that tickles me a little even as I write it), there may come a time that streamlining the action down to the two featured players will enable stronger and more well-crafted staging.

Final Thought

Considering the messages (intended or otherwise) that are being sent by our staging practices allows us to tap into the state of improv mindfulness that infuses most engaging performances. Both the *what* we are doing and saying, and the *how* we are doing and saying it, demand our equal attention as performers. A failure to sufficiently consider the latter will nearly always undermine the former. If you have a habit of just standing (or sitting) as a player, the first step toward remedying dull stage pictures can quite literally just be taking a first step or refusing to sit down in that beckoning chair in the first place.

Related Entries: Exits, Focus, Levels, Physicality, Side Support **Antonyms:** Split Focus, Sticky Feet, Talking Heads, Upstaging **Synonyms:** Blocking, Staging
Connected Game: They Said, They Said

STAGE VIOLENCE

A term used to describe simulated physical aggression on stage. Most modern improv practices agree that such choices (if they are welcome onstage at all) should occur in slow motion and with the "victim" controlling the pace and momentum. The safety of the players should always remain paramount, as should an awareness of how such acts might trigger or alienate members of the audience.

Related Entry: Consent

STAKES

There is an interesting inherent tension when it comes to stakes in improv. As players, it's healthy for us to nurture a low stakes performance environment where risks can be taken, slip-ups embraced, and lessons learned without the crippling fear of dire consequences. As characters, however, low stakes will rarely help us generate electricity and passion on the stage, so high stakes here are the lingua franca. **Stakes**, in this second context, are synonymous with the factors that are pushing our characters forward: what do they stand to gain if they are ultimately successful, or lose if their plans finally amount to naught? Writing of his Theatre of the Oppressed, Boal charges his actors:

> All can be changed, and at a moment's notice: the actors must always be ready to accept, without protest, any proposed action; they must simply act it out, to give a live view of its consequences and drawbacks.[16]

Just as a character without a dynamic **objective** or motivation often becomes rudderless within a scene and limps forward lacking clear direction, a desire devoid of stakes will lack sufficient fuel to drive you toward your goal in spite of the potential costs. There is a marked distinction between a student's efforts to pass a class, for example, if they are merely taking it as an elective in their first year as opposed to a classmate during their final semester of university who *must* get a passing grade to graduate. The class itself remains the same in both circumstances – it is the stakes that have changed and, in turn, added power to the resulting scene. (The **urgency** has also increased in this illustration, but that's a related topic for another day.)

Example

Players A and B are fellow low-level crooks who have found themselves embroiled in a mobster's machinations. As they carefully break into their target's mansion, they bemoan their situation.

Player A: (attaching the glass cutter to the windowpane) "You promised that the *last* heist was going to be our last..."

Player B: (assessing the perimeter through their binoculars) "Well, that was before we knew we were walking into a trap set up by the mob."

Player A: (carefully cutting a hole in the glass in a circular motion) "And now we have to do this job for them or else...."

Player B: (securing their binoculars in their backpack and checking the mansion schematics) "Or else, we're sleeping with the fishes."

Player A: (wiping the sweat from their brow) "And the boss will never let my sister see the light of day again either."

Player B: "I told you we should have got her safely out of town when things started to get hot."

Player A: "And I told you that something didn't feel right about that *last* job. But you insisted. And now there's no way out of this mess but forward..."

Raising the Stakes

There are many time-honored ways to make matters pointedly worse or better for your characters and their journeys...

1. **Increase the consequences.** The easiest way to up the stakes is to make the results of succeeding or failing more dire or desired. If I eat that donut that I know I shouldn't, but no one will ever know or care, the stakes of my struggle aren't very compelling. This internal and relatable turmoil might be enough to craft a charming two-minute scene but would be challenging as a contribution to a more robust dramatic arc. If I, instead, am tempted to steal that donut and will become a social pariah if I'm caught, the stakes click up a few notches. If, furthermore, I live in a totalitarian regime where even such petty crimes are publicly punished, the stakes rise again. And if the donut is not to satiate my sweet tooth but rather for my hungry child who hasn't eaten in several days, then we're now in the territory of a sugar-coated *Les Mis*. Even the most apparently benign offer can become invigorating when polished by this stakes-enhancing process.

2. **Increase the passion.** It's also viable to elevate the stakes through internal changes as opposed to adjustments in the external world of the play. Just mildly craving a donut (I should have eaten before writing this entry) is less likely to propel you to action than loving donuts above all else. If this desire moves to the level of an obsession or uncontrollable compulsion, then once more our seemingly innocuous treat has taken on epic proportions worthy of the stage. Leaning into an unexpected juxtaposition, as is presented by our trivial donut example, opens comedic and satiric pathways; substitute the donut for something of more profound or obvious value, and you've set your protagonist up for a riveting dramatic journey.

3. **Increase the obstacles.** Another stakes-raising angle emerges when you consider what stands in the way between you and your desired objective as a character. A conventional theatrical equation observes that "objective" plus "obstacle" equals "tactic" or action. After all, if nothing stands in the way of us and our wants it becomes a rather simple matter to just achieve our goals and then move on. Shifting our tempting donut from a counter in our private house, to a friend's kitchen table, or a public supermarket display, or even a top-of-the-line safe in a well-guarded mansion, provides increasing levels of obstacles that our characters must overcome in order to succeed. When we pace or stack these obstacles artistically and appropriately (not starting with the most impossible problem first), we set up the characters for exciting action as they must deploy well-chosen tactics to keep hopes of success alive. This reflects the "to make matters worse" narrative technique that serves as a helpful complication when crafting longer pieces.
4. **Increase the commitment.** These complementary and potentially cumulative ingredients won't amount to much without appropriate commitment on the part of the relevant characters (and the players underneath them). It's possible to have a dramatic goal, heightened emotion, and thwarting obstacles in your path, but ultimately, it's our commitment to the journey that elevates our characters and engages our patrons. Playing at the top of our intelligence, deploying a full array of imaginative tactics, and keeping the prize front of mind all can make the resulting action enticing. Yes, a character may certainly step away from the field of battle, momentarily turning their back on their dreams to lick their wounds or plot a new strategy. But if the character (or player) doesn't *care* and just passively plods forward, uses the same ineffective tactic time and time again, or ultimately gives in, they are adding little to the story or are cueing the finale of an epic tragedy as they embrace their loss or comeuppance. It predictably follows that if the onstage character doesn't care about the donut that we won't either.

Final Thought

Not to poke holes in my own donut example, but I've focused on largely negative outcomes and complications here – it's equally helpful to explore the "to make matters better" side of the coin, although this is less prevalent in the dramatic canon that tends to thrive on crisis rather than carefree wish fulfillment. If our donut is not just *any* donut, but rather your favorite, or has been declared the most delicious donut in your city, country, the world, or the history of all humanity, this provides a similarly successful but positive ladder toward greater stakes. Obstacles are a little trickier in this light as they, by definition, prevent you from easily getting your goal, but even these can be framed as whimsical distractions rather than ominous impediments. Or, to truly invert the formula, it may now be a case of former obstacles no longer being in play: you *used* to be gluten-free and living a donut-free life but just finally tested negative for the condition due to an experimental drug protocol…

Dynamic stakes act in tandem with an equally robust sense of **urgency** so consider exploring this later entry too.

Related Entries: Drama, Objective, Urgency
Antonym: Passivity **Synonym:** Heighten
Connected Game: Escalating Scene

STARTING SCENES

While there are many approaches to starting an improv scene, most schools of thought recommend tending to your foundational elements (such as the CROW or WWW) sooner rather than later to facilitate effortless play grounded in commonly understood assumptions.

Synonym: Initiation

STATEMENT

Often viewed as a preferred antidote to asking vague questions in improv as it accepts the responsibility for generating scenic facts rather than asking your partners to do all this creative work for you.

Synonym: Assumption

STATUS

Most of my thoughts and strategies about status inevitably lead back to the groundbreaking teachings of Johnstone. I'm confident much of what follows here found its genesis in *Impro: Improvisation and the Theatre* and would highly recommend reading his work for a deeper dive. Johnstone offers helpful framing words when he writes,

> Status is not confusing so long as we understand it as something we do, rather than our social position; for example, a king can play low status to a servant, while a servant can play high status to a king.[17]

When we acknowledge or play **Status** on the stage, we tap into the subtle and not-so-subtle power games and tensions that form the behavioral contracts of society. Do we say anything if someone cuts in front of us in a queue at the checkout counter? Who gives right of way when we encounter a stranger while walking in opposite directions on a narrow path? Which friend always rides shotgun in the communal car when we're going to the beach? It can seem that status is innately a struggle or covert in nature, but in many cases, everyone has tacitly agreed to play by these unspoken but widely known rules; in fact, the participants may actually find great joy in accepting their assigned status positions. Johnstone aptly notes that one definition of friendship involves a mutually agreed willingness to engage in playful status games and exchanges together: "You think *you* didn't get much sleep last night…"

Some cultures and social groups are more at peace with displaying and embracing status configurations than others which strive to hide or obfuscate these interpersonal systems. I've found students, accordingly, display a similar variety of attitudes ranging from great ease to squirming discomfort when faced with utilizing this tool on stage. In some cases, it can require facing disquieting realities in terms of how privilege or entitlement are embedded in everyday interactions. In others, pulling back the curtain feels empowering as previous behavioral mysteries are revealed for what they are. Once you are made aware of status and its implications, it can prove difficult to *not* see it play out *everywhere*. Even this entry wrestles for appropriate status as I seek to balance deferring to my improv forebears, simultaneously giving the reader comfort that I have sufficient expertise to weigh in on the subject, *and* maintaining my own stylistic preference for low status whimsy and irreverence.

Example

A wealthy business-type executive, Player A, paces in their sumptuous living room awaiting the tardy return of their miscreant child. After a few anxious moments, Player B enters with an unapologetic air.

Player A: (turning with a steely eye) "We've talked about this."

Player B stands casually in the doorway, throwing their keys into a dish on a decorative table.

Player B: "I'm going to my room."
Player A: (a bit taken aback – this is not their usual tone) "I'm sorry. That's not how you're going to talk to me in my house."
Player B: "That might have been the case in the past…"
Player A: "In the past?"
Player B: "Yeah, *before* I knew just what kind of person you really were…"

Some Common Status Misconceptions

1. **Status isn't permanent.** One of the most powerful and theatrically helpful aspects of status is that it is fluid and frequently contested. Although you might occupy the highest position in the pecking order one moment, the next you may have slid down several rungs only to regain some footing again soon after your stumble. Our parental figure likely entered the scene with the *intent* of assuming the higher authoritative position, but within a few moments, this has been challenged. If we were to then see this parent in a new scene exploring a different relationship, status will probably reset yet again. When we see status as static or definitive, we may enter the territory of the **bulldozer** or assume a **bulletproof** demeanor, unwilling to accept endowments or adjust our tactics based on the offers of our scene partners. An understanding of status demands flexibility and an awareness that change can (and should) occur in this interpersonal dynamic as much as any other facet of character. It may take a whole dramatic arc – as is the case in Greek tragedy – but it's an exceptional play where some form of status adjustment hasn't occurred by the time the curtain (or sun) descends.

2. **Status isn't synonymous with rank or class.** Johnstone remarks upon this nugget of wisdom in the opening quote when he observes that a king,

despite his elevated rank, can play low status to a servant. Now, if this regal figure played low status to *everyone* in their realm, a coup may not be too far away, but there is inherent beauty in seeing characters in atypical status configurations. Such a move can disrupt stereotypical or overly familiar plot points – instead of the king scolding their servant for poor service now the trusted servant scolds the king for their poor leadership. It's important that everyone involved understands that traditional boundaries are being blurred, and this needn't (shouldn't) necessarily be accepted as commonplace or acceptable. Such moves will nearly always invite an imaginative consideration and justification of the *why*. Is this free-speaking servant a holdover from the previous monarch and thus represents inherited parental authority? Additionally, while players should accept the offer that status has become fluid this doesn't (shouldn't) mean that there won't ultimately be a status reset or repercussions down the line for perceived injuries or infractions. The king (or our parent above) might play low status while being scolded so as to hear the servant's (child's) truth only to turn around and have them imprisoned (grounded) in the tower (their bedroom) for treason (treason) a few scenes later.

3. **High status doesn't imply bullishness.** Most of us have probably fallen into the trap of conflating high status with dictatorial power at one point or another. While this is undeniably *a* way to play status on stage, it's by no means the *only* pathway open to us and, frankly, it is seldom the most interesting or truthful. When you're the top scenic dog – or just a step above another character – it's important to remember that there are *many* different styles of leadership and ways to embody power. I cast the parent as an executive type as this conjures certain images of an investment in the "system" and governance hierarchies. In this schema, our parent is perhaps more traditional and programmed to have a bite reflex when their position is undermined. But this is obviously just one possibility for exploring status. They might rather assume a parental "best friend" style of communication, or be up to date on all the latest parenting manuals and subsequently over-analyze every exchange, or show their power and disapproval through ponderous silences… Petulant high status will quickly feel odd or forced if it isn't strongly connected to the truth of the character and premise. High status can be kind, aware, generous, patient, responsive…

4. **Low status doesn't imply powerlessness.** The power of a high-status persona is often reasonably obvious and comprehensible. Some players struggle to see equivalent sources of joy and agency when they don the role of a low status character. Yes, a high-status *character* might (initially) appear to have more control in the scene, but this is purely a social construct and the *player* under the persona is still bound by the improvisational edict to accept, justify, and change. As Johnstone's delightful Making Faces exercise illustrates, low status characters also have an ability to revel in secrecy and mischief. Nothing can upturn status quite so easily as knowledge and servants are often privy to swathes of information that their superiors would rather they didn't possess. Many players – myself included – also experience great joy from playing second or third fiddle as there is so much more to *do* when you're not the boss figure. These underlings may happily serve with no intent to advance, or subtly use their skills and wherewithal to situate themselves strategically for the moment the revolution begins. When our late teenager alludes to a scandalous discovery that they have chosen to leverage in their own favor, they are providing a keen example of this second instinct.

5. **Ultimately you can't mandate your own status.** To return a last time to Johnstone's cogent words, he acknowledges that status reflects something we *do* rather than something we *are*. Another common trap, especially when seeking an elevated stance, is to decide you're high status and then try to demand this position from your teammates. In reality, the more we fight or posture, the more likely it is that our intended status position will become questioned or undermined. A despotic ruler angrily barking orders probably has very little real status in this moment and will appear desperate and *out of control*. They might instill fear but are much less likely to inspire loyalty. Just as status must be negotiated and ultimately accepted on some level – if I hand my servant an empty glass only to have it thrown to the floor then we're off the races on a status battle – it is also most effective when it is playfully bestowed – I stand up on the bus to offer my seat to an octogenarian acknowledging their esteemed place in my society. High status, specifically, is very challenging to establish without others diligently ceding some ground, preparing the ornate throne, never turning their back on royalty, getting home before curfew… This is not to say that such deference will remain permanently unquestioned, but a tilt or break in the routine will land more resolutely when it's predicated on a clear status quo. If you ever feel

that your attempted status in a scene isn't landing or that there's a status struggle between the *improvisers* rather than the *characters*, consider reinforcing someone else's status intent rather than stubbornly pushing your own agenda. If you have to fight too long for high status in particular, you've already lost it.

Final Thought

For clarity, I've explored some rather extreme status contrasts above. Most scenes thrive equally (if not more fully) with less blatant distance between the characters: two co-workers in adjoining cubicles vying for the better desk chair, friends trying to equitably split the bill after an expensive meal out, wedding guests jostling to establish they are more connected to the happy couple… Even greater fun awaits when you level up from overt and obvious status battles (one-upping and one-downing games explore this amusing dynamic to great effect) and explore instead more subtly subversive maneuvers. And yet another element to contemplate is your status in terms of the environment: do you exert yourself over the room or is the inverse true?

To conclude: (in high status) this is all you'll ever need to know about status and how to use it in your scenes; (in low status) I really appreciate you taking the time to read my thoughts on this subject although I imagine you knew all of this anyway – let me know what I can improve; (and my preferred status somewhere in the middle) I hope this entry has provided you with some interesting tools for playfully incorporating more status into your future work.

> **Related Entries:** Character, Relationship
> **Antonyms:** Class, Rank, Station **Synonym:** Power
> **Connected Game:** High Card

STEAMROLLING

Leaving your scene partners flattened in your wake so that your choices can make it to the stage unimpeded.

> **Synonym:** Bulldozing

STEP OUT, STEP BACK IN

The strategic tool of momentarily abandoning or inverting your established game or deal just so that you can later return to it with added vim and vigor.

> **Related Entry:** Point of View

STEREOTYPE

Assuming a character lightly and usually with the express intent to grab at an easy laugh.

> **Antonym:** Archetype

STICKY FEET

"Speak the truth, but leave immediately after."
– Slovenian Proverb

This is a term I've adopted that may not be in wide circulation (yet): **Sticky Feet** provides a vivid way of describing an improviser inclination to get stuck onstage. The joy of participation can prove so enticing that players find themselves pulled onto the stage only to discover that they are not *particularly* needed. And then they stay on stage… for a long time. This habit isn't necessarily destructive – especially when compared to more egregious activities such as blocking or pimping – but left unaddressed, sticky feet can result in needless clutter, muddy focus, and declining scenic momentum.

Example

Player A enters the scene to deliver a previously mentioned pizza.

One minute later, Player A remains loitering by the door. They "briefly" considered that an exit might be in order, but that felt like a hassle and the wall they are now leaning against is rather comfortable.

Two minutes later, Player A is still standing, largely unnoticed in the corner of the room, their purpose (like their pizza) long-since served. But they are enjoying observing their teammates, so there's that.

Three minutes later…

Warning Signs You're About to Get Stuck

1. **You entered without a clear objective.** Characters (and the improvisers that inhabit them) who just sort of find themselves wandering into the action are prime contenders for sticky feet syndrome. If you don't have an objective, then you're unlikely to know when it's been achieved and that you can leave. This can operate at the character or player level: my character wants to squeeze out some extra overtime from my boss and finally succeeds or gives up; or as an improviser, I want to add a helpful set element to the environment for my teammates. More times than not, when you've accomplished this goal, you should probably leave. Without a purpose in mind, it becomes much easier to inadvertently become a non-contributing piece of the set yourself.
2. **You immediately got comfortable.** Although I refer to this loitering tendency as sticky feet it often manifests itself in the form of a sticky bum (to use my kiwi vernacular!) There is something about sitting down in an improv scene for any length of time that invariably prevents characters from moving or leaving when it's their time. So, I'd strongly advise that you avoid the temptation to get too settled in the first place, especially if your involvement in the scene is already a little marginal. If you've been seated for a while, get up; if you've been listlessly lying on the floor, get up; if you've been leaning on the door frame, maybe walk through it and get out! Frankly, if you've been inactive for so long that you've been able to get *really* comfortable, that probably indicates that your scenic contributions have precipitously declined and you probably won't be missed.
3. **Your energy levels are low.** Part of the risk of getting too complacent on stage is that, if you're not cautious, your energy level will easily and steadily diminish. Presence without passion or commitment will typically take more from the scene that it gives. And, to make matters worse, as your energy decreases so too does the momentum required to facilitate a timely exit. The only truly effective antidote to this dilemma is unfaltering vigilance: if you find your attention or investment waning, grab the next opportunity for a retreat. Improv is difficult enough without having to rally the energies of our fellow teammates. As I've noted elsewhere, when you're not really engaged, you're probably not particularly engaging either.

Final Thought

There are definitely worse things in improv than loitering a little too long, especially as this is often a side effect of basking in the creative joy and delight of the onstage chemistry. But there is a generous power in knowing when your job is done and not overstaying your welcome. And with that in mind…

Review my thoughts on **exits** for some additional pointers on "Should I stay, or should I go now…?"

> **Related Entries:** Entrances, Exits, Sharing Focus, Stage Picture **Antonyms:** Commitment, Energy
> **Synonym:** Passivity
> **Connected Game:** Relay Entrances and Exits

STRANGERS

The conventional wisdom when it comes to **Strangers** is to avoid them whenever you can (on the improv stage just as in real life). By definition, strangers don't tend to bring vital backstory or relationship details to the story. Subsequently, more times than not, these personae stall the action or lower the overall stakes. Such ill-defined characters are particularly irksome in short-form traditions as we may only see a person or relationship *once* and much of that time will be spent justifying and determining why we're seeing this random character combination in the first place. If you find yourself inadvertently falling into this trap, there are some "quick fixes" that can prove reasonably effective, such as recognizing your scene partner as someone significant (and justifying why you didn't do so initially), *needing* them in a concrete and emotionally grounded way, or finding a commonality that inextricably ties your fates together. "Wait a second, weren't we on that same dreadful math-letics team in high school…?" or "I know you don't know me, but I need you to be my alibi…," or "So I hear Omar broke your heart as well. Wanna help me get revenge?"

Example

An elderly character sits on a park bench consuming their lunch from a brown paper bag. After a few moments, they are joined by a teenager listening to their music on headphones. They glance at each other. They are strangers.

OR

A flustered shopper overladen with an armful of shopping bags struggles beside their car, trying to acquire their keys from an uncooperative jacket pocket. A teenager chuckles from their perch leaning on the wall of the convenience store and then quickly returns to scrolling through messages on their phone. They are strangers.

OR

In a line at the sports stadium, a bedecked fan excitedly purchases an over-processed and equally over-priced hotdog. Behind them, a teenager silently and indifferently observes, waiting their turn. They are strangers.

When Is a Stranger Not a Stranger?

Accepting as a given the pitfalls of assuming a stranger persona outlined above, there are (as has clearly become the norm in this dictionary) some notable exceptions. I'd offer that the techniques described below are better fits for a long-form modality where the payoff of a stranger character has much more time to gestate.

1. **When it's a plot device.** It's a common trope in theatre, film, and television to utilize a new or stranger character as a vehicle for introducing and establishing other foundational roles and relationships. When used in this manner, the stranger becomes a proxy for the audience, learning all the given circumstances that will prove necessary to get the dramatic ball rolling. As they meet each new character and engage in formal pleasantries, the audience also has a chance to get up to speed. It's likely that through this expositional process we'll *also* learn about the stranger character as well, and they may, in fact, be situated as the action's protagonist: they're the new doctor (and possibly vampire) in town just hired by the hospital, the reclusive transfer student (and possibly vampire) who suddenly arrives mid-term at the high school, or the up-and-coming legal aide (and possibly vampire) hoping to make their mark on the big city. Initially a stranger, these characters typically evolve alongside the action they facilitate.
2. **When it's a seed.** A stranger can serve as the ultimate shelved detail or curve ball. Especially in genre work that embraces suspense and a sense of mystery, a stranger may strategically appear with the explicit intent of initially remaining ill-defined and seemingly disconnected from the greater story arcs. Again, this is probably a little challenging to pull off effectively in a shorter production, but in pieces spanning multiple scenes, or even evenings, such a choice can add delightful potentials. Each appearance of the stranger might plant deliberately opaque or unwatered seeds, trusting that later improvisational moves will find prescient connections and justifications. There is an intoxicating and palpable risk in such a device – if the stranger doesn't ultimately prove vital to the story's climax with a dynamic reveal, the buildup to this choice will ultimately disappoint – but this is a brave and genre-specific way to deploy an embodiment of the unknown.
3. **When it's a ruse.** Strangers can provide dramatic opportunities for subterfuge. While these characters may initially *appear* as strangers to their scene partners, they are actually strongly connected to the known characters but are electing to hide their true identities (at least at first). They are, if you will, one-sided strangers as they know their scene partners even though they themselves are unknown. Such a choice could resemble the strategy above, but more often than not the ruse becomes shared with the audience as this provides the spice of the dynamic. (And in doing so, the improvisers will also know this information even while their characters remain in the dark which provides further opportunities for mischief and raising the stakes.) There are ample examples of such machinations in the classic dramatic canon – the ubiquitous tradition of cross-dressing heroines seeking agency leans into this energy mightily – and the contrast between what the audience knows and what the characters know provides rich contrasts and tensions.
4. **When it's a foil.** It's important to note that there are dramatic opportunities when a stranger's presence is actually needed to serve the needs of another significant character. Strangers can act as enabling foils assuming relationships with the featured character that are secondary to the information or heat that they can bestow. This can be the realm of teachers, doctors, lawyers, counselors, law enforcement, and the like – voice pieces of important institutions that have the power to offer up unexpected tilts or news. It's a trap to reduce such roles to *solely* their plot function, and equipped players will also imbue these personae with compelling energies and deals of their own, but they frequently appear in one-off encounters destined to influence the story arc and then vanish into the ether. Their gifts are more likely to travel with their defined scene partners than live on in later iterations of

their own journeys. Sometimes, such an outside character is the best vehicle for pushing the story along to that next substantial moment.

5. **When it's a game.** And in larger ensemble-based or non-realistic pieces, strangers may appear as part of a larger thematic gesture or serve as cogs in more broadly conceived games or staging dynamics. Side support and Canadian crosses are probably the most readily familiar examples of this impetus, where strangers can add to the environment or energy of a scene without any intent of becoming more indelibly connected to the dominant story threads. But we could also encounter a sea of strangers in a run, revolving door, or group scene that serves as a preamble to a relationship of note or increases the isolation of our protagonist by surrounding them with a swirl of anonymous faces so as to intensify the weight of their emotional plight. When the ensemble suspends the need for individuality and works as an organic but faceless whole, the persona of the stranger can become a truly evocative tool.

Final Thought

Onstage strangers are most dangerous when they are the product of nervousness – players warily avoiding naming each other or forging meaningful relationships as they are unsure if their idea is "good" enough or the "right" choice for this theatrical moment. The above exceptions all employ the device of the stranger from a place of deliberateness and strength: I am *not* defining this connection *now* as I know it will be more powerful later; I have a gift to bestow from the vantage point of this stranger and will trust you to exploit it; I am focusing on energy, mood, or style as I know that will serve us all well in the long run. So, when is a stranger not a stranger? When it's a purposeful opportunity for discovery.

Related Entries: Character, CROW, Curve Ball, Endowing, Relationship, Secrets
Antonym: Specificity **Synonyms:** Vagueness, Wimping
Connected Game: Pan Left, Pan Right

STRUCTURE

The mutually agreed upon parameters that helpfully shape, guide, and inspire spontaneous play.

Related Entries: Long-Form, Short-Form

SUBTEXT

Humans rarely say *exactly* what they mean or want – in many situations, we may not actually know or be able to clearly express our needs. For most of us, this level of unbridled transparency is reserved for a special handful of privileged relationships. When we fail to mirror this honest complexity on stage through the use of **Subtext** and its communicative kin **ambiguity**, our conversations can start to feel remedial or inauthentic. Paying attention to what is between and beneath our lines makes what may have otherwise been rather mundane dialogue sizzle with emotion and specificity.

Example

Two friends are hanging out together on a porch, dangling their feet over the edge of a swing couch for two.

Player A: "I like your shoes."

Getting to the Bottom of Subtext

The concept of subtext is rather simple – what you say shouldn't necessarily align exactly with what you mean or want. If this technique isn't commonly deployed in your scene work, here are some helpful pointers to help you escape the perils of **cartooning**.

1. **Don't say what you're thinking.** Or, if you prefer, don't think what you're saying! This is really just a textbook definition of the technique, but it's helpful to have this basic formula front of mind if your dialogue has become anemic. The lowest hanging fruit on this branch of the subtext tree tends to be sarcasm, which expresses the exact opposite of your truth, so "I like your shoes" really means "I *hate* your shoes." A *slightly* more subtle variant of this energy would be colloquially known in the United States as "southern charm," which tends to similarly disguise critique with the veneer of *apparent* politeness. But subtext needn't be oppositional to prove effective. "I like your shoes" could as easily mean "Aren't those *my* shoes?" or "I wish I could afford shoes like that."

2. **Communicate through the silences.** I think it's also a mistake to forget that subtext needn't exclusively accompany spoken dialogue but can also be powerfully expressed through silence, body language, and behavior. Maintaining an active inner monologue while you're onstage allows you to consciously process and react to material as it emerges. When your subtext is clear and rich, you're often able to achieve as much, if not more, with a look or gesture than a whole volume of words. Perhaps our friends have just come out the other side of a rather unpleasant argument, and A's observation serves as a peace offering of sorts. Player B's responding look, exhalation, or gesture (or lack thereof) is probably ample to reveal whether or not they are similarly ready to make amends.
3. **Tell a lie every now and then.** Perhaps not the best advice in our day-to-day transactions, but lies are such a provocative subset of subtext as they open great story potentials and relationship tensions. These are helpful if only the speaker is aware of the untruth – Player A's distaste for B's shoes is known only to them – but take on even greater utility when other characters, players, or the audience recognize our statements as false. Perhaps Player A has spent much of the current scene railing against this particular pair of shoes with B, in which case the compliment now lands as a shared outlandish joke. If A has established in a prior scene with a different friend how much they loath B's fashion sense but that they now need to butter them up to get an invite to that party of the season, the same lie takes on a more surreptitious hue.
4. **Explore subtlety and nuanced tactics.** Subtext is a great delivery system for exploring varied tactics. Yes, characters can just candidly ask for what they want, but this strikes me as the exception rather than the rule in most dramatic actions. There is a lot of fun and dynamism to be unearthed from playfully deploying subtle or mischievous moves. When tactics become too repetitive or transparent, they frequently lose any potential for success. But when our characters play at the top of their intelligence

Figure 15.3 Lies and subterfuge form the bedrock of many style pieces, such as *The Lost Comedies of William Shakespeare* (Improvising stage manager: Anastasia Herbert; Associate scenic designer: Rebecca Kleinman; Live Foley artist: Gabby Schiavenato). Photo credit: Tony Firriolo.

and infuse these choices into their subtext, even mundane transactions can become fresh. Perhaps Player B has been eating a delicious bag of chips without offering to share any. "I like your shoes" in this context could actually be a gentle move toward eventually securing a snack.

5. **Develop a taste for irony and ambiguity.** As subtext implies some form of tension between your words and meaning it's useful to develop a palate for irony and ambiguity. Specificity and clarity – two admirable improvisational goals – need not conflict with a subtextual inclination toward complexity. The concept of specific **ambiguity** creatively exploits this fruitful marriage. My above examples suggest some purposeful design on the part of Player A, but it's also exciting to just lace a strong emotion or energy under the dialogue trusting that the why will figure itself out eventually. In this way, you could make a very specific emotional choice (excitement) with an equally elusive intent that adds mystery to an otherwise pedestrian exchange. Just making *any* strong choice with conviction will usually set you on a scenic path toward discovery.

Final Thought

People are complicated beings with multiple competing agendas that are expressed through equally opaque speech acts. Our characters should reflect these realities too. It's a little sobering when you realize just how malleable text can become when it's infused with thoughtful or brave subtext. And perhaps a little surprising that we're ultimately able to communicate anything with definitive precision. So, with that in mind, "I like your shoes!"

> **Related Entries:** Ambiguity, Objective, Secrets, Specificity **Antonym:** Cartooning **Synonym:** Meaning **Connected Game:** Text/Subtext

SUGGESTION

An audience elicited prompt used to inspire the improvised action.

> **Synonym:** Ask-For

SUPER OBJECTIVE

The central desire or motivation that pushes a character into action for the duration of the theatrical event.

> **Related Entry:** Objective

SURPRISE

Embracing choices that organically bubble up through the spontaneous process that at first glance might seem pleasantly unexpected. Surprising from within the established context of a given scene or story arc (or exploring a choice that is connected to your world but in a slightly unique or peculiar way) can provide a helpful device for keeping the journey fresh and engaging.

> **Related Entry:** Curve Ball

SWEEP

Dashing across the stage – usually in front of the current performers – with the intent of editing the scene so that a new action can commence.

> **Related Entry:** Edits

NOTES

1. Charna Halpern et al., *Truth in Comedy. The Manual of Improvisation.* Colorado Springs: Meriwether, 1994. p. 125.
2. Hazel Smith and Roger Dean, *Improvisation, Hypermedia and the Arts since 1945.* Amsterdam: Overseas Publishing Association, 1997. p. 29.
3. Neva Leona Boyd, *Play and Game Theory in Group Work: A Collection of Papers.* Chicago: University of Illinois at Chicago Circle, 1971. p. 43.
4. Charna Halpern et al., *Truth in Comedy. The Manual of Improvisation.* Colorado Springs: Meriwether, 1994. p. 74.

5. Eugene Van Erven, *The Playful Revolution. Theatre and Liberation in Asia.* Bloomington, Indiana: Indiana UP, 1992. p. 232.
6. Amy E. Seham, *Whose Improv Is It Anyway: Beyond Second City*. Jackson, MS: U of Mississippi P, 2001. p. 112.
7. Rob Kozlowski, *The Art of Chicago Improv: Shortcuts to Long-Form Improvisation.* Portsmouth, NH: Heinemann, 2002. p. 116.
8. Viola Spolin, *Theatre Games for the Lone Actor: A Handbook.* Evanston, IL: Northwestern UP, 2001. pp. 163–164.
9. Viola Spolin, *Theatre Games for the Lone Actor: A Handbook.* Evanston, IL: Northwestern UP, 2001. p. 7.
10. Keith Johnstone, *Impro. Improvisation and the Theatre.* 1979. New York: Routledge, 1992. p. 29.
11. Jacques Lecoq, *The Moving Body.* [*Le Corps poétique*] Trans. David Bradby. New York: Routledge, 2001 [1997]. p. 31.
12. Jonathan Fox, *Acts of Service. Spontaneity, Commitment, Tradition in the Nonscripted Theatre.* New Paltz, NY: Tusitala Publishing, 1994. p. 216.
13. Augusto Boal, *Legislative Theatre.* Trans. Adrian Jackson. London: Routledge, 1998. p. 58.
14. Peg Jordan, "Zap! On the Improvisational Edge." *American Fitness* 9.1 (Jan–Feb 1991): 8(2).
15. Viola Spolin, *Improvisation for the Theater. A Handbook of Teaching and Directing Techniques.* 3rd ed. Evanston, IL: Northwestern UP, 1999. p. 147.
16. Augusto Boal, *Games for Actors and Non-Actors.* Trans. Adrian Jackson. London: Routledge, 1992. p. 134.
17. Keith Johnstone, *Impro for Storytellers.* New York: Routledge, 1999. p. 219.

T

TAG

Also referred to as a "tag out," this motion provides a means for adjusting the current player combination by tapping out and/or waving away superfluous characters so that a new or tangentially related scene can assume focus.

Synonym: Edits

TAKE

When it comes to moving focus around on the improv stage, you only really have iterations of two choices: you can **give** focus by directing it to another or **Take** focus by personally owning the next dramatic moment or step. In thriving scenes that have found their rhythm, the process of give and take will probably feel rather effortless and organic – the focus ball is likely passed around with joyous ease. In other instances, when the action has become more frenetic, stalled, or unsure, focus shifts need more robust attention and direction. In either case, "Each improviser shares a small portion of responsibility for the piece on stage. They must focus their concentration on the work of the group – *not* the work of any individual."[1]

When focus becomes fraught, giving can *appear* more generous – you are moving the focus to someone else after all – but scenes can suffer from too much deferring or "passing the buck," especially when the stage may be a little crowded or overwrought with potential next moves (or, alternatively, completely *absent* of any next idea). In such moments, a chorus of well-intended generosity can, in fact, drown the scene if no one is willing to captain the ship at least momentarily. A give, at the end of the day, that the recipient doesn't want or has no idea how to use in a timely fashion isn't really a gift so much as an awkward curse that they may bunt or outright reject. Frequently, the brave and constructive move is to take the reins during such moments of unsurety to unify the scene's direction.

Example

What began as an effective and playful game of various townsfolk gathering in the communal square to share a litany of woes has slowly devolved and lost its steam. The crowd scrambles to find a connected next move…

Ways to Take

Here are some seemingly basic but undeniably effective ways to own the focus in moments where the action may have become lost:

1. **Verbal takes.** An effective focus grab consists of a transparent vocal choice that communicates you're game to make the next story contribution. This may assume the form of loudly clearing your throat, making a brief utterance – a "hey," audible exhalation, or scream – or just announcing your intent: "Quiet down everyone, I've got something to say…" In smaller scenes that have established clear communicative patterns, you should be able to take just with your dialogue alone, but in crowded scenes, some form of preamble or warning helps you stand out from the verbal mumbling that may now characterize the scene as a whole. A little wind-up, especially if pitched through the chaos, allows your teammates a second to process your request and (hopefully) adjust accordingly. Regardless of your specific verbal choice, it needs to clearly display intent and hit the stage with

energy and conviction. The tradition of **speaking your truth** allies nicely with this strategy, providing a mechanism for you to acknowledge that you are experiencing split focus or waning energy and are now making a move to remedy this situation.

Player A slowly emerges from the churning mob.

Player A: (imploring) "Friends, friends, please! In truth, this chaos will get us nowhere. Our grumbling will never force change unless we organize and unite. I volunteer to take our concerns to the assembly…"

2. **Physical takes.** When you're trapped in verbal cacophony or a vignette characterized by a succession of interruptions and over-talking, a strictly verbal take will probably fail to stand out from the clatter. In these moments, leaning into a definitive physical offer will serve you better. Generally speaking, seek a way to stand out or separate yourself from the proverbial rabble. Move to the strongest stage position available – where the majority of your teammates can see you and throw you their attention. Assume a higher level atop a platform, chair, or table, place yourself firmly center stage, or dramatically embody a pose that disrupts the current staging norms. If everyone else is standing or sitting and you start passionately pacing, or building a barricade, or boldly recording complaints on an oversized parchment, this physical contrast should move eyes to you. When in focus, you can then elect to heighten your physical choice, add a verbal element, or redirect the energy to another suitable contender.

Player A, weakened by their subsistence living, gradually struggles forward, each step more painful and fatiguing than the last. Slowly, the other townsfolk become aware of their compatriot's plight, and gently make way for A's path. Finally, when they have arrived in the middle of the crowd, their body can no longer serve them, and they collapse with a gentle sigh. They pointedly reach toward a fellow player…

3. **Energy takes:** Whether you're leaning into a verbal, physical, or hybrid focus take, endeavor to exude an appropriate energy, emotional intensity, or urgency. High status characters are uniquely equipped to step up in times of division. If you currently hold or can reasonably adopt such a status position, you may be the best option for determining or voicing the logical next step. Be aware that when high status characters exert their power (if this power is accepted and uncontested by others in the scene) that it may largely silence or squelch other existing dynamics, so such an authoritative assertion should not be made lightly. It can be anticlimactic to circle back for any sustained amount of time to more trivial games or bits when the stakes have suddenly exploded, especially if the taking character holds a significant status advantage. So, if current dynamics have untapped potential, you might want to give them a little room to build. Similar focus shifts can also be heralded by new robust emotional offers that introduce deliberate and significant elements. This is a helpful equivalent to a high-status shift that plays equally well from a low-status initiator, such as an injured peasant who returns in terror having just been attacked at the assembly gates.

A previously anonymous figure in the crowd, Player A, steps forward while removing their hood and revealing their august identity as the leader of the assembly. The crowd audibly gasps with some instinctively bowing at the sight.

Player A: (calmly, perhaps eerily so) "My cousins, I have heard your concerns. I am not blind to your suffering and pain. I feel each wound myself…"

4. **Strategic takes.** In my companion entry on **gives**, I posit that sometimes the most gracious give is actually an exit. The complementary tactic in terms of taking would be a well-timed edit or entrance. A scene currently-in-progress may not have the self-awareness that it has outlived its usefulness or interest or may have realized this state of affairs but not be able to find a viable "out" from amidst the turmoil or growing malaise. Off-stage eyes can often recognize and diagnose needs that elude those currently lost in the weeds of creation. It can be risky adding *yet another* character to the stage if it's already overcrowded, but a well-timed entrance with that previously absent piece of information or integral character might be the most efficient way forward. Entrances, when offered with gusto, are, by definition, focus takes as the audience (and ideally other players) will naturally be drawn to the new appearance. If you're entering a cluttered scene, status, stakes, or emotional intensity will serve as your best friends as an undersold arrival could go largely ignored, thereby leaving you equally as stranded as the teammates you were hoping to rescue. If a scene has lost all momentum and agency, almost *any* committed energy will likely prove sufficient for the cause. Once you resolutely possess the focus,

you can then strategically move the scene to richer pastures, edit the action so that something new can rush to the stage, or pitch a culminating button to bring the current scene to a close.

Player A runs onstage from the direction previously established as the great assembly. They are out of breath and clearly panicked.

Player A: *(after a moment)* "They're coming... the guard... the assembly has sent the guard and they're going to arrest us all. I have a family to support. I can't afford to be found here fomenting revolution..."

Player A looks with fear behind them before launching themselves once more out of the town square. Others, now equally panicked, quickly follow Player A's cue and soon the square is empty as the lights transition...

Final Thought

It's a jarring experience having the focus suddenly thrown to you when you least expected or wanted it: the resulting nerve-shaking situation more closely resembles pimping or gagging than a generous give. Well-executed taking, on the other hand, allows a focus exchange born from confidence rather than panic. Aggressively taking too often or as your norm can come across as bullish or **bulldozing**, especially if such choices are routinely designed to shut down or silence the emerging ideas of others. This misguided use of the "taking" tool is as highly problematic as *always* throwing away your opportunity to participate so that you can ride along risk-free as a scenic **passenger**. But it's beneficial to hone this fundamental focus skill so that you can deploy it when it's needed by stepping into the fray and leading from strength for the good of all.

> **Related Entries:** Bulldozing, Commandment #2, Edits, Give, Stage Picture **Antonyms:** Passenger, Split Focus **Synonyms:** Entrances, Sharing Focus **Connected Game:** Tag-Team Monologue

TALKING HEADS

Talking Heads refers to the improvisational plague of performers essentially only acting from the neck up (not the highly physical 1970s rock band of the same name). Whether sitting or standing, these players – and the scenes they populate – are largely intellectual affairs devoid of dynamic staging, physicality, and subtext-infused body language. Although such players are typically squarely focused on their language (and wit), their resulting creations that lack embodied presence stop making sense on a deeper level as they fail to capture the electricity and complexity of theatricalized human behavior. The habit of talking heads frequently appears with its improv relatives, **commenting**, **telling**, and **sticky feet**.

Example

Player A, a nervous big retail store employee, enters their supervisor's office...

Player A: "Thanks for seeing me, Travis."
Player B: *(looking up from their desk)* "Have a seat, Mark. What did you want to talk about?"
Player A: "I've been working here for three years now..."

Both characters continue to sit and talk about what's on Mark's mind, and then they sit and talk some more...

Escaping the Road to Nowhere

1. **Add an activity.** It's *possible* to achieve sound scenic results while just chatting, but ignoring physicality invariably means missing opportunities to deepen and complicate your storytelling efforts. Adding almost *any* activity – no matter how mundane it might strike you at first – allows characters to now show rather than tell their subtext and choices. Burning down the house of the manager while asking for a raise would certainly elevate the heat, but even a simpler choice like Player B watering their office plants is enough to get someone out of their chair. And what begins as a perfunctory activity can evolve into more pointed action or a means for creating tension or irony. If B displays enormous care for their plants while showing entrenched indifference toward their workforce, the scene now has upped its game, perhaps without even altering a single line of dialogue.

Player A: "Thanks for seeing me, Travis."
Player B: *(standing with a clipboard)* "No worries, we'll just have to chat on the move as there's an inventory issue in the warehouse..."

2. **Add environment.** One of the unintended consequences of talking heads scenes is that once the characters become immovable the world around them quickly evaporates leaving few details intact save the two chairs or small ill-defined square on which the players are passively standing. If you find yourself in an overused or basic location – such as our anonymous office above – strive to add unique details. Is it so cluttered that you *can't* sit down or get comfortable? Does the boss have the air conditioning set so low that you can't help but shiver and have to yell to be heard above the constant white noise? Or even better, take me to the river, a bustling marketplace, or the hushed back shelves of a research library. Open new doors by having your everyday conversation in an exceptional locale (or everyday locale with an exceptional feature).

Player A: "Thanks for seeing me, Travis."

Player B hands their employee a large pile of sensitive tax documents that are apparently in tall piles on the floor.

Player B: "Start shredding our filings for 2010 and I'll do the same for the current year. Now, how can I help you...?"

3. **Add heat.** Talking head scenes may display patience and active listening but can also linger in stasis for most of the "action" as players search for (and often miss) the choice ripe for investigation. Rather than assume each interaction begins in a perfect world, take the joyful risk of offering up (or recognizing) an off-kilter story element. This technique has the bonus of providing a "starting in the middle" sense of energy and urgency: if we know we want the scene to result in some dramatic fire, why begin it with assembling the kindling when we have the option of benefiting from using a fire pit that already has some flickering flames? Incessant talking scenes tend to *reduce* the likelihood of heat if the players aren't extremely cognizant. When you find yourself about to enter a predictable exchange unlikely to easily yield new options, consider adding an "again" endowment as this can at least raise the stakes of this familiar encounter. If Mark *always* comes into the office with requests, there's now some backstory to encourage stronger emotions and actions.

Player A: "Thanks for seeing me, Travis."
Player B: (standing awkwardly) "HR has asked me to keep the door open when we meet from now on to prevent further misunderstandings... So, how can I help you, Mr. Gordon?"

4. **Add context.** Providing activity, environment, and heat are all subsets of the greater tool of refining context. Dull content will remain uninspiring if it is allowed to play out under dull circumstances. Well selected and executed framing choices can do much to alleviate and break passive patterns, thereby encouraging characters to explore storylines with their whole physical and emotional selves. A request for a raise is a fine starting point, but can quickly benefit from creative answers to the question of "why does this scene need to happen *now*?" If the answer elevates but is in keeping with our known reality, the scene gains heightening stakes and urgency. Perhaps Player A's significant other just lost their job, or they are expecting an addition to the family. Hopefully, these enhanced motivations can prod the character to a wider array of tactics. When the answer to the suggested riddle above questions, upturns, or surprisingly reframes the otherwise customary scene, the result can create delightfully satiric or deliberately jarring results. Player B could *be* Player A's significant other, or the zombie apocalypse could have a hoard of slippery people banging on the store's front door threatening to decrease the size of A's family (but corporate policy *still* won't budge for hazard pay).

Mark continues to hold his "unionize now!" sign high above his head as co-workers loudly chant the same refrain from the picket line outside of Player B's office window.

Player B: (getting up from behind their desk and trying in vain to block out the chanting) "How can I help you?"

Final Thought

I would speculate that a talking heads dynamic can surface as a side effect of players' misplaced efforts to craft "realistic" or subtle scene work that resembles (at least in theory) what they have seen on screen. But the stage is a different performance beast and does not have the benefit of camera angles, extreme close-ups, and refined editing to communicate the smallest choice or thought process to the audience. For the stage to capture the full wealth of this wild, wild life, talking heads scenes need the additional gifts that robust staging, elevated stakes, and thoughtful context can offer.

Related Entries: Environment, Stakes, Sticky Feet, Telling **Antonyms:** Physicality, Stage Picture
Synonym: Waffling
Connected Game: Contact

TARGET RHYMING

A technique whereby an improviser strategically saves the "better" rhyming word, utilizing a less obvious or preferred option as the setup so that a couplet or series of lyrics can end with a more impressive punch.

Related Entry: Rhyme

TEACHING SCENE

Teaching Scenes (much like transactional and stranger exchanges) are widely discouraged in most improv circles. The basic dynamic – that one character has all the knowledge and agency and must tell the other what to do – is rife with pitfalls while also inviting players to wander into other problematic habits, such as asking questions, conflating text and subtext, and becoming reduced to talking heads where you ponderously discuss action rather than engage in it. It's also challenging to find interest in what can become a fait accompli – the student will either follow the prescribed steps and blandly succeed, or (more often) they will prove inept and thwart the instructor. And yet, improvisers frequently find themselves falling into these potentially unproductive onstage relationships. As it's unlikely (and perhaps ultimately unhelpful) to completely eradicate such scenarios from your improv repertoire, it's wise to have some strategies in your pocket to make teaching scenes more than what immediately meets the eye.

Example

Based on the audience's suggestion of "oil change," Player A assumes the role of a parent and gestures for their teenage child, B, to join them at the car.

Player A: "OK, this is long overdue. I'm embarrassed that I haven't walked you through this yet."
Player B: "I'm here and I'm all ears."
Player A: "So, what's the first step…?"
Player B: "Listening closely to you!"
Player A: "Not what I was expecting, but I can't fault you that. We need to jack the car up so we can get underneath it."
Player B: (reluctantly) "Well, that sounds needlessly complicated and dirty."
Player A: "Here, take the car jack…"

Lessons Designed for Teaching Scenes

1. **Invert.** Part of the innate ineffectiveness of teaching scenes is that they are usually *so* obvious and predictable. It becomes difficult to sustain the interest of the audience (and probably the players, too) with these vignettes unless those in attendance are in desperate need of the lesson themselves. If you quickly invert or subvert expectations, there's a good chance this will enrich the core relationship and unlock some potential charm or spontaneity. If it becomes clear that Player B knows *a great deal* about car maintenance – much more than their parent – but only gently amends A's coaching as they understand this is an important albeit unnecessary act of parental love, our simple teaching scene will become much more. This concept of inverting where the know-how resides can also apply to the audience when a team bravely attempts to model a process that the audience (but not the players) knows intimately. Explored fearlessly, this tension provides joyful play and is, in many ways, the central conceit behind endowment games where an unknowing improviser must fumble their way to knowledge that the audience already happily possesses.

2. **Disrupt.** When you're a few steps (or, less ideally, minutes) into a teaching scene, another option to shock everyone out of uncreative patterns is to deploy a "fit-for-most-occasions" **CAD**. Well-timed revelations will quickly jolt a scene out of its complacency and provide new pathways for exploration. Perhaps Player B *confesses* that they have secretly been getting the neighbor – their parent's rival no less – to help them with their oil changes. Or the teenager *accuses* their parent of favoritism as all their siblings learned this lesson when they were much younger. Or, as one of our characters slides under the chassis, they *discover* an angry swarm of wasps has made their home there. If the teaching element of the scene continues (and in many instances, I'd recommend this

so that there is still some physical activity), it will now take on a very different tone through these sharpened stakes.

3. **Reframe.** Fully accepting an emotionally powerful CAD will typically change the context of the scene for the better, but this strategy of reframing the parameters of the action can also helpfully occur in the more incremental building blocks of story construction, particularly within the foundational **CROW** elements. If the teenager is actually a mechanic or the parent is a clueless intellectual *character*, we've made a move into less overwrought territory. This may be the parent's monthly weekend with their child after a messy divorce, which sheds new light on the status quo of the *relationship*. The backstory could include that B's last car was totaled due to a lack of basic maintenance, which would infuse both players' *objectives* in interesting ways. And changing the *where* to the family's auto repair shop, the parking lot of a police station, or a dimly lit roadside after the car has unexpectedly broken down at midnight adds exciting new potentials as well that – fully embraced – should make the scene about something greater than merely the visible teaching component.

4. **Map.** And the reframing could be deliberately taken even further to exploit irony, satire, and juxtaposition. Mapping is a riveting way to use the tropes and language of one situation to implicitly or explicitly reveal dynamics hidden in another (usually unrelated) scenario. Applying a mapping methodology, our bland oil change scene becomes a vehicle for revealing comedic truths and tensions elsewhere in the human experience. So even though the *words* will remain car-specific – this is a crucial component of the gimmick – the mean*ing* of these words changes dramatically. Now, Player A's efforts may metaphorically reflect their own strained relationship with their teenager, with each car part substituting for a facet of their lives together. The scene could be infused with the urgency and danger of a bomb disposal with the car standing in for an explosive device just moments away from detonation. Or the parent's language will become ripe with new overtones if this conversation serves as a long overdue attempt to explain love and the birds and the bees… You can read a little more about this concept (mapping that is) in my earlier **game of the scene** entry.

Final Thought

If you find yourself in a teaching scene, the best advice is to make sure it's not *just* a teaching scene.

Consciously altering just one or two constituent ingredients and then leaning into these specifics should provide ample opportunities for everyone to learn something new and unanticipated alongside the more mundane surface lesson.

Related Entries: CAD, CROW, Game of the Scene, Strangers, Talking Heads, Transaction Scene **Antonym:** Subtext
Connected Game: Expert Double Figures

TEAMWORK

Placing the good of the group over the success or joy of any one individual.

Synonym: Ensemble

TECHNICIANS

If you've had the unbridled joy of improvising in a venue with a strong technical setup and a gifted improvising **Technician**, you will deeply appreciate just how much such astute hands add to the work. From elegant transitions and mood-enhancing washes to rich ambient environments and mischievous sound effects, the stage action transforms under their watch. Reviewer Hettie Judah celebrates these elements when considering a production of *Lifegame*: "The mood can swing at the click of a finger, and as much credit for this must be given to the lighting and sound designers as to the actors themselves."[2] Hopefully, it goes without saying that these unseen members of the team are improvising just as fearlessly as the players on the stage, accepting and pitching offers and ideas to maximize the entertainment and energy. If you primarily work *on* the stage, as I do, it can be easy to inadvertently forget just *how much* artistic technical improvising elevates the performance event – it can be difficult to register in the moment the subtle shifts in light or sound that are supporting or inspiring your work and choices. But as you rehearse on the cold theatre boards under fluorescent lighting in the afternoon, the absence couldn't be more starkly palpable. So, in addition to serving as a love note to our technical magicians, this entry also aims to remind us all of some best practices for collaborating with these fellow improvisers.

Example

Host: "And let's see that scene based on a rain forest in 5, 4, 3, 2, 1…."

The stage lights fade as the host's voice echoes through the sound system. The countdown reaches its climax, and the stage becomes bathed in vibrant shadows evocative of a dense canopy. A steady storm can be heard pounding in the distance, punctuated by the cries of rambunctious unseen wildlife. As Players A and B emerge, the lights gently swell around them, and their body microphones are turned on. Their voices reverberate in the endless forest as they utter their first words…

Honoring Technical Improvisers

1. **Set them up for joy.** If your company has the good fortune to work regularly with an improvisational musician, it would be odd to routinely craft shows or play sets where they sat idly by for lengthy periods of time, their considerable gifts left untapped. The same holds true for the creative improvising technicians in our midst. Strive to include opportunities to feature their contributions in meaningful and joyous ways. It's important to have this voice and perspective in the development phase of projects as well as in green room pre-show planning sessions to assist in this endeavor. In a short-form show, it can be as simple as folding a game or two regularly in the mix that highlights design improv; in long-form, it may involve developing a greater awareness of how to best exploit latent technical potentials. Onstage and offstage improvisers alike thrive when challenged and are not asked to plod through the same routines in the same way time and again.
2. **Embrace their choices.** Be wary of viewing spontaneous design choices in a different light than you would a verbal or physical offer from a character. Just as a player might fumble or serve up a good idea in an inelegant or unclear manner, so too can a technician make a good faith call that lands wonkily or experience unknown equipment malfunctions that prevent them from fully realizing the potentials of the scene. The iteration of *Gorilla Theatre* that I've directed included a tradition of directly addressing all the improvisers in the space, so an opaque choice that pushes against the current director's intent was typically verbally addressed in the moment (with the technician often responding in a similar fashion and tone on the god mic). Generally, however, I'd advocate the same accepting "go with the flow" attitude that applies to any other unanticipated scenic offer, reserving any critique or discussion for the postmortem. Players should justify design offers with the same joyful spirit as any other improv addition.
3. **Communicate expectations.** Regardless of the skill and experience level of the improvising technicians in question, it's good practice to communicate show expectations clearly and consistently. If a planned short-form game or scene requires a special technical treatment or offers unique design opportunities, you're more likely to set your fellow improviser up for success if this isn't sprung upon them at the last moment, especially if what you're requiring involves behind the scenes preparation such as accessing specific sound effects or music files. Using pre-show notes to talk through any exciting new games or dynamics provides the technician advanced notice and gives ample time to troubleshoot the specifics or strategize an alternative course of action if this particular idea would be better served by some rehearsal without the presence of paying observers.
4. **Know the tools at their disposal.** Discussing show possibilities and creative needs also affords a chance for everyone to better understand what tools are – and aren't – in the technicians' tool belt. Players who keep walking into that one lighting blind spot expecting a spotlight aren't making anyone look good, least of all themselves. If you're fortunate enough to have more advanced programmable consoles and equipment, there may be aspects of the show that aren't particularly flexible from a technical perspective, or when something goes wrong a manual reset might have unavoidably noticeable onstage repercussions. Many of the most responsive technical improvisers I've collaborated with have more than a passing understanding of onstage improv practices. Pursuing some knowledge of the technical aspects of your venue not only allows you to exploit these rich tools more fully in your scene work but also builds empathy and ensemble.
5. **Don't expect miracles.** And finally, just as we wouldn't expect one preassigned onstage player to single-handedly execute the perfect move to rescue any flailing improv scene, we shouldn't have this unrealistic expectation of our technical teammates either. I see this tension most frequently swirl around the issue of scene endings. A well-timed blackout can do an awful lot to save a lethargic game or scene – as can the addition

Figure 16.1 Members of Rollins Improv Players acknowledge their collaborators in the booth after a show. Players routinely fill different roles as needed, improvising on the stage one performance, and then as a lighting or sound designer, assistant director, or member of house management the next. Scott Cook Photography.

of an appropriately uplifting soundtrack or well-crafted lighting steering our attention to where it's needed. But technical improvisers cannot create dynamic buttons out of *nothing*. We are all responsible for "saving" our own scenes, or to be frank, not allowing a scene to become such an unmitigated mess that it needs saving. If our booth colleague misses a panicked editing wave or sweep, it's quite likely the audience might not have experienced the moment in question as a resolute ending either.

Final Thought

I've referred to technical improvisers in the third person "they" for clarity in this entry, but in many venues, "they" are really "us" and "we" as improvisers often wear many hats (sometimes on the same night). One show you might play onstage, the next you take on the role of host, and the following you're steering the action from the computer or instrumental keyboard. There is great reciprocity in terms of learning, with strategies sharpened in one arena providing lessons and awareness for challenges encountered in another. So even if you've found yourself specializing in one area of the craft, there is much to be gleaned from appreciating how fellow improvisers approach their positions as well. As I noted in my earlier entry on material, interesting improvisers are interested improvisers, so be sure to extend this sense of creative fascination to your colleagues as well.

Related Entries: Ensemble, Hosting, Music
Synonyms: Lighting Improviser, Scenic Improviser, Sound Improviser, Stage Managing Improviser
Connected Game: Booth Torture

TELLING

In 99 out of 100 situations, **Telling** on our improv stages will prove inferior to its antithesis **showing**. To tell announces or describes a choice in lieu of committing to it with all your physical, emotional, and subtextual being. As Jonathan Fox reminds us, "Theatre is a bridge between the nonverbal and the literary arts."[3] Improvisers who favor telling tend to esteem more intellectual styles of play and might use verbal prowess to maintain distance from their characters and the worlds that they populate. (You can explore more perceived double-edged "benefits" of this tendency in my analysis of **commenting**.) Improvisers comfortable with a showing approach contrarily utilize their whole selves more freely, revealing characters and stories through behavior and action *as well as* words. We all have our own patterns and preferences as performers, so it's no easy task to move from one column to the other, but every journey starts with the desire to move. My earlier musing on **showing** provides some pointers to help you put on your walking shoes.

Example

A couple sit on their porch. They converse with an unintentional deadpan quality.

Player A: "It's raining."
Player B: "That dog is scrounging through the garbage, again."
Player A: "Someone needs to do something about that."
Player B: "It makes me livid."
Player A: "I'm thirsty."
Player B: "The rain does that to you..."

Tell Me About It

As a completely deadpan and exceptional scene, our couple could add delightful variety to a performance. As a stylistic norm, however, frequent appearances of such chill demeanors will cause stakes, momentum, and investment to plummet. Adding at least *some* showing to your largely telling scene will undoubtedly deepen and sharpen the work.

While most schools of improv elevate showing in general (a stance I also hold), there *are* moments when telling can get improvisers out of a pickle or enhance the work in other ways. So here are some "one out of a hundred" thoughtful exceptions to a common improv "rule."

1. **Speaking your truth.** Especially if onstage communication has become strained or ineffective – players are talking all over each other or oblivious to the ramifications of their choices – showing can prove ill-equipped to resolve issues in a timely fashion. In reality, fellow players have probably been *showing* their needs or discomfort for a while, only to have it go unnoticed. In these moments, explicitly telling your teammates what you're experiencing or require is more than appropriate. This is the rationale behind the tradition of **speaking your truth** or calling it onstage. If you're feeling nauseous (as the improviser, *not* the character) and need to make a hasty departure from the stage, telling will get the job done clearly (as opposed to risking showing more than you had intended).

   Player A: "In truth, mom, I've got to go to my room, and I probably won't be back..."

2. **Carving a path.** Immense delight can stem from volleys of initially disparate choices all accidentally hitting the stage at once; and, in fact, many games like Statues and Scene from Music are built on this concept, requiring players to creatively resolve these contradictions in real time much to the joy of the audience. Cumulative **justifying** that creatively puts random elements together stands as the optimal path, but there are moments where conflicting choices merely compound confusion rather than inspire spontaneity. If you're many scenes into a narrative long-form and previously widely accepted "facts" are in clumsy peril, or disagreement between the improvisers stalls any potential action between the characters, then telling can become your friend. A kind but unambiguous statement carves a unified way forward by getting everyone on the same page. You do need to be informed and cautious: a misguided player pushing for their perception of the given circumstances in spite of their obliviousness that the rest of the ensemble is in full agreement to the contrary will only worsen chaos by stubbornly asserting an unhelpful inconsistency. This is doubly so as I believe a named reality should take precedence over an implied one: my partner might have intended to be washing dishes, but if I (in good faith or even mischievously) see this as operating a photocopier, then the scene is now in the office. But if you're in possession of critical knowledge or a finesseful move that connects the scattered dots, then by all means *tell* your scene partners.

   Player A: "Alright class, just a few moments more putting the finishing touches on your individual projects and then it's time for our guest speaker and judge..."

3. **Painting the picture.** And then telling can be integral to your style or a particular production, often taking the form of narration or scene painting. It's difficult in many cases to implicitly show unseen environmental elements or give nuance to imagined set pieces that aren't within reach. Ideally, a little telling under these circumstances will then become supported by subsequently showing the effect and significance of the offered additions. One could argue that if narrated descriptions don't ultimately influence the mood, style, meaning, or action that these choices have either been blocked or weren't serving their intended purpose. It's helpful to keep in mind, then, that an overabundance of described offers – the equivalent to **waffling** – won't set teammates up for success in this regard as it decreases the likelihood that the plethora of shelved details will resurface. But especially in "design poor" venues, descriptive telling can truly honor the transformative powers of improv by reinventing the same modest stage again and again.

Player A: (scene painting) "A wall-sized mirror looms in the estate's grand foyer, demanding that all who enter must face their comparative insignificance…"

4. **Sealing the deal.** Finally, a little telling can serve as a powerful and successful scenic punctuation. Generally, naming the game currently underway is a big improv no-no: "Oh, I see, everyone is making clever puns with different world capitals…" These moves invariably and awkwardly release the air out of the game, thereby suffocating the very dynamic that was providing joy. But there are carefully directed moments when upending, inverting, or exploding the current scenic trajectory can effectively stick the landing. This is the basic idea behind a "rug pull" or surprise button, quick blackout, or edit. Perhaps the characters that have been plotting their big escape suddenly fall limp as the scene climaxes with a child turning on their playroom light, revealing the characters as anthropomorphic toys (courtesy of *Toy Story*). Explicit clarity is critical in these moments if they are to benefit from the advantage of concisely etched surprise. While it's possible to show such a move in some situations, telling typically prevents any uncertainty or player confusion, which can result in stepping on the intended tilt.

After a boardroom scene nears its ending that was replete with unexpected and inappropriate behavior among the apparently esteemed business leaders, Player A enters…

Player A: "Thanks for being so patient, kids. I can take you back to the play center now where your parents can pick you up…"

Blackout.

Final Thought

As a safety valve, descriptive tool, and dynamic reveal, telling can serve your improv needs successfully. As an evasive tactic to keep you detached and separated from your choices and fellow players, telling will hamstring your journey as an improviser and character.

> **Related Entry:** Talking Heads
> **Antonyms:** Emotional Truth, Showing
> **Synonyms:** Cartooning, Commenting
> **Connected Game:** Soundtrack

THEME

One of Aristotle's preferred three elements of tragedy (along with plot and character) that describes the deeper meaning and significance of the performed event.

> **Related Entry:** Material

THIRD ACT

In the scripted realm, this term refers to the climax and final phases of the dramatic action (in a three-act structure). In the improv realm, it can describe the tendency to unhelpfully lurch forward into only loosely connected terrain that, subsequently, edits or abridges the latent potential of the current moment.

> **Related Entry:** Chapter Two

THIRD THOUGHT

Johnstone describes an effortless and paradigmatic style of creativity:

> An artist who is inspired is being *obvious*. He's not making any decisions, he's not weighing one idea against another. He's accepting his first thoughts. How else could Dostoyevsky have dictated one novel in the morning and one in the afternoon for three weeks in order to fulfil his contracts.[4]

What can we do as improvisers when we are faced with similar scenic prompts again and again that invite the same obvious reactions again and again? The state of reactivity that Johnstone extols serves as an enticing exemplar, and most improvisers have experienced at least glimpses of this breathtaking effortlessness where obvious choices reign supreme. This is, simply put, "the zone" we all aspire to achieve. And then there are other times when you're working on the same structured longform or style piece night after night, exploring the same relationship onstage with the same teammate yet again, or facing down the barrel of getting that same suggestion from the audience for the umpteenth time as the countdown begins. In cases such as these, your **Third Thought** (rather than your first) might be the way to go.

To illustrate, if I'm responding to a fellow improviser in a word-association-type dynamic and they say "dog," my *first* thought is comprehending their offer "dog," my *second* association might be "house," and then my *third* thought responding to this new prompt could be "paint." In this way, while I'm still embracing obvious connections, I've "skipped a step" and now utilize this new, more typically tangentially related idea. When improvisers are first exposed to this creative technique, it's not uncommon for them to get in their heads – as it requires a *little* consideration, which we strive to avoid – but as you find more comfort it quickly becomes no more internal than a character finding the most fitting word to express their feelings or desire accurately.

Example

The audience suggests "teacher" for an improv scene.

As they step onto the stage, Player A's first thought is "teacher," their second thought is "a rowdy classroom," and their third thought is "decompressing at a bar." The scene now begins at a local tavern...

OR

Player B thinks "teacher," then their specific "third grade teacher," then connects it to a vivid memory of the time this teacher shared their lunch when they forgot their own. The scene starts with an anxious child not wanting to go outside for lunch with their classmates...

OR

Player C hears "teacher," associates "big brother mentor," and then connects a "latch-key child." They now initiate a scene from the perspective of a home alone 13-year-old sitting on their porch...

Three Thoughts on Third Thoughts

Used carelessly, a third thought approach can become a justification for retreating further into your planning brain, especially if you are prone to a more intellectual style of play to begin with. If *every* offer is met with this measured reaction, you're also likely to have a stalling and disconnected story arc. Instead, explore this tool in these moments that are particularly well-suited to this more thoughtful subset of acceptance...

1. **Brainstorming.** When you're warming up your creative juices during your development process, rehearsals, prior to a performance, or as part of the show itself, this technique can add levels and newfound discovery to well-worn association exercises. In my campus troupe, we have several long-form shows that seek to examine and complicate a central theme. A third thought approach to an ensemble warm-up greatly assists in the goal of looking at an issue or idea from a multitude of dynamic angles.
2. **Disrupting.** Routines and patterns are essential components of story building, but left unchallenged for *too* long, they can entrench a scene in uninteresting loops. In many cases, the power of a pattern is that it dramatically calls attention to the moment when it is broken or interrupted: this is, in fact, a solid definition of an ignition or inciting incident that marks the beginning of the rising action in linear scripted pieces. Deploying a third thought when a scene limps from cliché to cliché disrupts the status quo and reveals new unexplored terrain. Such a redirection will prove particularly useful if the current path is perpetuating problematic biases or lazily reinforcing uninterrogated stereotypes. An "obvious" next

move in such instances will usually leave such damaging choices unquestioned.

3. **Curve balling.** Looking beyond your first thought also elevates the potential for increased spontaneity and surprise. These dynamics are central to the idea of curve balling (examined in my entry of the same name), where a player deliberately seasons the scene with an offer that *at first glance* feels a little random. Used sparingly, these unexpected choices can add mystery and risk back into the improv equation when it may have otherwise lacked novelty or inspiration. Using a third thought provides a gentler variant of this impetus in that the initiator has made some tacit connection to the source material that can become more explicit as the scene progresses (not that this is strictly necessary on any level). Our child on the porch, for example, might soon be joined by a kindhearted neighbor who has taken to help them with their homework every afternoon. Or not.

Final Thought

While improv advocates trusting your instincts, going with the obvious, and finding an effortlessness in your actions – all admirable and noteworthy goals – in reality, our spontaneity finds shape through thoughtfulness and editing. Some reactive choices are best left unsaid; some stories require empathetic efforts and conscious adjustments in service of our greater goals at building community and pursuing representation. Viewed in this light, exploring your third thought provides a gateway to improvisational choices that push the boundaries and assumptions of the stage and the worlds in which we play.

> **Related Entries:** Abandon, Obvious
> **Antonym:** Over-Originality
> **Synonyms:** Care, Surprise
> **Connected Game:** Bad Rap

TIEBREAKER

A short-form game – usually some test of wit or skill – designed to find an ultimate winner at the end of a competition.

> **Synonym:** Decider

TILT

The practice of upending or disrupting an established routine, game, or balance. When this occurs near the beginning of a dramatic action, it may also serve as the ignition or inciting action.

> **Synonym:** Breaking Routines

TIP OF THE HAT

Playfully acknowledging to the audience a notable finesse, piece of improv mischief, or moment of metatheatrical folly. This brief pause in the onstage action may or may not involve the literally miming of tipping one's hat.

> **Related Entry:** Mugging

TRANSACTION SCENE

Theatre provides an engaging glimpse into human behavior and desires. With few stylistic exceptions – such as an extreme approach to "slice of life" naturalism – stories and their constituent moments are theatricalized with an eye toward maximizing dynamism and thus audience attention. There's a reason we don't see many movies, plays, or (successful) improv scenes where a character sits and watches television uninterrupted for several hours, or the duration of a nice refreshing midday nap despite how ubiquitous (or sought-after) such moments are in our real lives. Theatre edits and enhances lived experiences and, in doing so, sets the stage for enthralling the enthusiastic audience of which Sweet writes:

> In both improvisation and sport, what grips the audience is the fact that the outcome is truly in doubt. The players in both have, through arduous training, developed skills with which to deal with the unpredictable; but these skills cannot tame the unpredictable, they can only give the players a better chance of not being routed by it. And in both, the audience's enthusiasm is a major part of the experience.[5]

And therein lies the innate problem of **Transaction Scenes**. Yes, buying a cup of coffee in a drive-thru, returning a purchase at a customer service counter, or asking for help finding those perfect shoes in our size are familiar activities for many, but presented as is, they are the mundane life chores that performance traditions rightly ascribe to the cutting room floor. Purchases or routine negotiations hold little potential for sustained interest as the outcome is largely foreseeable and assured. To make matters worse, these predictable exchanges nearly always occur between **strangers**, another scenario trap; throw in the need for some help with the product in question and you've completed the holy trinity of improv blandness by *also* making it a **teaching scene**.

Example

Player A begins the scene by pushing on an imaginary shopping trolley (cart) and casually scanning the supermarket shelves. After a few beats, Player B enters and establishes themselves as a shelf stocker. They turn helpfully...

Player B: "Can I help you find something?"
Player A: "I can't seem to find the turkey gravy..."
Player B: (pleasantly) "It's actually in aisle five alongside the stuffing."
Player A: "That makes sense! Thank you so much."

A beat... as both contemplate what might be next...

Player B: "... can I help you with something else...?"

Several items later, the scene grinds to an awkward and unsatisfying end.

Exchange Your Transaction for This...

1. **Action.** It's possible that the above exchange could provide a workable scenic balance *for a moment or two* but left unignited there's not much brewing theatricality. When an everyday *activity* becomes synonymous with the stage *action*, you're in deep water (or actually very undramatic *shallow* water!) This is similar to making your text and subtext exactly the same in that it robs the scene of complexity and intrigue that should bubble under the "obvious" surface. While *activity* provides a helpful staging addition – offering players something to physically do together as the story develops – *action* is the domain of **objectives** and tactics, and describes the characters' efforts to grasp success. At the very least, if you find yourself dancing into the realm of a dispassionate and unimportant transaction, make sure there's something more vital at stake for your character and their world than the turkey gravy. Ideally, your scene partner is inextricably connected to this need as well. For example, Player A is shopping without the means to pay and is striving to build rapport with Player B in the hopes they will eventually come to their aid.

2. **Power.** While a transaction on the textual level will rarely add much to your story, a similar dynamic on the subtextual level holds interesting potential. **Status** inversions, in particular, can inspire playful games that maintain the *appearance* of the lackluster transaction while fueling it with energizing undercurrents. Status battles (such as one-upping ladders and one-downing slides) or unanticipated inversions (a disproportionate*ly* high-status shelf stocker assisting a low-status customer) provide promising variations that refresh the stale scenic template. When status positions are contested, this adds additional spice. Our customer may, in fact, have been fired from this very store recently and is testing their replacement's mettle in the hopes of getting their old job back. In this light, each seemingly transactional move is now a subtle power play toward a hidden end. A similar result can be achieved by establishing and exchanging strong emotional states: a carefree employee and anxious shopper might find themselves gradually swapping these climates by the end of the scene as prompted by their mutual choices and discoveries.

3. **Secrets.** A strategically selected secret can also spice up dispassionate transactions. By shifting the context of a **CROW** element, you will jumpstart subtextual tensions and perspectives. If Player A is a secret shopper or an undercover regional manager, this adjustment in *character* should make today's exchange at least a little more significant and out of the ordinary. Both characters could be passionate newlyweds who can't stand to be apart, so they hide their *relationship* in the supermarket and A pretends to need help finding an increasingly odd array of groceries. If Player A's *objective* isn't finding the gravy but rather reconnecting to their estranged child that they left as a baby, bolder energies beckon. Or perhaps both characters are expats in a foreign land – or *where* – and the turkey gravy is a palpable reminder of a lost home with all its holiday traditions. Placing a secret in any or a combination of these scenic elements will usually do the trick of adding heat.

4. **Style.** Another useful way to aid our troubled scene is to shift the context entirely so that our uninspired dialogue takes on new meaning. This is the central dynamic behind mapping (discussed in **game of the scene**), but layering on a distinct or contrasting time period, genre, or mood can also work wonders, especially if this perspective shift enables irony or a grander metaphor: our turkey gravy now stands in for something more significant or thematically engaging. Played with a Shakespearean overlay, as futuristic androids, or in the style of French expressionism, our meandering scene will at the very least gain an element of comedic estrangement, allowing the audience to witness a recognizable exchange through a jarringly different lens. It strikes me that the charm and audience goodwill earned from such an approach might be relatively short-lived – I still don't want to watch a commonplace transaction in Shakespearean poetry that never evolves beyond that simple premise for a protracted period of time – so the resulting scenes would benefit from applying one of the above strategies too.

Final Thought

When you find yourself having stumbled into a transactional dynamic – and you will – you'll be well served by heeding some of the above advice. A commercial transaction offers little of interest as they are so predictable and provides little opportunity for discovery and character-based revelations. The same is not true when the transaction in question focuses on pursuing desires, wrestling control, or exposing hidden truths.

> **Related Entries:** CROW, Objective, Secrets, Strangers, Subtext, Teaching Scene
> **Antonyms:** Breaking Routines, Change, Stakes, Urgency **Synonym:** Stasis
> **Connected Game:** Replay

TRUST

I'm a big fan of The Playground's mission statement.

> We believe that the value of improv goes beyond mere entertainment; rather, in a society filled with isolating and fragmenting influences, improv holds a societally valuable message: it demonstrates how teamwork, trust and support can make something wonderful out of absolutely nothing.[6]

Little of value occurs in any improv venue without a robust sense of **Trust**. If players aren't confident that the ensemble will lift them up in times of strife and make room for them in times of success, the rapid game of ping pong that is improvisation – with teammates instinctively and immediately exchanging creative volleys – will inevitably collapse. Without trust, improv becomes a rather inward focused or competitive solo affair where players just happen to share physical space and time but little else.

Example

While the lights fade, a company member makes eye contact with another in the opposite wing as an invitation to join them onstage for the next scene. Both players happily step into the darkness...

Times to Trust

1. **Trust yourself.** Trust definitely begins with yourself as an inability to see and esteem the contributions of others generally reflects a similar struggle to value our own gifts and attributes. "Trust your instincts" echoes as a common rallying cry in the rehearsal hall, although I'm inclined to adjust this to "Trust your *honed* instincts." Our raw or uninformed instincts may prove harmful, perpetuating personal and cultural biases. Our *honed* instincts, on the other hand, hopefully also embody previous lessons and discoveries that have helped us shape and sharpen the tools of spontaneity. When these informed creative choices hit the stage, it's important that they do so with an air of confidence and joy. If an aura of apology masks our offers – thereby announcing our distrust of our own idea – it naturally follows that others' trust will similarly dissipate.
2. **Bestow trust.** There's rarely time for players to slowly develop or earn foundational trust on the improv stage (although companies that have worked together for many years may certainly transform these assumed bonds into unshakable steel cables). Especially if you're working with unfamiliar or new company members, "testing the trust waters" could leave you still floundering at sea as the evening draws to a close. Rather, improvisers will suffer if they don't unconditionally bestow trust as the action begins. This is no small leap and requires an assumption of good faith on the part of all involved – a belief that

everyone is working on behalf of the ensemble and with the best interests of all participants at heart. A commonly held company improv ethos, philosophy, or a clear statement of guiding principles can jumpstart this dynamic. In the classroom, this document might be a syllabus that outlines the pedagogic mission and expectations for inclusive play. Regardless of whether such a code is informally assumed or codified in written form, a commitment to our peers forms the bedrock of a trust-filled environment.

3. **Repair trust.** It is understandable that unreservedly bestowing trust may result in moments of frustration or disappointment. Even if we are united in a common goal, each player will invariably have at least slightly different aesthetic or performance preferences. And improv as a fluid form itself pushes against boundaries and established norms. When missteps occur – and they will – it's crucial that injuries are noted and addressed in a timely fashion. Small cracks in the armor of trust can easily rust and spread when left unattended. Players can enlist a **speaking your truth** approach if an in-the-moment adjustment feels warranted, or a forthright but kind **postmortem** should hopefully provide the mechanism for repair and redress. If your team or company doesn't yet have transparent pathways for frank and constructive feedback, then this will compound otherwise minor fractures.

4. **Trust your audience.** To close, it's a common trap to not fully trust our audience either. I believe there are important contracts improv companies can and should forge with their host communities – I pontificate on this in my corresponding "A" entry – as an inability to serve, represent, and entertain our patrons is a surefire path to irrelevance. In our efforts to attract and maintain an audience, however, it can prove easy to become cynical or pander only to a lowest common denominator sense of what we think (fear?) they may want. This is often the justification for rather thoughtless or lazy work that ignores societal tensions or shortcomings in the name of "entertainment." Just as we should play to the top of our (honed) intelligence as improvisers, so too should we strive to play to the top of our audiences' intelligence. This is not to say we should happily present esoteric or self-serving work with no effort to provide our (paying) guests with sufficient tools for comprehension and enjoyment. But we should trust that our audience isn't and doesn't want *one thing*: we can invite them to laugh, think, feel, and contemplate change all within the same performance frame.

Final Thought

Take the leap. Trust.

> **Related Entries:** Audience, Postmortem, Speaking Your Truth **Antonyms:** Fear, Winning
> **Synonym:** Ensemble
> **Connected Game:** Creation Myth Scene

TRUTH

I turn to the inimitable Del Close to open this discussion:

> Coming here [to iO] to learn to make people laugh is […] absurd. To assume that making the audience laugh is the goal of improvisation is almost as absurd as assuming that you go to a dojo to learn how to kick somebody's face in. It's just not true! Still, they laugh. It is a side-effect of attempting to achieve something more beautiful, honest and truthful, something that has far more to do with the theatre – which puts your attention on what is important about being a human in a community – as opposed to television entertainment, which is designed to take your mind *off* what is more important about your lives.[7]

As improvisers, we are always in search of the next idea, the next move, and often (despite Close's observation above) the next laugh. Though an improvisational production might declare its intent as being primarily comedic or dramatic, realistic or stylized, contemporary or genre-based, entertaining or service-focused, I can think of few instances when our efforts are not elevated by a pursuit of **Truth** on stage. We may not always use this particular *word* – some companies might prefer honest, connected, authentic, or grounded – but without this ingredient, our theatrical efforts won't amount to much of substance. Truths, be they trivial, familiar, playful, or resoundingly difficult to face, link our various spontaneous efforts in an exploration of what it is to be "human in a community."

Example

Player A: (addressing the audience) "I'm looking for someone who'd be willing to share a story with us tonight that can inspire our play. Has anyone had a wonderful surprise this week…?"

Four Truths and a Lie

1. **Emotional truth.** Monochromatic emotional explorations onstage pale in comparison to the power and vibrancy of performances in technicolor. When we approximate, tell, or comment on our characters' feelings – rather than seek to earnestly and personally experience them alongside our dramatic creations – we needlessly undermine the effectiveness of our scenes. In improv striving toward more realistic ends, a small but connected emotion will serve better than an overt and passionate choice offered without sincerity. While overtly satiric or sillier work might exploit over-the-top energies, I would contend that this style of play *also* benefits from efforts to plumb deeper emotional truths as this will strengthen the players' and viewers' connection to the work.

2. **Personal truth.** When we bravely bring our own experiences to the stage, we'll likely add more dimensions to our scene work. Characters infused with the details of our own lives and experiences tend to ring truer and effortlessly reveal rich nuances and potentials missing from their lightly worn improvisational kin. Furthermore, such an approach to generating **material** and **character** tends to increase opportunities for vulnerability. Bringing yourself to the role enables more empathetic creations – characters that evade becoming reductive stereotypes – while simultaneously opening doors for your audience to connect to the work as they recognize their own lived truths in those they witness as well. Furthermore, when there is *nothing* of us in our onstage personae, the possibility for careless misrepresentations generally becomes problematically magnified.

3. **Dramatic truth.** It's common to talk about the **game of the scene**, which refers to the evolving and discovered rules of our theatricalized world: perhaps everyone speaks their subtext aloud, or children are in charge, or, for a darker hue, the State has absolute control over the individual and severely punishes anyone perceived as a miscreant. Improvisational truth, viewed in this context, refers to honoring and building upon the contracts and (implicit or explicit) promises of your central premise. This can involve applying the helpful improv mantra, "if this is true, what else would also be true?" For example, if babies ran everything, pubs would now serve juice boxes and apple sauce. Clumsily breaking these truths will jar as much as ignoring more conventional "facts" in a "realistic" setting. And if these fictional flights of fantasy are skillfully used to satirically reveal deeper human realities, that's even better. Which brings me to…

4. **Societal truth.** Close mentions the escapism of popular television, and while live spontaneous performance may certainly bow at this altar too, it's important to note that our art will always hold up some form of mirror to nature. This mirror might seek absolute fidelity, delightfully distort the source image, or aim to hide or exaggerate imperfections. The very act of determining the direction and bend of the glass, however, is innately political in nature. If we're inclined to frame our shows as "just entertainment," we must honestly wrestle with the reality that such a stance simultaneously serves the conserve or status quo in its willingness to turn away from critical tensions and realities of the day. Pursuing an escapist stance begs the question, "Who are we empowering to escape from what and why?" Societal truths will lurk under the surface of our performances whether we like it or not as every show occurs in the political specificity of the here and now. It's important we knowingly aim our mirrors accordingly.

5. **Truthful lies.** And here's the lie, or at least, the consideration of how we can powerfully use lies on the improv stage. The very construct of theatre has historically been the target of fear and restraint by powerful institutions due to its innately complex relationship with reality. When a Renaissance actor assumes the costume (and therefore the status) of royalty, the clergy, the ruling classes, or multiple genders, the very nature of these systems of power and oppression are called into question. Improvised theatre, with its innate ability to evade censorship and consistent hierarchical messaging, is uniquely situated to embody and interrogate these bigger lies we perpetuate and tell ourselves. Some practitioners more overtly commit to exposing blindnesses, façades, and harmful tropes through performance than others – Boal strikes me as a paradigmatic example of using improv as a tool for tackling harmful deceit. Non-critically replaying lies onstage (often done in the name of escapism) will merely reify stereotypes, but offered satirically the provocative truth behind such lies can be revealed and dismantled, or, at the very least, the possibility for such change can be imagined and rehearsed.

Final Thought

In exploring what it is to be "human in community," we potentially create the very humane communities we seek. In seeking to empathetically present truth on stage, we may, in fact, reveal its deeper shades and lessons.

> **Related Entries:** Comedy, Culpability, Drama, Emotional Truth, Material **Antonym:** Escapism
> **Synonyms:** Honesty, Integrity
> **Connected Game:** Lotus Monologues

NOTES

1. Charna Halpern et al., *Truth in Comedy. The Manual of Improvisation.* Colorado Springs: Meriwether, 1994. p. 39.
2. Hettie Judah review of *Lifegame*, "Added Twist to This Life." *The Times (London)* 19 May 1998.
3. Jonathan Fox, *Acts of Service. Spontaneity, Commitment, Tradition in the Nonscripted Theatre.* New Paltz, NY: Tusitala Publishing, 1994. p. 190.
4. Keith Johnstone, *Impro. Improvisation and the Theatre.* 1979. New York: Routledge, 1992. p. 88.
5. Jeffrey Sweet, *Something Wonderful Right Away.* 1996. New York: Limelight Editions, 1978. p. xxxix.
6. Mission of The Playground, quoted in Amy E. Seham's *Whose Improv Is It Anyway: Beyond Second City.* Jackson, MS: U of Mississippi P, 2001. p. 217.
7. Del Close in Charna Halpern et al.'s *Truth in Comedy. The Manual of Improvisation.* Colorado Springs: Meriwether, 1994. pp. 24–25.

U/V

UPSTAGING

This entry focuses on a more universal theatrical concept that is not particularly unique to improv, although it can disproportionately affect spontaneous performance as an attentive director can't quietly adjust staging in the privacy of the rehearsal hall. **Upstaging** refers to a performer's inability to remain "open" or seen by the audience, which, in turn, can create the additional challenge of making dialogue difficult to hear. It embodies an inelegant staging tendency that will undermine the dramatic action, increase the chances of miscommunication, and annoy your audience, who must strain to see what needs to be seen and hear what needs to be heard. As Spolin reminds us, "the actors must interrelate, communicate physically, and be seen and heard as they solve the acting problem. When an audience is restless, uninterested, the actors are responsible for this."[1] Inexperienced improvisers can fall into this trap of adopting a weak stage position, but often, players of all stripes inadvertently upstage their scene partners by literally performing behind them in a way that forces others to turn around and face upstage.

In a related sense, the term can also refer to stealing focus from fellow players in less-than-generous ways. For example, a *really* interesting crowd member can easily pull attention from the more central action occurring between featured characters who are positioned downstage of them. Whether you're upstaging yourself, absent mindedly forcing others to do the same, or grabbing unwarranted attention, this habit is counterproductive and distracting.

Example

A firefighter, police officer, and medic walk into a bar… They arrange themselves poorly, and only one of them can now be seen and heard.

What's Up with That Staging?

1. **Can you see the audience?** A simple truth is that if you can't see the audience, then they probably can't see you either (or at least your *eyes*). If you're performing on a more conventional stage, an equivalent adage is making sure you can feel the light on your face assuming that you're not exclusively using dramatic side lighting from the wings! When playing in more presentational modes where characters may directly address the crowd with great frequency, retaining this physical orientation, openness, and connection will likely remain more front of mind. In representational or "realistic" styles, it can become easy to lose sight of this responsibility as your focus resides more firmly behind the fourth wall. In these situations, nothing beats practice, a mindful coach, and kind-hearted teammates working to keep you seen.

> A sidenote: remember that the saying above also holds true when you're striving to create verisimilitude. Visibly loitering in the wings or the side of the stage when you're "offstage" might break this illusion by unduly drawing the audience's attention. In such cases, you *shouldn't* be able to see the audience while waiting for your moment to contribute.

2. **Are you standing toe-to-toe?** The closer we stand by our fellow players, the more likely it becomes that we might inadvertently close each other off. This is particularly true when characters stand toe-to-toe and in full profile (essentially forming a straight line parallel to the edge of the stage while facing each other). Angles and a little distance are an improviser's best friends unless you're playing affectionate or intimate scenes where you'll still want to explore angles, but inappropriate

distance would undermine the intended relationship. Rather than stand in strict profile so that the audience can only see half your face at best, cheat out a little to more of a three-quarters orientation: this will add visibility and a little staging variety. Flat angles (only standing in profile or full out to the audience) don't add much to our visual storytelling efforts. The same can be said for assuming monotonously uniform physical levels or postures. When we imaginatively endow our stage spaces with furniture and props, this also justifies stage business, which facilitates more interesting stage pictures and character configurations.

3. **Is your connection to your scene partner clearly established?** In our efforts to forge strong and emotional connections to other onstage characters, we can find ourselves almost locked in close eye contact. In truth, there is something understandably enticing about maintaining this bond – as they say, the eyes are the windows to the soul, and we can send and receive a *lot* of information through these portals. In larger venues, however, an over-reliance on this practice can easily become problematic, especially if it results in stasis or if your partner is located behind you, thus forcing an upstaging orientation. In the opening moments of a scene, rigorous eye contact makes sense as it helps both the players and characters get on the same page. Once this connection is strong, however, you can aesthetically utilize different angles – perhaps facing downstage and talking over your shoulder – without severing emotional bonds. Of course, check back in as needed if you'd like to see how a choice has landed or want to keep the emotional energy building. But don't forget that you should also create and maintain a connection with your audience, and they want to see your eyes too.

4. **Are you throwing focus to where it's needed?** Ceding the proverbial high ground receives consideration in my discussion on **stage picture**. When players become aware of their own upstaging habits and adjust accordingly, they often invariably nudge their teammates into less favorable positions and angles instead. If you have finished pitching your offer or are perhaps largely assuming a support function in general, it is an act of improv kindness to step into a weak or self-upstaging pose so that your partner remains strongly visible. Lowering yourself is particularly effective as this can keep sight lines open, elevate your scene partner's status, and help craft dynamic and multi-leveled staging. The same holds true if you are improvising with guests onstage or players with a less polished sense of stagecraft. When you witness another player struggling to find an effective stage position, there is a lot that a mindful improviser can do to gently help remedy the situation, much of which reflects an understanding and thoughtful application of the advice above.

Final Thought

If you're unfamiliar with the etymology of the term, upstage denotes moving toward the back wall of the theatre or away from the audience. European proscenium stages used to be built on a rake, so this traffic pattern would literally involve the performer moving "up" as opposed to traveling "down" the stage to be closer to their adoring fans. Nervous players tend to drift *up* to perceived safety, but this, more times than not, creates the "ideal" circumstances for problematic sightlines.

Related Entries: Acting, Levels, Physicality, Sharing Focus, Stage Picture **Antonyms:** Being Seen, Staying Open **Synonym:** Closing Yourself Off **Connected Game:** One-Voice Expert

URGENCY

"In certain trying circumstances, urgent circumstances, desperate circumstances, profanity furnishes a relief denied even to prayer."
– Mark Twain, American writer

Urgency (alongside **stakes**) provides an all-purpose tool to make our actions more intense and theatrical. While elevated stakes influence the consequences of failing or succeeding, urgency fuels the action by considering the question of "why now?" What factors are currently in play that make this choice or action critical in this given moment? When urgency is low, there are few, if any, repercussions for an unfavorable scenic result: characters could always just try again later. But when urgency has been dynamically crafted, characters will face a ticking clock that demands immediate action. Whether it is an asteroid just minutes away from smashing into a crowded campground, a train full of passengers uncontrollably speeding down the track just miles away from a washed-out rail bridge, or a student experiencing a panic attack moments before entering their final exam for the semester, the specter of time running out supplies great power to a scene by adding tension to an otherwise potentially mundane situation.

Example

Players A and B are bomb disposal experts on the scene of a looming disaster.

Player A: "OK, let's see what we have here…"

OR

Young siblings, Players C and D, are hard at work in the kitchen preparing a Mother's Day breakfast for their currently sleeping parent.

Player C: "OK, let's see what we have here…"

Intensifying the Urgency

To increase the urgency of your character's plight, consider implementing one or more of these helpful strategies:

1. **Decrease the time.** Even the most dramatic scenario, such as our bomb disposal premise above, will quickly lose steam if the anticipated calamity is placed too far off in the future. There's a reason bomb counters in movies rarely start counting down in weeks, opting instead for red flashing minutes or seconds. The wildly popular television series *24* was built on this heightened (perhaps ridiculously so) urgency: if each episode spanned the length of a month or year rather than one hour of a particularly bad day – with the looming disasters adjusting accordingly – the action would suffer greatly. Our simpler breakfast scene can likewise benefit from a tightened timeline. If the siblings know their mother always wakes up at 7:00 am. and the kitchen clock currently shows 6:57, then the stage is set for action. Unless you're looking to start the scene *at* the moment of crisis or working in a long-form mode with a sizeable arc and subsequently gentler pace, it's helpful to establish a time frame that will expire just before the scene culminates, or even sooner as the following strategy encourages…
2. **Decrease the preamble.** An effective way to further increase the urgency is to actively decrease the scenic preamble or inactive exposition. Frankly, this is sage advice for most scenes as a "starting in the middle" feel propels the story into the rising action and encourages activating any pertinent backstory. There is something safe and predictable about beginning a bomb disposal vignette back at headquarters, carefully assembling the needed equipment and receiving all the important instructions, or starting the breakfast scene discussing how much you love your mother and musing on what you should cook. When you skip these ponderous steps in lieu of jumping into (or at least *near*) the climactic event, the resulting story benefits enormously from this energy spike. This is not to say that you shouldn't *also* add relevant background information – whether you call it **CROW**, **WWW**, or context – as it's an essential component of a well-rounded performance. But now, these details accompany the action in progress rather than postpone it.
3. **Decrease your attempts.** An advantage of decreasing the amount of time you have available to achieve your goal is that this will necessarily decrease the number of attempts you can make, too. Screenwriters go to great lengths to justify why their protagonists can't just try and try again without suffering dire consequences. Such efforts may also deploy the "rule of threes," which generally involves two thwarted efforts or unanticipated complications before the third attempt ultimately proves triumphant or irreversibly disastrous. For our bomb disposal unit, this dramatic approach might be seen in the presence of potential trip switches, decoy panels, or secondary triggers and activation systems. For our cooking siblings, perhaps there are only enough ingredients for one batch of pancakes, the children can only reach one pan in the entire house, or the power company is about to turn off the electricity for late payments *any moment now*. The more attempts available to achieve your desire, the less dramatic the journey becomes.
4. **Decrease your skillset.** You can further ramp up the urgency by carefully considering the skillset of those engaged in the action at hand. You'll want to be wary of falling into the "I've never done this before" trope as, in novice hands, this will quickly translate into tepid choices, inactivity, or devolve the action into a teaching scene complete with a stalling litany of uninteresting questions. However, the urgency can become sapped if there is a sense that the obstacle is really no match at all for the characters. If the bomb expert has diffused this *exact* model many times before, or our young chefs are child prodigies who have won awards for their culinary prowess, there is now little doubt as to the eventual outcome of the story. Seasoning your scenes with a little strategic uncertainty can go a long way. If our disposal unit has never seen this particular device or is facing an adversary renowned for installing an array of complex and unique traps that could foil the team at any wrong move, the outcome of the scene is

no longer secure. Similarly, if our siblings have a reputation for causing kitchen disasters when left unattended, their scene takes on new levels of dynamism. In both cases, with the clock ticking, there's no time to bring in anyone else, so they must push forward regardless of their innate abilities or lack thereof.

5. **Decrease the acceptability of failure.** This final consideration tilts more firmly into the domain of **stakes**, but urgency declines if the projected outcome doesn't really matter to anyone. If the test you're racing to complete is just one of several practice exams that doesn't count toward your final grade, then all our efforts to increase the pressure of vanishing time won't succeed. Such an anticlimactic move can serve (and often does) as a "rug pull" maneuver whereby the intense stakes and urgency are pushed to the breaking point only to reveal that the bomb squad was defusing a dud or performing in a simulation, or our ill-equipped kids were playing make-believe in their toy kitchen all along and so the house didn't really burn down. This exceptional and sudden inversion keeps our characters safe to face the impossible another day, but generally, if the audience knows that failure is acceptable or inconsequential, the magnitude of the scene collapses. Instead, raise the stakes and enhance the urgency by moving the incendiary device from an abandoned building to a bustling metropolis, or make this celebratory breakfast the mother's first homecooked meal since returning home from surgery or time in the penitentiary.

Final Thought

Just as every improv scene won't have life and death stakes, it also follows that there won't always be an ominous ticking clock counting down the seconds until imminent disaster. But if you routinely engage in **talking heads** scenes or find yourself just wandering on and off the stage with little purpose or energy, bringing urgency to your work will unquestionably create more interest. Without any sense of urgency, dialogue tends to become ineffectual, action grinds to a halt, and characters lose their sense of direction and agency.

Urgency and **stakes** go hand in hand on stage, so check out my prior entry for more helpful tips.

Related Entries: Drama, Stakes
Antonym: Postponing **Synonym:** Repercussions
Connected Game: Starting in the Middle

VAGUENESS

The act of making tepid and safe choices that provide little detail or nuance and, thus, offer scant potential for discovery: a nondescript someone doing an ill-defined something in a featureless somewhere.

Antonym: Specificity

VERBAL SKILLS

Unless you're contributing in a musical or design capacity, our onstage improv offers essentially consist of **physicality**, **Verbal Skills**, or (ideally) a rich combination of these two components. How we vocalize our choices as characters can reveal hidden meanings, magnify dramatic tensions, increase the emotional stakes and connections, or – when things aren't going so well – obfuscate our intent and frustrate our scene partners and spectators. Offers that cannot be heard or comprehended beyond a surface level cannot be fully accepted and justified. Bernie Sahlins notes the immense power of an improviser's language: "Without a set, just a back wall with two doors, without costumes, with just words and our great actors, there is pure theatre magic on that stage."[2] Ironically, while many improv styles of play over-emphasize the spoken word in performance, problematically fewer pay equal attention to polishing and expanding the very verbal skills on which they rely so heavily.

Example

Two rather nervous improvisers begin a scene in the upstage corner of the stage based on the suggestion of "embarrassment." They sit down and begin to quietly talk about an issue of consequence. The scene may have been very poignant and moving, but sadly, no one will ever know as the majority of the dialogue was incomprehensible…

V Verbal V's

1. **Volume.** In smaller improv venues, a more filmic vocal style might pass muster, but even then, when you add some soundtrack enhancement, a little accidental over-talking or upstaging, and

(hopefully) some audience reactions, suddenly your realistic mumbled dialogue disappears beneath the everyday din. When we discuss appropriate onstage volume, this obviously doesn't mean bombastically yelling our dialogue regardless of the scenic needs – overtly loud improvisers can strip the story of any nuance and jar the nerves – but as I discuss in my **drama** entry, effective onstage dialogue does require consciously avoiding falling into the pitfalls of unsupported speech. There's a reason that the term "stage whisper" exists as *even* a whisper in the theatre is magnified so that its content is known to all in attendance: for this particular device, performers tend to *add* a breathiness rather than dramatically *subtract* volume. If you're fortunate enough to play in spaces with microphones and sound technicians, even here, under-energized vocals will create other issues, diminishing the onstage attack that is so crucially needed to create and shape action. Low volume usually reflects low stakes, urgency, commitment, and emotional potency, so in addition to staying open (letting the audience see your face) and coming downstage (rather than hiding against the back wall) also increase the amplitude in one or more of these aforementioned areas.

2. **Vocabulary.** A second "v" to consider on the stage is our vocabulary. As improvisers may be called upon to play a multitude of different characters, it would naturally follow that all these personae wouldn't utilize language in exactly the same way. A five-year-old is unlikely to wield the same vocabulary and speech patterns as an octogenarian crossword champion (although a deliberate inversion of these expectations would certainly craft amusing results too!) It can prove helpful as an improviser to practice a collector's attitude toward language, consciously seeking out unfamiliar words to expand your knowledge base so you have richer options at your disposal when the opportunity arises. A specific word choice, after all, communicates just as much as the way in which it is delivered. While rude, annoying, and persnickety are loosely synonyms, the tone and feeling of each word are quite unique and likely to inform or inspire different characters and dynamics. When we incline ourselves toward using our language deliberately, we also reduce the likelihood of "vague-prov" and empty dialogue that postpones or stalls the action. This is of particular import when we leap into stylistic pieces that demand a more robust verbal presence to provide a stark contrast with our daily idiom: a Shakespearean scene without *any* Elizabethan flair or wordplay probably won't land well. If you're looking for an accessible starting point, assuming a fearless **expert** approach with your verbal work provides one helpful pathway to this level of certitude and colorful finesse.

3. **Variety.** I've briefly discussed the potentials of applying Laban movement qualities to our work (in my complementary **physicality** musings) to introduce a wider array of character traits and options; this same philosophy can reap similar rewards with our verbal choices. Sometimes, embracing a seemingly random pattern or style at the top of the scene is enough to inspire a new character perspective or presence. If you're usually effusive with your language, explore a sparse vocal style where every word matters. Perhaps your norm is rapid-fire parlays, or leaning heavily into your alto speaking range, or you have your own natural speech rhythms or patterns that, left to their own devices, typically infuse most of your characters. Playfully switching up just one of these areas will encourage freshness. Once you have settled in on the basic communicative style of your character, it's equally important to find variety within their speech acts. Sure, you might get away with doing the same thing in slightly different ways for a short-form scene, but if your creations are to have depth and invite sustained interest, they will benefit greatly from pursuing a plethora of tactics. When the low-talker suddenly erupts, or the reserved character reveals their verbal acumen, or a naïve child unexpectedly utters wisdom beyond their years, such moments stand out as prior patterns have been disrupted in pleasing ways. Alternatively, when a character uses the same vocal tool again and again and again, it can lose its charm and effectiveness easily: how many clever sketches have you seen when the "bit" failed to evolve and the thing that once gave you joy eventually grated on your last nerve?

4. **Voracity.** One potential meaning of voracity is a "hunger," which works nearly as well as the intended meaning here, which is displaying a general eagerness in your work. Language without passion soon becomes empty rhetoric – passive sounds perhaps intended to persuade that ultimately have little sway on the speaker or audience. When our characters (and the improvisers inhabiting them) lack voracity – that hunger or consuming need – ineffective verbal choices can quickly follow. A dispassionate character is unlikely to fill the acoustic space, pursue every nuanced tactic available to them, or infuse their language with specificity and emotion. A powerful objective, on the other hand, coupled with a sense of true hunger or desire, fuels

the scenic action as characters emphatically chase their goals and ambitions. Players who routinely struggle with volume onstage benefit from exploring passions worthy of their time as this increased power essentially *demands* a greater vocal presence. Improvisers who habitually conflate text and subtext – commenting on the action or announcing their emotions without conviction or connection – can similarly profit from exploring their driving passions in new and complex ways. At the end of the day, if our characters don't actively and painfully *want* on the stage, then all the beautiful and well-chosen language in the world won't amount to much.

5. **Verisimilitude.** My final "v" is verisimilitude, a fancy term often used in scripted performance devoted to realism that refers to faithfully honoring our source material and presenting the world with an air of authenticity and familiarity. If you're hoping to expand your verbal storehouse, you really need to look no further than the world around you for an abundance of potential case studies and sources of inspiration. Observing others' speech patterns, tempos, and idiosyncrasies and then playfully applying them to your own stage work can provide a grounded anchor for new characterizations. Parodic traditions rely on such an approach of recreating the verbal tells of recognizable celebrities and politicians. But the same tool can be applied more gently as well, allowing observed vocal quirks to enrich your own verbal repertoire. Just as authors are encouraged to "write what they know," improvisers can gain effortless details by "improvising what (or who) they know." Finding inspiration from that memorable relative can be enough to level up your verbal game. On one end of the spectrum, the resulting work may read as impersonation (and there's nothing wrong with that). When applied more subtly, you may uncover whole new facets of yourself. As you playfully pursue verisimilitude one does have to wrestle with issues of representation and stereotyping, especially if you are wearing a dialect or regionalism as the totality of your character with little effort to incorporate empathy, connection, or integrity. Such choices when they are punching up at powerful public figures feel very different than when they are punching down at marginalized groups or demographics absent from your stage or company.

Final Thought

When we care about what we say *and* how we say it, it's more likely that others will care too. Offers not only consist of the what or raw content but also the how. Both parts are equally codependent on the other for meaning to be forged powerfully in our improvisational creations.

> **Related Entries:** Experts, Obvious, Physicality, Rhyme, Talking Heads **Antonyms:** Waffling, Wimping **Synonym:** Vocabulary
> **Connected Game:** Alphabet Game

VOLUNTEERS

From interactive street theatre and sociodramatic modalities to short-form competitive games and monologue-inspired long-forms, many improvisational practices invite or require the use of audience **Volunteers**, those who bravely offer up themselves or their stories to enable spontaneous play. Johnstone recalls a particularly playful example:

> Audience volunteers are sometimes conscripted: I once saw fifty people run on to the stage and lie down and make sucking noises while the improvisers pretended to be duck hunters wading through a swamp.[3]

While some might consider audience members in the same category as animals and children – artistic collaborators to be avoided if at all possible – utilizing the right volunteer in the right way can raise your performance to another level. There is something captivating about seeing "one of your own" cross the divide between the auditorium and stage, and many improv schools actively seek and celebrate this inclusive and participatory style of play.

Example

Player A: "For this next game, I'm looking for someone to come and join us on the stage who really likes to dance…"

Can I Have a Volunteer?

1. **Choose wisely.** There is an inherent risk in bringing an audience member to the stage or making them front and center in an interactive piece. A good choice can make the games or stories that follow feel effortless or magical; a less inspired selection can become an anchor around your

neck or scuttle the whole enterprise almost before it's even started. I've found that there are some telltale signs that you might be inviting challenge or disaster to the stage. Be wary of over-eager or aggressive candidates as this selfsame energy will easily overwhelm and audiences tend to root for and enjoy more humble or charming demeanors (the notable exception being if you're using your craft to address and diminish intense feelings among your constituency). The same holds true for overly reluctant guests often "volunteered" by the friend beside them. It *can* prove successful to enlist this vocal friend instead, but they sometimes belong to the former category of dominating volunteers, so don't make this a default choice. When volunteers will be closely interacting with improvisers on stage, it's important that they are fully in control of their faculties – there's nothing fun about bringing that belligerent drunk up only to then have to run interference for the whole scene or exchange. Everyone on the stage should feel safe. And volunteers with agendas or insider status can skewer the improv, too. Unless your format actively invites the involvement of other improvisers, bringing a friend or improv student to the stage generally adds an odd dynamic that alienates the rest of the audience who aren't "in the know." Such volunteers may also bring other agendas with them – such as a palpable desire to impress their coaches – which puts them unhelpfully further into their heads.

2. **Know what you're looking for.** Every improv game or situation is not created equally, and it's helpful to have a sense of what skills (or lack thereof) will best suit your needs. A young child might prove charming in a Puppets or Moving Bodies scene but quickly become overwhelmed or unresponsive in Audience Sound Effects, which requires a little more range and finesse. In many cases, it's wise to let your potential talent pool know the gist of what's to follow, especially if the task in question requires stamina or an ability to move without risk of injury. Harming an audience member (physically or emotionally) would be wrenching for all involved, so keep safety front of mind. If your performance frame has (or can have) multiple opportunities for audience involvement, take full advantage of this reality and strategize accordingly. While Playback Theatre culminates with volunteers sitting onstage in the teller's chair

Figure 17.1 Professional improvisers (center) work alongside audience volunteers (left and right) during a game of Moving Bodies during a *Duel of Fools* at Sak Comedy Lab. James Berkley Photography.

sharing an often rather personal narrative, the event starts with smaller bite-sized opportunities for participation that allow the company to get a read of the space and identify those who might need to develop some trust and comfort before offering themselves up. This patient and responsive practice provides a lovely model for welcoming volunteers in general.

3. **Make them shine.** Arguably, improvisers should *always* be working to elevate others on the stage, but this is doubly so when you incorporate audience members into the creative process. It's disconcerting if someone volunteers to play in a featured capacity only to then watch them become sidelined or largely forgotten by the very improvisers who originally courted them. Johnstone's example above provides a lovely illustration of an audience acting as a unified ensemble; oftentimes, though, one or two people join the cast and there's at least a tacit understanding that they will do *something* of note. It's standard practice not to throw volunteers truly into the improvisational deep end – it's smart to test the waters a little to see their aptitude and ability to play, for example – but quickly look for ways to make these brave souls look good. (A wise rule of thumb is that it should at least *look* like it's primarily the resident improvisers who are being messed with rather than the outsider if such a dynamic is being deployed at all.) Some helpful tips include assigning a cast member as a chaperone if the game involves some technical finesse, peculiar rules, or staging needs; finding a way to suitably challenge or feature guests during the scenic climax by giving them the final word or chance to make the last significant offer; and celebrating their involvement as the scene wraps up and they return to their former role as observers. A major pet peeve is watching audience members wandering awkwardly off the stage after they've lent a hand while improvisers obliviously stand by. When volunteers are used in competitive shows with a scoring system, it's also good form to stress that it's the *other* players that are being judged (or perhaps just give the volunteer a generous score all their own!).

Final Thought

I confess that I rarely slate games with my campus troupe that require audience volunteers, although we often elicit reasonably detailed stories to inspire our long-form, but this is a rather different dynamic. There is something innately tricky when improvisers who are just finding their own stride are then expected to confidently and kindly guide the efforts of novices (who, in this case, are also usually their peers and friends). This is a taxing balancing act that the most seasoned professional can find difficult at the best of times.

Most semesters, however, we'll schedule an "all play" show where company members play alongside audience members who have put their names in the hat to play random short-form games. Almost without exception, these shows reveal a generosity of spirit as the resident players work diligently to make sure our guests excel. While I can tend to view the use of volunteers as a little bit of a gimmick or public relations stunt (especially in commercial improv houses), such moments remind me that there is an important and innate value in (re)learning how to help others shine and succeed, and that this embracing and celebration of the "amateur" or everyday viewer sets improv apart from so many other forms of performance art where the tools and opportunities for participation are staunchly withheld.

Related Entries: Audience, Looking Good, Shining
Antonym: Ensemble **Synonyms:** Amateur, Guest
Connected Game: Moving Bodies

VULNERABILITY

The opposite of **bulletproof** armor onstage (and perhaps its antidote) consists of nurtured **Vulnerability**. While improvisers can accidentally reflect (Western) society's obsession with winning – thereby resisting opportunities for power inversions or undesirable changes in fortune – vulnerable players and characters happily embrace the exciting potential of such moments secure in the knowledge that accepting the "loss" holds a different creative power of its own. After all, "improv is exciting because it puts actors in vulnerable positions, either to soar or crash."[4] The same holds true for our characters. I fear that there are many deeply ingrained social psychoses that value victory at any cost and subsequently squelch honest confessions of wrongdoing. When this mindset frames onstage play, the theatrical results become argumentative, aggressive, and generally unproductive. Without willingly accepting chances for change, scenic work quickly mires itself in a quibbling rut.

Example

Player A: (angrily/desperately) "You don't love me anymore, do you?"

Player B: (after a pained moment of thought and without any malice) "Despite my best efforts, no, I'm sorry, I don't."

The Glorious Risks of Vulnerability

1. **Risk being wrong as the character.** Take the risk of being wrong onstage. Especially when faced with a **CAD** (confession, accusation, or discovery) that paints your character in an unflattering light, it can be human nature to respond with a bite reflex, lobbing back a similar charge immediately to even the score and playing field. This retaliatory instinct – as a familiar human behavior – certainly has a place on the stage; but if this becomes your standard or only reaction, scenes will struggle to move beyond matches of wit or anger. When you, instead, take that "gut check" and then assume **culpability**, exciting pathways will emerge. Yes, you *did* or *said* that thoughtless thing, and your conscience has been wracked with guilt ever since, or now you're relieved beyond compare that your secret is finally known. Being right is boring and resembles the bland trap of nice people doing nice things; being wrong as the character reveals flaws, blindnesses, and fault lines that are inherently more dramatic and worthy of theatrical treatment.
2. **Risk being wrong as the improviser.** Take the risk of being wrong backstage. Just as facing characters that are *always* right and unwilling to admit wrongdoing becomes exhausting, the same holds true for such a proclivity when it's routinely faced in the green room or note sessions. When we cling to a need to explain or justify our choices to prove that they were, in fact, correct despite others' experiences, we are falling into the same communicative hole that prevents progress, growth, and learning in our scenes. It's helpful to take a quiet "gut check" during these debriefing moments, too, sitting with feedback in an open way that acknowledges improvisers are flawed and evolving just like their dramatic doppelgangers.
3. **Risk showing weakness as the character.** Take the risk of revealing weakness onstage. In many ways, theatre is the embodied exploration of growth and change (or the epically tragic inability to do so). When we embrace weakness and fragility, we also set the scene for later strength and victory. The hard-earned successes for such characters taste all the sweeter when we have seen their honest struggles and embarrassments. The victory of the well-loved underdog is a common theatrical device for a reason. And the inverse holds true for the seemingly untouchable character or villain that after an arduous journey *finally* descends from their high-status perch and reveals their unprotected underbelly. This move from powerful to powerless (or vice versa) defines the concept of peripeteia so central to Greek tragedies, an effective dramatic conceit that has survived and thrived for millennia because it is so compelling and relatable.
4. **Risk showing weakness as the improviser.** Take the risk of revealing weakness backstage. An improviser who believes or projects that they have nothing to learn quickly becomes problematically just that and no more. My favorite teachers have always been those who embody an insatiable curiosity and are just as excited to discover something new as their student collaborators. Improv *is* process. The contributing factors always change regardless of how often we have played a particular game, character, or form. A new audience, unfamiliar cast combination, unexpected prompt, or provocative story in the headlines should re-contextualize our play together and offer new subtle or even profound lessons. When we fail to recognize that past wisdoms may not apply wholesale to present practices, we will quickly become out of step with the needs and gifts of the here and now.
5. **Risk embracing failure as the character.** Take the risk of failing onstage. Not every character can or should win every scene: generals don't typically vanquish every foe; surgeons don't generally save every patient; teachers don't miraculously break through to every troubled student. Significant or thwarting failures loom large for such characters and serve as new spurs to action, intensify objectives, and raise the stakes of the playing field as another failure could always be just around the corner. Losing is character forming and revealing. Embracing failure can provide moments of true profundity, comedy, or both. There's something delightfully unexpected about seeing a character revel in their mistakes and losses or using such occasions as emotional tactics to chart a new path toward hopeful success. In the scripted tradition, playwrights ultimately decide who will win or lose, but it's a rare play when *someone* doesn't lose. Our improv gains finesse when players celebrate well-played character stumbles as ardently as their strategic successes.
6. **Risk embracing failure as the improviser.** Take the risk of failing onstage (but as the improviser). In most improvisational practices, failure, or at

least the tacit potential for failure, is built into the greater performance event. I think it would be a fair argument to state that many patrons are attracted to the form *because* of the ever-present chance that everything could collapse at any given moment. The home runs seem even more impressive if you've seen a few strikes or foul balls first as these remind us of the requisite skill involved. Watching improvisers try and mess up with good grace, and then get back up again and happily try some more, is rather unique in the arts and is perhaps more reminiscent of the sports player who secures themselves in the spectators' hearts when they triumph over adversity. Now, an evening of *only* struggle is another matter entirely, but finding the joyful humility in acknowledging and laughing at your own missteps is a true gift worthy of cultivating. And if you don't at least occasionally skirt on the edge of improv failure, it is likely that you might be working from a place of complacency rather than expansive creativity.

Final Thought

While "strong" characters might seemingly provide energy, it is often self-contained and closed. Vulnerable characters, on the other hand, invite audiences and other players into their worlds and emotions. The former breed of personae (and improviser) can craft impressive moments and plot points; the latter variety forges lasting bonds and connections as well.

Related Entries: Change, Culpability, Emotional Truth, Postmortem
Antonyms: Bulletproof, Winning **Synonym:** Losing
Connected Game: Neighbors

NOTES

1. Viola Spolin, *Improvisation for the Theater. A Handbook of Teaching and Directing Techniques*. 3rd ed. Evanston, IL: Northwestern UP, 1999. p. 38.
2. Bernard Sahlins, *Days and Nights at the Second City. A Memoir, with Notes on Staging Review Theatre.* Chicago: Ivan R. Dee, 2001. p. 41.
3. Keith Johnstone, *Impro for Storytellers*. New York: Routledge, 1999. p. 5.
4. Laurie Stone, "70 Hill Lane. (P.S. 122, New York, New York)." *The Nation* 266.9 (9 March 1998): 34(3).

W

WAFFLING

To **Waffle** is to exert the might of your words clumsily and without finesse. Johnstone considers gossip as one variant of this tendency: "Gossip can be entertaining, but at its worst it's just a mass of waffling that drags on until the improvisers find 'a laugh to end on.'"[1] There are, in fact, many unique but related faces of voluminous verbosity, but they all share the common feature that – despite appearances – they tend to take more from the scene and teammates than they give.

Example

A scene begins in a dentist's office. Player A anxiously approaches the reception counter, clearly a first-time patient who has obviously avoided this moment at great personal cost. The dental assistant looks up from behind the counter and begins…

Player B: (only tangentially aware of A's established reality, if at all) "Welcome to the Smile Factory. I'm going to need you to fill out the following forms in triplicate before the doctor will be able to see you, although as we're so busy today – and a little understaffed – I can't guarantee that you'll make it into surgery in the next hour or so… so if you're in a rush you might want to set up a more formal appointment time online. You can find the link on the sign above the desk. Make sure you're firmly pressing with the pen, or it won't go through all the copies, and you'll want to list any preexisting conditions as a new patient, as well as any medications. And I wouldn't sit against the wall as the air conditioner duct blasts really cold air against it…"

Types of Wafflers That Might Show Up in Your Scene Work If You're Not Particularly Careful about Using Your Words Deliberately and Concisely

1. **The scattershot…** Random, thoughtless, unfiltered, disconnected, and over-original: the scattershot likely hasn't possessed a thought onstage that they haven't voiced immediately. While it's very important to embrace our spontaneous spirit and impulses, without self-awareness, it can become easy to flood the stage with a tsunami of half-formed ideas that may have little to do with the story threads already in play. Too many offers also make it exponentially more difficult to isolate *any* single idea for polishing and development. Improv often suffers from excess, which becomes fueled by a misplaced belief that there isn't *enough* happening. A scattershot approach of saying anything and everything invariably results in anything and everything becoming largely meaningless and nothing. Improv benefits from purposefulness.

Player B's unvoiced subtext: "If I say everything I'm thinking, something good must eventually come out."

2. **The overloader…** Effusive, eclipsing, cluttering, panicked, and unfocussed: while the scattershot improviser inclines toward randomness and disconnection, the overloader may provide more linear or related choices, but this waffler still uses their language unknowingly as a weapon rather than a constructive tool. The improv shelves will quickly become burdened by well-intended minutiae, too much for the scene or show to

ever possibly manage or utilize fully. This brand of panic privileges quantity over quality. Softer hues and more subtle potentials become suffocated in the verbal assault. Individual ideas, taken one at a time, could prove helpful and insightful, but taken en masse leave little room for others to add details of their own. Improv flourishes with moderation.

Player B's unvoiced subtext: "If I make a whole bunch of offers, everyone will see that I'm contributing."

3. **The staller...** Inactive, postponing, fearful, wimping, and under-energized: the staller doesn't so much control the action with their verbal meanderings so much as grind it to a halt altogether. If you talk incessantly about the pros and cons of a potential plot twist or action, after all, then you'll probably never have to do it. This vampiric tendency to drain the momentum out of a scene reveals a deep-seated fear of fully committing to an exploration of the unknown and in this sense is perhaps a more "run of the mill" embodiment of a **wimping** energy. Stallers enjoy the perceived safety of their intellectual musings and are experts at providing clever or witty reasons why *not* embarking on that exciting adventure is actually the "better" choice. Improv thrives on action.

Player B's unvoiced subtext: "If I hide behind these words long enough, then I won't have to actually pursue anything that might reveal something about me."

4. **The bulldozer...** Controlling, bulletproof, overwhelming, prescriptive, and unresponsive: although our prior wafflers' efforts might inadvertently result in taking some control over the scene, this is the raison d'etre of the bulldozer. This improviser often needs control over the action to quell their own anxieties. From this perspective, to stop talking is to allow for the possibility that the next major choice might come from somewhere else on the stage. There are clearly times when certitude and leadership are welcome and can steer an otherwise sinking story to calmer waters; but, as a stylistic norm, bulldozing cuts a clear path ahead at the cost of laying waste to your teammates whose own ideas might stand in the way. I discuss some ways to siphon the fuel from such a destructive energy in my entry devoted to this improv trap. Improv shines with collaborative give and take.

Player B's unvoiced subtext: "If I keep speaking, then I will also retain control over the scene and won't run the risk of looking foolish when I don't know how to respond to someone else's idea."

5. **The talking head...** Static, witty, overly intellectual, gossiping, and backstory-spewing: Johnstone alludes to this last waffling variant in his opening quote. When dialogue becomes the *only* focus of our work on stage, a **talking heads** scene will nearly always follow. Here, players ignore the communicative (and vulnerable) potentials of full-bodied expression in lieu of a "neck up" approach to theatre. Scenes may quickly become discussions about past events, or considerations of (never-to-be-seen) future actions, or dispassionate displays of wordplay that only comment on present possibilities. While our other four faces might also appear in this dynamic, talking heads frequently thrive in each other's company where there is safety (and stasis) in numbers. For some tips on escaping this "road to nowhere," explore my earlier full-length entry of the same title. Improv gains immeasurably from using our whole selves.

Player B's unvoiced subtext: "If I concentrate on my talking, then I won't need to feel anything real."

Final Thought

Talk less to say and do more. Talk less to enable others to contribute more. Talk less to experience and feel more honestly and deeply. Talk less.

Related Entries: Bulldozing, Commandment #6, Over-Originality, Postponing, Wimping
Antonyms: Action, Physicality
Synonyms: Commenting, Talking Heads
Connected Game: Chatterbox

WARM-UP

A public or private exercise designed to develop critical improv skills and prepare the players for the rehearsal or performance to follow. When time is tight, it can be tempting to omit this tradition. Most improvisers only make this mistake once.[2]

Related Entry: Ensemble

WEARING YOUR CHARACTER LIGHTLY

If someone observes that you are **Wearing Your Character Lightly**, they are encouraging you to dig deeper and find more grounded truths in your work. This is no small task and is, arguably, the pursuit of a lifetime in the performance arts. Scott Markwell, writing of Del Close's core philosophy, includes combating this unhelpful inclination as one of three critical skills an improviser should foster.

> Working with Elaine May at the Crystal Palace in Saint Louis, the Compass's satellite space, Close helped formulate three principles of improv: don't dispute what's been said (you've got to play along); assume the active voice instead of the passive; and find the character in your own inclinations, never wear it as something outside yourself.[3]

Many entries in this current project examine tools and techniques for enriching our onstage characterizations and finding ourselves more fully represented in their actions and desires. If you are concerned that you're nonchalantly slipping on your characters rather than bravely embodying them with all your being, explore some of the following...

In Search of Snugger-Fitting Clothes

1. **Eschewing two-dimensional acting.** Lightly worn characters can tend to comment on the action rather than roll up their sleeves and commit to the unfolding events. **Cartooning** examines ways to bring that third dimension to your scene work, while **subtext** provides pointers for infusing your dialogue with greater complexity.
2. **Embracing new character energies.** My prior entry on **character** looks at ways to break out of your old patterns and tempos so that you can mine deeper and more dynamic possibilities through considering elements such as age, occupation, and socio-economic background.
3. **Avoiding comfortable pitfalls.** There is safety in keeping your character (and scene partners) at arm's distance, and my consideration on **commenting** reflects on some familiar pitfalls that can foil an unaware improviser.
4. **Gaining strength through weakness.** Shallow characters avoid change to retain power or stasis. Exploring **culpability** and its many gifts (as described in this entry of the same name) reveals the true gift of embracing tilts and less-admirable qualities in your character work. **Vulnerability** further elucidates the related joys of accepting when you're wrong both on and off the improv stage.
5. **Enjoying the dramatic.** When we lean into dramatic moments (as opposed to leaning away from them in fear or undermining them with awkward commentary), our characters can reach new heights. **Drama** offers some time-tested techniques for avoiding performance traps that can stall these efforts at creating connected truth.
6. **Relishing your emotions.** Performance devoid of emotional honesty is likely lacking depth and nuance in general. My thoughts on **emotional truth** outline some helpful strategies for inviting more robust emotions into your work, while thoughts on **love**, and **material** also elucidate how to bring more of yourself to the stage.

Final Thought

Fear usually resides at the center of keeping your distance from your theatrical creations. When you assume such a stance, you're less likely to tap into your own feelings, reveal deeply held personal truths and experiences, or connect to your scene partners in an unguarded way. Taking the risk to bring more of yourself to your work is just that, a risk, but it also inspires work that can forge meaningful and lasting connections to your collaborators on both sides of the proscenium arch. That's a risk worth taking in my humble opinion.

Related Entries: Drama, Love, Material, Vulnerability **Antonyms:** Culpability, Emotional Truth, Subtext
Synonyms: Cartooning, Commenting
Connected Game: Four Square Relationships

WEAVING

In musical improvisation, this term refers to the pleasing harmonic or lyrical embellishment of the melody provided by fellow players. In nonmusical improvisation, weaving describes the similarly pleasing orchestration of previous offers and details as they are strategically spun into the tapestry of the emerging narrative.

Related Entry: Connections

WHAT

One of the three Ws in WWW. On the most basic level, this describes the actions or activities of the characters. On a more helpful level, it summarizes the deeper needs and desires that propel the dramatic personae forward into the world.

Related Entry: Objective

WHERE

While **Where** serves as the last letter of **CROW** and, for me, the final "W" in **WWW** (I say who, what, where), scenes suffer significantly when this element is sidelined or the last to meaningfully make it to the stage. Even if a scene has thrived with a riveting relationship and palpable objectives, the absence of an equally colorful locale potentially traps the improvisers in a nowhere land or **talking heads** dynamic in which action is almost purely psychological or verbal. A well-chosen and well-crafted where provides literal and metaphorical doorways for discovery. And, as improv historians Frost and Yarrow further observe,

> The 'who/where/what' discipline helps to remove these anxieties [of uncertainty and discomfort for the actor] and these blocks. It gives the performer a reassuring and familiar structure within which to operate, and it also insists that the creativity keep within the logical bounds of the initial idea. It's another way of taking pressure off, without losing genuine spontaneity.[4]

Example

As the lights fade, a flurry of improvisers strikes the remaining set pieces from the prior scene. They quickly and strategically place a few blocks and chairs in a provocative configuration. When the lights once again rise, the action is already in motion...

Where It's At

1. **Keep location front of mind.** Though it's not ideal, inattentiveness to a relationship or objective can typically become addressed later within a scene, thereby resolving any unhelpful ambiguities or vagueness. Due to the physical nature of our settings, it's difficult to adeptly and unobtrusively tend to location elements after the fact if they have been ignored for too long. When players have wandered all over the stage space and then suddenly decide to place an imagined (or real) table in the middle of this void, it will feel jarring and contradictory. If your staging vernacular includes actual set pieces, I'd advocate making bold placement choices as the lights are transitioning into focus. The best-case scenario is that *all* these elements will frame and inspire action; the typical scenario is that at least *some* will provide opportune details; and the worst-case scenario is that you'll end up with a talking heads scene with a few chairs scattered around it which is at least a little more interesting than a talking heads scene on an empty stage! The same philosophy holds true for mimed pieces and space objects. Commit to creating these scenic additions *as soon as you can* so that they can then add detail and context to your story without denying prior staging patterns and audience imaginings.
2. **Define your staging norms.** In venues with a "poor" aesthetic that primarily rely on pantomime and imagination to paint epic environments, it's common practice to just have a few chairs or blocks that can be used to assist. Generally, it's wise to use these as weight-bearing pieces as opposed to strictly decorative elements. Especially if you're moving quickly from scene to scene or game to game, struggling to arrange those cubes in a particular configuration to represent a table or counter or refrigerator that just "sits there" rarely adds much value and can just stall or prevent action. You can't safely overturn a table in a fit of passion when it's actually a clump of heavy blocks, or reach into the sink on a counter that is a solid mass, or open the approximated refrigerator in any meaningful way... Oftentimes, such pieces also impede sight lines and make swift transitions or cutaways all but impossible. Even if you perform with a "richer" aesthetic, I'd also caution against adopting an overtly sumptuous approach for the same reasons,

Figure 18.1 On one end of the spectrum, the realistic nature of *Murder We Wrote* demanded an expansive store of props and costumes (Props master: Lauren Cushman). While *Upton Abbey* still utilized realistic costumes and major furniture pieces, these were augmented through mimed hand props and creative imagining (Costume design: Katie Stine; Associate sound designer: Ellie Flaumenhaft). Photo credit: Tony Firriolo.

although if you're one of the few fortunate venues to deploy dedicated improvising scenographers, this makes grander but flexible stage design possible on a whole new level. Once the audience has seen and learned your in-house practices, they will happily accept how you frame your theatrical reality, so just seek consistency.

3. **Beware of a mix and match hodgepodge.** After establishing your design rules and vocabulary, be aware that accidental inconsistencies don't disappointingly dispel your ornate creations. If you've constructed an imaginary prop world and someone then whips out their actual cell phone, this will seem peculiar and probably take everyone out of the carefully crafted reality for at least a moment. You also can't put that *real* phone down on any of the imaginary set pieces that populate the space, which just compounds the awkwardness even further. I've constructed shows where *nothing* was mimed, formats when only costumes and major set pieces were real, and others where essentially everything was imagined into being. There's obviously no one path, but it's helpful to have some internal logic that everyone buys into or at least a collective company understanding that breaking the design norms of location is a *big* move. If *one* real prop suddenly appears in an otherwise pantomimic world, that one prop becomes extremely important (whether that was your initial intent or not!) Use such an out-of-the-box and powerful move with care and thoughtfulness.

4. **Go big first.** I also reference this technique in my companion game post as Spolin provides fantastic setting guidance with her "three large objects make a where" approach. The short and sweet summary of this philosophy is that most familiar locales can be effectively communicated to your fellow teammates and the audience through the careful creation and use of three substantial set pieces (as opposed to hand props). For example, if I first mime a sink, I could be offering up a wide range of possible locations: a paint shop, a gas station restroom, a Winnebago… When I add a second major element – perhaps a wall-mounted microwave – the range of options narrows: a mom-and-pop restaurant, an office break room, a dorm room… A third thoughtful addition provides enough of the puzzle to more confidently assess the greater intent: a luxurious king-sized bed now likely puts us in a hotel room, while a full-sized refrigerator might suggest a family kitchen. When you go beyond the basic "what" of each furniture piece and explore its unique qualities, the communicative potentials multiply tenfold.

Final Thought

I've explored hidden potentials lurking in the greater extended **environment** and the gifts of smaller **space objects** in prior entries. These additional tools augment the "big picture first" approach discussed above that offers a strong foundation on which to build and play. When we give location its due attention, our settings can delightfully become well-rounded characters in their own right, igniting technical and musical choices, exerting status and personality traits, and assisting or preventing the desires of the onstage personae. Improvisers need not find themselves and their characters restrained by those two ubiquitous black chairs resting against the back wall.

> **Related Entries:** Character, CROW, Environment, Levels, Objective, Space Objects, Stage Picture **Antonym:** Talking Heads
> **Synonyms:** Location, Locale
> **Connected Game:** Zones

WHO

A way of describing the characters that appear within the dramatic action; one of the three Ws in WWW that is a direct equivalent to the C and R in CROW.

> **Related Entries:** Character, Relationship

WIMPING

As a core "Ten Commandment" concept, the insidious ways that wimping can infect your improvisational play have already been discussed at length. **Wimping** describes a fear-based response characterized by the phrase "Yes, but…" that ultimately withholds energy and reduces the all-important drive that allows scenes to climb to new unexplored heights. Or, in the words of Johnstone, "We wimp when we accept ideas but refuse to add to them."[5] Left unchecked, teammates can find themselves subjected to an obstructive wimper-in-chief who needlessly stands in the way of the action, *any* action.

Example

During a critical moment as a surgery takes place, the surgeon (Player A) turns to their assistant (Player B):

Player A: "Hand me the scalpel…"
Player B: "Yes, but…"

When the Fear Strikes…

1. **Don't rationalize, feel.** When faced with an unanticipated offer or scenic direction, the temptation can easily emerge to talk about the path ahead. Yes, people in the real world will discuss major life decisions and so some representation of this process can belong onstage, but both bracing scripted and spontaneous works tend to edit such chats, weave them into the journey itself, place them in the offstage unseen action, or use them to propel the characters forward into an embodied choice. When rationalizing or discussing appears as an alternative to experiencing characters making choices – both good and bad – the stage action becomes ineffectively replaced by stage inaction. In lieu of intellectual discussion, a typically dispassionate stakes-lowering habit, allow your character to passionately *feel* as these emotions tend to inspire connected reactions that will propel them onwards.

    Player B: "Yes, doctor. I'm glad my mother is in such capable hands…"

2. **Don't obstruct, fuel.** Some players can find satisfaction in the dynamic of wimping as it seems as if they are adding conflict to the scene. Yes, initially, a wimping or contrarian attitude can *appear* to create pressure, but more often than not, a relentlessly oppositional dynamic between characters reveals a similarly dysfunctional energy between the players themselves, who are wrestling to determine where the scene will or won't go. Now, there is clearly a place for some obstacles in our protagonists' journeys – otherwise, they will just careen from one delightful twist of fate to another – but theatrical obstacles necessitate rather than eliminate action. Providing obstacles with incessant verbal pontificating ultimately stalls or burns action that could have proven exhilarating if it was seen without voluminous preamble. Helpful obstacles and conflict should raise the stakes and urgency with incendiary fuel rather than douse potential scenic embers with the calming waters of contemplation.

    Player B: "Yes, doctor. There are only two minutes left on the clock before we must resuscitate the patient. I'm not sure we'll have enough time…"

3. **Don't postpone, pounce.** Procrastination serves as a powerful force in most people's everyday lives, and the majority of us have put off many a difficult assignment or decision. Yes, we can use our dialogue to paint vivid pictures about our turmoil and complex options, but too much postponement will diminish rather than elevate the moment of crisis or conflict when (if?) it *finally* makes it to the stage. There's good dramaturgical precedence for the protagonist and antagonist *not* having their ultimate climactic confrontation in the opening beats of the dramatic action, and yet the action leading up to such moments rarely consists of lengthy static chats. The rising action consists of many smaller steps forward: it's important that we routinely see characters moving even (especially?) if their choices eventually backfire or push their goal further from their reach. When we postpone too much and discuss our tactics at length, this can also make the eventual enactment of these previewed actions rather predictable and anticlimactic.

    Player B: "Yes, doctor… you did promise that I would get to close today…"

4. **Don't solve, complicate.** When our wimping aligns with a tendency to advise or teach, the results are sadly even more lackluster. Yes, nice empathetic advice will make you feel good as the player, but this is yet another wimpy way of diffusing that ever-important potential for momentum. There is a reason that "to make matters worse" is much more common in the improvisational lexicon than "to make matters better." Complications dynamically prolong and intensify the electricity of the story; chatty solutions usually pull out the power cord leaving just a dark screen. If this particular dynamic is a personal wimping pitfall, consider, at the very least, giving *bad* advice that will result in epic consequences or adding framing information that makes the journey even more necessary and perilous.

    Player B: "Yes, but…" *(they pass the doctor the last scalpel that just moments before the audience saw them drop carelessly onto the floor…)*

Final Thought

When you find yourself deploying wimping devices to stall, prevent, or explain away the action, take a breath and perhaps explore a passionate emotional or physical response instead. Wimping is so pernicious as it not only pauses the action for usually inconsequential chatter, but it also allows energy and drive to evaporate while putting little of value in its place. Feel, fuel, pounce, and complicate.

> **Related Entries:** Commandment #8, Conflict, Waffling **Antonym:** Accepting
> **Synonyms:** Blocking, Negating, Postponing
> **Connected Game:** Yes Party

WINNING

How do we define winning in our improvisational communities? In the sporting arena, the answer is generally obvious: the team who leaves the playing field with the most points, tries, or touchdowns assumes the winner's title and trophy. While some improv franchises assume a similarly competitive frame, in most cases, this is pure conceit designed to give the punters some additional buy-in. A team might be announced as the winner, but this rarely (hopefully) has any real cachet or meaning. And yet competitiveness can lurk in the not-so-distant background of many an improv event if players aren't careful and, as Neva Boyd notes, can serve as a doorway for anti-social and anti-collaborative play.

> The greed for power, the hatred and dishonesty which have become associated with competitive games are not an inherent part of them but have found their way in them through a false sense of values. Prizes separate people, pit them against each other, discourage the less able and set the more able apart.[6]

So, I return to my opening question: how do we define **Winning** within our communities of play in a way that does not leave our fellow artists discouraged or discarded in the shadows? And are there new ways to frame this very issue of competitiveness that better serve the broad discipline that is improvisational theatre?

Example

The improv company takes a bow together...

Toward a Winning Formula

1. **Elevating the whole team.** When improvisers become solipsistic or overly concerned with the success of a smaller team unit, the greater chemistry and commitment to unrestrained collaboration suffer. Engaging improv demands that all participants are rowing in the same direction despite any structural conceits that might imply the opposite. When we're not working for the good of the whole, we're likely hampering the play that follows. If a competitive edge makes an improviser second guess entering a scene that needs an assist (or, equally as troubling, makes those already in the scene question the intent behind a "rival's" good faith contribution), then the company has lost a great deal already. Even (especially) in overtly team-based structures, there is something inspiring about watching players all truly rallying together to benefit the scene or show. The ensemble should really emerge as the only "team" of any consequence.

2. **Honoring your contract with the audience.** I'll admit openly that I'm about to espouse a product-centric assertion about a performance style renowned for its process-centric attitude, but an area where you can harness a winning temperament toward a fruitful end is when it's applied to the greater goals of the performance event. What contracts have been made with your audience, and have these been attempted with every sharpened spontaneous tool in your tool belt? In service-focused modes, this may look like modeling and forging an open and inclusive environment where participation is welcomed but not coerced. For long-form pieces, this success might resemble collectively crafting a playful narrative that smartly uses the pertinent stylistic tropes and structural elements. For competitive short-form shows, "winning" might involve skillfully playing a wide variety of games with abandon while giving the *impression* that a heated competition is taking place. From such a vantage point, spectacularly recognizing and embracing an epic "loss" with a healthy sense of performed passion could fit the bill. This last example also honors the overly theatricalized performance at the core of professional wrestling entertainment that served as a key source of inspiration for *Theatresports'* founder, Keith Johnstone.

3. **Privileging the process.** And to balance the above product-centric considerations, did your ensemble "win" when it came to the process of creation? This will also look different from company to company depending on your stated or implied mission. Was your play marked by a sense of abandon, acceptance, and active listening? (Or, to paint a less rosy picture, blocking, bulldozing, and bulletproof characters?) While there's no guarantee that a joyful process will necessarily result in an equally successful product, experience would strongly suggest that attention to the former greatly increases the likelihood of generating work of any lasting value. An ensemble fraught with interpersonal tensions and unattended injuries will struggle and undermine any elevated artistic intention. If you have inadvertently *created* this very dynamic in your pursuit of excellence, you might face a Pyrrhic victory at best. I've already written about making others look good on the improv stage (see **looking good**); this would be the much less discussed equivalent of making others *feel* good.
4. **Prioritizing personal and ensemble growth.** Personally, I find this variant the most palatable form of competitiveness in improvisation; namely, can I do better than my prior *self* as opposed to *others* involved in the performance event? In this context, "winning" really becomes synonymous with personal growth (or company growth, for that matter, when this lens is applied to collective hurdles that the ensemble is working to overcome). Perhaps I'm focusing on getting more comfortable with accepting and enjoying change onstage and in my characters, or avoiding rushing to inorganic conflict that stalls the action, or I'm striving to bring CROW ingredients more efficiently and elegantly to my scene starts. The added beauty of relocating competitiveness in this fashion is that one player's victory does not come at the expense of another nor preclude anyone else from enjoying similar highs. In fact, the opposite holds true as when we "beat" our own old habits or hindrances, we are probably simultaneously raising everyone's improv game. In my own ensembles, I'll often start a performance with players sharing a personal challenge to encourage this particular mindset.

Final Thought

True competitiveness encourages a style of play that promotes shining, upstaging, and one-upping. These dynamics can find a temporary home in deciders and tiebreakers where "winning" is part of the gimmick, but I've found in my own work that when such energies infect the evening as a whole, everyone ends up losing a little. When we're too invested in our own ideas and contributions, we can miss the brilliance that resides in the work of others or the magical potentials that become realities when ideas combine and blossom in the hands of a joyfully collaborating ensemble.

Related Entries: Commandment #3, Commandment #10, Looking Good
Antonym: Ensemble
Synonyms: Competitiveness, Shining
Connected Game: Slow Motion War

WWW

A handy-dandy way of summarizing the critical foundational choices of a scene – namely, the who, what, and where. Most improv scenes struggle when these elements are unintentionally ignored or poorly defined for too long.

Synonym: CROW

NOTES

1. Keith Johnstone, *Impro for Storytellers*. New York: Routledge, 1999. p. 119.
2. See the accompanying Game Library at www.improvdr.com for helpful examples.
3. Scott Markwell, "Comedy Mother." *Reader* 24.45 (11 August 1995): 1, 14–22. p. 18.
4. Anthony Frost and Ralph Yarrow, *Improvisation in Drama*. New York: St. Martin's Press, 1989. p. 127.
5. Keith Johnstone, *Impro for Storytellers*. New York: Routledge, 1999. p. 114.
6. Neva Leona Boyd quoted by Paul Simon, "Neva Leona Boyd, A Biographical Sketch." *Play and Game Theory in Group Work: A Collection of Papers*. Neva Leona Boyd. Chicago: University of Illinois at Chicago Circle, 1971, 7–19. p. 9.

X/Y/Z

X-RATED

Ever since humankind stumbled across improvisational performance, the resulting work has tended to gravitate toward bawdier hues and more populist content than much of the extant scripted canon, which prefers the tragic acts of nobility struggling to find their place in the world while appeasing the angry gods. Writing of the Dorian mimes, Frost and Yarrow remark,

> Probably its performances were crude, parodic and improvised. The masked performers were not possessed by the god; their burlesque provided a balancing, humanising version of the sacred events.[1]

There are unquestionably examples of august and serious improv, just as there are early examples of written buffoonery, but many spontaneous traditions – old and new alike – find humor and community through staging our most basic bodily functions, uncensored impulses, and carnal desires.

As I went looking for a suitable improv "X," the topic of ratings, content, and the carnivalesque spirit unsurprisingly came to mind. I've performed in a wide variety of venues, from makeshift barprov stages where the audience has had a few drinks, to custom-built Equity entertainment spaces where the audience has had a few drinks, to family-friendly traditional theatres where at least some of the audience has had a few drinks (or perhaps wishes they had…) The Bacchic spirit remains alive and well in many modern improvisational houses. Venues approach content parameters in different ways, and these often change or loosen as the evening gets longer and the paying public gets more raucous. I won't deny enjoying pushing the limits a little in my own work, although this entry will quickly reveal my preference for a specific breed and approach to mature, saucy, or **X-Rated** material.

I've found that when improvisers pursue primarily racy content, there can be a direct inverse correlation to the quality of work onstage. And, in a nutshell, that explains my general hesitancy for just completely letting loose: I value storytelling, connection, and patient inquisitiveness, all qualities that usually get trampled underfoot when the audience *expects* X-rated material. At best, overtly naughty or obscene scene work can quickly become a crutch rather than an embellishment; and, at worst, it may alienate and offend your audience, fellow company members, or both. If you're attracted to content on the wild side, it's worth weighing the pros and cons of such an approach to make sure your scene work is supporting your greater goals and mission. I've definitely seen some incredibly joyful raucous improv that would have made the ancient Dorians proud, but without exception, it displayed thoughtfulness.

Example

Player A: "Can I please have an occupation to inspire our next scene?"

The audience yells out a predictable array of inappropriate spoilers much to their own amusement…

X-amining Your X-Rated Tendencies

1. **Adult content is a one-way street.** My biggest concern with working in a *casually* X-rated way stems from my experiences in the classroom. In an effort to feel edgy or relevant, students can mistake profanity or gratuitous lewdness for *quality* as it tends to get that immediate audience reaction that most of us seek on some level. This perception subsequently encourages quantity: "If you thought *that* was funny, wait until you get

a load of *this!*" I've found that players who are hardwired to play and train in such a no-holds-barred manner *really struggle* when faced with other more family-oriented performance environments or scenic work that demands a more subtle set of skills. The same does not hold true moving in the opposite direction. Most improvisers accustomed to exploring more measured material find it's a much simpler matter to add some saltiness to the improv recipe than it is to remove it after-the-fact if that's all they've become accustomed to tasting. Hence, my preference as a teacher is to cook in a low-sodium improv kitchen (even if I routinely play in venues likely to spike your blood pressure).

2. **Saturation can dull the effect.** One of my major gigs for the last several decades has been teaching improv on university campuses, so this next piece of advice should be taken with that frame in mind. In some instances, this performance work publicly represents my home institution and may include parents, donors, and administrators in the audience. It's important to me that our content doesn't become saccharine or preachy and so I've never had a list of unsuitable words (although some, I trust, don't need to be put on a troupe list to be deemed off limits). My attitude has always been that strong language should be earned – the character is in such an extreme state of emotional stress or upheaval that the absence of some well-chosen words could feel trite. This frame has worked well, reserving colorful language, in particular, for just a handful of intense moments per show if it's used at all (and it usually isn't). Once you've let the lid off your content – whatever that may mean for you – it can create an unhelpful expectation for the audience that *everything* that follows will be on that same frequency. This is particularly problematic if your style of play values variety and softer moments alongside more comic or silly tomfoolery. It's easy for the stage to quickly feel unwelcoming to simpler truths once that crazy and foul-mouthed uncle character has come to town.

3. **Specific ambiguity applies to explicit ambiguity.** Specific ambiguity refers to the powerful skill of making strong choices that are meaningful and connected while simultaneously retaining a level of mystery or the potential for several different readings. When it comes to X-rated material, utilizing this same approach resembles the techniques of innuendo and double entendre, where racy ideas are presented with a wink rather than a sledgehammer. Disney and Pixar movies expertly take this high road, weaving in a handful of adult comments or situations that will appeal to older moviegoers while simultaneously flying over the heads of the intended market. English pantomime straddles a similar line. In addition to keeping your space family-friendly when that's an issue, choices that may feel crass or outright jarring can take on more playful hues when offered with a light touch. This cheeky style of wordplay and inference also reminds me of Shakespeare whose plays include some pretty filthy material but do so in such a clever way that it appealed to the widest contemporaneous demographic possible, literally spanning the full range from royalty to groundlings.

4. **Shocking choices still have consequences.** If you opt to improvise under a banner of "anything goes," this does not make you immune to the intended or unintended consequences of your art. When I improvised on Disney property, one of the only unbreakable rules was that no harm to a child could occur in our sets (the other was that we couldn't improvise illicit drug use on stage). Even though we were in a club setting with adult beverages flowing freely (at theme park prices), this line in the sand made sense to me. X-rated improv can become synonymous with blindly offensive improv, but this needn't be the case. If your primary goal is to shock or offend, you shouldn't be surprised if this starts to exclude patrons, especially if such a stance is really just a veiled justification for saying the most stereotypical or reductive things (usually from a position of unexamined privilege) that you'd think twice about saying anywhere else. Such choices can similarly breach trust and joy within the ensemble itself, especially if certain categories of players find themselves routinely objectified, marginalized, or presented as the punchline.

5. **Just because you can say or do something, doesn't mean you should.** Just because you *can* say or do something, doesn't mean you *should*.

Final Thought

As you would for any other improv production, it's important to have clear expectations, boundaries, and mechanisms for redress when you're committed to exploring the more adult facets of life and love. The traditions of **postmortems**, **consent**, and **speaking your truth** strike me as particularly vital, as does providing your audience with a clear sense of what they're in for and what is and isn't acceptable. X-rated needn't (shouldn't) become camouflage for careless collaborative creation; work under this moniker can (should) still interrogate societal taboos and norms with equal doses of whimsy, irreverence, and insight. Punching down shouldn't (shouldn't) become the valued currency.

Related Entries: Consent, Gagging, Material, Postmortem, Punching Up, Speaking Your Truth
Antonym: Family-Friendly **Synonyms:** Boundaries, Content, Mature
Connected Game: Pick-Up Lines

YES, AND...

The battle cry of the modern-day improviser. This core philosophy extols the virtue of carefully embracing the intent of your scene partner and then responding with a small, connected, and committed choice of your own.

Synonym: Accepting

YES, BUT...

The typically unintentional battle cry of the fearful modern-day improviser. It is the emblematic stalling phrase of the compulsive wimp.

Synonym: Wimping

YIELDING

A close kin to accepting (many consider these terms as synonyms). To yield is to give way to another's idea or place it above your own intent for a scene. Yielding is a critical act of improvisational generosity in that it acknowledges that the best paths generally reveal themselves when we joyfully follow and add onto the brilliance of our scene partners.

Related Entry: Accepting

YOU

For many of us, improv serves as an embodied exploration of our own humanity and communities.

> When we are in action, we open ourselves to more possibilities. Because others are interacting with us in ways that we have not planned, our feelings, thoughts, and how we would handle a situation emerge spontaneously and honestly.[2]

Compared to most other performance traditions, there are few immovable barriers preventing entry into the art of improv. This doesn't mean you can walk into that ensemble you admire or onto the biggest stage in your community without considerable effort – and even then, it may not happen at all – but the tools of improv *are* widely available to everyone, and the form itself welcomes amateurs and neophytes like few others. If you have an open space, a fellow player, and an idea or two, you can improvise: if someone else is willing to watch, then you have the semblance of an improv show. The *systems* supporting improv companies and governance, on the other hand, can reflect biases and toxicity, and we must be ever vigilant as a community that the core tenets of the craft are being upheld both on and off the stage. But if you see yourself finding joy or increasing your creativity through the tools of improv, it is highly likely that there can be a place for **You** (you just might have to make the first move in making it happen).

There Is a You in Improv

1. **You are enough.** We are all works in progress and it's healthy to have a sense of perspective about where you are in your own growth and journey. That being said, it's equally important to celebrate that you are where you are today. Using every performance to "prove" your worth (to yourself or others) will just put you unhelpfully in your head. Rather, use each new performance or workshop opportunity as a chance to connect, learn, and grow. If you remain open, in the moment, and receptive to feedback and discovery, the "you" of today won't be the same "you" of tomorrow. But also remember that doesn't mean that you can't enjoy where you are currently in this time and place and with these specific collaborators. Don't become so lost in the pursuit of greatness that you can't see what's already great right now.

2. **Your experiences are important.** Your experiences, struggles, and dreams belong on the stages you populate. These facets of your life are what make you unique and interesting in addition to making your "obvious" different than everyone else's "obvious." If you're working in an environment that doesn't actively invite and value your truths, that is something that needs to be addressed; spending your stage time obfuscating or hiding your hard-earned stories robs everyone of opportunities to develop empathy and understanding. The fluidity of improv allows previously unheard voices to stand proudly front and center and it would be a shame to throw away this power, especially if you haven't typically seen yourself honestly represented in mainstream art. Or, if you belong to the well-represented majority, remember to model allyship by elevating others through stepping aside freely and frequently.
3. **Your feelings are valid.** As improv is, by design, essentially a staged rehearsal that is always looking to evolve and deepen, there will undoubtedly be moments where the results don't live up to our expectations or ideals. When stumbling occurs (or, for that matter, "success" that is tone deaf or exclusive in nature) your feelings are valid. Whenever you can, **speak your truth** on stage or during post-show reflections. Give the ensemble the benefit of your perspective and wisdom; allow the audience to see a subject from a hitherto unconsidered angle. Your voice has a vibrancy and place as improv is only greater than the sum of its parts when all of its parts are empowered to participate fully and openly. Don't let the machine consume you in the name of groupmind or unquestioning acceptance.
4. **Your journey is your own.** Not everyone who finds improvisation is looking for the same thing, and that's more than okay. You are on your own journey, and you don't have to be on the same path as others nor do you need to compare your progression or goals to find validation. Savor every step as you climb. Soak up the view on your way up (and down) the improv mountain! It's certainly helpful to ally yourself with a company or fellow players that share some facet or your vision, but you should use the tools of improv to construct your own individualized edifice. Enjoy the process of finding out about your own artistry and expression, train where and with whom you want that speaks to your soul, surround yourself with those who will support and challenge you. Authenticity is a much more valuable currency in improv than misguided efforts to do what you think some hypothetical (or perhaps real) improv council wants from you.

Final Thought

One of the awkward truths of many Western-style improv theatres is that their education wings are revenue drivers in a way that is less common for our scripted kin who rely more heavily on subscribers, donors, and fundraising to keep the doors open. A potential side effect of this training-dependent model is that companies can peddle dreams a little: look at these photos of some of our famous alums on our walls – you can be like them if you study here long enough. And maybe you can be if the stars align. In my traditional acting classroom, we talk a lot about playable objectives. "To be famous," by most standards, would be considered a problematic "want" as it is passive, vague, and doesn't invite clear actionable steps. While I hope such a fate awaits over the horizon if that is what you seek, in the spirit of improv, don't lose sight of the lessons of this current moment and these particular players. If you spend too much time looking to an unknown future, you'll miss out on the amazing *now* that makes improv such a vibrant and enriching art. Give your fellow improvisers the unabashed creative presence that is the incomparable *you*.

Related Entries: Commandment #1, Commandment #9, Consent, Ensemble, Groupmind, Inclusiveness, Looking Good
Antonym: Over-Originality **Synonym:** Obvious
Connected Game: You Look…

ZOOMPROV

It's fitting that I conclude this "A" to "Z" of improv where this journey started for me. This project began in response to unexpectedly finding myself isolated from my improv community during the lost years that were 2020 and 2021. Like so many others, I turned to writing and technology to fill this spontaneous void. My in-progress spring university classes – all performance or improv-based – suddenly had to convert to online formats. I also faced a sabbatical where one after another exciting improv project vanished into the COVID ether. Like countless other artists around the world, I toyed with creating workshops and shows online: enter Zoomprov.

Figure 19.1 The effects of COVID exerted a lasting influence on performances on my home campus. In 2022, we presented our 17th installment of *ImprOvientation* in masks but were largely playing without them by the end of the academic year. Scott Cook Photography [top]; Photo credit: Kalani Senior [bottom].

Seham describes a prevalent pre-pandemic view of non-live improv:

> Most [Chicago players] agreed that real improvisation was incompatible with television. Television would never capture the spontaneity, audiences wouldn't feel the connection, and network executives would never take the chance.[3]

As I revise this final entry, I'm unsure if online or broadcast improv will remain a permanent part of the live improv landscape. As life returns to our collective new normal, it remains unclear if such experiments will retreat to the shadows and become a forgotten footnote in the ever-evolving history of our art form. Most of us encountered steep and unforgiving learning curves when it came to housing the spirit of improvisation on our computer screens. I think it would be fair to say that while a few companies experienced some success, the resulting work both is and isn't improv as we knew it prior to these odd times. In most instances, streamed performances are devoid of any live laughter or perceivable audience reactions save those seen fleetingly in a chat box. There is also something equally exciting and off-putting in the knowledge that most pieces are being viewed live while also being recorded for future observers. And then there is the reality that often players are now boxed into a talking heads dynamic unless they have the technical means and bandwidth to set up a home studio of sorts. (Am I allowed to voice I won't miss any of these particular realities?)

In my own experiments, the issue of focus quickly emerged as a critical new challenge. Communicative pitfalls, such as over-talking, under-energizing, and middle-of-the-road waffling, became magnified in the online realm. The thoughts that follow are offered with this particular lens in mind as lessons from Zoom also reinforce and polish best practices for real-time embodied improv too. And so, I close my dictionary with...

Zip, Zap, Zoom: Focus and Online Improv

1. **Keep it small.** At first when I was faced with the sea change that was 2020, I aimed to keep my syllabus and structures as planned. But I quickly found that the more students or improvisers that we used in a scene, the more likely communication missteps undermined the integrity and flow of the action. When I simplified nearly all my scenic work into pairs (sometimes with a third waiting with their "camera off" in the proverbial wings in case they were needed), the process and results became noticeably stronger. In this way, actors can also set their scene partner as their exclusive focus on the screen and have a fighting chance to make a more honest and fruitful connection. If you are playing in a larger group, turning off your camera as your character leaves is an obvious but helpful choice to minimize visual clutter as well.

2. **Don't ramble.** A move online, for many of us, made us rely too heavily on our verbal gifts as improvisers: on the screen it's easy for our bodies to become disengaged and for our words to lose specificity and agency. If we are cognizant that our words must carry the majority of our meaning and offers, then we must be economical and deliberate with those words. We should use each word with care, and make sure that we are providing clear and dramatic final punctuation. As our partner awaits behind their monitor, it doesn't forebode success if they are constantly unsure if we have, in fact, finished our sentences… or if… we're still contemplating… how we might finish… our sentence. You get the (online) picture.

3. **Use old-fashioned gives.** My introductory improv classes always include a unit on giving and taking focus as, I note, without a playwright or director in the traditional sense of those terms, we are responsible for always knowing where the focus should be on stage at any given moment. Especially if you're in a larger group, throwing the focus carelessly into the air will typically create either a prolonged awkward silence or a cascade of overlapping dialogue as your teammates try to figure out who was organically next in the scene. Use character names liberally (or familial equivalents such as honey, son, sis…) to mark the next likely speaker especially as the scene is being established. Clearly shift your focus and the target of your emotion on the screen to designate your focus throw and explore tonal shifts to provide clues to your partners: most of us don't talk to our parents with the same energy or voice that we talk to our significant other, and we can mine these distinctions to help share focus around.

4. **Scenic painting can help.** If you can find simple ways to refer to your environment, and the people in it, you can set each other up for clear entrances and initial dialogue exchanges. If we've been sitting at that restaurant table waiting to be served for what feels like an eternity, observing the carefree waiter who seems to be avoiding us, when we note that "I've finally caught their eye" and "they're coming over," we have set this improviser up for a clear focus transition. If you

don't have the technology or skill to make clever green-screen background changes or add ambient sounds, heightened scene painting strikes me as a must in general as it allows for more fully fleshed out worlds to play within.

5. **Err on the side of interruption.** This may be a personal preference, but the dead air between speech acts in Zoom-based improv is one of the features that makes it most uncomfortable for me as an observer. If we're using some of the strategies above, we then need to jump into scenes with abandon thereby risking cutting off our partner(s). If someone interrupts you, embrace that they clearly thought you were wrapping up (or that you should have been wrapping up). If, as a group, this becomes too caustic or combative, check in afterward and adjust the aggressiveness of your takes accordingly. Connected to this strategy is making sure that your scenes have an energy that would justify such a strong approach to focus gives and takes. Deadpan or under-energized characters are equally as problematic on the screen as they are on the stage.

6. **Use the technology.** For good or evil, if you're improvising online then that is your reality with all its inherent promise and complications. If your audio cuts out, that needs to be justified. If you didn't catch what someone said, you need to honor that and ask them to repeat it or make an assumption. If you're a professional at changing backgrounds or have someone who is adept at wrangling different improvisers and screens onto a common online stage, then make sure that person is deeply thanked and use those dynamics to the best of your abilities. Again, perhaps a personal preference, just note that meta scenes about characters using Zoom have largely been played out so look for content elsewhere. And if your performance is so dependent upon perfect technology showing up then the battle to fearlessly play and improvise may have already been lost.

Final Thought

This entry is based on one of my first ImprovDr blog posts and it's interesting to rework these ideas several years after I first tackled this issue. I'm particularly struck by the fact that most of this advice transcends the site of the virtual stage. Uncluttered scenes, deliberately concise dialogue, and clear gives are all important skills to hone and have served as worthy entry subjects in their own rights. And perhaps this is the biggest takeaway of all from the online years that many might view as at least partially lost: improvisation finds a way even in the most trying times and becomes enriched when we're open to viewing old techniques from a new perspective.

Related Entries: Focus, Give, Sharing Focus, Stage Picture, Take, Talking Heads
Antonyms: Split Focus, Waffling
Synonym: Online Improv
Connected Game: Camera, Narrator, Actor, Actor

NOTES

1. Anthony Frost and Ralph Yarrow, *Improvisation in Drama.* New York: St. Martin's Press, 1989. p. 6.
2. Patricia Sternberg and Antonina Garcia, *Sociodrama: Who's in Your Shoes?* 2nd ed. Westport, CT: Praeger, 2000. p. 19.
3. Amy E. Seham, *Whose Improv Is It Anyway: Beyond Second City.* Jackson, MS: U of Mississippi P, 2001. p. 221.

For Product Safety Concerns and Information please contact our EU
representative GPSR@taylorandfrancis.com
Taylor & Francis Verlag GmbH, Kaufingerstraße 24, 80331 München, Germany

www.ingramcontent.com/pod-product-compliance
Lightning Source LLC
Chambersburg PA
CBHW081759300426
44116CB00014B/2174